Contents

Introduction

This study text is the ACCA's official text for Paper 3.6 *Advanced Corporate Reporting*, and is part of the ACCA's official series produced for students taking the ACCA examinations.

This new 2004 edition has been produced with direct guidance from the examiner. It covers the syllabus and study guide in great detail, giving appropriate weighting to the various topics. Targeted very closely on the examination, this study text is written in a way that will help you assimilate the information easily. Numerous practice questions and exam-type questions at the end of each chapter reinforce your knowledge.

DEFINITION

- **Definitions.** The text defines key words and concepts, placing them in the margin, with a clear heading, as on the left. The purpose of including these definitions is to focus your attention on the point being covered.

KEY POINT

- **Key points**. In the margin you will see key points at regular intervals. The purpose of these is to summarise concisely the key material being covered.

ACTIVITY 1

- **Activities**. The text involves you in the learning process with a series of activities designed to catch your attention and make you concentrate and respond. The feedback to activities is at the end of each chapter.

SELF-TEST QUESTIONS

- **Self-test questions**. At the end of each chapter there is a series of self-test questions. The purpose of these is to help you revise some of the key elements of the chapter. All the answers to these questions can be found in the text.

EXAM-TYPE QUESTIONS

- **End of chapter questions**. At the end of each chapter we include examination-type questions. These will give you a very good idea of the sort of thing the examiner will ask and will test your understanding of what has been covered.

Syllabus and study guide

Objectives of the study guide

This study guide is designed to help you plan your studies and to provide a more detailed interpretation of the syllabus for Paper 3.6 *Advanced Corporate Reporting*. It contains both the syllabus and the study guide, which you can follow when preparing for the examination.

The syllabus outlines the content of the paper. The study guide takes the syllabus content and expands it into study sessions of similar length. These sessions indicate what the examiner expects of candidates for each part of the syllabus, and therefore gives you guidance in the skills you are expected to demonstrate in the examinations.

Syllabus content

1 THE UK REGULATORY FRAMEWORK

a   Financial Reporting Standards, Financial Reporting Exposure Drafts, Discussion Papers, Urgent Issues Task Force pronouncements including accounting for equity and liabilities, assets, provisions and contingencies, segments, related parties, financial instruments, taxes, leases, retirement benefits.

b   The content of the UK regulatory framework in a given range of practical situations.

c   The problems with the current and proposed changes to the UK regulatory framework including measurement and recognition issues.

d   The impact of current and proposed regulations on the financial statements of the entity.

e   The effect of business decisions and proposed changes in accounting practice by the entity on the financial statements.

f   The legitimacy of current accounting practice and its relevance to users of corporate financial statements.

2 PREPARATION OF THE FINANCIAL STATEMENTS OF COMPLEX BUSINESS ENTITIES

a   The financial statements of complex groups including vertical and mixed groups.

b   Group cash flow statements.

c   Accounting for group reorganisations and restructuring including demergers, take-overs and group schemes.

d   Accounting for foreign currency transactions and entities.

3 PREPARATION OF REPORTS FOR EXTERNAL AND INTERNAL USERS

a   Appraisal of financial and related information, the purchase of a business entity, the valuation of shares and the reorganisation of an entity.

b   Appraisal of the impact of changes in accounting policies and the regulatory framework on shareholder value.

c   Appraisal of the business performance of the entity including quantitative and qualitative measures of performance and the potential for corporate failure.

d   The assessment of the impact of price level changes and available methods of valuation on business decisions and performance.

e   The effectiveness of corporate governance within an entity.

4 CURRENT ISSUES AND DEVELOPMENTS

a   The accounting impact of environmental, cultural and social factors on the entity.

b   The impact of the content of financial statements on users including changes in design and content of interim and year-end financial statements and alternate ways of communicating results to users.

c   Proposed changes in the structure of national and international regulation and the impact on global harmonisation and standardisation.

d   The applicability of the regulatory framework to small- and medium-sized entities.

e   Current developments in corporate reporting.

5 ETHICAL CONSIDERATIONS

a   Ethics and business conduct.

Excluded topics

The syllabus content outlines the areas for assessment. No areas of knowledge are specifically excluded from the syllabus.

Key areas of the syllabus

Key topic areas are as follows:

- group accounting, group cash flow statements and foreign currency translation

- discussion papers, financial reporting exposure drafts and recent financial reporting standards

- problems with current accounting standards and the impact of changes therein on the entity

- preparation of reports in an advisory capacity including share valuation, and purchase of a business

- changes in organisational structure, reconstructions, demergers, etc

- the potential for business failure and problems with the business including financial analysis, corporate failure prediction and measurement of corporate performance

- environmental and social accounting and the impact of culture

- corporate governance and the dissemination of information to users

- the move to the use of International Accounting Standards

- current issues.

The main thrust of the syllabus will be the preparation of a set of group financial statements, advising clients on current standards and changes therein, reporting business performance including environmental and social reporting and corporate governance, and appraising current issues. It is important to realise that other areas of the syllabus will be also examined.

Additional information

Candidates need to be aware that questions involving knowledge of new examinable regulations will not be set until at least six months after the last day of the month in which the regulation was issued.

The study guide provides more detailed guidance on the syllabus. Examinable documents are listed in the 'Exam Notes' section of the *Student Accountant*.

Study guide

Chapter where covered

1 OVERVIEW OF UK GAAP　　　1

- Discuss the nature of UK GAAP

- Describe the applicability of UK GAAP for small companies

- Outline the Financial Reporting Standard for Smaller Entities (FRSSE)

- Discuss the solutions to differential financial reporting

- Discuss the implications of the first-time application of International Financial Reporting standards to financial statements drawn up under UK GAAP

Chapter where covered

2 CORPORATE GOVERNANCE　　　2

- Discuss the role and need for the reform of corporate governance

- Describe the nature of reporting under the combined code

- Discuss the need for corporate governance in small companies

- Describe the nature and content of the Operating and Financial Review (OFR)

3 GROUP FINANCIAL STATEMENTS I　　3, 4

- Review the basic principles of acquisition accounting

- Explain and illustrate the principles of measurement relating to the fair value of the consideration and the net assets acquired

- Discuss the nature of step by step acquisitions

- Prepare consolidated financial statements where control is established by a step by step acquisition

- Account for complex group structures

4 GROUP FINANCIAL STATEMENTS II　　　4

- Explain and illustrate the basic principles relating to the disposal of group companies

- Discuss and illustrate the treatment of goodwill on disposal

- Apply the principles of accounting for partial and deemed disposals

5 MERGERS　　　5

- Explain the basic principles and philosophy of merger accounting

- Account for equity eliminations, expenses and dividends of the subsidiary

- Prepare consolidated financial statements utilising merger accounting techniques

- Determine whether merger accounting could be used in specific circumstances and the relative merits of different methods of accounting for business combinations

6 GROUP RE-ORGANISATIONS AND RESTRUCTURING　　　6

- Discuss the creation of a new holding company

- Explain changes in the ownership of companies within a group

- Discuss the nature of demergers and divisionalisation

**Chapter where
covered**

- Discuss the different approaches used to disclose segmental information
- Discuss the importance of segmental information to users of financial statements

17 ACCOUNTING FOR RETIREMENT BENEFITS 16

- Describe the nature of defined contribution, multi-employers and defined benefits schemes
- Explain the recognition of defined benefit schemes under current proposals
- Discuss the measurement of defined benefit schemes under current proposals
- Account for defined benefit schemes including the amounts shown in the balance sheet, statement of total recognised gains and losses, profit and loss account and notes to the account
- Discuss perceived problems with current proposals on accounting for retirement benefits

18 TAXATION 17

- Discuss the different approaches to accounting for deferred taxation
- Discuss the recognition of deferred taxation in the balance sheet and performance statements under current proposals including revaluations, unremitted earnings of group companies and deferred tax assets
- Explain the nature of the measurement of deferred taxation under current proposals including tax rates and discounting
- Calculate deferred tax amounts in financial statements under current proposals

19 REPORTING FINANCIAL PERFORMANCE AND EARNINGS PER SHARE 18

- Discuss proposed changes to reporting financial performance
- Explain the rationale behind the proposed changes in reporting financial performance
- Calculate diluted earnings per share by reference to dilutive potential ordinary shares, loss per share and particular types of dilutive instruments including partly paid shares, employee incentive schemes and contingently issuable shares

20 POST BALANCE SHEET EVENTS, PROVISIONS AND CONTINGENCIES 19

- Discuss the problems of accounting for post balance sheet events including reclassification, window dressing etc

**Chapter where
covered**

- Discuss the issues relating to recognition and measurement of provisions including 'best estimates', discounting, future events
- Explain the use of restructuring provisions and other practical uses of provisioning
- Discuss the problems with current standards on provisions and contingencies including definitional and discounting problems

21 RELATED PARTIES AND SHARE-BASED PAYMENT 20

- Discuss the related party issue
- Identify related parties (including deemed and presumed) and the disclosure of related party transactions
- Discuss the effectiveness of current regulations on disclosure of related party transactions
- Describe the current proposals for the recognition and measurement of share-based payment
- Show the impact of the proposals on the performance statements of the entity

22 PREPARE REPORTS I 21

- Calculate and appraise a range of acceptable values for shares in an unquoted company
- Advise a client on the purchase of a business entity
- Analyse the impact of accounting policy changes on the value and performance of an entity

23 PREPARATION OF REPORTS II 22

- Discuss the financial and non-financial measures of performance
- Describe the procedures in designing an accounting based performance measurement system
- Appraise the different performance measures including return on investment, residual income and economic value added
- Compare target levels of performance with actual performance

24 PREPARATION OF REPORTS III 22, 23

- Discuss alternative definitions of capital employed and measurement bases for assets
- Discuss the impact of price level changes on business performance
- Appraise the alternative methods of accounting for price level changes
- Evaluate the potential for corporate failure

Examinable documents

Prior to each sitting of the examination, the ACCA issues Exam Notes setting out which official documents are examinable.

The documents examinable for Paper 3.6 (UK) are set out below. We recommend that students read the *Student Accountant* to keep up-to-date. Documents denoted by an asterisk (*) are also examinable in Paper 2.5.

Statements of Standard Accounting Practice (SSAPs)

No	Title	Issue date
	* Foreword to Accounting Standards	Jun 1993
4*	Accounting for government grants (revised)	July 1990
5*	Accounting for value added tax	Jan 1974
9*	Stocks and long-term contracts (revised)	Sept 1988
13*	Accounting for research and development (revised)	Jan 1989
17*	Accounting for post balance sheet events	Sept 1980
19*	Accounting for investment properties	July 1981
	Amendment to SSAP 19	July 1994
20	Foreign currency translation (including aspects on consolidated financial statements)	April 1983
21*	Accounting for leases and hire purchase contracts (amended March 1997)	July 1984
25*	Segmental reporting	July 1990

Financial Reporting Standards (FRSs)

No	Title	Issue date
FRS 1*	Cash flow statements (**including** group cash flow statements) (revised)	Oct 1996
FRS 2*	Accounting for subsidiary undertakings	July 1992
FRS 3*	Reporting financial performance (**including** group aspects)	Oct 1992
FRS 4*	Capital instruments	Dec 1993
FRS 5*	Reporting the substance of transactions	April 1994
FRS 6*	Acquisitions and mergers	Sept 1994
FRS 7*	Fair values in acquisition accounting	Sept 1994
FRS 8*	Related party disclosures	Oct 1995
FRS 9*	Associates and joint ventures	Nov 1997
FRS 10*	Goodwill and intangible assets	Dec 1997
FRS 11*	Impairment of fixed assets and goodwill	July 1998
FRS 12*	Provisions, contingent liabilities and contingent assets	Sept 1998
FRS 13	Derivatives and other Financial instruments: Disclosures	Sept 1998
FRS 14*	Earnings per share	Oct 1998
FRS 15*	Tangible fixed assets	Feb 1999
FRS 16*	Current tax	Dec 1999
FRS 17	Retirement benefits	Dec 2000
FRS 18*	Accounting policies	Dec 2000
FRS 19*	Deferred tax	Dec 2000
FRS 20	Share-based payment	April 2004

Other Statements

Title	Issue date
*Operating and Financial Review	July 1993
*Statement of Principles for Financial Reporting	Dec 1999
Interim reports	Sept 1997
Financial Reporting Standard for smaller entities (FRSSE)	Dec 2001

Urgent Issues Task Force (UITF) Abstracts

Students sitting Paper 3.6 are expected to be aware of the issues/reasons which have led to the publication of a UITF abstract indicated as examinable in the list below, and their principal requirements.

No	Title	Issue date
	Foreword to UITF Abstracts	Feb 1994
UITF Abstract 4*	Presentation of long-term debtors in current assets	July 1992
UITF Abstract 5*	Transfers from current assets to fixed assets	July 1992
UITF Abstract 9	Accounting for operations in hyper-inflationary economies	June 1993
UITF Abstract 11	Capital instruments: issuer call options	Sept 1994
UITF Abstract 13	Accounting for ESOP Trusts (superseded by Abstract 38)	June 1995
UITF Abstract 15*	Disclosure of substantial acquisitions (revised)	Feb 1999
UITF Abstract 19	Tax on gains and losses on foreign currency borrowings that hedge an investment in a foreign enterprise	Feb 1998
UITF Abstract 21	Accounting issues arising from the proposed introduction of the Euro	Mar 1998
UITF Abstract 21	Appendix	Aug 1998
UITF Abstract 23	Application of the transitional rules in FRS 15	May 2000

No	Title	Issue date
UITF Abstract 24	Accounting for start-up costs	June 2000
UITF Abstract 25	National Insurance contributions on share option gains	July 2000
UITF Abstract 27	Revisions to estimates of the useful economic life of goodwill and intangible assets	Dec 2000
UITF Abstract 28	Operating lease incentives	Feb 2001
UITF Abstract 29	Website development costs	Feb 2001
UITF Abstract 30	Date of award to employees of shares or rights to shares (withdrawn by FRS 20)	Mar 2001
UITF Abstract 31	Exchanges of businesses or other non-monetary assets for an interest in a subsidiary, joint venture or associate	Oct 2001
UITF Abstract 32	Employee benefit trusts and other intermediate payment arrangements	Dec 2001
UITF Abstract 33	Obligations in capital instruments	Feb 2002
UITF Abstract 34	Pre-contract costs	May 2002
UITF Abstract 35	Death in service and incapacity benefits	May 2002
UITF Abstract 36	Contracts for sales of capacity	Mar 2003
UITF Abstract 37*	Purchases and sales of own shares	Oct 2003
UITF Abstract 38	Accounting for ESOP Trusts	Dec 2003

Financial Reporting Exposure Drafts (FREDs), Discussion Papers, Financial Reporting Review Panel (FRRP) Pronouncements and Statements

Students sitting Paper 3.6 are expected to be aware of the issues/reasons which have led to the publication of a DP or FRED, indicated as examinable in the list below, and to appreciate the main thrust of these documents.

Financial Reporting Exposure Drafts (FREDs)

No	Title	Issue date
FRED 22	Review of FRS 3 'Reporting financial performance'	Dec 2000
FRED 23	Financial instruments: hedge accounting	May 2002
FRED 31	Share-based payment (now FRS 20)	Nov 2002
FRED 32	Disposal of non-current assets and presentation of discontinued operations	July 2003

FREDs 24 to 30 and IASB Proposals to amend certain International Accounting Standards will be examined on the basis of the effect of the main changes proposed to existing UK requirements.

FRED 24	The effects of changes in foreign exchange rates. Financial reporting in hyperinflationary economies	May 2002
FRED 25	Related party disclosures	May 2002
FRED 26	Earnings per share	May 2002
FRED 27	Events after the balance sheet date	May 2002
FRED 29	Property, plant and equipment; borrowing costs	May 2002
FRED 30	Financial instruments: disclosure and presentation, recognition and measurement	May 2002
IASB Proposals to amend certain International Accounting Standards (consultation paper)		May 2002
IASB Proposals on business combinations, impairment and intangible assets (now IFRS 3)		Dec 2002

Discussion Papers and other documents

Title	Issue date
Year-end Financial Reports: Improving Communication	Feb 2000
The Combined Code on Corporate Governance	July 2003
Revenue recognition (now Application Note G to FRS 5)	July 2001
Statement of Principles: Interpretation for Public Benefit Entities	May 2003
IFRS 1* First-time Adoption of International Financial Reporting Standards	June 2003
A 'One-stop Shop' FRSSE	Mar 2004
UK Accounting Standards: A Strategy for Convergence	Mar 2004

FRRP Pronouncement

Students sitting Paper 3.6 need to understand the role of the FRRP which is to examine companies' accounts to determine whether, in its opinion, the accounts should be revised. The FRRP has reviewed the accounts of a number of companies and students should be aware of the comments issued by the FRRP.

The examination

Format of the examination

	Number of marks
Section A: One compulsory question	25
Section B: Choice of 3 from 4 questions (25 marks each)	75
	100

Total time allowed: 3 hours

Section A will normally comprise one compulsory question on group financial statements including group cash flows and foreign currency translation. The questions in Section B will involve advising, discussing and reporting on issues and topics in corporate financial reporting.

Examination tips: paper-based exam

- Spend the first few minutes of the examination **reading the exam paper**.

- Where you have a **choice of questions**, decide which ones you will do.

- **Divide the time** you spend on questions in proportion to the marks on offer. One suggestion is to allocate 1½ minutes to each mark available, so a 10-mark question should be completed in 15 minutes.

- Unless you know exactly how to answer the question, spend some time **planning** your answer. Stick to the question and **tailor your answer** to what you are asked.

- **Fully explain** all your points but be **concise**. Set out all workings **clearly and neatly**, and state briefly what you are doing. Don't write out the question.

- If you do not understand what a question is asking, **state your assumptions**. Even if you do not answer precisely in the way the examiner hoped, you should be given some credit, if your assumptions are reasonable.

- If you **get completely stuck** with a question, leave space in your answer book and **return to it later.**

- Towards the end of the examination spend the last **five minutes** reading through your answers and **making any additions or corrections**.

- Before you finish, you must fill in the required information on the front of your answer booklet.

Answering the questions

- **Essay questions**: Make a quick plan in your answer book and under each main point list all the relevant facts you can think of. Then write out your answer developing each point fully. Your essay should have a clear structure; it should contain a brief introduction, a main section and a conclusion. Be concise. It is better to write a little about a lot of different points than a great deal about one or two points.

- **Computations**: It is essential to include all your workings in your answers. Many computational questions require the use of a standard format: company profit and loss account, balance sheet and cash flow statement for example. Be sure you know these formats thoroughly before the examination and use the layouts that you see in the answers given in this book and in model answers.

  If you are asked to comment or make recommendations on a computation, you must do so. There are important marks to be gained here. Even if your computation contains mistakes, you may still gain marks if your reasoning is correct.

- **Reports, memos and other documents**: Some questions ask you to present your answer in the form of a report or a memorandum or other document. Use the correct format – there could be easy marks to gain here.

Study skills and revision guidance

This section aims to give guidance on how to study for your ACCA exams and to give ideas on how to improve your existing study techniques.

Preparing to study

Set your objectives

Before starting to study decide what you want to achieve – the type of pass you wish to obtain. This will decide the level of commitment and time you need to dedicate to your studies.

Devise a study plan

- Determine which times of the week you will study.

- Split these times into sessions of at least one hour for study of new material. Any shorter periods could be used for revision or practice.

- Put the times you plan to study onto a study plan for the weeks from now until the exam and set yourself targets for each period of study – in your sessions make sure you cover the course, course assignments and revision.

- If you are studying for more than one paper at a time, try to vary your subjects; this can help you to keep interested and see subjects as part of wider knowledge.

- When working through your course, compare your progress with your plan and, if necessary, re-plan your work (perhaps including extra sessions) or, if you are ahead, do some extra revision/practice questions.

Effective studying

Active reading

You are not expected to learn the text by rote, rather, you must understand what you are reading and be able to use it to pass the exam and develop good practice. A good technique to use is SQ3Rs – Survey, Question, Read, Recall, Review:

1 **Survey** the chapter – look at the headings and read the introduction, summary and objectives, so as to get an overview of what the chapter deals with.

2 **Question** – whilst undertaking the survey, ask yourself the questions that you hope the chapter will answer for you.

3 **Read** through the chapter thoroughly, answering the questions and making sure you can meet the objectives. Attempt the exercises and activities in the text, and work through all the examples.

4 **Recall** – at the end of each section and at the end of the chapter, try to recall the main ideas of the section/chapter without referring to the text. This is best done after a short break of a couple of minutes after the reading stage.

5 **Review** – check that your recall notes are correct.

You may also find it helpful to reread the chapter and try to see the topic(s) it deals with as a whole.

Note-taking

Taking notes is a useful way of learning, but do not simply copy out the text. The notes must:

- be in your own words
- be concise
- cover the key points
- be well-organised
- be modified as you study further chapters in this text or in related ones.

Trying to summarise a chapter without referring to the text can be a useful way of determining which areas you know and which you don't.

Three ways of taking notes:

- **Summarise the key points** of a chapter.

- **Make linear notes** – a list of headings, divided up with subheadings listing the key points. If you use linear notes, you can use different colours to highlight key points and keep topic areas together. Use plenty of space to make your notes easy to follow.

- **Try a diagrammatic form** – the most common of which is a mind-map. To make a mind-map, put the main heading in the centre of the paper and put a circle around it. Then draw short lines radiating from this to the main sub-headings, which again have circles around them. Then continue the process from the sub-headings to sub-sub-headings, advantages, disadvantages, etc.

Highlighting and underlining

You may find it useful to underline or highlight key points in your study text – but do be selective. You may also wish to make notes in the margins.

Revision

The best approach to revision is to revise the course as you work through it. Also try to leave four to six weeks before the exam for final revision. Make sure you cover the whole syllabus and pay special attention to those areas where your knowledge is weak. Here are some recommendations:

- **Read through the text and your notes again** and condense your notes into key phrases. It may help to put key revision points onto index cards to look at when you have a few minutes to spare.

- **Review any assignments** you have completed and look at where you lost marks – put more work into those areas where you were weak.

- **Practise exam standard questions** under timed conditions. If you are short of time, list the points that you would cover in your answer and then read the model answer, but do try and complete at least a few questions under exam conditions.

- Also **practise producing answer plans** and comparing them to the model answer.

- If you are stuck on a topic find somebody (a colleague or a tutor) to explain it to you.

- **Read good newspapers and professional journals**, especially ACCA's *Student Accountant* – this can give you an advantage in the exam.

- Ensure you **know the structure of the exam** – how many questions and of what type you will be expected to answer. During your revision attempt all the different styles of questions you may be asked.

Chapter 1

OVERVIEW OF UK GAAP

This chapter begins by discussing the nature of UK GAAP. Some of this material should be familiar from your earlier studies.

Much of the detail of this chapter is concerned with the ASB's Statement of Principles. This should also be familiar from your earlier studies and should help you to understand the reasons why the ASB has required or proposed particular accounting treatments. You will probably find it useful to return to this material at intervals as you study accounting standards and exposure drafts later in the text.

Lastly, the chapter considers reporting requirements for small companies.

Objectives

When you have studied this chapter you should be able to:

- understand and discuss the nature of UK GAAP

- describe the applicability of UK GAAP for small companies

- outline the reporting exemptions available to small companies, including the Financial Reporting Standard for Smaller Entities (FRSSE)

- discuss the solutions to differential financial reporting.

1   The nature of UK GAAP

1.1   The Companies Act and UK GAAP

GAAP stands for 'generally accepted accounting principles' or 'generally accepted accounting practice'.

Unlike US GAAP (generally accepted accounting principles in the United States) UK GAAP has no official definition.

The Companies Act 1985 (CA85) refers to GAAP in two instances.

- In order for a business combination to be treated as a merger, the accounting method adopted must accord with 'generally accepted accounting principles or practice'.

- Realised profits and losses are defined as 'such profits or losses of the company as fall to be treated as realised in accordance with principles generally accepted, at the time when the accounts are prepared with respect to the determination for accounting purposes of realised profits or losses'.

However, GAAP is not defined in the Act.

1.2   The meaning of GAAP

Most people would accept that the requirements of the Companies Acts and accounting standards represent GAAP. However, some areas of financial accounting and reporting are not covered by accounting standards. For example, there is still no standard that deals with the general principles of share-based payment.

A wider definition of GAAP is contained in a US Auditing Standard. Although it refers to US GAAP it could apply equally to UK GAAP.

The definition reproduced in the margin implies two things.

* UK GAAP extends beyond the requirements of company law and accounting standards to include all generally acceptable accounting treatments, whether or not they are set out in statute, accounting standards or any other applicable regulations.

* GAAP is a dynamic concept. It evolves over time, in response to changing business practices and new economic developments.

It has been suggested that UK GAAP includes any accounting practice which is regarded as legitimate by the accounting profession. Whether a particular accounting practice is legitimate depends on the circumstances in which it has been applied.

2   Sources of UK GAAP

2.1   Introduction

There are several actual and potential sources of UK GAAP. The main ones are as follows.

* company law
* UK accounting standards
* EC directives
* Stock Exchange requirements
* International Accounting Standards (IASs) and International Financial Reporting Standards (IFRSs)
* the ASB's Statement of Principles for Financial Reporting
* other generally accepted concepts and principles (e.g. substance over form, objectivity, the entity concept).

Limited company financial statements must comply with the requirements of the Companies Acts and all applicable accounting standards. Listed company financial statements must also comply with Stock Exchange requirements. Other sources of GAAP may be relevant where a particular transaction is not covered by company law or by an accounting standard.

2.2   Company law

The regulatory framework of accounting is affected by company law in a number of areas.

* Financial statements of companies must show a 'true and fair view'.

* Accounting standards issued by the ASB are given legal authority as recognised accounting standards.

* Prescribed formats for the profit and loss account and balance sheet are required.

* Detailed disclosures of information are required.

* A company is limited in the amounts of profits it can distribute to its shareholders.

* Various provisions have to be satisfied if a company wishes to increase or reduce its share capital.

Arguably the most important way in which company legislation influences financial reporting is the requirement for accounts to show a 'true and fair view'. This requirement overrides all other regulatory requirements, including those of accounting standards. There is no absolute definition of 'true and fair', which is a legal concept. In extreme cases, its meaning may be decided by the courts. It is now widely accepted that the meaning of 'true and fair' evolves over time and in accordance with changes in generally accepted accounting practice.

2.3 UK accounting standards

Accounting standards are authoritative statements of how particular types of transactions and other events should be reflected in the financial statements. Compliance with accounting standards is normally necessary for financial statements to give a true and fair view.

The current standard setting regime was introduced in 1990 and is as follows.

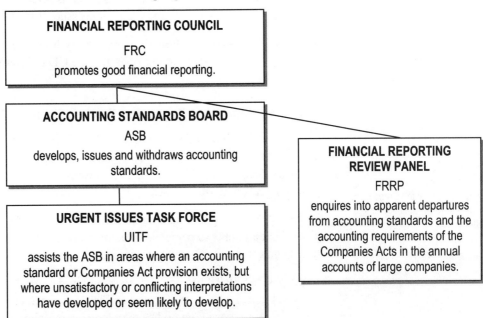

The roles of the main bodies are examined in more detail below.

2.4 The Accounting Standards Board (ASB)

The aims of the Accounting Standards Board (ASB) are to establish and improve standards of financial accounting and reporting for the benefit of users, preparers, and auditors of financial information.

The ASB works to achieve its aims by:

- developing principles to guide it in establishing standards and to provide a framework within which others can exercise judgement in resolving accounting issues (see the Statement of Principles)

- issuing new accounting standards, or amending existing ones, in response to evolving business practices, new economic developments and deficiencies being identified in current practice (see SSAPs and FRSs)

- addressing urgent issues promptly (see the work of the UITF).

The current standard setting process was introduced at a time when public confidence in the accounting profession was low and UK financial reporting lacked credibility. In its first few years of existence the ASB concentrated on preventing abuses and reducing the scope for 'creative accounting'.

The need for international harmonisation of accounting standards has now become the principal influence on the ASB's work and this is discussed in a later chapter.

2.5   The Financial Reporting Council (FRC)

The Financial Reporting Council (FRC) guides the standard setting process and ensures that the ASB's work is properly funded. It is ultimately responsible for the enforcement of standards, and achieves this enforcement through the work of the Review Panel.

The FRC is the 'political' front to the bodies involved in the standard setting process and produces an annual review which summarises recent events and likely action by the ASB, the Review Panel and the Urgent Issues Task Force (UITF).

The FRC's main contribution to the regulatory framework has been the support and authority that it has given to the ASB and the UITF through the Financial Reporting Review Panel.

2.6   The Financial Reporting Review Panel (FRRP)

The Financial Reporting Review Panel (FRRP) examines apparent departures from the accounting requirements of the Companies Acts and relevant accounting standards. It normally deals with public and large private companies; the Department of Trade and Industry deals with other cases.

The FRRP has the power to seek a court order to remedy defective accounts. Wherever possible, it attempts to persuade directors to revise defective accounts voluntarily and to date no court orders have been sought.

In the past the FRRP has not actively monitored company accounts for possible defects, but has investigated matters which have been brought to its attention. Individuals and corporate bodies may lodge complaints with the FRRP, but approximately 60% of investigations have resulted from a qualified audit report or from press comment. In the future the FRRP will try to take a more proactive approach, itself seeking out matters to be investigated.

The FRRP issues reports on the accounts of companies that it has investigated and quite early in its life there were a number of highly publicised cases (notably concerning Trafalgar House plc). More recently there have been fewer cases, but companies are still occasionally asked to revise their accounts.

Referrals to the FRRP occur for a number of reasons. Normally they arise from breach of an accounting standard, but there have been a few instances where companies have been asked to correct errors in the cash flow statement. Accounts can be referred where it is believed that they do not give a true and fair view, even if no regulations have been breached. Many cases involve inadequate disclosure, rather than actual adjustments. One commentator has pointed out that many of the cases concern the implementation of new accounting standards or changes in accounting policy.

One possible weakness of the FRRP is that it can only take action where there has been an apparent breach of legislation or of an accounting standard. It cannot deal with cases of creative accounting as such.

2.7   Consensus pronouncements of the UITF

The UITF issues consensus pronouncements (called Abstracts) covering areas where an accounting standard or a Companies Act provision exists, but where unsatisfactory or conflicting interpretations have developed or seem likely to develop.

Consensus pronouncements are applicable to financial statements of a reporting entity that are intended to give a true and fair view. They need not be applied to immaterial items.

Consensus pronouncements should be considered to be part of the corpus of practices forming the basis for determining what constitutes a true and fair view (i.e. they form part of UK GAAP). They may be taken into consideration by the Financial Reporting Review Panel in deciding whether financial statements call for review.

2.8   EC Directives

It is the aim of the European Union (EU) that its member states will eventually become parts of a single economic entity. To achieve this goal, businesses must operate under the same legal and accounting requirements.

- The **Fourth Directive** resulted in accounts formats and detailed disclosure requirements being contained in Sch 4 CA85.

- The **Seventh Directive** on group accounts was passed by the EU council in June 1983. The provisions are contained in CA89.

Because the EC Directives have been enacted in UK law, all UK limited companies must comply with them. Other EU members have passed similar legislation.

2.9   Stock Exchange requirements

The London Stock Exchange is a market place for trading in the securities of companies. The purpose of the Listing Rules publication is to set out and explain the requirements which apply to applicants for 'listing' (i.e. admission to the Official List of the Stock Exchange), the manner in which any proposed marketing of securities is to be conducted and the continuing obligations of issuers.

A most important condition for listing is acceptance of the continuing obligations which will apply following admission. These obligations form the basis of the relationship between an issuer and the Stock Exchange, governing the disclosure of information necessary to protect investors and maintain an orderly market.

The Stock Exchange has the power to withdraw a company's listing if it fails to comply with the Listing Rules. It is therefore in a position to have considerable influence on the financial statements of listed companies.

The Stock Exchange requirements in some areas are more extensive than the Companies Acts requirements. In addition, the Stock Exchange has responded to the recent public concerns about corporate governance and ethical standards in business by requiring listed companies to state whether they have complied with the Combined Code of Best Practice on corporate governance matters.

2.10   International Accounting Standards (IASs)

International Accounting Standards (IASs) were issued by the International Accounting Standards Committee (IASC). This has now been replaced by the International Accounting Standards Board (IASB) which now issues International Financial Reporting Standards (IFRSs).

By 2005, all listed EU companies must prepare their consolidated financial statements in accordance with international accounting standards. To avoid differences in practice between listed and unlisted companies, the ASB is incorporating all relevant IASs and IFRSs into UK FRSs. This will require revision to the Companies Act as well. Therefore, by 2005, the IASB will be the most important influence on UK GAAP.

3   The Statement of Principles for Financial Reporting

3.1   The purpose of the Statement

The Statement of Principles is an attempt to formulate a conceptual framework within which accounting standards can be issued.

In detail the intended role of the Statement is:

- to assist the ASB in the development of future accounting standards and in its review of existing accounting standards

- to assist the ASB by providing a basis for reducing the number of alternative accounting treatments permitted by law and accounting standards

- to assist preparers of financial statements in applying accounting standards and in dealing with topics that do not form the subject of an accounting standard

- to assist auditors in forming an opinion on whether financial statements conform with accounting standards

- to assist users of financial statements in interpreting the information contained in financial statements prepared in conformity with accounting standards

- to provide those who are interested in the work of the ASB with information about its approach to the formulation of accounting standards.

Almost all commentators recognise the need for a conceptual framework. However, several aspects of the Statement have been controversial. When the first draft of the Statement was issued in 1995, it had such a hostile reception that it was revised and a second Exposure Draft issued. The final version of the Statement was issued in December 1999.

The ASB has set itself five principal objectives:

- exclude from the balance sheet items that are neither assets nor liabilities

- make 'off balance sheet' assets and liabilities more visible by putting them on the balance sheet wherever possible

- ensure that all gains and losses are reported prominently so that nothing can be overlooked

- reverse the 'bottom line' mentality by focusing performance reporting on the components of income

- use up-to-date measures, where appropriate, if other measures such as historical cost are ineffective.

The ASB believes that implementing principles based on these objectives will result in evolutionary change in financial reporting rather than revolutionary change.

3.2   Status and scope of the Statement

The Statement of Principles is not an accounting standard nor does it have a status that is equivalent to an accounting standard.

It is intended to be relevant to the financial statements of profit-oriented entities, including public sector profit-oriented entities, regardless of their size. The Statement is also relevant to not-for-profit entities, but some of the principles would need to be re-expressed and others would need changes of emphasis before they could be applied to that sector (see below).

3.3   True and fair

The Introduction to the Statement of Principles states that it is not intended to be a definition or an explanation of the meaning of true and fair. Detailed legal requirements, accounting standards and other evidence of generally accepted accounting practice normally determine the content of financial statements intended to give a true and fair view.

However, the Introduction acknowledges that the concept of a true and fair view lies at the heart of financial reporting in the UK. Although the Statement of Principles does not discuss the true and fair view, that does not mean that the concept has been abandoned.

3.4   Contents of the Statement of Principles

The Statement of Principles is made up of eight chapters which are discussed in the following sections:

- Chapter 1   The objective of financial statements

- Chapter 2   The reporting entity

- Chapter 3   The qualitative characteristics of financial information

- Chapter 4   The elements of financial statements

- Chapter 5   Recognition in financial statements

- Chapter 6   Measurement in financial statements

- Chapter 7   Presentation of financial information

- Chapter 8   Accounting for interests in other entities

3.5   Applicability to public benefit entities

DEFINITION

Public benefit entities are reporting entities whose primary objective is to provide goods or services for the general public or social benefit.

It was noted above that the Statement of Principles is primarily intended to be relevant to profit-oriented entities in the private and public sectors. In May 2003 the ASB issued a discussion paper: *Statement of Principles for Financial Reporting: Proposed Interpretation for Public Benefit Entities* seeking comments on their view that a common set of principles should underlie the financial reporting by all entities, whether profit-seeking or not-for-profit. The contents of the original Statement of Principles is not amended, but guidance is offered in a new document on how these principles can be extended and interpreted to apply to public benefit entities (including charities and other not-for-profit bodies). The ASB therefore intends to publish in due course a separate Statement of Principles applicable to public benefit entities, while remaining as loyal as possible to the wording in the original statement.

4   The objective of financial statements

4.1   Users of financial statements and their needs

The Statement of Principles identifies the objective of financial statements as providing information about the reporting entity's financial performance and financial position that is useful to a wide range of users for assessing the stewardship of the entity's management and for making economic decisions.

Investors (providers of risk capital) are interested in information that:

- helps them to assess how effectively management has fulfilled its stewardship role (i.e. the safekeeping of the entity's resources and their proper, efficient and profitable use)

- is useful in taking decisions about their investment or potential investment in the entity.

They are, as a result, concerned with the risk inherent in, and return provided by, their investments and need information on the entity's financial performance and financial position that helps them to assess its cash generation abilities and its financial adaptability.

Other users of financial statements, and their information needs, include the following.

- **Lenders** are interested in information that enables them to determine whether their loans will be repaid, and the interest attaching to them paid, when due. Potential lenders are interested in information that helps them to decide whether to lend to the entity and on what terms.

- **Suppliers and other trade creditors** are interested in information that enables them to decide whether to sell to the entity and to assess the likelihood that amounts owing to them will be paid when due.

- **Employees** are interested in information about the stability and profitability of their employers. They are also interested in information that enables them to assess the ability of their employer to provide remuneration, employment opportunities and retirement benefits.

- **Customers** are interested in information about the entity's continued existence. This is especially so when they are dependent on the entity (e.g. if product warranties are involved or if specialised replacement parts may be needed).

- **Governments and their agencies** are interested in the allocation of resources and, therefore, the activities of entities. They also require information in order to regulate the activities of entities, assess taxation and provide a basis for national statistics.

- **The public** may be interested in information about the trends and recent developments in the prosperity of the entity and the range of its activities (for example, an entity may make a substantial contribution to a local economy by providing employment and using local suppliers).

4.2   Limitations of financial statements

The inherent limitations of financial statements are as follows.

- They involve a substantial degree of classification and aggregation and the allocation of the effects of continuous operations to discrete reporting periods.

- They focus on the financial effects of transactions and other events and do not focus to any significant extent on their non-financial effects or on non-financial information in general.

- They provide information that is largely historical. They do not reflect future events or transactions, nor do they anticipate the impact of changes in the economic or potential environment.

4.3   Information required by investors

Investors (and other users of the financial statements) require information that focuses on four key areas.

- The **financial performance** of an entity comprises the return it obtains on the resources it controls, the components of that return and the characteristics of those components.

- The **financial position** of an entity encompasses:

    (a)   the economic resources it controls
    (b)   its financial structure
    (c)   its liquidity and solvency
    (d)   its risk profile and risk management approach
    (e)   its capacity to adapt to changes in the environment in which it operates.

- Information about the ways in which an entity **generates and uses cash** in its operations, its investment activities and its financing activities provides an additional perspective on its financial performance – one that is largely free from allocation and valuation issues.

- An entity's **financial adaptability** is its ability to take effective action to alter the amount and timing of its cash flows so that it can respond to unexpected needs or opportunities.

4.4   The reporting entity

An entity should prepare and publish financial statements if there is a legitimate demand for the information that its financial statements would provide and it is a cohesive economic unit.

The boundary of the reporting entity is determined by the scope of its control.

Control has two aspects:

- the ability to deploy the economic resources involved

- the ability to benefit (or to suffer) from their deployment.

To have control, an entity must have both these abilities.

FRS 2 *Accounting for subsidiary undertakings* uses the concept of the reporting entity described in this chapter.

4.5   Control

DEFINITION

Control is the ability of an undertaking to direct the financial and operating policies of another undertaking with a view to gaining economic benefits from its activities.

An entity will have control of a second entity if it has the ability to direct that entity's operating and financial policies with a view to gaining economic benefits from its activities. Control will be evidenced in a variety of ways depending on its basis (for example ownership or other rights) and the way in which it is exercised (interventionist or not). Control does not necessarily involve share ownership or voting rights.

5 The qualitative characteristics of financial information

The qualitative characteristics of financial information are the qualities that it has that make it useful to users.

The Statement of Principles identifies four characteristics:

- relevance
- reliability
- comparability
- understandability.

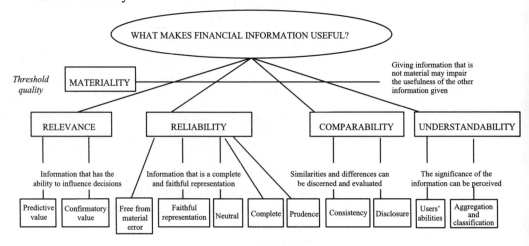

DEFINITION

Qualitative characteristics are the qualities that make the information provided in the financial statements useful to users for assessing the financial position, performance and financial adaptability of an enterprise.

5.1 Relevance

Information is **relevant** if it has the ability to influence the economic decisions of users and is provided in time to influence those decisions.

Information provided by the financial statements needs to be relevant. Where choices have to be made between mutually exclusive options, the option selected should be the one that results in the relevance of the information being maximised – in other words, the one that would be of most use in taking economic decisions.

Information that is relevant has predictive value or confirmatory value. It has predictive value if it enables users to evaluate or assess past, present or future events. It has confirmatory value if it helps users to confirm or correct their past evaluations and assessments.

DEFINITION

Information is **relevant** if it has the ability to influence the economic decisions of users and is provided in time to influence those decisions.

5.2 Reliability

Information provided by the financial statements must be reliable, i.e. it must give a complete and faithful representation of the true situation.

Faithful representation

If information is to represent faithfully the transactions and other events that it purports to represent, it is necessary that they are accounted for and presented in accordance with their substance and economic reality and not merely their legal form.

Neutrality

Information must be neutral, that is free from bias. Financial statements are not neutral if, by the selection or presentation of information, they influence the making of a decision or judgement in order to achieve a predetermined result or outcome.

DEFINITION

Information is **reliable** when:

- it can be depended upon by users to represent faithfully what it either purports to represent or could reasonably be expected to represent
- it is free from deliberate or systematic bias (i.e. it is neutral)
- it is free from material error
- it is complete within the bounds of materiality
- in conditions of uncertainty, a degree of caution (i.e. prudence) has been applied in exercising judgement and making the necessary estimates.

Completeness

The information must be complete and free from error within the bounds of materiality. A material error or an omission can cause the financial statements to be false or misleading and thus unreliable and deficient in terms of their relevance.

Prudence

Uncertainty surrounds many of the events and circumstances that are reported on in the financial statements and it is dealt with in those statements by disclosing the nature and extent of the uncertainty involved and by exercising prudence.

Prudence is the inclusion of a degree of caution in the exercise of the judgements needed in making the estimates required under conditions of uncertainty, such that gains and losses are not overstated and losses and liabilities are not understated. More confirmatory evidence is required about the existence of, and greater reliability of measurement for assets and gains than is required for liabilities and losses.

It is not necessary to exercise prudence where there is no uncertainty.

5.3 Comparability

DEFINITION

Information is **comparable** if it can be compared with similar information obtained elsewhere.

Users must be able to compare the financial statements of an entity over time to identify trends in its financial position and performance. Users must also be able to compare the financial statements of different entities to evaluate their relative financial position, performance and financial adaptability. Consistency and disclosure of accounting policies are therefore required.

Consistency

Consistency is not an end in itself nor should it be allowed to become an impediment to the introduction of improved accounting practices. Consistency can be useful in enhancing comparability between entities, but it should not be confused with a need for absolute uniformity.

Disclosure

Users need to be able to identify differences between:

(a)   the accounting policies adopted to account for like transactions and other events

(b)   the accounting policies adopted from period to period

(c)   the accounting policies adopted by different entities.

Therefore, disclosure of the accounting policies adopted, and any changes to them, enhances the usefulness of financial statements.

5.4 Understandability

DEFINITION

Information is **understandable** if users can perceive its significance.

Information needs to be understandable; users need to be able to perceive its significance.

Understandability depends on:

*   the way in which the effects of transactions and other events are characterised, aggregated and classified

*   the way in which information is presented

*   the capabilities of users.

It is assumed that users have a reasonable knowledge of business and economic activities and are willing to study the information provided with reasonable diligence.

5.5 Materiality

Information is material if its misstatement or omission might reasonably be expected to influence the economic decisions of users.

Materiality is a threshold quality that is demanded of all information given in the financial statements.

Information that is material needs to be given in the financial statements and information that is not material need not be given.

Whether information is material will depend upon the size and nature of the item in question judged in the particular circumstances of the case.

5.6 Constraints on the qualitative characteristics

Conflicts may arise between the key qualitative characteristics. In these circumstances a trade off needs to be found that still enables the objective of the financial statements to be met.

Relevance and reliability

Where there is a conflict, it is usually appropriate to use the information that is the most relevant of whichever information is available.

Conflicts may arise over timeliness. A delay in providing information can make it out of date and less relevant, but reporting on transactions and other events before all the uncertainties are resolved may make information less reliable. Financial information should not be provided until it is sufficiently reliable.

Neutrality and prudence

Neutrality involves freedom from bias. Prudence is potentially biased because it seeks to ensure that gains and assets are not overstated and losses or liabilities are not understated in conditions of uncertainty. It is necessary to find a balance that ensures that deliberate understatement of assets or gains and overstatement of liabilities or losses does not occur.

Understandability

Information that is relevant and reliable should not be excluded from the financial statements simply because it is too difficult for some users to understand.

5.7 The way that the Statement has influenced accounting standards

Many of the ideas in the first three chapters of the Statement have already influenced the development of accounting standards.

Here are some examples.

- Information may be relevant because it has predictive value. FRS 1 *Cash flow statements* and FRS 3 *Reporting financial performance* both increase the predictive value of financial information. FRS 3 requires reporting entities to analyse results between continuing operations, acquisitions and discontinued operations and to disclose details of unusual and infrequent items of income and expenditure.

- Information is reliable if it reports the substance of transactions rather than their strict legal form. FRS 5 *Reporting the substance of transactions* now requires all reporting entities to do this.

- One of the more controversial parts of the Statement of Principles has been its attitude to prudence. Some commentators express fears that the ASB's approach will require a radical re-appraisal of the way in which the prudence concept is applied. Time will show whether these fears are well founded.

6   Recognition in financial statements

6.1   The elements of financial statements

Seven elements of financial statements are identified, all of which are seen to be interrelated. In order for an item to be included in financial statements it must fall within one of the definitions of elements, and meet the recognition criteria. The definitions of assets and liabilities are the same as those used in FRS 5.

Assets

Assets are rights or other access to future economic benefits controlled by an entity as a result of past transactions or events.

- **Rights or other access**

  For example property is only an asset because of the rights (shared or sole) deriving from ownership or the other rights of occupation and use.

- **Future economic benefits**

  These are evidenced by the prospective receipt of cash. This could be cash itself, a debt receivable or any item which may be sold. Although, for example, a factory may not be sold (on a going concern basis) it houses the manufacture of goods. When these goods are sold the economic benefit resulting from the use of the factory is realised as cash.

- **Controlled by an entity**

  Control is the ability to obtain the economic benefits and to restrict the access of others (e.g. by a company being the sole user of its plant and machinery, or by selling surplus plant and machinery).

- **Past transactions or events**

  The transaction or event must be 'past' before an asset can arise.

Liabilities

Liabilities are obligations of an entity to transfer economic benefits as a result of past transactions or events.

- **Obligations**

  These may be legal or not. For example an entity may have no realistic alternative to refunding the price of goods that fail to meet the expectations of customers, even though there is no legal requirement to do so.

  Obligation implies that the outflow of resources is unavoidable. Costs to be incurred in the future do not represent liabilities as long as the entity can choose to avoid the expenditure. For example, decisions of the board of directors cannot, in themselves, create a liability, because the board of directors has the power to rescind its own decisions.

- **Transfer of economic benefits**

  This could be a transfer of cash, or other property, the provision of a service, or the refraining from activities which would otherwise be profitable.

DEFINITION

Assets are rights or other access to future economic benefits controlled by an entity as a result of past transactions or events.

DEFINITION

Liabilities are obligations of an entity to transfer economic benefits as a result of past transactions or events.

- **Past transactions or events**

  The obligation must have arisen from a *past* transaction or event.

Ownership interest

Ownership interest is the residual amount found by deducting all of the entity's liabilities from all of the entity's assets.

Owners invest in an entity in the hope of a return (for example, the payment of dividends). Unlike creditors, owners cannot insist that a transfer is made to them regardless of the circumstances. Their interest is in the assets of the entity after all the liabilities have been deducted.

Gains and losses

These are counted as two of the seven elements.

Gains are increases in ownership interest, not resulting from contributions from owners.

Losses are decreases in ownership interest, not resulting from distributions to owners.

Contributions from owners

Contributions from owners are increases in ownership interest resulting from transfers from owners in their capacity as owners.

Owners contribute to entities by transferring assets, performing services or accepting ownership interest in satisfaction of liabilities. Rights in the ownership interest are usually granted in return for a contribution from owners. For example, owners may provide cash (additional capital) to an entity in return for additional shares.

Distributions to owners

Distributions to owners are decreases in ownership interest resulting from transfers to owners in their capacity as owners.

Distributions to owners include the payment of dividends and the return of capital. For example, when a company purchases its own shares, this is reflected by reducing the amount of ownership interest.

6.2 The recognition process

Recognition involves depicting an item in words (with additional disclosure if necessary) and by a monetary amount within the financial statements.

The recognition process has the following stages:

(a) initial recognition, which is where an item is depicted in the primary financial statements for the first time (e.g. the purchase of an asset)

(b) subsequent re-measurement, which involves changing the amount at which an already recognised asset or liability is stated in the primary financial statements (e.g. revaluation)

(c) de-recognition, which is where an item that was until then recognised ceases to be recognised (e.g. the sale of an asset).

DEFINITION

Ownership interest is the residual amount found by deducting all of the entity's liabilities from all of the entity's assets.

DEFINITION

Gains are increases in ownership interest, not resulting from contributions from owners. **Losses** are decreases in ownership interest, not resulting from distributions to owners.

DEFINITION

Contributions from owners are increases in ownership interest resulting from transfers from owners in their capacity as owners.

DEFINITION

Distributions to owners are decreases in ownership interest resulting from transfers to owners in their capacity as owners.

6.3   Recognition and de-recognition

If a transaction or other event has created a new asset or liability or added to an existing asset or liability, that effect is recognised if:

(a) sufficient evidence exists that the new asset or liability has been created or that there has been an addition to an existing asset or liability, and

(b) the new asset or liability or the addition to the existing asset or liability can be measured at a monetary amount with sufficient reliability.

An asset or liability is wholly or partly de-recognised if:

(a) sufficient evidence exists that a transaction or other past event has eliminated all or part of a previously recognised asset or liability, or

(b) although an item continues to be an asset or liability, the criteria for recognition are no longer met.

6.4   Revenue recognition

The starting point for the recognition process is always the effect that the transaction or other event involved has had on the reporting entity's assets and liabilities. Assuming that no contribution from owners or transfer to owners is involved:

(a) if net assets increase, a gain is recognised

(b) if previously recognised assets are reduced or eliminated, a loss is recognised.

When goods or services are sold, the recognition criteria are met on the occurrence of the critical event in the operating cycle involved. (This is usually, but not always, the delivery of the goods.)

6.5   Effect on accounting standards

There are several important things to note in relation to the ideas in this part of the Statement.

(a) The principles of FRS 5 (and to some extent FRS 4 *Capital instruments*) are based on the recognition criteria set out above. More recently, FRS 12 *Provisions, contingent liabilities and contingent assets* has also used the definition of a liability and the principles for recognising liabilities.

(b) Two important points are made which have implications for recent accounting standards.

- Costs intended to be incurred in the future do not represent liabilities now.

- The event which triggers recognition of an asset or a liability must be a past event.

    For example, the ASB's recent requirement that deferred tax must be calculated on a full provision basis is partly based on the idea that partial provision is inadequate because it allows for the taxation effects of future events. (FRS 19 *Deferred tax* is covered in a later chapter of this text.)

    These two points are also at the heart of FRS 12.

(c) The Statement of Principles is balance sheet orientated. Gains and losses arise from a change in assets or liabilities. A profit and loss account based approach would concentrate on the transactions undertaken by a reporting entity and allocate them to the accounting period in which they belong. The balance sheet would then consist of residual amounts arising from this allocation.

    This is another highly controversial idea and has caused a great deal of adverse comment from professional firms (notably Ernst and Young) and other interested parties.

ACTIVITY 1

The approach followed in the ASB's Statement of Principles is balance sheet orientated.

(a) Why is this approach controversial?

(b) Are there any advantages to a balance sheet based approach?

Feedback to this activity is at the end of the chapter.

6.6 Measurement in financial statements

Once it has been decided to recognise an asset or liability, next a measurement basis must be decided on for that category of assets or liabilities.

The Statement considers various possible bases:

- historical cost

- net realisable value

- current cost (i.e. value to the business = deprival value).

No particular basis is required by the Statement. The basis selected should be the one that best meets the objective of financial statements.

7 Presentation of financial information

7.1 The financial statements

KEY POINT

The primary financial statements are:

- the profit and loss account

- the STRGL

- the balance sheet

- the cash flow statement.

Financial statements consist of primary financial statements and supporting notes. The primary financial statements are:

- the statements of financial performance (profit and loss account and statement of total recognised gains and losses)

- the statement of financial position (balance sheet)

- the cash flow statement.

The presentation of information on **financial performance** focuses on the components of financial performance and their characteristics.

The presentation of information on **financial position** focuses on the types and functions of assets and liabilities held and on the relationships between them.

The presentation of **cash flow information** shows the extent to which the entity's various activities generate and use cash.

7.2 Presentation

Financial statements should communicate clearly and effectively and in as straightforward a manner as possible without loss of relevance or reliability and without unnecessarily increasing the length of the financial statements.

Structure and aggregation

The mass of detail would obscure the message if financial statements reported every single aspect of every relevant transaction and event. Greater knowledge results from an orderly **loss** of information.

Aggregating information:

- conveys information that would otherwise have been obscured
- highlights significant items and relationships between items
- facilitates comparability between different entities
- is more understandable to users.

The notes and primary financial statements form an integrated whole. The notes amplify and explain the financial statements by providing more detailed information on items recognised in the primary financial statements.

Disclosure of information in the notes to the financial statements is not a substitute for recognition. It does not correct or justify any misrepresentation or omission in the primary financial statements.

Classification

Items that are similar should be presented together and distinguished from dissimilar items. Classification should enable the consideration of the relationships between different classes of items, for example the relative sizes of profits and capital employed or debtors and sales.

7.3   Financial performance

Information on financial performance should focus attention on the components of financial performance and on their key characteristics. This typically involves:

- recognising only gains and losses in the statements of financial performance
- classifying components by reference to a combination of function (such as production, selling and administrative) and by the nature of the item (such as employment costs, interest payable and amounts written off investments)
- distinguishing amounts that are affected in different ways by changes in economic conditions or by business activity (for example, by providing segmental information or by presenting income from continuing and discontinued operations as separate components).

Gains and losses are generally not offset in presenting information on financial performance.

7.4   Financial position

Information on financial position should be presented in a way that focuses attention on the types of assets and liabilities held and the relationship between them, and in the function of the various assets.

Assets are not offset against liabilities.

7.5   Cash flow statement

Cash flow information should show the extent to which the entity's activities generate and use cash. It should distinguish cash flows that are the result of operations from cash flows that result from other activities. For example, cash received from trading activities should be shown separately from cash used to repay debt, cash used to distribute dividends and cash reinvested.

7.6   Accompanying information

Financial statements are often accompanied by other information, for example, five year trend information, operating and financial reviews, directors' reports and

KEY POINTS

Gains and losses are generally not offset in presenting information on financial performance.

Assets are not offset against liabilities.

statements by the chairman. This information should not be inconsistent with the financial statements.

The more complex an entity and its transactions become, the more users need an objective and comprehensive analysis and explanation of the main features underlying the entity's financial performance and position. These disclosures (normally included in the operating and financial review) are best presented in the context of a discussion of the business as a whole and are most useful if they discuss:

- the main factors underlying the reporting entity's financial performance, including the principal risks, uncertainties and trends involved in each of the main business areas and how the entity is responding to them

- the dynamics of the reporting entity's financial position, including the strategies being adopted on capital structure and treasury policy

- the activities and expenditure (other than capital expenditure) of the period that can be regarded as a form of investment in the future.

7.7　Highlights and summary indicators

These may include amounts, ratios and other computations that attempt to distil key information about the reporting entity's financial performance and financial position. By itself, this type of information cannot adequately describe an entity's financial performance or financial position and as a result is not a basis for meaningful analysis or prudent decision making. The presentation of such information will therefore need to avoid exaggerating its importance.

7.8　Effect on accounting standards

The 'presentation' chapter was one of the first chapters of the Statement to be developed and the original version was issued at the same time as the exposure draft of what became FRS 3 *Reporting financial performance*. FRS 3 provides users of the financial statements with information that assists them in analysing the components of an entity's financial performance.

The ideas in this chapter have also influenced the following:

- FRS 1 *Cash flow statements* (separate reporting of cash flows resulting from different activities)

- FRS 4 *Capital instruments* (analysis of shareholders' funds and long-term debt)

- The Statement on Operating and Financial Review.

ACTIVITY 2	What are the potential disadvantages of adopting a 'principles based' approach to standard setting?

Feedback to this activity is at the end of the chapter.

7.9　Accounting for interests in other entities

The final chapter of the Statement of Principles considers the appropriate accounting for investments in single entity financial statements and consolidated financial statements. There are no surprises. In the consolidated statements:

- an interest that involves control should be consolidated

- an interest that involves joint control or significant influence should be accounted for by recognising the investor's share of the investee's results and resources

- an interest that involves neither control nor significant influence should be accounted for like any other asset.

8 The Financial Reporting Standard for Smaller Entities (FRSSE)

8.1 Introduction to the small companies debate

The number and complexity of accounting standards is increasing. Within the profession there is currently a debate as to whether accounting standards place an unnecessary burden on small companies. One view is that accounting standards should apply to all financial statements which are intended to show a true and fair view. Another view is that small companies should be exempted from the requirements of certain standards. A third view is that there should be a completely different set of accounting standards for small companies.

8.2 The traditional position

Small companies are already exempt from certain requirements of the Companies Act and of accounting standards.

The Companies Act

- Companies which meet the definition of 'small' or 'medium-sized' contained in the Act may file abbreviated accounts with the Registrar of Companies. Abbreviated accounts for 'small' companies consist of a simplified balance sheet and limited notes.

- 'Small' companies may circulate simplified accounts to shareholders.

- 'Small' and 'medium-sized' companies are not required to state whether they have complied with accounting standards.

- 'Small' and 'medium-sized' groups are exempt from preparing group accounts.

Accounting standards

- A company which meets the Companies Act definition of a 'small' company is exempt from the requirement to prepare a cash flow statement under FRS 1.

- Companies which fall below the criteria multiplied by ten for defining a 'medium-sized' company are exempt from making certain disclosures required by SSAP 13 *Accounting for research and development* and SSAP 25 *Segmental reporting*.

8.3 Financial Reporting Standard for Smaller Entities (FRSSE)

In 1997 the ASB issued the first version of the Financial Reporting Standard for Smaller Entities (FRSSE) and it has been regularly revised since then.

In issuing the FRSSE, the ASB recognised that many of the provisions of existing accounting standards are not relevant to smaller entities. The FRSSE is a comprehensive standard containing the measurement and disclosure requirements in existing accounting standards and UITF Abstracts that are relevant to most smaller entities, in a simplified form.

Scope

The FRSSE applies to:

(a) companies incorporated under companies legislation and entitled to the exemptions available for small companies or small groups when filing accounts with the Registrar of Companies

(b) entities that would have come into category (a) above had they been companies incorporated under companies legislation.

A company meets the Companies Act definition of 'small' if it meets two of the following three criteria:

- turnover not more than £5.6 million
- balance sheet total not more than £2.8 million
- number of employees not more than 50.

Public companies, banks, building societies, insurance and financial services companies cannot qualify as 'small', regardless of their size. This also applies to members of groups containing any of the above.

Entities falling within the scope of the FRSSE may either produce their financial statements as normal following FRSs, SSAPs, UITF Abstracts, etc or may choose to produce simplified statements in compliance with the FRSSE.

True and fair view

The FRSSE requires that financial statements should present a true and fair view of the results for the period and of the state of affairs at the end of the period. To achieve such a view, regard should be had to the substance of any arrangement or transaction into which the entity has entered. To determine the substance of a transaction it is necessary to identify whether the transaction has given rise to new assets or liabilities for the reporting entity and whether it has changed the entity's existing assets or liabilities.

Therefore the requirement to present a true and fair view is explicitly linked with the requirement to have regard to the substance of transactions.

Measurement

The measurement bases required are the same as those in existing standards, but they have been simplified. Here are two examples.

- For a finance lease, an asset and liability should be recorded by the lessee at the fair value of the leased asset (SSAP 21 requires them to be stated at the present value of the minimum lease payments).
- Finance charges on finance leases may be charged on a straight-line basis (SSAP 21 normally requires the actuarial method or the sum of the digits method).

Disclosure

The financial statements should state that they have been prepared in accordance with the FRSSE.

Many disclosures currently required under existing accounting standards are not required by the FRSSE. Examples of disclosures not required include the following:

- analysis of turnover, costs and results into continuing operations, acquisitions and discontinued operations (FRS 3)
- analysis of stocks into raw materials, work in progress and finished goods (SSAP 9).

Groups

The FRSSE applies to small groups (as defined by the Companies Acts). Under the Companies Acts, small groups are not required to prepare consolidated accounts, but may choose to do so. In practice, few small groups do prepare consolidated accounts.

As a result, the FRSSE does not cover consolidated accounts and small groups preparing consolidated financial statements are required to comply with the accounting practices and disclosure requirements in FRSs 2, 6, 7, 9 and 10 in their present form.

Cash flow statements

The FRSSE encourages, but does not require small entities to prepare a cash flow statement. It has been argued that a cash flow statement is of limited value for small companies for the following reasons.

- If transactions are normally straightforward, a cash flow statement adds little to the picture already given by the profit and loss account and the balance sheet.

- The gap between the period-end and the date on which the financial statements are finalised may be so long that the usefulness of cash flow information is limited.

- Managers in small businesses are well aware of the need to manage cash effectively.

Small companies are currently exempt from the requirements of FRS 1 *Cash flow statements.*

This has been one of the more controversial areas of the FRSSE. The argument for requiring small companies to prepare a cash flow statement is that management of cash is crucial in small, as well as large businesses. Potential lenders and other users of the financial statements believe that a cash flow statement provides a useful focus for discussion with management as well as a reference point for subsequent more detailed analysis that they might require.

Related party disclosures

The FRSSE requires the disclosure of material related party transactions and includes most of the requirements of FRS 8 *Related party disclosures.* The definition of a related party is the same as that in FRS 8.

Some commentators have argued that the requirements of the Companies Acts provide adequate protection for users of the financial statements of a small entity. However, the ASB believes that related party transactions are often more common and more material in smaller entities than in large ones. For example, directors often give personal guarantees in respect of borrowings of the reporting entity.

8.4   Evaluation of the FRSSE

Many commentators welcomed the FRSSE as a pragmatic step in the right direction, in so far as it attempts to reduce the regulatory burden on small companies.

There has been some debate as to whether the FRSSE actually does achieve its aims in practice. It has been argued that many of the more onerous disclosure requirements excluded from the FRSSE were never relevant to small companies in any case. It has also been argued that the FRSSE may actually increase the burden on practitioners, because there are now two sets of reporting requirements, instead of one.

There is also a wider debate about the basis of differential financial reporting (developing different GAAP for large and small companies). As we have seen, in practice there is now a separate GAAP for small companies. Most commentators now accept that this is desirable. However, some commentators believe that 'small GAAP' has been approached in the wrong way. They make the following points.

- The real issue is not whether small companies find accounting standards onerous, but whether existing accounting standards produce financial statements that meet the information needs of the owners of small businesses and other users.

- The current definition of 'small companies' is based on size. But a small company is not simply a smaller version of a large company. It is fundamentally different in nature.

- Large company financial statements are used by a wide range of people: existing and potential investors; their advisers; loan creditors; the press; and the general public. Small company financial statements are used by a very different and limited range of people: normally the owners of the business; the Inland Revenue; and the bank.

- The owners of large companies are not usually involved in managing the company, but small companies are normally managed by their owners. Financial Reporting Standards are designed to ensure that managers are accountable to investors (stewardship), but this is not relevant for a smaller company.

The Statement of Principles assumes that the objectives of all general purpose financial statements are the same and that financial statements that meet the needs of investors will meet the needs of all users. This is not necessarily the case.

8.5   Review of the FRSSE

When the FRSSE was first issued in November 1997, the ASB stated that it would review how it was working in practice after two full years of effective operation. The ASB has commissioned research into the operation of the FRSSE and in February 2001 it issued a Discussion Paper: *Review of the Financial Reporting Standard for Smaller Entities (FRSSE)*. The Paper made no firm proposals, but sought the views of interested parties on the following issues:

- Should there continue to be a FRSSE?
- Can a single FRSSE cater for the range of smaller entities?
- How and when should the FRSSE be updated?
- Which aspects of smaller entities' reporting should the FRSSE cover?
- How should the requirements of the FRSSE be determined?
- How should the FRSSE be drafted and presented?

The ASB believes that the FRSSE (or something like it) should continue to exist, but that it was an appropriate time to consider what changes, if any, might be made to the existing regime.

8.6   A 'one-stop shop' future for the FRSSE

The current approach for the FRSSE is that it contains the simplified versions of UK accounting standards that small companies can choose to follow, while preparers of small company accounts must refer to companies legislation separately to find out the requirements from that source. The ASB received strong support from the 2001 consultation exercise for the idea that the FRSSE should contain both the applicable requirements of accounting standards and companies legislation, i.e. it should be a 'one-stop shop' for preparers of small company accounts in listing out all the requirements to be followed.

The ASB therefore issued a Discussion Paper: *A 'One-stop Shop' Financial Reporting Standard for Smaller Entities (FRSSE)* in March 2004 seeking further feedback on this proposal. The ASB believes that such a development could be of significant benefit by easing the burden on preparers of small company accounts, by offering a single source of accounting and reporting requirements. If the ASB receives positive feedback to this proposal, it is likely that the next routine updating of the FRSSE will be drafted to include the applicable requirements of company law as well as accounting standards.

8.7 Possible future developments

A wide-ranging review of company law is currently in progress. One of the proposals is that there should be a completely separate reporting regime for small companies, rather than one adapted from the large company requirements. If this is adopted, it would be logical to replace the FRSSE with alternative accounting standards specially developed for smaller companies. However, the proposed definition of a small company is still based purely on size.

The ASB has also undertaken a review of the year-end financial reporting requirements. This mainly addresses the ways in which financial information is disseminated to users, rather than the small company regime. However, this does indicate growing awareness that the information required by large institutional investors is not necessarily helpful or relevant to all users.

These proposals are discussed in more detail in a later chapter.

SELF-TEST
QUESTIONS

The nature of UK GAAP

1   What is meant by US GAAP? How does it differ in principle from UK GAAP? (1.1)

Sources of UK GAAP

2   Describe the accounting standard setting system in the UK. (2.3)

3   What is the status of a UITF consensus pronouncement? (2.7)

The Statement of Principles for Financial Reporting

4   What is the ASB's Statement of Principles and what is its intended role? (3.1)

The objective of financial statements

5   What is the Statement's definition of the objective of financial statements? (4.1)

6   When will an entity be said to have control of another entity? (4.5)

The qualitative characteristics of financial information

7   When can information be said to be reliable? (5.2)

8   Define materiality. (5.5)

Recognition in financial statements

9   What are the seven elements of financial statements identified by the Statement of Principles? (6.1)

10   Give the Statement of Principles' definition of assets and liabilities. (6.1)

11   How are 'future economic benefits' evidenced? (6.1)

12   What are the stages of the recognition process? (6.2)

13   What is the effect of the Statement of Principles being balance sheet oriented? (6.5)

Presentation of financial information

14   Which are the primary financial statements? (7.1)

15   How should information on each of financial performance and financial position be presented? (7.3, 7.4)

The Financial Reporting Standard for Smaller Entities (FRSSE)

16   What are the scope and the main provisions of the FRSSE? (8.3)

PRACTICE
QUESTION

Accounting framework for small companies

The administrative and legislative burdens which have been imposed on small companies have been the subject of debate for several years. The application of accounting standards to small companies has been the subject of considerable research. It is the view of some accountants that accounting standards should apply to all financial statements whilst others feel that small companies should have a completely different set of accounting standards. In response to the continuing debate in this area, the Accounting Standards Board has issued a Financial Reporting Standard 'Financial Reporting Standard for Smaller Entities'.

Required:

Discuss the main issues in the development of an accounting framework for small companies with reference to the Financial Reporting Standard 'Financial Reporting Standard for Smaller Entities'.　　　　　　　　**(10 marks)**

For the answer to this question see the 'Answers' section at the end of the book.

FEEDBACK TO
ACTIVITY **1**

(a) **Reasons for controversy**

(i) The balance sheet is unsatisfactory in its present format. Most assets are included at historical cost; others may be included at a valuation, but not all companies revalue their assets. Internally generated intangible assets, such as brand names, may represent a significant part of the value of a company, but under current accounting practice they are not normally recognised.

(ii) Many commentators believe that a balance sheet based approach implies a move towards a system of current value accounting. This is likely to cause immense practical problems; the profession has been attempting to find a satisfactory system of inflation accounting for years, without success.

(iii) Investors are recognised as the most important users of accounts. Investors normally regard the level of profit as the most important information within the financial statements. This implies that the profit and loss account should be given primacy.

(b) **Advantages of a balance sheet based approach**

(i) Emphasis on the 'bottom line' encourages preparers of accounts to manipulate figures and users to adopt a simplistic approach to financial information. If the focus is on the balance sheet, it will be less tempting to manipulate the profit and loss account.

(ii) Financial statements are supposed to provide information on the stewardship of management. Stewardship implies the management of assets and liabilities, as well as the generation of profit. Management of working capital (for example) can be critical to the survival of a company. Focusing on the balance sheet allows a wider appreciation of the performance of management; 'growth' is a wider concept than profit.

(iii) It can be argued that the balance sheet is forward looking. Assets are rights to **future** economic benefits; liabilities will give rise to cash outflows **in the future**. Information in the balance sheet often has predictive value and should focus attention on the adaptability of an enterprise.

(iv)   In theory, auditors may find a balance sheet based approach more helpful than a profit and loss account based approach. It is normally easier to audit a balance sheet than to audit a profit and loss account.

FEEDBACK TO ACTIVITY 2

The potential disadvantages of adopting a 'principles based' approach to standard setting are:

(a)   Accounting standards derived from a conceptual framework are likely to be complex and to rely on specialised terminology. The ASB has already been criticised for producing 'unintelligible' standards.

(b)   Some users and preparers of accounts may prefer a prescriptive approach. There may be a belief that 'creative accounting' can only be prevented by a detailed 'cookbook' of rules.

(c)   There are no definitive right answers to many accounting problems. Conflicts will always exist (for example, between accruals and prudence and between relevance and reliability) and choices will still have to be made. The existence of a conceptual framework, by itself, will not solve problems such as accounting for complex financial instruments. It may, however, raise unrealistic expectations.

Chapter 2

CORPORATE GOVERNANCE

The directors of UK listed companies are required to ensure that their company complies with the Combined Code on corporate governance. This is a code of best practice which covers matters such as the procedures by which directors' remuneration is fixed, the way in which they communicate with shareholders and the ways in which they safeguard the company's assets. Directors must include a statement in the annual report and accounts describing the procedures that they follow in order to comply with the Code, and giving details of any non-compliance.

This chapter focuses on reports to shareholders (and other users of the financial statements) under the Combined Code.

Objectives

When you have studied this chapter you should be able to:

- understand the role, and the need for reform, of corporate governance

- describe the nature of reporting under the Combined Code

- discuss the need for corporate governance in small companies

- describe the nature and content of the Operating and Financial Review.

1   The need for reform of corporate governance

1.1   Introduction

During the late 1980s a number of large UK public companies failed, some of them as a result of large-scale fraud by directors. These companies included Polly Peck, Maxwell Communications, and BCCI.

KEY POINT

Company failures in the 1980s led to a reduction in public confidence in UK financial reporting.

These failures reduced public confidence in financial reporting and auditing. Many people believed that company directors regarded accounting standards as a set of rules to be circumvented and 'creative accounting' was implicated in several company liquidations. For example, the accounts of Polly Peck showed that the company was apparently in a healthy position while in fact it was on the verge of collapse. Directors were putting auditors under increasing commercial pressure to accept the use of 'creative accounting' schemes.

These problems were addressed by the introduction of new standard setting regimes for both financial reporting and auditing. There were other concerns about the accountability of directors, as follows.

- There was no clear framework for ensuring that directors reviewed internal controls in their companies.

DEFINITION

Corporate governance is 'the system by which companies are directed and controlled'. It is concerned with the role of the board of directors and accountability throughout the company.

- There was a perceived lack of accountability for directors' remuneration, which in some cases was believed to be excessive. In addition, there was increasing public concern that financial statements did not adequately reflect directors' remuneration.

A general need was perceived for a strengthening of the systems of corporate governance used by UK companies.

1.2 The Cadbury Report

The Cadbury Committee was set up in 1991 by the FRC, the Stock Exchange and the accountancy profession to examine the reporting and control functions of boards of directors, and the role of auditors and shareholders. Its full title was 'The Committee on the Financial Aspects of Corporate Governance', chaired by Sir Adrian Cadbury.

The Cadbury Report, entitled '*The Financial Aspects of Corporate Governance*', was issued in December 1992.

The committee issued a code of best practice for company directors. Compliance with the code was voluntary. However, the London Stock Exchange Listing Rules required UK-incorporated listed companies to include a statement in their annual report and accounts as to whether they had complied with the code. Non-compliance had to be explained.

Broadly the Cadbury Code covered the following areas:

- membership of the board with effective division of responsibility (combination of executive and non-executive directors)

- independence of the board (no financial connection with the company except fees and shareholdings)

- remuneration committees to be established and service contracts in excess of three years to be approved by shareholders

- reporting and disclosure (including disclosure of directors' emoluments and reporting on internal control systems)

- establishment of audit committees (with at least three non-executive directors, at least two being independent).

The Cadbury Committee recommended that directors should state in their report and accounts that the business is a going concern. In November 1994 the Cadbury Committee issued a paper, *Going Concern and Financial Reporting*, to give guidance to help directors in complying with this recommendation.

The Committee also recommended that directors of listed companies should report on the effectiveness of the company's system of internal control. This requirement was incorporated into the Combined Code (see below).

1.3 The Greenbury Report: directors' remuneration

Early in 1995 the CBI set up a committee to draw up guidelines on directors' remuneration. The committee was headed by Sir Richard Greenbury. This move was a response to increasing public concern that financial statements still did not adequately reflect management remuneration. The committee included members from the Institute of Directors, the National Association of Pension Funds and the Stock Exchange.

The committee reported in September 1995. The report set out a code of best practice in determining and accounting for directors' remuneration. The detailed provisions were prepared with large companies mainly in mind, but the committee stated that the principles apply equally to small companies.

All listed companies registered in the UK were required to comply with the Greenbury Code from 1995 onwards. They had to include a statement about their compliance in the annual report to shareholders or in the annual report of the remuneration committee. Any areas of non-compliance were to be explained and justified.

1.4   The Hampel Report

In January 1998 another report on corporate governance was issued, this time from a committee under the chairmanship of Sir Ronnie Hampel. While both the Cadbury and Greenbury reports concentrated on preventing abuses, the Hampel report 'is concerned with the positive contribution which good corporate governance can make'. Throughout, it aims to restrict the regulatory burden facing companies and substitute broad principles where practicable.

Each company's circumstances are different. A 'one-size-fits-all' approach to corporate governance issues is rejected. Instead, each listed company must include in the annual report a narrative explaining how the broad principles of corporate governance have been applied.

The general message of Hampel is that a board must not approach the various corporate governance requirements in a compliance mentality: the so-called 'tick-box' approach. Good corporate governance is not achieved by satisfying a checklist. Directors must comply with the substance as well as the letter of all best practice pronouncements.

1.5   Subsequent developments

After publishing its report, the Hampel Committee drew up a single Combined Code of Best Practice, incorporating the Cadbury, Greenbury and Hampel recommendations, and submitted this to the Stock Exchange, recommending that it should be incorporated into the Listing Rules, after consultation on the details.

2   The Combined Code

2.1   Introduction

KEY POINT

The Combined Code consists of 17 principles and a number of more detailed provisions. The principles and provisions cover five topics:
- directors
- remuneration
- accountability and audit
- relations with shareholders
- institutional shareholders.

The final version of the Hampel *Principles of Good Governance and Code of Best Practice* (the 'Combined Code') was published in 1998 and slightly amended in July 2003. The Combined Code consists of 17 principles and, under the heading of each principle, a number of more detailed provisions. The principles and provisions cover five topics: directors, remuneration, accountability and audit, relations with shareholders and institutional shareholders.

The Stock Exchange Listing Rules require a listed company in the UK to include the following in its annual report and accounts.

- A narrative statement of how it has applied the principles set out in the Combined Code, providing explanation which enables its shareholders to evaluate how the principles have been applied.

- A statement as to whether or not it has complied throughout the accounting period with the Combined Code provisions. A company that has not complied with the Combined Code provisions, or complied with only some of the Combined Code provisions, or complied with it for only part of an accounting period, must specify the provisions with which it has not complied, and give reasons for any non-compliance.

The principles are listed below.

2.2 Directors

Every company should be headed by an effective board, which is collectively responsible for the success of the company.

There should be a clear division of responsibilities at the head of the company between the running of the board and the executive responsibility for the running of the company's business. No one individual should have unfettered powers of decision.

The board should include a balance of executive and non-executive directors (and in particular independent non-executive directors), such that no individual or small group of individuals can dominate the board's decision taking.

There should be a formal rigorous and transparent procedure for the appointment of new directors to the board.

The board should be supplied in a timely manner with information in a form and of a quality appropriate to enable it to discharge its duties. All directors should receive induction on joining the board and should regularly update and refresh their skills and knowledge.

The board should undertake a formal and rigorous annual evaluation of its own performance and that of its committees and individual directors.

All directors should be submitted for re-election at regular intervals, subject to continued satisfactory performance. The board should ensure planned and progressive refreshing of the board.

2.3 Directors' remuneration

Levels of remuneration should be sufficient to attract, retain and motivate directors of the quality required to run the company successfully, but a company should avoid paying more than is necessary for this purpose. A significant proportion of executive directors' remuneration should be structured so as to link rewards to corporate and individual performance.

There should be a formal and transparent procedure for developing policy on executive remuneration and for fixing the remuneration packages of individual directors. No director should be involved in deciding his or her own remuneration.

2.4 Accountability and audit

Financial reporting

The board should present a balanced and understandable assessment of the company's position and prospects.

This assessment is usually given in the Operating and Financial Review, which is discussed later in this chapter.

Internal control

The board should maintain a sound system of internal control to safeguard shareholders' investment and the company's assets. The relevant provision is as follows.

- The board should, at least annually, conduct a review of the effectiveness of the group's system of internal controls and should report to shareholders that they have done so. The review should cover all material controls, including financial, operational and compliance controls and risk management systems.

The profession believed that additional guidance was needed on how this provision should be implemented, so the Institute of Chartered Accountants in England and Wales agreed with the Stock Exchange to set up a working party to produce guidance for directors on the scope, extent, nature and review of internal controls under the Combined Code. The working party was chaired by Nigel Turnbull and it produced, in September 1999, a report entitled *Internal Control: Guidance for Directors on the Combined Code* (known as the 'Turnbull Report').

Audit committee and auditors

The board should establish formal and transparent arrangements for considering how they should apply the financial reporting and internal control principles and for maintaining an appropriate relationship with the company's auditors.

2.5   Relations with shareholders

There should be a dialogue with shareholders based on the mutual understanding of objectives. The board as a whole has responsibility for ensuring that a satisfactory dialogue with shareholders takes place.

The board should use the AGM to communicate with investors and to encourage their participation.

2.6   Institutional shareholders

Institutional shareholders should enter into a dialogue with companies based on the mutual understanding of objectives.

When evaluating companies' governance arrangements, particularly those relating to board structure and composition, institutional shareholders should give due weight to all relevant factors drawn to their attention.

Institutional shareholders have a responsibility to make considered use of their votes.

KEY POINT

The directors are required to report that the business is a going concern.

2.7   Going concern statement

One of the Combined Code provisions in the 'Accountability and audit' section states that the directors should report that the business is a going concern, with supporting assumptions or qualifications as necessary. The guidance in the Cadbury Committee paper, *Going Concern and Financial Reporting*, is still relevant.

The paper explains the significance of going concern in relation to the financial statements. It refers to the requirements of the CA85 and of SSAP 2 (now replaced by FRS 18). It also discusses the term 'foreseeable future', making the following points.

- The foreseeable future depends on the specific circumstances at a point in time, including the nature of the company's business, its associated risks and external influences.

- Any judgement made, whilst reasonable at the time, can be valid only at that time and can be overturned by subsequent events.

- In assessing going concern, directors should take account of all information of which they are aware at the time. It is not possible to specify a minimum period to which they should pay particular attention in assessing going concern. Where the period considered has been limited, for example, to a period of less than one year from the date of approval of the financial statements, additional disclosure may be necessary in order to explain the assumptions that underlie the adoption of the going concern basis.

2.8   Procedures in assessing going concern

The paper describes the procedures that an explicit statement regarding going concern may entail. The procedures are described in broad terms, with more detailed suggestions in an appendix.

Directors are best placed to know which factors are likely to be of greater significance in relation to their company. These factors will vary by industry, and from company to company within a particular industry. Major areas in which procedures are likely to be appropriate are:

- forecasts and budgets
- borrowing requirements
- liability management
- contingent liabilities
- products and markets
- financial risk management
- financial adaptability.

The directors should consider the range of potential outcomes and their probability in order to determine the likely commercial outcome.

If the directors become aware of factors that cast doubt on the ability of the company to continue in operational existence, then they will need to carry out more detailed investigations. Such work will provide evidence in support of their statement on going concern and additional disclosure in their statement may be appropriate.

2.9   Disclosure by directors

Directors should include their statement on going concern in the Operating and Financial Review (OFR), if they include an OFR in their accounts. There are three possibilities as follows.

- **Going concern presumption appropriate** – The directors should make a basic statement to that effect. The following form of words has been suggested:

  'After making enquiries, the directors have a reasonable expectation that the company has adequate resources to continue in operational existence for the foreseeable future. For this reason, they continue to adopt the going concern basis in preparing the accounts.'

- **Going concern basis used despite doubts on going concern presumption** – The directors should explain the circumstances so as to identify the factors which give rise to the problems (including any external factors outside their control which may affect the outcome) and an explanation of how they intend to deal with the problem so as to resolve it.

- **Going concern basis not appropriate** – The directors should state that, in their opinion, the company is no longer a going concern. They should consider taking legal advice on the wording of the statement.

  Where the company is not a going concern, the company is not necessarily insolvent (unable to pay its debts as they fall due). The directors should consider whether the company is or may become insolvent. Section 214 of the Insolvency Act states that an action for wrongful trading may be brought against a director if, at some time before the commencement of the winding up of the company, he knew or ought to have concluded that there was no reasonable prospect that the company would avoid going into insolvent liquidation.

2.10 Evaluating the Combined Code

The Combined Code is a set of principles, rather than a set of rules. Directors are required to describe in their own words the way in which they have applied the general principles of corporate governance. There are several advantages to this approach.

- Because the directors report on the actual circumstances of their own company, in theory the report should be more meaningful than one based on specific detailed requirements.

- Requirements based on statute might be difficult to interpret, or be open to different interpretations.

- A code of practice can be changed much more easily than statutory requirements. This means that the Combined Code can be updated to respond to changing conditions and changing expectations of shareholders and others.

ACTIVITY 1

Are there any potential disadvantages in having a Combined Code that consists of principles, rather than rules?

Feedback to this activity is at the end of the chapter.

3   The need for corporate governance in smaller quoted companies

3.1   The Combined Code and smaller companies

KEY POINT

The Combined Code applies to all listed companies, whether they are large or small.

The Combined Code applies to all listed companies, whether they are large or small. The Hampel Committee decided not to draw a distinction between large and small quoted companies, although it recognised that smaller companies might have difficulty in complying with some of the provisions. The Committee concluded that:

(a) any distinction based on size would be arbitrary; and

(b) high standards of governance are as important for smaller listed companies as for larger ones.

It said that those considering corporate governance in smaller listed companies should do so with 'flexibility and a proper regard to individual circumstances'.

In practice, the Code is not intended to be prescriptive. If the board of a small quoted company does not believe that a particular provision is appropriate, it should disclose this fact and the reasons for non-compliance. This enables readers of the annual report to consider the performance of the board based on the individual circumstances of the company.

3.2   Guidance for smaller companies

The City Group for Smaller Companies (CISCO) has prepared guidance for smaller quoted companies. This identifies areas of the Combined Code which may prove difficult for smaller companies to implement and suggests appropriate alternative recommendations, which mainly relate to non-executive directors and audit committees.

The CISCO guidelines are not intended to be an alternative to the Combined Code. A listed company must report any non-compliance with the Combined Code, and the reasons for it, in its annual report. However, if companies comply with the CISCO guidelines they comply with all the provisions of the Combined Code that they could reasonably be expected to implement. This is preferable to them doing nothing at all.

4 Operating and Financial Review (OFR)

4.1 Introduction

The ASB issued a Statement in July 1993 (revised slightly in January 2003) recommending that an Operating and Financial Review (OFR) should be included in the annual reports of large companies. The Statement was originally issued in response to the Cadbury Committee's recommendation that boards should present a balanced and understandable assessment of the company's position and prospects. This recommendation has now become a principle of the Combined Code.

The purpose of an OFR is to give the directors of a company the opportunity to discuss and explain, in a structured and comprehensive way, some of the main factors underlying the company's financial statements, and thus to help users to understand more fully the business and environment in which the company operates.

The ASB recognises that many listed companies' annual reports already include detailed discussion of operations and financing, often in the Chairman's Report. The Statement provides general guidelines to indicate what should be covered in such a review to ensure that it is balanced and complete.

4.2 Characteristics of the OFR

The main characteristics of the OFR are that it should:

- be written in a clear style and as succinctly as possible, and should focus on matters of significance to investors, so that it should be readily understandable by the general reader of annual reports

- be fair, in the sense of being a balanced and objective statement of both good and bad news

- refer to comments made in previous statements where these have not been borne out by events

- contain analytical discussion rather than merely numerical analysis

- follow a 'top down' structure, discussing individual aspects of the business in the context of a discussion of the business as a whole

- explain the reason for, and the effect of, any changes in accounting policies

- make it clear how any ratios or other numerical information given relate to the financial statements

- include discussion of: trends and factors underlying the business that have affected the results but are not expected to continue in the future; known events, trends and uncertainties that are expected to have an impact on the business in the future. It is not suggested that the OFR should forecast the outcome of any uncertainties.

Where the directors decide not to disclose information on the grounds that it is commercially sensitive or confidential, the OFR should ensure that the user is not misled by a discussion that is no longer complete and balanced.

It is for boards of directors to decide how best the information should be presented within a company's annual report; it is not part of the Statement that a particular format should be followed. The ASB believes, however, that it is important that the OFR should clearly be seen to be the responsibility of the board of directors as a whole.

The ASB takes the view that much of the material to be included in the OFR is not suitable for inclusion in notes to accounts, and should therefore not be made a requirement of an accounting standard. The Statement on Operating and Financial Review is therefore not mandatory but sets out a generally accepted view on what should be regarded as best practice in this area.

The OFR covers three main areas: a description of the business and its objectives, to provide a context for the review sections; the operating review; and the financial review.

4.3   Description of the business and its objectives

This provides a context for the directors' discussion of the company's performance and financial position. Areas that might be covered would include:

- the industries in which the business operates

- the main products and services supplied

- the main operating facilities and their location

- the objectives of the business, and management's strategy for achieving those objectives

- the measures used by management to assess the achievement of objectives.

4.4   The operating review

The operating review should enable the user to understand the dynamics of the various lines of business undertaken – that is, the main influences on the overall results, and how these interrelate. It needs to explain the main factors that underlie the business and in particular those which have either varied in the past or are expected to change in the future.

It normally includes the following.

(a) A discussion of the operating results for the period, including the significant features and covering all aspects of the profit and loss account to the level of profit on ordinary activities before taxation. This should focus on both the overall business and on segments. It should also cover changes in the industry or the environment in which the business operates, developments within the business and their effect on the results, for example:

- changes in market conditions

- new products and services introduced or announced

- changes in market share or position

- changes in turnover and margins

- changes in exchange rates and inflation rates

- new activities, discontinued activities and other acquisitions and disposals.

(b) Returns to shareholders: a discussion of the directors' dividend policy, any share repurchases, and movements in the share price in comparison with competitor companies.

(c) The dynamics of the business: a discussion of the main factors and influences that may have a major effect on future results, whether or not they were significant in the period under review. This should include the principal risks and uncertainties in the main lines of business and the approach to managing these risks. Examples of matters that may be relevant include: scarcity of raw materials; skill shortages; dependence on major suppliers or customers; environmental protection costs and potential environmental liabilities; exchange rate fluctuations.

(d) Investment for the future: the extent to which the directors have sought to maintain and enhance future income or profits, such as:

- capital expenditure

- marketing and advertising campaigns

- training programmes

- pure and applied research which may lead to potential new products and services

- development of new products and services.

4.5   The financial review

The financial review explains the capital structure of the business, its treasury policy and the dynamics of its financial position – its sources of liquidity and their application, including the implications of the financing requirements arising from its capital expenditure plans. It should normally include the following.

(a) A discussion of the capital structure of the business, in terms of the maturity profile of debt, type of capital instruments used, currency, and interest rate structure. This should include comments on relevant ratios such as interest cover and debt/equity ratios.

(b) A discussion of capital funding, treasury policies and objectives, covering the management of interest rate risk, the maturity profile of borrowings and the management of exchange rate risk. The OFR should also discuss the implementation of these policies in the period under review, in terms of:

- the manner in which treasury activities are controlled

- the currencies in which borrowings are made and in which cash and cash equivalents are held

- the extent to which borrowings are at fixed interest rates

- the use of financial instruments, for hedging purposes and otherwise

- the extent to which foreign currency net investments are hedged by currency borrowings and other hedging instruments.

The purpose and effect of major financing transactions undertaken up to the date of approval of the financial statements should be explained. The effect of interest costs on profits and the potential impact of interest rate changes should also be discussed.

(c) A discussion of the cash inflows and outflows during the period, commenting on any special factors that influenced these. Where segmental cash flows are significantly out of line with segmental profits, this should be indicated and explained.

(d) A discussion of the business's liquidity at the end of the period. This should include comment on the level of borrowings at the end of the period, the seasonality of borrowing requirements and the maturity profile of both borrowings and committed borrowing facilities. The discussion should refer to any restrictions on the ability to transfer funds from one part of the group to meet the obligations of another part of the group, where these represent, or might foreseeably come to represent, a significant restraint on the group.

(e) A statement that the business is a going concern (as required by the Combined Code).

Much of the information in points (a) and (b) above is now required by FRS 13 *Derivatives and other financial instruments: disclosures.*

4.6   Statement of compliance

The OFR Statement represents best practice and compliance is voluntary. Therefore the directors are not expected to include any formal statement of compliance. However, comment on the extent to which the Statement has been followed may be helpful to the user. Where it is implied, through the use of the words 'operating and financial review', that the directors have endeavoured to follow the principles set out in the Statement, they should signal any fundamental departure from it.

5   Revision to the Combined Code: Non-executives and Audit Committees

5.1   Introduction

The Combined Code has been under constant review since its initial publication. The latest changes were made in July 2003 following the Higgs Report and the Smith Report.

In January 2003 Derek Higgs presented his *Review of the Role and Effectiveness of Non-Executive Director*s. The Report had been commissioned by the Department of Trade and Industry. At the same time Sir Robert Smith delivered his report on Audit Committees.

Higgs said that the aim of his review was to 'let in some daylight on the role of the non-executive director in the boardroom and to make recommendations to enhance their effectiveness'. His review led him to believe that, thanks to the Combined Code, the fundamentals of corporate governance in the UK were sound. He opposed the calls for stricter legal control over directors, because the brittleness and rigidity of legislation cannot dictate the behaviour or foster the trust that was necessary for good corporate governance. He also supported the unitary board structure, and saw no reason to adopt the split management board and supervisory board common in Europe.

Despite Higgs' praise of the existing system, his own report was met with outright hostility from members of the FRC, the LSE, the FSA and others. The main criticisms were that the report was generally too prescriptive, and that the specific demands to split the roles of chairman and chief executive, and for half of the board to consist of non-executives, were impractical. The revised code (see below) relaxed the rule on non-executive directors.

In July 2003, the FRC agreed a final text for the new Combined Code. This incorporated a revised version of the Higgs Report along with the recommendations made by Sir Robert Smith in his report on Audit Committees.

5.2   Amendments to The Combined Code

The revised Combined Code has additional requirements for the Board, the Chairman, Executive and Non-executive Directors (following the Higgs Report), and the Audit Committee (following the Smith Report). These are set out below:

The board

The board is collectively responsible for promoting the success of the company's affairs. The performance of a board and of its committees should be evaluated.

The Chairman

The role of Chairman and Chief Executive should not be combined. Their respective roles should be set out in writing. The Chairman's role is to provide leadership for the non-executive directors and to communicate shareholders' views to the Board. The Chairman should develop a close relationship with the senior independent director and the other non-executives.

A Chief Executive should not become the Chairman of the same company.

Directors

A nomination committee (with a majority of independent non-executives) should recommend future executive and non-executive directors. There should be open and rigorous procedures for the appointment of directors. Directors should be subject to a professional development programme and an annual evaluation of their performance.

Non-executive directors

At least half the board of the top 350 listed companies must be independent non-executive directors. Smaller listed companies must have at least two independent non-executives.

The audit committee

Sir Robert Smith's report into audit committees stated that the 'audit committee has a peculiar role, acting independently from the executive, to ensure that the interests of shareholders are properly protected in relation to financial reporting and internal control'.

The role, responsibilities and activities of the audit committee should be noted in the Annual Report. The committee itself should contain a majority of non-executives. The role of the audit committee continues to grow. The committee will be responsible for monitoring the integrity of financial reports, supporting the independence of the external auditor and reviewing the management of financial (and other) risks.

Some experts think that the audit committee will evolve into a sort of 'Supervisory Board' as seen on the Continent. However, neither Sir Robert nor Derek Higgs saw any need to replace the UK–style Unitary board with the 'Management' and 'Supervisory Boards' of Europe.

SELF-TEST
QUESTIONS

The need for reform of corporate governance

1   What was the focus of (a) the Cadbury Report, (b) the Greenbury Report and (c) the Hampel Report? (1.2, 1.3, 1.4)

The Combined Code

2   In the light of the Combined Code, what statements do the Stock Exchange Listing Rules require a listed UK company to include in its annual report and accounts concerning compliance with the Code? (2.1)

3   What are the Combined Code's requirements relating to the size of directors' remuneration? (2.3)

4   What responsibility does the board have in relation to internal control? (2.4)

5   Describe the procedures that should typically be undertaken in order for directors to make the required statement on going concern. (2.8)

6   Describe the three possible conclusions available for the going concern statement. (2.9)

Operating and Financial Review (OFR)

7   What are the desirable characteristics of an Operating and Financial Review? (4.2)

Revision to the Combined Code

8   Which of Higgs's recommendations attracted the most opposition? (5.1)

EXAM TYPE
QUESTION

Daxon plc

Daxon plc is a listed company that carries on business as a book wholesaler. In the financial year ended 31 October 20X5, the growth in sales turnover to £25m has continued to match the rate of inflation; costs have been contained by reducing staff from 96 to 90; the asset turnover rate has been maintained at five times.

The Daxon plc accountant has prepared draft accounts for the year ended 31 October 20X5, and included the following directors' responsibilities statement:

'The directors are required by UK company law to prepare financial statements for each financial period which give a true and fair view of the state of affairs of the group as at the end of the financial period and of the profit and loss for that period. In preparing the financial statements, suitable accounting policies have been used and applied consistently, and reasonable and prudent judgements and estimates have been made. Applicable accounting standards have been followed. The directors are also responsible for maintaining adequate accounting records, for safeguarding the assets of the group, and for preventing and detecting fraud and other irregularities.'

On receiving the statement, one of Daxon plc's directors commented that the statement included aspects that he had always assumed were the responsibility of the auditor and complained about the apparent proliferation of irrelevant new rules.

He requested that the accountant should prepare a memo for the board to explain certain of the items.

Required:

(a)   Assuming that you are the accountant of Daxon plc, draft a memo to the board of directors explaining:

    (i)   The background to the inclusion in the annual report of a directors' responsibilities statement.

    (ii)   What is meant by true and fair and how the board can determine whether the financial statements give a true and fair view.

(b)   (i)   Explain briefly the principal aim of the financial review section of an operating and financial review prepared in accordance with the ASB statement *Operating and Financial Review*.

    (ii)   Explain briefly the matters that should be considered when discussing capital structure and treasury policy.

(20 marks)

For the answer to this question see the 'Answers' section at the end of the book.

FEEDBACK TO
ACTIVITY 1

Disadvantages of a Combined Code based on principles:

- Describing procedures (as opposed to making specific disclosures) may be challenging for some boards of directors.

- There is a danger that the directors' statement might be drafted in very general terms, so that it becomes almost meaningless. (This has already happened to some of the disclosures in the directors' report, for example those concerning disabled employees.)

Chapter 3

SIMPLE GROUPS

DEFINITION

An undertaking is the **subsidiary** of another undertaking if: the parent holds a majority of voting rights; or the parent can appoint directors holding a majority of voting rights; or the parent can control the undertaking by other means; or the parent has a participating interest and actually exercises a dominant influence.

DEFINITION

A **participating interest** means an interest in shares, held for the long term, to secure a contribution to its activities by the exercise of control or influence. A holding of 20% or more is presumed to be a participating interest unless the contrary can be shown.

DEFINITION

A **parent company** is a company that owns a subsidiary undertaking.

This chapter begins by revising the basic principles of group accounts, including the legal and professional requirements as set out in the Companies Act and FRS 2 *Accounting for subsidiary undertakings*. It then looks at the requirements of FRS 7 *Fair values in acquisition accounting*.

Finally, we look at the preparation of consolidated accounts where there has been a step-by-step acquisition. As the name suggests, step-by-step acquisitions involve acquiring control of a company in stages.

Objectives

When you have studied this chapter you should be able to:

- understand the basic principles of acquisition accounting

- explain the principles of measurement relating to the fair value of the consideration and the net assets acquired

- discuss the nature of step-by-step acquisitions

- prepare consolidated financial statements where control is established by a step-by-step acquisition.

1   Companies Act and FRS 2 definitions

1.1   Definition of subsidiary undertaking

The CA89 extended the definition of a subsidiary beyond the previous (CA85) definition to implement the EC Seventh Directive. FRS 2 assists in interpreting the legal definition.

It is important to note that the definitions for accounting purposes refer to a subsidiary undertaking rather than a subsidiary company. A subsidiary undertaking may include a partnership or an unincorporated business.

An undertaking is the **subsidiary** of another undertaking in any of the following circumstances:

(a) the parent holds a majority of the rights to vote at general meetings of the undertaking/company on all or substantially all matters

(b) the parent is a member and has a right to appoint or remove directors having a majority of the rights to vote at board meetings of the undertaking/company on all or substantially all matters

(c) the parent is a member and has the right to control alone a majority of the rights to vote at general meetings of the undertaking/company pursuant to an agreement with other shareholders

(d) the parent has a right to exercise a dominant influence over the undertaking by virtue of provisions in the memorandum or articles or by a lawful contract

(e) the parent has a participating interest and actually exercises a dominant influence or the parent and subsidiary undertaking are managed on a unified basis.

For definition (d) above the existence of a dominant influence is only deemed to apply if the parent has a right to give directions on operating or financial policies and the subsidiary directors are obliged to comply with those directions whether or not they are for the benefit of the subsidiary.

FRS 2 gives guidance on the meaning of the CA 1989 definitions.

(i) For definition (e) the result of the actual exercise of dominant influence is that major decisions will be taken in accordance with the wishes of the dominant party whether these are expressed or perceived. Two or more undertakings are managed on a unified basis if the whole of their operations are integrated and managed as a single unit. An interest should be considered as held on a long-term basis where it is held other than exclusively with a view to subsequent resale.

(ii) For definition (d) the phrase 'dominant influence' is defined in the Act and is a more restrictive definition than the interpretation given for the actual exercise of dominant influence in definition (e). FRS 2 makes it clear that they are two separate definitions.

1.2   Why the definitions need to be so complex

The definition of a subsidiary under the old CA85 applied when either:

(a) more than 50% of the equity shares were held; or

(b) there was control over the composition of the board of directors.

This definition caused difficulties mainly owing to the possibilities of creating a dependent company which was not legally a subsidiary and which could then be used for various 'off balance sheet' activities.

The CA89 fundamentally changed the definition and brought most of these dependent companies into the group accounts.

1.3   Statement of Principles – accounting for interests in other entities

Chapter 8 of the ASB's Statement of Principles covers the accounting treatment of subsidiaries, associates, joint ventures and simple investments. The main points are summarised below.

(a) Single entity financial statements and consolidated financial statements present the reporting entity's interests in other entities from different perspectives.

(b) In single entity financial statements, interests in other entities are dealt with by focusing on the income and capital growth arising from the interest (e.g. dividends received and changes in market value).

(c) In consolidated financial statements, the way in which interests in other entities are dealt with depends on the degree of influence involved.

- An interest in another entity that involves control of that other entity's operating and financial policies is dealt with by incorporating the controlled entity as part of the reporting entity (i.e. by consolidation).

- An interest in another entity that involves joint control of, or significant influence over, that other entity's operating and financial policies is dealt with by recognising the reporting entity's share of that other entity's results and resources in a way that does not imply that they are controlled by the reporting entity (e.g. by the equity method or gross equity method).

- Other interests in other entities (simple investments) are dealt with in the same way as any other asset.

(d) Although consolidated financial statements are the financial statements of the group as a whole, they are prepared from the perspective of the parent's shareholders. As a result, they ultimately focus on the parent's ownership interest in its subsidiaries. The effect on benefit flows of any outside equity interest in the subsidiaries (minority interest) is therefore separately identified.

(e) Consolidated financial statements reflect the whole of the parent's investment in its subsidiaries, including purchased goodwill.

(f) A business combination is reflected in the consolidated financial statements in accordance with its character. Therefore, a transaction that is in the character of:

- an acquisition is reflected in the consolidated financial statements as if the acquirer purchased the acquiree's assets and liabilities as a bundle of assets and liabilities on the open market

- a merger is reflected in the consolidated financial statements as if a new reporting entity, comprising all the parties to the transaction, had been formed.

The Statement of Principles effectively restates generally accepted accounting principles.

2   Requirements relating to the preparation of consolidated accounts

2.1   FRS 2's regulations in relation to acquisition accounting

In most cases, group accounts should be presented as consolidated accounts which may be prepared under the acquisition or merger methods. These methods are dealt with in FRS 6 later in this book.

FRS 2 covers such matters as the following:

- purpose of group accounts

- definition of group members (see above)

- exemptions from preparing group accounts

- exclusions of subsidiaries from consolidation

- consolidation adjustments

- changes in composition of a group and changes in stake.

2.2   Purpose of consolidated accounts

The CA85 requires group accounts to be in the form of consolidated accounts which give a 'true and fair' view.

FRS 2 *Accounting for subsidiary undertakings* states that the purpose of consolidated accounts is to:

'present financial information about a parent undertaking and its subsidiary undertakings as a single economic entity to show the economic resources controlled by the group, the obligations of the group and the results the group achieves with its resources'.

2.3   The usefulness and problems of the current requirements

It is generally accepted that consolidated accounts provide useful information to users of the financial statements. They reflect the economic substance of the group as a single economic entity rather than the individual accounts of the group companies as separate legal entities.

Consolidated accounts reflect the fact that the group controls 100% of the assets and liabilities of the subsidiaries because group assets and liabilities are included. They also show the proportion of shareholders' funds and the result for the year owned by the group.

This is reflected by the disclosure of minority interest in the consolidated profit and loss account and the consolidated balance sheet. Intra-group transactions are eliminated, meaning that distortion of the view of the group's financial performance is avoided.

However, the requirement to prepare consolidated accounts may also cause problems. Consolidated accounts may obscure information about the separate assets, liabilities and results of individual subsidiaries. (The parent undertaking does not have to present its own profit and loss account if group accounts are prepared.) For example, consolidated accounts may hide a situation in which one subsidiary is making losses because the other subsidiaries are making profits or a situation in which one subsidiary has a dangerous liquidity problem.

The acquisition method results in the 'freezing' of the pre-acquisition reserves of subsidiaries and means that shareholders' funds in the consolidated accounts may be very much lower than the aggregate of shareholders' funds in the individual accounts. Because consolidated accounts include all the liabilities of the group, it may appear very much more highly geared than any of the individual companies.

2.4   Consolidation techniques

The CA89 introduced into the law various rules on consolidation accounting. FRS 2 confirms the rules or reduces the choice in some instances. There are three main areas.

*   **Accounting policies** – Uniform group accounting policies should be used for determining the amounts to be included in the consolidated financial statements. In exceptional cases different policies may be used with disclosure.

    Clearly if the aggregate figures are to make sense they should have been derived using common policies.

*   **Accounting periods and dates** – The accounts of all subsidiaries to be used in preparing consolidated financial statements should have the same financial year-end and be for the same accounting period as those of the parent company. Where the financial year of a subsidiary differs from that of the parent company, interim financial statements for that subsidiary prepared to the parent company's accounting date should be used. If this is impracticable, earlier financial statements of the subsidiary undertaking may be used, provided they are prepared for a financial year that ended not more than three months earlier.

*   **Intra-group transactions** – In the past there has been a variety of methods adjusting for the effect of intra-group transactions. Such transactions may result in profits or losses being included in the book value of assets in the consolidation. This area is dealt with in detail in the next section.

3   Adjustments for intra-group trading

3.1   Reasons for adjustments

Presenting information about the economic activities of the group as a single economic entity in consolidated financial statements requires adjustment for intra-group transactions of the amounts reported in the individual financial statements of the parent and its subsidiary undertakings. Intra-group transactions may result in a profit or loss that is included at least temporarily in the book value of group assets. To the extent that such assets are still held in the undertakings included in the consolidation at the balance sheet date, the related profits or losses recorded in the individual financial statements have not arisen for the group as a whole and must therefore be eliminated from group results and asset values. The elimination should be in full, even where the transactions involve subsidiaries with minority interests.

3.2   Situations where intra-group profits occur

Intra-group profits occur in two situations:

*   goods are sold by one member of the group to another and the items are used as raw materials in the receiving company or sold on by the receiving company

*   goods are sold by one member of the group to another and the items are used as fixed assets by the receiving company.

Each situation is dealt with below.

3.3 Stock

Where goods have been sold by one group company to another at a profit and some of these goods are unsold at the year end, then the profit loading on these goods is unrealised from the viewpoint of the group as a whole.

- **Wholly-owned subsidiary** – Where goods are sold by S Ltd (a wholly-owned subsidiary) to H Ltd (its parent company), or by H Ltd to S Ltd, and some of the goods are in stock at the year end, there are two steps:

    (a) calculate the unrealised profit in closing stock; and

    (b) Dr   Consolidated revenue reserves

          Cr   Consolidated stock

  with the unrealised profit. This reduces stock to cost and removes unrealised profit from the group reserves.

- **Partly-owned subsidiary** – Suppose H Ltd owns 90% of S Ltd. During the year S Ltd sells goods to H Ltd at cost plus 25%. At the year end the closing stock of H Ltd includes £8,000 of goods, at invoice value, acquired originally from S Ltd. What adjustments are required in the consolidation working papers?

  In the past this was an area in which opinions differed. The CA 1989 requires intra-group profits to be eliminated but where a subsidiary is partly owned it allows the elimination to be either of the whole of the profit or in proportion to the group's shareholding in the subsidiary.

3.4 The treatment of intra-group profits as required by FRS 2

FRS 2 removes the choice as to who should suffer the deduction of intra-group profit and requires that 'the profits should be eliminated against both the group's interest and the minority's interest in proportion to their interest in the company whose individual accounts recorded the profits'.

Thus, sales from the parent company to the subsidiary produce profits in the parent company. Any unrealised profits should be charged against the group. Sales from the subsidiary to the parent company produce profits in the subsidiary company. The unrealised profits should be split between the group and the minority.

Returning to the above example of H Ltd and S Ltd, the total unrealised profit is:

$$\frac{25}{125} \times £8,000 = £1,600$$

(Note the denominator in the fraction. The £8,000 is at selling price to S Ltd, i.e. 100 + 25.)

Consolidated stock must be reduced (credited) with £1,600.

The debit to this credit is split between consolidated reserves and minority interests as the subsidiary recorded the original profit. The journal entry required is thus:

		£	£
Dr	Consolidated revenue reserves 90% × 1,600	1,440	
Dr	Minority interests 10% × 1,600	160	
	Cr Consolidated stock		1,600

A note to the accounts would show 'Provision has been made for the whole of the unrealised profit in stock'. This note should appear in the statement on accounting policies.

If H Ltd had sold the goods to S Ltd the journal entry required would be

		£	£
		£	£
Dr	Consolidated revenue reserves	1,600	
	Cr Consolidated stock		1,600

3.5   Fixed assets

The problems involved are similar to those considered under stock, but there is the added complication of depreciation on the fixed assets.

Example – fixed assets

At the beginning of the year S Ltd (60% owned by H Ltd) sells goods costing £20,000 to H Ltd. H Ltd pays £25,000 for the goods and uses them as fixed assets, depreciating over five years with a nil scrap value at the end of the period using the straight line basis.

Solution

There are two points here.

(a) There is an unrealised profit of £5,000 in the transfer price of the fixed asset.

(b) During the first year in which the fixed asset is used H Ltd is incurring a depreciation charge of 20% of £25,000. Had the goods been transferred at cost, the depreciation charge would have been only £4,000. This, of course, works in the opposite direction to (a) from the group's viewpoint.

Step 1

Calculate the cost and accumulated depreciation on the transferred asset as it stands in the balance sheet.

	Per balance sheet
	£
Cost	25,000
Accumulated depreciation	5,000
NBV	20,000

Step 2

Compare these figures with how the fixed asset would appear had there been no transfer (i.e. how the asset should appear).

	Per balance sheet	Should be
	£	£
Cost	25,000	20,000
Accumulated depreciation	5,000	4,000
	20,000	16,000

Step 3

Calculate the adjustments required.

	Per balance sheet	Should be	Adjustment	
	£	£	£	
Cost	25,000	20,000	5,000	(a) Unrealised profit
Accumulated depreciation	5,000	4,000	1,000	(b) Depreciation overcharge
NBV	20,000	16,000		

Step 4

Deal with the adjustments.

(a) Unrealised profit on transfer

A provision for unrealised profit will be made, which reduces the cost of the fixed asset from its transfer value to the original cost to the group. The debit will either be wholly to consolidated reserves or shared between the group and minority interest depending upon where the original profit was recorded. In this case:

		£	£
Dr	Consolidated profit and loss account (60% × 5,000)	3,000	
Dr	Minority interest (40% × 5,000)	2,000	
	Cr Fixed asset cost (provision for unrealised profit)		5,000

(b) Each year the provision for unrealised profit will be reduced by £1,000 to adjust for the excess depreciation charged. The consolidated reserves, and minority interest when appropriate, will be credited. After five years, at the end of the useful life of the asset, the provision for unrealised profit will be fully written back. In this particular case, the depreciation is charged in H Ltd, and therefore the profit adjustment is wholly attributable to the group:

		£	£
Dr	Provision for depreciation (provision for unrealised profit)	1,000	
	Cr Consolidated profit and loss account		1,000

Step 5

The fixed assets section of the balance sheet will show:

	Cost £	Depn £	£
Fixed assets			
Plant (25,000 − 5,000)	20,000		
(5,000 − 1,000)		4,000	16,000

ACTIVITY 1	A plc owns 80% of the equity shares in Z Ltd. During the year ended 31 December 20X4 Z Ltd sold goods to A plc for £100,000 making a profit of 20% on selling price.

At the balance sheet date £30,000 of these goods remained in the stocks of A plc.

What is the unrealised profit in stock at 31 December 20X4 and how will this be dealt with in the consolidated accounts?

Feedback to this activity is at the end of the chapter.

3.6   Alternative treatments for eliminating intra-group unrealised profits

The alternative treatments that have been used in the past include the following:

• eliminating the unrealised profit from group reserves in all circumstances

• eliminating the group share only.

Using the above activity, the adjustments would therefore be as follows.

			£	£
(a)	Dr	Consolidated reserves	6,000	
	Cr	Consolidated stocks		6,000
(b)	Dr	Consolidated reserves	4,800	
	Cr	Consolidated stocks		4,800

The second alternative is easier to criticise than the first.

Transactions between undertakings included in the consolidation deal with the assets and liabilities that are wholly within the group's control, even if they are not wholly owned. From the perspective of the group as a single entity no profit or loss arises on intra-group transactions because no increase or decrease in the group's net assets has occurred.

The treatment leaves stock at a value which is above cost to the group.

The first alternative has the support of some commentators on the grounds of prudence. Legally the minority interests have made a profit on the transaction as the goods have been properly sold to the other company. The group should therefore suffer the full adjustment. However FRS 2 views the adjustment on a matching basis. Group accounts are being prepared and from a group perspective the transaction is deemed not to have taken place. If it is so deemed then profit must be removed from where it has been included.

4   Exemptions from preparing group accounts

4.1   Exemptions for intermediate parent companies

An intermediate parent company is a company which has a subsidiary but is also itself a subsidiary of another company.

For example:

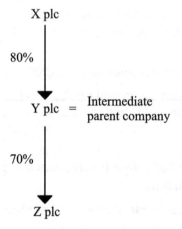

An intermediate parent company is exempt from the requirement to prepare group accounts if:

(a) none of its securities is listed anywhere in the EC; and

(b) its immediate holding company is incorporated in the EC.

Providing that:

(a) it is wholly owned by that immediate parent; or

(b) its immediate parent holds more than 50% and notice for the preparation of group accounts has not been served from shareholders owning either more than one half of the remaining shares or 5% of the total shares.

Various detailed conditions apply for this exemption including the need for the intermediate parent company to be included in the group accounts of an EC parent. A copy of these accounts must be filed with the Registrar of Companies together with an English translation.

4.2   Exemptions for small- and medium-sized groups

A parent company need not prepare group accounts if the group headed by that parent satisfies at least two of the following conditions.

Annual turnover	£27.36m gross or £22.8m net
Balance sheet assets	£13.68m gross or £11.4m net
Average employees	250

The 'gross' figures are those calculated prior to any consolidation adjustments whereas the 'net' figures are those after the consolidation adjustments, such as the elimination of intra-group balances, have been made. A company may satisfy the relevant limits on either a net or a gross basis or by a mixture of the two.

The purpose of allowing the calculations to be made using the higher gross figures is to prevent a parent company from having to prepare group accounts in order to discover that it does not need to prepare group accounts.

Surprisingly, if the accounting period is more or less than one year the turnover limit specified is not adjusted on a pro-rata basis as it is for individual company abbreviated accounts limits.

The right to the exemption from preparing group accounts does not apply if any company in the group is:

(a) a public company; or

(b) a banking or insurance company; or

(c) a company authorised under the Financial Services Act.

5   The exclusion of subsidiary undertakings from consolidation

5.1   Introduction

Under the CA85 there are cases where subsidiary undertakings need not or must not be included in the consolidation. Where all of the subsidiaries fall within the exclusions, group accounts are not required.

FRS 2 is based on the premise that the value of the information provided by the consolidated accounts depends on the extent to which the information about the group is complete, i.e. all undertakings are consolidated. Thus a subsidiary should only be excluded in exceptional circumstances. Where such exceptional circumstances are identified FRS 2 makes exclusions mandatory rather than optional.

5.2   Different activities

Subsidiaries must be excluded from consolidation where their activities are so different from other undertakings in the consolidation that their inclusion would be incompatible with the obligation to give a true and fair view. The exclusion does not apply merely because some of the undertakings are industrial, some commercial and some provide services or because they carry on industrial or commercial activities involving different products or providing different services.

This is the only mandatory exclusion under the Companies Act.

Where a subsidiary is excluded because of dissimilar activities, the group accounts should include separate financial statements for that subsidiary. They may be combined with the financial statements of other subsidiaries with similar operations if appropriate.

In the group accounts the investment in the subsidiary should be stated using the equity method of accounting.

5.3   Materiality

The Companies Act states that a subsidiary undertaking may be excluded from the consolidation where its inclusion is not material for the purpose of giving a true and fair view.

Two or more undertakings may be excluded on these grounds only if they are not material when taken together.

FRS 2 (like any Accounting Standard) does not deal with immaterial items and therefore does not cover this exclusion.

5.4   Severe long-term restrictions

A subsidiary should be excluded from the consolidation where severe long-term restrictions substantially hinder the exercise of the rights of the parent company over the assets or management of that undertaking.

Subsidiaries excluded from consolidation are to be treated as fixed asset investments. They are to be included at their carrying amount when the restrictions came into force, subject to any write down for impairment in value, and no further accruals are to be made for profits or losses of those subsidiary undertakings, unless the parent undertaking still exercises significant influence. In the latter case they are to be treated as associates.

5.5   Disproportionate expense or undue delay

In the CA85 a subsidiary may be excluded from the consolidation where the information necessary for the preparation of group accounts cannot be obtained without disproportionate expense or undue delay. Whether the expense is disproportionate or the delay undue should be judged in the context of that information to the group accounts.

FRS 2, however, states that neither reason can justify excluding a subsidiary.

5.6   Temporary investment

A subsidiary should be excluded from the consolidation where the interest of the parent company is held exclusively with a view to subsequent resale and the undertaking has not previously been included in consolidated group accounts prepared by the parent company.

The investment in the subsidiary will be shown as a current asset at the lower of cost and net realisable value.

5.7   Summary

Reason	CA89	FRS 2	Treatment
Different activities	Mandatory	Mandatory (in exceptional circumstances only)	Equity accounting
Severe long-term restrictions	Optional	Mandatory	If restrictions in force at date of acquisition carry initially at cost. If restrictions came into force at a later date equity account at date when restrictions came into force. Consider need for provisions for impairment in value.
Immaterial	Optional	Not applicable	–
Disproportionate expense or undue delay	Optional	Not permissible	–
Temporary investment	Optional	Mandatory	Current asset at the lower of cost and NRV

ACTIVITY 2

(a)   X plc, an international manufacturing group, has a subsidiary undertaking, Z Ltd, which is an insurance company. Can the group be exempted from consolidating Z Ltd on the grounds of different activities?

(b)   A plc owns a subsidiary undertaking, P Ltd, which is located in an African state where the Government has for a number of years frozen all remittances out of the country by private individuals and companies.

Does A plc need to include P Ltd in its consolidated accounts?

(c)   The N group has the following group figures at its current year end.

Annual turnover £28m gross and net.

Balance sheet assets £11m net £13m gross.

Average employees 245.

Do group accounts need to be prepared?

Answer the above questions giving reasons.

Feedback to this activity is at the end of the chapter.

5.8   The validity of the arguments for non-consolidation of subsidiary undertakings

FRS 2 requires the consolidation of subsidiaries in situations based on full control of the net assets of the subsidiary and the intention to hold the subsidiary as a long-term investment. If there is no or insufficient control, it is misleading to prepare group accounts on a basis which implies full control as does the consolidation basis. Similarly if there is no intention to retain the subsidiary, it is misleading to treat it as an integral part of the group by consolidation of its assets and liabilities.

The main area where it is arguable whether a subsidiary should be excluded from consolidation relates to dissimilar activities. Consolidation does not imply that all businesses within the group are in similar trades. The consolidation accounts merely show the collective assets under the control of the parent company. Segmental analysis shows the split between different activities where appropriate. Therefore, it could be argued that there are no situations in which this exclusion is merited.

FRS 2 does however stress that cases of different activities are exceptional. For example it states in its explanatory notes that the contrast between banking and insurance companies and other companies is not sufficient of itself to justify non-consolidation.

6   FRS 7 *Fair values in acquisition accounting*

6.1   Introduction

In order to account for an acquisition, the acquiring company must measure the cost of what it is accounting for, which will normally represent:

- the cost of the investment in its own balance sheet; and

- the amount to be allocated between the identifiable net assets of the subsidiary and goodwill in the consolidated financial statements.

The subsidiary's identifiable assets and liabilities are included in the consolidated accounts at their fair values for the following reasons.

- Consolidated accounts are prepared from the perspective of the group, rather than from the perspectives of the individual companies. The book values of the subsidiary's assets and liabilities are largely irrelevant, because the consolidated accounts must reflect their cost to the group (i.e. to the parent), not their original cost to the subsidiary. The cost to the group is their fair value.

- Purchased goodwill is the difference between the cost of an acquired entity and the aggregate of the fair values of that entity's identifiable assets and liabilities. If fair values are not used, the value of goodwill will be meaningless.

6.2   Objective of FRS 7

The objective of FRS 7 is as follows:

- To ensure that when a business entity is acquired by another, all the assets and liabilities that existed in the acquired entity at the date of acquisition are recorded at fair values reflecting their condition at that date.

FRS 7 was intended to solve two main problems.

- For acquisition accounting, the CA89, FRS 2 and FRS 6 require the cost of investment to be based on the fair value of the consideration given. The subsidiary's identifiable assets and liabilities must be included in the consolidated accounts at their fair values. However, before FRS 7 was issued there was very little guidance as to how fair values should be determined.

- During the 1980s, one of the more common creative accounting abuses concerned the valuation of assets and liabilities of subsidiaries at the date of acquisition.

An acquiring company would set up a large provision for future reorganisation costs/operating losses among the net assets acquired. Setting up the provision had no effect on profits. It increased the purchased goodwill figure, so increased the amount debited directly to reserves on acquisition. (Before the issue of FRS 10, immediate elimination against reserves was the preferred method of accounting for goodwill.) However, after acquisition, losses or costs that would have been charged against profits could then be charged directly against the provision, thus increasing the reported profit figure. The larger the provision, the higher the reported profits figure could be. Many UK companies appeared to be abusing this principle in the 1980s and setting up large contingent provisions for expenses that were not known at the date of the acquisition. FRS 7 effectively prohibited this practice.

6.3 Main requirements of FRS 7

- The assets and liabilities recognised in the allocation of fair values should be those of the acquired entity that existed at the date of acquisition. They should be measured at fair values that reflect the conditions at the date of the acquisition.

- The liabilities of the acquired entity should not include provisions for future operating losses. Changes in the assets and liabilities resulting from the acquirer's intentions or from events after the acquisition should be dealt with as post-acquisition items. Similarly, costs of reorganisation and integrating the business acquired, whether they relate to the acquired entity or the acquiring group, should be dealt with as post-acquisition costs and do not affect the fair values at the date of acquisition.

- Fair values should be based on the value at which an asset or liability could be exchanged in an arm's length transaction. The fair value of monetary items should take into account the amounts expected to be received or paid and their timing.

- Unless they can be measured at market value, the fair values of non-monetary assets will normally be based on replacement cost, but should not exceed their recoverable amount as at the date of acquisition. The recoverable amount reflects the condition of the assets on acquisition but not any impairments resulting from subsequent events.

Provisions for future reorganisation costs/losses should not be established as part of the fair values of the net assets of a subsidiary acquired. The costs/losses relate to the post-acquisition period and no 'liability' exists at the acquisition date which complies with the definition of a liability in the Statement of Principles.

6.4 Allocation of fair values to assets and liabilities

- **Tangible fixed assets** – The fair value of a tangible fixed asset should be based on:
  - (a) market value, if assets similar in type and condition are bought and sold on an open market; or
  - (b) depreciated replacement cost, otherwise.

  The fair value should not exceed the recoverable amount of the asset.

- **Intangible assets** – The fair value should be based on the asset's replacement cost, which is normally its estimated market value.

- **Stocks and work-in-progress** – Stocks that the acquired company trades on a market in which it participates as both a buyer and a seller should be valued at current market prices. Other stocks should be valued at the lower of replacement cost and net realisable value.

- **Quoted investments** – Quoted investments should be valued at market price.

- **Monetary assets and liabilities** – The fair value should take into account the amounts expected to be received or paid and their timing. Fair value should be determined by reference to market prices, where available, by reference to the current price at which the business could acquire similar assets or enter into similar obligations, or by discounting to present value.

- **Contingencies** – Contingent assets and liabilities should be measured at fair values where these can be determined (reasonable estimates of the expected outcome may be used).

  Note: FRS 12 prohibits the recognition of contingent assets and liabilities in individual financial statements.

- **Pensions and other post retirement benefits** – The fair value of a deficiency or (if it can be recovered through reduced contributions) a surplus in a pension or other post retirement benefits scheme, should be recognised as a liability or an asset of the acquiring group.

- **Deferred tax** – Deferred tax on adjustments to record assets and liabilities at their fair values should be recognised in accordance with the requirements of FRS 19 *Deferred tax*.

  Deferred tax assets that were not recognised because they were not recoverable may become recoverable as a result of the acquisition. Deferred tax assets of the acquired entity should be recognised. Deferred tax assets of the acquirer or other group companies should be recognised as a credit to the tax charge in the post-acquisition period.

ACTIVITY 3

X plc acquired 80% of the ordinary share capital of Y Ltd on 30 September 20X4 for £320,000.

The net assets of Y Ltd at that date had a book value of £350,000.

The following information is relevant.

(a) Y Ltd's freehold factory is included in the accounts at £100,000 and no adjustment has been made to recognise the valuation of £120,000 put on the property when it was professionally revalued on 15 September 20X4.

(b) The fair value of Y Ltd's stock at 30 September 20X4 is estimated to be £4,000 less than its book value at that date.

(c) In August 20X4 Y Ltd made a decision to close down a small workshop with the loss of some jobs. The net costs of closure are estimated at £10,000. No provision has been made at 30 September 20X4.

What is the goodwill arising on the acquisition of Y Ltd?

Feedback to this activity is at the end of the chapter.

6.5   Investigation period and goodwill adjustments

Because the 'fair value exercise' is complex, it might be necessary to use provisional values in the first post-acquisition financial statements of the acquirer. Any necessary adjustments to these provisional values should be made by the date that the financial statements for the first full financial year following the acquisition are approved by the directors. There must also be a corresponding adjustment to purchased goodwill.

Thereafter, any adjustments should be recognised in the profit and loss account as they occur. The exception to this is the correction of fundamental errors, which should be treated as prior period adjustments as required by FRS 3.

6.6   Fair value of the cost of acquisition

The cost of acquisition is:

(a) the amount of cash paid; plus

(b) the fair value of other purchase consideration given by the acquirer; plus

(c) the expenses of acquisition.

FRS 7 lays down the following rules.

- When settlement of cash consideration is deferred, the amount expected to be payable should be discounted to its present value. The discount rate used should be the rate at which the acquirer could obtain a similar borrowing.

- Where shares (and other capital instruments) issued by the acquirer are quoted on a ready market, the market price on the date of acquisition normally provides the most reliable measure of fair value.

Where, owing to unusual fluctuations, the market price on one particular date is an unreliable measure of fair value, market prices for a reasonable period before the date of acquisition, during which acceptances could be made, would need to be considered.

- Where securities issued by the acquirer are not quoted or, if they are quoted, the market price is unreliable owing, for example, to the lack of an active market in the quantities involved, it is necessary to make a valuation of those securities. The fair value is estimated by taking into account items such as:

  (a) the value of similar securities that are quoted

  (b) the present value of the future cash flows of the instrument issued

  (c) any cash alternative to the issue of securities

  (d) the value of any underlying security into which there is an option to convert.

- When the amount of purchase consideration is contingent on one or more future events, the cost of acquisition should include a reasonable estimate of the fair value of amounts expected to be payable in the future. The cost of acquisition (and therefore the goodwill arising) should be adjusted to reflect changes in this estimate until the amount payable is known with certainty.

- Fees and similar incremental costs incurred directly in making an acquisition should be included in the cost of acquisition. (These might include fees paid to merchant banks, accountants, legal advisers, etc.)

- Issue costs of shares are not included in the cost of acquisition. These are deducted from the proceeds of the issue, as required by FRS 4 (see the relevant chapter of this text).

- Internal costs and other expenses that cannot be directly attributed to the acquisition cannot be included in the cost of acquisition. They should be charged to the profit and loss account.

7 Changes in composition of a group

7.1 Date of change in composition of a group

The date on which an undertaking becomes or ceases to be another undertaking's subsidiary undertaking marks the point at which a new accounting treatment for that undertaking is applied. The relevant date is the date on which control passes. The date on which control passes is a matter of fact and cannot be backdated or otherwise altered.

- Where control is transferred by a public offer, the date control is transferred is the date the offer becomes unconditional, usually as a result of a sufficient number of acceptances being received. For private treaties, the date control is transferred is generally the date an unconditional offer is accepted.

- Where an undertaking becomes or ceases to be a subsidiary undertaking as a result of the issue or cancellation of shares, the date control is transferred is the date of issue or cancellation.

The date that control passes may be indicated by the acquiring party commencing its direction of the operating and financial policies of the acquired undertaking or by changes in the flow of economic benefits. The date on which the consideration for the transfer of control is paid is often an important indication of the date.

8 Step-by-step acquisitions

8.1 The problems caused by step-by-step acquisitions

A step-by-step or piecemeal acquisition arises when shares in the subsidiary are acquired over a period of time. The question arises as to whether goodwill should be computed by reference to each slice of share capital acquired, i.e. whether the fair value of assets is considered on each acquisition of shares.

FRS 2 takes the simpler approach: the computation of goodwill will be one computation by reference to the fair value of the net assets of the subsidiary at the date the subsidiary becomes part of the group. This complies with Sch 4A para 9 CA85.

However, there are two situations in which problems may arise:

- when a group increases its stake in an undertaking that is already a subsidiary
- when an increase in stake results in an associate becoming a subsidiary.

When a group increases its interest in an undertaking that is already its subsidiary, FRS 2 states that the identifiable assets and liabilities of that subsidiary should be revalued to fair value and goodwill arising on the increase in interest should be calculated by reference to that fair value. This revaluation is not required if the difference between fair values and carrying amounts of the identifiable assets and liabilities attributable to the increase in stake is not material.

Illustration

A Ltd acquires shares in B Ltd over a period of time as follows:

Date	% acquired	Cost	Net assets of B Ltd at fair value
		£	£
31/3/20X6	10%	40,000	100,000
31/3/20X7	60%	250,000	300,000
31/3/20X8	30%	150,000	400,000

B Ltd becomes a subsidiary of A Ltd for the first time at 31 March 20X7. Goodwill is calculated as follows:

	£
Cost (40,000 + 250,000)	290,000
Net assets acquired (70% × 300,000)	(210,000)
Goodwill	80,000

When A Ltd increases its stake in B Ltd on 31 March 20X8, B Ltd is already a subsidiary and goodwill is calculated separately on the additional interest acquired:

		31/3/X7 acquisition	31/3/X8 acquisition
		£	£
Cost		290,000	150,000
Net assets acquired	(70% × 300,000)	(210,000)	
	(30% × 400,000)		(120,000)
		80,000	30,000

Total goodwill is £110,000.

8.2   Step-by-step acquisitions involving an associate

When a subsidiary undertaking is acquired in stages, goodwill is normally calculated on the basis of the fair value of the net assets acquired *at the date on which control is gained*.

This may present problems where an existing investment is increased so that an associate becomes a subsidiary. The normal goodwill calculation as required by FRS 2 and the Companies Act ignores the fact that the investing company's share of post-acquisition results has already been included in group reserves from the date on which the investment became an associate. Under the normal rules, these post-acquisition results must be reclassified as goodwill.

FRS 2 addresses this situation by stating that, in cases where the normal calculation would be misleading, goodwill should be calculated on each separate purchase. Where an associate becomes a subsidiary, goodwill must be calculated on each separate purchase in order to give a true and fair view.

KEY POINT

Where an associate becomes a subsidiary, goodwill must be calculated on each separate purchase in order to give a true and fair view.

Illustration

A Ltd acquires shares in B Ltd over a period of time as follows:

Date	% acquired	Cost £	Net assets of B Ltd at fair value £
31/3/20X6	30%	100,000	100,000
31/3/20X7	60%	250,000	300,000

B Ltd becomes an associate at 31 March 20X6 and a subsidiary at 31 March 20X7. Goodwill is calculated as follows.

		31/3/X6 acquisition £	31/3/X7 acquisition £
Cost		100,000	250,000
Net assets acquired	(30% × 100,000)	(30,000)	
	(60% × 300,000)		(180,000)
		70,000	70,000

Total goodwill is £140,000.

Note: This method of calculating goodwill contravenes the Companies Act and therefore 'true and fair view' override disclosures are required.

ACTIVITY 4

Company X acquires an 80% holding in Company Y over a number of years as shown below:

Holding acquired %	Fair value of net assets of Y £m	Price paid £m
10	8	1.00
20	10	2.50
25	12	3.10
25	16	5.95
80		12.55

The investee's balance sheet at the consolidation date shows:

	£m
Net assets	20
Share capital	4
Reserves	6
	20

The amount of issued share capital has remained unchanged.

The goodwill is held at cost without amortisation.

Calculate:

* the goodwill arising from X's investment in Y
* the group's share of Y's post-acquisition reserves.

Feedback to this activity is at the end of the chapter.

8.3 The effects of a subsequent bonus issue or a capital reduction of a subsidiary company

There may be changes to the share capital of a subsidiary following its acquisition. Either may appear as a complication in an examination question.

Bonus issue – A bonus issue is a transfer of reserves to share capital. It therefore should not affect the financial statements of the group. The net assets of the group are the same and the parent company has the same percentage interest in the subsidiary. Care needs to be taken to consider properly the 'reserves at acquisition' figure supplied to you in the question however.

If the bonus issue is less than the amount of reserves which existed at the date of acquisition, then reduce the reserves at acquisition by the bonus issue when calculating goodwill. Goodwill remains the same as the share capital increases by the group share of the bonus issue.

If the bonus issue is more than the amount of reserves which existed at the date of acquisition, then as far as the group is concerned, the post-acquisition profits recorded in group reserves should be the same as before the issue. Therefore the group share of all the remaining reserves of the subsidiary needs to go to consolidated reserves and in addition the group share of the post-acquisition profits which have been turned into share capital needs to be included in consolidated reserves rather than the goodwill calculation.

Capital reduction – A capital reduction normally arises when a company has got into financial difficulties. The normal feature is that some of the share capital is written off so that a debit balance on the profit and loss account is eliminated. In addition however, further write-offs may be required due to the write down in value of assets.

It is thus similar to a bonus issue to the extent that it effectively represents a transfer from share capital **to** reserves. There should thus be no effect on the consolidated balance sheet. It will however be easier to compute goodwill which arose on the original acquisition by using the original figures for share capital and reserves.

If there has been an asset write down, then the group share of the asset write down must be charged against group reserves.

The easiest way to account for the effect on the group financial statements is to compute the allocation of share capital and reserves before the effect of the capital reduction on these items.

Example

A plc has an 80% interest in Y Ltd which is undertaking a capital reduction scheme. The balance sheet before the capital reduction is as follows:

	£
Net assets	500,000
Share capital	650,000
Profit and loss	(150,000)
	500,000

The capital reduction scheme will eliminate the debit balance on the profit and loss account and reduce assets by £100,000.

A plc paid £800,000 for its investment when the reserves of Y Ltd were £200,000. Goodwill arising on the acquisition has been fully amortised.

Show how the relevant items would be included in the consolidated balance sheet.

Step 1

Put through the capital reduction scheme.

	£
Net assets	400,000
Share capital	400,000
Profit and loss	-
	400,000

Step 2

Minority interests

$$20\% \times 400,000 \quad = \quad £80,000$$

Step 3

Goodwill: calculate using original figures.

	£	£
Cost of investment		800,000
Less: Share of net assets acquired		
Share capital	650,000	
Reserves	200,000	
	850,000	680,000
	(80%)	
Goodwill – fully amortised		120,000

Step 4

Compute post acquisition reserves to go to group reserves.

	£
Reserves at acquisition	200,000
Loss at time of capital reduction	150,000
Post acquisition loss	350,000
Add asset write down	100,000
	450,000
Loss to group reserves 80%	360,000
Add goodwill fully amortised	120,000
	480,000

Effect on consolidated balance sheet:

	£
Net assets	400,000
MI	(80,000)
	320,000
Group reserves reduced by	480,000
Elimination of cost of investment	800,000

9   Reverse acquisitions

Reverse acquisitions occur when a parent acquires a subsidiary by issuing new shares, and then issues so many new shares that the former shareholders of the subsidiary end up controlling the parent. Reverse acquisitions can be used as a cheap way of gaining access to the stock exchange. The unlisted subsidiary reverses into and takes control of a quoted parent.

Under International Accounting Standards, the substance of the transaction is reported; the legal subsidiary is treated as the acquirer, and the legal parent is treated as the subsidiary (IAS 22 Paragraph 12). However, this is not allowed under UK law, and so it is not addressed by FRS 6. UITF Information Sheet Number 17 states that there might be occasions when the true and fair override could be invoked to allow the subsidiary to be treated as the parent, but that each case would have to be taken on its merits.

10   IFRS 3 *Business Combinations*

You should be aware that, in the future, the accounting for groups is likely to be revised. Traditional UK accounting is now that:

- acquisitions are consolidated using acquisition accounting (the usual situation) while mergers are consolidated using merger accounting

- positive goodwill arising on consolidating an acquisition is capitalised on the consolidated balance sheet as an intangible fixed asset and amortised over its useful life.

This is set to change in the future. Standard-setters have never been comfortable with leaving preparers to accounts to decide whether a particular business combination is an acquisition or a merger, suspecting that many combinations that are accounted for as mergers are really acquisitions. After all, if there is no dominant party in the combination, why did it take place at all?

A Position Paper by the G4+1 group proposed to ban the merger method (also known as the pooling of interests method). This idea was picked up by the IASB and developed into ED 3 which has now become IFRS 3 (issued in March 2004).

The key points of IFRS 3 are as follows.

- All business combinations must be accounted for using the acquisition method (also called the purchase method). The merger method is prohibited.

- Positive goodwill arising on consolidating an acquisition is capitalised on the consolidated balance sheet as an intangible fixed asset. It is not routinely amortised. Instead it must be tested for impairment annually, and only written down if found to be impaired.

The days of the merger method in the UK are numbered. In due course UK accounting will follow the lead of IFRS 3 and ban merger accounting.

SELF-TEST **QUESTIONS**	**The exclusion of subsidiary undertakings from consolidation**

The exclusion of subsidiary undertakings from consolidation

1   Define 'subsidiary undertaking'. (1.1)

2   What are the main points covered by Chapter 8 of the Statement of Principles on the accounting treatment of subsidiaries, associates, joint ventures and investments? (1.3)

Adjustments for intra-group trading

3   How are intra-group profits on stock accounted for? What are the requirements of FRS 2 on this point? (3.3, 3.4)

Exemptions from preparing group accounts

4   What exemptions from preparing group accounts are possible? (4)

The exclusion of subsidiary undertakings from consolidation

5   When can a subsidiary undertaking be excluded from consolidated accounts? (5)

Fair values in acquisition accounting

6   What is the objective of FRS 7 and what two problems was it explicitly intended to address? (6.2)

7   What is the definition of fair value? (6.3)

8   How should fair values be allocated to (a) tangible fixed assets, (b) stocks and work-in-progress and (c) monetary assets and liabilities? (6.4)

Step-by-step acquisitions

9   How does FRS 2 approach the computation of goodwill in a step-by-step acquisition? (8.1)

10   What are the effects on goodwill and reserves where a subsidiary makes a bonus issue or a capital reduction following acquisition? (8.3)

IFRS 3 *Business combinations*

11   How will goodwill arising on consolidation be treated if the rules in the IASB's IFRS 3 are adopted in the UK? (10)

P Group

The balance sheets of P Ltd and its subsidiaries Q Ltd and R Ltd at 31 December 20X7 are given below:

	P Ltd	Q Ltd	R Ltd
	£	£	£
Tangible fixed assets	775,000	125,750	67,920
Investments			
in Q Ltd	95,000		
in R Ltd	79,000		
Stock	22,950	11,890	7,440
Debtors	55,960	12,530	6,510
Bank	1,250	–	750
	1,029,160	150,170	82,620
Ordinary share capital			
(all £1 shares)	800,000	80,000	49,000
Profit and loss account	197,450	42,950	22,760
Creditors	31,710	27,220	10,860
	1,029,160	150,170	82,620

Additional information

1   P Ltd acquired 75% of the shares of Q Ltd on 1 January 20X0 when Q Ltd's reserves stood at £20,000.

2   Q Ltd acquired 80% of the shares of R Ltd on 1 April 20X4 for £50,000 when R Ltd's reserves stood at £12,000. These shares were transferred to P Ltd on 1 January 20X7 when R Ltd's reserves stood at £20,000. The relevant profit on sale is included in the reserves of Q Ltd.

3   Items purchased by Q Ltd from P Ltd and remaining in stock at 31 December 20X7 amounted to £7,000. P Ltd's profit margin is 20% of selling price.

4   Included in the tangible fixed assets of P Ltd is a machine purchased for £30,000 from Q Ltd on 1 January 20X6, when it had a remaining useful life of four years. Q Ltd purchased the machine on 1 January 20X5 and recorded a profit of £5,000 on the sale of the machine. Both companies depreciate assets using the straight-line method.

5   The following balances are included in debtors and creditors respectively.

   P Ltd   Debtors   - Q Ltd   £25,000
   Q Ltd   Creditors - P Ltd   £17,500

6   A cheque drawn by Q Ltd for £7,500 on 27 December 20X7 was received by P Ltd on 2 January 20X8.

7   It is the policy of the group to capitalise and amortise goodwill over its useful economic life. All goodwill had been completely amortised at 31 December 20X7.

Required:

(a)   Prepare a schedule detailing all the necessary adjustments for 1 to 7 above.

(30 marks)

(b)   Prepare, in a format suitable for inclusion in the annual report of the P Group, the consolidated balance sheet at 31 December 20X7.   **(5 marks)**

(c) Explain the way in which consolidated accounts reflect control and ownership.

(5 marks)

(Total: 40 marks)

EXAM-TYPE
QUESTION 2

A plc

The balance sheets of A plc and its investee undertakings, B Ltd and C Ltd, at 30 September 20X6 (the accounting date of all three companies) are given below:

	A plc		B Ltd		C Ltd	
	£'000	£'000	£'000	£'000	£'000	£'000
Fixed assets (notes 1 and 3):						
Tangible assets	9,100		9,000		8,000	
Investments	8,900		-		-	
		18,000		9,000		8,000
Current assets (note 3):						
Stocks	4,000		3,000		2,500	
Debtors	3,000		2,500		2,000	
Cash in hand	800		700		600	
	7,800		6,200		5,100	
Current liabilities (note 3):						
Trade creditors	2,500		2,000		1,700	
Taxation	600		500		450	
Proposed dividend	600		500			
Bank overdraft	3,200		2,800		2,450	
	6,900		5,800		4,600	
Net current assets		900		400		500
Long-term loans (note 3)		(8,000)		(2,000)		(2,000)
		10,900		7,400		6,500
Capital and reserves:						
Called up share capital						
(£1 shares)		5,000		4,000		4,000
Profit and loss account		5,900		3,400		2,500
		10,900		7,400		6,500

Notes

1 On 15 June 20X0 (the date of incorporation of B Ltd) A plc subscribed for 3.2 million shares in B Ltd at par. No new shares have been issued by B Ltd since its incorporation.

2 On 1 June 20X6 A plc purchased 3 million shares in C Ltd at an agreed value of £1.90 per share. The purchase was financed by an additional issue of loan stock, carrying an interest rate of 10%.

3   C Ltd produced interim financial statements, drawn up as at 1 June 20X6, in connection with the acquisition by A plc. The balance sheet of C Ltd at that date showed the following:

	£'000		£'000
Tangible fixed assets *(note 4)*	7,875	Trade creditors	1,600
Stocks *(note 5)*	2,000	Taxation	300
Debtors	1,450	Bank overdraft	1,825
Cash in hand	600	Long-term loans *(note 6)*	2,000
		Share capital (£1 shares)	4,000
		Profit and loss account	2,200
	11,925		11,925

4   The following information relates to the tangible fixed assets of C Ltd at 1 June 20X6.

	£'000
Gross replacement cost	14,220
Net replacement cost	8,295
Economic value	9,000
Net realisable value	4,000

The fixed assets of C Ltd at 1 June 20X6 had a total purchase cost to C Ltd of £13.5 million. They were all being depreciated at 25% per annum pro rata on that cost. This policy is also appropriate for the consolidated financial statements of A plc. No fixed assets of C Ltd which were included in the interim financial statements drawn up as at 1 June 20X6 were disposed of by C Ltd prior to 30 September 20X6. No fixed asset was fully depreciated by 30 September 20X6.

5   The stocks of C Ltd which were shown in the interim financial statements at cost to C Ltd of £2 million would have cost £2.1 million to replace at 1 June 20X6 and had an estimated net realisable value at that date of £2.4 million. Of the stock of C Ltd in hand at 1 June 20X6, goods costing C Ltd £1.5 million were sold for £1.8 million between 1 June 20X6 and 30 September 20X6.

6   The long-term loan of C Ltd carries a rate of interest of 10% per annum, payable on 31 May annually in arrears. The loan is redeemable at par on 31 May 20X9. The interest cost is representative of current market rates. The accrued interest payable by C Ltd at 30 September 20X6 is included in the trade creditors of C Ltd at that date.

7   On 1 June 20X6 A plc took a decision to rationalise the group so as to integrate C Ltd. The costs of the rationalisation (which were to be borne by A plc) were estimated to total £1.5 million and the process was publicly announced on 1 August 20X6 and due to start on 1 December 20X6. No provision for these costs has been made in any of the financial statements given in this question.

Required:

(a)   Compute the goodwill on consolidation of C Ltd that will be included in the consolidated financial statements of the A plc group for the year ended 30 September 20X6, explaining your treatment of the items mentioned in Notes 2 to 7. You should refer to the provisions of relevant Accounting Standards.

(12 marks)

(b) Prepare the consolidated balance sheet of the A plc group at 30 September 20X6, assuming that A plc deals with investment income on an accruals basis and that goodwill is capitalised and amortised over four years, with a full year's charge in the year of acquisition. **(18 marks)**

Note: ALL your numerical workings can be rounded to the nearest £000.

(Total: 30 marks)

For the answers to these questions see the 'Answers' section at the end of the book.

FEEDBACK TO ACTIVITY 1

Step 1   Calculate the unrealised profit.

£30,000 × 20% = £6,000

Step 2   Calculate minority share of unrealised profit.

£6,000 × 20% = £1,200

Step 3   Show adjustments in consolidated accounts.

		£	£
Dr	Consolidated reserves	4,800	
	Minority interest	1,200	
	Cr Consolidated stocks		6,000

FEEDBACK TO ACTIVITY 2

(a) Z Ltd must be included unless to do so would impair the true and fair view.

(b) P Ltd can be said to be operating under severe long-term restrictions. Its results should not be consolidated and it should be equity accounted at the date restrictions came into force.

(c) No group accounts need to be prepared as the group meets two of the three size criteria for exemption.

FEEDBACK TO ACTIVITY 3

Step 1   Adjust the value of Y Ltd's net assets at 30 September 20X4 to fair value.

	£
Net assets per question	350,000
Revaluation of property	20,000
Write-off of stock	(4,000)
Provision for reorganisation costs*	(10,000)
	356,000

(*Note that since Y Ltd made the decision to close, and the decision was made before the date of acquisition, this is a valid provision.)

Step 2   Calculate goodwill.

	£
Fair value of consideration	320,000
Net assets acquired 80% × £356,000	284,800
Goodwill arising	35,200

FEEDBACK TO ACTIVITY 4		

Step 1 Determine whether the company is a subsidiary at the date of consolidation and, if so, consolidate assets and liabilities with minority being allocated their share of share capital and reserves at that date.

MI 20% × £20m = £4m

Step 2 Perform separate calculations of goodwill as at:

(a) date investee became associate (if applicable)

(b) date investee became subsidiary

(c) date further investments made.

		Transaction		Total
	2	3	4	
	£m	£m	£m	£m
Cost of investment	3.5	3.1	5.95	
Share of net assets acquired at each relevant date:				
30% × £10m	3.0			
25% × £12m		3.0		
25% × £16m			4.00	
Goodwill	0.5	0.1	1.95	2.55
Post acquisition reserves				
30% × (16 – (10 – 4))	3.0			
25% × (16 – (12 – 4))		2.0		
25% × (16 – (16 – 4))			1.0	6.0

Step 3 Effect on group balance sheet

	£m
Goodwill	2.55
Consolidated net assets	20
MI	(4)
	18.55
Addition to group reserves	(6.00)
Elimination of cost of investment	12.55

Chapter 4
COMPLEX GROUP STRUCTURES

Until now, you have only dealt with simple group structures in which one parent owns one or more subsidiaries or associates. This chapter covers more complex group structures in which subsidiaries themselves have investments in subsidiary companies.

It then moves on to cover another important topic, the disposal of a subsidiary. A parent could sell its entire shareholding (full disposal) or part of its shareholding (partial disposal). Following a partial disposal a subsidiary may remain as a subsidiary or become an associate or a simple investment. The group balance sheet is relatively easy to prepare where there has been a disposal, as it simply reflects the position at the balance sheet date. For this reason, exam questions almost always feature the group profit and loss account.

Objectives

When you have studied this chapter you should be able to:

- account for complex group structures

- understand the basic principles relating to the disposal of group companies

- understand the treatment of goodwill on disposal

- account for full, partial and deemed disposals.

1 Mixed and vertical groups

1.1 The different possible structures of a group

More complex group structures exist where a subsidiary of a parent company owns all or part of the shareholding which makes another company also a subsidiary of the parent company. The structures can be classified under two headings.

- vertical groups

- mixed groups.

Examples of both are illustrated below.

Vertical groups

(a) Suppose H Ltd owns 70% of A Ltd. A Ltd is thus a subsidiary of H Ltd.

(b) If, in addition, A Ltd owns 60% of B Ltd, then B Ltd is a subsidiary of A Ltd. Furthermore, B Ltd is said to be a sub-subsidiary of H Ltd.

(c) H Ltd has a direct interest in A Ltd and an indirect interest in B Ltd (exercised via A Ltd's holding in B Ltd). H Ltd has an effective interest of only 42% (70% × 60%) in B Ltd. Nevertheless, B Ltd is a sub-subsidiary of H Ltd because H Ltd has a controlling interest in A Ltd and A Ltd has a controlling interest in B Ltd. There is now a 'vertical group' consisting of H Ltd, A Ltd and B Ltd.

H's interest in B Ltd:

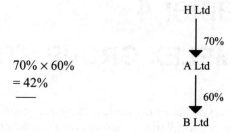

$$70\% \times 60\% = 42\%$$

Where a parent company owns a controlling interest in a subsidiary which in turn owns a controlling interest in a sub-subsidiary, then the group accounts of the ultimate parent company must disclose the parent company's share of the underlying net assets and earnings of both the subsidiary and the sub-subsidiary companies.

Mixed groups

In a mixed group situation the parent company has a controlling interest in at least one subsidiary. In addition, the parent company and the subsidiary together hold a controlling interest in a further company.

For example, H Ltd owns 80% of S Ltd, H Ltd owns 40% of W Ltd, S Ltd owns 30% of W Ltd.

This is a mixed group situation.

(a) S Ltd is a subsidiary of H Ltd.

(b) H Ltd and S Ltd between them own more than 50% of W Ltd (the fact that S Ltd is not a wholly-owned subsidiary of H Ltd is irrelevant).

W Ltd is thus a member of the H Ltd group and must, therefore, be included in the consolidated balance sheet.

Diagrammatically, the situation is as follows.

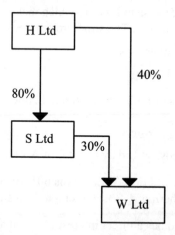

H Ltd's interest in W Ltd = (80% × 30%) + 40% = 64%

Example

H Ltd owns 35% of S Ltd, S Ltd owns 40% of W Ltd and H Ltd owns 40% of W Ltd.

Solution

This is not a mixed group situation. Neither S Ltd nor W Ltd is a member of the H Ltd group, although S Ltd and W Ltd may both be 'associates' of H Ltd.

H Ltd's interest in W Ltd might be calculated as before as (35% × 40%) + 40% = 54%. Although H Ltd has an arithmetic interest in W Ltd which is more than 50%, it does not have parent company control of W Ltd, as it does not control S Ltd's 40% stake in W Ltd.

ACTIVITY 1

H Ltd owns 60% of S Ltd, S Ltd owns 25% of W Ltd, H Ltd owns 30% of W Ltd.

Is W Ltd a subsidiary company of H Ltd?

Feedback to this activity is at the end of the chapter.

2　The direct and indirect methods to consolidate sub-subsidiaries

2.1　Methods of consolidation

Calculations of the goodwill on consolidation, the minority shareholders' interest and so on become more complicated. Nevertheless, the normal approach is used, subject to certain modifications.

There are two methods which can be used for dealing with sub-subsidiaries, each giving different results for particular items.

- **The direct method** – this approach will be followed here.

- **The indirect method** – this requires sub-consolidations to be made. In the example in the previous section B Ltd would be consolidated with A to produce the A group accounts. H Ltd and the A group would then be consolidated.

This method is generally more time consuming (in an examination question).

Two situations will be considered in turn.

(a) Situation 1 – where the subsidiary is acquired first and then the sub-subsidiary.

(b) Situation 2 – where the subsidiary acquires the sub-subsidiary first and is subsequently taken over by the parent company.

Example 1 – Subsidiary acquired first

The draft balance sheets of H Ltd, S Ltd and T Ltd, as at 31 December 20X4, are as follows.

	H Ltd £'000	S Ltd £'000	T Ltd £'000		H Ltd £'000	S Ltd £'000	T Ltd £'000
Net assets	180	80	80	Share capital (£1 shares)	200	100	50
Shares in subsidiary	120	80		Profit and loss a/c	100	60	30
	300	160	80		300	160	80

You ascertain that H Ltd acquired 75,000 £1 shares in S Ltd on 1 January 20X4 when the revenue reserves of S Ltd amounted to £40,000. S Ltd acquired 40,000 £1 shares in T Ltd on 30 June 20X4 when the revenue reserves of T Ltd amounted to £25,000; they had been £20,000 on the date of H Ltd's acquisition of S Ltd. Goodwill is amortised over five years from the date of acquisition, with a full year's charge in the year of acquisition.

Solution

Step 1

Draw a diagram of the group structure and then set out the respective interests of the parent company and the minority, distinguishing between direct (D) and indirect (I) interests.

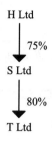

H Ltd

75%

S Ltd

80%

T Ltd

	S Ltd			*T Ltd*
Interest of:				
H Ltd shareholders	75% (D)	75% × 80% =		60% (I)
Minority shareholders	25% (D)		20% (D)	
		25% × 80% =	20% (I)	
				40%
	100%			100%

Make sure that you understand the above calculations. The main difficulty lies in the calculation of the minority interest in T Ltd. The effective figure of 40% consists of two distinct elements.

(i)   The direct minority of 20% – i.e. the 20% of the share capital of T Ltd not owned by S Ltd.

(ii) 25% of S Ltd is not owned by H Ltd. This 25% minority of S Ltd thus have a stake in T Ltd via their company's holding in T Ltd, equivalent to 25% of 80%, i.e. 20%. This is the indirect minority in T Ltd.

Step 2

Draw a diagram setting out the relationship between the various companies, and show the revenue reserves at key dates:

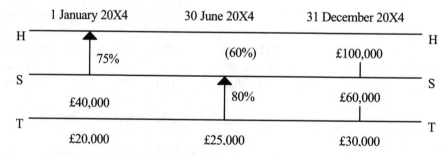

1 January 20X4   30 June 20X4   31 December 20X4

H   H

75%   (60%)   £100,000

S   S

£40,000   80%   £60,000

T   T

£20,000   £25,000   £30,000

Step 3

Goodwill.

Two calculations are required, one for each subsidiary. They are performed separately as goodwill/negative goodwill is determined for each subsidiary.

	Notes	S Ltd		T Ltd	
		£'000	£'000	£'000	£'000
Cost of investment					
(75% × 80)	(1)		120		60
Less: Share of net assets					
at acquisition date					
Share capital		100		50	
Profit and loss account	(2)	40		25	
	(3)	140 (75%)	(105)	75 (60%)	(45)
	(4)		15		15
Amortisation			(3)		(3)
			12		12

Notes

(1)   The cost of H Ltd's investment in S Ltd is £120,000, and this figure is used in the calculation. The cost of S Ltd's investment in T Ltd is £80,000. However, H Ltd owns only 75% of S Ltd, so the 'effective' cost to H Ltd of its indirect holding is T Ltd is £60,000 (75% × £80,000).

(2)   Care must be taken in determining the date for the split between post-acquisition and pre-acquisition reserves. The parent company acquired control of S Ltd on 1 January 20X4, so this is the relevant date: but what about S Ltd's acquisition of shares in T Ltd? When talking about the pre-acquisition/post-acquisition split, the problem is considered from the viewpoint of the ultimate parent company, H Ltd. The test is to ask the question 'When did T Ltd become a member of the H Ltd group?'

The answer is 30 June 20X4. Profits of T Ltd arising after this date are post-acquisition as regards the H Ltd group. The information given regarding T Ltd's reserves at 1 January 20X4 is irrelevant in this context.

(3)   The interest of H Ltd in S Ltd and the effective interest of H Ltd in T Ltd are taken from the table in Step 1. Whilst S Ltd owns 80% of T Ltd's share capital and reserves, H Ltd only owns 75% of S Ltd. Thus, the effective interest of 60% (75% × 80%) is used.

Step 4

Consolidated profit and loss account

	£'000
H Ltd	100
S Ltd 75% (60 – 40) (see note 3 above)	15
T Ltd 60% (30 – 25) (see notes 2 and 3 above)	3
Less: Goodwill amortised (30 ÷ 5)	(6)
	112

Step 5

Minority interest

		Notes	£'000	£'000
S Ltd:	Net assets at balance sheet date			
	Share capital		100	
	Profit and loss account		60	
			160	
Less: Cost of investment in T Ltd		(5)	(80)	
		(6)	80 (25%)	20
T Ltd:	Net assets at balance sheet date			
	Share capital		50	
	Profit and loss account		30	
		(6)	80 (40%)	32
				52

Notes

(5) The minority shareholders in S Ltd are entitled to their share of the net assets of S Ltd. However, one of the assets of S Ltd is the cost of the investment in T Ltd which, in the consolidation process, is replaced with the net assets of T Ltd. The minority shareholders in S Ltd are entitled to their share of these also. They receive their share of T Ltd's net assets as the minority interest in S Ltd form the indirect minority interest in T Ltd. So, the minority in S Ltd receive their share of the net assets of S Ltd after having deducted the cost of the investment in T Ltd, and their share of the net assets of T Ltd as they form the indirect part of the minority interest in T Ltd.

(6) The percentage interests are taken from the table in Step 1.

Step 6

The consolidated balance sheet can now be prepared:

**Summarised consolidated balance sheet of H Ltd
and its subsidiary companies as at 31 December 20X4**

	£
Goodwill	24,000
Net assets	340,000
Minority interests	(52,000)
	312,000
Capital and reserves.	
Called up share capital	200,000
Profit and loss account	112,000
	312,000

ACTIVITY 2

The balance sheets of H Ltd, S Ltd and M Ltd as at 31 December 20X5 were as follows:

	H Ltd £	S Ltd £	M Ltd £
Ordinary share capital (£1 shares)	120,000	60,000	40,000
Reserves	95,000	75,000	35,000
	215,000	135,000	75,000
45,000 shares in S Ltd	72,000		
16,000 shares in M Ltd	25,000		
12,000 shares in M Ltd		20,000	
Sundry net assets	118,000	115,000	75,000
	215,000	135,000	75,000

All shares were acquired on 31 December 20X2 when S reserves amounted to £30,000 and M reserves amounted to £10,000.

You are required to calculate the goodwill arising on the consolidation of S Ltd and M Ltd.

Feedback to this activity is at the end of the chapter.

Example – Subsidiary acquires sub-subsidiary first

The draft balance sheets of H Ltd, S Ltd and T Ltd as at 31 December 20X4 are as follows:

	H Ltd £'000	S Ltd £'000	T Ltd £'000		H Ltd £'000	S Ltd £'000	T Ltd £'000
Net assets	180	80	80	Share capital	200	100	50
Shares in subsidiary	120	80		Revenue reserves	100	60	30
	300	160	80		300	160	80

S Ltd acquired 40,000 £1 shares in T Ltd on 1 January 20X4 when the revenue reserves of T Ltd amounted to £25,000. H Ltd acquired 75,000 £1 shares in S Ltd on 30 June 20X4 when the revenue reserves of S Ltd amounted to £40,000 and those of T Ltd amounted to £30,000. Goodwill is amortised over 5 years from the date of acquisition, with a full year's charge in the year of acquisition.

Solution

The main area of difficulty lies in the allocation of the reserves of the subsidiary companies between pre-acquisition and post-acquisition. (Remember that the object of the exercise is to prepare a consolidated balance sheet of the **H Ltd group**.)

(a) **Revenue reserves of S Ltd**

When did S Ltd become a member of the H Ltd group? Answer: 30 June 20X4 – so only revenue reserves of S Ltd arising after 30 June 20X4 can be regarded as post-acquisition from the viewpoint of the H Ltd group.

(b) **Revenue reserves of T Ltd**

Care must be taken here! When did T Ltd become a member of the H Ltd group? Certainly not on 1 January 20X4, because S Ltd was not a subsidiary of H Ltd at that time. The answer is 30 June 20X4, because only from that time was T Ltd a subsidiary of S Ltd **and** a member of the H Ltd group. Hence, only revenue reserves of T Ltd arising after 30 June 20X4 can be viewed as post-acquisition as regards the H Ltd group.

The same procedures as outlined above can now be performed for the consolidation, dealing with the two acquisitions separately. The detailed workings are left for the student to do.

The only difference from the earlier example is that the revenue reserves of T Ltd were £5,000 more at the date when H Ltd became T Ltd's ultimate parent company. Hence, 'goodwill on consolidation' will be reduced by £3,000 (H's interest in T × £5,000) = £3,000.

Goodwill (at cost)	£27,000
Consolidated reserves	£115,000

2.2 The effect on the group financial statements of using the direct and indirect methods

As we have seen, the direct method computes the group accounts of the holding company using the effective interest of the parent company in the subsidiary to allocate share capital and reserves. The indirect method would consolidate the sub-subsidiary with the subsidiary to produce the group accounts of the subsidiary and then the accounts of the parent company and the accounts of the subsidiary group can be consolidated (i.e. by this stage the subsidiary group can be dealt with as one accounting entity).

The two approaches will not make any difference to the assets and liabilities recorded in the parent company group balance sheet, nor a difference in the gross turnover and costs in the consolidated profit and loss account.

There may however be differences in the amounts of goodwill, minority interests, and group reserves due to the different way in which the reserves of the sub-subsidiary are allocated. The nature and size of the differences will depend on the precise circumstances of each case.

3 The consolidation of mixed groups

3.1 Approach

The approach is similar to the direct method of dealing with sub-subsidiaries, i.e. an effective interest is computed and used to allocate share capital and reserves. The approach will be illustrated by the following example.

Example

The following are the summarised balance sheets of T Ltd, P Ltd and A Ltd as at 31 December 20X4.

	T Ltd	P Ltd	A Ltd
	£	£	£
Fixed assets	140,000	61,000	170,000
Investments (see notes)	200,000	65,000	-
Net current assets	10,000	14,000	10,000
	350,000	140,000	180,000
Ordinary shares of £1 each	200,000	80,000	100,000
Profit and loss account	150,000	60,000	80,000
	350,000	140,000	180,000

You ascertain the following information.

(a) On 1 January 20X3 P Ltd acquired 35,000 ordinary shares in A Ltd at a cost of £65,000 when the revenue reserves of A Ltd amounted to £40,000.

(b) On 1 January 20X4 T Ltd acquired 64,000 ordinary shares in P Ltd at a cost of £120,000 and 40,000 shares in A Ltd at a cost of £80,000. The revenue reserves of P Ltd and A Ltd amounted to £50,000 and £60,000 respectively on 1 January 20X4.

You are required to prepare the consolidated balance sheet of the T Ltd group as at 31 December 20X4. Goodwill is amortised over four years from the date of acquisition, with a full year's charge in the year of acquisition.

Solution

Step 1

Basic approach is similar to that used in vertical groups.

Group structure

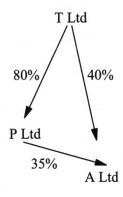

Respective interest in P Ltd and A Ltd.

	P Ltd			*A Ltd*	
T Ltd shareholders	80%	(D) Direct	=	40%	
		Indirect 80% × 35%	=	28%	
					68%
Minority shareholders	20%	(D) Direct	=	25%	
		Indirect 20% × 35%	=	7%	
					32%
	100%				100%

Notes

(a) T Ltd effectively owns 68% of A Ltd. This comprises a direct holding of 40% and an indirect holding (exercised through T Ltd's controlling interest in P Ltd) of 28%.

(b) A Ltd is a member of the T Ltd group because T Ltd and P Ltd (a subsidiary of T Ltd) together own more than 50% of the share capital of A Ltd (in fact, together they hold 75%).

Diagrammatic representation of shareholdings and revenue reserves

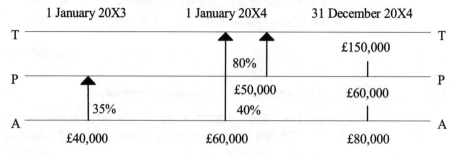

Step 2

Prepare consolidation schedules:

Goodwill

		P Ltd			*A Ltd*	
		£		£	£		£

Cost of investment

		£	£	£	£
T:		120,000			80,000
P: 80% × 65,000					52,000
					132,000

Less: Share of net assets acquired

	£	£	£	£	£	£
Share capital	80,000			100,000		
Profit and loss account	50,000			60,000		
	130,000 (80%)	(104,000)	160,000 (68%)	(108,800)

Goodwill	16,000	23,200
Amortisation charge	(4,000)	(5,800)
	12,000	17,400

Consolidated profit and loss account reserve

			£
T Ltd:			150,000
P Ltd:	80% (60,000 – 50,000)		8,000
A Ltd:	68% (80,000 – 60,000)		13,600
Less:	Goodwill amortised	P	(4,000)
		A	(5,800)
			161,800

Minority interest

		£	£
P Ltd:	Share capital	80,000	
	Profit and loss account	60,000	
		140,000	
	Less: Cost of investment in A	(65,000)	
		75,000 (20%)	15,000
A Ltd:	Share capital	100,000	
	Profit and loss account	80,000	
		180,000 (32%)	57,600
			72,600

Step 3

Consolidated balance sheet of T Ltd and its subsidiary companies as at 31 December 20X4

	£	£
Fixed assets		
Intangible assets		29,400
Tangible assets		371,000
Net current assets		34,000
Total assets less current liabilities		434,400
Minority interests		72,600
Capital and reserves		
Called up share capital, allotted and fully paid	200,000	
Profit and loss account	161,800	
		361,800
		434,400

Having worked through the solution to this question, try working it on your own.

4   Disposals of subsidiaries

4.1   Introduction

During the year, a parent company may decide to sell all or part of its shareholding in an individual company. Possible situations may include:

- the disposal of all the shares held in the subsidiary

- the disposal of part of the shareholding, still leaving a controlling interest after the sale

- the disposal of part of the shareholding, leaving a residual holding after the sale which is regarded either as an associated company investment or a trade investment.

Each of the situations will be examined in this chapter. In each case it has been assumed that acquisition accounting was originally used for the business combination.

Disposals of subsidiaries which have previously been consolidated using merger accounting are not considered by FRS 2.

4.2   FRS 2's accounting and disclosure requirements

Where there is a material disposal (i.e. sale of a substantial shareholding), the consolidated profit and loss account should include:

- the appropriate proportion of the results (i.e. turnover and profit) of the subsidiary up to the date of sale. The results of the subsidiary are likely to be separately disclosed on the face of the profit and loss account as they may constitute a 'discontinued operation' under FRS 3

- the gain or loss (usually treated as an exceptional item) on the sale of the investment. The calculation of the gain or loss is rather tricky. It is the difference between:

  (a)   the proceeds of sale; and

  (b)   the parent company share of the net assets of the subsidiary, at the date of sale, plus the goodwill on consolidation to the extent that it has not been written off (amortised) through the profit and loss account.

4.3   Preparing group accounts following a disposal of shares

First we shall examine the situation where a parent company disposes of its entire shareholding in a subsidiary (a 'total disposal'). Consider the following balance sheets.

Balance sheet at 31 December 20X8

	H Ltd £'000	S Ltd £'000
Shares in S Ltd at cost (75%)	82.5	-
Other sundry assets	257.5	100
	340.0	100
Called up share capital – £1 ordinary	200.0	60
Profit and loss account	140.0	40
	340.0	100

H Ltd acquired the shares in 20X3 when S Ltd's profit and loss account stood at £10,000. The whole holding was sold for £115,000 on 31 December 20X8.

Assume that goodwill is carried as a permanent item.

Ignore taxation.

Prepare the consolidated balance sheet before the disposal and analyse the gain which will be reported on the sale.

Solution

Consolidated balance sheet before disposal

	£'000	£'000
Goodwill on consolidation $(82.5 - 75\% \times (60 + 10))$		30.0
Other sundry net assets		357.5
		387.5
Called up share capital – £1 ordinary		200.0
Consolidated reserves		
H Ltd	140.0	
S Ltd $(75\% \times (40 - 10))$	22.5	162.5
		362.5
Minority interests $(25\% \times 100)$		25.0
		387.5

The gain on sale would be computed as follows:　　　　　£'000

(a) Separate accounts of H Ltd

	£'000
Proceeds	115.0
Carrying amount – cost	(82.5)
	32.5

(b) Consolidated accounts

	£'000
Proceeds	115.0
Less: Share of net assets $(75\% \times 100)$	(75.0)
Goodwill not yet written off	(30.0)
	10.0

The difference between the gains represents the profits relating to the shares sold retained in the subsidiary, i.e. £22,500 which are included in consolidated reserves.

Thus the gain may be computed using an alternative method.　　　£'000

		£'000
(a)	Gain in separate accounts of H Ltd (as above)	32.5
	Less: Post-acquisition profits to date of disposal	(22.5)
(b)	Gain to group	10.0

Example illustrating FRS 3 disclosure

Balance sheets as before. The profit and loss accounts for the year ended 31 December 20X8 are as follows:

	H Ltd Group (excluding S Ltd)	S Ltd
	£'000	£'000
Turnover	300	200
Cost of sales	(190)	(120)
Gross profit	110	80
Administrative expenses	(30)	(25)

Distribution costs	(20)	(15)
Profit before taxation	60	40
Taxation	(21)	(14)
Profit after taxation	39	26
Dividends payable	(10)	-
Retained for the year	29	26
Brought forward	111	14
Carried forward	140	40

The entire holding in S Ltd is sold on 30 September 20X8 for £135,000. Taxation on any gain is to be ignored. Goodwill arising on consolidation is carried as a permanent item in the consolidated balance sheet. H Ltd has not yet accounted for the disposal. H Ltd has other, 100%, subsidiaries.

Prepare the consolidated profit and loss account for the year in accordance with FRS 3, incorporating the gain on the disposal.

Work to the nearest £.

Solution

Step 1

The gain on sale would be computed as follows:

H Ltd's accounts

		£
Proceeds		135,000
Cost		(82,500)
Gain to H Ltd		52,500

Consolidated accounts	£	£
Proceeds		135,000
Less: Share of net assets at disposal		
B/d (60 + 14 [40 – 26])	74,000	
In year up to disposal ($26 \times \frac{9}{12}$)	19,500	
Group share (75%)	93,500	(70,125)
		64,875
Less: Goodwill not yet written off		(30,000)
Gain to group		£34,875

Step 2

Consolidated profit and loss account would be as follows:

H Ltd Consolidated profit and loss account
for the year ended 31 December 20X8

	Continuing operations £	*Discontinued operations* £	*Total* £
Turnover (200,000 × $\frac{9}{12}$)	300,000	150,000	450,000
Cost of sales (120,000 × $\frac{9}{12}$)	(190,000)	(90,000)	(280,000)
Gross profit	110,000	60,000	170,000
Administrative expenses (25,000 × $\frac{9}{12}$)	(30,000)	(18,750)	(48,750)
Distribution costs (15,000 × $\frac{9}{12}$)	(20,000)	(11,250)	(31,250)
Operating profit	60,000	30,000	90,000
Profit on disposal of discontinued operations	-	34,875	34,875
Profit on ordinary activities before taxation	60,000	64,875	124,875
Tax on profit on ordinary activities (21,000 + $\frac{9}{12}$ × 14,000)			(31,500)
Profit on ordinary activities after taxation			93,375
Minority interest (25% × £26,000 × $\frac{9}{12}$)			(4,875)
Profit for the financial year			88,500
Dividends			(10,000)
Retained profit for the financial year			78,500

Note to the financial statements

Reserves

	Profit and loss account H Ltd £	*Profit and loss account* Group £
At beginning of year	111,000	114,000
Transfer from profit and loss account of the year (29,000 + 52,500)	81,500	78,500
At end of year	192,500	192,500

The split of the operating expenses could be shown as a note rather than on the face of the profit and loss account as illustrated in FRS 3, but for exam purposes the above method is the quickest.

4.4   Effect of goodwill

(a)   Goodwill carried as a permanent item

In the example above it was assumed that goodwill arising on consolidation had been carried as a permanent item in the consolidated balance sheet. FRS 10 allows goodwill to be retained in the balance sheet, provided that certain conditions are met and subject to annual impairment reviews.

However, remember that the gain to the group was calculated as follows:

			Consolidated
		£	£
Proceeds			135,000
Less: Share of net assets at disposal			
B/d (60 + 14)		74,000	
In year up to disposal (26 × 9/12)		19,500	
Group share 75%		93,500	(70,125)
			64,875
Less: Goodwill			(30,000)
Gain to group			34,875

At the moment of disposal, the goodwill relating to that part (all) of the original holding disposed of was written off as part of the gain on sale, thereby passing through the consolidated profit and loss account.

(b) **Goodwill amortised over time**

In accordance with FRS 10, purchased goodwill is normally amortised through the profit and loss account over its useful economic life. If only part of the goodwill has been written off prior to disposal only part will have passed through the consolidated profit and loss account. The **remainder** should be made to pass through the profit and loss account as part of the gain on sale.

For example, if in the example above, £18,000 out of the total goodwill of £30,000 had been written off by the date of disposal, the group gain on disposal would be calculated as follows:

	Consolidated
	£
Proceeds	135,000
Less: Share of net assets at disposal (as above)	(70,125)
Less: Goodwill not yet written off relating to disposal	
(30,000 – 18,000)	(12,000)
	52,875

This is clearly a different figure. Whereas previously £30,000 was written off as part of the group gain on sale, here £12,000 has been written off as part of the gain on sale and the other £18,000 as part of the amortisation of goodwill. Nevertheless the total amount passing through the consolidated profit and loss account is still £30,000.

5 Partial disposals

5.1 Partial disposal – subsidiary to associate

KEY POINT

Where the shareholding is reduced to between 20% and 50%, the entity will be fully consolidated up to the date of disposal and equity accounted from the date of disposal.

In this situation the disposal will reduce the shareholding below 50%. The entity will be consolidated up to the date of disposal and equity accounted from the date of disposal. Any gain or loss is computed as previously.

Example

Profit and loss accounts for the year ended 31 December 20X9

	H Ltd	S Ltd	A Ltd
	£	£	£
Profit before tax	100,000	80,000	30,000
Corporation tax	35,000	28,000	10,500
	65,000	52,000	19,500
Proposed dividend	20,000		
Retained for year	£45,000		

H Ltd acquired its investments on the following dates.

Company	%	Date	Cost	Share capital	Reserves at acquisition	Goodwill on consolidation
			£	£	£	£
S Ltd	80	20X0	110,000	100,000	12,000	20,400
A Ltd	60	20X5	60,000	70,000	10,000	12,000

One third of H Ltd's shares in A Ltd were sold on 31 March 20X9 for £35,000. Goodwill on consolidation has been fully amortised. A Ltd's reserves at 1 January 20X9 amounted to £25,000.

Solution

Step 1

The gain on sale would be computed as follows:

		£
H Ltd		
Proceeds		35,000
Cost 20/60 × £60,000		(20,000)
		£15,000

	£	£
Group		
Proceeds		35,000
Share of net assets at date of disposal		
Brought forward – share capital	70,000	
– reserves	25,000	
In year up to disposal 3/12 × £19,500	4,875	
20% ×	£99,875	(19,975)
Group gain		15,025

Step 2

A consolidation schedule could be prepared as follows:

	H Ltd	S Ltd	A Ltd Subsidiary (3/12)	A Ltd As associate (9/12 × 40%)	Consolidated
	£	£	£	£	£
Profit before tax	100,000	80,000	7,500		187,500
Share of associate				9,000	9,000
					196,500
Corporation tax	(35,000)	(28,000)	(2,625)		(65,625)
Share of associate				(3,150)	(3,150)
	65,000	52,000	4,875	5,850	127,725
Minority		(10,400)	(1,950)		(12,350)
		41,600	2,925		£115,375

Step 3

The consolidated profit and loss account would be as follows:

H Ltd Consolidated profit and loss account for 20X9

	£	£
Profit before tax		187,500
Income from interests in associated undertakings		9,000
Profit on disposal of continuing operations		15,025
		211,525
Taxation		
Group	(65,625)	
Share of associated undertaking	(3,150)	
		(68,775)
Profit after tax		142,750
Minority interests		(12,350)
Profit attributable to members of H Ltd		130,400
Proposed dividend		(20,000)
Retained for year		£110,400

Since all operations are continuing, the disclosure is considerably simplified.

5.2 Partial disposal – subsidiary to trade investment

A subsidiary would normally become a trade investment if the parent's interest fell below 20%. The subsidiary's results are included in the profit and loss account until the date of disposal.

A trade investment is normally included in the balance sheet at cost. However, the group has included its share of the subsidiary's post-acquisition results in consolidated reserves. Arguably, it still owns a small share of these profits, even after the disposal. There are two possible ways of dealing with this situation:

- include the investment in the balance sheet at cost and eliminate all the post-acquisition profits from consolidated reserves

- include the investment in the balance sheet at a valuation based on the remaining share of the net assets at the date of disposal (that is, value it under the equity method).

FRS 2 is silent on this matter, but FRS 9 *Associates and joint ventures* states that when an investment in a company ceases to be an associate, the initial carrying amount of any interest retained in the entity is based on the percentage retained of the final carrying amount for the former associate at the date the entity ceased to qualify as such (i.e. the carrying amount under the equity method). This treatment is consistent with the accounting treatment used where a subsidiary is excluded from consolidation on the grounds that the parent can no longer control it.

5.3 Accounting for a partial disposal of shares in a remaining subsidiary

Although there will be a gain or loss on sale, the subsidiary will be consolidated for the whole year, only the % holding will change, not the entity's status as a subsidiary.

Example

Facts as before except that only 5% of A Ltd's issued shares were sold on 31 March 20X9 for £12,000.

Solution

Step 1

The gain on sale would be computed as follows:

H Ltd		£
Proceeds		12,000
Cost $^{5}/_{60} \times £60,000$		(5,000)
		7,000

Group	£	£
Proceeds		12,000
Share of net assets at date of disposal		
Brought forward – share capital	70,000	
– reserves	25,000	
In year up to disposal $^{3}/_{12} \times £19,500$	4,875	
$5\% \times 99,875$		(4,994)
Group gain		7,006

Step 2

A consolidation schedule could be prepared as follows:

	H Ltd	*S Ltd*	*A Ltd*	*Consolidated*
	£	£	£	£
Profit before tax	100,000	80,000	30,000	210,000
Tax	(35,000)	(28,000)	(10,500)	(73,500)
PAT		52,000	19,500	
Minority interest			£	
In S Ltd	20% × 52,000		10,400	
In A Ltd	40% × $^{3}/_{12}$ × £19,500		1,950	
	45% × $^{9}/_{12}$ × £19,500		6,581	
			18,931	

Step 3

The consolidated profit and loss account would be as follows:

H Ltd Consolidated profit and loss account for 20X9

	£
Profit before tax	210,000
Profit on disposal of continuing operations	7,006
	217,006
Taxation	(73,500)
Profit after tax	143,506
Minority interests	(18,931)
Profit attributable to members of H Ltd	124,575
Proposed dividend	(20,000)
Retained for year	104,575

Again, since all operations are continuing, the disclosure is considerably simplified.

5.4 Treatment of dividends

The treatment is straightforward and does not involve any pro-rating calculations. There are two alternatives.

- The dividend has been paid prior to disposal, so the net assets of the subsidiary will have been reduced by the cash payment. Thus the full amount paid is taken out.

- The dividend is paid after the date of disposal or it is merely proposed. In either of these cases, the net assets have not been reduced by a cash payment prior to disposal. Therefore the dividend may be ignored.

Example

S Ltd has the following summary profit and loss account for the year ended 31 December 20X8.

	£'000
Profit after tax	240
Dividend paid in April	(50)
Dividend proposed	(70)

Retained profit	120
Retained profit b/d	580
Retained profit c/d	700

H Ltd acquired 80% of S Ltd four years ago when S Ltd had share capital of £200,000 and reserves of £250,000. Ignore goodwill.

H Ltd disposed of half of its holding in S Ltd on 1 July 20X8 for £400,000.

Calculate the profit on disposal for the group.

Ignore taxation.

Solution

	£	£
Sale proceeds		400,000
Share of net assets at disposal		
Brought forward (580 + 200)	780,000	
In year (½ × £240,000) − *50,000	70,000	
40% × 850,000		(340,000)
		£60,000

*The dividend paid is deducted from the profits for the first half of the year and the proposed dividend is ignored.

5.5   Taxation

The corporation tax payable on the gain is based on the gain in the parent company books, not the gain in the group accounts.

	£
Sale proceeds	X
Less: Cost	X
Gross gain	X
Tax computed as corporate tax rate × gross gain	X

This tax is then included in the tax charge relating to the discontinued activity.

ACTIVITY 3

H Ltd purchased 80% of the ordinary share capital of S Ltd on 30 September 20X4 for £15,000. S Ltd's share capital and reserves at that date were as follows.

	£
Share capital	10,000
Reserves	5,000
	15,000

Goodwill arising on consolidation was amortised over 10 years from the date of acquisition. On 30 September 20X8, H Ltd sold 25% of its holding in S Ltd for £10,000. S Ltd's profit after tax for the year ended 31 December 20X8 is £6,000, its opening reserves for 20X8 being £24,000.

What is the profit or loss arising on the disposal of S Ltd to be included in the consolidated accounts for the year ended 31 December 20X8?

Feedback to this activity is at the end of the chapter.

6   Deemed disposals

So far, we have considered direct disposals, that is, situations where a parent disposes of a subsidiary by selling shares. A company can cease to be a subsidiary in other ways.

- The subsidiary issues shares to third parties.

- The group does not take up its full allocation in a rights issue.

- The subsidiary declares scrip dividends which are not taken up by the parent.

- A third party exercises options or warrants.

All these situations would effectively reduce the parent's interest in the subsidiary, resulting in a 'deemed disposal'.

Because subsidiary and associate status depend on control, rather than the proportion of shares held by the parent, it is possible for a disposal to take place without the parent's percentage interest actually changing. For example, voting rights may change, or a parent may lose the power to appoint or remove directors.

KEY POINT

FRS 2 states that deemed disposals should be treated in exactly the same way as direct disposals.

FRS 2 states that deemed disposals should be treated in exactly the same way as direct disposals. In other words, the profit or loss on disposal is calculated by comparing the group share of the subsidiary's net assets before the disposal with the group share of the subsidiary's net assets after the disposal.

Example

Profit and loss accounts for the year ended 31 December 20X8

	X Ltd £	Y Ltd £	Z Ltd £
Profit before tax	200,000	160,000	60,000
Corporation tax	70,000	56,000	21,000
	130,000	104,000	39,000
Proposed dividend	40,000		
Retained for year	£90,000		

X Ltd has owned 100% of Y Ltd and 80% of Z Ltd since their incorporation. At 1 January 20X8 both subsidiaries had issued share capital of £100,000. On 31 March 20X8 Z Ltd issued 100,000 £1 ordinary shares to third parties for a consideration of £100,000. At 1 January 20X8 Z Ltd's reserves amounted to £50,000. All goodwill arising on consolidation has been fully amortised through the profit and loss account.

Prepare the consolidated profit and loss account for the year ended 31 December 20X8.

Solution

Step 1

Calculate the profit or loss on disposal

X Ltd has received no consideration for the disposal, so there is no profit or loss on disposal in the accounts of the individual company.

The profit or loss to the group is calculated as follows.

		£	£
Share of net assets immediately before disposal			
	Share capital	100,000	
	Reserves brought forward	50,000	
	In year up to disposal 3/12 × £39,000	9,750	
	80% ×	£159,750	127,800
Share of net assets immediately after disposal			
	Share capital	200,000	
	Reserves brought forward	50,000	
	In year up to disposal 3/12 × £39,000	9,750	
	40% ×	£259,750	103,900
Loss on disposal			23,900

Step 2

Prepare the consolidation schedule

	X Ltd	Y Ltd	Z Ltd Subsidiary (3/12)	Z Ltd As associate (9/12 × 40%)	Consolidated
	£	£	£	£	£
Profit before tax	200,000	160,000	15,000		375,000
Share of associate				18,000	18,000
					393,000
Corporation tax	(70,000)	(56,000)	(5,250)		(131,250)
Share of associate				(6,300)	(6,300)
	130,000	104,000	9,750	11,700	255,450
Minority	(20%)		(1,950)		(1,950)
			7,800		253,500

Step 3

Prepare the consolidated profit and loss account

X Ltd Consolidated profit and loss account for 20X8

	£	£
Profit before tax		375,000
Income from interests in associated undertakings		18,000
Loss on disposal of continuing operations		(23,900)
		369,100
Taxation		
Group	(131,250)	
Share of associated undertaking	(6,300)	
		(137,550)
Profit after tax		231,550
Minority interests		(1,950)
Profit attributable to members of X Ltd		229,600
Proposed dividend		(40,000)
Retained for year		189,600

SELF-TEST
QUESTIONS

The direct and indirect methods to consolidate sub-subsidiaries

1   What assets and liabilities will be affected by the decision as to whether to use the direct or the indirect methods? (2.2)

The consolidation of mixed groups

2   What is the difference in accounting treatment between sub-subsidiaries in (a) vertical groups and (b) mixed groups? (3)

Disposals of subsidiaries

3   What disclosures are required in the consolidated profit and loss account when there has been a sale of a substantial shareholding in a subsidiary which has been accounted for using acquisition accounting? (4.2)

4   How is goodwill on acquisition accounted for when it has not been fully amortised before disposal of the subsidiary? (4.4)

Partial disposals

5   When a parent disposes of part of a shareholding so that a subsidiary becomes an associate, what are the accounting effects? (5.1)

6   When a parent disposes of part of a shareholding so that a subsidiary becomes a trade investment, what are the accounting effects? (5.2)

7   What is the treatment for dividends from subsidiaries paid before disposal? (5.4)

Deemed disposals

8   Describe the circumstances under which there may be a deemed disposal. (6)

EXAM-TYPE
QUESTION 1

H Ltd

The balance sheets of H Ltd, S Ltd and T Ltd, as at 31 December 20X8 were as follows.

	H Ltd £	S Ltd £	T Ltd £
Ordinary share capital (£1 shares)	100,000	75,000	50,000
Reserves	120,000	60,000	40,000
	220,000	135,000	90,000
60,000 shares in S Ltd	95,000		
30,000 shares in T Ltd		48,000	
Sundry net assets	125,000	87,000	90,000
	220,000	135,000	90,000

The investments were acquired as follows:

	Balances on: S Ltd Reserves £	T Ltd Reserves £
(a) Both investments acquired 31 December 20X1	10,000	8,000
(b) H Ltd in S Ltd on 31 December 20X2	12,000	15,000
S Ltd in T Ltd on 31 December 20X4	20,000	18,000
(c) S Ltd in T Ltd on 31 December 20X5	30,000	25,000
H Ltd in S Ltd on 31 December 20X7	40,000	32,000

You are required to prepare the consolidated balance sheet of H Ltd and its subsidiary companies, as at 31 December 20X8 for each of the three possible situations. Show goodwill as a permanent asset.   **(25 marks)**

Hale, Rein and Snowe

The summarised balances extracted from the accounting records of Hale (H) Ltd, Rein (R) Ltd and Snowe (S) Ltd at 30 November 20X7 are given below:

	H Ltd £	R Ltd £	S Ltd £
Land and buildings		447,500	230,950
	52,000		
Plant and machinery	600,500		61,750
Fixtures and fittings	54,500	41,000	8,800
Investments at cost			
420,000 shares in Rein Ltd	367,500		
70,000 shares in Snowe Ltd	49,000		
35,000 shares in Snowe Ltd		24,500	
Stock and work in progress	526,610	163,290	85,700
Debtors	241,920	129,680	29,750
Cash and bank balances	88,200	4,725	8,105
Creditors	(95,480)	(86,645)	(88,605)
	2,280,250	507,500	157,500
Capital and reserves			
£1 shares	1,750,000		175,000
75p shares		420,000	
Other reserves	350,000	70,000	
Profit and loss account	180,250	17,500	(17,500)
	2,280,250	507,500	157,500

Further information

1   Hale Ltd purchased its interest in Rein Ltd and Snowe Ltd on 1 December 20X4 at which date there was an adverse balance on Snowe Ltd's profit and loss account of £35,000, and a credit balance of the same amount on the profit and loss account of Rein Ltd.

2   On 30 November 20X7 Hale Ltd despatched and invoiced goods for £12,500 to Rein Ltd which were not recorded by the latter until 3 December 20X7. A mark-up of 25% is added by Hale Ltd to arrive at selling price. Rein Ltd already had goods in stock which had been invoiced to them by Hale Ltd at £10,400.

3   Since its acquisition Rein Ltd has paid dividends of £70,000 of which half were paid out of pre-acquisition profits. Hale Ltd has credited all dividends received to profit and loss account.

4   Snowe Ltd had an adverse balance of £52,500 on profit and loss account when Rein Ltd purchased 35,000 shares in 20X3.

5   Hale Ltd received a remittance of £8,000 on 2 December 20X7 which had been sent by Rein Ltd on 29 November 20X7.

6   Included in Hale's debtors was a balance of £25,500 owed by Rein Ltd.

7   Neither Rein Ltd nor Snowe Ltd had any other reserves when their shares were purchased by Hale Ltd and Rein Ltd.

8   Creditors of Rein Ltd included an amount of £5,000 due to Hale Ltd.

You are required: to prepare the consolidated balance sheet of Hale Ltd and its subsidiaries at 30 November 20X7. You may assume that all goodwill arising on acquisition was fully amortised at this date.   **(30 marks)**

Apricot

The summarised balance sheets of A plc and its two subsidiaries, B Ltd and C Ltd, at 31 December 20X2 are shown below.

Summarised balance sheets at 31 December 20X2

	A plc £'000	B Ltd £'000	C Ltd £'000
Investment in subsidiaries:			
A plc in B Ltd	1,164		
A plc in C Ltd	1,120		
Other net assets	2,516	1,260	1,400
	4,800	1,260	1,400
Ordinary share capital (£1 shares)	1,500	500	400
Revenue reserves	3,300	760	1,000
	4,800	1,260	1,400

The summarised profit and loss accounts for A plc and B Ltd for the year ended 31 December 20X3 are as follows:

	A plc £'000	B Ltd £'000
Operating profit	1,200	250
Taxation	360	60
Profit after tax	840	190
Dividends paid	50	20
Retained profit for year	790	170
Retained profit b/fwd	3,300	760
Retained profits c/fwd	4,090	930

Additional information

1   A plc acquired 80% of the ordinary share capital of B Ltd on 1 January 20W4 when the reserves of B Ltd were £420,000.

2   A plc acquired 90% of the ordinary share capital of C Ltd on 1 January 20W5 when the reserves of C Ltd were £320,000.

3   It is the policy of A plc to write off goodwill to profit and loss over five years.

4   On 1 January 20X3, A plc disposed of 350,000 shares in C Ltd for £1,925,000. The relevant profit on sale has NOT been included in the profit and loss account of A plc.

5   Assume a rate of corporation tax on capital gains of 25%.

6   A plc accounts for dividends on a received basis.

7   There were no changes in the issued share capital of the subsidiaries since acquisition by A plc.

Required:

(a)   Prepare the consolidated profit and loss account and balance sheet of the A plc group at 31 December 20X3.   **(24 marks)**

(b)   Prepare a reconciliation of opening and closing consolidated reserves.   **(6 marks)**

(Show all your workings.)   **(Total: 30 marks)**

For the answers to these questions see the 'Answers' section at the end of the book.

Diagrammatically, the situation is as follows:

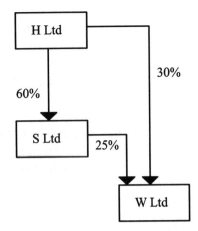

H Ltd's arithmetic interest in W Ltd = (60% × 25%) + 30% = 45%.

W Ltd is a subsidiary of H Ltd. H Ltd effectively controls S Ltd, and thus S Ltd's use of all its shares in W Ltd. Added to its own shares, H Ltd is then able to control the voting of 25% (through S Ltd) plus 30% of W Ltd's shares, i.e. 55%. For computational purposes, however, the group interest must be taken as 45% with a minority interest, as always the difference between 100% and the group interest, of 55%.

Step 1   Calculate group shareholdings.

In S Ltd

$$\frac{45,000}{60,000} \times 100\% = \qquad\qquad\qquad 75\%$$

In M Ltd

Direct $\dfrac{16,000}{40,000} \times 100\% =$ 40%

Indirect $75\% \times \dfrac{12,000}{40,000} \times 100\% =$ 22.5%

                                    62.5%

Step 2   Calculate goodwill arising on S Ltd.

	£	£
Cost of investment		72,000
Less: Share of net assets acquired		
Share capital	60,000	
Profit and loss account	30,000	
	90,000 (75%)	67,500
Goodwill		4,500

Step 3   Calculate goodwill arising on M Ltd.

	£	£
Cost of investment		
By H Ltd		25,000
By S Ltd		
75% × £20,000		15,000
		40,000
Less: Share of net assets acquired		
Share capital	40,000	
Profit and loss account	10,000	
	50,000 (62.5%)	31,250
		8,750

FEEDBACK TO
ACTIVITY 3

Step 1   Calculate consolidated goodwill.

	£
Cost	15,000
80% net assets acquired	12,000
Goodwill	3,000
Amortisation (3,000 ÷ 10 × 4)	(1,200)
	1,800

Step 2   Calculate gain/loss.

		£	£
Proceeds			10,000
Less: Net assets sold:			
Share capital		10,000	
Opening reserves		24,000	
Nine months profits	*9/12 × £6,000*	4,500	
		38,500	
Shares sold		20%	(7,700)
Less: Goodwill sold	*£1,800 × 25%*		(450)
Gain on disposal			**£1,850**

20% of the net assets have been sold.

The goodwill relating to this is 20/80^{ths}, which is 25%.

Chapter 5
MERGERS

Merger accounting and acquisition accounting are alternative methods of recording the acquisition of a subsidiary by a parent undertaking. Merger accounting is only appropriate if certain conditions are satisfied. The CA89 contains one set of conditions; these are tightened still further by the provisions of FRS 6.

Objectives

When you have studied this chapter you should be able to:

- understand the basic principles and philosophy of merger accounting

- account for equity eliminations, expenses and dividends of the subsidiary

- prepare consolidated financial statements using merger accounting techniques

- determine whether merger accounting could be used in specific circumstances

- understand the relative merits of different methods of accounting for business combinations.

1 Mergers and takeovers

1.1 The conceptual difference between an acquisition and a merger

Business combinations arise when one or more companies become subsidiaries of another company. Two different methods have been developed to account for business combinations – acquisition accounting and merger accounting.

In an acquisition, one party to the combination can be identified as having the role of an acquirer. FRS 6 requires the use of acquisition accounting in such circumstances.

In a merger, two or more companies are combining to pool their interests on an equal footing, and no acquirer can be identified. FRS 6 requires the use of merger accounting in such circumstances.

One key criterion employed to determine the appropriate method or methods of accounting is whether or not the combination is based principally on a share-for-share exchange. Merger accounting is considered to be an appropriate method of accounting when two groups of shareholders continue, or are in a position to continue, their shareholdings as before but on a combined basis. Acquisition accounting is, therefore, required when there is a transfer of the ownership of at least one of the combining companies, and substantial resources leave the group as consideration for that transfer. Conversely, when only limited resources leave the group, merger accounting may be used.

We will consider the other criteria later.

1.2   The requirements of the Companies Act and FRS 6 relating to merger accounting

FRS 6 *Acquisitions and mergers* deals only with accounting in the consolidated accounts and not with accounting in the individual company accounts (although some guidance is provided in an appendix to the standard). However, the entries at the individual company stage can affect the entries at the consolidated accounts stage and thus the accounts of the parent company are dealt with first.

1.3   Accounts of the parent undertaking – basic situation

The investment in a new subsidiary will be shown as a fixed asset investment in the parent company's own accounts. The amount at which this investment will be stated will depend upon which method of accounting is to be used on consolidation.

- If acquisition accounting is to be used, then the investment will be recorded at cost, which will normally be the fair value of the consideration given.

- If merger accounting is to be used, then the investment will be recorded at the nominal value of the shares issued as purchase consideration plus the fair value of any additional consideration.

Example

A plc makes an offer to all the shareholders of B plc to acquire their shares on the basis of one new £1 share (market value £3) plus 25p for every two £1 shares (market value £1.10 each) in B plc. The holders of 95,000 shares in B plc (representing 95% of the total shares) accept this offer.

Solution

The investment in B plc will be recorded in the books of A plc as follows:

(a) **If acquisition accounting is to be used on consolidation**

		£	£
Dr	Investment in B plc	154,375	
Cr	£1 ordinary shares		47,500
Cr	Share premium		95,000
Cr	Cash		11,875
		154,375	154,375

(b) **If merger accounting is to be used on consolidation**

		£	£
Dr	Investment in B plc	59,375	
Cr	£1 ordinary shares		47,500
Cr	Cash		11,875
		59,375	59,375

1.4   Accounts of the parent undertaking – the effect of merger relief

S130 CA85 states that if a company issues shares at a premium, whether for cash or otherwise, a sum equal to the aggregate amount or value of the premium on those shares shall be transferred to a share premium account.

KEY POINT

If a company issues shares at a premium, a sum equal to the aggregate amount or value of the premium on those shares is transferred to a share premium account (S130 CA85).

S131 CA85 provides that where a company has, by an arrangement including the exchange of shares, secured at least a 90% equity holding in another company then S130 CA85 shall not apply to the premium on any shares which are included in the purchase consideration. This provision is known as the 'merger relief' provision.

In the example above A plc did, by an arrangement including the exchange of shares, secure at least a 90% equity holding in another company and hence would not transfer £95,000 to the share premium account, and could then record the investment in B plc at £59,375 – exactly the same figure as arrived at if merger accounting were to be used on consolidation. If however A plc has decided that acquisition accounting is to be used on consolidation, the holding company would credit the share premium to a merger reserve, as follows:

		£	£
Dr	Investment in B plc	154,375	
	Cr £1 ordinary shares		47,500
	Cr Merger reserve		95,000
	Cr Cash		11,875
		154,375	154,375

A plc is relieved by S131 from setting up a share premium account, but wants to state the investment at its fair value, in order to use acquisition accounting on consolidation. The merger reserve is therefore set up to enable the investment to be stated at its fair value.

1.5   Conditions necessary to apply merger accounting

Both CA89 and FRS 6 allow merger accounting to be used only in specified circumstances. These circumstances are listed below and should be learnt.

CA89 conditions

(a) The subsidiary was acquired by an arrangement providing for the issue of equity shares by the parent company or its subsidiaries.

(b) The group has obtained at least 90% of the 'relevant shares' in the subsidiary (being shares with unrestricted rights to participate in distributions and on liquidation).

(c) The fair value of consideration given other than equity shares does not exceed 10% of the nominal value of the equity shares issued.

(d) The adoption of merger accounting complies with generally accepted accounting principles or practice.

If these conditions are met, the CA89 permits that the merger method of accounting may be used.

FRS 6 criteria

FRS 6 contains five criteria that must be satisfied before merger accounting can be used.

(a) No party to the combination is portrayed as either acquirer or acquired, either by its own board or management or by that of another party to the combination.

(b) All parties to the combination participate in establishing the management structure for the combined entity and in selecting the management personnel.

(c) The relative sizes of the combining entities are not so disparate that one party dominates the combined entity by virtue of its relative size.

(d) The consideration received by the equity shareholders of each party to the combination, in relation to their equity shareholding, comprises primarily equity shares in the combined entity. Any non-equity consideration represents an immaterial proportion of the fair value of the consideration received by the equity shareholders of that party.

(e) No equity shareholders of any of the combining entities retain any material interest in the future performance of only part of the combined entity.

If a business combination meets all five of these criteria, and the use of merger accounting is not prohibited by companies legislation, FRS 6 requires that merger accounting must be used for that combination.

The following points can be made:

(a) Condition (d) of the CA89 effectively gives statutory backing to FRS 6 or any other revised standard on this topic in the future.

(b) FRS 6 explains criterion (c) by stating that one party would be presumed to dominate if it is more than 50% larger than each of the other parties to the combination, judged by considering the proportion of the equity of the combined entity attributable to the shareholders of each of the combining parties. However this presumption may be rebutted if it can be clearly shown that there is no such dominance.

(c) No further guidance is given on the interpretation of 'immaterial proportion' in criterion (d) of FRS 6.

ACTIVITY 1

P is a parent company about to make an offer to acquire another company S.

The initial proposal is to issue 1,000 ordinary shares of £1 each worth £3 per share together with £200 cash.

Demonstrate whether these proposals meet the CA89 conditions for merger accounting.

Feedback to this activity is at the end of the chapter.

1.6 Consolidated accounts – acquisition accounting

Where a business combination is accounted for as an acquisition, the fair value of the purchase consideration should, for the purpose of consolidated financial statements, be allocated between the underlying net tangible and intangible assets other than goodwill, on the basis of the fair value to the acquiring company in accordance with the requirements of FRS 2.

Any difference between the fair value of the consideration and the aggregate of the fair values of the separable net assets including identifiable intangibles such as patents, licences and trade marks will represent goodwill, which should be accounted for in accordance with the provisions of FRS 10.

KEY POINT

In an acquisition the results of the acquired company should be brought into the group accounts from the date of acquisition only.

In an acquisition the results of the acquired company should be brought into the group accounts from the date of acquisition only.

1.7   Consolidated accounts – merger accounting

In merger accounting it is not necessary to adjust the carrying values of the assets and liabilities of the subsidiary to fair value either in its own books or on consolidation. However, appropriate adjustments should be made to achieve uniformity of accounting policies between the combining companies.

In the group accounts for the period in which the merger takes place, the profits or losses of subsidiaries brought in for the first time should be included for the entire period without any adjustment in respect of that part of the period prior to the merger. Corresponding amounts should be presented as if the companies had been combined throughout the previous period and at the previous balance sheet date.

A difference may arise on consolidation between the carrying value of the investment in the subsidiary (which will normally be the nominal value of the shares issued as consideration plus the fair value of any additional consideration) and the nominal value of the shares transferred to the issuing company.

- Where the carrying value of the investment is less than the nominal value of the shares transferred, the difference should be treated as a reserve arising on consolidation.

- Where the carrying value of the investment is greater than the nominal value of the shares transferred, the difference is the extent to which reserves have been in effect capitalised as a result of the merger and it should therefore be treated on consolidation as a reduction of reserves.

1.8   Merger accounting – further points

Expenses of the merger

FRS 6 requires that all expenses of the merger should be written off to the profit and loss account at the effective date of the merger. Merger expenses are disclosed as costs of a fundamental reorganisation or restructuring, in other words, as exceptional items under FRS 3.

One possible exception to this rule is share issue expenses. If the parent has a share premium account, the expenses may qualify to be written off against this (one of the few uses of the share premium account permitted by the Companies Act). Once the share issue costs have been charged against the profit and loss account they may be taken to the share premium account by means of a reserve transfer.

Dividends of the subsidiary

Dividends paid after the merger are treated in exactly the same way as in acquisition accounting. They are intra-group transactions and are therefore eliminated on consolidation. Only dividends paid post-merger by the parent appear in the profit and loss account.

In merger accounting, the profit and loss accounts of the parent and the subsidiary are added together as if the two companies had always been combined. This creates a problem, because dividends paid by the subsidiary before the merger were paid to third parties. They cannot be eliminated on consolidation, but must be shown as distributions in the consolidated profit and loss account. Pre-merger dividends of the subsidiary should be disclosed separately from those of the parent, either on the face of the profit and loss account or in a note.

2 Comparison of consolidated financial statements prepared under merger accounting and acquisition accounting

2.1 Example

On 31 December 20X6 F plc purchased 29,000 shares in B Ltd by issuing 58,000 shares as consideration. The market value of F plc's shares on that date was £2.50 each.

The balance sheets of the two companies immediately before the share exchange were as follows:

	F plc £'000	B Ltd £'000
Sundry net assets	220	120
£1 ordinary shares	100	30
Profit and loss account	120	90
	220	120

As at 31 December 20X6, the fair value of B Ltd's sundry net assets was £15,000 in excess of their book value.

You are required to prepare consolidated balance sheets as at 31 December 20X6 reflecting the above information, on the basis of:

(a) acquisition accounting

(b) merger accounting.

Solution

Step 1

(a) Acquisition accounting

For consolidation purposes the investment in B Ltd must be recorded at its fair value.

		£	£
Dr	Cost of investment	145,000	
	Cr £1 ordinary shares (58,000 @ £1)		58,000
	Cr Merger reserve (58,000 @ £1.50)		87,000
		145,000	145,000

Alternatively the merger reserve would be established as a consolidation adjustment only.

Step 2

If acquisition accounting is to be used, assets must be recorded at their fair value.

	£	£
Dr Sundry net assets	15,000	
Cr Revaluation reserve		15,000

This may be done in the subsidiary's books or as a consolidation adjustment.

Step 3

Consolidation schedules

Goodwill

	£	£
Cost of investment		145,000
Less: Share of net assets acquired		
Share capital	30,000	
Revaluation reserve	15,000	
Profit and loss account	90,000	
	135,000 (29/30)	130,500
Goodwill		14,500

Consolidated profit and loss account reserve

	£
F plc:	120,000
B Ltd: 29/30 (90,000 – 90,000)	0
	120,000

Minority interest

	£	£
Share of net assets		
Share capital	30,000	
Revaluation reserve	15,000	
Profit and loss account	90,000	
	135,000 (1/30)	4,500

Step 4

Consolidated balance sheet as at 31 December 20X6

	£'000
Sundry net assets	355.0
Goodwill	14.5
	369.5
£1 ordinary shares	158.0
Consolidated revenue reserves	120.0
Merger reserve	87.0
Minority interests	4.5
	369.5

(b) **Merger accounting**

Step 1

The investment in B Ltd is recorded as the nominal value of shares issued by F plc.

	£	£
Dr Cost of investment	58,000	
Cr £1 ordinary shares		58,000

Assets are not restated to their fair value.

Step 2

Consolidation schedules

'Difference' on consolidation

	£
Nominal value of shares issued	58,000
Less: Nominal value of shares acquired	29,000
Positive difference – write off to consolidated reserves	29,000

Consolidated profit and loss account reserve

	£
F Ltd:	120,000
B Ltd: $29/30 \times £90,000$	87,000
Less: Difference on consolidation written off	(29,000)
	178,000

Minority interest

	£
$1/30 \times £120,000$	4,000

Step 3

Consolidated balance sheet as at 31 December 20X6

	£'000
Sundry net assets	340
£1 ordinary shares	158
Consolidated revenue reserves	178
Minority interests	4
	340

2.2 Notes on comparison

Although consolidated revenue reserves have been recorded as £178,000 under merger accounting and £120,000 under acquisition accounting, this does not mean that distributable reserves are greater. Distributions are made from the profits of individual companies, not by groups.

Differences which are sometimes described as goodwill can arise in merger accounting, but these differences are not goodwill as they are not based on the fair values of the consideration given and the separable net assets acquired. Such differences should always be adjusted against consolidated reserves.

The summarised balance sheet of G Ltd at 28 February 20X6 was as follows:

	£		£
Fixed assets	180,000	Ordinary share capital	
Current assets	565,000	(25p ordinary shares)	245,000
		Reserves	300,000
		Current liabilities	200,000
	745,000		745,000

At that date the company acquired the whole issued share capital of C Ltd by the issue of 120,000 new ordinary shares at the day's market price of 80p.

The summarised balance sheet of C immediately prior to acquisition was as follows:

	£		£
Fixed assets	40,000	Ordinary share capital	
Current assets	55,000	(£1 ordinary shares)	20,000
		Reserves	50,000
		Current liabilities	25,000
	95,000		95,000

The fixed assets of C were revalued two weeks before the acquisition at £50,000 but no entry had yet been made in the books of C.

You are required to prepare the consolidated balance sheet at 28 February 20X6 using:

(a) acquisition accounting

(b) merger accounting.

Feedback to this activity is at the end of the chapter.

2.3 UITF Abstract 15 *Disclosure of substantial acquisitions*

FRS 6 requires detailed disclosures in respect of substantial acquisitions arising during the accounting period. For listed companies FRS 6 defines 'substantial' by reference to Class 1 or Super Class 1 transactions under the Stock Exchange Listing Rules. These classify transactions by assessing their size relative to that of the company making the transaction. It does this by ascertaining whether any of a number of ratios (e.g. the net assets of the target to the net assets of the offeror) exceeds a given percentage.

UITF Abstract 15 was issued in order to clarify the definition of 'substantial' in respect of listed companies, as the Listing Rules have changed since FRS 6 was issued. An acquisition is now defined as substantial if it is a transaction in which any of the ratios set out in the London Stock Exchange Listing Rules defining Class 1 transactions exceeds 15%.

For other entities, an acquisition is 'substantial':

- where the net assets or operating profits of the acquired entity exceed 15% of those of the acquiring entity; or

- where the fair value of the consideration given exceeds 15% of the net assets of the acquiring entity.

For substantial acquisitions, the following information must be disclosed:

- the summarised profit and loss account and statement of total recognised gains and losses of the acquired entity for the period from the beginning of its financial year to the effective date of acquisition, giving the date on which this period began

- the profit after tax and minority interests for the acquired entity's previous financial year.

3 Acquisition accounting and merger accounting compared

3.1 The reasoning behind the different methods

The two methods are compared below.

- **Pre-acquisition profits** – There is no concept of pre-acquisition profit under merger accounting as there is under the acquisition method. The parent and the subsidiary are deemed to have been together since incorporation and therefore, conceptually, there can be no profits earned before acquisition.

- **Fair value of assets** – Under the acquisition method, the net assets of the subsidiary are revalued to fair value on acquisition so that goodwill is correctly computed and the true cost of the purchase of the stake by the parent company is recorded.

  There is no acquisition under merger accounting and therefore fair values at the date of acquisition are irrelevant.

- **Corresponding amounts** – Under merger accounting the comparative figures disclosed in the financial statements in the year of the merger are restated to include the relevant amounts from the subsidiary. Once again, there is conceptually no date of acquisition and therefore all historical data should reflect the assumption that the two entities have always been combined.

- **Intra-group transactions** – Under both acquisition and merger accounting, intra-group transactions and balances are cancelled out on consolidation, reflecting the fact that a single entity cannot trade with itself.

Each method reflects the substance of the relationship between the parent and the subsidiary. However, because they can produce such different results, preparers of accounts may wish to use one method in preference to others.

3.2 Advantages of the different methods

Acquisition method

This normally enhances the balance sheet because:

(a) assets and liabilities are revalued to fair value

(b) goodwill is capitalised.

However, earnings may be reduced due to higher depreciation charges and amortisation of goodwill.

Merger method

(a) Reserves are normally higher than under the acquisition method, because all the reserves of the subsidiary are brought into the consolidated accounts. There are no pre-acquisition reserves.

(b) Earnings are normally higher than under the acquisition method, because the subsidiary's profits are included for the entire year, regardless of the date of combination. Because there is no goodwill, there is no amortisation charge. Because assets are stated at book value, depreciation charges may be lower than under the acquisition method.

(c) Although the balance sheet may appear 'weaker' than under the acquisition method, particularly if a large 'difference' has to be written off to reserves, capital employed is lower.

These factors mean that merger accounting usually results in higher earnings per share and higher ROCE than the acquisition method. In addition, distributable reserves appear to be higher, although this is misleading as distributions are made by the parent, not by the group as a whole.

These comparisons illustrate the incentives, which preparers of accounts might have, to adopt particular methods of consolidation. One of the most significant 'creative accounting' abuses of the 1980s was the use of merger accounting for combinations that were in substance acquisitions.

However, it is important to remember that in practice there is no longer any choice. FRS 6 sets out clearly the situations in which merger accounting is to be used.

4   IFRS 3 *Business combinations*

The IASB's IFRS 3 has banned the use of the merger method in accounts prepared in accordance with IASs, as discussed earlier in this text. In due course the UK will follow suit, so you should be aware that the days of the merger method are numbered. In the future, all group accounting will be carried out using the acquisition method.

Mergers and takeovers

1 What is the difference between a merger and an acquisition? (1.1)

2 How is a merger accounted for in the parent company's accounts? (1.3)

3 What effect does merger relief have on the parent company's accounts? (1.4)

4 When can merger accounting be used, according to (a) the Companies Act and (b) FRS 6? (1.5)

5 What are the main differences between merger accounting and acquisition accounting? (1.6, 1.7)

6 How are merger expenses and subsidiary company dividends treated under merger accounting? (1.8)

Comparison of consolidated financial statements prepared under merger accounting and acquisition accounting

7 Under UITF Abstract 15, when is an acquisition substantial and what information about it must be disclosed? (2.3)

Acquisition accounting and merger accounting compared

8 What are the relative advantages and disadvantages of merger accounting and acquisition accounting? (3.2)

IFRS 3 *Business combinations*

9 What are the main requirements in the IASB's IFRS 3 *Business combinations*? (4)

Charlie plc

Charlie plc is negotiating to acquire all the issued equity and voting shares of Alex Ltd. It is proposed that the consideration offered to the shareholders of Alex Ltd comprises a 2 for 1 share-for-share exchange and 25 pence cash per share. The current share price of Charlie plc is £3.

Although the two companies are in competition, both management teams have agreed that by merging the two companies the new entity will be in a better position to counter increased foreign competition. It is expected that the two management teams will be able to work together.

The shareholders of Alex Ltd are not hostile to the combination as it will improve the liquidity of their share price.

Inevitably as a result of the combination there will be some reorganisation to eliminate common overheads. At present, rationalisation plans would result in the closure of Alex Ltd's regional distribution network at an estimated cost of £4,500,000, including redundancy costs of £500,000 and losses on the disposal of various fixed assets of £3,750,000.

The balance sheets of both companies as at 31 December 20X5 are set out below:

	Charlie plc		Alex Ltd	
	£'000	£'000	£'000	£'000
Fixed assets				
Tangible		9,715		14,250
Current assets				
Stock	8,000		2,000	
Long-term debtors	-		1,500	
Investments	-		500	
Debtors	600		875	
	8,600		4,875	
Current liabilities	(1,100)		(3,200)	
Net current assets		7,500		1,675
Long-term liabilities		(1,000)		(4,000)
		16,215		11,925
Called up share capital				
(ordinary shares of £1)		12,000		5,000
Reserves		4,215		6,925
		16,215		11,925

The following information relates to Alex Ltd.

1 Fixed assets

These comprise:

	Freehold offices	Plant
Net book value	£8,000,000	£6,250,000

The freehold offices have a market value of £10 million.

A lot of the plant will be scrapped under the reorganisation plans and has an estimated value on that basis of £2,500,000. The net replacement cost of the plant is £5 million. The amount Alex Ltd would have expected to recover from its future use is at least £5 million.

2 Stock

Stocks are carried at the lower of cost and net realisable value.

	£'000
Cost	2,000
Net realisable value	6,000
Replacement cost	2,500

3 The long-term debtors are receivable at the 20X7 year end.

4 The investments are carried in the balance sheet at the lower of cost and net realisable value. They cost £500,000 and have a net realisable value of £980,000.

5 The long-term liability is a loan carrying 10% pa interest and is repayable on 31 December 20X8. The current interest rate available on loans is 12%.

You are required to:

(a) explain whether the combination should be treated as an acquisition or a merger, according to the conditions set out in the CA85 and in FRS 6

(b) prepare the consolidated balance sheet of the Charlie plc group at 31 December 20X5 together with a table of fair values as required by FRS 6 *Acquisitions and mergers*

(c) explain your treatment of the reorganisation costs which are expected to arise as a result of the combination.

Assume a corporation tax rate of 40%.

Present value factors to discount from end of year.

End of year	10%	11%	12%	13%	14%	
1	0.909	0.901	0.893	0.885	0.877	
2	0.826	0.812	0.797	0.783	0.769	
3	0.751	0.731	0.712	0.693	0.675	
4	0.683	0.659	0.636	0.613	0.592	
5	0.621	0.593	0.567	0.543	0.519	**(20 marks)**

For the answer to this question see the 'Answers' section at the end of the book.

FEEDBACK TO ACTIVITY **1**	The proposals do not meet the requirements of CA89 as the cash element is more than 10% of the nominal value of the equity shares.

	Nominal value	
	£	%
Equity shares 1,000 @ £1	1,000	100
Cash	200	20

This problem could be overcome by P making a bonus issue of 1 for 1 held and then offering to issue 2,000 equity shares worth £1.50 each to the shareholders of S.

	Nominal value	
	£	%
Equity shares 2,000 @ £1	2,000	100
Cash	200	10

FEEDBACK TO ACTIVITY **2**

(a) Acquisition accounting balance sheet

	£	£
Fixed assets (230,000 + 16,000 (W2))		246,000
Current assets	620,000	
Creditors – amounts falling due within one year	225,000	
Net current assets		395,000
Total assets less current liabilities		641,000
Capital and reserves		
Called up share capital (W3)		275,000
Merger reserve (W1) (Allowed by Companies Act)		66,000
Profit and loss account		300,000
		641,000

Workings

(W1) Issue of shares at a premium

	Dr £	Cr £
Dr Cost of investment 120,000 × 80p	96,000	
Cr Ordinary share capital		30,000
Cr Merger reserve		66,000

(W2) Calculation of goodwill on consolidation

	£	£
Cost of investment		96,000
Net assets at acquisition		
Equity interest	70,000	
Surplus on revaluation	10,000	
		(80,000)
Goodwill		16,000

(W3) **Share capital**

	£
Previously in issue	245,000
Consideration for acquisition	30,000
	275,000

(b) **Merger accounting balance sheet**

	£	£
Fixed assets		220,000
Current assets	620,000	
Creditors – amounts falling due within one year	225,000	
Net current assets		395,000
		615,000
Capital and reserves		
Called up share capital		275,000
Profit and loss account (W)		340,000
		615,000

Working

	£	£
G Ltd reserves		300,000
C Ltd reserves		50,000
Difference arising		
Nominal value of shares issued	30,000	
Nominal value of shares acquired	20,000	
		(10,000)
Consolidated reserves		340,000

Chapter 6

GROUP REORGANISATIONS AND RESTRUCTURING

Group reorganisations involve the changing of relationships between companies in a group. There are several ways in which this can take place, for example by setting up a new holding company or by changing the direct ownership of a subsidiary within a group. This chapter looks at the accounting treatment of group re-organisations.

Objectives

When you have studied this chapter you should be able to:

- discuss the creation of a new holding company

- explain changes in the ownership of companies within a group

- understand the nature of demergers and divisionalisation

- prepare group financial statements after re-organisation and reconstruction

- appraise the benefits of a reorganisation and restructuring.

1   Group reorganisations

1.1   The reasons why groups change their internal structures

The legal structure tends to reflect the way the group wants to manage the total operations and the way the individual sections report.

Thus a group may have a pyramid structure as below.

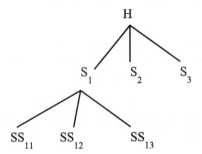

The bottom level companies (sub-subsidiaries) report to the next level (subsidiaries) which in turn report to the holding company. This structure supports a hierarchical style of management.

Other groups may prefer a flatter organisational structure with perhaps the number of subsidiaries being reduced and most subsidiaries being directly owned by the holding company.

Clearly with changes in management at the top of a group or changes in the operating environment for a group, changes may be thought necessary in the legal structure of a group. It is of course possible for the reporting and management structure to operate in a different way from the legal structure but, in the long run, it is easier if the two coincide.

Further reasons why a group may change its structure include taxation (the total taxation borne by the group can be affected by the legal structure of the group) and overseas operations (which may need to be operated as separate subsidiaries to comply with local laws).

1.2   FRS 6 and group reconstructions

FRS 6 defines a group reconstruction as reproduced in the margin.

FRS 6 allows merger accounting to be used to account for group reconstructions, even if there is no business combination meeting the definition of a merger, provided:

- the use of merger accounting is not prohibited by companies legislation

- the ultimate shareholders remain the same, and the rights of each such shareholder, relative to the others, are unchanged

- no minority's interest in the net assets of the group is altered by the transfer.

2   Creating a new holding company

2.1   Introduction

A group might set up a new holding company for an existing group in order to improve co-ordination within the group or as a vehicle for flotation.

A typical situation would be as shown below:

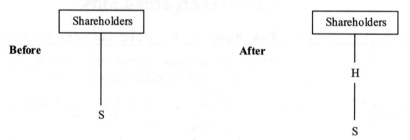

H becomes the new holding company of S. Usually H issues shares to the shareholders of S in exchange for shares of S, but occasionally the shareholders of S may subscribe for shares in H and H may pay cash for S.

A new holding company can also be set up as a means of returning capital to the shareholders. In this situation, H issues shareholders in S with cash or debentures in exchange for their existing shares.

2.2   Accounting treatment

This type of reorganisation meets the definition of a group reconstruction under FRS 6. If the reorganisation is carried out by means of a share-for-share exchange then merger accounting can be used to account for the combination.

Note that merger accounting is optional in this situation, but it is likely to be the method used because it tends to present a more favourable view of a group's performance and position than acquisition accounting.

If H pays cash for S, the combination does not meet the Companies Act criteria for merger accounting and should therefore be treated as an acquisition. This will also normally be the case where a new holding company is used to return capital to the shareholders, because the cash consideration usually exceeds 10% of the nominal value of the shares issued.

However, some companies have treated these combinations as mergers. FRS 6 states that acquisition accounting is likely to be inappropriate in the case of a transaction that does not alter the relative rights of the ultimate shareholders. These companies invoke the 'true and fair view override' and use the merger method for this reason.

ACTIVITY 1

X plc has owned 100% of Y Ltd since its incorporation. The balance sheets of X plc and Y Ltd at 31 December 20X2 are shown below:

	X plc £m	Y Ltd £m
Tangible fixed assets	400	200
Investment in Y Ltd	100	
Net current assets	100	100
	600	300
Share capital (ordinary shares of £1 each)	100	100
Profit and loss account	500	200
	600	300

On 1 January 20X3 a new holding company, H plc, is set up. H plc issues 500 million £1 ordinary shares to the shareholders of X plc in return for the whole of the issued share capital of that company.

Show how the accounts of all three individual group companies and the group accounts will appear immediately after this transaction.

Feedback to this activity is at the end of the chapter.

3   Changing direct ownership of a company within a group

3.1   The effects of changes in the direct ownership of subsidiaries

The reorganisation of the group should not result in any changes to the group financial statements. The reorganisations are achieved by transferring the shareholdings from one group company to another. No assets leave or are added to the group as a result.

However, accounting problems may arise in the individual company(ies) which originally held the investment(s). The transferor company has disposed of an asset.

3.2   Types of re-organisation

(a) Subsidiary moved up

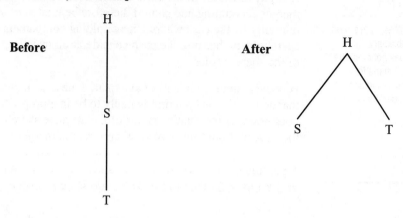

(b) Subsidiary moved down

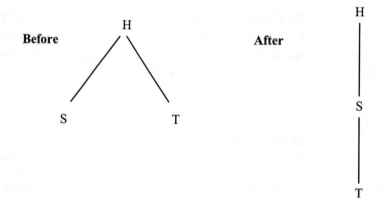

(c) Subsidiary moved along

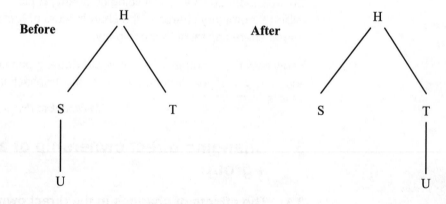

ACTIVITY 2	X owns 100% of Y and Y owns 100% of Z. Y's investment in Z is transferred to X, so that Z becomes a direct subsidiary of X. Suggest reasons why the group might have carried out this reorganisation.

Feedback to this activity is at the end of the chapter.

3.3   Subsidiary moved up

This can be achieved in one of two ways.

- S transfers its investment in T to H as a dividend *in specie*. If this is done then S must have sufficient distributable profits to pay the dividend.

- H purchases the investment in T from S for cash. In practice the purchase price often equals the carrying value of the investment, so that no gain or loss arises on the transaction.

A parent cannot issue shares to a subsidiary and so this type of reorganisation cannot be carried out by means of a share-for-share exchange.

Example

A plc has owned 100% of B Ltd since its incorporation. B Ltd acquired 100% of C Ltd many years ago when the balance on C Ltd's reserves was £5 million. Goodwill arising on the acquisition has been fully amortised.

The balance sheets of the three companies at 31 December 20X2 are as follows:

	A plc £m	B Ltd £m	C Ltd £m
Tangible fixed assets	300	100	20
Investment in B Ltd	30		
Investment in C Ltd		35	
Net current assets	80	50	10
	410	185	30
Share capital	60	30	20
Profit and loss account	350	155	10
	410	185	30

On 1 January 20X3 A plc purchased the whole of B Ltd's investment in C Ltd for £35 million in cash.

Show how the accounts of the three individual companies and the group would appear immediately after this transaction.

Solution

	A plc £m	B Ltd £m	C Ltd £m	Group £m
Tangible fixed assets	300	100	20	420
Investment in B Ltd	30	–	–	
Investment in C Ltd	35	–	–	
Net current assets	45	85	10	140
	410	185	30	560
Share capital	60	30	20	60
Profit and loss account (W)	350	155	10	500
	410	185	30	560

Working

Group profit and loss account:	£m
A plc	350
B Ltd (all post-acquisition)	155
C Ltd (post-acquisition)	5
	510
Goodwill on acquisition of C Ltd (35 − 25)	(10)
	500

Notice that the group accounts are exactly the same after the reorganisation as they were before. From the perspective of the group nothing has changed. The group has not made an acquisition or a disposal and the fact that C Ltd is now a subsidiary of A plc rather than a subsidiary of B Ltd does not affect the amount of pre-acquisition reserves. These are 'frozen' at the date that C Ltd first became a member of the group.

The purchase consideration is exactly the same as the carrying value of the investment in C Ltd. Suppose that it had been £25 million, rather than £35 million. There are three implications.

- B Ltd would record a loss on sale of £10 million. This would reduce its own profit and loss account reserve, but would be eliminated on consolidation (as an intra-group item) and would not affect group reserves.

- A transfer at less than the fair value of the investment might be regarded as a distribution to A plc. There could be legal problems if B Ltd did not have sufficient distributable reserves.

- If the purpose of the reorganisation is to allow B Ltd to leave the group, the purchase price paid by A plc should not be less than the fair value of the investment in C Ltd. If the purchase price is less than fair value, this could be construed as financial assistance to B Ltd for the purchase of its own shares, which is prohibited by the CA85 unless certain conditions are met. If B Ltd is not acquired by another company it will have to purchase its own shares in order to leave the group.

3.4 Subsidiary moved down

This reorganisation may be carried out where there are tax advantages in establishing a 'sub-group', or where two or more subsidiaries are linked geographically.

This can be carried out either by:

- a share-for-share exchange (S issues shares to H in return for the shares in T); or

- a cash transaction (S pays cash to H).

If there is a share-for-share exchange, S132 CA85 gives partial relief from the requirement to set up a share premium account. Only the 'minimum premium value' is taken to the share premium account.

Shares cannot be issued at a discount. This means that the investment in T must be worth at least the nominal value of the shares issued by S.

DEFINITION

The **minimum premium value** is the amount by which the book value of the investment (or cost, if lower) exceeds the nominal value of the shares issued.

KEY POINT

Shares cannot be issued at a discount. This means that an investment must be worth at least the nominal value of the shares issued in consideration.

Example

A plc has owned 100% of B Ltd since its incorporation. A plc acquired 100% of C Ltd many years ago when the balance on C Ltd's reserves was £5 million. Goodwill arising on the acquisition has been fully amortised.

The balance sheets of the three companies at 31 December 20X2 are as follows:

	A plc £m	B Ltd £m	C Ltd £m
Tangible fixed assets	480	160	40
Investment in B Ltd	50		
Investment in C Ltd	60		
Net current assets	130	80	20
	720	240	60
Share capital	100	50	50
Profit and loss account	620	190	10
	720	240	60

On 1 January 20X3 B Ltd purchased the whole of A plc's investment in C Ltd by issuing 50 million £1 ordinary shares as consideration.

Show how the accounts of the three individual companies and the group would appear immediately after this transaction.

Solution

	A plc £m	B Ltd £m	C Ltd £m	Group £m
Tangible fixed assets	480	160	40	680
Investment in B Ltd (50 + 60) (note 1)	110	–	–	
Investment in C Ltd	–	60	–	
Net current assets	130	80	20	230
	720	300	60	910
Share capital (note 2)	100	100	50	100
Share premium (note 2)		10		
Profit and loss account (W)	620	190	10	810
	720	300	60	910

Notes

(1) A plc's investment in B Ltd is increased by the value placed on the shares issued by B Ltd.

(2) The minimum premium value is £10 million (the difference between the book value of the investment in C Ltd and the nominal value of the shares issued in consideration. This is taken to the share premium account. Note that the shares cannot be issued at a discount.

Again, the group accounts are exactly the same after the reorganisation as they were before.

Working

Group profit and loss account:	£m
A plc	620
B Ltd (all post-acquisition)	190
C Ltd (post-acquisition)	5
	815
Goodwill on acquisition of C Ltd (60 – 55)	(5)
	810

3.5 Subsidiary moved along

This is carried out by T paying cash (or other assets) to S. The consideration cannot be in the form of shares because T might then become a subsidiary or an associate of S and therefore retain an indirect interest in U.

If the purpose of the reorganisation is to allow S to leave the group, the purchase price paid by T should not be less than the fair value of the investment in U otherwise S may be deemed to be receiving financial assistance for the purchase of its own shares.

4 Demergers and divisionalisation

4.1 Why a company may demerge some of its subsidiaries

A demerger is the splitting of a group into two or more parts, each of which continues to be owned by the original shareholders.

A demerger is an extreme form of internal restructuring. The group becomes two groups but from the shareholders' point of view it is a restructuring as they retain the same effective interest in the two groups as they had in the original group.

The main reason given for demergers is to 'enhance shareholder value'. In the view of the directors making the decision, the stock market has a history of placing a value on the old group which does not equal the true value of the group. Splitting the group results in two publicly quoted groups which may be valued by the stock market at more than the former combined entity. This seems to have been the case with the demergers that have been done in the past but it is not a common type of reorganisation.

The impetus for demerging may be an unwanted bid by another company and it is thus a means of defending the group from takeover.

Demergers may also be carried out in order to improve the focus of management and thus promote growth.

4.2 Preparing the financial statements after a demerger

The preparation of financial statements after a demerger is quite straightforward provided you understand the nature of the transactions. In accounting terms a group is giving some of its assets, i.e. investments in subsidiaries, to its shareholders by distributing the shareholdings to them. This may be done directly or through the medium of another company. The end effect to the shareholders is the same.

DEFINITION

A **demerger** is the splitting of a group into two or more parts, each of which continues to be owned by the original shareholders but with no legal relationship with the former other parts of the group.

A direct distribution of the investment is a distribution *in specie* as in the illustration below.

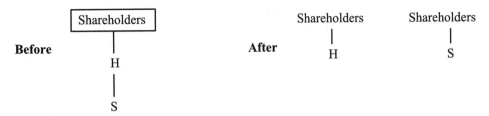

In accounting terms, the company is paying a dividend in the form of shares rather than cash. The entry in the holding company books is therefore as follows:

Dr   Profit and loss account (or directly to reserves)

Cr   Cost of investment

with the book value (probably) of the investment.

Alternatively a new company may be formed and the shares issued to the shareholders in the existing group. The investment (or subsidiary) is transferred to the new company as below.

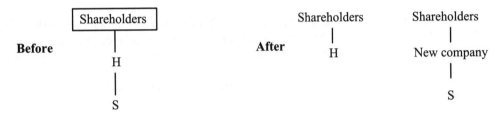

In the old parent company, the transaction is dealt with in the same way as for a direct distribution, i.e. a 'dividend' is being paid to the shareholders, the value of which is (probably) made to be equivalent to the book value of the net assets transferred to the new company or the cost of investment of the subsidiary being transferred.

Example

The summarised consolidated balance sheet of the X Group is shown below, together with the individual summarised balance sheets of X plc and its wholly owned subsidiary Y Ltd at 31 December 20X6.

	X Group	X plc	Y Ltd
	£'000	£'000	£'000
Investment in Y Ltd	-	800	-
Other net assets	3,600	2,200	1,400
	3,600	3,000	1,400
Share capital	2,000	2,000	800
Profit and loss account	1,600	1,000	600
	3,600	3,000	1,400

On 1 January 20X7, X plc forms a new company, Z Ltd. Z Ltd issues 800,000 £1 ordinary shares to the shareholders of X plc in exchange for X plc's investment in Y Ltd, so that Y Ltd is demerged.

Prepare the summarised financial statements of X plc and the X Group immediately after the demerger.

Solution

Tutorial note: X plc has effectively made a distribution of £800,000 to its shareholders. The group's net assets are reduced by £1,400,000 and X plc's net assets by £800,000. The reduction is disclosed as a movement on retained earnings.

	X Group £'000	X plc £'000
Net assets	2,200	2,200
Share capital	2,000	2,000
Profit and loss account b/f	1,600	1,000
Demerger	(1,400)	(800)
	2,200	2,200

In practice, merger accounting can normally be used for demerger transactions of this type, provided that they meet the definition of a group reconstruction and all the conditions under FRS 6.

ACTIVITY 3

S plc has owned 100% of T Ltd since its incorporation. S plc also acquired 100% of U Ltd many years ago when the balance on U Ltd's reserves was £25 million. Goodwill arising on the acquisition has been fully amortised.

The balance sheets of the three companies at 31 December 20X2 are as follows:

	S plc £m	T Ltd £m	U Ltd £m
Tangible fixed assets	720	240	60
Investment in T Ltd	80		
Investment in U Ltd	80		
Net current assets	190	120	20
	1,070	360	80
Share capital (£1 ordinary shares)	150	80	50
Profit and loss account	920	280	30
	1,070	360	80

On 1 January 20X3 a new company, R plc was set up. R plc issued 160 million £1 shares to the shareholders of S plc in exchange for the shares held in T Ltd and U Ltd.

Show how the accounts of S plc and the R plc group would appear immediately after this transaction.

Feedback to this activity is at the end of the chapter.

4.3 Divisionalisation

Divisionalisation is the transfer of the assets and trades of a number of subsidiaries into one company.

Divisionalisation may be carried out in order to simplify the group structure and to save costs.

Typically, one subsidiary purchases the business of another for cash. The other company becomes a dormant shell. The accounting treatment is normally straightforward, but two main problems can arise.

- The group's investment in the shell company may become impaired and need to be written down. This is likely to be an issue if goodwill arose on the original acquisition of the investment in the shell company and the business is transferred at a price that reflects only the value of the net tangible assets. The goodwill remains in the shell company, but the business to which it relates now belongs to another company. For this reason, the value of the parent's investment in the 'shell' company falls below its cost.

- Because the shell company ceases trading, the purchase transaction may never actually be settled in cash. This means that there is an inter-company balance that must be eliminated on consolidation.

Example

X plc has owned 100% of Y Ltd since its incorporation. It also acquired 100% of Z Ltd many years ago when the balance on Z Ltd's reserves was £30 million. Goodwill arising on the acquisition has been fully amortised.

The balance sheets of the three companies at 31 December 20X2 are as follows:

	X plc £m	Y Ltd £m	Z Ltd £m
Tangible fixed assets	900	300	90
Investment in Y Ltd	90		
Investment in Z Ltd	105		
Net current assets	240	150	30
	1,335	450	120
Share capital	180	90	50
Profit and loss account	1,155	360	70
	1,335	450	120

On 1 January 20X3 the assets and trade of Z Ltd were transferred to Y Ltd at their book value. The consideration for the transfer was £100 million. In practice, this amount will remain as a debtor in the books of Z Ltd, as this company will not trade after the reorganisation.

Show how the accounts of the three individual companies and the group would appear immediately after this transaction.

Solution

	X plc £m	Y Ltd £m	Z Ltd £m	Group £m
Tangible fixed assets	900	390	–	1,290
Investment in Y Ltd	90	–	–	
Investment in Z Ltd (note 1)	100	–	–	
Net current assets	240	80	100	420
	1,330	470	100	1,710
Share capital	180	90	50	180
Revaluation reserve (note 2)		20		
Profit and loss account (note 3) (W)	1,150	360	50	1,530
	1,330	470	100	1,710

Notes

(1) X plc's investment in Z Ltd is impaired and is written down.

(2) The revaluation reserve is the gain on the purchase of the assets from Z Ltd (120 – 100).

(3) The profit and loss account of X plc reflects the impairment loss on the investment in Z Ltd. Z Ltd records a loss on disposal of £20 million (the difference between the carrying value of its assets and the consideration received).

Working

This is as it would have been before the divisionalisation as all the transactions involved are intra-group items and are therefore eliminated on consolidation.

Group profit and loss account:

X plc	1,155
Y Ltd (all post-acquisition)	360
Z Ltd (post-acquisition)	40
	1,555
Goodwill on acquisition of Z Ltd (105 – 80)	(25)
	1,530

Group reorganisations

1 How does FRS 6 define a group reconstruction? (1.2)

2 What conditions does FRS 6 impose on a reconstruction being accounted for as a merger? (1.2)

Changing direct ownership of a company within a group

3 When can a reconstruction give rise to partial relief from the requirement to set up a share premium account? (3.4)

Demergers and divisionalisation

4 What is a demerger and why do companies demerge? (4.1)

5 What is the accounting effect of a demerger? (4.2)

6   Define divisionalisation. (4.3)

7   How is divisionalisation accounted for? What problems can it present? (4.3)

EXAM-TYPE
QUESTION

S plc

The following financial statements relate to S plc, T plc, U Ltd and V Ltd for the year ended 31 May 20X7.

	S plc £m	T plc £m	U Ltd £m	V Ltd £m
Fixed assets:				
Tangible fixed assets	4,200	660	72	108
Investment in T	1,080			
Investment in U		108		
Investment in V	60			
	5,340	768	72	108
Net current assets	2,196	480	84	72
Creditors falling due after 1 year	(156)	(36)	(12)	(6)
	7,380	1,212	144	174
Capital and reserves				
Called up share capital of £1	1,620	120	36	24
Share premium account	1,860	120	12	24
Profit and loss account	3,900	972	96	126
	7,380	1,212	144	174

Profit and loss accounts for the year ended 31 May 20X7

	S plc £m	T plc £m	U Ltd £m	V Ltd £m
Turnover	9,600	3,600	390	636
Cost of sales	6,000	2,400	234	384
Gross profit	3,600	1,200	156	252
Administrative and distribution costs	2,400	480	42	150
Income from group companies	16	5	–	
Operating profit before taxation	1,216	725	114	102
Taxation	360	240	48	30
Profit on ordinary activities after tax	856	485	66	72
Dividends paid	36	12	6	6
Retained profit for year	820	473	60	66

(i)   The directors of S plc decided to reconstruct the group at 31 May 20X7. Under the scheme the existing group of companies was split into two separate groups in order to separate their different trades. S plc has disposed of its shareholding in T plc to another company W plc. In return the shares in W plc were distributed to the shareholders in S plc. No profit or loss arose on the disposal of the shares in T plc as the 'demerger' simply involved a distribution to the shareholders of S plc of the shares of W plc.

(ii) After the 'demerger', there were two separate groups controlled by S plc and W plc. S plc and V Ltd formed one group. W plc and the T group plc formed another group. W plc issued 360 million ordinary shares of £1 in exchange for S plc's investment in T plc. The transaction took place on 31 May 20X7.

(iii) The following information relates to the dates of acquisition of the investments in group companies:

Holding company	Co. acquired	% acquired	Dates	£m Share premium account	£m Profit/Loss account
S plc	T plc	100	1.1.20X4	100	300
S plc	V Ltd	60	1.5.20X5	24	108
T plc	U Ltd	80	1.6.20X5	12	72

(iv) The group's policy is not to amortise goodwill arising on acquisition of a subsidiary unless annual impairment reviews show that a write-down is necessary. No fair value adjustments have been required.

(v) Dividends paid by group companies have been accounted for by the recipient companies. S group plc has decided to show the effect of the distribution of the shares in W plc and the demerger of T group plc in its profit and loss account and not as a movement on reserves.

(vi) The group is to take advantage of the provisions of the CA85 regarding group reconstruction relief and the transaction qualifies as a merger.

Required:

(a) Prepare the consolidated balance sheet of the T group plc as at 31 May 20X7.

(6 marks)

(b) Prepare the consolidated profit and loss account and balance sheet of S Group plc for the year ended 31 May 20X7 after accounting for the demerger.

(16 marks)

(You should prepare the financial statements in accordance with FRS 3 Reporting Financial Performance).

(c) Show the share capital and reserves of W Group plc at 31 May 20X7.

(3 marks)

(Total: 25 marks)

For the answer to this question see the 'Answers' section at the end of the book.

FEEDBACK TO ACTIVITY 1

	H plc £m	X plc £m	Y Ltd £m	Group £m
Tangible fixed assets	–	400	200	600
Investment in X plc	500	–	–	
Investment in Y Ltd	–	100	–	
Net current assets	–	100	100	200
	500	600	300	800
Share capital	500	100	100	500
Profit and loss account (W)	–	500	200	300
	500	600	300	800

Working

Merger accounting is used, as this meets the FRS 6 definition of a group reconstruction and the conditions are met.

Group profit and loss account:	£m
X plc	500
Y Ltd	200
	700
'Difference' (500 – 100)	(400)
	300

<table>
<tr><td>FEEDBACK TO ACTIVITY 2</td><td>If Y and Z are in different businesses this restructuring enables the different businesses to be carried out through directly owned subsidiaries.

The change would also allow X to sell Y without disposing of Z.</td></tr>
</table>

FEEDBACK TO ACTIVITY 3

	S plc	R Group
	£m	£m
Tangible fixed assets	720	300
Net current assets	190	140
	910	440
Share capital	150	160
Profit and loss account (W)	760	280
	910	440

Note: Merger accounting is used.

Workings	£m	£m
Profit and loss account: S plc		
Per accounts		920
Less distribution *in specie*		(160)
		760
Profit and loss account: R Group		
T Ltd		280
U Ltd		30
		310
Shares issued by R	160	
Nominal value of shares in T Ltd	(80)	
Nominal value of shares in U Ltd	(50)	
'Difference'		(30)
		280

Chapter 7

ASSOCIATES, JOINT VENTURES AND JOINT ARRANGEMENTS THAT ARE NOT ENTITIES

DEFINITION

An entity over which an investor can exercise significant influence is called an **associate**.

DEFINITION

A **joint venture** is an entity which is jointly controlled by one or more other entities.

In this chapter we look at situations where a company may not be able to exercise control over an investee, but can influence its operating and financial policies. An entity over which an investor can exercise significant influence is called an associate. A joint venture is an entity which is jointly controlled by one or more other entities. Much of the material in this chapter should already be familiar to you.

Objectives

When you have studied this chapter you should be able to:

- account for associates, joint ventures and joint arrangements that are not entities (JANEs)

- apply the equity and gross equity methods of accounting

- prepare group financial statements including accounting for associates, joint ventures and JANEs.

1 Associated undertakings – introduction

1.1 Introduction

Where a company owns more than 50% of the voting shares of another company, the CA85 requires group accounts. The law in effect recognises the influence which a parent company may exert over a subsidiary company and the existence of an economic unit, the group. If a parent company's accounts were to show only dividends received or receivable from subsidiaries, the shareholders of the parent company would not be given sufficient information regarding the underlying profitability of the unit, the group. Consequently, group accounts normally include the parent company's share of the post-acquisition profits of subsidiaries.

However, if a company, H Ltd, which has subsidiaries, owns (say) 40% of the ordinary share capital of another company, A Ltd, then A Ltd does not come within the legal definition of subsidiary company. H Ltd may nevertheless be able to exert considerable influence over A Ltd. It would thus seem sensible to allow H Ltd to show information in its accounts about its share of the profits of A Ltd.

FRS 9 provides rules for accounting for associated companies, i.e. companies which fall into the position described above.

The CA89 introduced into law the requirement for associated undertakings to be included in group accounts under the equity method. The equity method is the method detailed by FRS 9.

The term undertakings includes companies and unincorporated businesses. FRS 9 also applies to all undertakings (not just companies). As the CA89 requires the word 'undertaking' to be used in the published accounts, the rest of this section will follow the CA89 terminology, where it is sensible to do so.

1.2 What is an 'associated undertaking'?

Company law

The CA89 states that an **associated undertaking** is an undertaking in which an undertaking included in the consolidation has a participating interest and over whose operating and financial policy it exercises a significant influence, and which is not:

- a subsidiary undertaking; or

- a joint venture.

The CA89 further states that a **participating interest** is an interest in shares held on a long-term basis for the purpose of securing a contribution to the investor's activities. A holding of 20% or more is presumed to be a participating interest unless the contrary is shown.

FRS 9

An associate is an entity (other than a subsidiary) in which another entity (the investor) has a participating interest and over whose operating and financial policies the investor exercises a significant influence.

The exercise of significant influence means that the investor is actively involved and is influential in the direction of its investee through its participation in policy decisions covering aspects of policy relevant to the investor, including decisions on strategic issues such as:

- the expansion or contraction of the business, participation in other entities or changes in products, markets and activities of its investee

- determining the balance between dividend and reinvestment.

The FRS 9 definition is quite complex, but is essentially very similar to the company law definition.

The main thing to note is that the emphasis of the FRS 9 definition is different to that in the Companies Act. Under the Companies Act, a long-term holding of 20% or more is presumed to be an associate unless it can clearly be demonstrated otherwise. SSAP 1 (which preceded FRS 9) used a similar definition. In practice, this meant that the 20% threshold was normally the only factor taken into account, so that many investments were treated as associates when the investee did not actually exercise significant influence.

The FRS 9 definition centres on the actual substance of the relationship between the parties (i.e. whether significant influence is exercised in practice) rather than its strict legal form (the size of the shareholding).

An investing company's ability to exercise significant influence may depend on the other shareholdings as well as its own. For example, if A Ltd holds 30% of the shares in B Ltd, but the remaining 70% of the shares in B Ltd are held by C plc, then A Ltd is extremely unlikely to be able to exercise significant influence over B Ltd.

However, in questions you should assume that a shareholding of between 20% and 50% is an associate unless you are given information which suggests otherwise.

2   Joint ventures

The term 'joint venture' is used very widely in practice to cover all types of jointly controlled activity. Jointly controlled operations, assets and entities may all be described as joint ventures. FRS 9 defines 'joint venture' in a much narrower sense.

A **joint venture** is an entity in which the reporting entity holds an interest on a long-term basis and is jointly controlled by the reporting entity and by one or more other venturers under a contractual arrangement.

For an investment to qualify as a joint venture, there must be:

(a) a separate entity

(b) which carries on a trade or business of its own.

This means that the joint venture must have some independence to pursue its own commercial strategy and it must generally be able to buy and sell on the same terms as are available in the market.

FRS 9 provides further examples of indications that the arrangement is not carrying on a trade or business of its own.

- The participants derive their benefit from products or services taken in kind rather than by receiving a share in the results of trading.

- Each participant's share of the output or result of the joint activity is determined by its supply of key inputs to the process producing that output or result.

A cost or risk sharing means of carrying out a process in the participants' own trades or businesses (e.g. a joint marketing or distribution network or a shared production facility) is not a joint venture.

A joint arrangement to carry out a single project is unlikely to meet the definition of a joint venture.

(a) A (a builder) and B (an estate agent) together buy a house which they let to tenants. A is responsible for the initial refurbishment and maintenance of the house and B finds the tenants and collects the rents. A and B each take an agreed share of the rental income from the house.

(b) A and B enter into an agreement to manufacture and sell a new product. They set up a company which carries out these activities. A and B each own 50% of the equity share capital of the company and are its only directors. They share equally in major policy decisions and are each entitled to 50% of the profits of the company.

Are these two joint activities joint ventures or joint arrangements?

Feedback to this activity is at the end of the chapter.

3   Accounting for associates

3.1   Possible accounting methods

There are two possible methods of dealing with associates and joint ventures in the consolidated financial statements.

DEFINITION

A **joint venture** is an entity in which the reporting entity holds an interest on a long-term basis and is jointly controlled by the reporting entity and by one or more other venturers under a contractual arrangement.

DEFINITION

A reporting entity **jointly controls** a venture with one or more other entities if none of the entities alone can control that entity but all together can do so and decisions on financial and operating policy essential to the activities, economic performance and financial position of that venture require each venturer's consent.

DEFINITION

A **joint arrangement that is not an entity** is a contractual arrangement under which the participants engage in joint activities that do not create an entity because it would not be carrying on a trade or business of its own.

ACTIVITY 1

The equity method

The equity method requires the group balance sheet to record the investor's share of the net assets of the associate but does not mislead the user into thinking that the associate is a part of the group as the assets are not combined with the group assets.

The main disadvantage of the equity method is that it fails to reveal the underlying assets and liabilities. This is why its use is not regarded as a valid method of showing group accounts in the majority of situations, and it is therefore only used when, for some reason, consolidation is regarded as inappropriate.

The proportional consolidation method

The proportional consolidation method has the advantage of showing the group's share of the underlying assets and liabilities.

However, it does not clearly distinguish the assets of the associate or joint venture from those of the group. This treatment implies that the investing group can control the assets and liabilities of the entity. Therefore proportional consolidation would be potentially misleading if it were used for an associate.

The ASB considered proportional consolidation for joint ventures, but rejected it on the grounds that it would be inconsistent with the accounting treatment of both associates and subsidiaries. It argues that in most cases, the venturer controls an interest in the joint venture, rather than its share in individual assets and liabilities.

Proportional consolidation would also be inconsistent with the requirements of the Companies Act in most cases. Under CA89 proportional consolidation can only be used for unincorporated joint ventures.

3.2 The requirements of FRS 9

FRS 9 requires the equity method to be used to account for an associated undertaking in the consolidated financial statements. Where the investing company does not prepare group accounts (perhaps because it has no subsidiaries) the associate is accounted for as an ordinary trade investment, i.e. dividends received/receivable in the profit and loss account and cost or valuation less amounts written off in the balance sheet.

3.3 Equity accounting in the consolidated balance sheet

(a) **Calculation**

The investment in the associate is stated at:

	(i)	cost
plus	(ii)	group share of retained post-acquisition profits
less	(iii)	amounts written off (e.g. goodwill).

Where goodwill has been fully amortised, the valuation will be equal to the investing company's share of net assets in the associate.

Example

Eagle plc acquired 25% of the ordinary share capital of Hawk plc for £640,000 when the reserves of Hawk plc stood at £720,000. Eagle plc appointed two directors to the board of Hawk plc and the investment is regarded as long-term. Both companies prepare accounts to 31 December each year. The summarised balance sheet of Hawk plc on 31 December 20X4 is as follows:

	£'000
Sundry net assets	2,390
Capital and reserves	
Called up share capital	800
Share premium	450
Profit and loss account	1,140
	2,390

Hawk plc has made no new issues of shares nor has there been any movement in the share premium account since Eagle plc acquired its holding.

Show at what amount the investment in Hawk plc will be shown in the consolidated balance sheet of Eagle plc as on 31 December 20X4. Assume that goodwill arising on the acquisition has been fully amortised.

Investment in associated undertaking

	£
Cost	640,000
Add: group share of post acquisition reserves	
25% × £(1,140 – 720)	105,000
Less: goodwill fully amortised (W1)	(147,500)
Alternatively 25% × £2,390,000	597,500

(W1)   Goodwill

		£	£
Cost			640,000
Less: Share of net assets at acquisition			
	Share capital	800,000	
	Share premium	450,000	
	Reserves	720,000	
	25% ×	1,970,000	(492,500)
Goodwill			147,500

(b) **Disclosure**

Using the above figures

Investments

Interests in associated undertakings   £597,500

3.4   Equity accounting in the consolidated profit and loss account

(a) **Calculation**

The group share of the associate's following items is brought in and disclosed in the consolidated profit and loss account:

(i)   operating profit

(ii)   exceptional items

(iii) interest receivable

(iv) interest payable

(v) taxation.

Amortisation of goodwill is charged against the group share of operating profit of associates, and must be separately disclosed.

Notional total turnover for the business (i.e. group turnover plus the group share of associates' turnover) may be disclosed as a memorandum item in the profit and loss account. This disclosure enables users of the financial statements to appreciate the size of the business as a whole.

Example

Following on from the facts above, the consolidated profit and loss account of Eagle plc (before including any amounts for Hawk plc) and the profit and loss account of Hawk plc for the year ended 31 December 20X4 are as follows:

	Eagle plc £'000	Hawk plc £'000
Turnover	11,000	4,000
Cost of sales	(6,500)	(3,000)
Gross profit	4,500	1,000
Distribution costs	(1,000)	(500)
Administrative expenses	(700)	(300)
Operating profit	2,800	200
Interest receivable	300	200
Interest payable	(100)	(100)
Profit on ordinary activities before taxation	3,000	300
Taxation	(1,200)	(60)
Profit on ordinary activities after taxation	1,800	240
Minority interests	(300)	–
Profit attributable to the group	1,500	240
Dividends proposed	(300)	(50)
Retained profit for the year	1,200	190
Retained profit b/f	6,300	950
Retained profit c/f	7,500	1,140

Prepare the consolidated profit and loss account for Eagle plc for the year ended 31 December 20X4.

(b) **Disclosure (and solution to example)**

	£'000	£'000
Turnover: group and share of associate	12,000	
Less: share of associate's turnover (25% × 4,000)	(1,000)	
Group turnover		11,000
Cost of sales		(6,500)
Gross profit		4,500

Distribution costs		(1,000)
Administrative expenses		(700)
		———
Group operating profit		2,800
Share of operating profit in associates (25% × 200)		50
Interest receivable		
Group	300	
Associates (25% × 200)	50	
	———	
		350
Interest payable		
Group	100	
Associates (25% × 100)	25	
	———	
		(125)
		———
Profit on ordinary activities before taxation		3,075
Taxation		
Group	1,200	
Associates (25% × 60)	15	
	———	
		(1,215)
		———
Profit on ordinary activities after taxation		1,860
Minority interests		(300)
		———
Profit attributable to the group		1,560
Dividends		(300)
		———
Retained profit for the year		1,260
Retained at 1 January 20X4 (W)		6,210
		———
Retained at 31 December 20X4		7,470
		———

Working

Eagle	6,300
Hawk (25% × (950 – 720))	58
Less: goodwill fully amortised (per previous example)	(148)
	———
	6,210
	———

A C T I V I T Y **2**	What are the headings in the CA85 group account formats for the balance sheet and the profit and loss account which are used for associated undertakings?

Feedback to this activity is at the end of the chapter.

3.5   Transactions between the group and the associate

Trading transactions and/or loans may be made between member companies of the group (i.e. parent company and subsidiaries) and the associate. As the associate is not consolidated it follows that these transactions are not cancelled out. For example a loan made by the parent company to an associate will remain as a loan on the consolidated balance sheet (as an asset). The liability recorded in the associate's balance sheet will merely reduce the net assets (which are recorded as one figure – share of net assets – on the consolidated balance sheet).

(a) Trading between group and associate

An adjustment will only be required if there is unrealised profit at the balance sheet date, i.e. stocks exist as a result of the trading. FRS 9 requires an adjustment for the group's share of the unrealised profit. The elimination should be taken in the consolidated profit and loss account against either the group or the associate according to which of them recorded the profit on the transaction. The adjustment in the balance sheet should be made against:

(i)   consolidated stock (if the unrealised profit is in respect of part of this stock); or

(ii)   investment in associate (if the stock is in the associate).

(b) Loans and inter-company balances

The table below states the position. Remember that the asset or liability recorded by the associate will automatically be reflected in the net asset calculation.

Treatment in the consolidated balance sheet

Item	Treatment
(a) Loans between associated undertakings and the group.	(1) These should be disclosed separately, but:
	(i) if long-term, they may appear in the same balance sheet section as 'investment in associate'
	(ii) otherwise they should appear as current assets or liabilities.
	(2) Loans to and from should not be netted off.
(b) Debtors and creditors arising from trading transactions with associated undertakings.	(1) Include under respective current assets or liabilities without netting off.
	(2) Disclose separately if material.

3.6 Applying the equity method – further points

Statement of total recognised gains and losses

The investor's share of the total recognised gains and losses of its associates should be included in the consolidated statement of total recognised gains and losses. If the amounts are material, they should be shown separately under each heading either in the statement or in a note to the statement.

General principles

* The consideration paid for the acquisition and the goodwill arising should be calculated using fair values.

* Investor and associate should apply the same accounting policies.

* The accounts of the associate should have the same financial year-end as those of the investor. If this is impracticable, earlier financial statements of the associate may be used, provided they are prepared for a financial year that ended not more than three months earlier.

* The date on which an investment becomes an associate is the date on which the investor begins to hold a participating interest and to exercise significant influence.

* The date on which an investment ceases to be an associate is the date on which the investor ceases to hold a participating interest and to exercise significant influence.

4   Accounting for joint ventures and joint arrangements that are not entities

4.1   The requirements of FRS 9

(a)   Joint arrangements that are not entities

Participants in a joint arrangement that is not an entity should account for their own assets, liabilities and cash flows, measured according to the terms of the agreement governing the arrangement.

(b)   Joint ventures

In the investor's **individual financial statements**, investments in joint ventures should be treated as fixed asset investments and shown either at cost, less any amounts written off, or at valuation.

In the **consolidated financial statements** joint ventures should be included using the gross equity method.

The treatment is the same as for associates, but with additional disclosure.

- The investor's share of turnover is shown in the consolidated profit and loss account (but not as part of group turnover).

- The investor's share of the gross assets and liabilities is shown in the consolidated balance sheet (instead of the investor's share of the net assets).

(c)   Structures with the form but not the substance of a joint venture

A structure has the form but not the substance of a joint venture when it is a separate entity in which the participants hold a long-term interest and exercise joint management, but which operates as a means for each participant to carry on its own business, with each venturer able to identify and control its share of the assets, liabilities and cash flows of the venture.

In this situation, each entity should account directly for its part of the assets, liabilities and cash flows held within that structure. (This is very similar to proportional consolidation.)

4.2   Illustration

FRS 9 gives examples of how information about joint ventures could be disclosed. Example 1 from FRS 9 is shown below. This example also includes associates.

Consolidated profit and loss account

	£m	£m
Turnover: group and share of joint ventures	320	
Less: share of joint ventures' turnover	(120)	
Group turnover	—	200
Cost of sales		(120)
Gross profit		80
Administrative expenses		(40)
Group operating profit		40
Share of operating profit in		
Joint ventures	30	
Associates	24	
	—	54
		94

Interest receivable (group)		6
Interest payable		
Group	(26)	
Joint ventures	(10)	
Associates	(12)	
	—	(48)
		—
Profit on ordinary activities before tax		52
Tax on profit on ordinary activities*		(12)
		—
Profit on ordinary activities after tax		40
Minority interests		(6)
		—
Profit on ordinary activities after taxation		
and minority interest		34
Equity dividends		(10)
		—
Retained profit for group and its share of		
associates and joint ventures		24
		—

* Tax relates to the following:	Parent and subsidiaries	(5)
	Joint ventures	(5)
	Associates	(2)

Consolidated balance sheet

	£m	£m	£m
Fixed assets			
Tangible assets		480	
Investments			
Investments in joint ventures			
Share of gross assets	130		
Share of gross liabilities	(80)		
	—	50	
Investments in associates		20	
		—	550
Current assets			
Stock		15	
Debtors		75	
Cash at bank and in hand		10	
		——	
		100	
Creditors (due within one year)		(50)	
		——	
Net current assets			50
			—
Total assets less current liabilities			600
Creditors (due after more than one year)			(250)
Provisions for liabilities and charges			(10)
Equity minority interest			(40)
			——
			300
			——

Capital and reserves

Called up share capital	50
Share premium account	150
Profit and loss account	100
	——
Shareholders' funds (all equity)	300
	——

5 Disclosure requirements for associates and joint ventures

5.1 All associates and joint ventures

For each associate or joint venture included in the financial statements of the investing group, disclose the following:

(a) name

(b) proportion of the issued shares in each class held by the investing group

(c) accounting period or date of the financial statements used if different from those of the investing group

(d) an indication of the nature of its business.

Disclose any notes relating to the financial statements of associates that are material to understanding the effect on the investor of its investments.

Indicate the extent of any statutory, contractual or exchange control restrictions on the ability of an associate to distribute its reserves.

Disclose the amounts owing and owed between the investor and its associates or joint ventures, analysed into amounts relating to loans and amounts relating to trading balances.

Where an investor holding 20% or more of the voting rights of another entity does not treat it as an associate, a note should explain the reasons for this.

5.2 Detailed disclosures where associates and joint ventures are material to the investing group

One of the disadvantages of the equity method is that it only provides limited information about associates and joint ventures. In particular, only one figure is included in the balance sheet, representing the group share of the associates' net assets. It is possible for material liabilities to be hidden in this figure, enabling investors to use equity accounted entities as a form of off balance sheet finance.

For this reason, FRS 9 requires additional disclosures where size thresholds are exceeded. The thresholds are applied by comparing the investor's share of its associates or joint ventures of any of the following with the corresponding amounts for the investor group (excluding associates and joint ventures):

- gross assets
- gross liabilities
- turnover
- operating results (on a three year average).

(a) Where the aggregate of the investor's share in its associates or its joint ventures exceeds a 15% threshold with respect to the investor group, a note should give the aggregate of the investor's share of each of the following:

  - turnover (associates only; for joint ventures it must always be disclosed)
  - fixed assets
  - current assets

- liabilities due within one year
- liabilities due after one year or more.

(b) Where the investor's share in any individual associate or joint venture exceeds a 25% threshold with respect to the investor group, a note should name that associate or joint venture and give its share of each of the following:

- turnover
- profit before tax
- taxation
- profit after tax
- fixed assets
- current assets
- liabilities due within one year
- liabilities due after one year or more.

ACTIVITY 3

You are provided with the following information about H plc and its associated undertaking, A Ltd for the year ended 30 June 20X8.

	H plc	A Ltd
	£'000	£'000
Turnover	110,000	60,000
Operating profit	30,000	16,000
Profit before tax	25,000	12,000
Taxation	10,000	4,000
Profit after tax	15,000	8,000
Fixed assets	250,000	160,000
Current assets	40,000	24,000
Creditors due within one year	45,000	24,000
Creditors due after more than one year	110,000	40,000

H plc holds 25% of the equity share capital of A Ltd.

Show the additional disclosures required in respect of A Ltd in the consolidated financial statements of the H plc group for the year ended 30 June 20X8.

Feedback to this activity is at the end of the chapter.

6 Evaluation of FRS 9

6.1 Advantages of the requirements

- The definitions of an associate and of significant influence are consistent with those in the Companies Act and ensure that the financial statements reflect the economic substance of the relationship.

- The extended disclosure requirements should reduce the scope for using associates as a form of 'off balance sheet finance'.

- The accounting and reporting of joint ventures is fully covered for the first time and the use of the gross equity method should provide useful information to users of the financial statements.

6.2 Criticisms of the requirements

- Many people believe that joint ventures are so commercially distinct from associates that they should be dealt with in a separate accounting standard. A separate standard would also have enabled the ASB to deal with jointly-controlled assets and operations and to explore the different shareholdings that might arise in a joint venture. (This would have been consistent with the position taken by the IASC.)

- The disclosure requirements might be onerous in practice and add to an already extensive list of additional disclosures introduced by recent FRSs.

6.3 Proportional consolidation

Some commentators believe that proportional consolidation should be used to account for all joint ventures. They argue that because joint control means a sharing of risks and rewards it gives a higher level of influence than mere significant influence. It is therefore appropriate to recognise the venturer's share of individual assets and liabilities. Proportional consolidation would give a better representation of the economic substance of the investment and would be consistent with international practice. It is argued that this would also be consistent with the requirements of FRS 5 (recognition of interests in assets).

7 UITF Abstract 31 *Exchanges of businesses or other non-monetary assets for an interest in a subsidiary, joint venture or associate*

7.1 The issue

An entity (A) exchanges a business or other non-monetary assets for an interest in another entity (B), which becomes A's subsidiary or which is or becomes A's joint venture or associate.

- Should businesses or other non-monetary assets exchanged for an interest in a subsidiary, joint venture or associate be accounted for:

  - at their fair value at the date of the transaction; or

  - at their previous book values?

  This affects the amounts of profits or losses and goodwill that are recognised by A.

- How should any gain or loss arising on the transaction be reported in the consolidated accounts of A?

7.2 UITF Consensus

The following accounting treatment should apply in A's consolidated financial statements:

(a) If A retains an ownership interest in a business or non-monetary asset that it has exchanged for an interest in B, then after the transaction, that retained interest, including any goodwill, should be included in A's consolidated financial statements at its pre-acquisition carrying amount (i.e. at its previous book value).

(b) A's share of net assets acquired through its new interest in B should be accounted for at fair value. The difference between the net assets acquired and the fair value of the consideration given is accounted for as goodwill. (This is consistent with FRS 7 *Fair values in acquisition accounting*.)

(c) If the fair value of the consideration received by A exceeds the book value of the part of the business or non-monetary asset no longer owned by A together with any cash given up, A should recognise a gain. Any gain arising on the exchange that is not realised should be reported in the statement of total recognised gains and losses.

(d) Where the fair value of the consideration received by A is less than the book value of the part of the business or non-monetary asset no longer owned by A, together with any cash given up, A should recognise a loss. The loss should either be recognised as an impairment in accordance with FRS 11 *Impairment of fixed assets and goodwill* or, for any loss remaining after an impairment review of the relevant assets, in A's profit and loss account.

8   International Accounting Standards

IAS 28 *Accounting for investments in associates* requires the equity method of consolidation, as does FRS 9. The only difference is that IAS 28 includes the profits of the associate from Profit before Tax rather than from Operating Profits. Therefore, IAS 28 will not reveal the group's share of the associate's finance costs and so on.

The group share of the associate's reserves should be disclosed separately. They are not controlled by the group, and so they should not be lumped together with the reserves of the parent and its subsidiaries.

A proposed revision to IAS 28 will require a company with associates but no subsidiaries to prepare consolidated accounts incorporating its associates using the equity method.

IAS 31 *Financial reporting of interests in joint ventures* sets out two methods. The benchmark method is to use proportional consolidation. This means that the group's share of every item of income and expenditure, asset and liability will be consolidated. This is illegal in the UK. The allowed alternative is to consolidate the joint venture using the equity method as for an associate. (The gross equity method is not required.)

SELF-TEST
QUESTIONS

Associated undertakings

1   What is an associated undertaking according to (a) company law and (b) FRS 9? (1.2)

2   What is a participating interest? (1.2)

3   When is significant influence exercised? (1.2)

Joint ventures

4   How does FRS 9 define a joint venture? How is a joint venture different from a joint arrangement? (2)

Accounting for associates

5   Describe the two ways in which it is possible to account for associates and joint ventures. (3.1)

6   Why did the ASB reject proportional consolidation? (3.1)

7   What is equity accounting? How is the value of an investment in an associate calculated for inclusion in the consolidated balance sheet? (3.3)

8   The group share of which items are brought into the consolidated profit and loss account under equity accounting? (3.4)

9   How are transactions between the group and the associate accounted for? (3.5)

10 How do associates affect the statement of recognised gains and losses? (3.6)

Accounting for joint ventures and joint arrangements that are not entities

11 Under FRS 9, how should investments in joint ventures be treated in (a) the investor's individual financial statements and (b) the consolidated financial statements? (4.1)

Disclosure requirements for associates and joint ventures

12 What detailed disclosures need to be made where an associate is material to the investing group? (5.2)

Evaluation of FRS 9

13 List the successes and the failings of FRS 9. (6)

Bold plc

Bold plc, the parent company of the Bold Group, acquired 25% of the ordinary shares of Face plc on 1 September 20X0 for £54,000. Face plc carried on business as a property investment company. The draft accounts as at 31 August 20X1 are as follows:

Profit and loss accounts for the year ended 31 August 20X1

	Bold Group £'000	Face plc £'000
Sales	175	200
Profit before tax	88	60
Taxation	22	20
	66	40
Profit on sale of property to Face plc	13	
	79	
Proposed dividends	61	-
	18	40

Balance sheets as at 31 August 20X1

	Bold Group £'000	Face plc £'000
Fixed assets		
Tangible fixed assets	135	200
Investment in Face plc	54	
Current assets		
Stock	72	210
Debtors	105	50
Current liabilities		
Creditors	(95)	(20)
Overdraft	(14)	(100)
Net current assets	68	140
Total assets less current liabilities	257	340
Ordinary shares of £1 each	135	50
Reserves	122	90
10% loan	-	200
	257	340

On 1 September 20X0 Bold plc sold a property with a book value of £40,000 to Face plc at its market value of £60,000. Face plc obtained the funds to pay the £60,000 by raising a loan which is included in the 10% loan that appears in its balance sheet at 31 August 20X1.

Goodwill arising on acquisition is amortised through the profit and loss account over 5 years from the date of acquisition.

Required:

(a) (i)   Prepare the consolidated profit and loss account of the Bold group for the year ended 31 August 20X1 and a consolidated balance sheet as at that date.

   (ii)   Prepare relevant notes to comply with the requirements of FRS 9 *Associates and joint ventures*.   **(8 marks)**

(b)   Explain two defects of simple equity accounting and the remedies that you would propose to overcome these defects, illustrating your answer with the data from the Bold Group.   **(4 marks)**

(c)   If Face plc issued 30,000 ordinary shares, each of £1 value, to a third party on 1 September 20X1, for a cash consideration of £4 per share:

   (i)   explain any matters to be taken into consideration in finalising the 20X1 consolidated accounts; and

   (ii)   calculate the carrying value of the investment in Face plc in the consolidated balance sheet at 31 August 20X2 and comment upon any related items.   **(8 marks)**

(Total: 20 marks)

For the answer to this question see the 'Answers' section at the end of the book.

FEEDBACK TO
ACTIVITY **1**

(a)   This is a joint arrangement that is not an entity because:
   - no separate entity exists
   - the arrangement is a single project
   - it appears to be simply a means of carrying out A and B's own businesses.

(b)   This appears to be a joint venture because:
   - there is a separate entity
   - the entity appears to be carrying out a business of its own
   - the participants share in the profits of the business.

FEEDBACK TO
ACTIVITY **2**

In the balance sheet under Fixed Asset Investments:

   'Interests in associated undertakings'

In the profit and loss account after arriving at group operating profit:

   'Income from interests in associated undertakings'.

Additional disclosures for associates

	£'000	£'000
Share of turnover of associates (25% × 60,000)		15,000
Share of assets		
Share of fixed assets (25% × 160,000)	40,000	
Share of current assets (25% × 24,000)	6,000	
		46,000
Share of liabilities		
Liabilities due within one year or less (25% × 24,000)	6,000	
Liabilities due after more than one year (25% × 40,000)	10,000	
		(16,000)
Share of net assets		30,000

Working

H plc's share of the total assets of the associate exceeds 15%. (Note that the disclosures have to be made if **any** of the thresholds are exceeded.)

Turnover $\dfrac{25\% \times 60,000}{110,000} = 14\%$

Operating profit $\dfrac{25\% \times 16,000}{30,000} = 13\%$

Total assets $\dfrac{25\% \times 184,000}{290,000} = 16\%$

Total liabilities $\dfrac{25\% \times 64,000}{155,000} = 10\%$

Chapter 8

FOREIGN CURRENCY

This chapter looks at the topic of foreign currency translation. It begins by covering the technique for translating transactions in the accounts of a single company.

We then consider the problem which is most likely to feature in the exam - translation of the accounts of a foreign subsidiary into sterling so that they can then be consolidated into the group financial statements.

Lastly, we look at two situations which present special problems: the treatment of foreign loans where they finance foreign equity investments and translating the accounts of a subsidiary operating in a country where there is hyper-inflation.

Objectives

When you have studied this chapter you should be able to:

- understand the recording of transactions and re-translation of monetary/non-monetary items at the balance sheet date for individual entities

- account for the treatment of exchange differences re the above

- understand the nature of the closing rate/net investment method and the temporal method

- account for foreign equity investments financed by borrowings

- prepare group financial statements incorporating a foreign subsidiary

- discuss the problem areas in foreign currency transactions for individual and group companies.

1   SSAP 20 *Foreign currency translation*

1.1   Introduction

SSAP 20 identifies two sets of circumstances in which a business must consider how to deal with foreign currency amounts within its accounts: direct business transactions and operations conducted through a foreign entity.

1.2   Direct business transactions

Whenever a UK business enters into a contract where the consideration is expressed in a foreign currency, it will be necessary to translate that foreign currency amount at some stage into sterling for inclusion into its own accounts. Examples include the following.

- imports of raw materials

- exports of finished goods

- importation of foreign-manufactured fixed assets

- investments in foreign securities

- raising an overseas loan.

Translation may be necessary at more than one time. For example, the import of raw materials creates a foreign currency liability when the goods are supplied and for which a sterling value must be incorporated in the books. Where settlement is delayed because of normal credit terms, the actual sterling cost of settlement may differ from the liability initially recorded.

Similarly, the sterling value of a long-term foreign currency loan is likely to fluctuate from one period to another.

1.3　Operations conducted through a foreign entity

Companies frequently establish local subsidiaries in foreign countries through which to conduct their operations. These subsidiaries will maintain full accounts in the local currency and these accounts must clearly be translated into the currency of the parent before they can be consolidated.

This chapter deals firstly with the translation of direct business transactions (the individual company stage) and then with the translation of the accounts of foreign subsidiaries (the consolidated financial statements stage).

1.4　Foreign currency conversion and translation

An individual converts currency when he buys, say, Swiss francs for sterling at the start of a holiday. If he has any money left at the end of the holiday, he reconverts the francs to sterling. If the exchange rate has changed in the meantime he will make a gain or loss on the transaction less the costs of commission and the buy/sell price spread.

A business will also convert currencies when it has to pay for an item which it has purchased which is denominated in another currency. For example a UK business may purchase goods from a Swiss supplier and agree to pay a certain number of francs. When it comes to pay for the goods, it is likely to have to convert sterling into francs to pay for the goods.

From a business viewpoint however, the need to **translate** items denominated in a foreign currency is more important.

1.5　The temporal and closing rate methods of translation

There are two exchange rates which can generally be used to translate any foreign currency balance. These are:

- **the historical rate** – this is simply the exchange rate which applied at the date of the transaction

- **the closing rate** – this is the rate of exchange ruling at the balance sheet date.

Thus, a fixed asset acquired for Euros 100,000 when the exchange rate was Euros 2 = £1 and now translated for inclusion in a balance sheet when the exchange rate has moved to Euros 1.5 = £1 could be shown at either of the following rates.

- historical rate – £50,000

- closing rate – £66,667.

These two rates are used in the two methods as follows.

- **Closing rate method** – All assets and liabilities are translated at the closing rate.

- **Temporal method** – Transactions are initially recorded at the historical rate. If a monetary item denominated in a foreign currency exists at the balance sheet date, that item is re-translated to closing rate.

Under the temporal method, the re-translation of monetary items, such as debtors and creditors, accords with the historical cost convention that monetary items are recorded at the latest estimate of amounts receivable or payable in cash.

DEFINITION

Foreign currency conversion is the process of physically exchanging one currency for another currency.

DEFINITION

Foreign currency translation is the statement of an item denominated in a foreign currency in terms of the domestic reporting currency.

KEY POINT

Closing rate method – all assets and liabilities are translated at the closing rate.

KEY POINT

Temporal method – transactions are initially recorded at the historical rate. If a monetary item denominated in a foreign currency exists at the balance sheet date, that item is re-translated to closing rate.

It should be clear that selection of an appropriate translation rate will have a significant impact on balance sheet values and on reported profits. Where the historical rate is employed, the value of the asset is unchanging. However, if the closing rate is applied, the book value of the fixed asset above is increased by £16,667 and this must be reflected either in reported profits or as a movement in reserves.

2   The requirements of SSAP 20 as they relate to individual companies

2.1   Basic principles

This stage concerns the translation of business transactions in an individual company.

It is quite likely that during an accounting period, a company (whether situated in the UK or abroad) will enter into transactions in a currency other than its own domestic (i.e. functional) currency. The results of these transactions should be translated and recorded in the company's accounting records:

- at the date the transaction occurred

- using the rate of exchange in operation on that date (or where appropriate, at the rate of exchange at which it is contracted to settle the transaction in the future).

No further translation will be required for non-monetary assets (e.g. fixed assets or stocks) carried at historical costs. However, monetary items at the balance sheet date are re-translated at the closing rate of exchange with differences taken to profit and loss account. This would include debtors, creditors, bank balances and loans, where any of these amounts is expressed in a foreign currency.

2.2   Fixed assets

Once these assets have been translated at the historical rate and recorded they are carried in terms of the currency of the individual company.

Thus where a UK company purchases plant and machinery, for its own use in the UK, from an American supplier on 30 June 20X7 for $90,000 when the rate of exchange was £1 = $1.80, it will record the asset at £50,000 ($90,000 @ 1.80). No further translation will occur. All depreciation charged on this asset will be based on £50,000.

2.3   Debtors

Where goods are sold to overseas customers and payment is received in a currency other than the functional currency, the following transactions must be recorded:

- the sale – at the rate of exchange applicable at the time of sale

- the receipt of cash – the actual proceeds.

Any exchange difference (the balance on the debtors' account) will be reported as part of the profit for the period from normal operations.

If on 7 May 20X6 a UK company sells goods to a German company for Euros 48,000 when the rate of exchange was £1 = Euros 3.2, the sale will be recorded as follows:

	£	£
Dr Customer Euros 48,000 @ 3.2	15,000	
Cr Sales		15,000

Assuming on 20 July 20X6 the customer remits a draft for Euros 48,000 which realises £15,150 the following entries will be needed.

		£	£
Dr	Bank	15,150	
	Cr Customer		15,150

The credit balance of £150 on the debtor's account will represent a profit on exchange to be taken to profit and loss account as part of the operating profit for the year.

2.4 Creditors

The same principles as those set out for debtors apply to creditors.

ACTIVITY 1

A British company buys goods from a Swiss supplier for SFr 8,700 when the rate of exchange was £1 = SFr 3. The British company settled the amount due with a bankers draft for SFr 8,700 when the rate of exchange was £1 = SFr 2.8. Prepare the supplier's account.

Feedback to this activity is at the end of the chapter.

2.5 Loans

KEY POINT

Where a company raises a loan abroad, denominated in a currency other than its own currency, the amount outstanding must be re-translated at the closing rate at each year end.

Where a company raises a loan abroad, denominated in a currency other than its own currency, the amount outstanding must be re-translated at the closing rate at each year end. Again, this is because a loan is a monetary item. Any difference on exchange must form part of the profit from normal operations.

Example

A UK company takes out a five year loan of $1m from an American bank. The sterling proceeds amounted to £555,556 (when rate of exchange was £1 = $1.80). At the balance sheet date the rate had moved to £1 = $1.70.

The loan must be translated at this rate to £588,235. The loss on exchange of £(588,235 – 555,556) = £32,679 will be reported as part of profit from normal operations. Re-translation will occur at each balance sheet date.

2.6 Contracted rate of exchange

KEY POINT

Where a transaction is to be settled at a contracted rate of exchange, that rate should be used.

Where a transaction is to be settled at a contracted rate of exchange, that rate should be used.

Example

A UK company purchased an item of plant from a German manufacturer for Euros 100,000, when the rate was £1 = Euros 3.18 but the contract specified settlement in three months at an exchange rate of £1 = Euros 3.2. At the time of settlement, the actual exchange rate was £1 = Euros 3.19.

The effect of the specified rate is to freeze the sterling cost of the plant *ab initio*. Accordingly, it will be debited in the accounts at the certain sterling cost of:

Euros 100,000 ÷ 3.2 = £31,250

2.7   Use of forward contracts

Where a trading transaction is covered by a related or matching forward contract, the rate of exchange specified in that contract may be used.

Example

A UK company sells goods to a US corporation on 30 June for $200,000. The contract provides for settlement on 30 September. The UK company sells $200,000 forward three months on 30 June.

Rates of exchange are as follows:

	Spot	3 months forward
30 June	1.75	1.78
30 September	1.72	

How will the sale and debtor be reflected?

Solution

By selling dollars forward, the UK company guarantees the ultimate sterling receipt, irrespective of exchange rate movements. Accordingly, these ultimate proceeds may be reflected immediately as a sale and as a debtor.

$200,000 \div 1.78 = £112,360$

In this case, no exchange differences will arise.

2.8   Individual companies that engage in foreign currency transactions

Summary of entries

Transactions during accounting period – These should be translated and recorded at the rate of exchange ruling at the date of the transaction. In practice, an average rate might be used.

Monetary items at balance sheet date – Where these items (debtors, creditors, bank balances, loans) are denominated in a foreign currency they should be translated and recorded at the closing rate (or, if appropriate, at the rate at which the transaction is contracted to be settled).

Exchange differences – Except to the extent that they relate to extraordinary items, all exchange differences should be reported as part of normal operating profit.

2.9   The conflict between SSAP 20 and the Companies Act

All the exchange differences that we have calculated in this section are included in the profit and loss account and thus affect reported earnings. Consideration needs to be given to whether this effect is valid, i.e. are they 'proper' gains and losses which should be included in the profit and loss account? The general principle for inclusion of items in the profit and loss account is that gains should be realised (as in the Companies Act concept of realisation).

For transactions which have been settled in the accounting period, the inclusion of exchange gains and losses is valid as the gains/losses are already reflected in local currency cash flows. A settled transaction means the debtor, for example, has paid his debt or the business has paid a creditor.

Where a transaction has not been settled by the end of the accounting period we need to distinguish between short-term and long-term monetary items.

- A short-term trade debtor or creditor will be received or paid in cash shortly after the year end. The amount received or paid may be different from the rate of exchange ruling at the balance sheet date but, in most cases, not materially so. As the exchange difference is likely to be reflected in cash flows, the exchange gain/loss is validly reported as part of earnings.

- A long-term item, for example a foreign currency loan, is re-translated to closing rate at the end of each accounting period. This may result in reported gains in one period followed by a compensatory loss in the following accounting period as the exchange rates fluctuate. It is therefore uncertain whether a calculated gain or loss will eventually be reflected in cash flows.

SSAP 20 agrees that there is uncertainty but argues that exchange differences on long-term monetary items need to be reflected in the profit and loss account in accordance with the accruals concept. However in cases where there is doubt about the convertibility of the currency in question, exchange gains on long-term monetary items should be restricted, i.e. prudence overtakes the accruals concept.

2.10 Equity investment financed by foreign currency loan – hedging

It is not unusual for UK companies making overseas investments to raise the funds locally in an overseas currency. Such loans are known as **hedging loans** as they are designed to hedge against foreign currency movements since the sterling equivalent of both the equity investment and the overseas currency loans will move in the same direction – either both up or both down.

Were it not for special rules which cover hedging loans, the requirements of SSAP 20 would apply unfairly and illogically where companies had financed equity investments by foreign currency loans.

Without them, the normal rules of SSAP 20 would apply, with the following effect.

In the separate accounts of the investing company:

- the loan as a monetary item would be re-translated at the closing rate of exchange and any resulting profit or loss would be taken to the profit and loss account

- the investment in the foreign entity is a non-monetary item and would therefore be carried at the historical exchange rate with no subsequent exchange differences arising.

Assuming a weakening parent company functional currency, the deteriorating exchange rate will give:

- an increased cost of repaying the foreign loan – charged to the profit and loss account; and

- no increase in value for the fixed asset investment.

The economic reality is that the foreign loan matches the investment in the foreign entity. It will be repaid either out of the sale proceeds of the foreign investment or, more likely, out of cash flows – presumably dividends – from the investment. Logic therefore demands that the corresponding gains and losses should in some way be matched by offset and this is what SSAP 20 permits.

SSAP 20 permits the investing company to treat the equity investment as a monetary item and translate the carrying amount (cost or value) at each balance sheet date at the closing rate of exchange. Differences arising are taken to reserves and the differences on translating the loan are taken to the same reserve for offset. The offset is subject to the following conditions.

- In any accounting period exchange differences on the borrowings are offset only to the extent of differences on translating the investment (any excess must be dealt with in the profit and loss account).

- The foreign currency borrowings should not exceed the total cash that the investments are expected to be able to generate (dividends plus sale value).

- The offset procedure should be applied consistently.

- The loans need not be in the same currency as the investment.

- The offset is available on any overseas equity investment (not merely subsidiary and associate relationships) financed by foreign borrowings.

Example

On 1 January 20X8 100% of a French subsidiary was acquired by H plc at a cost of Euros 960,000 when the rate was Euros 6 = £1. Assume that the whole of the purchase price was borrowed from a Swiss bank when the rate was SFr 4 = £1.

The following is the draft balance sheet of H plc at 31 December 20X8.

	£'000		£'000
Shares in subsidiary		Share capital	1,800
(Euros 960,000 @ 6 = £1)	160	P&L a/c	1,200
Sundry net assets	3,000	Loan (160,000 × 4 = SFr640,000)	160
	3,160		3,160

Rates at 31 December 20X8

£1 = 5 Euros = SFr 3.2.

Show the carrying value of the investment, loan and any offset at 31 December 20X8.

Solution

	€(000)	Rate	£'000
(a) Investment carrying value – purchase	960	6	160
– 31.12.X8	960	5	192
Gain on restating investment			32

	SFr(000)		
(b) Loan – at borrowing date	640	4	160
– at 31.12.X8	640	3.2	200
Loss on restating loan			(40)

(c) Offset of £40,000 loss on loan

(i) Reserve movement (limited to gain on investment)	(32)
(ii) Profit and loss account – excess	(8)
	(40)

Where offset has occurred additional disclosure is required.

(a) The amount offset against reserves (of the differences on translating the loan), i.e. £32,000.

(b) The net amount charged or credited to the profit and loss account, i.e. £8,000.

ACTIVITY 2

T Ltd sold a block booking of holidays in Spain to a German travel agent on 16 April 20X8 for Euros 1,980,000. An invoice was raised for this amount with sums payable by the travel agent to be as follows:

30 August	Euros 980,000
30 September	Euros 1,000,000.

The amounts were paid on the due dates. T Ltd took out a forward cover contract to sell Euros 980,000 on 30 August at Euros 3.16 = £1 and Euros 1,000,000 on 30 September at Euros 3.17 = £1.

Relevant exchange rates for the year are as follows:

Date	Euros = £1
16 April 20X8	3.12
30 August 20X8	2.96
30 September 20X8	3.24

Write up the sales and debtor accounts to record these transactions for the year ended 31 October 20X8.

Feedback to this activity is at the end of the chapter.

2.11 The adequacy of the current regulations governing the treatment of foreign exchange losses

Under the hedging concept described (also known as the cover concept), losses on borrowings can go direct to reserves. There is a risk that the losses may not end up being covered from cash flows from the investment when the loan is repaid although SSAP 20 tries to set conditions which limit the likelihood of such an occurrence.

Under the CA85 the computation of a loss at the year end on a liability is a 'provision' and provisions, under company law, are realised losses (see the text dealing with distributable profits). As a consequence, the argument is that the loss should be recognised in the profit and loss account.

KEY POINT

SSAP 20 is trying to record economic reality.

The arguments in support of SSAP 20 have been explained in the previous section. SSAP 20 is trying to record economic reality.

3 Foreign subsidiary undertakings

3.1 Introduction

Companies frequently establish local branches or subsidiaries in foreign countries through which to conduct their operations. These will maintain full accounts in the local currency and these must clearly be translated into the currency of the parent before they can be consolidated.

The translation method to be used depends on the relationship between parent and foreign entity.

- **Quasi-autonomous foreign entity** – Where the foreign entity is relatively independent of its parent, its transactions do not impinge directly on cash flows and profits of the parent. Accordingly, it is the **net investment** in the foreign entity which is of interest rather than the individual assets and liabilities. This net investment is translated at the **closing rate** of exchange and the resulting exchange difference dealt with in reserves.

- **Foreign entity as an extension of the parent** – Where the foreign entity is, in reality, the parent company operating abroad, foreign transactions will impinge directly on cash flows and profits of the parent. Accordingly, the foreign entity's transactions should be accounted for as if they were those of the parent by translation according to the **temporal method**.

3.2   When the net investment concept is appropriate

One of the general principles of SSAP 20 is the adoption of the closing rate/net investment method for the consolidation of foreign subsidiaries. Although this approach is widely supported, a small minority oppose it on the grounds that it displays an inconsistency in two areas. They consider that the net investment concept conflicts with the single entity approach which FRS 2 applies to consolidation procedures and that it is inappropriate to apply the closing rate to historical cost figures. SSAP 20 considers, however, that the principle is appropriate for the following reasons.

- The parent company's investment is normally in the net worth of a business operation rather than in its individual assets and liabilities.

- The method of translation ensures that the translated results and relationships do not differ significantly from those reported prior to translation.

- The method acknowledges the fact that operations which are conducted in currencies and in economic environments other than those of the parent are essentially different from the parent's own operations.

- Translation of the historical cost accounts at closing rates is merely a restatement of assets and liabilities for the purposes of consolidation and does not constitute a revaluation.

3.3   When the temporal method of translation should be used

In exceptional circumstances, the subsidiary may be regarded as an extension of the trade of the parent company. This would apply where the cash flows of the subsidiary impact directly on the cash flows of the parent company. Here are some examples of such situations.

- The subsidiary acts as a selling agency, receiving stocks from the parent company, selling them locally and remitting the proceeds to the parent company.

- The subsidiary is a supplier of raw materials or components to the parent company.

- The subsidiary is located overseas for tax, exchange control or similar reasons to act as a means of raising finance for other companies in the group.

In such cases the historical temporal method should be used. This is the method you have seen at the individual company stage.

It is important to appreciate that identification of the relationship between parent and subsidiary will not always be clear cut. Many situations may require a balancing of criteria and the application of judgement.

SSAP 20 considers the following factors to be relevant:

- the extent to which cash flows of the foreign entity impact directly on the parent

- the extent to which functioning of the entity is directly dependent on the parent

- the currency in which the majority of trading transactions are denominated

- the major currency to which the operation is exposed in its financial structure.

It is important to appreciate that SSAP 20 does not give a company the freedom to choose which method of translation should be used. It lays down the circumstances in which each particular method must be used.

3.4 Arguments for and against the temporal and closing rate methods

The debate about the advantages and disadvantages of the two methods dates back to the time when many considered that a choice had to be made between one method or the other for all circumstances. SSAP 20 neatly defused this argument by putting forward the proposition that the two methods have different objectives and therefore both should be used. Which one is used in a particular situation depends on the individual circumstances as we have seen in the previous section.

The arguments for the temporal method reflect its objectives.

- It is compatible with the HC convention as non-monetary assets are stated at original cost and monetary assets and liabilities at their current worth.

- At the consolidation stage it uses the same rates as apply at the individual stage. Therefore it is closer to the normal concept of consolidation by assuming the group is one entity.

These arguments for the temporal method are arguments against the closing rate method.

The argument for the closing rate method also reflects its objective. Economic reality is reflected in the accounting treatment, i.e. the investment of the parent company is the net worth of its foreign subsidiary.

4 Consolidated financial statements incorporating a foreign subsidiary

4.1 Closing rate method

(a) **Balance sheet**

All assets and liabilities are translated into the reporting currency at the closing rate. Where there is an intermediate foreign parent company the consolidation will be in two stages:

(i) overseas consolidation – to the **reporting currency** of the overseas intermediate parent company

(ii) UK consolidation – to sterling.

(b) **Profit and loss account**

Amounts in the profit and loss account must be translated at either:

(i) the closing rate for the period; or

(ii) an average rate for the accounting period.

Advantages can be claimed for both methods of translating profits. The closing rate does maintain the relationships shown in the financial statements of the overseas enterprise. The average rate better reflects the impact of cash flows throughout the period from the group viewpoint.

To be a true average it must reflect all factors involved, such as seasonal activity levels, wide fluctuations in the exchange rate, etc. For many companies that prepare monthly/quarterly profit statements for the group the best estimate of the sterling annual profit will be the aggregate of those statements.

(c) **Exchange differences**

All exchange differences arising on consolidation should be accounted for as reserve movements.

4.2   Sources of exchange differences

Exchange differences arise because items are translated at different points in time at different rates of exchange.

It must be remembered that:

Opening equity	+	Profit	=	Closing equity
(Opening net assets)	+	(Increase in net assets)	=	(Closing net assets)

(a) **Opening equity (= opening net assets)**

These will have been translated for the purpose of last year's accounts at last year's closing rate of exchange. For the purposes of the current year's accounts these items are translated at this year's closing rate of exchange since the opening net assets will be included within the closing net assets which are translated at the closing rate.

(b) **Profit for year (where average rate is used)**

The net assets generated by the profit must be translated at this year's closing rate (again within the closing net assets).

Thus the exchange difference will arise from the translation of:

(i)   **opening equity** – from last year's closing rate to this year's closing rate

(ii)   **profit** – from the average rate to the closing rate (no difference arises where profit is translated at the closing rate).

4.3   Special points on consolidation

(a) **Goodwill on consolidation**

This must be computed using the principles set out in FRS 2 and FRS 10 by comparing:

(i)   the fair value of the cost of investment, with

(ii)   the fair value of net assets at acquisition.

For a foreign subsidiary, the net assets at acquisition are determined by translating the share capital and pre-acquisition reserves at the rate of exchange at the date of acquisition of the shares in the subsidiary.

(b) Minority interests

(i) Profit for the year

The minority interests in the profit for the year will be their share of the sterling equivalent of the profit shown by the separate accounts of the subsidiary (whichever method of translation has been used).

(ii) Net assets

The minority interests for balance sheet purposes will be computed by reference to their interest in the net assets of the subsidiary translated at the closing rate at the balance sheet date. In effect the minority interests are credited (or debited) with their share of all exchange differences.

Example

The following draft financial statements are produced by a French subsidiary S Ltd at 31 December.

Balance sheets

	20X8 €'000	20X9 €'000		20X8 €'000	20X9 €'000
Fixed assets	960	1,250	Share capital	750	750
Net current assets	720	1,080	Reserves	330	980
			Long-term loan	600	600
	1,680	2,330		1,680	2,330

Profit and loss account for 20X9

	€'000
Profit on ordinary activities before taxation	1,050
Taxation	(400)
	650

Further information

(a) The loan was raised from a US bank in the sum of $165,000. There have been no repayments during the year.

(b) The UK parent company acquired a 100% interest on 1 January 20X8 at a cost of Euros 960,000, when the subsidiary's reserves amounted to Euros 120,000.

(c) The rates of exchange were

At	1 January	20X8	£1 = Euros 6	
	31 December	20X8	£1 = Euros 8	= $2.20
	31 December	20X9	£1 = Euros 10	= $2.40
Average		20X8	£1 = Euros 7.2	
Average		20X9	£1 = Euros 9	

(d) Profits are translated at average rate.

Solution

(a) Separate accounts of S Ltd

The loan shown in the balance sheet at 31 December 20X8 is the dollar liability translated at the closing rate at that date (i.e. Euros 8 = $2.20).

At 31 December 20X9 this liability must be translated at the year end closing rate (i.e. Euros 10 = $2.40) = Euros 687,500. The exchange loss of Euros 87,500 must be charged against profit from normal operations.

The profit before tax will become Euros 962,500 reducing the total retained profits to Euros 892,500.

(b) Consolidation

The translation at 31 December 20X8 would have been as follows

	€'000	Rate	£'000
Fixed assets	960	8	120
Net current assets	720	8	90
Long-term loan	(600)	8	(75)
	1,080		135

The net assets at acquisition would have been represented by share capital and reserves at that date. In order to compute the goodwill on consolidation, these net assets would have been translated at the rate of exchange at that date of acquisition (i.e. £1 = Euros 6).

	€'000	Rate	£'000
Share capital	750	6	125
Pre-acquisition profits	120	6	20
	870		145
Cost of shares	960	6	160
Goodwill	90		15

The equity interest at 31 December 20X8 would have been translated as follows:

	€'000	Rate	£'000
Share capital	750	6	125.00
Reserves			
Pre-acquisition	120	6	20.00
Profit for year	210	7.2	29.17
		(average)	
	1,080		174.17
Exchange loss (balance)			(39.17)
Represented by net assets (i.e. net investment)	1,080	8	135.00

The exchange difference relates to:

		£'000	£'000
(i)	Equity interest at beginning of accounting period (Euros 870,000)		
	At opening rate (£1 = Euros 6)	145.00	
	At closing rate (£1 = Euros 8)	108.75	(36.25)
(ii)	Profit for year (Euros 210,000)		
	At average rate (£1 = Euros 7.2)	29.17	
	At closing rate (£1 = Euros 8)	26.25	(2.92)
			(39.17)

In the accounts to 31 December 20X8 (the first year of consolidation) this exchange difference of £39,170 would be taken to reserves. This does not imply a separate reserve. The loss is adjusted in the **statement of total recognised gains and losses** rather than directly in the profit and loss account.

The translation at 31 December 20X9 would be as follows:

	€'000	*Rate*	£'000
Fixed assets	1,250.0	10	125.00
Net current assets	1,080.0	10	108.00
Long-term loan (as adjusted)	(687.5)	10	(68.75)
Net investment 31.12.20X9	1,642.5		164.25

The equity interest must be analysed

	€'000	*Rate*	£'000
Share capital	750.0	6	125.00
Reserves			
Pre-acquisition	120.0	6	20.00
Post-acquisition b/d (net of exchange loss (29.17 – 39.17))	210.0	actual	(10.00)
Profit for 20X9 (650 – 87.5)	562.5	9	62.50
Exchange loss (balance)	-	-	(33.25)
	1,642.5		164.25

The exchange loss for the current year can be reconciled as follows:

		£'000	£'000
(i)	Equity interest at beginning of accounting period (Euros1,080,000)		
	At opening rate (£1 = Euros 8)	135.00	
	At closing rate (£1 = Euros 10)	108.00	(27.00)
(ii)	Profit for year (Euros 562,500)		
	At average rate (£1 = Euros 9)	62.50	
	At closing rate (£1 = Euros 10)	56.25	(6.25)
			(33.25)

4.4   Principles – closing rate method

- **Separate accounts**

  Monetary items denominated in a foreign currency (i.e. the dollar loan) must be recorded in the separate accounts at the closing rate at each balance sheet date.

- **Goodwill on consolidation**

  In order to compute the goodwill, the share capital and pre-acquisition profits must always be translated at the rate ruling at the date of acquisition of the subsidiary.

- **Post-acquisition profits**

  The sterling equivalent of the accumulated profit will be brought forward each year for incorporation in the current year's trial balance. No one exchange rate would be appropriate for translation purposes. The total includes past exchange differences.

- **Exchange differences**

  (a)   **Separate accounts stage**

  Any difference arising at the separate accounts stage (of the subsidiary, or if appropriate, of the parent company) must be dealt with as part of the profit from normal operations.

  (b)   **Consolidation stage**

  All exchange differences arising on consolidation must be dealt with as reserve movements in the profit and loss account reserve.

Statement of total recognised gains and losses

	£'000
Profit for the financial year	X
Currency translation differences on foreign currency net investment	X
Total gains and losses recognised since last annual report	X

4.5   Consolidation stage – temporal method

If the trade of the subsidiary is regarded as an extension of the trade of the parent company, the temporal method MUST be used. This means that the fixed assets must be translated at the rate ruling when the asset was acquired. For **consolidation** purposes this will be as follows:

- **owned at acquisition of shares by H plc** – at the rate ruling at that date (not the rate when the assets were acquired) – i.e. cost to the group will be the fair value attributed at acquisition

- **acquired since acquisition** – at the rate when each asset was acquired.

Depreciation must be translated at the same rate as that applied to the relevant assets. Consequently the profit for the year will be translated as follows:

Profit before depreciation (strictly rate when transaction occurs) – Average rate
Depreciation – Asset rates

Example

Facts as above. The fixed assets may be reconciled as follows:

	€'000
At 1.1.20X8	1,200.0
Depreciation 20X8 (20% × 1,200)	(240.0)
At 31.12.20X8	960.0
Additions (30.6.20X9 – £1 = Euros 9)	662.5
Depreciation 20X9 (20% × (1,200 + 662.5))	(372.5)
At 31.12.20X9	1,250.0

Show the translation of the subsidiary's balance sheet into sterling:

(a) at 31 December 20X8

(b) at 31 December 20X9.

Solution

(a) **Translation at 31.12.20X8**

	€'000	Rate	£'000
Fixed assets	960	6	160
Net current assets	720	8	90
Loan	(600)	8	(75)
	1,080		175
Share capital	750	6	125.00
Reserves			
Pre-acquisition	120	6	20.00
Post-acquisition	210	(see below)	22.50
	1,080		167.50
Exchange (balance)			7.50
	1,080		175.00
Profit for year after depreciation	210		
Depreciation	240		
Profit before depreciation	450	7.2	62.50
Depreciation	(240)	6	(40.00)
Profit before taxation	210		22.50

Strictly there is no need to identify separately the exchange difference since it must be dealt with in arriving at the profit for the year from normal operations. Thus the profit for the year could be taken as the balancing figure in the translation process, i.e. (£22,500 + £7,500) £30,000.

(b) Translation at 31.12.20X9

	Cost	Depreciation			
	€'000	€'000	€'000	Rate	£'000
Fixed assets					
Deemed purchase					
1.1.20X8	1,200.0	480.0	720.0	6	120.00
Acquired 30.6.20X9	662.5	132.5	530.0	9	58.89
	1,862.5	612.5	1,250.0		178.89
Net current assets			1,080.0	10	108.00
Loan			(687.5)	10	(68.75)
			1,642.5		218.14
Share capital			750.0	6	125.00
Reserves					
Pre-acquisition			120.0	6	20.00
Post-acquisition brought forward			210.0	actual	30.00
Profit for year			562.5	(balance)	43.14
			1,642.5		218.14

4.6   Hedging at the consolidated financial statements stage

You have already dealt with hedging in the individual company's financial statements.

- Without hedging

  - **loan** as a monetary item is translated at closing rate of exchange and exchange difference is taken to profit and loss account

  - **investment** as a non-monetary item is recorded and left at the historical rate.

- With hedging

  - both are re-translated to closing rate and an offset (subject to certain limitations) achieved in reserves.

If this seems unfamiliar you should at this stage refer back to earlier in the chapter.

Where the **closing rate method** is used on consolidation, hedging is also available in the consolidated accounts. However, this works in a slightly different way.

- Cost of investment

  - this must, as you have seen, be translated at the historical rate, otherwise the calculation of goodwill will change each year

  - if, therefore, this has been re-translated in the individual (holding) company's books, those entries must be reversed so that the cost of investment is ready, at its historical amount, for consolidation.

- Loan

  - as for the individual company stage this is re-translated to the closing rate.

- Offset

  - the offset is available between the exchange difference arising on the loan and that arising on the re-translation of the net investment in the subsidiary (i.e. the exchange differences arising on consolidation).

The conditions which apply now are similar.

- The investment must be one for which the closing rate method is applicable.

- The differences on the borrowings are offset only to the extent of the differences on re-translating the investment.

- The total borrowings do not exceed the cash flows that would be generated from the investment (i.e. dividends due plus sale value).

- The treatment is consistently applied.

The SSAP makes it quite clear that the offset is available for all classes of investment.

- Subsidiaries – where the annual exchange difference (group share) is available for offset.

- Associates – same as subsidiaries.

- Other equity investments – reproduce the effect applied at separate accounts stage.

Example

Facts as in Example in paragraph 2.10.

The subsidiary balance sheet at 31 December 20X8 is as follows:

	€'000		€'000
Sundry net assets	1,200	Share capital	500
		Profit – 1 January 20X8	300
		– for 20X8	400
	1,200		1,200

The group translates profit at the closing rate.

Show the offset for 20X8.

Solution

	£'000
(a) **Loss on loan (see solution to example earlier)**	40

(b) **Translation of net investment**

	€'000		Rate	£'000
Sundry net assets	1,200		5	240.0
Share capital	500	Acquisition	6	83.3
Pre-acquisition profit	300	Acquisition	6	50.0
	800			133.3

Profit for 20X8	400	Closing	5	80.0
				213.3
Gain in translation (balance)				26.7*
	1,200			240.0

*Representing	€'000		£'000
Opening net assets	800	@ 6	133.3
Restated		@ 5	160.0
			26.7

(c) Offset

The offset is now

	£'000
Loss on loan	(40.0)
Gain on translation	26.7
Charge to consolidated profit	(13.3)

(d) Accounting adjustment

Since at the separate accounts stage £8,000 was charged to profit the adjustment will be to charge consolidated profit and loss with the additional £5,300.

Note:

The difference can be identified as the goodwill on consolidation.

	€'000	*Rate*	£'000
Cost of shares	960		
Pre-acquisition capital	800		
Goodwill	160 at cost 6		26.7
Restated (as part of investment cost)		5	32.0
Gain			5.3

ACTIVITY 3

R plc purchased equity shares in H Inc a US company for US$3,500,000 on 30 June 20X7 when the exchange rate was £1 = $1.50. This purchase was partially financed by means of a Swiss Franc loan of SFr 4,000,000 taken out on the same date at a rate of £1 = SFr 2.2.

R plc's year end is 31 March. Exchange rates at 31 March 20X8 were £1= $1.60 and £1 = SFr 2.4.

Calculate the exchange differences arising on the investment and loan at 31 March 20X8 and indicate how these will be dealt with in the financial statements to that date.

Feedback to this activity is at the end of the chapter.

4.7   Problem areas in foreign currency translation

There are a number of issues on which SSAP 20 is either silent or fails to give adequate guidance.

(a) Transactions should be recorded at the rate ruling at the date the transaction occurred, but in some cases this date is difficult to establish. For example, it could be the order date, the date of invoice or the date on which the goods were received.

(b) SSAP 20 states that average rates can be used if these do not fluctuate significantly, but what period should be used to calculate average rates? Should the average rate be adjusted to take account of material transactions?

(c) SSAP 20 does not provide any guidance where there are two or more exchange rates for a particular currency or where an exchange rate is suspended. It has been suggested that companies should use whichever rate seems appropriate given the nature of the transaction and have regard to prudence if necessary.

(d) SSAP 20 makes a distinction between the translation of monetary and non-monetary items, but in practice some items (such as progress payments paid against fixed assets or stocks and debt securities held as investments) may have characteristics of both.

(e) The guidance on the appropriate translation rates to use in hedge accounting and forward contracts is generally regarded as being insufficient. It does not take account of the variety of (often) complex contracts that exist. The ASB is developing standards on the measurement of derivatives and other financial instruments and this project will cover hedging and forward contracts.

(f) SSAP 20 does not address various issues relating to group accounts.

- Should the closing rate or the average rate be used when eliminating inter-group profits?

- How should cumulative exchange differences be treated when an investment in a foreign subsidiary is sold?

- Should the historical rate or the current rate be used to calculate goodwill on consolidation?

- Where the accounts of a subsidiary are translated using the closing rate method and the year-end of the subsidiary is different from the parent, which closing rate should be used?

There are additional problems.

(a) Large exchange differences go direct to reserves under the closing rate method. The reasoning behind this is that these exchange differences do not result from the operations of the group. To include them in the profit and loss account would be to distort the results of the group's trading operations. However, some commentators consider that all such gains and losses are part of a group's profit and should go through the profit and loss account.

FRS 3 requires that exchange differences taken to reserves are disclosed in the statement of total recognised gains and losses.

(b) The standard permits choices in some areas.

- Where a company has a forward contract, use of the contract rate is optional. Companies can ignore the existence of the contract and account for transactions using the average rate as usual if they wish.

- Use of hedge accounting (sometimes called the cover method) is optional, even when the criteria are met.

These choices may lead to lack of comparability between the financial statements of different entities.

(c) The rules for hedge accounting are problematic for the following reasons.

- Borrowings may be in a different currency from that of the investment. This means that exchange differences on the borrowings are not always covered by those on the investment. In order to eliminate exchange risk completely the borrowings must be in the same currency as the investment.

- The fact that the borrowings may be in a different currency from the investment can lead to inconsistent treatment from period to period. In some periods the SSAP 20 criteria may be met and exchange differences are taken to reserves. In other periods the criteria may not be met and all or part of the exchange differences will be taken to the profit and loss account.

5   UITF abstracts relating to foreign currency translation

5.1   UITF Abstract 9 *Accounting for operations in hyper-inflationary economies*

Where a foreign enterprise operates in a country in which a very high rate of inflation exists ('hyper-inflation') it may not be possible to present fairly in historical cost accounts the financial position of a foreign enterprise simply by a translation process. In such circumstances the local currency financial statements should be adjusted where possible to reflect current price levels before the translation process is undertaken.

UITF Abstract 9 *Accounting for operations in hyper-inflationary economies* was issued due to uncertainty as to when the adjustment above should be made.

The Task Force reached a consensus that adjustments are required where the distortions caused by hyper-inflation are such as to affect the true and fair view given by the group financial statements. In any event adjustments are required where the cumulative inflation rate over three years is approaching, or exceeds, 100% and the operations in the hyper-inflationary economies are material.

The following two methods of eliminating the distortions are consistent with SSAP 20 and therefore acceptable.

- As per the SSAP 20 rules, adjusting the overseas financial statements to reflect current price levels before the translation process is undertaken. This includes taking any gain or loss on the net monetary position through the profit and loss account.

- Using a relatively stable currency as the functional currency (i.e. the currency of measurement) for the relevant foreign operations. For example in certain businesses operating in Latin American territories the US dollar acts effectively as the functional currency for business operations. The functional currency would in effect be the 'local currency'.

If the transactions are not recorded in that stable currency, they must first be translated into that currency using the temporal method. The effect is that the movement between the original currency and the stable currency is used as proxy for the inflation index.

KEY POINT

Adjustments are required where the cumulative inflation rate over three years is approaching, or exceeds, 100% and the operations in the hyper-inflationary economies are material (UITF Abstract 9).

ADVANCED CORPORATE REPORTING

Example

On 1 January 20X1 Cinnamon plc set up a subsidiary, Anise Ltd, in a country which suffered from high rates of inflation. The currency of this country is measured in Tambala (T). On the same date Anise Ltd acquired freehold land for T400,000.

Relevant exchange rates are as follows:

1 January 20X1	T5 = £1
1 January 20X1	US$2.5 = £1
31 December 20X4	T25 = £1
31 December 20X4	US$1.75 = £1

The relevant price index was 100 at 1 January 20X1 and 550 at 31 December 20X4.

Show the value at which the freehold land would be included in the consolidated financial statements of Cinnamon plc at 31 December 20X4:

(a) using normal translation rules (the closing rate method)

(b) adjusting to reflect current price levels

(c) using US Dollars as a 'functional currency'.

Solution

Tutorial note: The difference between the sterling value of the land at acquisition and at 31 December 20X4 illustrates the problems caused by hyper-inflation. Hyper-inflation gives rise to an exchange loss of £64,000.

	T	Rate	Inflation adjusted/US$	Rate	£
At 1 January 20X1	400,000			5	80,000
(a) Closing rate	400,000			25	16,000
(b) Current prices	400,000	550/100	2,200,000	25	88,000
(c) US Dollars	400,000	2.5	160,000	1.75	91,429

5.2 UITF Abstract 19 *Tax on gains and losses on foreign currency borrowings that hedge an investment in a foreign enterprise*

Gains and losses on re-translation of foreign currency borrowings that hedge an investment in a foreign enterprise may now be taxable, following changes to UK tax legislation.

Exchange differences on foreign currency borrowings that have been used to provide a hedge against equity investments in foreign enterprises are taken to reserves and reported in the statement of total recognised gains and losses.

The UITF consensus is that tax charges or credits that are directly and solely attributable to such exchange differences should also be taken to reserves and reported in the statement of total recognised gains and losses.

The amount of tax charges and credits accounted for in this way should be disclosed.

5.3　UITF Abstract 21 *Accounting issues arising from the proposed introduction of the euro*

This Abstract addresses the accounting for external and internal costs of the changeover to the euro (the single European currency).

- Costs of making the necessary modifications to assets to deal with the euro should be written off to the profit and loss account unless:

    (a)　the entity already has an accounting policy to capitalise assets of the relevant type; or

    (b)　the expenditure clearly results in enhancement of an asset, rather than merely maintaining its service potential.

- Other costs associated with the introduction of the euro should be written off to the profit and loss account.

- Expenditure incurred in preparing for the changeover to the euro and regarded as exceptional should be disclosed in accordance with FRS 3.

- Particulars of commitments at the balance sheet date in respect of costs to be incurred should be disclosed where they are regarded as relevant to assessing the entity's state of affairs.

- Cumulative foreign exchange translation differences recognised in the statement of total recognised gains and losses in accordance with SSAP 20 should remain in reserves after the introduction of the euro. They should not be reported in the profit and loss account.

6　Convergence and FRED 24

FRED 24 will replace SSAP 20 and UITF 9. It is based on the proposals to revise IAS 21, and it will bring UK GAAP into line with international practice.

The main changes that FRED 24 will introduce are:

1　A subsidiary's profit and loss account must be translated using the actual (average) rate for the year. The option to use the closing rate is eliminated.

2　Goodwill should be retranslated using the closing rate method, rather than being left fixed at its historic rate as it is at present. This requires goodwill to be regarded as the subsidiary's asset rather than the parent's.

3　The terms *functional* and *presentation* currency:

   Functional currency: 'The currency of the primary economic environment in which the enterprise operates'. This is a stricter definition than before.

   Presentation currency: Whatever currency is used for presenting the financial statements. There is a completely free choice of presentation currency. (For example, South African Breweries does most of its trade in Africa, but it is listed in the UK and presents its accounts in US$.)

4　Entities operating in hyper-inflationary currencies should restate their statements using appropriate indices before translation. The option to use a surrogate hard currency is withdrawn.

FRED 24 does not adopt the international proposal to recycle translation gains and losses back through the profit and loss account when a subsidiary is sold and the gains (or losses) realised.

SSAP 20 *Foreign currency translation*

1 Give examples of direct business transactions which may cause a company to translate foreign currency. (1.2)

2 Define foreign currency conversion. (1.4)

3 What are (a) the historical rate and (b) the closing rate? Which is used in the temporal method? (1.5)

The requirements of SSAP 20 as they relate to individual companies

4 At what rate are fixed assets translated in the accounts of an individual company? (2.2)

5 How are foreign currency loans outstanding at the year end accounted for in the accounts of an individual company? (2.5)

6 Must the rate specified in a matching forward contract be used to translate a trading transaction? (2.7)

7 How does SSAP 20 conflict with the Companies Act? (2.9)

8 Why are there special rules on offset for hedging loans? What are they? (2.10)

Foreign subsidiary undertakings

9 How is a quasi-autonomous foreign subsidiary accounted for in consolidated financial statements? (3.1)

10 When should the temporal method of translation be used for a foreign subsidiary undertaking? (3.3)

Consolidated financial statements incorporating a foreign subsidiary

11 When is hedging available in consolidated accounts? For which classes of investment is it available? (4.6)

UITF abstracts relating to foreign currency translation

12 In what circumstances has the UITF decided that adjustments are required for the effects of hyper-inflation? (5.1)

UK plc

The balance sheets of UK plc and its subsidiaries France SA and US Inc at 30 September 20X8 (the accounting date for all three companies) are given below.

	UK plc		France SA		US Inc	
	£'000	£'000	€'000	€'000	$'000	$'000
Fixed assets:						
Tangible assets	26,000		95,000		56,000	
Investments	25,500		–		–	
(Notes 1 & 2)						
		51,500		95,000		56,000
Current assets:						
Stocks (Note 3)	15,000		44,000		25,000	
Debtors (Note 4)	10,000		30,000		16,000	
Cash in hand	2,000		6,000		3,000	
	27,000		80,000		44,000	
Current liabilities:						
Trade creditors						
(Note 4)	6,000		12,000		8,000	
Taxation	3,000		6,000		4,000	
Proposed dividend	2,000		8,000		3,000	
Bank overdraft	8,000		10,000		9,000	
	19,000		36,000		24,000	

Net current assets	8,000	44,000	20,000
Long-term loans	(20,000)	–	(25,000)
	39,500	139,000	51,000

Capital and reserves:			
Share capital (Note 5)	20,000	80,000	32,000
Profit and loss account	19,500	59,000	19,000
	39,500	139,000	51,000

Notes to the financial statements

Note 1

UK plc has owned 100% of the ordinary share capital of France SA since incorporation, subscribing for it at par. The date of incorporation of France SA was 25 May 20X0. France SA acts as a selling agent for products manufactured in the UK by UK plc and has no manufacturing capacity of its own. UK plc has negotiated an overdraft facility for France SA and has guaranteed the overdraft. Apart from this overdraft, France SA receives all its funding from UK plc.

Note 2

On 30 September 20X2, when the reserves of US Inc stood at $8 million, UK plc purchased 24 million shares in US Inc for $35 million. US Inc has a product range which is similar to that of UK plc and France SA, but is targeted more specifically towards the needs of the US market. The stock is manufactured in the USA, and US Inc negotiates its own day-to-day financing needs with US financial institutions. The $25 million loan which was outstanding at 30 September 20X8 was originally taken out on 30 June 20V6 for a 30-year period. The accounting policy of UK plc is to amortise premiums on acquisition over a 20-year period. In the case of US Inc, the first write-off took place in the year ended 30 September 20X3.

Note 3

The stocks of France SA were acquired from UK plc on 31 August 20X8. They represent a consignment which cost UK plc £3.6 million to manufacture but were invoiced to France SA at a price of Euros 44 million. This price represented the sterling transfer price of £4 million translated at the spot rate of exchange in force at 31 August 20X8. The stocks of US Inc were all manufactured locally. The stock in hand of US Inc at 30 September 20X8 represents six months' production.

Note 4

(a) The debtors of UK plc include dividends receivable from France SA and US Inc. These debtors have been translated into sterling using the rate of exchange in force at 30 September 20X8.

(b) The trade creditors of France SA comprise Euros 12 million payable to UK plc. UK plc's debtors include the equivalent asset translated into sterling using the rate of exchange in force at 30 September 20X8.

(c) There was no other inter-company trading.

Note 5

(i) The shares of UK plc are £1 shares.

(ii) The shares of France SA are €1 shares.

(iii) The shares of US Inc are $1 shares.

Note 6

The dates of acquisition of the tangible fixed assets of France SA and US Inc were as follows:

30 September 20X8 – Net Book Value of Fixed Assets

Date	France SA €'000	US Inc $'000
25 May 20X0	10,000	2,000
30 September 20X3	45,000	20,000
30 September 20X7	40,000	34,000
	95,000	56,000

Note 7

Exchange rates at relevant dates were as follows:

Date	£/€ rate	£/$ rate
25 May 20X0	10	2.4
30 September 20X2	9.5	2.0
30 September 20X3	9	1.7
30 September 20X7	10	1.6
31 March 20X8	10.5	1.7
31 August 20X8	11	1.8
30 September 20X8	12	1.8

Required:

(a) Explain how the financial statements [profit and loss account and balance sheet] of France SA and US Inc will be translated into sterling for the purposes of the consolidated financial statements of UK plc. Your answer should refer to relevant Accounting Standards and should explain the treatment of the exchange difference on translation in each case. **(10 marks)**

(b) Prepare the working schedule for the consolidated balance sheet of the UK plc group at 30 September 20X8. Your schedule needs to show only ONE figure for consolidated reserves, so a separate analysis of the exchange differences is NOT required. **(30 marks)**

(Total: 40 marks)

For the answer to this question see the 'Answers' section at the end of the book.

FEEDBACK TO ACTIVITY 1

The supplier's account would appear as follows:

Supplier's account

	£		£
Bank account (remittance (2.8))	3,107	Purchases account (3)	2,900
		P&L a/c (loss on exchange)	207
	3,107		3,107

A sale was made of holidays in April 20X8. Therefore at that date:

Dr   Debtors

Cr   Sales

with Euros 1,980,000 at forward exchange rates

as T Ltd knows it can sell the Euros at the forward rates. There is thus no exchange difference when the Euros are received on the respective dates. The ledger accounts will therefore be as follows:

Sales

	£			£
		16.4.X8	$\frac{980,000}{3.16}$ Debtor	310,127
			$\frac{1,000,000}{3.17}$ Debtor	315,457

Debtor

	£			£
16.4.X8 Sales	310,127	30.8.X8	$\frac{980,000}{3.16}$ Cash	310,127
	315,457	30.9.X8	$\frac{1,000,000}{3.17}$ Cash	315,457
	625,584			625,584

	£
Investment	
@ 30.6.X7	2,333,333
@ 31.3.X8	2,187,500
Loss on investment	(145,833)
Loan	
@ 30.6.X7	1,818,182
@ 31.3.X8	1,666,667
Gain on loan	151,515

£145,833 will be offset in reserves. The balance of £5,682 being the excess gain on the loan will be credited to the profit and loss account.

Chapter 9

GROUP CASH FLOW STATEMENTS

This chapter begins by discussing whether or not cash flow information is useful. We also revise the preparation of a cash flow statement for a single company, which you have covered as part of your earlier studies.

We then cover the preparation of cash flow statements for a group of companies, including the treatment of associates, mid year acquisitions and disposals and foreign currency transactions. Exam questions at this level will feature a group, rather than a single company, and will almost certainly include an acquisition or a disposal.

Objectives

When you have studied this chapter you should be able to:

- discuss the usefulness of cash flow information

- prepare a group cash flow statement classifying cash flows by standard headings and including acquisition and disposal of subsidiaries

- deal with associates, joint ventures, joint arrangements and foreign currencies.

1   Cash flow information

1.1   The benefits of producing a cash flow statement

In order to survive, a business depends on its ability to generate cash. There have been numerous examples of apparently highly profitable companies which have failed as a result of liquidity problems.

Cash flow statements enable users of the financial statements to assess the liquidity, solvency and financial adaptability of a business. A cash flow statement provides information that is not available from the balance sheet and the profit and loss account.

A cash flow statement is believed to provide useful information to users of the financial statements for the following reasons.

- Unlike profits, cash flows are not affected by an entity's choice of accounting policies or by the exercise of judgement. Cash flows can be verified objectively and therefore they allow little scope for 'creative accounting'.

- Cash flow information is thought to have predictive value. It may assist users of financial statements in making judgements on the amount, timing and degree of certainty of future cash flows.

- It gives an indication of the relationship between profitability and cash generating ability, and thus of the quality of the profit earned. The reconciliation of operating profit to the net cash flow generated by operating activities is particularly useful in this context and highlights movements in working capital.

- Cash flow may be more easily understood than profit, particularly by users who are unfamiliar with the technical aspects of financial reporting.

- The cash flow statement provides information which may be useful in interpreting the profit and loss account and balance sheet. For example, it shows cash flow from capital transactions as well as from revenue transactions. It may highlight a company's financial adaptability (for example, its ability to generate future profits and cash flows by selling fixed assets or by issuing shares).

- FRS 1 *Cash flow statements* requires entities to present cash flow information in a standard format. This format highlights the significant components of cash flow in a way that facilitates comparison of the cash flow performance of different businesses. All aspects of cash flow performance are shown, including treasury management (stewardship) and the effect of the methods used to finance the entity's operations.

1.2 Are cash flows and balances difficult to manipulate?

It is often argued that cash flows and balances cannot be manipulated because cash flow is a matter of fact. It is not subject to estimates and it can only be treated in one way. However, there is still some scope for manipulation of cash flows.

Cash balances are measured at a point in time. This means that it is possible to arrange receipts and payments of cash so that the cash balance is some particular amount. A business may make a special effort to collect debts just before the year end, likewise, it may also delay paying creditors until just after the year end.

A business may also structure transactions so that the cash balance is favourably affected. For example, if assets are acquired under leasing agreements cash outflows are spread over several accounting periods rather than one accounting period.

These practices are legitimate ways of managing cash. Cash management is an important aspect of stewardship and therefore desirable. However, more deliberate manipulation is possible. Loans may be raised and repaid immediately after the year-end. Assets may be sold and then immediately repurchased. The disclosures required by FRS 5 *Reporting the substance of transactions* and SSAP 17 *Post balance sheet events* may alert users of the financial statements to the existence of such arrangements.

1.3 The dangers of concentrating on cash

Cash flow cannot be regarded as equivalent to earnings. Cash flow is necessary for survival in the short term, but in order to survive in the long term a business must be profitable. Profits generate cash flow.

Cash management may result in a healthy bank balance at the expense of profits. For example, if a company offers discounts as an incentive to pay promptly, profits are reduced. More significantly, it is often necessary to sacrifice cash flow in the short term in order to generate profits in the long term. Most businesses need to invest in fixed assets in order to generate profits, but this normally results in a temporary cash outflow. A huge cash balance is not a sign of good management if the cash could be invested elsewhere to generate profit.

It has been stated that cash flow information is particularly useful because it has some predictive value. However, cash flow statements are based on historical information and therefore do not provide complete information for assessing future cash flows.

KEY POINT

Neither cash flow nor profit provide a complete picture of a company's performance when looked at in isolation.

It should also be remembered that cash flows result from earlier activities. Because the profit and loss account matches income and expenditure with the periods in which they occur, there are often significant timing differences (for example) between sales and the resulting cash inflow. Present cash flows may not be a reliable indicator of future cash flows. Neither cash flow nor profit provide a complete picture of a company's performance when looked at in isolation. The component parts of the financial statements interrelate because they reflect different aspects of the same transactions.

2   The requirements of FRS 1

2.1   Objective of cash flow statements

The objective of FRS 1 (revised) is to ensure that reporting entities falling within its scope:

- report their cash generation and cash absorption for a period by highlighting the significant components of cash flow in a way that facilitates comparison of the cash flow performance of different businesses

- provide information that assists in the assessment of their liquidity, solvency and financial adaptability.

To help to achieve the objective of cash flow reporting, the FRS requires that individual cash flows should be classified under certain standard headings according to the activity that gave rise to them. The standard headings required in a cash flow statement are listed below.

- operating activities
- dividends from joint ventures and associates
- returns on investments and servicing of finance
- taxation
- capital expenditure and financial investment
- acquisitions and disposals
- equity dividends paid
- management of liquid resources
- financing.

The objective of the standard headings is to ensure that cash flows are reported in a form that highlights the significant components of cash flow and facilitates comparison of the cash flow performance of different businesses.

Cash flows relating to the management of liquid resources and financing can be combined under a single heading provided that the cash flows relating to each are shown separately and separate subtotals are given.

Each cash flow should be classified according to the substance of the transaction giving rise to it. The substance of a transaction determines the most appropriate standard heading under which to report cash flows that are not specified in the standard categories.

2.2   Scope of FRS 1

FRS 1 applies to all financial statements intended to give a true and fair view of the financial position and profit or loss (or income and expenditure), except those of entities in the following categories.

(a) Subsidiary undertakings where 90 per cent or more of the voting rights are controlled within the group, provided that consolidated financial statements in which the subsidiary undertakings are included are publicly available.

(b) Companies incorporated under companies legislation and entitled to the exemptions available in the legislation for small companies when filing accounts with the Registrar of Companies.

(c) Entities that would have been in category (b) above if they were companies incorporated under companies legislation.

(d) Mutual life assurance companies, pension funds, some open-ended investment funds and some building societies.

The FRSSE encourages, but does not require, small entities to prepare a cash flow statement.

FRS 1 exempts subsidiary undertakings where 90% or more of the voting rights in the subsidiary are controlled within its group. In this situation, it is likely that the liquidity, solvency and financial adaptability of the subsidiary will depend upon the group, rather than its own cash flows. Groups often have centralised cash management operations and cash balances can be moved around a group rapidly. For this reason, historical cash flow information of individual group companies does not always contribute to an assessment of future cash flows.

DEFINITIONS

Cash is cash in hand and deposits repayable on demand with any qualifying financial institution, less overdrafts from any qualifying financial institution repayable on demand. Deposits are repayable on demand if they can be withdrawn at any time without notice and without penalty or if a maturity or period of notice of not more than 24 hours or one working day has been agreed. Cash includes cash in hand and deposits denominated in foreign currencies.

An **overdraft** is a borrowing facility repayable on demand that is used by drawing on a current account with a qualifying financial institution.

A **qualifying financial institution** is an entity that as part of its business receives deposits or other repayable funds and grants credits for its own account.

Cash flow is an increase or decrease in an amount of cash.

2.3 The meaning of cash

The definition of cash is central to the preparation and interpretation of cash flow statements. The bottom line in the cash flow statement is the **total cash flow** for the period, in other words, the total increase or decrease in the amount of cash.

The practical effect of these definitions is that the cash flow statement reports inflows and outflows of 'pure' cash. Short-term deposits and loans are not included within the definitions.

2.4 Advantages of the strict cash approach

The ASB decided to use pure cash as the basis of the cash flows reported in the cash flow statement. However, it has also introduced a section for cash flows relating to the management of liquid resources. It believes that this approach has the following advantages.

- It avoids an arbitrary cut-off point in the definition of cash equivalents.

- It distinguishes cash flows arising from accumulating or using liquid resources from those for other investing activities.

- It provides information about an entity's treasury activities that was not previously available to the extent that the instruments dealt in fell within the definition of cash equivalents.

The ASB believes that focusing on cash (rather than on a broader measure such as net debt):

- highlights the significant components of cash that make up a cash flow statement

- shows as cash flow movements transactions that would not be captured by a broader measure such as net debt (e.g. redemption of debentures for cash)

- facilitates comparison of the cash flow performances of different entities

- is in line with the international focus on cash (e.g. with IAS 7).

Illustration

The following illustration is included in FRS 1. It shows a cash flow statement for a single company. It illustrates the standard headings and examples of items within the standard headings.

The illustration includes the reconciliations and notes required by FRS 1. The reconciliations may be shown adjoining the cash flow statement or in the notes. If they adjoin the cash flow statement they should be clearly labelled and kept separate.

Note 1 gives the components of the net cash flows reported under each heading. These can be shown on the face of the cash flow statement or in the notes.

XYZ Ltd Cash flow statement for the year ended 31 December 20X6

Reconciliation of operating profit to net cash inflow from operating activities

	£'000
Operating profit	6,022
Depreciation charge	899
Increase in stocks	(194)
Increase in debtors	(72)
Increase in creditors	234
Net cash inflow from operating activities	6,889

Cash flow statement

	£'000
Net cash inflow from operating activities	6,889
Returns on investments and servicing of finance (note 1)	2,999
Taxation	(2,922)
Capital expenditure (note 1)	(1,525)
	5,441
Equity dividends paid	(2,417)
	3,024
Management of liquid resources (note 1)	(450)
Financing (note 1)	57
Increase in cash	2,631

Reconciliation of net cash flow to movement in net debt (note 2)

	£'000
Increase in cash in the period	2,631
Cash to repurchase debenture	149
Cash used to increase liquid resources	450
Change in net debt	3,230
Net debt at 1 January 20X6	(2,903)
Net funds at 31 December 20X6	327

Notes to cash flow statement

(1) Gross cash flows

	£'000	£'000
Returns on investments and servicing of finance		
Interest received	3,011	
Interest paid	(12)	
	———	2,999
Capital expenditure		
Payments to acquire intangible fixed assets	(71)	
Payments to acquire tangible fixed assets	(1,496)	
Receipts from sales of tangible fixed assets	42	
	———	(1,525)
Management of liquid resources		
Purchase of treasury bills	(650)	
Sale of treasury bills	200	
	———	(450)
Financing		
Issue of ordinary share capital	211	
Repurchase of debenture loan	(149)	
Expenses paid in connection with share issues	(5)	
	———	57

(2) Analysis of changes in net debt

	At 1 Jan 20X6 £'000	Cash flows £'000	Other changes £'000	At 31 Dec 20X6 £'000
Cash in hand, at bank	42	847		889
Overdrafts	(1,784)	1,784		
		———		
		2,631		
Debts due within 1 year	(149)	149	(230)	(230)
Debts due after 1 year	(1,262)		230	(1,032)
Current asset investments	250	450		700
Total	(2,903)	3,230	-	327

2.5   Net cash flow from operating activities

KEY POINT

FRS 1 permits either the direct method or the indirect method to be used in reporting the cash flow from operating activities.

There are two possible methods for reporting net cash flow from operating activities.

The **direct method** shows operating cash receipts and payments (including, in particular, cash receipts from customers, cash payments to suppliers and cash payments to and on behalf of employees), aggregating to the net cash flow from operating activities.

The **indirect method** starts with operating profit and adjusts it for non-cash charges and credits to reconcile it to the net cash flow from operating activities.

FRS 1 permits either method to be used.

2.6   The utility of the direct and indirect methods of presentation

The principal advantage of the direct method is that it shows operating cash receipts and payments. Knowledge of the specific sources of cash receipts and the purposes for which cash payments were made in past periods may be useful in assessing future cash flows. However, the ASB does not believe at present that in all cases the benefits to users of this information outweigh the costs to the reporting entity of providing it and, therefore, has not required the information to be given.

The principal advantage of the indirect method is that it highlights the differences between operating profit and net cash flow from operating activities. Many users of financial statements believe that such a reconciliation is essential to give an indication of the quality of the reporting entity's earnings. Some investors and creditors assess future cash flows by estimating future income and then allowing for accruals adjustments; thus information about past accruals adjustments may be useful to help estimate future adjustments.

Accordingly, the FRS requires the cash flow statement to show the net cash flow from operating activities, supplemented by a note reconciling this to the reporting entity's operating profit for the period. This reconciliation should not be given in the primary cash flow statement, in order to avoid confusing operating profit and the reconciling items with cash flows. The result is that reporting entities must always give the information required by the indirect method.

3   Classification of cash flows

3.1   Returns on investments and servicing of finance

Returns on investments and servicing of finance are receipts resulting from the ownership of an investment and payments to providers of finance, non-equity shareholders (e.g. the holders of preference shares) and minority interests, excluding those items required to be classified under another heading.

Cash inflows from returns on investments and servicing of finance include:

(a)   interest received, including any related tax recovered

(b)   dividends received, net of any tax credits (except dividends from any equity accounted entities).

Cash outflows from returns on investments and servicing of finance include:

(a)   interest paid (even if capitalised), including any tax deducted and paid to the relevant tax authority

(b)   cash flows that are treated as finance costs under FRS 4 (this will include issue costs on debt and non-equity share capital)

(c)   the interest element of finance lease rental payments

(d)   dividends paid on non-equity shares of the entity

(e)   dividends paid to minority interests.

3.2   Taxation

The cash flows included under this heading are cash flows to or from the taxation authorities in respect of the reporting entity's revenue and capital profits. (In practice, this is normally the amount paid for UK corporation tax.)

Value added tax (VAT) is not included under this heading. Cash flows should be shown net of any attributable VAT unless the tax is irrecoverable. The net movement on the VAT account should normally be allocated to cash flows from operating activities (i.e. it is treated as a normal movement in working capital).

3.3 Capital expenditure and financial investment

The cash flows included in 'capital expenditure and financial investment' are those related to the acquisition or disposal of any fixed asset other than one required to be classified under 'acquisitions and disposals' and any current asset investment not included in liquid resources. (Acquisitions and disposals and liquid resources are explained below.)

If no cash flows relating to financial investment fall to be included under this heading the caption may be reduced to 'capital expenditure'.

Cash inflows from capital expenditure and financial investment include:

(a)   receipts from sales or disposals of property, plant or equipment

(b)   receipts from the repayment of the reporting entity's loans to other entities or sales of debt instruments of other entities other than receipts forming part of an acquisition or disposal or a movement in liquid resources.

Cash outflows from capital expenditure and financial investment include:

(a)   payments to acquire property, plant or equipment

(b)   loans made by the reporting entity and payments to acquire debt instruments of other entities other than payments forming part of an acquisition or disposal or a movement in liquid resources.

3.4 Acquisitions and disposals

The cash flows included in 'acquisitions and disposals' are those related to the acquisition or disposal of any trade or business, or of an investment in an entity that is, or, as a result of the transaction, becomes or ceases to be either an associate, a joint venture, or a subsidiary undertaking.

Cash inflows from acquisitions and disposals include:

(a)   receipts from sales of investments in subsidiary undertakings, showing separately any balances of cash and overdrafts transferred as part of the sale

(b)   receipts from sales of investments in associates or joint ventures

(c)   receipts from sales of trades or businesses.

Cash outflows from acquisitions and disposals include:

(a)   payments to acquire investments in subsidiary undertakings, showing separately any balances of cash and overdrafts acquired

(b)   payments to acquire investments in associates and joint ventures

(c)   payments to acquire trades or businesses.

It follows that this caption does not normally appear in the cash flow statement of a single company. The exception would be if a company had acquired or disposed of an unincorporated business during the period.

Under the previous version of FRS 1, capital expenditure and acquisitions and disposals were reported together under the same caption, 'investing activities'.

Entities undertake investing activities in order to maintain the current level of operations and sometimes to expand the current level of operations. The cash flow statement does not distinguish between different types of investing activity, on the grounds that this is not feasible.

However, when the ASB revised FRS 1, it recognised that useful information would be provided by analysing investing activities into capital expenditure and acquisitions and disposals of investments. The notes to the FRS state that 'this distinction should not be interpreted as reflecting on the one hand maintenance expenditure and on the other expenditure for expansion because, depending on the circumstances, these may be included under either heading'.

3.5   Equity dividends paid

The cash outflows included in 'equity dividends paid' are dividends paid on the reporting entity's, or, in a group, the parent's equity shares.

This is another change introduced by the revised FRS. Previously, all dividends paid or received were reported under 'returns on investments and servicing of finance'.

Equity dividends paid are now reported separately from interest and other dividends paid to highlight the fact that payment of equity dividends is discretionary. In contrast, an entity has no discretion over the amount or the timing of interest payable and no discretion over the amount of non-equity dividends.

Equity and non-equity shares are defined in accordance with FRS 4 *Capital instruments*.

3.6   Management of liquid resources

The 'management of liquid resources' section includes cash flows in respect of liquid resources as defined in the margin.

The definition opposite does not specify the type of investment that would be classed as a liquid resource. Instead it has been drafted in general terms, in order to emphasise the liquidity of the investment and its function as a readily disposable store of value. In practice, term deposits, government securities, loan stock, equities and derivatives might form part of an entity's liquid resources. Short-term deposits would also fall within the definition. Because of the requirement that they should be readily convertible into known amounts of cash at or close to their carrying amount, deposits that are more than one year from maturity on acquisition would not normally be classed as liquid resources.

Each entity should explain what it includes as liquid resources and any changes in its policy.

Cash inflows in management of liquid resources include:

(a)   withdrawals from short-term deposits not qualifying as cash in so far as not netted (see below)

(b)   inflows from disposal or redemption of any other investments held as liquid resources.

Cash outflows in management of liquid resources include:

(a)   payments into short-term deposits not qualifying as cash in so far as not netted

(b)   outflows to acquire any other investments held as liquid resources.

DEFINITION

Liquid resources are current asset investments held in readily disposable stores of value. A readily disposable investment is one that is disposable by the reporting entity without curtailing or disrupting its business and is either:

(a) readily convertible into known amounts of cash at or close to its carrying amount; or

(b) traded in an active market.

Cash inflows and outflows within the management of liquid resources may be netted against each other if they are due to short maturities and high turnover occurring from rollover or re-issue (for example, short-term deposits).

This section of the cash flow statement has been introduced by the revised version of FRS 1. It is designed to provide information about the way that entities manage their cash and similar assets. It distinguishes cash flows in relation to cash management from cash flows arising from other investment decisions (for example, the acquisition and disposal of fixed asset investments).

3.7   Financing

Financing cash flows comprise receipts or repayments of principal from or to external providers of finance.

Financing cash inflows include:

(a) receipts from issuing shares or other equity instruments

(b) receipts from issuing debentures, loans, notes and bonds from other long-term and short-term borrowings (other than overdrafts).

Financing cash outflows include:

(a) repayments of amounts borrowed (other than overdrafts)

(b) the capital element of finance lease payments

(c) payments to re-acquire or redeem the entity's shares

(d) payments of expenses or commissions on any issue of equity shares.

The amounts of any financing cash flows received from or paid to equity accounted entities should be disclosed separately.

ACTIVITY 1

Prepare a cash flow statement (using the indirect method) in accordance with FRS 1 from the following information for the year ended 30 June 20X3:

Hubert Ltd

Balance sheet as at 30 June

	20X2 £m	20X3 £m
Fixed assets:		
Cost	170	238
Depreciation	52	74
	118	164
Current assets and liabilities:		
Stocks	68	80
Debtors	52	48
Cash at bank	20	26
Trade creditors	(30)	(46)
Taxation	(24)	(30)
Dividend	(26)	(34)
	60	44
Long-term liabilities:		
10% debentures	(40)	(20)
	138	188

Share capital and reserves		
Ordinary shares of £1 each	52	56
Share premium	24	26
Profit and loss account	62	106
	138	188

Notes

1   No fixed assets were disposed of during the year.

2   Of the 10% debentures £20m was redeemed at par on 30 June 20X3.

3   The profit and loss account for the year ended 30 June 20X3 showed a tax charge of £30m and total dividends of £34m.

4   Notes to the cash flow statement are not required.

Feedback to this activity is at the end of the chapter.

4   Net debt and non-cash transactions

4.1   Reconciliation of movements in net debt

DEFINITION

Net debt is the borrowings of the reporting entity (comprising debt as defined in FRS 4, together with related derivatives and obligations under finance leases) less cash and liquid resources. Where cash and liquid resources exceed the borrowings of the entity reference should be made to 'net funds' rather than to 'net debt'.

KEY POINT

Non-equity shares of the entity are excluded from net debt because, although these have features that may be similar to those of borrowings, they are not actually liabilities of the entity.

FRS 1 (revised) requires a note reconciling the movement of cash in the period with the movement in net debt. (An example of this reconciliation was illustrated earlier in the chapter.) This reconciliation can be given either adjoining the cash flow statement or in a note. If the reconciliation adjoins the cash flow statement, it should be clearly labelled and kept separate.

The objective of the reconciliation is to provide information that assists in the assessment of liquidity, solvency and financial adaptability.

Non-equity shares of the entity are excluded from net debt because, although these have features that may be similar to those of borrowings, they are not actually liabilities of the entity. (This distinction between liabilities and non-equity shares is consistent with the requirements of FRS 4.)

The definition also excludes debtors and creditors because, while these are short-term claims on and sources of finance to the entity, their main role is as part of the entity's trading activities. (Movements in debtors and creditors are dealt with as part of operating activities.)

The changes in net debt should be analysed from the opening to the closing component amounts showing separately, where material, changes resulting from:

- the cash flows of the entity
- the acquisition or disposal of subsidiary undertakings
- other non-cash changes
- the recognition of changes in market value and exchange rate movements.

Where several balance sheet amounts or parts thereof have to be combined to form the components of opening and closing net debt, sufficient detail should be shown to enable the cash and other components of net debt to be traced back to amounts shown under the equivalent captions in the balance sheet. This is done by means of a note analysing net debt.

4.2 Cash, liquid resources and net debt

The cash flow statement presents information about the components of cash flow (i.e. the increase or decrease in an entity's cash resulting from transactions during the accounting period). The definition of cash was stated at the beginning of the chapter.

Cash is very narrowly defined. It includes cash in hand, deposits repayable on demand and overdrafts. It does not include investments, however liquid or near maturity. The effect of this definition is that the bottom line of the cash flow statement shows the increase or decrease in 'pure' cash for the period.

In theory, there are alternatives to the strict cash approach.

- Use a wider definition of cash which includes some liquid resources.
- Alternatively, change the focus of the statement from cash to movements in net funds or net debt.

A wider definition of cash

Entities may borrow on a short-term basis. Alternatively, they may invest cash in short-term liquid investments. Many entities would argue that these activities form an important part of their cash management. For these entities, the distinction between pure cash, short-term loans and liquid investments is artificial and means that the cash flow statement does not reflect the economic reality of their situation.

Under the original version of FRS 1, the cash flow statement showed the movement in cash and cash equivalents. Cash equivalents were defined as 'short-term, highly liquid investments which are readily convertible into known amounts of cash without notice and which were within three months of maturity when acquired'.

This definition was widely criticised by commentators and by preparers of financial statements. In particular, the three-month limit was regarded as arbitrary. Deposits which in practice were used as part of treasury management had to be classified as investments, thus presenting a potentially misleading picture to users of the financial statements.

It would be difficult to draft a definition which did not depend on some kind of arbitrary limit. It would also be unacceptable to allow entities to determine their own basis for defining cash equivalents.

A focus on net funds or net debt

One of the objectives of the cash flow statement is to provide information to assist users in assessing the liquidity, solvency and financial adaptability of an entity. Some commentators have argued that a cash flow statement cannot provide information about an entity's liquidity because it focuses only on changes in cash. Net debt is a widely used financial indicator and a statement which focused on net debt or net funds would provide more useful information.

4.3 Major non-cash transactions

Standard accounting practice

'Material transactions not resulting in movements of cash of the reporting entity should be disclosed in the notes to the cash flow statement if disclosure is necessary for an understanding of the underlying transactions.'

Consideration for transactions may be in a form other than cash. The purpose of a cash flow statement is to report cash flows and non-cash transactions should, therefore, not be reported in a cash flow statement. However, to obtain a full picture of the alterations in financial position caused by the transactions for the period, separate disclosure of material non-cash transactions is also necessary.

Examples of non-cash transactions are given below:

- certain acquisitions and disposals of subsidiaries by a group
- finance leases
- certain changes in debt and equity.

4.4   HP and finance leases

Hire purchase and finance leases are accounted for by the lessee/purchaser capitalising the present value of the minimum lease payments. A liability and a corresponding asset are produced which do not reflect cash flows in the accounting period.

The cash flow statement records the cash flow, i.e. the rentals paid. As each rental represents a payment of interest and capital FRS 1 requires a split between the two elements:

- the interest element is shown under servicing of finance
- the capital element is shown under financing.

The interest element will already be computed as it is charged (and disclosed in the financial statements) in arriving at profit before taxation. Deducting the interest charge from rentals paid provides the capital paid in the year.

The non-cash flow elements of a finance lease may need to be disclosed:

- if the finance lease is of such significance that it is classified as a major non-cash transaction
- in the reconciliation of net cash flow to movement in net debt (as the finance lease liability may have been aggregated with, for example, bank loans on the balance sheet).

4.5   Exceptional items

KEY POINT

Where cash flows relate to items that are classed as exceptional or extraordinary items in the profit and loss account the cash flows should be shown separately under the appropriate standard headings, according to the nature of each item.

Where cash flows relate to items that are classed as exceptional or extraordinary items in the profit and loss account the cash flows should be shown separately under the appropriate standard headings, according to the nature of each item. Disclosure of the nature of the cash flows should be given in a note to the cash flow statement.

These disclosures allow users of the financial statements to gain an understanding of the effect of the underlying transactions on the cash flows.

Re-organisation charges that are exceptional must be disclosed separately and explained.

Cash flows in respect of operating items relating to provisions are included in operating activities, even if the provision was not included in operating profit. Examples of such cash flows are redundancy payments falling under a provision for the termination of an operation or for a fundamental reorganisation or restructuring, also operating item cash flows provided for on an acquisition.

KEY POINT

Where cash flows are exceptional because of their size or incidence but are not related to items that are treated as exceptional or extraordinary in the profit and loss account, sufficient disclosure should be given to explain their cause and nature.

Exceptional cash flows

Where cash flows are exceptional because of their size or incidence but are not related to items that are treated as exceptional or extraordinary in the profit and loss account, sufficient disclosure should be given to explain their cause and nature.

For a cash flow to be exceptional on the grounds of its size alone, it must be exceptional in relation to cash flows of a similar nature. A large prepayment against a pension liability is an example of a possible exceptional cash flow unrelated to an exceptional or extraordinary item in the profit and loss account.

4.6 Further optional disclosure

FRS 1 suggests that the standard cash flow classifications could be subdivided further to give a fuller description of the activities of the reporting entity or to provide segmental information. One of the illustrative examples to the FRS shows a possible format for further optional disclosures based on the requirements of FRS 3.

Reconciliation of operating profit to net cash inflow from operating activities

	Continuing	*Discontinued*	*Total*
	£'000	£'000	£'000
Operating profit	18,829	(1,616)	17,213
Depreciation charges	3,108	380	3,488
Cash flow relating to previous year restructuring provision		(560)	(560)
Increase in stocks	(11,193)	(87)	(11,280)
Increase in debtors	(3,754)	(20)	(3,774)
Increase in creditors	9,672	913	10,585
Net cash inflow from continuing operating activities	16,662		
Net cash outflow in respect of discontinued activities		(990)	
Net cash inflow from operating activities			15,672

This illustration also includes an exceptional item (the cash flow relating to previous year restructuring provision).

5 Applying FRS 1 to the preparation of consolidated cash flows

5.1 FRS 1 as it relates to consolidated cash flows

Where a company has subsidiaries, cash flow statements should be based on the group accounts, and the starting figure should therefore be the group operating net cash inflow.

Cash flows that are internal to the group should be eliminated in the preparation of a consolidated cash flow statement.

The standard has specific requirements in relation to minority interests, associates and acquisitions and disposals of subsidiaries. These are examined in the following sections.

5.2 Minority interests – standard accounting practice

Dividends paid to minority interests are disclosed separately under 'returns on investments and servicing of finance'.

Example

The following information has been extracted from the consolidated financial statements of WG plc for the years ended 31 December.

	20X6 £'000	20X5 £'000
Dividends payable to minority shareholders	100	160
Minority interest in group net assets	780	690
Minority interest in consolidated profit after taxation	120	230

What is the dividend paid to minority interests in the year 20X6?

Solution

Minority interests

	£'000		£'000
Dividends paid (bal fig)	90	Balance b/d dividends payable	160
Balance c/d dividends payable	100	Balance b/d minority interest	690
Balance c/d minority interest	780	Share of profits in year	120
	———		———
	970		970

5.3 Associates, joint ventures and joint arrangements that are not entities

Associates and joint ventures reflect a cash flow in or out of the group to the extent that:

- dividends are paid or payable out of the profits of the associate/joint venture

- trading occurs between the group and the associate/joint venture

- further investment is made in the associate/joint venture.

Associates and joint ventures are dealt with under the equity method of accounting and FRS 1 uses this terminology.

Standard accounting practice

'The cash flows of any equity accounted entity should be included in the group cash flow statement only to the extent of the actual cash flows between the group and the entity concerned, for example dividends received in cash and loans made or repaid.'

Dividends

It is only dividends paid which represent a cash inflow. Proposed dividends represent an increase in group debtors (i.e. the share of the dividend payable which is received by the investing company will not form part of the asset 'Investment in associates and joint ventures' but will be included in group debtors).

Thus, in reconciling group net cash inflow to group operating profit the balance sheet movement in debtors must exclude proposed dividends from the associate/joint venture so that dividends received can be shown in the cash flow statement.

Dividends received from associates and joint ventures should be included as a separate item in the consolidated cash flow statement between operating activities and returns on investments and servicing of finance.

Trading between group and associate or joint venture

Trading between the group and an associate or joint venture will give rise to inter-company balances on the group balance sheet at the year end. The balances will be treated in the same way as any other trading debtors and creditors, i.e. the balance sheet movement forms part of the reconciliation between group operating profit and group net cash inflow from operating activities.

If the direct method is used it follows that when cash is paid/received in respect of inter-company balances the cash is included in the 'cash received from customers/cash payments to suppliers' section of the cash flow statement. It may, however, be appropriate to show the cash outflow/inflow separately from the group customers and suppliers.

Change in investment in associate or joint venture

A change in investment in the associate or joint venture can arise when:

- an additional shareholding is purchased or part of the shareholding is sold
- loans are made to/from the associate/joint venture or amounts previously loaned are repaid.

Provided cash consideration is involved, any change will be shown under the acquisitions and disposals section of the cash flow statement.

Joint arrangements that are not entities

Participants in a joint arrangement that is not an entity should account for their own cash flows, measured according to the terms of the agreement. This is because each participant is effectively operating its own business independently of the others.

Example of a cash flow statement involving an associate

The following information has been extracted from the consolidated financial statements of H plc for the year ended 31 December 20X1.

Group profit and loss account

	£'000	£'000
Operating profit		734
Share of profit of associated undertaking		122
Tax on profit on ordinary activities		
UK corporation tax	(324)	
Share of tax of associated undertaking	(54)	
	——	(378)
Profit on ordinary activities after tax		478

Group balance sheet

	20X1	20X0
	£'000	£'000
Investment in associated undertaking		
Share of net assets	466	456
Loan to associate	380	300
Current assets		
Debtors	260	190

Included with group debtors are the following amounts.

Dividend receivable from associate	48	29
Current account with associate	40	70

Show the relevant figures to be included in the group cash flow statement for the year ended 31 December 20X1 and the amount at which debtors will be shown in the reconciliation of operating profit to net cash inflow.

Solution

Extracts from cash flow statement

	£'000
Reconciliation of operating profit to net cash inflow	
from operating activities	
Operating profit	734
Increase in debtors (W2)	(51)
Cash flow statement	
Dividend received from associate (W1)	39
Capital expenditure and financial investment	
Loan to associated undertaking	(80)

Workings

(W1)   **Associate**

	£'000		£'000
Balance b/d		Share of tax	54
Share of net assets	456	Dividend received (bal fig)	39
Dividend receivable	29	Balance c/d	
Share of profits	122	Share of net assets	466
		Dividend receivable	48
	607		607

Tutorial note

An alternative approach to the above working is to construct initially a profit and loss account showing profit information relating to the associate.

	£'000
Share of profits	122
Share of tax	54
	68
Dividends from 20X1 profits (bal fig)	58
Increase in share of net assets (i.e. share of retained profits 466 – 456)	10

Then adjust £58,000 by the opening and closing dividend receivable

(29 + 58 – 48) £39,000.

(W2)   **Increase in debtor**

	20X0 £'000	20X1 £'000
Debtors per balance sheet	190	260
Less: Dividend receivable	(29)	(48)
	161	212
Increase		£51,000

5.4 Acquisition of subsidiaries during the year – standard accounting practice

Where a subsidiary undertaking joins or leaves a group during a financial year the cash flows of the group should include the cash flows of the subsidiary undertaking concerned for the same period as that for which the group's profit and loss account includes the results of the subsidiary undertaking.

A note to the cash flow statement should show a summary of the effects of acquisitions and disposals of subsidiary undertakings indicating how much of the consideration comprised cash.

Material effects reported under each of the standard headings reflecting the cash flows of a subsidiary undertaking acquired or disposed of during the period should be disclosed, as far as practicable. This information could be given by dividing cash flows between continuing and discontinued operations and acquisitions.

Payments to acquire subsidiaries and receipts from disposals of subsidiaries are reported under 'acquisitions and disposals'. Any balances of cash and overdrafts acquired or transferred should be shown separately.

5.5 Computational aspects of dealing with acquisitions and disposals

The substance of an acquisition of a subsidiary is that the group has purchased the assets of the subsidiary. However, in the cash flow statement we only wish to record the actual cash flow. Thus, for example, the additional fixed assets under the control of the group as a result of the acquisition will not be included under the heading 'capital expenditure'. Care needs to be taken when expenditure on fixed assets is derived as a balancing figure. Fixed assets of the subsidiary at acquisition must be included in the ledger account used to derive the balancing figure.

Similar care needs to be applied in relation to other assets and liabilities in the subsidiary at acquisition.

For example, the balance sheet movement in stock needs to be computed and shown as a reconciling item between operating profit and net cash inflow. Where there has been an acquisition the movement in stock can be analysed:

Beginning of year	*Part-way through year*	*End of year*
Group stock excluding subsidiary not yet acquired	Subsidiary acquired (£9,384 stock included in net assets acquired)	Group stock including subsidiary acquired in year
[£53,019]	[Increase in stock]	[£74,666]

Increase in stock = £74,666 – (53,019 + 9,384) = £12,263.

X plc acquired Y plc in the current accounting period. Extracts from the group accounts of X plc show:

	Last year £'000	This year £'000
NBV fixed assets	10,000	16,000

Depreciation charged in the group profit and loss account is £2,600,000, and the NBV of disposals is £600,000. The fair value of Y plc's fixed assets when Y plc was acquired by X plc is £4,800,000.

What was the expenditure on fixed assets during the current accounting period?

Feedback to this activity is at the end of the chapter.

5.6   Partly-owned subsidiary acquired in current year

This is not as complicated as it sounds. The note to the cash flow statement summarising the net assets acquired and for what consideration will include an item 'minority interest'. The amount will be the minority interests' share of net assets of the subsidiary at the date of acquisition. It will have no direct bearing on the figures shown in the cash flow statement except where dividends paid to minority interests have to be computed as a balancing figure. In such an event the minority interests' share of net assets at acquisition will be a credit in the minority interest account constructed to derive dividends paid.

5.7   Disposal of subsidiary

A disposal is treated using the same principles as for an acquisition. The cash consideration received will be shown as a receipt under 'acquisitions and disposals'.

If any group assets or liabilities are being analysed to determine a cash inflow or outflow the book value of the subsidiary's assets/liabilities will need to form part of the analysis. For example tax liabilities in the subsidiary at the date of disposal will represent a debit in a taxation account being written up to determine tax paid.

Tax account

	£		£
Cash paid (bal fig)	X	Balance b/d: group (P + S) liability	X
Tax liability in subsidiary		Tax charge for year	X
at date of disposal	X		
Balance c/d: group (P) liability	X		
	X		X

The debit entry for the tax liability in the subsidiary is equivalent to the balance c/d at the end of the accounting period for the remaining part of the group liability.

5.8   Detailed example

Several years ago H plc acquired 80% of the ordinary share capital of S Ltd. It also acquired a 25% shareholding in A Ltd and the company is regarded as an associated company. On 1 January 20X8 H plc acquired the entire share capital of J Ltd. You are provided with the following information regarding the group accounts.

Consolidated profit and loss account for the year ended 31 December 20X8

Note		£	£
(1)	Group operating profit		3,976,300
	Share of operating profit of associate		59,000
(2)	Sale of freehold property		500,000
	Interest received		9,800
	Premium on redemption of preference shares		(15,000)
	Interest paid		(12,100)
	Profit before taxation		4,518,000
(3)	Taxation		2,247,160
	Profit after taxation		2,270,840
	Minority interest		41,664
	Profit attributable to members of H plc		2,229,176

Dividends

Interim (paid)	250,000	
Final (proposed)	300,000	
		550,000
Retained profit for year		1,679,176

Consolidated balance sheets (summarised)

Notes		31 Dec 20X7 £	31 Dec 20X8 £
(2)	Freehold property	8,276,718	9,744,658
(4)	Plant and machinery	2,673,400	3,955,400
	Goodwill on consolidation	66,500	192,500
(5)	Associated undertaking	80,750	98,570
	Stock	2,065,000	3,400,100
	Debtors	854,200	1,250,000
	Cash	21,100	136,750
		14,037,668	18,777,978
	Ordinary share capital (£1 shares)	3,000,000	4,200,000
(6)	Reserves	5,661,850	7,941,026
(7)	Preference shares	300,000	-
	Long-term loan	-	150,000
	Creditors	984,500	1,640,640
	Corporation tax	3,226,318	3,903,848
	Dividends	245,000	300,000
	Minority interest	620,000	642,464
		14,037,668	18,777,978

You are provided with the following additional information.

(1) Operating profit

Operating profit is arrived at after charging depreciation amounting to £558,000. Interest paid is after adjusting for an opening accrual of £600 and a closing accrual of £4,600.

(2) Exceptional item

This represents profit on sale of freehold property. The property was in the books at £940,000. Property is not depreciated.

(3) Taxation

	£
Group companies	2,216,480
Associate	30,680
	2,247,160

(4) Plant and machinery

	Cost £	Agg. depn. £	NBV £
At 1 January 20X8	3,500,000	826,600	2,673,400
Additions			
J Ltd	1,100,000	240,000	860,000
Others	980,000	-	980,000
Depreciation – charge for year		558,000	(558,000)
	5,580,000	1,624,600	3,955,400

(5) Associate

At 31 December

	20X7 £	20X8 £
Cost	72,000	72,000
Accumulated profit	8,750	26,570
	80,750	98,570

Included within debtors are dividends receivable from associate: 31 December 20X7, £29,000; 31 December 20X8, Nil.

(6) Reserves

	Revenue £	Capital redemption £	Share premium £	Total £
At 1 January 20X8	5,586,850	-	75,000	5,661,850
Retained profit	1,679,176	-	-	1,679,176
Issue of ordinary shares	-	-	600,000	600,000
Redemption of preference shares	(300,000)	300,000	-	-
At 31 December 20X8	6,966,026	300,000	675,000	7,941,026

(7) Preference shares

The preference shares were redeemed during the year at a premium of 5%. Ordinary shares were issued to finance the redemption.

(8) Acquisition of J Ltd

	£	£
Consideration		
800,000 shares at £1.50		1,200,000
Cash		600,000
		1,800,000

Assets acquired

Plant and machinery	860,000
Stock	836,500
Debtors	449,300
Creditors	(262,000)
Cash	532,400
Corporation tax	(742,200)

1,674,000

Goodwill	126,000

You are required to prepare a consolidated cash flow statement in a form suitable for publication. Ignore amortisation of goodwill.

Solution

Step 1

Working capital movements

	Start of year £	Subsidiary £	End of year £	Movement £
Stock	2,065,000	836,500	3,400,100	498,600
Debtors	854,200	449,300	1,250,000	(24,500)
Dividend from associate	(29,000)		-	
Creditors	984,500	262,000	1,640,640	390,140
Interest accrual	(600)		(4,600)	

Step 2

Associate

As the dividends received from the associate have not been given, reconstruct the group's share of profits from the associate from available information.

	£
Profit	59,000
Tax	30,680
	28,320
Dividend (bal. fig.)	10,500
Retained profit	17,820
Dividend receivable b/d	29,000
Dividends out of current year's profit	10,500
Less: Dividend receivable c/d	-
Dividends paid	39,500

Step 3

Minority interests

Profits earned by subsidiaries are retained within the group, except to the extent that a dividend is paid to the minority shareholders.

Minority interest account

	£		£
Cash (bal fig)	19,200	Balance b/d	620,000
Balance c/d	642,464	Profit and loss	41,664
	661,664		661,664

It is assumed that there are no amounts in creditors relating to proposed dividends due to minority interests.

Step 4

Taxation

Corporation tax account excluding associate

	£		£
Cash (bal fig)	2,281,150	Balance b/d	3,226,318
		Profit and loss (note 3)	2,216,480
		Corporation tax – balance on J at acquisition	742,200
Balance c/d	3,903,848		
	6,184,998		6,184,998

The tax paid is normally arrived at as a balancing figure. As the subsidiary had a tax creditor at acquisition, the amount must be brought into the group corporation tax account because when the liability is paid, it will form part of group tax paid.

Step 5

Property

Property account – NBV

	£		£
Balance b/d	8,276,718	Disposals account (NBV)	940,000
Additions (bal fig)	2,407,940	Balance c/d	9,744,658
	10,684,658		10,684,658

Property disposals account

	£		£
Property at NBV	940,000	Cash proceeds	1,440,000
Profit on sale (exceptional item)	500,000		
	1,440,000		1,440,000

As the exceptional item relates to a disposal of a fixed asset, the sale proceeds are shown under capital expenditure.

Step 6

Purchase of subsidiary

Only the net cash effect of the purchase should be shown. Non-cash consideration is thus excluded and any cash in the subsidiary at acquisition reduces the cash price paid. The opposite would apply if there were an overdraft in the subsidiary at acquisition.

	£
Cash paid	600,000
Cash in subsidiary	532,400
	67,600

Step 7

Ordinary shares

	Nominal value £	Premium £
Increase in year	1,200,000	600,000
To purchase subsidiary	800,000	400,000
For cash	400,000	200,000

Step 8

Prepare cash flow statement

H plc

Consolidated cash flow statement for year ended 31 December 20X8

	£
Reconciliation of operating profit to net cash inflow from operating activities	
Operating profit	3,976,300
Depreciation charges	558,000
Increase in stocks	(498,600)
Decrease in debtors	24,500
Increase in creditors	390,140
Net cash inflow from operating activities	4,450,340
Cash flow statement	
Net cash inflow from operating activities	4,450,340
Dividends received from associate	39,500
Returns on investments and servicing of finance (Note 1)	(17,500)
Taxation: Corporation tax paid (W4)	(2,281,150)
Capital expenditure (Note 1)	(1,947,940)
Acquisitions and disposals (Note 1)	(67,600)
Equity dividends paid (245 + 250)	(495,000)
Cash outflow before financing	(319,350)
Financing (Note 1)	435,000
Increase in cash for the period	115,650

Reconciliation of net cash flow to movement in net debt (Note 2)

Increase in cash for the period	115,650
Cash inflow from issue of long-term loan	(150,000)
Change in net debt	(34,350)
Net funds at 1 January 20X8	21,100
Net debt at 31 December 20X8	(13,250)

Notes to the cash flow statement

1　**Gross cash flows**

	£	£
Returns on investments and servicing of finance		
Interest received	9,800	
Interest paid (600 + 12,100 – 4,600)	(8,100)	
Dividends paid to minority interest	(19,200)	
		(17,500)
Capital expenditure		
Payments to acquire tangible fixed assets		
(980,000 + 2,407,940)	(3,387,940)	
Receipts from sales of tangible fixed assets	1,440,000	
		(1,947,940)
Acquisitions and disposals		
Cash consideration	(600,000)	
Cash in subsidiary at acquisition	532,400	
		(67,600)
Financing		
Issue of ordinary share capital	600,000	
Issue of loan	150,000	
Redemption of preference shares (300 × 105%)	(315,000)	
		435,000

2　**Analysis of changes in net debt**

	At 1 Jan 20X8 £	Cash flows £	At 31 Dec 20X8 £
Cash at bank	21,100	115,650	136,750
Long-term loan	-	(150,000)	(150,000)
Total	21,100	(34,350)	(13,250)

3　**Major non-cash transactions**

Part of the consideration for the purchase of a subsidiary during the year comprised ordinary shares. The net assets acquired and the consideration given are shown below.

	£		£
Net assets acquired:		Discharged by	
Fixed assets	860,000	Shares issued	1,200,000
Goodwill	126,000	Cash	600,000
Stock	836,500		
Debtors	449,300		
Creditors	(262,000)		
Taxation	(742,200)		
Cash	532,400		
	1,800,000		1,800,000

6 Foreign exchange gains and losses in cash flow statements

6.1 Introduction

The treatment of foreign currencies is only mentioned in one paragraph of FRS 1, which deals with the treatment of foreign subsidiaries or associates.

Before considering group accounts, we will deal with the foreign currency transactions entered into directly by a company – the individual company stage per SSAP 20.

6.2 Individual company stage

Exchange differences arising at the individual company stage are in most instances reported as part of operating profit. If the foreign currency transaction has been settled in the year the cash flows will reflect the reporting currency cash receipt or payment and thus no problem arises. An unsettled foreign currency transaction will however give rise to an exchange difference for which there is no cash flow effect in the current year. Such exchange differences therefore need to be eliminated in computing net cash flows from operating activities.

Fortunately this will not require much work if the unsettled foreign currency transaction is in working capital. Adjusting profit by balance sheet movements in working capital will automatically adjust correctly for the non-cash flow exchange gains and losses.

Example

A company purchases raw materials for $200,000. These are translated into its books at £100,000. By the year end it has paid for half the goods (£48,000) and the remaining creditor is retranslated to closing rate at £45,000. The purchase ledger control account is as follows:

Purchase ledger control

	£		£
Cash	743,000	Balance b/d	300,000
Exchange gains		Purchases	910,000
On settled transaction			
(50,000 – 48,000)	2,000		
On unsettled transaction			
(50,000 – 45,000)	5,000		
Balance c/d			
Foreign currency creditor	45,000		
Other	415,000		
	£1,210,000		£1,210,000

Sales are for cash and amount to £1,003,000.

The company also has a US dollar loan which was recorded in last year's balance sheet at £235,000 and this year at £245,000.

Balance sheets

	Last year £	This year £
Fixed assets	-	-
Current assets		
Stock	300,000	300,000
Cash	335,000	595,000
Trade creditors	(300,000)	(460,000)
Loan	(235,000)	(245,000)
	£100,000	£190,000
Capital and reserves	£100,000	£190,000

Profit and loss account for the year

	£	£
Sales		1,003,000
Cost of sales		(910,000)
Operating profit before exchange differences		93,000
Exchange differences		
Trading	7,000	
Loan	(10,000)	
		(3,000)
Operating profit		90,000
Tax		-
Dividends		-
Retained for year		£90,000

Show the gross cash flows (i.e. cash flows under the direct method) from operating activities and other elements of the cash flow statement for the year together with:

(a) reconciliation of operating profit to net cash inflow from operating activities

(b) reconciliation of net cash flow to movement in net debt/funds.

Ignore VAT.

Solution

Cash flow statement for the year

	£	£
Cash received from customers	1,003,000	
Cash payments to suppliers	743,000	
Net cash inflow from operations		260,000
Increase in cash		260,000

Reconciliation of operating profit to net cash inflow from operating activities

	£
Operating profit	90,000
Exchange loss on foreign currency loan	10,000
Increase in creditors	160,000
Net cash inflow from operations	£260,000

Reconciliation of net cash flow to movement in net funds (Note)

	£
Increase in cash for the period	260,000
Exchange difference	(10,000)
Change in net funds	250,000
Net funds at beginning of year (335 – 235)	100,000
Net funds at end of year (595 – 245)	350,000

6.3 Preparation of consolidated cash flow statements involving a foreign subsidiary

Standard accounting practice

- Where a portion of a reporting entity's business is undertaken by a foreign entity, the cash flows of that entity are to be included in the cash flow statement on the basis used for translating the results of those activities in the profit and loss account of the reporting entity.

- The same basis should be used in presenting the movements in stocks, debtors and creditors in the reconciliation between operating profit and cash from operating activities.

- Where intra-group cash flows are separately identifiable and the actual rate of exchange at which they took place is known, that rate, or an approximation thereto, may be used to translate the cash flows in order to ensure that they cancel on consolidation.

The key to the preparation of a group cash flow statement involving a foreign subsidiary is an understanding of the make up of the foreign exchange differences themselves. This make up will vary depending on whether the closing rate/net investment method or the temporal method is used for translating the results of the foreign enterprise.

None of the differences under either method reflects a cash inflow/outflow to the group however. The main concern therefore is to determine the real cash flows particularly if they have to be derived as balancing figures from the opening and closing balance sheets.

If cash balances are partly denominated in a foreign currency, the change in cash will be stated in the cash flow statement before the effect of foreign exchange rate changes. The reconciliation of net cash flow to movement in net debt and the note analysing changes in net debt will therefore show the effect of foreign exchange rate changes.

6.4   Temporal method

Using the temporal method, the exchange difference on translating the statements of the foreign enterprise will relate to the opening net monetary assets of that enterprise (i.e. debtors, creditors, cash and loans). Under the temporal method all exchange differences pass through the profit and loss account.

Example – Temporal method

A gain of £100,000 was made on the translation of the financial statements of an 80% owned foreign subsidiary for the year ended 31 December 20X7. This gain is found to be made up as follows:

	£
Gain on opening net monetary assets	
Debtors	80,000
Cash	70,000
Creditors	(50,000)
	£100,000

A loss of £40,000 was made on the parent company's foreign currency loan.

Consolidated financial statements are as follows:

Balance sheets as at 31 December

	20X7 £'000	20X6 £'000
Fixed assets	1,000	800
Stocks	600	400
Debtors	700	550
Cash	650	420
Creditors	(690)	(500)
Minority interest	(450)	(300)
Long-term loan	(200)	(160)
	1,610	1,210
Share capital	1,000	1,000
Consolidated revenue reserves	610	210
	1,610	1,210

There were no fixed asset disposals during the year.

Profit and loss account for the year ended 31 December 20X7

	£'000
Group profit before tax (after depreciation of £150,000)	2,900
Taxation	(800)
Group profit after tax	2,100
Minority interest	(300)
Profit attributable to members of parent undertaking	1,800
Dividend paid	(1,400)
Retained profit	400

Prepare a cash flow statement for the year ended 31 December 20X7.

Solution

Cash flow statement for the year ended 31 December 20X7

Reconciliation of operating profit to net cash inflow from operating activities

	Either	*Or*
	£'000	£'000
Operating profit	2,900	2,900
Depreciation charges	150	150
Exchange differences on working capital £(80 – 50)	-	(30)
Exchange differences on loan and cash £(70 – 40)	(30)	(30)
Increase in stocks	(200)	(200)
Increase in debtors £(150 – 80)	(150)	(70)
Increase in creditors £(190 – 50)	190	140
Net cash inflow from operating activities	2,860	2,860

Tutorial note: all exchange differences under the temporal method are included in operating profit. None represent a cash flow and thus should be adjusted for. For those items already appearing in the reconciliation statement – debtors and creditors – either the exchange differences are ignored thus allowing the full balance sheet movement to be recorded, or the exchange differences and the 'real' balance sheet movements are shown.

Cash flow statement	£'000
Net cash inflow from operating activities	2,860
Returns on investments and servicing of finance	
Dividends paid to minority interests (W)	(150)
Taxation	
Corporation tax paid	(800)
(no other information given in the example)	
Capital expenditure	
Purchase of fixed assets £(200 + 150)	(350)
Equity dividends paid	(1,400)
Net cash inflow before financing	160
Financing	-
Increase in cash	160

Note

Reconciliation of net cash flow to movement in net funds

	£'000
Increase in cash for the period	160
Exchange differences	30
Change in net funds	190
Net funds at 1 January 20X7	260
Net funds at 31 December 20X7	450

Note

Analysis of changes in net funds

	At 1 Jan 20X7 £'000	Cash flows £'000	Exchange differences £'000	At 31 Dec 20X7 £'000
Cash	420	160	70	650
Long-term loan	(160)		(40)	(200)
Total	260	160	30	450

Working

Minority interest			
	£'000		£'000
Dividend paid (bal fig)	150	Balance b/d	300
Balance c/d	450	P&L charge	300
	600		600

6.5 Closing rate/net investment method

Using the closing rate/net investment method, the exchange difference on translating the statements of the foreign enterprise will relate to the opening net assets of that enterprise (i.e. fixed assets, stocks, debtors, cash, creditors and loans) and also to the difference between the average and the closing rates of exchange on translation of the profit and loss account, if an average rate has been used for translating the profit and loss account.

Under the closing rate/net investment method the group's share of the translation exchange differences will go directly to reserves. If there are foreign currency loans in the books of the parent company the exchange differences on the loan would normally pass through the profit and loss account, unless the parent company takes advantage of the 'cover' concept and offsets these exchange differences against the translation differences in the reserves.

Care needs to be taken in two areas.

- **Analysis of fixed assets** – Fixed assets may require analysis in order to determine cash expenditure. Part of the movement in fixed assets may reflect an exchange gain/loss.

- **Analysis of minority interests** – If minority interests require analysis to determine dividends paid, it must be remembered that they have a share in the exchange gain/loss arising from the translation of the subsidiary's accounts.

Example

A gain of £160,000 was made on the translation of the financial statements of a 75% owned foreign subsidiary for the year ended 31 December 20X7. This gain is found to be made up as follows:

Gain on opening net assets	£
Fixed assets	90,000
Stocks	30,000
Debtors	50,000
Creditors	(40,000)
Cash	30,000
	160,000

A loss of £70,000 was made on the parent company's foreign currency loan and this has been taken to consolidated reserves in accordance with the cover concept of SSAP 20.

Balance sheets as at 31 December

	20X7	20X6
	£'000	£'000
Fixed assets	2,100	1,700
Stocks	650	480
Debtors	990	800
Cash	500	160
Creditors	(870)	(820)
Minority interest	(520)	(370)
Long-term loan	(250)	(180)
	2,600	1,770
Share capital	1,000	1,000
Consolidated revenue reserves	1,600	770
	2,600	1,770

There were no fixed asset disposals during the year.

Profit and loss account for the year ended 31 December 20X7

	£'000
Group profit before tax (after depreciation of £220,000)	2,170
Taxation	(650)
Group profit after tax	1,520
Minority interests	(260)
Profit attributable to members of parent undertaking	1,260
Dividend paid	(480)
Retained profit	780

Prepare a cash flow statement for the year ended 31 December 20X7.

Solution

The first stage is to produce a statement of reserves so as to analyse the movements during the year.

Statement of reserves

	£'000
Reserves brought forward	770
Retained profit	780
Exchange gain £((160,000 × 75%) 120,000 − 70,000)	50
Reserves carried forward	1,600

Cash flow statement for the year ended 31 December 20X7

Reconciliation of operating profit to net cash inflow from operating activities

	£'000
Operating profit	2,170
Depreciation charges	220
Increase in stock £(170 – 30)	(140)
Increase in debtors £(190 – 50)	(140)
Increase in creditors £(50 – 40)	10
Net cash inflow from operating activities	2,120

Tutorial note: since the group's share of all exchange differences goes straight to reserves, there are no foreign exchange adjustments.

Cash flow statement

	£'000
Net cash inflow from operating activities	2,120
Returns on investments and servicing of finance	
Dividends paid to minority interests (W1)	(150)
Taxation	
Corporation tax paid	(650)
(no other information supplied in the example)	
Capital expenditure	
Purchase of fixed assets (W2)	(530)
Equity dividends paid	(480)
Net cash inflow before financing	310
Financing	-
Increase in cash £(340 – 30)	310

Reconciliation of net cash flow to movement in net debt (Note)

	£'000
Increase in cash for the period	310
Exchange differences	(40)
Change in net debt	270
Net debt at 1 January 20X7	(20)
Net funds at 31 December 20X7	250

Note

Analysis of changes in net debt

	At 1 Jan 20X7 £'000	Cash flows £'000	Exchange differences £'000	At 31 Dec 20X7 £'000
Cash	160	310	30	500
Long-term loan	(180)		(70)	(250)
Total	(20)	310	(40)	250

Workings

(W1)

Minority interest

	£'000		£'000
Dividend paid (bal. fig.)	150	Balance b/d	370
Balance c/d	520	P&L charge	260
		Exchange gain ($160 \times 25\%$)	40
	670		670

(W2)

Fixed assets

	£'000		£'000
Balance b/d	1,700	Depreciation	220
Exchange gain	90		
Additions (bal. fig.)	530	Balance c/d	2,100
	2,320		2,320

SELF-TEST QUESTIONS

Cash flow information

1 How useful is the information provided in a cash flow statement? (1.1)

The requirements of FRS 1

2 What are the objectives of FRS 1? (2.1)

3 What are the standard headings required in a cash flow statement? (2.1)

4 What entities are outside the scope of FRS 1? (2.2)

5 Define (a) cash, (b) overdraft and (c) cash flow. (2.3)

6 Distinguish between the direct and the indirect methods for reporting net cash flow from operating activities. (2.5)

Classification of cash flows

7 Where does the net movement on the VAT account normally appear in a cash flow statement? (3.2)

8 Define 'liquid resources'. (3.6)

Net debt and non cash transactions

9 What is net debt? Where should the reconciliation of movements in net debt appear? (4.1)

10 How does FRS 1 require cash payments for HP and leases to be split? (4.4)

11 How do exceptional items affect the cash flow statement? (4.5)

Applying FRS 1 to the preparation of consolidated cash flows

12 How do the presence of (a) minority interests, (b) associates and (c) acquisitions and disposals of subsidiaries affect the group cash flow statement? (5.2, 5.3, 5.4)

Orchard group

Orchard plc is a fruit packaging company operating in the United Kingdom. The company has an 80% interest in a foreign subsidiary that carries on business as a fruit producer. Consolidated accounts are prepared at 31 December each year. All sales are to wholesalers and are on 90 days credit.

A draft consolidated profit and loss account and balance sheet have been prepared for the year ended 31 December 20X0. The directors have requested the accountant to prepare forecast accounts for 20X1 on the assumption that there is to be major capital expenditure on the replacement of the packaging plant in the United Kingdom. Obsolete machinery which cost £690,000 with a book value at 31 December 20X0 of £345,000 is to be sold and new machinery is to be purchased.

The draft consolidated profit and loss accounts and balance sheets for the years ended 31 December 20X0 and 20X1 are as follows:

Consolidated profit and loss accounts

	20X0		20X1	
	£'000	£'000	£'000	£'000
Sales		3,680		4,600
Cost of sales: Material	1,840		2,300	
Labour	690		805	
Expenses	230		345	
		2,760		3,450
		920		1,150
Expenses	460		518	
Depreciation	115		161	
Loss of sale of plant	-		172	
		575		851
		345		299
Other income		55		55
Profit on ordinary activities before tax		400		354
Tax		140		105
Profit on ordinary activities after tax		260		249
Minority interest		45		42
Profit attributable to shareholders		215		207
Dividends		170		200
Profit retained for the financial year		45		7

Consolidated balance sheets

	20X0		20X1	
	£'000	£'000	£'000	£'000
Fixed assets				
Land and buildings		920		920
Plant - at cost	1,150		1,610	
- depreciation	690		506	
		460		1,104

Current assets

Stock	403		576	
Investments	737		804	
Debtors	919		1,145	
Bank	58		(805)	
		2,117		1,720

Current liabilities

Trade creditors	550		681	
Taxation	140		125	
		(690)		(806)
		2,807		2,938

Share capital	1,150	1,150
Consolidated reserves	1,207	1,264
Minority interest	300	344
Long-term loan	150	180
	2,807	2,938

The group uses the closing rate method for translating the financial statements of the foreign subsidiary and the accountant estimated that there would be a gain arising on translating the opening net investment made up as follows:

	£
Plant	60,000
Stocks	20,000
Debtors	42,000
Cash	25,000
Creditors	(47,000)

An estimated loss of £30,000 made on the parent company's foreign currency loan has been charged against the consolidated reserves.

Required:

(a) Prepare a cash flow statement for the Orchard group for the year ended 31 December 20X1 in accordance with FRS 1 (Revised), using the direct method.

(b) Assuming that the profit and loss account has been translated using the average rate and that there is a translation gain of £10,000 arising from the difference between the average and the closing rates, explain how the gain would be dealt with in the cash flow statement for the year ending 31 December 20X1 and its effect on the amounts that have been calculated under (a) above. **(25 marks)**

For the answer to this question see the 'Answers' section at the end of the book.

Hubert Ltd

Cash flow statement for the year ended 30 June 20X3

	£m	£m
Reconciliation of operating profit to net cash inflow from operating activities		
Operating profit (W4)		112
Depreciation (74 – 52)		22
Increase in stocks		(12)
Decrease in debtors		4
Increase in creditors		16
		⎯⎯
		142
		⎯⎯

Cash flow statement

	£m	£m
Net cash inflow from operating activities		142
Returns on investments and servicing of finance:		
Interest paid (40m x 10%)		(4)
Taxation:		
Corporation tax paid (W2)		(24)
Capital expenditure:		
Payments to acquire tangible fixed assets (W1)		(68)
Equity dividends paid (W3)		(26)
		⎯⎯
Net cash outflow before financing		20
Financing:		
Issue of ordinary share capital	6	
Redemption of debentures	(20)	
	⎯⎯	
		(14)
		⎯⎯
Increase in cash		6
		⎯⎯

Workings

1   Fixed assets

Fixed assets at cost

Balance b/f	170		
Purchases (bal. fig.)	68	Balance c/f	238
	⎯⎯		⎯⎯
	238		238
	⎯⎯		⎯⎯

2 Tax paid

Taxation

Tax paid (bal. fig.)	24	Balance b/f	24
Balance c/f	30	P and L account	30
	⎯⎯		⎯⎯
	54		54
	⎯⎯		⎯⎯

3 Dividends

Dividends

Dividends paid (bal. fig.)	26	Balance b/f	26
Balance c/f	34	P and L account	34
	60		60

4 Operating profit

Profit and loss account

Taxation	30	Balance b/f	62
Dividends	34	Profit for the year	108
Balance c/f	106	(bal. fig.)	
	170		170

Profit for the year is after charging interest on debentures of £4m. Therefore operating profit is 108 + 4 = £112m.

FEEDBACK TO
ACTIVITY **2**

Fixed assets – NBV

	£'000		£'000
Balance b/d	10,000	Depreciation charge	2,600
In subsidiary at acquisition	4,800	Disposals	600
Additions (bal. fig.)	4,400	Balance c/d	16,000
	19,200		19,200

Expenditure is £4,400,000

Chapter 10

INTANGIBLE FIXED ASSETS AND IMPAIRMENT

This chapter covers two important accounting standards that deal with fixed assets.

- FRS 11 *Impairment of fixed assets and goodwill*
- FRS 10 *Goodwill and intangible assets.*

You should already be familiar with the main requirements of these standards. At this level, exam questions will cover the more complicated or problematic areas and often ask you to apply the requirements of standards to a practical problem or to respond to a proposed accounting treatment.

Objectives

When you have studied this chapter you should be able to:

- understand the nature of impairment and the impairment review
- apply the impairment review and deal with losses on assets
- account for the amortisation of goodwill and intangible assets including impairment
- explain and apply the provisions of FRS 11.

1 FRS 11 *Impairment of fixed assets and goodwill*

1.1 Impairment

It is accepted practice that a fixed asset should not be carried in financial statements at more than its recoverable amount, but traditionally there was little guidance as to how recoverable amount should be identified or measured.

The Companies Act requires provision to be made for permanent diminutions in the value of fixed assets, but does not include guidance as to:

- what constitutes a permanent (as opposed to a temporary) diminution
- the way in which diminutions should be presented in the financial statements.

SSAP 12 (the predecessor of FRS 15 *Tangible fixed assets*) required that where there was a permanent diminution in value, the asset should be immediately written down to its recoverable amount and then depreciated over its remaining useful economic life. This meant that in most cases the diminution was charged immediately to the profit and loss account and was treated as additional depreciation. However, the issue is more complicated where a fixed asset has been revalued.

Example

An asset costing £100,000 was purchased on 1 January 20X1 and has a useful economic life of 10 years. On 1 January 20X3 it was revalued to £150,000. On 1 January 20X5 it was estimated that the recoverable amount of the asset was only £100,000.

How could this impairment be treated in the financial statements for the year ended 31 December 20X5?

Solution

There are several possibilities. In theory (provided that the asset is not an investment property), the preparers of the financial statements could decide not to recognise the impairment on the grounds that it is temporary, but this would be unlikely to give a true and fair view.

In practice, there are two options.

(a) Treat the impairment as a fall in value.

Dr	Revaluation reserve	£12,500	
	Cr	Fixed assets	£12,500

The impairment is recorded in the statement of total recognised gains and losses, but does not affect the results for the year. This is similar to the treatment of a temporary diminution required by SSAP 19.

(b) Treat the impairment as additional depreciation.

Dr	Depreciation expense	£12,500	
	Cr	Fixed assets	£12,500

This is similar to the treatment of a permanent diminution required by SSAP 19 and results in a charge to the profit and loss account for the year.

From this we can see that this lack of guidance reduced the comparability of financial statements. In addition, impairment losses were not always recognised as soon as they occurred.

The need for guidance on how to calculate and recognise impairment has become more urgent with the issue of recent accounting standards.

KEY POINT

FRS 10 *Goodwill and intangible assets* requires annual impairment reviews where goodwill and intangible assets have a useful life exceeding 20 years.

- FRS 10 *Goodwill and intangible assets* requires annual impairment reviews where goodwill and intangible assets have a useful life exceeding 20 years.

- FRS 15 *Tangible fixed assets* requires annual impairment reviews where:

  - no depreciation charge is made on the grounds that it would be immaterial; or

  - the estimated remaining useful economic life of an asset is more than 50 years.

1.2 Scope

FRS 11 applies to purchased goodwill that is recognised in the balance sheet and all fixed assets except:

- investment properties as defined by SSAP 19

- fixed assets falling within the scope of FRS 13 (e.g. investments)

- an entity's own shares held by an ESOP and shown as a fixed asset in the entity's balance sheet under UITF Abstract 13 *Accounting for ESOP trusts*.

Note that FRS 11 applies to investments in subsidiaries, associates and joint ventures because these are outside the scope of FRS 13.

1.3 The basic principle

Impairment is measured by comparing the carrying value of the asset with its recoverable amount. If the carrying amount exceeds the recoverable amount, the asset is impaired and should be written down. (Note that this effectively abolishes the distinction between temporary and permanent diminutions in value by treating all diminutions as permanent.)

DEFINITIONS

Net realisable value is the amount at which an asset could be disposed of, less any direct selling costs.

Value in use is the present value of the future cash flows obtainable as a result of an asset's continued use, including those resulting from its ultimate disposal.

ACTIVITY 1

The following information relates to three assets.

	A £'000	B £'000	C £'000
Net book value	100	150	120
Net realisable value	110	125	100
Value in use	120	130	90

(a) What is the recoverable amount of each asset?

(b) Calculate the impairment provision for each of the three assets.

Feedback to this activity is at the end of the chapter.

1.4 When to carry out an impairment review

Impairment reviews should be carried out if:

(a) events or changes in circumstances indicate that the carrying amount of an asset may not be recoverable; or

(b) when required by FRS 10 or by FRS 15.

They are not required otherwise.

Indications that assets may have become impaired include:

- a current period operating loss in the business in which the fixed asset or goodwill is involved or a net cash outflow from the operating activities of the business, combined with either past or expected future operating losses or net cash outflows from operating activities

- a significant decline in a fixed asset's market value during the period

- evidence of obsolescence or physical damage to the fixed asset

- a significant adverse change in the business or the market in which the fixed asset or goodwill is involved (e.g. the entrance of a major competitor)

- a commitment by management to undertake a significant re-organisation

- a major loss of key employees

- a significant increase in market interest rates or other market rates of return that are likely to affect materially the fixed asset's recoverable amount.

1.5   Net realisable value

The net realisable value of an asset that is traded on an active market should be based on market value.

Net realisable value is the amount at which an asset could be disposed of, less any direct selling costs. Direct selling costs might include:

- legal costs
- stamp duty
- costs relating to the removal of a sitting tenant (in the case of a building).

Redundancy and reorganisation costs (e.g. following the sale of a business) are not direct selling costs.

1.6   Value in use

Value in use is the present value of the future cash flows obtainable as a result of an asset's continued use.

Therefore there are two steps to the calculation.

1   Estimate future cash flows.

2   Discount them to arrive at their present value.

Where possible, value in use should be estimated for individual assets. However, it may not always be possible to identify cash flows arising from individual fixed assets. If this is the case, value in use is calculated for income generating units (groups of assets that produce independent income streams).

Future cash flows should normally be estimated for individual fixed assets or income generating units in their current condition. They should not include future cash outflows or future capital expenditure (for example, the cost of future reorganisations). The exception to this rule is when a newly acquired income generating unit, such as a subsidiary, is being reviewed for impairment. In these cases, the cost of the asset (the purchase price) reflects the fact that the acquirer may have to bear the cost of future capital expenditure or future reorganisations. Therefore planned future expenditure may be taken into account up to the end of the first full year after acquisition.

The discount rate

The discount rate used to arrive at the present value of the expected future cash flows should be the rate of return that the market would expect from an equally risky investment. It should exclude the effects of any risk for which the cash flows have been adjusted and should be calculated on a pre-tax basis.

In practice, the discount rate can be estimated using:

- the rate implicit in market transactions of similar assets
- the current weighted average cost of capital of a listed company whose cash flows have similar risk profiles to those of the income generating unit; or
- the weighted average cost of capital for the entity but only if adjusted for the particular risks associated with the income generating unit.

DEFINITION

An **income generating unit** is a group of assets, liabilities and associated goodwill that generates income that is largely independent of the reporting entity's other income streams. The assets and liabilities include those directly involved in generating the income and an appropriate portion of those used to generate more than one income stream.

1.7   Income generating units

It may not be possible to estimate the value in use for individual fixed assets. If this is the case, it is necessary to base the calculation on income generating units.

Income generating units are identified by dividing the total income of the entity into as many largely independent income streams as is reasonably practicable.

Income generating units should be as small as is reasonably practicable, but the income stream underlying the future cash flows of the unit should be largely independent of other income streams of the entity and should be capable of being monitored separately.

Where there are a large number of small income generating units, it may be appropriate to consider groups of units together.

Example

An entity has a chain of restaurants, each of which is an individual income generating unit. Impairment of individual restaurants is unlikely to be material, but a material impairment may occur if a number of restaurants are affected together by the same economic factors.

In practice, income streams can often be identified by reference to major products or services and unique intangible assets that generate income independently of each other, such as brands.

1.8   Allocating assets and liabilities to income generating units

Each of the identifiable assets and liabilities of the entity, excluding deferred tax balances, interest bearing debt, dividends payable and other items relating wholly to financing, are allocated to an income generating unit.

Central assets

Central assets (for example, assets used by the head office) may have to be apportioned across the units on a logical and systematic basis.

Example

An entity has three independent income streams. The net assets of the income streams are as follows:

A	£500,000
B	£750,000
C	£1,000,000

In addition, there are head office net assets whose carrying amount totals £90,000. The income streams use head office resources in the proportion 2:3:4.

The income generating units are as follows:

	A £'000	B £'000	C £'000	Total £'000
Net assets directly attributable to income generating unit	500	750	1,000	2,250
Head office net assets	20	30	40	90
Total	520	780	1,040	2,340

If there were an indication that a fixed asset in unit A was impaired, the recoverable amount of A would be compared with £520,000, rather than £500,000. The cash flows upon which the value in use of A is based should include the relevant portion of any cash outflows arising from central overheads.

Alternative approach to central assets

If it is not possible to apportion central assets meaningfully between income generating units, they may be excluded. If this approach is followed, an additional impairment review must be performed on the excluded central assets. In the example above, if the head office assets were not apportioned between units A, B and C, two separate impairment reviews would be necessary. The recoverable amounts of the individual units would be compared with the carrying amounts of £500,000, £750,000 and £1,000,000 respectively. The recoverable amount of the whole entity would then be compared with its total carrying value of £2,340,000.

Goodwill

Capitalised goodwill should be apportioned between income generating units in the same way as other assets. In practice, where several similar income generating units have been acquired as part of the same investment and are involved in similar parts of the business these may be combined to assess the recoverability of the goodwill.

Example

An entity acquires a business comprising three income generating units, D, E and F. After three years the carrying amount and the value in use of the net assets in the income generating units and the purchased goodwill are as follows:

	D £'000	E £'000	F £'000	Goodwill £'000	Total £'000
Carrying amount	240	360	420	150	1,170
Value in use	300	420	360		1,080

No reliable estimates of net realisable value are available.

An impairment loss of £60,000 is recognised on unit F. This reduces its carrying amount to £360,000 and the total carrying amount to £1,110,000 (1,170,000 – 60,000). A further impairment loss of £30,000 must then be recognised in respect of the goodwill (1,110,000 – 1,080,000).

1.9 Allocating impairment losses

Impairment losses may arise in relation to income generating units, rather than individual assets. Sometimes it may be obvious that specific assets are impaired (for example, they may be known to be damaged or obsolete). Otherwise, the loss is allocated to the assets in the income generating unit in the following order:

1   goodwill

2   other intangible assets

3   tangible assets (on a pro-rata or more appropriate basis).

This means that the loss is allocated to assets with the most subjective valuations first.

No intangible asset with a readily ascertainable market value should be written down below its net realisable value.

No tangible asset with a net realisable value that can be measured reliably should be written down below its net realisable value.

ACTIVITY 2

An impairment loss of £60,000 arises in connection with an income generating unit. The carrying amount of the assets in the income generating unit, before the impairment, is as follows:

	£'000
Goodwill	20
Patent (with no market value)	10
Tangible fixed assets	40
	——
	70
	——

How would the impairment loss be allocated?

Feedback to this activity is at the end of the chapter.

1.10 Allocation where acquired businesses are merged with existing operations

When an acquired business is merged with an existing business, this may result in an income generating unit that contains both purchased and (unrecognised) internally generated goodwill. In this case, the impairment loss should be allocated as follows.

(a) Estimate the value of the internally generated goodwill of the existing business at the date of merger and add it to the carrying amount of the income generating unit.

(b) Allocate any impairment arising on merging the businesses solely to purchased goodwill within the newly acquired business.

(c) Allocate subsequent impairments pro-rata between the goodwill of the acquired business and that of the existing business.

(d) The impairment allocated to the existing business should be allocated first to the (notional) internally generated goodwill.

(e) Only the impairments allocated to purchased goodwill (and, if necessary, to any other assets) should be charged in the profit and loss account.

Example

An entity has net assets with a carrying amount of £210,000. Value in use has been calculated as £240,000. Several years earlier, the entity had acquired another business. The carrying amount of the purchased goodwill arising on this acquisition is now £20,000. At the time of the acquisition, the original business had internally generated goodwill of £100,000.

Solution

Step 1

Calculate the impairment loss

	£'000
Carrying amount of net assets	210
Carrying amount of purchased goodwill	20
Notional carrying amount of internally generated goodwill	100
	——
	330
Less: value in use	(240)
	——
Impairment loss	90
	——

Step 2

Allocate the loss

	Before impairment £'000	Loss £'000	After impairment £'000
Net assets	210		210
Purchased goodwill	20	(15)	5
Internally generated goodwill	100	(75)	25
	330	(90)	240

The impairment loss of £15,000 relating to purchased goodwill is recognised in the profit and loss account. The loss on internally generated goodwill does not affect the financial statements.

1.11 Subsequent monitoring of cash flows

For the five years following each impairment review where the recoverable amount has been based on value in use, the cash flows achieved should be compared with those forecast. If the actual cash flows are so much less than those forecast that use of the actual cash flows could have required recognition of an impairment in previous periods, the calculation should be re-performed using actual cash flows. Any impairment identified should be recognised in the current period.

1.12 Recognising impairment losses in the financial statements

- **Assets carried at historic cost** – Impairment losses are recognised in the profit and loss account. The impairment is effectively treated as additional depreciation.

- **Assets which have been revalued** – Impairment losses are normally recognised in the statement of total recognised gains and losses until the carrying value of the asset falls below depreciated historical cost. Impairments below depreciated historical cost are recognised in the profit and loss account. The impairment is treated as a downward revaluation.

  Where a fixed asset has been revalued but the impairment is caused by a clear consumption of economic benefits (e.g. because it is damaged) the loss is recognised in the profit and loss account. This type of impairment is treated as additional depreciation, rather than as a loss in value.

A C T I V I T Y   3

At 1 January 20X7 a fixed asset had a carrying value of £20,000, based on its revalued amount, and a depreciated historical cost of £10,000. An impairment loss of £12,000 arose in the year ended 31 December 20X7.

How should this loss be reported in the financial statements for the year ended 31 December 20X7?

Feedback to this activity is at the end of the chapter.

1.13 Reversal of past impairments

After an impairment loss has been recognised, it may reverse. The reversal can only be recognised under certain conditions.

- **Tangible fixed assets and investments in subsidiaries, associates and joint ventures**

  The reversal of past impairment losses should be recognised only when the recoverable amount has increased because of a change in economic conditions or in the expected use of the asset.

The reversal should be recognised in the current period's profit and loss account, unless it arises on a previously revalued fixed asset, in which case the reversal should be credited to the revaluation reserve and shown in the statement of total recognised gains and losses.

- **Goodwill and intangible assets**

  The reversal of an impairment loss should be recognised in the current period, if and only if:

  (i) the original loss was caused by an external event and subsequent external events clearly and demonstrably reverse the effects of that event in a way that was not foreseen in the original impairment calculations; or

  (ii) the loss related to an intangible asset with a readily ascertainable market value and this has increased to above the intangible asset's impaired carrying amount.

  In all cases, the reversal of the loss should be recognised to the extent that it increases the carrying amount of the asset up to the amount that it would have been had the original impairment not occurred.

ACTIVITY 4

An impairment loss of £40 million has arisen in connection with an income generating unit and has been allocated to the net assets in the unit as follows:

	Before impairment £m	Loss £m	After impairment £m
Goodwill	20	(20)	–
Patent (with no market value)	10	(10)	–
Tangible fixed assets	40	(10)	30
	70	(40)	30

The original loss arose because the product made by the entity had been overtaken by a technologically more advanced model produced by a competitor. Three years later, the entity develops a technologically more advanced product of its own and the recoverable amount of the income generating unit increases to £45 million. The carrying amount of the tangible fixed assets would have been £35 million had the impairment not occurred.

How is the reversal of the impairment loss recognised in the financial statements?

Feedback to this activity is at the end of the chapter.

1.14 Presentation and disclosure

KEY POINT

Impairment losses are normally recognised in the statement of total recognised gains and losses if the asset has been revalued and the impairment is not due to a consumption of economic benefits. Otherwise impairment losses are recognised in the profit and loss account.

Impairment losses recognised in the profit and loss account should be included within operating profit under the appropriate statutory heading. They should be disclosed as an exceptional item if appropriate.

Impairment losses recognised in the statement of total recognised gains and losses should be disclosed separately on the face of that statement.

In the notes to the financial statements in the accounting periods after the impairment, the impairment loss should be treated as follows.

(a) For assets held on a historical cost basis, the impairment loss should be included within cumulative depreciation: the cost of the asset should not be reduced.

(b) For revalued assets held at a market value, the impairment loss should be included within the revalued carrying amount.

(c) For revalued assets held at depreciated replacement cost, an impairment loss charged to the profit and loss account should be included within cumulative depreciation: the carrying amount of the asset should not be reduced. An impairment loss charged to the statement of total recognised gains and losses should be deducted from the carrying amount of the asset.

Other required disclosures include:

(a) the discount rate applied (where the impairment loss is based on value in use)

(b) the reason for any reversal of an impairment loss recognised in a previous period, including any changes in the assumptions upon which the calculation of recoverable amount is based.

1.15 FRS 11 in practice

Most preparers and users of financial statements support the general principles of FRS 11. In particular, the recoverable amount test means that there is no need to judge whether a diminution is permanent or temporary. Users of financial statements are made aware of losses which otherwise might not have been recognised on the grounds that they were 'temporary'.

Impairment reviews may be complex, time consuming and subjective, as they involve forecasting future cash flows. However, the ASB believes that in practice they are likely to be comparatively rare for tangible fixed assets as they are only required if there is some indication of impairment. Where impairment reviews are required, it will only be necessary to calculate value in use if net realisable value is lower than the carrying amount. The impairment review procedures were satisfactorily field tested by selected large companies as part of the development of the FRS.

However, FRS 11 has been criticised on the following grounds.

*   Impairments are classified as additional depreciation or as downward revaluations depending on their cause. This determines whether they are taken to the profit and loss account or to the statement of total recognised gains and losses. In practice, this distinction is likely to be extremely subjective.

*   The allocation of assets and liabilities to income generating units is also bound to be subjective.

*   Impairment must be assessed by reference to discounted cash flow. This implies that assets must be included in the balance sheet at amounts that are expected to earn at least a satisfactory rate of return. Some commentators have suggested that even profitable companies may have to write down their assets if they earn a poor rate of return, which seems illogical.

*   There are inconsistencies with FRS 12 *Provisions, contingent liabilities and contingent assets* (discussed in a later chapter). FRS 12 prohibits the setting up of provisions for future losses (unless these are specifically required by another accounting standard). FRS 11 requires that future cash flows should be taken into account in calculating value in use. This means that projected future losses may be reflected in asset values.

*   Some critics of the ASB believe that in practice impairment reviews will need to be far more common than it has suggested.

2   Problems of accounting for goodwill and intangible assets

2.1   Nature of goodwill

There is an important distinction between purchased goodwill and non-purchased goodwill (sometimes called inherent goodwill or internally generated goodwill).

Purchased goodwill arises as a result of a purchase transaction (e.g. when one business acquires another as a going concern). The term therefore includes goodwill arising on the inclusion of a subsidiary or associate in the consolidated accounts. Purchased goodwill will be recognised within the accounts because at a specific point in time the fact of purchase has established a figure of value for the business as a whole which can be compared with the fair value of the individual net assets acquired, and this figure will be incorporated in the accounts of the acquiring company as the cost of the acquisition.

Non-purchased, or **inherent goodwill** is any other goodwill. It will not be recognised in the accounts because no event has occurred to identify the value of the business as a whole.

Goodwill has been described as an accounting anomaly. Purchased goodwill arises from a distinct transaction and must be accounted for, yet each method of accounting for it results in inconsistencies with other aspects of financial reporting. No single method is universally accepted as being the correct one.

2.2   The effect of alternative treatments on performance ratios

Under SSAP 22 (which preceded FRS 10) purchased goodwill could be treated in one of two ways. The alternatives were immediate write off against reserves (therefore removing the asset from the balance sheet but no effect on earnings) and amortisation (therefore leaving the NBV of the asset on the balance sheet and reducing earnings).

- **Earnings per share** – Amortisation charges decrease the earnings per share.

  Thus EPS will be lower if a policy of amortisation is adopted rather than a policy of immediate write off.

- **Return on capital employed** – Write off of purchased goodwill reduces capital employed and thus the return on capital employed is higher than when the goodwill is capitalised.

  This effect is made more marked by amortisation charges reducing the return.

- **Net assets per share** – Net assets per share decreases when goodwill is written off directly to reserves. The ratio can be used as an indication of the extent to which the asset base supports the value of the shares. The goodwill write off can thus cause a misleading impression as the goodwill itself has not fallen in value.

Investment analysts normally overcame the lack of comparability between entities in the past by removing the effects of goodwill from the accounts, i.e. applying the preferred approach of SSAP 22 in all circumstances and eliminating goodwill in full.

2.3   Intangible assets

Intangible assets may comprise brands, patents, licences, publishing titles, franchises, quotas and other types of asset. Some intangible assets, such as brands, are very similar in nature to goodwill, so that it can be difficult to distinguish between them. The important difference between goodwill and intangible assets is that an identifiable intangible asset can be disposed of separately without disposing of the business of the entity. If this is not the case, it is effectively part of goodwill.

The term 'brand' is difficult to define precisely. The constituents of a brand include a recognised name, a product or range of products, an established operation and market position, marketing and other specialist know-how, and trading connections.

It is a wider term than 'trade name' as if a brand is purchased, the acquisition often involves the acquisition of many of the supporting functions which make the brands produce profits.

Thus a brand is a combination of factors expected to produce enhanced earnings just like goodwill. This analysis is further supported by the fact that brands and goodwill are both commonly valued using earnings multiples.

The accounting treatment of intangible assets has been the subject of controversy in recent years. To understand the problem it is necessary to consider the context which gave rise to it.

(a) Some companies, following an acquisition, assigned fair values to intangible assets of various types rather than to goodwill.

Companies who made such a classification avoided having to apply the treatment required for accounting for goodwill to the assets thus identified. Until the issue of FRS 10 in 1997 there was no accounting standard dealing with intangible assets other than development expenditure and so intangible assets could be carried forward in the balance sheet indefinitely without mandatory review.

(b) There was the possibility that it would become widespread practice to incorporate similar assets in the balance sheet by revaluation rather than by acquisition.

The balance sheet would thus include 'home-grown' intangibles as well as those which had been acquired at a known cost or an assigned fair value.

ACTIVITY 5

A case can be made for putting brands on to the balance sheet to disclose to shareholders and others the true value of the assets in the business.

What are the arguments for and against including a value for brand names in the balance sheet?

Feedback to this activity is at the end of the chapter.

2.4 The Companies Act requirements relating to intangible fixed assets

Company law has special provisions relating to development expenditure (see later) and goodwill.

KEY POINT

The CA85 states that only goodwill which was purchased (rather than internally generated) may be carried as an asset.

The amount of goodwill carried in the balance sheet is subject to special restrictive rules. Only goodwill which was purchased (rather than internally generated) may be carried as an asset. Goodwill cannot be restated under the alternative accounting rules.

As goodwill comes within the heading of fixed assets, it must be written off through the profit and loss account over its useful economic life. In addition the period over which it has been written off and the reasons for choosing that period must be disclosed in a note to the accounts.

3 FRS 10 *Goodwill and intangible assets*

3.1 Why FRS 10 was necessary

FRS 10 was issued in 1997 to replace SSAP 22 *Accounting for goodwill*. Most commentators regarded SSAP 22 as unsatisfactory because it permitted a choice between two different accounting treatments. Entities chose the accounting treatment which gave the most favourable view of earnings and net assets. The preferred alternative, immediate elimination against reserves, was criticised for two main reasons.

- It gave the impression that the acquirer's net worth had been depleted or eliminated.

- The financial statements overstated the rate of return on acquired investments.

In addition, there was clearly a need for an accounting standard which dealt with other intangible fixed assets. The similarities between goodwill and certain intangible assets such as brand names made it appropriate to consider the two together.

3.2 Objective

The objective of FRS 10 is to ensure that:

- capitalised goodwill and intangible assets are charged in the profit and loss account in the periods in which they are depleted

- sufficient information is disclosed in the financial statements to enable users to determine the impact of goodwill and intangible assets on the financial position and performance of the reporting entity.

Note that the FRS applies to all intangible assets with the exception of:

- oil and gas exploration and development costs

- research and development costs (already covered by SSAP 13)

- any other intangible assets that are specifically addressed by another accounting standard.

3.3 Goodwill

- Positive purchased goodwill should be capitalised and classified as an intangible fixed asset on the balance sheet.

- Internally generated goodwill should not be capitalised.

3.4 Other intangible assets

- An intangible asset purchased separately from a business should be capitalised at its cost.

  Examples of assets which might be purchased separately from a business include copyrights, patents and licences.

- An intangible asset acquired as part of the acquisition of a business should be capitalised separately from goodwill if its value can be measured reliably on initial recognition. It should initially be recorded at its fair value.

- If its value cannot be measured reliably, an intangible asset purchased as part of the acquisition of a business should be subsumed within the amount of the purchase price attributable to goodwill.

  Most purchased brand names are likely to be subsumed within goodwill, but the ASB has not specifically prohibited their recognition.

- An internally developed intangible asset may be capitalised only if it has a readily ascertainable market value.

In practice, very few internally generated intangibles have a readily ascertainable market value. The ASB does not believe that it is possible to determine a market value for unique intangible assets such as brands and publishing titles and so the recognition of internally generated brand names is effectively prohibited.

This treatment of internally generated intangible assets is consistent with the treatment of internally generated goodwill. If it is accepted that internally generated goodwill is never recognised because it cannot be valued objectively, it follows that internally generated brand names should not be recognised either.

A C T I V I T Y   **6**

How should the following intangible assets be treated in the financial statements?

(a) A publishing title acquired as part of a subsidiary company.

(b) A licence to market a new product.

Feedback to this activity is at the end of the chapter.

3.5   Amortisation

Once they have been recognised, FRS 10 requires that intangible assets are treated in exactly the same way as goodwill. There are two reasons for this.

- Even if assets such as brand names are not part of goodwill, they are so similar to goodwill that they should be accounted for in the same way.

- If intangibles must be treated in the same way as goodwill, there is no longer any advantage in separately recognising brand names and similar assets.

Standard accounting practice

- Where goodwill and intangible assets are regarded as having limited useful economic lives, they should be amortised on a systematic basis over those lives.

- There is a rebuttable presumption that the useful economic lives of purchased goodwill and intangible assets are limited to 20 years or less.

- Where access to the economic benefits associated with an intangible asset is achieved through legal rights that have been granted for a finite period, the economic life of the asset may extend beyond that period only if the legal rights are renewable and renewal is assured.

- A residual value may be assigned to an intangible asset only if the residual value can be measured reliably. No residual value may be assigned to goodwill.

- The straight line method of amortisation should normally be used unless another method can be demonstrated to be more appropriate.

- The useful economic lives of goodwill and intangible assets should be reviewed at the end of each reporting period and revised if necessary.

- If a useful economic life is revised, the carrying value of the goodwill or intangible asset at the date of revision should be amortised over the remaining useful economic life.

3.6   Where useful economic life is longer than 20 years

In most cases, goodwill and intangible assets will be amortised over a period of less than 20 years. However, FRS 10 does recognise that they may occasionally have longer useful economic lives or that their lives may even be indefinite.

A useful economic life may be regarded as longer than 20 years or indefinite if:

- the durability of the acquired business or intangible asset can be demonstrated and justifies estimating the useful economic life to exceed 20 years; and

- the goodwill or intangible asset is capable of continued measurement (so that annual impairment reviews will be feasible).

Where goodwill and intangible assets are regarded as having indefinite useful economic lives, they should not be amortised.

Note that the Companies Acts do not allow purchased goodwill or intangible assets to be carried indefinitely as assets in the balance sheet. If goodwill and intangible assets are not amortised it will be necessary to make the additional disclosures required by FRS 18 *Accounting policies*, as the 'true and fair view override' will be invoked.

KEY POINT

There is a rebuttable presumption that the useful economic lives of purchased goodwill and intangible assets are limited to 20 years or less.

KEY POINT

Where goodwill and intangible assets are regarded as having indefinite useful economic lives, they should not be amortised.

3.7   Impairment reviews

Impairment reviews are required as follows:

(a) **Where goodwill and intangible assets are amortised over 20 years or less**

- at the end of the first full financial year following the acquisition

- in other periods if events or changes in circumstances indicate that the carrying value may not be recoverable.

(b) **Where goodwill and intangible assets are amortised over more than 20 years**

- impairment reviews are required at the end of each reporting period.

If the review indicates that there has been a diminution in value, the goodwill and intangible assets must be written down accordingly. The revised carrying value should be amortised over the current estimate of the remaining useful economic life (unless the asset is not being amortised because it has an indefinite life). This is similar to the treatment of tangible fixed assets where there has been an impairment in value.

Impairment reviews should be carried out in accordance with the requirements of FRS 11 *Impairment of fixed assets and goodwill*.

3.8   Revaluation and restoration of past losses

Goodwill and intangible assets should not be revalued, either to increase the carrying value above original cost or to reverse prior period losses arising from impairment or amortisation, unless:

- the asset has a readily ascertainable market value; or

- an impairment loss was caused by an external event (e.g. a change in economic conditions) and subsequent external events clearly and demonstrably reverse the loss in a way that was not foreseen in the original impairment calculations. (If the recoverable amount is increased above the asset's carrying value, the increase must be recognised in the current period.)

If one intangible asset is revalued, all assets of the same class should be revalued. Once an intangible asset has been revalued, further revaluations should be performed regularly.

The amortisation charge for revalued assets should be based on the revalued amount and the remaining useful economic lives (as for tangible fixed assets).

3.9   Negative goodwill

- Negative goodwill should be recognised and separately disclosed on the face of the balance sheet, immediately below the goodwill heading and followed by a subtotal showing the net amount of the positive and negative goodwill.

- Negative goodwill up to the fair values of the non-monetary assets (fixed assets and stocks) acquired should be recognised in the profit and loss account in the periods in which the non-monetary assets are recovered, whether through depreciation or sale.

- Any negative goodwill in excess of the fair values of the non-monetary assets acquired should be recognised in the profit and loss account in the periods expected to be benefited.

Negative goodwill is not expected to arise frequently.

ACTIVITY **7**

On 1 January 20X6 A plc acquires the whole of the share capital of B Ltd for £100,000. The summarised net assets of B Ltd at the date of acquisition are as follows:

	£
Fixed assets (depreciated over 5 years)	130,000
Stocks	30,000
Other current assets	10,000
Current liabilities	(20,000)
	150,000

What is the credit to the profit and loss account for negative goodwill for the year ended 31 December 20X6?

Feedback to this activity is at the end of the chapter.

3.10 Disclosures

Recognition and measurement

(a) Describe the method used to value intangible assets.

(b) Disclose the following information separately for positive goodwill, negative goodwill and each class of intangible asset included on the balance sheet.

   (i)   cost or revalued amount at the beginning of the financial period and at the balance sheet date

   (ii) the cumulative amount of provisions for amortisation and impairment at the beginning of the financial period and at the balance sheet date

   (iii) a reconciliation of the movements

   (iv) the net carrying amount at the balance sheet date.

(c) The profit and loss on each material disposal of a previously acquired business or business segment.

Amortisation

Disclose the following:

(a) methods and periods of amortisation of goodwill and intangible assets and the reasons for choosing those periods

(b) details of changes in amortisation period or method

(c) grounds for amortising goodwill or intangible assets over a period that exceeds 20 years (if applicable).

Revaluation

Where assets have been revalued, disclose:

(a) the year in which the assets were valued, the values and the bases of valuation

(b) the original cost or fair value and the amount of any provision for amortisation that would have been recognised if the assets had been valued at their original cost or fair value

(c) the name and qualifications of the valuer (where the revaluation has taken place during the year).

Negative goodwill

(a) Disclose the periods in which negative goodwill is being written back in the profit and loss account.

(b) Where negative goodwill exceeds the fair values of the non-monetary assets acquired, the amount and source of the 'excess' negative goodwill and the periods in which it is being written back should be explained.

FRS 6 *Acquisitions and mergers* requires the following additional disclosures.

(a) A table should be provided showing, for each class of assets and liabilities of the acquired entity:

    (i)   the book values, as recorded in the acquired entity's books immediately before the acquisition and before any fair value adjustments

    (ii)   the fair value adjustments, analysed into

- revaluations
- adjustments to achieve consistency of accounting policies
- any other significant adjustments

       giving the reasons for the adjustments

    (iii) the fair values at the date of acquisition.

The table should include a statement of the amount of purchased goodwill or negative goodwill arising on the acquisition.

(b) Where the fair values of the identifiable assets or liabilities, or the purchase consideration, can be determined only on a provisional basis at the end of the accounting period in which the acquisition took place, this should be stated and the reasons given. Any subsequent material adjustments to such provisional fair values, with corresponding adjustments to goodwill, should be disclosed and explained.

4   Evaluation of FRS 10

4.1   Introduction

The issue of FRS 10 followed years of heated debate. Many people believed that the ASB would be unable to produce an accounting standard which would gain the support of preparers and users of accounts.

In order to attempt to obtain a consensus, the ASB discussed its proposals with interested parties at a series of public meetings. In addition, some large companies tested the proposed accounting treatments, including the impairment review procedures. Perhaps because of these attempts, FRS 10 turned out to be cautiously welcomed.

4.2   Advantages

- FRS 10 recognises that purchased goodwill is neither an identifiable asset nor an immediate loss in value.

- In theory, goodwill can be carried forward indefinitely. It can be argued that this approach reflects economic reality. Entities can avoid an amortisation charge to the profit and loss account by carrying out impairment reviews.

- FRS 10 recognises that there are many different types of intangible asset with different characteristics. Some of these can be measured reliably and are clearly separable from goodwill.

- There is consistency between the treatment of goodwill and other intangible assets.

- The introduction of an accounting standard dealing with intangibles will reduce the scope for creative accounting. Entities will not be able to recognise internally generated intangibles.

4.3   Criticisms

- Only for large public companies will the benefit of maintaining goodwill on the balance sheet outweigh the costs and practical problems of carrying out annual impairment reviews. Smaller companies will almost certainly amortise goodwill. The ultimate success of the standard may depend on the effectiveness of the impairment review procedures if they are widely applied.

- The tests for impairment are subjective and might provide entities with scope for creative accounting.

- It may be difficult to compare the financial statements of entities which amortise goodwill and intangibles and those which carry out impairment tests.

- Where entities opt to carry out impairment tests, earnings may be volatile.

- The treatment of negative goodwill has been criticised in that it effectively creates a 'dangling credit' in the balance sheet. The 'amortisation' of negative goodwill may also be complicated to apply in practice.

5   UITF Abstract 27 *Revision to estimates of the useful economic life of goodwill and intangible assets*

5.1   The issue

FRS 10 requires the useful economic lives of goodwill and intangible assets to be reviewed at the end of each reporting period and revised if necessary. If a useful economic life is revised, the carrying value should be amortised over the remaining useful economic life.

An entity may rebut the presumption that goodwill or an intangible asset has a useful economic life of 20 years or less because there is evidence that it has an indefinite life. In a subsequent period, it may decide that this is no longer the case. This means that there is a change from non-amortisation to amortisation over less than 20 years.

Should the change be treated as a change in accounting policy (resulting in a prior period adjustment) or as a change in useful economic life (with amortisation over the remaining useful economic life)?

5.2   UITF Consensus

- Where estimates of the useful economic lives of goodwill or intangible assets are revised, the carrying value should be amortised over the revised remaining useful economic life, as required by FRS 10.

- This applies equally where the presumption of a 20 year life has been rebutted, as it does to other revisions of estimates of the useful economic life of goodwill and intangible assets.

6   IFRS 3 *Business combinations*

The convergence programme will see the eventual adoption of the requirements of IFRS 3 into UK accounting. The effects on goodwill arising on consolidation will be as follows.

Positive goodwill will be capitalised and held in the balance sheet forever, subject to an annual impairment review.

If **negative goodwill** arises, then first of all the fair values of the net assets acquired should be reviewed to ensure that there have been no mistakes. If there is still negative goodwill then it should be credited to the profit and loss account immediately.

SELF-TEST
QUESTIONS

FRS 11 *Impairment of fixed assets and goodwill*

1   Define impairment. (1.1)

2   To which types of goodwill and fixed assets does FRS 11 apply? (1.2)

3   Define (a) recoverable amount, (b) net realisable value and (c) value in use. (1.3)

4   List four factors that indicate that assets may have become impaired. (1.4)

5   What discount rate should be used to arrive at the present value of the expected future cash flows of an investment? (1.6)

6   When is an income generating unit used in estimating value in use? (1.7)

7   Where in the financial statements are impairment losses recognised for (a) assets carried at historic cost, (b) assets which have been revalued? (1.12)

Problems of accounting for goodwill and intangible assets

8   Define (a) purchased goodwill, (b) identifiable assets and liabilities. (2.1)

FRS 10 *Goodwill and intangible assets*

9   What is the objective of FRS 10? Which intangible assets are excepted from FRS 10? (3.2)

10   Under FRS 10, how should purchased goodwill be accounted for? (3.3)

11   What method should be used to amortise goodwill and intangible assets, and over what periods? (3.5)

12   When does FRS 10 require impairment reviews to be carried out? (3.7)

13   Under what limited circumstances can goodwill be revalued? (3.8)

14   How is negative goodwill accounted for? (3.9)

Evaluation of FRS 10

15   State the merits and the weaknesses of FRS 10. (4.2, 4.3)

Invest plc

FRS 10 *Goodwill and intangible assets* was issued in December 1997. At the same time, SSAP 22, the previous Accounting Standard which dealt with accounting for goodwill, was withdrawn. SSAP 22 allowed purchased goodwill to be written off directly to reserves as one amount in the accounting period of purchase. FRS 10 does not permit this treatment.

Invest plc has a number of subsidiaries. The accounting date of Invest plc and all its subsidiaries is 30 April. On 1 May 20X8, Invest plc purchased 80% of the issued equity shares of Target Ltd. This purchase made Target Ltd a subsidiary of Invest plc from May 20X8. Invest plc made a cash payment of £31 million for the shares in Target Ltd. On 1 May 20X8, the net assets which were included in the balance sheet of Target Ltd had a fair value to Invest plc of £30 million. Target Ltd sells a well-known branded product and has taken steps to protect itself legally against unauthorised use of the brand name. A reliable estimate of the value of this brand to the Invest group is £3 million. It is further considered that the value of the brand can be maintained or even increased for the foreseeable future. The value of the brand is not included in the balance sheet of Target Ltd.

For the purposes of preparing the consolidated financial statements, the Directors of Invest plc wish to ensure that the charge to the profit and loss account for the amortisation of intangible assets is kept to a minimum. They estimate that the useful economic life of the purchased goodwill (or premium on acquisition) of Target Ltd is 40 years.

Required:

(a) Outline the key factors which lay behind the decision of the Accounting Standards Board to prohibit the write off of purchased goodwill to reserves.

(11 marks)

(b) Compute the charge to the consolidated profit and loss account in respect of the goodwill on the acquisition of Target Ltd for its year ended 30 April 20X9.

(5 marks)

(c) Explain the action which Invest plc must take in 20X8/X9 and in future years arising from the chosen accounting treatment of the goodwill on acquisition of Target Ltd.

(4 marks)

(Total: 20 marks)

For the answer to this question see the 'Answers' section at the end of the book.

(a) A: £120,000, B: £130,000, C: £100,000

(b) A: Nil, B: £20,000, C: £20,000

The impairment loss is allocated as follows:

	Before impairment £'000	Loss £'000	After impairment £'000
Goodwill	20	(20)	–
Patent (with no market value)	10	(10)	–
Tangible fixed assets	40	(30)	10
	70	(60)	10

FEEDBACK TO ACTIVITY 3	Assuming that the loss is not a reduction in the service potential of the asset, a loss of £10,000 will be recognised in the statement of total recognised gains and losses and the remaining loss of £2,000 will be recognised in the profit and loss account.

FEEDBACK TO ACTIVITY 4	The carrying amount of the tangible fixed assets is increased to £35 million, which is the amount that it would have been had the original impairment not occurred. A gain of £5 million is recognised in the profit and loss account.
	No reversal of the impairment is recognised in relation to the goodwill and the patent, because the effect of the external event that caused the original impairment has not reversed. The original product has still been overtaken by a more advanced model.

FEEDBACK TO ACTIVITY 5	The main arguments in favour of including brand names in a company's balance sheet centre on the idea that inclusion will give a fairer presentation of the 'real' value of the company's assets. This inclusion is favoured by companies who consider that the following advantages will follow.

- They expect an increase in the share price. (**Note:** this expectation is unfounded if the efficient market hypothesis is accepted, because in that case the share price will already reflect the fact that a company has brand names of value.)

- The risk of unwelcome take-over bids is reduced.

- The cost of raising new capital can be reduced (in 'cost of capital' terms).

- It is easier to borrow long-term finance because the reserves created by the valuation of brand names reduce the gearing of a company.

- The problems of having to account for what would inevitably be a higher goodwill value are avoided (in the case of purchased brand names).

The arguments against including a value for brand names in the balance sheet centre on two main points.

- It is not possible to comply with the basic accounting concepts in reaching a value for brand names, particularly for non-purchased brands. The methodology is likely to be too subjective and not verifiable.

- The balance sheet, as it is produced in normal historical cost accounting systems, does not purport to show the 'real' value of a company's net assets.

FEEDBACK TO ACTIVITY 6	(a) The answer depends on whether the asset can be valued reliably. Although the ASB believes that unique intangible assets cannot have a market value it acknowledges that there are techniques that can be used for estimating values indirectly (e.g. indicators based on multiples of turnover). If this is possible, the title will be recognised at its fair value, otherwise it will be treated as part of goodwill.
	(b) Assuming that the licence has been purchased separately from a business, it should be capitalised at cost.

Negative goodwill is £50,000 (150,000 – 100,000).

	£
Non-monetary assets recovered in 20X6:	
Fixed assets (depreciated over 5 years)	26,000
Stocks (assumed sold during the year)	30,000
	56,000

Amortisation: $\dfrac{56}{160} \times 50,000 = £17,500$

Chapter 11

TANGIBLE FIXED ASSETS

This chapter looks at tangible fixed assets, in particular at issues relating to revaluation. It also covers other problematic areas: initial measurement of fixed assets, subsequent expenditure and capitalisation of interest.

Objectives

When you have studied this chapter you should be able to:

*   account for revaluation gains and losses and the depreciation of revalued assets

*   account for the disposal of revalued assets

*   discuss the effect of revaluations on distributable profits

*   understand the problem areas in accounting for fixed assets.

1   Valuation of fixed assets

1.1   Introduction

The Companies Act 1985 allows tangible fixed assets to be carried either at historical cost or at a valuation (and also requires disclosure in the directors' report where the market value of land is substantially different from book value).

The ASB wishes to encourage the use of current value in financial statements as it believes that this provides relevant information to users.

ACTIVITY 1

What are the arguments for carrying assets at current values?

Feedback to this activity is at the end of the chapter.

1.2   The basic rules contained in FRS 15

DEFINITION

A **class of tangible fixed assets** is a category of tangible fixed assets having a similar nature, function or use in the business of the entity.

*   Revaluation of fixed assets is optional.

*   If one tangible fixed asset is revalued, all tangible fixed assets of the same class must be revalued. (This means that it is now impossible to 'cherry pick', for example, by revaluing some freehold properties and not others.)

*   Where an entity adopts a policy of revaluation it need not be applied to all classes of tangible fixed assets held by the entity.

DEFINITION

The **current value** of a tangible fixed asset to the business (also known as **deprival value**) is the lower of replacement cost and recoverable amount.

In practice a class of tangible fixed assets might be determined by the Companies Act balance sheet formats, for example: land and buildings; plant and machinery; and fixtures, fittings, tools and equipment. However, narrower classes are allowed, for example: specialised properties; non-specialised properties; and short leasehold properties.

*   The carrying amount of a revalued fixed asset should be its current value at the balance sheet date.

1.3   Frequency and basis of valuation

Frequency

Before the issue of FRS 15 many entities did not keep valuations up to date (particularly if property prices were falling). FRS 15 does not insist on annual revaluations, but instead requires the following.

(a) Non-specialised properties

- a full valuation every five years with an interim valuation in Year 3 or in other years where there has been a material change in value; or

- full valuation on a rolling basis over five year cycles with an interim valuation on the remaining portfolio where there has been a material change in value.

(b) Specialised properties: valuation at least every five years and in the intervening years where there has been a material change in value.

(c) Other tangible fixed assets

- annual valuation where market comparisons or appropriate indices exist

- otherwise, valuation at least every five years and in the intervening years where there has been a material change in value.

Five-yearly valuations should be carried out by a qualified external or internal valuer. If an internal valuer is used, the valuation should be reviewed by a qualified external valuer.

Basis

The following valuation bases should be used for revalued properties that are not impaired.

- Non-specialised properties: existing use value plus directly attributable acquisition costs if material. Disclose open market value where this is materially different.

- Specialised properties: depreciated replacement cost.

- Properties surplus to an entity's requirements: open market value less expected direct selling costs where these are material.

Tangible fixed assets other than properties should be valued using market value, where possible. Where market value is not obtainable, depreciated replacement cost should be used.

1.4   Reporting gains and losses on revaluation

Gains

- Revaluation gains should normally be recognised in the statement of total recognised gains and losses (this is also required by FRS 3). They cannot be recognised in the profit and loss account because they are not yet realised.

- Revaluation gains are only recognised in the profit and loss account if they reverse revaluation losses on the same asset.

Losses

A revaluation loss may be caused either:

- by a fall in prices (e.g. a slump in the property market); or

- by consumption of economic benefits (e.g. physical damage or deterioration).

DEFINITION

An **internal valuer** is a director, officer or employee of the entity. An **external valuer** is not an internal valuer and does not have a significant financial interest in the entity.

KEY POINT

Revaluation gains are only recognised in the profit and loss account if they reverse revaluation losses on the same asset.

Unless there is evidence to the contrary, it is assumed that a loss is caused by a fall in prices.

- Revaluation losses that are caused by a clear consumption of economic benefits should be recognised in the profit and loss account.

- Other revaluation losses should normally be recognised in the statement of total recognised gains and losses until the carrying amount reaches its depreciated historical cost. Thereafter they should be recognised in the profit and loss account.

- The exception to this rule is where the recoverable amount of the asset is greater than its revalued amount. The loss should then be recognised in the statement of total recognised gains and losses to the extent that the recoverable amount of the asset is greater than its revalued amount.

- In determining in which performance statement gains and losses on revaluation should be recognised, material gains and losses on individual assets should not be aggregated (in other words, gains and losses cannot be netted off against each other).

Losses caused by a fall in prices are valuation adjustments, are unrealised and are therefore reported in the statement of total recognised gains and losses. On the other hand, losses caused by a consumption of economic benefits are similar to depreciation and must therefore be reported in the profit and loss account. Where the recoverable amount of an asset is greater than its revalued amount the difference between the two amounts is not an impairment but a valuation adjustment and should therefore be recognised in the statement of total recognised gains and losses, rather than in the profit and loss account.

ACTIVITY 2

A property costing £500,000 was purchased on 1 January 20X4 and was depreciated over its useful economic life of 10 years. It had no residual value.

At 31 December 20X4 the property was valued at £540,000 and at 31 December 20X5 it was valued at £350,000.

How should these revaluations be treated in the accounts for the years ended 31 December 20X4 and 31 December 20X5 if:

(a) the recoverable amount at 31 December 20X5 was £350,000?
(b) the recoverable amount at 31 December 20X5 was £380,000?

Feedback to this activity is at the end of the chapter.

1.5   Disclosures where assets have been revalued

(a) For each class of revalued assets

- name and qualifications of the valuer(s)

- bases of valuation

- date and amounts of the valuation

- depreciated historical cost

- whether the valuer(s) is (are) internal or external

- if the valuation has not been updated because the directors are not aware of any material change, a statement to that effect

- date of the last full valuation (if not in the current period).

(b) For revalued properties

- • Where properties have been valued as fully equipped operational entities having regard to their trading potential, a statement to that effect and the carrying amount of those properties.

- • The total amount of notional directly attributable acquisition costs included in the carrying amount, where material.

DEFINITIONS

Depreciation is the measure of the cost or revalued amount of the economic benefits of the tangible fixed asset that have been consumed during the period.

The **depreciable amount** is the cost of a tangible fixed asset (or, where an asset is revalued, the revalued amount) less its residual value.

Residual value is the net realisable value of an asset at the end of its useful economic life.

The **useful economic life** of a tangible fixed asset is the period over which the entity expects to derive economic benefit from that asset.

2   Depreciation and disposal of revalued assets

2.1   Depreciable amount

Depreciation is a measure of the consumption of a fixed asset.

Consumption includes the wearing out, using up or other reduction in the useful economic life of a tangible fixed asset whether arising from use, effluxion of time or obsolescence through either changes in technology or demand for the goods and services produced by the asset.

FRS 15 requires that the depreciable amount of a tangible fixed asset should be allocated on a systematic basis over its useful economic life.

The depreciation method used should reflect as fairly as possible the pattern in which the asset's economic benefits are consumed by the entity.

The depreciation charge for each period should be recognised as an expense in the profit and loss account unless it is permitted to be included in the carrying amount of another asset (for example, where it is part of development expenditure that is capitalised).

ACTIVITY 3

A company revalues its buildings and decides to incorporate the revaluation into the books of account. The following information is relevant:

(a)   Extract from the balance sheet at 31 December 20X7.

	£
Buildings	
Cost	1,500,000
Depreciation	450,000
	1,050,000

(b)   Depreciation has been provided at 2% per annum on a straight line.

(c)   The building is revalued at 30 June 20X8 at £1,380,000. There is no change in its remaining estimated future life.

Show the relevant extracts from the final accounts at 31 December 20X8.

Feedback to this activity is at the end of the chapter.

2.2   Subsequent expenditure

Some entities in the past did not charge depreciation on revalued properties on the grounds that the assets were being maintained or refurbished regularly so that the economic life of the property was limitless. This treatment has been common in the hotel, brewing, public house and retail sectors.

FRS 15 states that subsequent expenditure on a tangible fixed asset that maintains or enhances the previously assessed standard of performance of the asset does not negate the need to charge depreciation.

2.3   Impairment reviews

FRS 15 states that when either:

- a tangible fixed asset is not depreciated on the grounds that the charge would be immaterial (either because of the length of the estimated remaining useful economic life or because the estimated residual value of the tangible fixed asset is not materially different from the carrying amount of the asset); or

- the estimated remaining useful economic life of the tangible fixed asset exceeds 50 years, then the asset should be reviewed for impairment, in accordance with FRS 11, at the end of each reporting period. (This does not apply to non-depreciable land.)

It was widely expected that FRS 15 would require that all fixed assets were depreciated, thereby closing what many perceived to be a 'loophole' in its predecessor, SSAP 12. However, the ASB has recognised that in rare cases, some tangible fixed assets may have very long useful economic lives. Entities can still avoid charging depreciation on the grounds that the charge is immaterial but they must carry out annual impairment reviews. This may discourage non-depreciation as impairment reviews can be time consuming, complicated and costly and may result in reduced profits (if an impairment loss has to be recognised in the profit and loss account).

2.4   Split depreciation

The ASB has considered allowing 'split depreciation' (i.e. charging depreciation based on historical cost to the profit and loss account and charging the extra depreciation on the revalued amount to the statement of total recognised gains and losses). Split depreciation has two main advantages.

- It increases the comparability of financial statements and removes a disincentive to revaluations.

- Depreciation charged to the profit and loss account represents an allocation of the actual cash outlay.

However, split depreciation would result in the profit and loss account not showing the full cost of the economic benefits consumed during the period. Depreciation based on current value reflects the cost that the entity could have avoided if it had not used the asset. Split depreciation would also be contrary to the Companies Act, which requires depreciation of revalued fixed assets to be calculated on the current cost or market value and based on the revalued amount. For these reasons, the ASB has concluded that split depreciation should not be allowed.

2.5   Reporting gains and losses on disposal

The profit or loss on the disposal of a revalued fixed asset should be calculated as the difference between the net sale proceeds and the carrying amount (this is also required by FRS 3). It should be accounted for in the profit and loss account of the period in which the disposal occurs and disclosed in accordance with FRS 3.

The gain or loss on revaluation has already been included in the accounts (in the statement of total recognised gains and losses) when the asset was revalued. Unless the profit or loss on disposal is based on the carrying amount, the gain or loss on revaluation will be recognised twice.

Note that any unrealised revaluation gains are now realised and should be transferred from the revaluation reserve to the profit and loss account reserve as required by FRS 3.

2.6   Evaluation of the requirements of FRS 15

On the whole, FRS 15 has been welcomed by users and preparers of financial statements. The requirement for regular revaluations has undoubted advantages in that it increases the comparability of financial statements and reduces opportunities for 'creative accounting'. (For example, many entities revalued assets during the 1980s and continued to use those valuations in their financial statements, despite the fact that property values subsequently fell.)

The requirement to revalue all assets within a class means that entities will not be able to 'cherry pick' certain assets for revaluation while carrying others at historical cost. This will also increase comparability between entities.

Entities still have the choice of whether to revalue fixed assets. The ASB has accepted that enforcing the use of current values would not be practical, given that there is widespread resistance to the idea of current value accounting.

The most controversial aspect of the FRS has probably been its failure to prohibit non-depreciation of revalued fixed assets (although it discourages the practice by requiring impairment reviews). Many commentators are concerned that this failure will lead to 'creative accounting' abuses.

The ASB wishes to encourage the use of current values as this provides relevant information to users of the financial statements. However, a few commentators fear that some entities could revert to using historical cost in order to avoid costly annual revaluations and the other disadvantages associated with using current values (for example, the higher depreciation charge and the requirement to 'report the bad news as well as the good' if market values fall).

3   The effect of revaluations on distributable profits

3.1   The statutory rules

All companies, including private companies, are prohibited from paying dividends (making a distribution) except out of profits available for that purpose.

The definition of 'profits available' permits the distribution as dividend of a **capital profit**, i.e. a surplus over book value realised on sale of a fixed asset. But the key words are:

- **accumulated** – which means that the balance of profit or loss from previous years must be brought into account in the current period; and

- **realised** – which prohibits the inclusion of unrealised profits arising from, e.g. the revaluation of fixed assets retained by the company.

A public company may not pay a dividend unless its net assets are at least equal to the aggregate amount of its called-up share capital and undistributable reserves.

The effect of this provision is that any excess of unrealised losses over unrealised profits must be deducted from realised profits in arriving at the amount available for distribution.

Note that distributions are made by individual companies and not by groups.

3.2 Further rules

There are the following rules in CA85.

- A revaluation surplus is an unrealised profit.

- If fixed assets are revalued and as a result more has to be provided for depreciation than would have been necessary if the original value had been retained, the additional depreciation may be treated as part of the realised profit for dividend purposes. This effectively means the depreciation based on the revaluation surplus can be added back notionally to the profit and loss account for the determination of realised profits. This adjustment can be put through the accounts as a transfer between reserves.

Example

A Ltd purchased freehold land and buildings on 30 June 20X4 for £200,000 (land £60,000, buildings £140,000). The net book value of the buildings at 31 December 20X7 is £121,386. On 1 January 20X8 the land was revalued to £75,000 and the buildings to £135,000. Depreciation on buildings is computed at 4% reducing balance. Accounts are prepared on a calendar year basis.

The entries to the revaluation reserve on 1 January 20X8 should be:

	£
Re land	15,000
Re buildings £(135,000 – 121,386)	13,614
	28,614

The depreciation charge for the year ended 31 December 20X8 = 4% × £135,000 = £5,400. This amount is the charge to P&L account (FRS 15) although CA85 requires only the HC depreciation (4% × £121,386 = £4,855).

However, to show the realised part of the revaluation reserve a transfer from the reserve to distributable reserves may be made.

Revaluation reserve

	£
Balance at 1 January 20X8	28,614
Transfer to distributable reserves £(5,400 – 4,855)	545
Balance at 31 December 20X8	28,069

FRS 3 now legitimises this treatment by adopting it in its illustrative examples.

- On the disposal of a revalued asset any unrealised surplus or loss on valuation immediately becomes realised.

3.3 Revaluation deficits

The CA85 stipulates the following.

- A provision made in the accounts is a realised loss. A revaluation deficit is a provision for a loss in value and is therefore a realised loss.

- If a revaluation deficit arises on a revaluation of all fixed assets (or on a revaluation of all fixed assets except for goodwill) the revaluation deficit is an unrealised loss.

Consequently, where a company undertakes a partial revaluation of fixed assets, a deficit on one asset is a realised loss and cannot therefore be offset against a surplus on another asset (an unrealised profit) for the purposes of arriving at distributable profits. This is despite the fact that all surpluses and deficits can be accounted for in the revaluation reserve.

- A partial remedy to this problem is contained in the CA85. Deficits arising on an asset where there has been a partial revaluation of the assets are to be treated as unrealised losses provided that:

    (a) the directors have 'considered' the aggregate value of the fixed assets which have not been revalued at the date of the partial revaluation, and

    (b) the directors are satisfied that their aggregate value is not less than their aggregate book value, and

    (c) a note to the accounts states the above two facts.

Example

X Ltd has the following capital and reserves:

	£'000
Share capital	100
Share premium	50
Revaluation reserve	70
Profit and loss account	80

Two of the company's assets were revalued during the year, one giving rise to a surplus of £100,000, the other a deficit of £30,000.

The profits available for dividend are as follows:

	£'000
Net realised profits – Profit and loss account	80
Less: Realised losses – Revaluation deficit	30
	50

If all the company's assets had been revalued or the directors had 'considered' the value of the assets not revalued, the revaluation deficit would be unrealised and therefore the profits available for distribution would be £80,000.

3.4 Revaluation surpluses

Revaluation surpluses are unrealised profits in the accounting period in which the revaluation takes place. The only exception to this rule is where the same asset was previously revalued giving rise to a deficit, and the deficit was treated as a realised loss. In such a case, the revaluation surplus will be a realised profit to the extent that it makes good the realised loss.

It should be noted that company law does not specify this but current accounting practice requires this treatment. (See the FRS 15 rules for recognising revaluation gains and losses discussed earlier in this chapter.)

4   Initial measurement of fixed assets

4.1   Cost

FRS 15 recognises that fixed assets may be acquired in a number of ways. They may be purchased or the entity may construct them for its own use. Occasionally they may be donated to an entity (for example, if the entity is a charity).

FRS 15 lays down the following rules:

- A tangible fixed asset should initially be measured at its cost.

- Only those costs that are directly attributable to bringing the asset into working condition for its intended use should be included in its measurement.

  Directly attributable costs are:

  (a) labour costs of the entity's own employees arising directly from the construction, or acquisition, of the specific tangible fixed asset

  (b) incremental costs that would have been avoided only if the tangible fixed asset had not been constructed or acquired.

  Administration and other general overhead costs should not be included, nor should abnormal costs (for example, costs caused by design errors, industrial disputes, idle capacity, wasted materials and production delays).

- Capitalisation of directly attributable costs should cease when substantially all the activities that are necessary to get the tangible fixed asset ready for use are complete, even if the asset has not yet been brought into use. A tangible fixed asset is ready for use when its physical construction is complete.

- The costs associated with a start up or commissioning period should be included in the cost of the tangible fixed asset only where the asset is available for use but incapable of operating at normal levels without such a start up or commissioning period.

  Example

  A machine has to be run in and tested before it can be used for producing goods. The costs associated with this are included in the cost of the machine.

  After the machine has been run in, there is a further period during which it is operated below its capacity. The machine is capable of operating at full capacity, but demand for the product it makes has not yet built up. Costs associated with this period cannot be included in the cost of the machine.

- The initial carrying amount of tangible fixed assets received as gifts and donations by charities should be the current value of the assets at the date that they are received.

ACTIVITY 4	An entity incurred the following costs in constructing a building for its own use:

	£'000
Purchase price of land	250,000
Stamp duty	5,000
Legal fees	10,000
Site preparation and clearance	18,000
Materials	100,000
Labour (period 1 April 20X7 to 30 September 20X8)	150,000
Architect's fees	20,000
General overheads	30,000
	—
	583,000
	—

The following information is also relevant:

(1) Material costs were greater than anticipated. On investigation, it was found that material costing £10 million had been spoiled and therefore was wasted and a further £15 million was incurred as a result of faulty design work.

(2) As a result of these problems, work on the building ceased for a fortnight during October 20X7 and it is estimated that approximately £9 million of the labour costs relate to this period.

(3) The building was completed on 1 July 20X8 and occupied on 1 September 20X8.

Required:

Calculate the cost of the building that will be included in tangible fixed asset additions.

Feedback to this activity is at the end of the chapter.

4.2 Subsequent expenditure

As well as the initial cost of acquiring a fixed asset, an entity may also incur additional costs in relation to the asset during its life. There are two main categories of subsequent expenditure:

(a) expenditure to maintain or service the asset (an expense of the period)

(b) expenditure to improve or upgrade the asset (effectively an addition to fixed assets).

FRS 15 sets out three circumstances in which subsequent expenditure should be capitalised.

(a) Where it provides an enhancement of the economic benefits of the tangible fixed asset in excess of its previously assessed standard of performance.

Examples given in FRS 15:

- modification of an item of plant to extend its useful economic life or increase its capacity

- upgrading machine parts to achieve a substantial improvement in the quality of output.

(b) Where a component of the tangible fixed asset that has been treated separately for depreciation purposes and depreciated over its individual useful economic life is replaced or restored.

(c) Where it relates to a major inspection or overhaul of a tangible fixed asset that restores the economic benefits of the asset that have been consumed by the entity and have already been reflected in depreciation.

All other subsequent expenditure must be recognised in the profit and loss account as it is incurred.

Points (b) and (c) above deal with the situation in which an asset requires substantial expenditure every few years for overhauling and restoring major components. Examples include:

- the replacing of the lining of a blast furnace

- the dry docking of a ship

- the replacing of the roof of a building.

Previously, some entities dealt with this situation by setting up a provision for the expenditure, but FRS 12 *Provisions, contingent liabilities and contingent assets* has now prohibited this treatment (see later). Instead, the part of the asset that needs regular replacement should be depreciated separately over its individual useful economic life.

Where a tangible fixed asset comprises two or more major components with substantially different useful economic lives, each component should be depreciated separately over its individual useful economic life.

Example

An aircraft is required by law to be overhauled every three years. The cost of the overhaul is estimated at £150,000. How is this expenditure treated in the accounts?

Solution

The overhaul costs of £150,000 are depreciated separately from the rest of the aircraft, so that depreciation of £50,000 is charged each year until the next overhaul. When the expenditure is incurred, at the end of the three year period, it is capitalised and depreciated over the three years until the next major overhaul.

Note the requirement to depreciate major components of the asset separately before the refurbishment/restoration expenditure can be capitalised. Where a fixed asset is not accounted for as several different components, this kind of subsequent expenditure must be treated as normal repairs and maintenance and charged to the profit and loss account as it is incurred.

4.3   UITF Abstract 23 *Application of the transitional rules in FRS 15*

The issue

As we have seen, FRS 15 requires that where a tangible fixed asset comprises two or more major components with different lives, each component should be accounted for separately for depreciation purposes and depreciated over its individual useful economic life.

FRS 15 also explains the arrangements for introducing this rule. Where entities separate tangible fixed assets into different components on adopting FRS 15, the changes should be dealt with as prior period adjustments, as a change in accounting policy. However this requirement is slightly unclear, as there are two possible implications of introducing component accounting:

(a) identifying the various separate components with different lives

(b) amending the residual value and/or useful life of the remainder of the asset.

Should the effect of both (a) and (b) be combined into a single prior period adjustment, or should the prior period adjustment only incorporate item (a), with item (b) treated as normal in FRS 15 and therefore not giving rise to a prior period adjustment?

UITF Consensus

The UITF decided on the second of these options. When component accounting is first introduced to comply with FRS 15, the prior period adjustment should reflect the identification of the separate components. Any change to the useful economic life or residual value of the remainder of the asset should be accounted for prospectively as normally required by FRS 15, and should not give rise to a prior period adjustment.

5 Capitalisation of finance costs

5.1 Introduction

Interest on borrowings is often a very significant cost of acquiring or constructing an asset. Opinion is divided on whether or not finance costs should be included in the cost of a tangible fixed asset. Property companies are the most significant advocates of capitalisation – indeed, most of them capitalise interest on loans used to finance the construction of properties. Many supermarket chains have also capitalised finance costs relating to the construction of large 'superstores'.

5.2 Arguments for capitalising finance costs

- Finance costs are just as much a cost of constructing a tangible fixed asset as other directly attributable costs.

- Capitalising finance costs results in a tangible fixed asset cost that more closely matches the market price of completed assets. Treating the finance cost as an expense distorts the choice between purchasing and constructing a tangible fixed asset. Capitalisation also means that users of the financial statements can more easily compare companies which construct their fixed assets themselves and those which purchase them from third parties.

- The accounts are more likely to reflect the true success or failure of projects involving the construction of assets.

- Failure to capitalise borrowing costs means that profits may be reduced in periods when fixed assets are acquired. This is misleading as capital investment should increase profits in the long term.

5.3 Arguments against capitalising finance costs

- Borrowing costs are incurred in support of the whole of the activities of an enterprise. Any attempt to associate borrowing costs with a particular asset is necessarily arbitrary.

- Capitalisation of borrowing costs results in the same type of asset having a different carrying amount, depending on the method of financing adopted by the enterprise.

- Treating borrowing costs as a charge against income results in financial statements giving more comparable results from period to period. This provides a better indication of the future cash flows of an enterprise. Interest remains a period cost of financing the business and its treatment should not change merely as a result of the completion of a tangible fixed asset.

- Capitalisation leads to higher tangible fixed asset costs, which are more likely to exceed the recoverable amount of the asset.

5.4   Standard accounting practice

Capitalisation of finance costs is optional. FRS 15 does, however, set out rules that must be followed if interest is capitalised.

- If an entity adopts a policy of capitalising finance costs it should be applied consistently (i.e. the entity cannot decide to capitalise finance costs in relation to some assets and not others).

- Only finance costs that are directly attributable to the construction of a tangible fixed asset should be capitalised as part of the cost of that asset. In other words, an entity should only capitalise those costs that would have been avoided if the asset had not been acquired or constructed.

- The total amount of finance costs capitalised during a period should not exceed the total amount of finance costs incurred during that period.

- Capitalisation should begin when:

    (a)   finance costs are being incurred; and
    (b)   expenditures for the asset are being incurred; and
    (c)   activities that are necessary to get the asset ready for use are in progress.

- Capitalisation should be suspended during extended periods in which active development is interrupted.

    The basic principle here is that finance costs should only be capitalised while activity that will change the asset's condition is actually taking place. They cannot be capitalised while the asset is simply being held, for example for future development, or while partially completed. However, the activity need not be actual physical construction. Activities necessary to get the asset ready for use include technical and administrative work such as obtaining permits.

- Capitalisation should cease when substantially all the activities that are necessary to get the tangible fixed asset ready for use are complete.

- When construction of a tangible fixed asset is completed in parts and each part is capable of being used while construction continues on other parts, capitalisation of finance costs relating to a part should cease when substantially all the activities that are necessary to get that part ready for use are completed.

Example

On 1 January 20X8 A Ltd takes out a loan to finance the construction of a housing estate. There are to be six separate houses and construction begins immediately. Although work takes place on all six houses simultaneously, House 1 is completed and is capable of being occupied on 30 September 20X8. The house was actually occupied on 1 December 20X8. At 31 December 20X8 the remaining five houses were still under construction.

If interest on the loan for the year to 31 December 20X8 is £600,000, what is the amount that should actually be capitalised?

Solution

Assuming that the loan interest can be apportioned equally between the six houses, the loan interest relating to House 1 should only be capitalised for the nine months to 30 September 20X8. Note that capitalisation of costs must cease when the house is complete and capable of being occupied, regardless of when it actually is occupied. Therefore finance costs of £575,000 are capitalised for the year ended 31 December 20X8.

5.5 Disclosures

Where finance costs are capitalised, the following disclosures are required.

- the accounting policy adopted

- the aggregate amount of finance costs included in the cost of tangible fixed assets

- the amount of finance costs capitalised during the period

- the amount of finance costs recognised in the profit and loss account during the period

- the capitalisation (interest) rate used to determine the amount of finance costs capitalised during the period.

Given that capitalisation of borrowing costs is optional, FRS 15 provides users of the financial statements with information to help them to compare the financial statements of different entities.

5.6 How to calculate the interest cost

In some cases, a loan is taken out specifically to construct an asset and therefore the amount to be capitalised is the interest payable on that loan.

Arriving at the interest cost is more complicated when the acquisition or construction of an asset is financed from an entity's general borrowings. In this situation it is necessary to calculate the finance cost by applying a notional rate of interest (the capitalisation rate) to the expenditure on the asset. FRS 15 provides the following guidance.

- The expenditure on the asset is the weighted average carrying amount of the asset during the period, including finance costs previously capitalised.

- The capitalisation rate is the weighted average of rates applicable to general borrowings outstanding in the period.

- General borrowings should not include loans for other specific purposes such as constructing other fixed assets, finance leases and hedging foreign investments.

Where an entity has a lot of different loans this could be a very complex and quite subjective calculation and FRS 15 acknowledges that judgement will have to be used in determining which borrowings should be included.

5.7 Why capitalisation is still optional

The ASB would have preferred either to make capitalisation compulsory or to prohibit it altogether, and has been convinced that there are strong arguments for capitalisation.

However, if capitalisation became compulsory, there would be practical problems. Capitalisation of borrowing costs results in the same type of asset having a different carrying amount, depending on whether the entity is funded by debt or funded by equity. The ASB believes that equity funded entities should be allowed to include the cost of capital in the cost of an asset if debt funded entities are required to capitalise interest costs. The ASB is exploring the idea of capitalising notional interest on equity, but until a consensus can be reached as to how to do this, capitalisation of finance costs will continue to be optional.

KEY POINT

Capitalisation of borrowing costs results in the same type of asset having a different carrying amount, depending on whether the entity is funded by debt or funded by equity.

6   Depreciation: further problem areas

6.1   Depreciation methods

FRS 15 does not prescribe a method of depreciation. It does say that the method chosen should result in a depreciation charge throughout the asset's economic life and not just towards the end of its useful economic life or when the asset is falling in value. It also briefly discusses the straight line and reducing balance methods and states that where the pattern of consumption of an asset's economic benefits is uncertain, a straight line method of depreciation is usually adopted.

Some methods of depreciation are designed to take into account the time value of money. The best known example of this type of method is the annuity method.

Suppose that an asset costs £10,000 and has an estimated useful economic life of five years with no residual value. Depreciation would be charged at £2,000 per year using the straight line method.

However, the £10,000 cash outflow occurs when the asset is purchased. This means that the economic cost of the benefits consumed in later years is greater, because of the implicit interest costs of paying for those benefits some years in advance of their consumption. An interest method of depreciation would take this implicit interest cost into account, so that notional interest and the depreciation charge combined are approximately the same for each of the five years of the asset's life. This has the effect of reducing the depreciation charge in earlier years and increasing it in later years.

There are arguments for using interest methods of depreciation.

- In principle they more fairly reflect the economic cost of the benefits consumed in the period.

- They are appropriate for assets that are financed by debt.

- They may be appropriate in certain other situations, e.g. for assets such as mineral reserves. This is because arguably the value of the asset only declines significantly towards the end of its life.

The ASB has issued an Exposure Draft of an amendment to FRS 15 that proposes that interest methods of depreciation should not be allowed. The reasoning behind this is that interest methods of depreciation do not provide an appropriate reflection of the consumption of the asset's economic benefits.

The ASB has considered the arguments for using interest methods and rejected most of them. For example, it has rejected the argument that interest methods of depreciation are appropriate for assets that are financed by debt. Interest methods of depreciation take into account the implicit interest cost relating to the timing of when economic benefits are expected to be consumed, rather than the actual interest cost incurred by financing the purchase of the asset. Economic benefits will be consumed as the fixed asset it used, regardless of how it was financed.

The work on the Exposure Draft has now been incorporated into the wider project on leasing, so no revised FRS 15 is expected in the near future.

6.2   Change in method

KEY POINT

A change from one method of providing depreciation to another does not constitute a change in accounting policy.

A change from one method of providing depreciation to another is permissible only on the grounds that the new method will give a fairer presentation of the results and of the financial position.

This does not constitute a change in accounting policy. The carrying amount of the tangible fixed asset is depreciated using the revised method over the remaining useful economic life, beginning in the period in which the change is made.

6.3 Review of useful economic life and residual value

- Useful economic life should be reviewed at the end of each reporting period and revised if expectations are significantly different from previous estimates. If a useful economic life is revised, the carrying amount of the asset at the date of revision should be depreciated over the revised remaining useful economic life.

- Where the residual value is material it should be reviewed at the end of each reporting period to take account of reasonably expected technological changes based on prices prevailing at the date of acquisition (or revaluation). Any change should be accounted for prospectively over the asset's remaining useful economic life.

6.4 Renewals accounting

Some entities, such as utility companies, own assets such as pipelines, roads, sewers, dams and tunnels, which they use to provide a service to the public. These assets are known as infrastructure assets. Many utility companies have not depreciated these assets, but instead have provided annually for the cost of maintaining them. FRS 12 has now prohibited the setting up of provisions for future costs.

Provided that certain conditions are met, FRS 15 allows 'renewals accounting' for infrastructure assets. Under renewals accounting, annual expenditure required to maintain the operating capacity of the infrastructure asset is charged as depreciation and is deducted from the carrying amount of the asset as accumulated depreciation. Actual expenditure is capitalised as part of the cost of the asset as it is incurred.

The conditions, all of which must be satisfied, are as follows.

- The infrastructure asset is a system or network that as a whole is intended to be maintained at a specified level by the continuing replacement and refurbishment of its components.

- The level of annual expenditure required to maintain the operating capacity of the asset is calculated from an asset management plan that is certified by a person who is appropriately qualified and independent.

- The system or network is in a mature or steady state (that is, not being expanded or run down).

6.5 Disclosure

As well as the disclosures required by the Companies Act (the tangible fixed asset note) FRS 15 requires the following disclosures for each class of tangible fixed assets:

- the depreciation methods used

- the useful economic lives or the depreciation rates used

- total depreciation charged for the period

- the effect of a change in useful economic lives or residual value in the period, where material.

Where there has been a change in the depreciation method used in the period, the effect should be disclosed, if material. The reason for the change should also be disclosed.

7   Investment properties

7.1   The requirements of SSAP 19 and the Companies Act

Under the general requirements of FRS 15 all fixed assets having a finite useful life should be subject to a depreciation charge. Investment property companies objected to this requirement when it was first published in SSAP 12 and as the ASC conceded they had reasonable grounds for objecting, investment properties were exempted from the SSAP 12 rules (and later from the FRS 15 rules). SSAP 19 *Accounting for investment properties* provides a solution, and should be looked at as an addition to FRS 15.

SSAP 19 regards an investment property as an asset which is held as a disposable investment rather than an asset consumed in the business operations of a company over a number of years. With such a property the most useful information to give a user of the accounts is the current value of the investment. Systematic annual depreciation would be of little relevance.

SSAP 19 requires therefore that investment properties should not suffer a depreciation charge and must be stated at their current values.

There are no special requirements of the CA85 with respect to investment properties. The requirement is to depreciate assets with a finite useful life.

7.2   Standard accounting practice in SSAP 19

- Investment properties should not be subject to periodic charges for depreciation on the basis set out in FRS 15, except for properties held on lease which should be depreciated on the basis set out in FRS 15 at least over the period when the unexpired term is 20 years or less.

- Investment properties should be included in the balance sheet at their open market value.

- The names of the persons making the valuation, or particulars of their qualifications, should be disclosed together with the bases of valuation used by them. If a person making a valuation is an employee or officer of the company or group which owns the property this fact should be disclosed.

- Changes in the market value of investment properties should not be taken to the profit and loss account but should be taken to the statement of total recognised gains and losses (being a movement on an investment revaluation reserve), unless a deficit (or its reversal) on an individual investment property is expected to be permanent in which case it should be charged (or credited) in the profit and loss account of the period.

The following are not regarded as an investment property:

- a property which is owned and occupied by a company for its own purposes is not an investment property

- a property let to and occupied by another group company is not an investment property for the purposes of its own accounts or the group accounts.

7.3 Applying the requirements of SSAP 19 and the Companies Act

Industrial Ltd produces accounts to 31 December. On 1 January 20X8 it moved from its factory in Bolton to a new purpose-built factory in Rochdale (expected life of fifty years). The old premises were available for letting from 1 January 20X8 and a lease was granted on 30 September 20X8 to B Ltd at an annual rental of £8,000. A valuation of the old premises at 31 December 20X8 was £160,000.

Extracts from the balance sheet as at 31 December 20X7 are given below.

Fixed assets

	Cost £	Depreciation £	NBV £
Land and buildings			
Old premises	200,000	80,000	120,000
New premises	450,000		450,000

Solution

Extracts from the balance sheet as at 31 December 20X8 would be as follows:

Fixed assets

	Cost £	Depreciation £	NBV £
Land and buildings	450,000	9,000	441,000
Investment property at valuation			160,000

Reserves

Investment revaluation reserve	40,000

7.4 Treatment of annual valuations

SSAP 19 regards the total investment property revaluation reserve as being available to cover deficits. Amounts only need to be charged to the profit and loss account in respect of permanent deficits on revaluation.

Example

Newline Investment Co Ltd purchased three investment properties on 31 December 20X1, and the following valuations have been made during the period to 31 December 20X4.

	31 Dec 20X1 £'000	31 Dec 20X2 £'000	31 Dec 20X3 £'000	31 Dec 20X4 £'000
Property A	200	180	120	90
Property B	300	330	340	340
Property C	400	440	450	450
Total	900	950	910	880

All revaluation deficits are expected to be temporary.

Show the balance on the investment revaluation reserve for each balance sheet date.

Solution

The investment revaluation reserve would be disclosed for the various years as follows:

	Year ended 31 December		
	20X2	*20X3*	*20X4*
	£'000	£'000	£'000
Balance b/d	Nil	50	10
Net revaluation	50	(40)	(10)
Balance c/d	50	10	Nil

The deficit of £20,000 not covered in the year ended 31 December 20X4 would normally be charged through the profit and loss account on the grounds of prudence, though SSAP 19 permits a debit balance on the investment revaluation reserve as long as it has arisen from temporary write-downs only.

7.5   The conflict between SSAP 19 and the Companies Act

The legality of SSAP 19 is questioned as the requirement not to depreciate is in conflict with the requirement of the CA85 to depreciate assets with a finite useful life.

SSAP 19 states however that the treatment is necessary in order to show a true and fair view and thus use is made of the overriding provisions of the CA85 to show such a true and fair view. (FRS 18 sets out the disclosures that must be made when the true and fair view override is invoked.)

SSAP 19 justifies the different accounting treatment for investment properties on the following grounds. It concludes that such assets are not held for consumption within the operations of the business but are held as investments. Therefore to the user of the financial statements, the most important information about such assets relates to their current value. Calculation of depreciation in such circumstances does not benefit the user from a balance sheet perspective nor from a profit and loss account perspective as the asset is not consumed in the business operations.

7.6   The weaknesses in SSAP 19

The justification of the different treatment of investment properties was explained earlier. Some commentators argue however that despite such arguments, SSAP 19 does not represent a valid treatment and is merely an example of the ASC giving way to the demands of pressure groups (i.e. the property investment companies).

Other weaknesses relate to the subjective nature of the standard. No guidance is given on the distinction between temporary and permanent diminutions in value, nor whether the measurement of a deficit should be in relation to the revalued carrying amount. FRS 11 treats all diminutions as permanent, but it does not apply to investment properties.

FRED 17, which eventually became FRS 15, would have replaced SSAP 19, but did not propose any major changes in the accounting treatment of investment properties. The ASB has decided to consider the accounting treatment of investment properties in future with special regard to the International Accounting Standard on investment properties. For the time being, SSAP 19 will remain in force.

8   UITF Abstract 5 *Transfers from current assets to fixed assets*

8.1   The issue

Where at a date subsequent to its original acquisition a current asset is retained for use on a continuing basis in the company's activities it becomes a fixed asset and the question arises as to the appropriate transfer value. An example is a property which is reclassified from trading properties to investment properties.

Of particular concern is the possibility that companies could avoid charging the profit and loss account with write-downs to net realisable value arising on unsold trading assets. This could be done by transferring the relevant assets from current assets to fixed assets at above net realisable value, as a result of which any later write-down might be debited to revaluation reserve.

8.2   UITF Consensus

Where assets are transferred from current to fixed, the current asset accounting rules should be applied up to the effective date of transfer, which is the date of management's change of intent. Consequently the transfer should be made at the lower of cost and net realisable value, and accordingly an assessment should be made of the net realisable value at the date of the transfer and if this is less than its previous carrying value the diminution should be charged in the profit and loss account, reflecting the loss to the company while the asset was held as a current asset.

9   FRED 29

FRED 29 proposes to incorporate IAS 16 *Property, plant and equipment* and IAS 23 *Borrowing costs* into UK accounting practice. These changes will not cause any significant differences in practice, because the two most contentious areas (borrowing costs and revaluations) are left unresolved. Both the new and the old standards give reporting entities the option to revalue and the option to capitalise borrowing costs. The basis of revaluation though will change. FRS 15 uses value to the business whereas the international standard uses a fair value model.

SELF-TEST QUESTIONS

Valuation of fixed assets

1   What are the basic rules in FRS 15 for the revaluation of fixed assets? (1.2)

2   How frequently should non-specialised properties, specialised properties and other tangible fixed assets be revalued? (1.3)

3   In which accounting statements should revaluation gains and losses be reported? (1.4)

Depreciation and disposal of revalued assets

4   Define depreciation, depreciable amount, residual value and useful economic life. (2.1)

The effect of revaluations on distributable profits

5   How do revaluations affect distributable profits? (3)

Initial measurement of fixed assets

6   How should tangible fixed assets be initially valued? (4.1)

7   When can subsequent expenditure be capitalised? (4.2)

Capitalisation of finance costs

8   What are the arguments for and against capitalising finance costs? Does FRS 15 require them to be capitalised? (5)

Depreciation: further problem areas

9   On what grounds is it permissible to change the method adopted for charging depreciation? (6.2)

Investment properties

10   At what amount should investment properties be included in the balance sheet? (7.2)

EXAM-TYPE QUESTION

Properties (London) Ltd

Properties (London) Ltd formed a subsidiary company on 1 January 20X6 called Properties (Brighton) Ltd to purchase and renovate office premises.

During the year ended 31 December 20X6 Properties (Brighton) Ltd obtained a loan of £175,000 from its parent company and used part of these funds to acquire an office block at an address in Brighton.

It proposed to sub-divide this office block into 16 separate units. The following information was available at 31 December 20X6.

(i)   A loan was obtained from Properties (London) Ltd on 1 January 20X6 of £175,000.

(ii)   The Brighton property was acquired for £100,000 of which £35,000 was the value of the land.

(iii)   Ten units were renovated at a cost of £60,000.

(iv)   Interest of £17,500 was paid to Properties (London) Ltd.

(v)   The open market valuation of the partially renovated property in Brighton at 31 December 20X6 was £200,000 of which £50,000 was the value of the land.

(vi)   It was estimated that a further £40,000 would be spent by 30 April 20X7 to complete the renovation of the remaining six units.

(vii)   An additional loan had been agreed with Properties (London) Ltd of £65,000 receivable on 1 January 20X7 at 10% per annum interest.

(viii)   There was estimated interest of £24,000 per year payable to Properties (London) Ltd for the years ended 31 December 20X7 and 20X8.

(ix)   Agents advised that they could arrange tenancies for these units at a rental of £2,500 per annum per unit as follows

	4 units on 30 September 20X7
a further	6 units on 31 December 20X7
and the final	6 units on 30 April 20X8

(x)   It is estimated that the open market value of the Brighton property will be £275,000 on 31 December 20X7 and £320,000 on 31 December 20X8.

(xi)   The balance sheet of the holding company, Properties (London) Ltd, as at 31 December 20X6 showed that the holding company had not raised any new finance from loans during the year. The directors of the holding company advise that they do not intend to raise additional loans during 20X7 and 20X8.

The assistant accountant was requested by the finance director to prepare profit and loss account and balance sheet entries on the basis that Properties (Brighton) Ltd would use the office premises in Brighton as its own head office accommodation. He prepared the following draft entries.

Balance sheet entries as at 31 December 20X6

	Notes	£
Fixed assets		
Property at valuation	(1)	200,000
Less: Depreciation	(2)	2,500
		197,500
Revaluation reserve		40,000

Profit and loss entries for year ended 31 December 20X6

	£
Depreciation	2,500
Interest payable	17,500

Notes

(1) The property was valued by Messrs Hews on 31 December 20X6.

(2) Depreciation is calculated at 2% of the cost of the buildings (£65,000 + £60,000).

(3) The company does not capitalise finance costs incurred in the construction of tangible fixed assets.

Required:

(a) Explain how far you agree with the draft entries prepared by the assistant accountant and calculate the appropriate entries for 20X6 and 20X7. **(6 marks)**

(b) (i) Show the appropriate entries that would appear in the profit and loss accounts for the years ended 31 December 20X6 and 20X7 and the balance sheets as at those dates in relation to:

- rental income
- interest payable
- depreciation
- cost of acquisition
- cost of renovation
- revenue amounts
- differences on revaluation.

Give a brief note to explain your treatment on the assumption that Properties (Brighton) Ltd decide to let the units and not use them for their own head office. **(13 marks)**

(ii) Draft the accounting policies for the accounting year ended 31 December 20X6 in respect of:

- income available for distribution
- properties
- depreciation

on the assumption that the units are let. **(6 marks)**

(Total: 25 marks)

For the answer to this question see the 'Answers' section at the end of the book.

FEEDBACK TO
ACTIVITY **1**

(a) If the balance sheet reflects the current value of an entity's assets, users of the financial statements are aware of the 'true' value of the capital employed in the business.

(b) The performance statements also reflect gains and losses on revaluation. These are part of an entity's performance, whether they are realised or unrealised. Information about gains and losses on revaluation provides users with information about an entity's financial adaptability (e.g. the amount of cash that could be realised by selling the assets).

(c) Revaluation of fixed assets produces a more realistic profit figure because it results in a higher depreciation charge. Although depreciation is a means of matching costs with revenues, rather than a means of setting aside funds to replace assets, depreciation based on current values helps to ensure that distributions to shareholders are kept at a level which maintains the operating capacity of the business.

FEEDBACK TO
ACTIVITY **2**

Year ended 31 December 20X4: a revaluation gain of £90,000 is reported in the statement of total recognised gains and losses.

Year ended 31 December 20X5: a revaluation loss of £130,000 occurs and is dealt with as follows:

		£'000
(a)	Recoverable amount £350,000	
	Statement of total recognised gains and losses (480 – 400)	80
	Profit and loss account	50
		130

		£'000
(b)	Recoverable amount £380,000	
	Statement of total recognised gains and losses	
	Net book value less depreciated historical cost (480 – 400)	80
	Recoverable amount less revalued amount (380 – 350)	30
		110
	Profit and loss account	
	Depreciated historical cost less recoverable amount (400 – 380)	20
		130

Working

	£'000
Cost at 1 January 20X4	500
Less: depreciation (500 ÷ 10)	(50)
	450
Revaluation gain	90
Valuation at 31 December 20X4	540
Less: depreciation (540 ÷ 9)	(60)
	480
Revaluation loss	(130)
Valuation at 31 December 20X5	350
Depreciated historical cost at 31 December 20X5 (500 – 100)	400

Profit and loss account – depreciation charge

	£
Based on original cost	30,000
Based on increase in valuation	5,000
Total	35,000

Balance sheet

	£
Buildings	
Valuation 30 June 20X8	1,380,000
Accumulated depreciation	20,000
	1,360,000

Workings

(a)
Buildings account (NBV)

20X8		£	20X8		£
1 Jan.	Balance b/d	1,050,000	30 Jun.	Profit and loss depreciation first half year	15,000
30 Jun.	Revaluation surplus (Bal. fig.)	345,000	30 Jun.	Balance c/d	1,380,000
		1,395,000			1,395,000
30 Jun.	Balance b/d	1,380,000	31 Dec.	Profit and loss depreciation second half year	20,000
			31 Dec.	Balance c/d	1,360,000
		1,380,000			1,380,000

(b) **Depreciation calculations**

	£
First half year $0.5 \times 2\% \times 1,500,000$	15,000
Second half year $0.5 \times \dfrac{1,380,000}{34.5**}$	20,000
	35,000

Had this building not been revalued, the charge for the year would have been £30,000.

**   This is arrived at as follows:

	Years	
Total number of years before building fully depreciated		50.0
Less: Depreciation in years to		
31 December 20X7 $\dfrac{450,000}{30,000}$	15.0	
Depreciation 1 January 20X8 to 30 June 20X8	0.5	
		15.5
Number of years for depreciation to run		34.5

FEEDBACK TO ACTIVITY 4

Only those costs which are directly attributable to bringing the asset into working condition for its intended use should be included. You may find it helpful to remember the rules for stocks in SSAP 9: abnormal costs are not included, nor are general overheads.

Labour costs are only included for the period to 1 July 20X8. The building was available for use on that date, regardless of the fact that it was not actually in use until three months later.

	£'000
Purchase price of land	250,000
Stamp duty	5,000
Legal fees	10,000
Site preparation and clearance	18,000
Materials (100 – 10 – 15)	75,000
Labour (150 × 15/18 – 9)	116,000
Architect's fees	20,000
	494,000

Chapter 12

FINANCIAL INSTRUMENTS

Capital instruments and financial instruments have become increasingly important in recent years. Companies use sophisticated and complex instruments in order to finance their activities. This can cause many problems for preparers and users of financial statements.

FRS 4 *Capital instruments* is concerned with the way in which complex capital instruments are treated and disclosed in financial statements. More recently, the ASB has turned its attention to derivatives and has issued a Discussion Paper *Derivatives and other financial instruments* and FRS 13 *Derivatives and other financial instruments: disclosures*.

Objectives

When you have studied this chapter you should be able to:

- account for debt instruments, share capital and the allocation of finance costs

- account for fixed interest rate and convertible bonds

- understand the measurement issues relating to complex instruments

- understand the definition and classification of a financial instrument

- explain the current measurement proposals for financial instruments

- describe the nature of the disclosure requirements relating to financial instruments

- discuss the key areas where consensus is required on the accounting treatment of financial instruments.

1 FRS 4 *Capital instruments*

1.1 Introduction

FRS 4 was issued in December 1993 to cover accounting for capital instruments. Its issue was primarily due to the increase in use of often complex forms of issues designed, in part, to allow companies to show an issue as equity rather than debt, and also to avoid charging the profit and loss account with interest until the accounting period in which the issue was redeemed. Companies were therefore manipulating their gearing ratio either from the balance sheet or the profit and loss account perspective.

1.2 Objectives of FRS 4

FRS 4 aims to standardise the following areas:

- the circumstances in which capital instruments should alternatively be reported as debt – that is, amongst liabilities – and as shares

- the methods by which the amounts representing such instruments and transactions in respect of them, such as payments of interest and the costs of issuing them, should be stated in the accounts

- disclosure requirements.

DEFINITION

A **capital instrument** is any type of share, loan stock or other instrument issued as a means of raising finance.

1.3 The classification of capital instruments

It is sometimes suggested that examples of instruments which seem not to be easy to classify as liabilities or as shares require either the abandonment of the distinction or the introduction of a new category into the balance sheet. FRS 4 does not propose this course should be taken. It is required instead that the distinction between shares and debt be maintained, and that guidance be given for accounting for capital instruments within these categories. In the case of group accounts, minority interests represent a third category.

Extract from FRS 4 (para 24)

'Capital instruments should be classified as liabilities if they contain an obligation to transfer economic benefits (including a contingent obligation to transfer economic benefits). Capital instruments that do not contain an obligation to transfer economic benefits should be reported within shareholders' funds.'

The FRS is thus following the definition of a liability in the Statement of Principles.

Effect of legal status of shares

The above classification is not used to determine how a company's shares should be accounted for. Shares have a distinct legal status reflected in the limitations imposed by company legislation on the circumstances in which payments may be made in respect of them. It is also impossible to classify shares as liabilities within the constraints of the statutory formats for the balance sheet.

Although there are practical and legal difficulties in classifying shares as liabilities, another distinction – that between equity and non-equity shares – is practicable.

1.4 Summary of classification

The principal distinctions envisaged by the FRS may be summarised as follows:

Item	Analysed between	
Shareholders' funds	Equity interests	Non-equity interests
Minority interests in subsidiaries	Equity interests in subsidiaries	Non-equity interests in subsidiaries
Liabilities	Convertible liabilities	Non-convertible liabilities

Examples

(a) Although convertible debt may be settled by the issue of shares, the company remains liable to repay it until such time as the holder elects to convert. It is therefore required that:

'Convertible debt should be reported within liabilities, but in order that the reader can assess the prospective cash flows relating to the instrument, the amount attributable to convertible debt should be stated separately from that of other liabilities.'

(b) The law requires that shares are reported separately from liabilities, but some kinds of share have features which resemble debt in some respects. It is therefore required that:

'Shareholders' funds should be analysed between the amount attributable to equity interests and the amount attributable to non-equity interests. Non-equity shares are essentially defined in terms of the amounts of dividends or participation in a winding up or payment in respect of redemption being independent of the company's assets or profits, or of a requirement that they be redeemed.'

(c) Outside interests in shares in subsidiaries are normally reported as minority interests in subsidiaries. Since such shares, like those issued by the company itself, may either be equity or non-equity, it is also required that:

'The amount of minority interests shown in the balance sheet should be analysed between the aggregate amount attributable to equity interests and amounts attributable to non-equity interests.'

1.5   Accounting for capital instruments

There are two main issues:

(a) the amount at which the instrument is recorded in the balance sheet (the carrying amount)

(b) calculation of the finance costs and their allocation between accounting periods.

(a) and (b) are to a large extent interdependent. The first step is to calculate the initial carrying amount. This will be the fair value of the consideration less issue costs. Fair value is not defined and thus general principles should be used.

1.6   Accounting for issue costs

It is required that:

'The direct costs incurred in connection with the issue of capital instruments should be deducted from the proceeds of the issue.'

The effect of this requirement is that, where material costs are incurred in the issue of debt, the amount at which the debt is initially stated will be less than it would otherwise be.

In the case of an issue of equity shares, the requirement is consistent with the provisions of the Companies Act that the costs of issue be taken to the share premium account. Where there is no share premium account, the cost of issuing shares should be taken directly to reserves. The issue costs will be reported in the statement of total recognised gains and losses.

1.7   Accounting for finance costs

Once the initial carrying amount has been determined the capital instrument will be stated at that amount on the balance sheet. If the instrument is equity shares this amount will not change in subsequent accounting periods. For other instruments the carrying amount may well change because of the allocation of finance costs.

The finance costs for liabilities and non-equity shares should be allocated to periods at a constant rate based on the carrying amount (i.e. the same requirement as in SSAP 21 for lessees accounting for their obligations under finance leases).

Example
Debt is issued for £1,000. The debt is redeemable at £1,250. The term of the debt is five years and interest is payable each year at 5.9%.

The debt would initially be recognised at £1,000. The total finance cost of the debt is the difference between the payments required by the debt which total £1,545 ((5 × £59) + £1,250) and the proceeds of £1,000, that is £545. In order to allocate these costs over the term of the debt at a constant rate on the carrying amount they must be allocated at the rate of 10%. The movements on the carrying amount of the debt over its term would therefore be as follows:

Year	Balance at beginning of year	Finance cost for year (10%)	Cash paid during year	Balance at end of year
	£	£	£	£
1	1,000	100	(59)	1,041
2	1,041	104	(59)	1,086
3	1,086	109	(59)	1,136
4	1,136	113	(59)	1,190
5	1,190	119	(1,250 + 59)	-

1.8 Other matters

- **Repurchase of debt** – Gains and losses arising on the repurchase or early settlement of debt should be recognised in the profit and loss account in the period during which the repurchase or early settlement is made.

- **The maturity of debt** – An analysis of the maturity of debt should be presented showing amounts falling due:

    (i)   in one year or less, or on demand

    (ii) in more than one year but not more than two years

    (iii) in more than two years but not more than five years

    (iv) in more than five years.

    The maturity of debt should be determined by reference to the earliest date on which the lender can require repayment.

- **Scrip dividends** – Where shares are issued (or proposed to be issued) as an alternative to cash dividends, the value of such shares should be deemed to be the amount receivable if the alternative of cash had been chosen. Where the number of shareholders who will elect to receive the shares is uncertain, the whole amount should be treated as a liability to pay cash dividends.

- **Equity shares and warrants** – The net proceeds from the issue of equity shares and warrants for equity shares should be credited direct to shareholders' funds. The amount attributed to equity shares or warrants should not be subsequently adjusted to reflect changes in the value of the shares or warrants.

    When a warrant is exercised, the amount previously recognised in respect of the warrant should be included in the net proceeds of the shares issued.

    When a warrant lapses unexercised, the amount previously recognised in respect of the warrant should be reported in the statement of total recognised gains and losses.

1.9 Disclosures

- **Disclosures relating to shares** – An analysis should be given of the total amount of non-equity interests in shareholders' funds relating to each class of non-equity shares and series of warrants for non-equity shares.

    A brief summary of the rights of each class of shares should be given. This should include:

    (a) the rights to dividends

    (b) the dates at which the shares are redeemable and the amounts payable in respect of redemption

(c)   their priority and the amounts receivable on a winding up

(d)   their voting rights.

This information will usually make clear why a class of share has been classified as equity or non-equity but, if necessary, additional information should be given to explain the classification.

The aggregate dividends for each class of share should be disclosed including the total amount in respect of each of: dividends on equity shares; participating dividends; and other dividends on non-equity shares.

- **Disclosures relating to debt** – In respect of convertible debt, details of the dates of redemption and the amount payable on redemption should be disclosed. The number and class of shares into which the debt may be converted and the dates at or periods within which the conversion may take place should be stated. It should also be stated whether conversion is at the option of the issuer or at that of the holder.

  A brief description should be given of the legal nature of any instrument included in debt where it is different from that normally associated with debt, for example where the debt is subordinated or where the obligation to repay is conditional.

  Gains and losses arising on the repurchase or early settlement of debt should be disclosed in the profit and loss account as separate items within or adjacent to 'interest payable and similar charges'.

1.10 UITF Abstract 11 *Capital instruments: issuer call options*

Different practices arose to account for issuer call options in accordance with FRS 4, so the UITF issued Abstract 11 on this topic.

The issue

The terms of a capital instrument may include an issuer call option, i.e. a right of the issuer (but not the investor) to redeem the instrument early, usually on the payment of a premium. The question arises as to how to account for an instrument that includes an issuer call option following FRS 4.

Principal requirements

Issuers of capital instruments should not have to account for possible payments that they are not obliged to make, and may very well elect not to make. Payment of a premium on exercise of an issuer call option is a cost that stems directly from the decision to exercise the option and should therefore be reported in the period in which exercise takes place.

The payment required on exercise of such an option does not form part of the finance costs which have to be spread over the instrument's term in accordance with FRS 4.

1.11 UITF Abstract 33 *Obligations in capital instruments*

The issues

FRS 4 *Capital instruments* states that capital instruments should be presented in the balance sheet in a way that reflects the obligations of the issuer. Capital instruments other than shares must be reported as liabilities if they contain an obligation to transfer economic benefits.

This Abstract considers several issues relating to the classification of capital instruments.

UITF Consensus

(a) A capital instrument, other than a share, which involves an obligation to transfer economic benefits is treated as a liability in the single entity financial statements of the issuer, unless that obligation would not be considered in accordance with the going concern concept (i.e. the obligation would only arise on the insolvency of the issuing company).

(b) A capital instrument other than a share should be treated as a liability if it contains an obligation to issue another capital instrument and that other instrument contains an obligation to transfer economic benefits.

(c) If a capital instrument other than a share contains an obligation that can be settled at the issuer's discretion either by transferring economic benefits or by issuing equity shares and:

– there is no genuine commercial possibility that the option to issue the shares will be exercised, the capital instrument should be treated as a liability

– there is no genuine commercial possibility that the option to transfer economic benefits will be exercised, the instrument should be reported as part of shareholders' funds

– if neither of these applies, the capital instrument should be treated as a liability if the number of equity shares that would need to be issued to settle the obligation will vary with changes in their fair value so that the total fair value of the shares issued will always equal the amount of the obligation.

2 Application notes

2.1 Introduction

Application notes specify how some of the requirements of FRS 4 are to be applied to transactions that have certain features. However, the notes are not an exhaustive guide to all the requirements that may be relevant and should therefore be read in conjunction with the FRS itself.

Capital instruments may have a combination of features and accordingly more than one note may be relevant to a single capital instrument.

2.2 Auction Market Preferred Shares (AMPS)

AMPS are preference shares that are entitled to dividends determined in accordance with an auction process in which a panel of investors participates, the shares being transferred at a fixed price to the investor who will accept the lowest dividend. If the auction process fails – for example because no bids are received – the shares remain in the ownership of the former holder and the dividend is increased to a rate, known as the default rate, that is calculated in accordance with a prescribed formula.

Analysis and required accounting

KEY POINT

Because they are redeemable at a fixed amount, and because the dividend rights are limited, AMPS constitute non-equity shares.

As AMPS are shares, dividends cannot be paid in respect of them except out of distributable profits, nor can they be redeemed unless the redemption is financed out of distributable profits or by a fresh issue of shares. Because they are redeemable at a fixed amount, and because the dividend rights are limited, AMPS constitute non-equity shares.

In accordance with the requirements of the FRS, AMPS should be reported within shareholders' funds as non-equity shares and included in the amount attributable to non-equity shares. The finance cost for each period should be the dividend rights accruing in respect of the period.

2.3   Convertible capital bonds

Convertible capital bonds are debt instruments on which interest is paid periodically, typically issued by a special purpose subsidiary incorporated outside the UK. Prior to maturity they may be exchanged for shares of the subsidiary which, at the option of the bondholder, are either immediately redeemed or immediately exchanged for ordinary shares of the parent. The bonds and payments in respect of the shares of the subsidiary are guaranteed by the parent. The parent has the right to issue convertible redeemable preference shares of its own in substitution for the bonds should it wish to do so.

Analysis and required accounting

From the standpoint of the subsidiary, convertible capital bonds are clearly debt since the obligation to pay interest is an obligation to transfer economic benefits. In addition, FRS 4 requires that conversion of debt should not be anticipated. In the subsidiary's financial statements the bonds should therefore be accounted for as debt.

From the standpoint of the group they are also liabilities. Even though the parent has the option to issue convertible preference shares in substitution for the bonds, the requirements of FRS 4 again entail that such conversion should not be anticipated.

Since the liabilities are convertible, the amount attributable to convertible capital bonds should be included in the amount of convertible debt, which should be stated separately from other liabilities.

2.4   Convertible debt with a premium put option

Convertible debt with a premium put option contains an option for the holder to demand redemption (either at the maturity of the debt or at some earlier date) for an amount that is in excess of the amount originally received for the debt. At the time the debt is issued, it is uncertain whether the debt will be converted before the redemption option may be exercised, and hence whether the premium on redemption will be paid.

Analysis and required accounting

The premium put option provides a higher guaranteed return to the holder of the debt than would be received on identical debt without such a put option. Often this higher return corresponds to that which the holder would have expected to receive on non-convertible debt. The holder's decision as to whether to exercise the option will depend on the relative values of the shares to which he would be entitled on conversion and the cash receivable, including the premium, on exercise of the option.

The term of convertible debt with a premium put option should be considered to end on the earliest date at which the holder has the option to require redemption. The premium payable on exercise of the premium put option falls to be included in the calculation of the finance costs for the debt.

On conversion the proceeds of the shares issued should be deemed to be the carrying amount of the debt, including accrued premium, immediately prior to conversion.

2.5   Convertible debt with enhanced interest

As an alternative to the premium put structure discussed above, convertible debt may contain an undertaking that the interest will be increased at a date in the future. At the time the debt is issued, it is uncertain whether the debt will be converted before the enhanced interest is payable.

Analysis and required accounting

The enhanced rate of interest increases the guaranteed return to the holder. Often this higher return corresponds to that which the holder would have expected to receive on non-convertible debt. The holders' decision as to whether to convert the debt will take into account the interest forgone by such a decision.

The interest for the full term of the convertible debt should be taken into account in the allocation of finance costs, which should be allocated at a constant rate.

Example

Convertible debt is issued on 1 January 2000 for £1,000 and is redeemable at the same amount on 31 December 2014. It carries interest of £59 a year (a nominal rate of 5.9%) for the first five years, after which the rate rises to £141 a year (a nominal rate of 14.1%).

In order to comply with FRS 4 the finance costs should be allocated to accounting periods at the rate of 10% a year. The movements on the carrying amount over the term of the debt would be as follows:

Year ending	Balance at beginning of year £	Finance costs for year (10%) £	Cash paid during year £	Balance at end of year £
31.12.2000	1,000	100	(59)	1,041
31.12.2001	1,041	104	(59)	1,086
31.12.2002	1,086	109	(59)	1,136
31.12.2003	1,136	113	(59)	1,190
31.12.2004	1,190	119	(59)	1,250
31.12.2005	1,250	125	(141)	1,234
31.12.2006	1,234	124	(141)	1,217
31.12.2007	1,217	122	(141)	1,198
31.12.2008	1,198	120	(141)	1,177
31.12.2009	1,177	118	(141)	1,154
31.12.2010	1,154	116	(141)	1,129
31.12.2011	1,129	113	(141)	1,101
31.12.2012	1,101	110	(141)	1,070
31.12.2013	1,070	107	(141)	1,036
31.12.2014	1,036	105*	(141 + 1,000)	-

* Increased by £1 rounding difference

2.6 Index linked loans

Sometimes loan agreements do not state a specific amount for the payments; instead they include a formula to be used for their calculation. For example, in the case of floating rate loans, the amount of periodic payments of interest will be calculated by reference to a base rate, e.g. LIBOR + 2 per cent.

Another example is that of index linked loans which may be redeemable at the principal amount multiplied by an index.

Analysis and required accounting

FRS 4 requires that finance costs contingent on uncertain events such as changes in an index should be adjusted to reflect those events only once they have occurred. The effect is that the initial carrying amount will take no account of those events but the carrying amount at each subsequent balance sheet date will be recalculated to take account of the changes occurring in that reporting period. The resulting change in carrying amount is accounted for as an increase or decrease in finance costs for the period.

Example

A loan of £1,250 is issued on 1 January 2000 on which interest of 4% (£50) is paid annually and the principal amount is repayable based on an index. The balance at the end of each year is found by multiplying the original principal amount by the index at the end of the year: the change in the amount is treated as additional finance costs. The movements on the carrying amount over the term of the debt would be as follows:

Year ending	Balance at beginning of year £	Finance costs for year £	Cash paid during year £	Balance at end of year £	Index at end of year
31.12.2000	1,250	125	(50)	1,325	106
31.12.2001	1,325	100	(50)	1,375	110
31.12.2002	1,375	75	(50)	1,400	112
31.12.2003	1,400	150	(50)	1,500	120
31.12.2004	1,500	175	(1,625 + 50)	-	130

2.7   Perpetual debt

Perpetual debt is debt in respect of which the issuer has neither the right nor the obligation to repay the principal amount of the debt. Usually, interest is paid at a constant rate, or at a fixed margin over a benchmark rate such as LIBOR.

Analysis and required accounting

Sometimes it is suggested that, as the principal amount will never be repaid, there is no need for the balance sheet to reflect a liability in respect of the debt. However, the obligation to pay interest is an obligation to transfer economic benefits and hence the instrument is a liability. As there are no repayments of principal the burden of this liability never diminishes.

The FRS is based on the principle that debt should be accounted for having regard to all the payments required by the debt, irrespective of their legal description, in the determination of the appropriate finance charge and capital repayment for each accounting period. In the case of perpetual debt where interest is paid at a constant rate, or at a fixed margin over a benchmark, the correct finance charge will be equal to the coupon payable for each period. Hence no part of the repayments will reduce the carrying amount and the debt will always be shown at the amount of net proceeds.

3   Measurement issues relating to complex capital instruments

3.1   Split accounting

FRS 4 requires that convertible debt be treated as a liability, despite the fact that it has characteristics of both debt and equity. Some commentators have suggested that this treatment does not reflect the economic substance of the arrangement.

One alternative would be to recognise that a convertible bond is a hybrid: a combination of debt and an option warrant. This means that the bond would be 'split' and each of the elements would be accounted for separately. 'Split accounting' involves the following steps.

(a) Analyse the net proceeds from the issue between the amount that represents the liability and the amount that represents the conversion rights. This is done by discounting the interest payments and the amount payable on redemption to their net present values. The difference between net present values and the proceeds of the issue is the amount that represents the conversion rights; the remainder is the liability.

(b) Treat the liability in the same way as any other debt. The amount repayable on redemption normally exceeds the amount allocated to the debt at the time of issue. Therefore a finance cost must be accrued in each accounting period, in addition to the interest actually paid.

(c) Treat the amount that represents the conversion rights as a warrant.

(d) If conversion takes place, debit the liability and credit share capital and share premium with the carrying amount of the liability.

One advantage of split accounting is that it results in a 'proper' finance charge in the profit and loss account. It can be argued that the FRS 4 treatment understates the finance charge. A further disadvantage of the current rules is that the finance cost can be manipulated according to the terms of the instrument.

The IASC has adopted 'split accounting', but at the time that FRS 4 was issued it was considered to be too radical. Some commentators believe that the ASB should now look again at the idea of subdividing complex capital instruments into their component parts and accounting for them separately.

Example

A company issues a bond for £10 million. The bond's interest rate is 6% per annum, but the market rate for borrowing is 10%. The bond is convertible into equity shares after five years and is otherwise redeemable at par.

The split between the liability and the conversion rights is calculated as follows:

	£'000	£'000
Proceeds		10,000
Interest (10,000 × 6% × 3.791)	2,275	
Principal (10,000 × 0.621)	6,210	
Liability		(8,485)
Conversion rights (warrant)		1,515

The net present value of the interest and the principal are based on the market rate of 10%, rather than the actual rate of 6%. This is because the split between the liability and the conversion rights must reflect the rate that would have been charged if the company had simply issued a debt instrument, rather than a convertible bond.

The amount representing the warrant is taken to a capital reserve. The amount representing the liability is built up to the redemption value of £10 million by an additional finance cost charged in the profit and loss account (this is allocated over the life of the instrument in the same way as usual).

4   The problems of accounting for derivatives and other financial instruments

4.1   Derivatives

Examples of derivatives include the following.

- **Forward contracts** – Derivatives that oblige the holder to buy or sell a defined amount of a specific underlying asset at a specified future date. For example, under a forward contract for foreign currency, the holder might contract to exchange £100,000 for $150,000 on 25 October.

- **Forward rate agreements** – Two parties agree the interest rate to be paid on a notional deposit with a specified maturity at an agreed future date. At the agreed future date, the seller pays the buyer if rates have risen above the contracted rate and, conversely, the buyer pays the seller if rates have fallen. The payment is the difference between the market rate and the contracted rate multiplied by the notional principal amount.

- **Futures contracts** – Derivatives that oblige the holder to buy or sell a standard quantity of a specific underlying item at a specified future date. Futures contracts are very similar to forward contracts, the distinction being that futures contracts have standardised terms and are traded on a financial exchange whereas the terms of a forward contract are tailored to meet the needs of the transacting parties, and forward contracts are not traded on a financial exchange.

- **Swaps** – Two parties agree to exchange periodic payments at specified intervals over a specified time period. For example, in an interest rate swap, the parties may agree to exchange fixed and floating interest payments calculated by reference to a notional principal amount (e.g. to swap 8% for LIBOR on a notional principal of £100 million at six monthly intervals for a period of five years). In a currency swap, the parties agree to exchange interest payments on principal amounts in different currencies and, sometimes, also to exchange the principal amounts themselves either at the date the swap is entered into and/or its maturity.

- **Options** – These give the holder the right, but not the obligation, to buy or sell a specific underlying asset on or before a specified future date.

4.2 The need for an accounting standard

Large companies are making increasing use of derivatives to finance their activities. Derivatives can be easily acquired, often for little or no cost, but their values can change very rapidly, exposing companies to the risk of large profits or losses. Because many derivatives have no cost, they might not appear in the balance sheet, even if they represent substantial assets or liabilities of the company. Gains and losses are traditionally not recorded until cash is exchanged. Gains and losses can be easily realised, often simply by making a telephone call, and this enables management to choose when to report gains and losses on realisation.

Derivatives can rapidly transform the position, performance and risk profile of a company, but this is not usually apparent from the financial statements and there may be little or no disclosure of the risks arising from using derivatives.

4.3 Risks associated with financial instruments

Because the value of derivatives depends on movements in underlying items, if an entity uses derivatives, it is exposed to risk.

Entities may use derivatives in order to manage risk.

Example

On 1 January 20X9 a UK company buys goods from a Swiss company. This results in a liability for SFr8 million which must be settled on 31 March 20X9. The exchange rate on 1 January is SFr8 = £1. The company takes out a forward exchange contract to buy SFr8 million for £1 million on 31 March 20X9. This is at the exchange rate ruling at 1 January (i.e. SFr8 = £1).

At 31 March the exchange rate is actually SFr8.5 = £1 so the contract is redeemable at £8,000,000/SFr8.5 = £941,176. If the UK company had not taken out the forward exchange contract it would have made an exchange gain of £58,824 (1,000,000 – 941,176). By taking out the forward exchange contract it has given up the chance to make this gain, but has also protected itself against the possibility of making a loss. In other words, it has used the forward exchange contract to eliminate exchange rate risk.

DEFINITION

Credit risk is the possibility that a loss may occur from the failure of another party to perform according to the terms of a contract.

DEFINITION

Liquidity risk (or funding risk) is the risk that an entity will encounter difficulty in realising assets or otherwise raising funds to meet commitments associated with financial instruments.

However, in recent years there have been several cases in which companies have failed as a result of using derivatives, sometimes as a result of speculating on price, exchange or interest rate changes.

An Appendix to FRS 13 describes the types of risk associated with financial instruments. The two most familiar of these are credit risk and liquidity risk.

Credit risk can be assessed from the nature of an entity's business and the numerical disclosures of gross debtors and provisions.

Liquidity risk can be deduced from the current and quick ratios and from disclosure of the terms and conditions of borrowing.

Two other important types of risk are associated with financial instruments – cash flow risk and market price risk.

Cash flow risk is the risk that future cash flows generated by a monetary financial instrument will fluctuate in amount.

Market price risk is the possibility that future changes in market prices may change the value, or the burden, of a financial instrument.

The main components of market price risk likely to affect most entities are as follows.

(a) **Interest rate risk** – the risk that the value of a financial instrument will fluctuate because of changes in market interest rates.

(b) **Currency risk** – the risk that the value of a financial instrument will fluctuate because of changes in foreign exchange rates.

(c) **Other market price risk** – the risk that the value of a financial instrument will fluctuate as a result of changes in market prices caused by factors other than interest rates or currencies. This category includes risks stemming from commodity prices and share prices.

The relationship between cash flow risk and market price risk can have a significant effect on the risk profile of the entity. Transactions to reduce one of these risks may have the effect of increasing the other risk.

ACTIVITY 1

An entity has two interest bearing investments. One of the investments earns interest at a fixed rate of 8% per annum. The rate of interest earned on the other is 1% above base rate.

The base rate rises to 10%. What happens to:

(a)   the market price of the two investments; and

(b)   the cash flow of the entity?

Feedback to this activity is at the end of the chapter.

4.4   The ASB's approach to the financial instruments problem

The ASB is tackling this problem in two stages. It has issued FRS 13, which requires detailed disclosures that will enable users of the financial statements to assess the risks that the entity has assumed in connection with financial instruments. It is also looking at the issues surrounding the measurement of financial instruments. As the issue of an FRS on the measurement of derivatives will probably involve far-reaching changes to present practice, the ASB wishes to allow ample time for preparers, users and auditors of accounts to debate the issues. It may be several years before a new standard is issued.

5   FRS 13 *Derivatives and other financial instruments: disclosures*

5.1   Objectives

FRS 13 was issued in order to ensure that reporting entities disclose information that enables users to assess:

A **financial instrument** is any contract that gives rise to both a financial asset of one entity and a financial liability or equity instrument of another entity.

A **derivative financial instrument** is a financial instrument that derives its value from the price or rate of some underlying item, such as interest rates, exchange rates and stock market and other indices.

- the risk profile of the entity for each of the main financial risks arising in connection with financial instruments; and

- the significance of such instruments and contracts to the entity's financial position, performance and cash flows.

Derivative financial instruments include futures, options, forward contracts, interest rate and currency swaps, interest rate caps, collars and floors, forward interest rate agreements, and commitments to purchase shares or bonds.

Underlying items include equities, bonds, interest rates, exchange rates and stock market and other indices.

5.2   Scope of FRS 13

A **financial asset** is any asset that is:
- cash
- a contractual right to receive cash or another financial asset from another entity
- a contractual right to exchange financial instruments with another entity under conditions that are potentially favourable; or
- an equity instrument of another entity.

(a) **Entities** – FRS 13 applies to public and listed companies.

(b) **Instruments to be dealt with in the disclosures** – FRS 13 applies to all financial instruments (except those specifically excluded), not just to derivatives. Financial instruments give rise to both a financial asset of one entity and a financial liability or equity instrument of another entity.

The following items are excluded from the disclosures:

- interests in subsidiary, quasi-subsidiary and associated undertakings, partnerships and joint ventures (unless held exclusively with a view to subsequent resale)

- employers' obligations to employees under employee share option and employee share schemes

- pension and similar assets and liabilities

- rights and obligations under operating leases

- equity shares and options and warrants relating to equity shares issued by the reporting entity.

A **financial liability** is any liability that is a contractual obligation:
- to deliver cash or another financial asset to another entity; or
- to exchange financial instruments with another entity under conditions that are potentially unfavourable.

(c) **Short-term debtors and creditors** – Either all or none of short-term debtors and creditors should be excluded from the disclosures. Although technically short-term debtors and creditors fall within the definition of financial instruments, the focus of FRS 13 is on financial instruments that are complex or have a significant impact on the risk profile of the entity. Therefore they do not have to be included in the disclosures, but the FRS acknowledges that some entities may wish to include them. An explanation of how these items have been dealt with should be provided.

(d) **Non-equity shares** – Non-equity shares should be dealt with in the disclosures in the same way as financial liabilities, but should be disclosed separately.

Which of the following items are financial instruments?

(a) debentures to be settled in cash

(b) plant and equipment

(c) goodwill

(d) warrants or options to subscribe for shares of the issuing entity

(e) a forward contract that will be settled in another financial instrument

(f) prepayments for goods or services

(g) stocks

(h) a forward contract that will be settled by the delivery of goods

Feedback to this activity is at the end of the chapter.

5.3 Narrative disclosures

(a) An explanation should be provided of the role that financial instruments have had during the period in creating or changing the risks the entity faces in its activities. This should include:

- an explanation of the objectives and policies for holding or issuing financial instruments and similar contracts; and

- the strategies for achieving those objectives (in both cases as agreed by the directors) that have been followed during the period.

(b) If these disclosures reflect a significant change from the explanations provided for the previous accounting period, this should be disclosed and the reasons for the change explained.

(c) If the directors agreed, before the date of approval of the financial statements, to make a significant change to the role that financial instruments will have in creating or changing the risks of the entity, that change should be explained.

(d) An explanation should be provided of how the period end numerical disclosures shown in the financial statements reflect the objectives, policies and strategies disclosed.

These disclosures should be given in the financial statements or in some other statement available with the financial statements, e.g. the operating and financial review.

5.4 Numerical disclosures

(a) **Interest rate risk** – Analyse the aggregate carrying amount of financial liabilities, by principal currency, between liabilities:

- at fixed interest rates

- at floating interest rates

- on which no interest is paid.

(b) **Currency risk** – Provide an analysis of the net amount of monetary assets and liabilities at the balance sheet date, showing the amount denominated in each currency, analysed by reference to the functional currencies of the operations involved.

(c) **Liquidity** – Present a maturity profile of the carrying amount of financial liabilities, showing amounts falling due:

- in one year or less, or on demand
- in more than one year but not more than two years
- in more than two years but not more than five years
- in more than five years.

Determine the maturity profile by reference to the earliest date on which payment can be required or on which the liability falls due.

Analyse any material undrawn committed borrowing facilities, showing amounts expiring:

- in one year or less
- in more than one year but not more than two years
- in more than two years.

(d) **Fair values** – Group the financial assets and financial liabilities (whether recognised or unrecognised) into appropriate categories and for each category disclose either:

- the aggregate fair value at the balance sheet date together with the aggregate carrying amount; or
- the aggregate fair value of items with a positive fair value and, separately, the aggregate fair value of items with a negative fair value, in both cases as at the balance sheet date and in each case accompanied by the relevant aggregate carrying amount.

Disclose the methods and any significant assumptions used in determining fair value.

Fair values need not be disclosed if it is not practicable to estimate them with sufficient reliability. The following should be provided instead:

- a description of the item and its carrying amount
- the reasons why it is not practicable to estimate fair value with sufficient reliability
- information about the principal characteristics of the underlying financial asset or liability that is pertinent to estimating its fair value.

(e) **Other disclosure requirements** – These concern:

- financial assets and financial liabilities held or issued for trading
- financial liabilities and financial assets used as hedges
- commodity contracts.

5.5   Effect of FRS 13

Most commentators accept the need for greater disclosure regarding derivatives and for this reason FRS 13 has proved relatively non-controversial. Although it could be argued that the additional disclosures contribute still further to an 'information overload', most commentators believe that the extra cost is justified.

The disclosures have the further advantage that gathering and preparing the information will provide preparers of the accounts with useful experience of the problems involved in accounting for derivatives. This will enable interested parties to participate in the debate over the next stage of the ASB's proposals.

6 Discussion Paper: *Derivatives and other financial instruments*

6.1 Introduction

In July 1996 the ASB issued a Discussion Paper: *Derivatives and other financial instruments*. The Discussion Paper deals with both disclosure and measurement issues; the disclosure proposals have since been developed into FRS 13.

As we have seen, the use of derivatives poses problems for preparers and users of financial statements for the following reasons.

- Many derivatives, such as futures and forward contracts, do not have a meaningful 'cost' that can be recognised in the financial statements.

- Gains and losses are traditionally not recorded until cash is exchanged, despite the fact that potential gains and losses often occur almost immediately. Under current accounting principles, gains and losses cannot be included in the profit and loss account before they are realised. Although SSAP 20 provides some guidance on forward exchange contracts used for trading (the forward exchange rate may be used to translate assets and liabilities into sterling) there is no guidance in any accounting standard on when to recognise gains and losses on other forms of derivative, especially where these are used for speculation, rather than for trading purposes.

The Discussion Paper attempts to address these problems, and would apply to listed and similar public interest companies only.

6.2 Measurement

The main proposal is that all financial instruments should be measured at current value.

Current value would be used for all derivatives, for holdings of shares or debt instruments of other entities and for the entity's own borrowings. The entity's own equity shares would continue to be measured at historic cost. All gains and losses would be recognised as they occur.

6.3 Arguments for using current value

The ASB believes that historic cost is no longer viable for financial instruments because:

- it does not report the actual transactions entered into

- unrealised gains and losses are not reported

- it does not actively reflect the management of risk

- it gives rise to a need for hedge accounting (which would be greatly reduced if all financial instruments were measured at current value)

- it results in a lack of comparability in that identical instruments that were acquired at different times may be recorded at different amounts.

Current value has other advantages.

- It provides relevant, up to date information about performance and stewardship.

- Current value information has predictive value.

- It is increasingly used for internal management information.

- It reflects the readily realisable nature of financial instruments (they are very similar to actual cash).

- It is practical, because many financial instruments are traded in an active market (and can therefore be easily valued).

6.4   Arguments against current value

- Assets and liabilities would be measured on different bases, because assets are likely to be non-financial and measured on the cost basis, while most liabilities are likely to be financial instruments.

- It might result in volatile profits.

- It reflects opportunity costs for transactions that may not be undertaken, rather than actual costs, and gains which may never be realised.

- It may be impractical (some instruments may be difficult to value).

- It would result in far-reaching changes to accounting practice.

6.5   Approaches to current value accounting

The ASB considered several different approaches to current value accounting. One was that all financial instruments and derivatives should be included in the balance sheet at current value at the balance sheet date. The others were 'halfway house' approaches, under which some instruments would be measured at current value and others at cost. The following 'halfway houses' were considered.

- **Basing the distinction on the kind of entity** – 'Simple' companies would use historic cost, while 'sophisticated' companies (i.e. those that actively managed risk by buying and selling derivatives in response to market movements) would use current value.

  It would be difficult to draw distinctions between the two types of company in practice. This approach would also result in non-comparability between entities that actively managed risk and those that did not.

  In practice most large companies would end up using current value because most large companies actively manage risk. The ASB has recognised this by proposing that a new accounting standard would only apply to listed and public interest companies.

- **Basing the distinction on management intent** – Historic cost would be used for instruments that management intended to hold to maturity while current value would be used for instruments that the entity intended to trade in the near future.

  An approach based on management intent would be subjective and would lead to inconsistencies with other accounting standards (for example FRS 12). It would also provide scope for deliberate manipulation of gains and losses.

  This approach would also result in a lack of comparability because identical items may be accounted for differently, depending on management's intent in respect of them. Management intent may change, resulting in a different accounting treatment that does not reflect a change in the economic position of the entity.

- **Basing the distinction on whether the instrument is a derivative** – Current value would be used for derivatives, while historic cost would be used for other financial instruments.

  This approach has little conceptual logic as the same effects can be achieved with both derivatives and non-derivatives. Therefore it would be more logical to account for them in the same way.

The ASB concluded that the anomalies that would result from such halfway houses are such as to rule them out, even as an interim solution.

6.6   Reporting gains and losses arising on financial instruments

In theory, there are several ways in which gains and losses on financial instruments could be reported.

(a) **All gains and losses could be reported in the profit and loss account**

Arguments for:

- All gains and losses represent the performance of management who are responsible for the decision to buy or sell instruments.

- If all changes in value are taken to the profit and loss account the scope for manipulation of profit is reduced.

Arguments against:

- Gains and losses on financial instruments have different characteristics from trading profits and losses. If gains and losses on financial instruments were reported outside the profit and loss account this would emphasise their different nature.

- If unrealised gains and losses on fixed rate debt were reported in the profit and loss account this would imply that fixed rate debt carried risk (because its value changes as interest rates move) and that floating rate debt is risk-free. This might mislead users.

(b) **Report certain gains in the profit and loss account and others in the statement of total recognised gains and losses (STRGL)**

Arguments for:

- Different types of gain and loss would be reported separately. For example, gains and losses on long-term instruments could be reported in the STRGL and those on short-term investments in the profit and loss account. This would highlight their different natures.

- The profit and loss account would be protected from volatility.

Arguments against:

- The main argument against this approach is that there would be problems in drawing a distinction between those gains and losses to be reported in the profit and loss account and those to be reported in the STRGL. The need to draw up principles for distinguishing the two has resulted in the ASB's separate project on reporting financial performance.

(c) **Defer changes in value in a balance sheet caption and transfer them to the profit and loss account in a future period**

Arguments for:

- Gains and losses could be 'recycled' to the profit and loss account once they were realised or gradually over the term of the instrument. This approach has the advantage of avoiding volatility in the profit and loss account. There would also be little change to present practice.

Arguments against:

- Gains and losses would not be reported in the period in which they occurred. This would provide opportunities for manipulation of the earnings figure.

- The amounts recorded in the balance sheet would be meaningless as the deferred debits and credits are not assets and liabilities. Losses would give rise to assets and gains to liabilities. Gains and losses could be shown as part of shareholders' funds, but this would effectively amount to reserve accounting and is difficult to justify.

(d) **Report some gains and losses in the STRGL and recycle them to the profit and loss account in a future period**

Arguments for:

- This is a similar method to (c) above and again, items could be recycled when they are realised or over the life of the instrument. The main advantage is that all gains and losses would be recorded in the period in which they occur.

Arguments against:

- Reported figures can be meaningless as an item can be reported in two performance statements at different times For example, if a loss on an instrument is initially reported in the STRGL and is recycled to the profit and loss account in a later period, the STRGL will then include a gain relating to an instrument on which only losses have arisen in a previous period. This effect is difficult to explain.

- The STRGL becomes a 'holding tank' for gains and losses that have not yet been reported in the profit and loss account. This is contrary to the way in which the statement is used for other items.

- The approach is inconsistent with FRS 3 *Reporting financial performance*. FRS 3 requires that a gain arising on the revaluation of a fixed asset that is initially recorded in the STRGL should not be reported again in the profit and loss account when the gain is realised.

The Discussion Paper recommends the second approach described above – report certain gains in the profit and loss account and others in the statement of total recognised gains and losses (STRGL).

It proposes that changes in the value of:

- fixed rate borrowings

- related derivatives used to manage the interest basis of borrowings (e.g. an interest rate swap that serves to 'convert' a borrowing from fixed rate to floating); and

- borrowings and derivatives that hedge a net investment in an overseas operation (this would be consistent with the requirements of SSAP 20)

would be reported in the statement of total recognised gains and losses. All other changes in value, whether realised or unrealised, would be recognised in the profit and loss account.

These proposals are likely to be modified in the light of the ASB's project on reporting financial performance. This proposes that the profit and loss account and statement of total recognised gains and losses should be amalgamated into one single performance statement.

6.7 Hedge accounting

The aim of hedging is to compensate for the risk associated with the hedged position. A hedged position can include recognised assets and liabilities, commitments under firm contracts and expected, but not firmly contracted, future transactions. (For example, a foreign currency investment can be hedged against a foreign currency loan.)

Hedge accounting involves linking separate transactions for accounting purposes because one of these is designed to offset exposures arising on the other. For example, a company that has ordered a fixed asset from a foreign supplier for delivery in the next financial year might take out a forward contract this year to buy the required amount of foreign currency so as to fix the sterling cost of the asset.

Hedge accounting may cause the following problems:

- it can be used to defer reporting losses

- it is discretionary (being based on management intent)

- it can result in losses being reported as gains and assets being reported as liabilities.

Some members of the ASB believe that hedge accounting should not be allowed. Gains and losses should be shown in the year in which they arise, with disclosures being used to explain gains and losses that 'hedge' transactions of other years. Other members favour its use in certain circumstances, such as the situation described below.

Example

A company has a contract to buy a certain quantity of raw materials from a German supplier for Euros on 30 June 20X3. Shortly before its year-end of 30 April 20X3 it takes out a forward contract to buy Euros on 30 June 20X3.

Solution

If there is no hedge accounting

At 30 April 20X3 the forward contract would be included in the balance sheet at current value (as proposed). The resulting gain or loss would be recognised in the profit and loss account for the year.

In the year to 30 April 20X4, the purchase of raw materials is recorded at the spot rate for Euros ruling on 30 June 20X3 and the same amount is recorded as the cost of the stock. Any further gain or loss on closing out the forward contract is taken to the profit and loss account for the year.

With hedge accounting

The gain or loss on valuing the forward contract on 30 June 20X3 would be deferred and recognised in the year to 30 June 20X4. This matches the gain or loss with the transaction that it hedges.

This is consistent with the current requirements of SSAP 20, which allows trading transactions to be recorded at the rate specified in a matching forward contract.

Some members of the ASB would also allow hedge accounting to be used where an entity is 'commercially committed' to a transaction. For example, suppose that the company above did not have a firm contract to purchase the raw materials, but fully expected to make the purchase. Because the raw materials were essential to its business and could only be purchased from a German supplier the purchase could not take place without exposing the company to currency risk. In this situation it could be argued that the company is 'commercially committed' to the transaction. It would be difficult to define 'commercial commitment' in practice.

The ASB is considering whether there are any circumstances in which hedge accounting should be permitted. The Discussion Paper concludes that the use of hedge accounting techniques should probably either be restricted in some way or prohibited.

7   FRED 23 and FRED 30

These two FREDs are part of the 2005 convergence project. The main changes introduced by these proposals are:

1   Hedging

Hedge accounting will only be allowed in the following circumstances:

- there is formal documentation identifying the hedge and the items being hedged
- the hedge is expected to be highly effective
- the effectiveness of the hedge can be measured reliably
- the effectiveness of the hedge is monitored continuously.

2   Measurement

Financial assets (including derivatives that are assets) should be measured at fair value, except for:

- loans and receivables originated by the entity, which must be measured at amortised cost
- held-to-maturity investments, which must be measured at amortised cost
- investments in equity instruments where fair value cannot be reliably measured, which must be measured at cost.

Financial liabilities should be measured at amortised cost, except for:

- liabilities that are held for trading, which must be measured at fair value
- derivatives that are liabilities, which must be measured at fair value.

3   Classification

The traditional split of shares into equity shares and non-equity shares is no more. All shares must be classified as either equity or liabilities, depending on the substance of the instrument. For example, normal ordinary shares would continue to be shown as equity on the balance sheet. However, a redeemable preference share would now be shown as a liability on the balance sheet, since there is a contractual obligation to deliver cash at a fixed date in the future.

4   Compound instruments

Instruments such as convertible bonds have both a liability and an equity element. 'Split accounting' is required on the balance sheet, showing the equity element as part of equity and the liability element amongst the liabilities on the balance sheet.

SELF-TEST QUESTIONS

FRS 4 *Capital instruments*

1   Define a capital instrument. (1.1)

2   What are the objectives of FRS 4? (1.2)

3   At what amount should a capital instrument be initially carried? (1.5)

4   What analysis of the maturity of debt does FRS 4 require to be presented? (1.8)

Application notes

5   What are AMPS and how should they be accounted for? (2.2)

6   How should perpetual debt be accounted for? (2.7)

Measurement issues relating to complex capital instruments

7   What steps are involved in split accounting? (3.1)

The problems of accounting for derivatives and other financial instruments

8   What is a derivative, and what are they normally used for? (4.1)

9   How does FRS 13 define credit risk and liquidity risk? (4.3)

FRS 13 *Derivatives and other financial instruments: disclosures*

10   What are the objectives of FRS 13? To which entities does it apply? (5.1, 5.2)

11   Define (a) a financial asset and (b) a financial liability. (5.2)

12   What narrative disclosures need to be made regarding the role of financial instruments? (5.3)

Discussion Paper: *Derivatives and other financial instruments*

13   What are the arguments for and against the idea of measuring financial instruments at current value? (6.3, 6.4)

14   How does the ASB's Discussion Paper recommend that gains and losses on financial instruments be reported? (6.6)

EXAM-TYPE
QUESTION

Hartington plc

Hartington plc is a manufacturing company which is listed on the London Stock Exchange. During recent years the company's operations have expanded rapidly and this expansion has chiefly been financed by loans from third parties.

During the year ended 30 June 20X3 the company entered into the following transactions.

(1) On 1 July 20X2 it obtained an index-linked loan of £2 million on which interest of 5% is paid annually. The loan is repayable on 30 June 20X5 and the amount to be repaid is the principal amount multiplied by an index. This index stood at 105 on 1 July 20X2 and at 110 on 30 June 20X3.

(2) On 1 July 20X2 it issued £5 million zero coupon bonds. The bonds are redeemable at £8,051,000 on 30 June 20X7. This represents the only payment to the holders of the bonds.

Discount table extract: Present value of £1 to be received after *t* years:

Number of years

	8%	10%	12%
1	0.926	0.909	0.893
2	0.857	0.826	0.797
3	0.794	0.751	0.712
4	0.735	0.683	0.636
5	0.681	0.621	0.567

Required:

(a) Explain why it became necessary to develop a financial reporting standard on derivatives and other financial instruments.   **(10 marks)**

(b) Explain how the loans (1) and (2) above should be treated in the financial statements of Hartington plc for the year ended 30 June 20X3.   **(4 marks)**

(c) Show how the loans should be disclosed in the notes to the balance sheet of Hartington plc for the year ended 30 June 20X3. (Note: you are NOT required to produce a narrative explanation of the role of financial instruments during the period.)   **(6 marks)**

(Total: 20 marks)

For the answer to this question see the 'Answers' section at the end of the book.

FEEDBACK TO ACTIVITY **1**	Fixed rate investment: the market price will probably fall, so that the entity may make a loss when it sells the investment, but the amount of interest and therefore cash received stays the same. In other words, there is market price risk, but no immediate cash flow risk.

Floating rate investment: the market price is likely to stay about the same, but the interest and cash receivable increases. This investment exposes the entity to cash flow risk, but not to significant market price risk.

Tutorial note:

From this example we can see that the choice of which risk the management seeks to reduce will have an important bearing on the entity's financial position, financial results and cash flows. Historically, however, users of the financial statements have had very little information about an entity's exposure to these risks.

FEEDBACK TO ACTIVITY **2**	Items (a), (d) and (e) are financial instruments.

Chapter 13

'OFF BALANCE SHEET' TRANSACTIONS

'Off balance sheet' finance is a form of creative accounting. It involves the manipulation of items in the financial statements so that they are excluded or changed in amount so as to present a more favourable picture of the entity.

FRS 5 *Reporting the substance of transactions* requires entities to report the economic substance of transactions in their financial statements. This standard has been heavily influenced by the ideas in the Statement of Principles.

Objectives

When you have studied this chapter you should be able to:

- explain the nature of the 'off balance sheet' problem and the principle of substance over form

- understand common forms of 'off balance sheet' finance and apply current regulatory requirements

- discuss the perceived problems of current regulatory requirements.

1   The 'off balance sheet' problem

1.1   The perceived advantages of off balance sheet finance schemes

The perceived benefits include the following.

- Apparent lower level of gearing.

- There may be a breach of loan covenants if further liabilities are recorded on balance sheet.

- In most cases, off balance sheet finance schemes result in assets also being reduced, so a higher ROCE may result.

- Specialised activities, e.g. leasing and financial services (which have high gearing) can be removed from a group balance sheet.

1.2   The concept of substance over form

The concept prevents off balance sheet finance because if the commercial reality is that the company has a financial commitment, that commitment should be included on the balance sheet.

The first major area where an accounting standard introduced a change from legal form to substance was SSAP 21 on leases and hire purchase. This standard is examined in detail in the next chapter but should already be familiar.

Finance leases give rights over the use of assets for a period which covers all or a substantial part of their useful life. Such leases are effectively an alternative to hire purchase and loan financing. Hence failure to capitalise such leases would give rise to

DEFINITION

Off balance sheet finance is the organisation of transactions such that financial commitments are not included in the balance sheet of a company or a group.

DEFINITION

Substance over form requires that transactions and other events should be accounted for and presented in accordance with their substance and financial reality and not merely with their legal form.

a disparity of accounting treatment which could distort comparisons between companies; in particular, comparisons of:

- return on capital employed
- debt/equity ratio

could be misleading.

Since the introduction of SSAP 21, companies have developed other means of providing off balance sheet finance, some of which were stopped by the revised definition of a subsidiary under CA89 (quasi-subsidiaries) and the rest (it is hoped by the ASB) by the issue of FRS 5.

2   FRS 5 *Reporting the substance of transactions*

2.1   Introduction

FRS 5 was issued in April 1994. Its main thrust is to ensure that financial statements report the substance of transactions and not merely their legal form. The view held by the ASB was that, previously, users could be left unaware of the total assets employed in a business and of its overall financing. Detailed disclosures in the notes are no substitute for inclusion in the accounts.

2.2   General principles

FRS 5 sets out general principles covering the following areas:

- what is excluded from the scope of the Standard
- how to determine the substance of a transaction
- whether any resulting assets and liabilities should be included in the balance sheet
- at what point there should be changes in previously recognised assets
- what disclosures are necessary
- whether any 'vehicle' companies incorporated into a transaction should be consolidated
- under what circumstances a 'linked' presentation is appropriate.

The FRS also contains notes showing how its requirements are to be applied to seven specific transaction types as we shall see below.

2.3   Scope of the standard

Certain transactions are excluded from the standard because of their special nature. The main exclusions relate to financing arrangements such as forward contracts, futures, foreign exchange and interest rate swaps. We have seen that FRS 13 requires entities to disclose information about financial instruments, and that the ASB is developing a further accounting standard on their measurement.

Where the general principles of the standard seem to apply to an asset or liability which is subject to the requirements of a more specific standard (e.g. SSAP 9 covers stocks), the specific requirements of the other standard apply.

2.4   Determining the substance of a transaction

Common features of transactions whose substance is not readily apparent are:

- separation of the legal title to an item from the ability to enjoy the principal benefits and exposure to the principal risks associated with it
- linking of a transaction with one or more others in such a way that the commercial effect cannot be understood without reference to the series as a whole; and

- inclusion in a transaction of one or more options whose terms make it highly likely that the option will be exercised.

A key step in determining the substance of a transaction is to identify its effect on the assets and liabilities of the entity. Assets are, broadly, rights or other access to future economic benefits controlled by an entity. Liabilities are, broadly, an entity's obligations to transfer economic benefits.

Risk often indicates which party has an asset. Risk is important, as the party which has access to benefits (and hence an asset) will usually also be the one to suffer or gain if the benefits ultimately differ from those expected.

These points are considered in detail in Chapters 4 and 5 of the ASB's Statement of Principles.

2.5   Inclusion of assets and liabilities in the balance sheet

Assets and liabilities should be included in the balance sheet where there is both:

- sufficient evidence that an asset or liability exists; and

- the asset or liability can be measured at a monetary amount with sufficient reliability.

2.6   Transactions in previously recognised assets

An asset should cease to be recognised only where two conditions are both fulfilled – that the entity retains no significant access to material benefits, and that any risk it retains is immaterial in relation to the variation in benefits likely to occur in practice.

2.7   Disclosures

Disclosure of a transaction should be sufficiently detailed to enable the user of the financial statements to understand its commercial effect.

A transaction may need to be disclosed whether or not it results in additional assets and liabilities being recognised. Where assets or liabilities are recognised but their nature differs from that of items usually found under the relevant balance sheet heading, the differences should be explained. For example certain assets may not be available for use as security for liabilities.

To the extent that a transaction has not resulted in the recognition of assets or liabilities it is still necessary to consider whether disclosure of its nature and effect is required in order to give a true and fair view. For example the transaction may give rise to guarantees or other obligations.

2.8   'Vehicle' companies

Some off balance sheet financing arrangements include the use of another entity (a 'vehicle') to house certain assets and liabilities. Normally, the arrangement will be structured so that the vehicle does not meet the legal definition of a subsidiary. Where the commercial effect is no different from that which would result were the vehicle a subsidiary, then the vehicle will meet FRS 5's definition of a 'quasi-subsidiary'. FRS 5 requires such quasi-subsidiaries to be included in consolidated accounts in the same way as if they were subsidiaries.

2.9   Linked presentation and offset

Parts of FRS 5 require certain assets and liabilities to be linked together (i.e. the gross amount of assets and liabilities are shown but are also netted off) or offset (i.e. only the net amount is shown).

Linked presentation

The linked presentation is available for certain non-recourse finance arrangements. Non-recourse finance involves selling an asset such as a debtor to a third party. If the seller does not have to make any payments to the purchaser if the debtor does not eventually pay the debt, the seller no longer has an asset (i.e. the debtor) as it does not meet the recognition criteria in the FRS (all significant benefits and risks have been transferred).

In some non-recourse finance arrangements however, an entity retains significant benefits and risks associated with a specific item, but the maximum loss it can suffer is limited to a fixed monetary amount. In such circumstances a 'linked' presentation is required to present the nature of such an arrangement.

Example
Extract from balance sheet

	£
Debtor	80,000
Less: Non-returnable amounts received on sale of debtor	80,000
	-

Pressure for the above approach came from certain financial institutions (e.g. banks) which wanted to show their gross 'assets' (e.g. mortgages advanced) even though they had passed on the assets, in this particular form, to another entity.

Offset

Offsetting of an asset and liability is generally not allowed, but here also the FRS is attempting to respond to special cases. It allows offset when the items do not constitute 'separate assets and liabilities'. Its main area of use would be certain types of bank balance and overdraft.

3   Applying FRS 5

3.1   Introduction

FRS 5 includes detailed application notes on the most common types of 'special purpose' transactions as follows:

- consignment stock
- sale and repurchase agreements
- factoring of debts
- securitised mortgages
- loan transfers
- Private Finance Initiative (PFI) and similar contracts
- revenue recognition.

The notes are meant to clarify, rather than to override, the general principles of the FRS but they are mandatory.

3.2 Consignment stock

Legal title on consignment stock may pass when one of a number of events has occurred, for example, when the dealer has held the stock for a specified period such as six months, or when the dealer has sold the goods. The sales price may be determined at the date of supply, or it may vary with the length of the period between supply and purchase, or it may be the manufacturer's factory price at sale.

Other terms of such arrangements include a requirement for the dealer to pay a deposit, and responsibility for insurance. The arrangement should be analysed to determine whether the dealer has in substance acquired the stock before the date of transfer of legal title.

FRS 5 states that the key factor will be who bears the risk of slow-moving stock. The risk involved is the cost of financing the stock for the period it is held. In a simple arrangement where stock is supplied for a fixed price that will be charged whenever the title is transferred and there is no deposit, the manufacturer bears the slow movement risk. If, however, the price to be paid increases by a factor that varies with interest rates and the time the stock is held, then the dealer bears the risk. If the price charged to the dealer is the manufacturer's list price at the date of sale, then again the risks associated with the stock fall on the manufacturer. Whoever bears the slow movement risk should recognise the stock on the balance sheet.

Consignment stock arrangements are most common in the motor trade.

ACTIVITY 1

On 1 January 20X6 Gillingham plc, a manufacturer, entered into an agreement to provide Canterbury plc, a retailer, with machines for resale. Under the terms of the agreement Canterbury plc pays a fixed rental per month for each machine that it holds and also pays the cost of insuring and maintaining the machines. The company can display the machines in its showrooms and use them as demonstration models.

When a machine is sold to a customer, Canterbury plc pays Gillingham plc the factory price at the time the machine was originally delivered. All machines remaining unsold six months after their original delivery must be purchased by Canterbury plc at the factory price at the time of delivery.

Gillingham plc can require Canterbury plc to return the machines at any time within the six month period. In practice, this right has never been exercised. Canterbury plc can return unsold machines to Gillingham plc at any time during the six month period, without penalty. In practice, this has never happened.

At 31 December 20X6 the agreement is still in force and Canterbury plc holds several machines which were delivered less than six months earlier. How should these machines be treated in the accounts for the year ended 31 December 20X6?

Feedback to this activity is at the end of the chapter.

3.3 Sale and re-purchase agreements

In such agreements the sale may be at market value or at some agreed percentage of market value. The re-purchase arrangement may take a number of forms, such as an unconditional commitment for both parties, an option granted to the seller to repurchase (a call option) or an option granted to the buyer to require re-purchase (a put option). The arrangements often contain provisions to enable the seller to make use of the asset during its ownership by the buyer.

The re-purchase price may be variable (depending on the original price and the period during which the asset has been held by the purchaser), agreed at the time of re-purchase or subject to market price movements. The re-purchase price may also be designed to permit the purchaser to recover incidental holding costs if these do not continue to be met by the seller.

FRS 5 states that the key question is whether the commercial effect is that of a sale or of a secured loan. A secured loan transaction will usually have the following features:

- the seller will secure access to all future benefits inherent in the asset, often through call options

- the buyer will secure adequate return on the purchase (interest on the loan, often through adjustment of the re-purchase price) and appropriate protection against loss in value of the asset bought (often through put options).

The analysis should look at all features of the agreement that are likely to have a commercial effect in practice.

Sale and re-purchase arrangements are common in property development and in maturing whisky stocks.

3.4 Debt factoring

Factoring of debts is a well-established method of obtaining finance. In most forms of factoring, debts are sold to the factor, but the latter's degree of control over, and responsibility for, those debts will vary from one arrangement to another. A significant accounting question is only likely to arise where the factoring arrangement leads to the receipt of cash earlier than would have been the case had the debts been unfactored. If this is so, the question to be answered is whether the seller has in substance received either a loan on the security of his debtors or receipts that are appropriately credited to reduce a debtor.

If the seller is in essence a borrower, and the factor a lender, then the arrangements will be such as to provide that the seller pays the equivalent of interest to the factor on the timing difference between amounts received by him from the factor and those collected by the factor from the debtor. Such payment would be in addition to any other charges.

FRS 5 states that the key factor in the analysis will be who bears the risk (of slow payment) and the benefit (of early payment) from the debtors. If the finance cost reflects events subsequent to transfer, then the transfer is likely to be equivalent to obtaining finance because the seller is bearing the risks and rewards of the debtors. If the cost is determined when the transfer is made, with no other variable costs, then it is likely to be a straightforward sale.

The risk of bad debts is unlikely to be relevant to the analysis, as the exposure to such risk is agreed between the seller and the factor and charges will reflect this, just as in a normal credit insurance contract.

A C T I V I T Y   2

On 1 January 20X6 Lewis plc entered into an agreement with Factoring plc whereby it transferred title to its debtors to Factoring plc subject to a reduction for bad debts based on past experience. Lewis plc received a payment of 90% of the total of net debtors. Under the terms of the agreement, the company had the right to a future sum the amount of which depended on whether and when the debtors paid. Factoring plc had the right of recourse against Lewis plc for any additional losses up to an agreed maximum amount.

At 31 December 20X6, title had been transferred to debtors with an invoice value of £10 million less a bad debt provision of £300,000 and Lewis plc was subject under the agreement to a maximum potential debit of £100,000 to cover losses.

What is the appropriate accounting treatment for this transaction in the balance sheet of Lewis plc at 31 December 20X6?

Feedback to this activity is at the end of the chapter.

3.5   Securitised assets

The assets transferred in a securitisation may be property, or stock or receivables such as trade debts. However this type of arrangement is most common in the UK for mortgages.

Suppose Company A issues mortgages to home buyers. It is responsible for setting the mortgage rate and term and for credit control. A is known as the 'originator' as it originates the mortgages.

A packages together a group of mortgages and 'sells' them to Company B. B issues loan notes offering the mortgages as security. Then B uses the proceeds from issuing the loan notes to settle with A. B is known as the 'issuer'.

B usually has negligible equity, and the shares that it has are usually owned by a charitable trust or by a 'friend' of A. A does not control the friendly party and thus B is not a legal subsidiary of A.

A will usually continue to service the mortgages and will extract profit from B by a servicing fee.

Where the originator retains significant benefits or risks then the mortgages remain as an asset and the money it received is shown as a liability.

The amounts may be shown under a linked presentation (see above) if the necessary conditions are satisfied.

Derecognition of the asset is only appropriate where the originator has not retained any significant benefits.

3.6   Loan transfers

Loan transfers involve transferring the benefits and risks of a loan to a third party. Effectively the loan is 'sold' like a tangible asset.

The same principles apply here as for securitised assets.

3.7   Quasi-subsidiaries

Identifying quasi-subsidiaries is very similar to identifying assets. As for other types of 'special purpose' transaction, the key factors are risks and benefits.

The flow of benefits from the other entity is not normally the critical factor. Benefits obtained from subsidiaries (e.g. dividends) may not differ substantially from those obtained from other forms of investment.

Evidence of which party is exposed to benefits and risks is often given by determining which party stands to suffer or gain from the financial performance of an entity.

Control is also a key factor. Control is defined as the ability to direct the financial and operating policies of an entity with a view to gaining economic benefit from its activities. The existence of control normally distinguishes a quasi-subsidiary from other forms of investment.

If one party controls another, but does not obtain benefits from the other's net assets, it is effectively managing that party on behalf of another. There must be a flow of benefits in order to distinguish control from management.

Where the operating and financial policies of an entity have been determined in advance, then the company which obtains the benefits will be deemed to have control on those grounds alone.

It is important to look at the situation that arises in practice and not merely at the notional rights that may be held by various investors.

ACTIVITY 3

On 1 January 20X6 Sarton plc sold a factory that it owned to Bypass plc, a wholly owned subsidiary of the National Investment Bank plc. The sale proceeds were £15 million. The factory had a book value of £12 million. Bypass plc was financed by a loan of £15 million from the National Investment Bank plc. Sarton plc was paid a fee by Bypass plc to continue to operate the factory. This fee represented the balance of profit remaining after Bypass plc had paid its parent company loan interest set at a level that represented current interest rates. If there was an operating loss, Sarton plc would be charged a fee that would cover the operating losses and interest payable.

How should these transactions be treated in the financial statements of Sarton plc for the year ended 31 December 20X6?

Feedback to this activity is at the end of the chapter.

3.8   Joint ventures

An entity may enter into joint ventures with other entities, in order to carry out specific projects. A joint venture may be a quasi-subsidiary of one of the venturers. Only if the two parties are genuine equals will a quasi-subsidiary relationship not exist.

Again, it is necessary to look at both control and benefits.

KEY POINT

Only if the two venturers in a joint venture are genuine equals will a quasi-subsidiary relationship not exist.

The key factor which dictates the substance of a joint venture arrangement is normally the identity of the two investors and their objectives in entering into the arrangement. If one of the parties to the venture is a bank or other financial institution, seeking a lender's return on the venture, it is likely that the joint venture is a quasi-subsidiary of the other party.

If one of the parties stands to gain or lose more than the other from the financial performance of the venture, then the venture is probably a quasi-subsidiary of that party. Gains and losses do not only arise from actual profit sharing. They may arise through interest, management charges, guarantees or options to transfer assets. As usual, it is important to look at the situation which is likely to arise in practice.

3.9   The Private Finance Initiative (PFI) and similar contracts

In September 1998 the ASB issued a further Application Note to FRS 5. This Application Note covers transactions subject to the Private Finance Initiative (PFI).

Under a typical PFI contract, a private sector 'operator' constructs a capital asset (e.g. a road, bridge, hospital, school) and uses that asset to provide services to a public sector 'purchaser'. The accounting issues are:

- whether the purchaser has an asset (the property used to provide the contracted services) and a corresponding liability to pay the operator for it; or

- whether the operator has an asset of the property used to provide the contracted services and a debt due from the purchaser.

A PFI contract should be analysed in two stages.

(a) Exclude any separable elements of the contract that relate only to services (these are not relevant to deciding which party has the asset).

(b) Assess the remainder of the contract.

Where all that remains is payments for the property that are akin to a stand-alone lease, SSAP 21 should be applied. This means that where the purchaser has substantially all of the risks and rewards of ownership of the property, the purchaser has an asset and a liability to pay for it.

In all other cases, FRS 5 should be applied. This means that the asset is recorded by the party that bears the profits or losses (risks and rewards) relating to the asset.

These requirements have proved controversial, the main issue being the separation of the services from the remainder of the contract. The Treasury view of PFI contracts is that they are essentially contracts for services rather than buildings and that the property and the service elements must be considered as a whole. This view normally results in the assets and liabilities being kept off the purchaser's balance sheet.

The ASB view is that transactions which give rise to assets and liabilities for the government should be reported as such.

3.10 PFI-related issues for service providers; UITF Abstract 34

Companies bidding to supply products or services often incur substantial costs before any contract is awarded. UITF Abstract 34 states that these costs should be charged as an expense immediately, unless it is virtually certain that the contract will be obtained. Once it is virtually certain that the contract will be obtained, then any directly attributable costs should be capitalised and then expensed over the life of the contract. Costs previously charged must not be reinstated as an asset.

3.11 Revenue recognition

In November 2003 the ASB issued one more Application Note to FRS 5, this time covering the topic of revenue recognition.

Revenue is the inflow of economic benefits during the period arising in the course of the ordinary activities of the enterprise. The Statement of Principles considers the principles of when revenue should be recognised in the performance statements, but the ASB wanted to include guidance in a mandatory FRS. The starting point for the recognition process is always the effect that the transaction involved has had on the reporting entity's assets and liabilities. In principle, therefore, revenue should be recognised when the transaction has increased the entity's recognised net assets.

For example, a seller should recognise revenue under a sale transaction with a customer when, and to the extent that, it obtains the right to consideration for the sale. At that time the seller will recognise a new asset, the debtor.

Revenue should be measured at the fair value of the right to consideration. This will be the price specified in the contractual arrangement, net of discounts, value added tax and similar sales taxes.

In addition to these basic rules, the Application Note gives specific guidance in a number of areas:

- long-term contractual performance (building on the rules in SSAP 9)

- separation and linking of contractual arrangements

- bill and hold arrangements (where there is transfer of title but physical delivery is deferred to a later date)

- sales with rights of return

- presentation of turnover as principal or as agent.

3.12 UITF Abstract 38 *Accounting for ESOP trusts*

Abstract 38 replaces the earlier Abstract 13, that dealt with the same topic.

Employee share ownership plans (ESOPs) are often used as vehicles for distributing shares to employees under remuneration schemes. The main features of ESOPs are often as follows.

- The ESOP trust provides a 'warehouse' for the sponsoring company's shares, acquiring and holding shares that are to be transferred to employees in the future. Purchase of the shares by the trust may be financed by the sponsoring company and/or a third party bank loan.

- Where an ESOP trust borrows from a third party, the sponsoring company will normally guarantee the loan.

- Shares held by the ESOP trust are distributed to employees through an employee share scheme.

- Most ESOP trusts are designed to serve the purposes of the sponsoring company, and to ensure that there will be minimal risk of any conflict arising between the duties of the trustees and the interest of the company. Where this is so, the sponsoring company has *de facto* control.

UITF Consensus

Where the sponsoring company effectively controls the shares held by an ESOP trust, the principles of FRS 5 require that it recognises certain assets and liabilities of the trust in its own accounts.

Until such time as the shares held by the ESOP trust vest unconditionally in employees, they should be recognised in the sponsoring company's accounts as a deduction from shareholders' funds. They cannot be shown as an asset since they do not meet the definition of an asset in the Statement of Principles: no economic benefit will be received from a third party arising from the shares.

Sufficient information should be disclosed in the financial statements of the sponsoring company to enable readers to understand the significance of the ESOP trust in the context of the sponsoring company. This should include:

- a description of the main features of the ESOP trust including the arrangements for distributing shares to employees

- the number and market values of the shares held by the ESOP trust which have not yet vested unconditionally with employees, and the corresponding deduction from shareholders' funds

- the extent to which these shares are under option to employees, or have been conditionally gifted to them.

3.13 UITF Abstract 32 *Employee benefit trusts and other intermediate payment arrangements*

The issue

Some entities establish and provide funds to employee benefit trusts. The trusts' accumulated assets are then used to pay the entities' employees for their services. There are two important issues:

– Should a payment to the intermediary (the trust) be charged as an expense when the payment is made?

– If the payment is not an expense, what are the nature and extent of the sponsoring entities' assets and liabilities after the payment?

UITF Consensus

This Abstract does not apply to intermediate payment arrangements dealt with in UITF Abstract 38 (ESOP Trusts) and FRS 17 *Retirement benefits* (pension schemes).

When an entity transfers funds to an intermediary (such as a trust), there should be a rebuttable presumption that the sponsoring entity has exchanged one asset (usually cash) for another (such as restricted cash or a prepayment) and that the payment itself does not represent an immediate expense.

When the sponsoring entity will continue to benefit from the assets transferred and has control of that benefit, the intermediary's assets, and any liabilities that it has, should be recognised as assets and liabilities of the sponsoring entity.

When an entity recognises the assets and liabilities held by an intermediary on its balance sheet, it should disclose sufficient information in the notes to its financial statements to enable readers to understand any restrictions relating to those assets and liabilities.

4 Problem areas

4.1 Recognition of transactions – evidence of existence

Traditional accounting practice recognises most transactions only when they have been performed, for example when goods have been despatched by the seller and received by the purchaser. However, if the principles in FRS 5 are applied it can be difficult to identify the point in time at which assets and liabilities should be recognised.

It is possible to interpret the recognition criteria to mean that entering into a purchase contract should result in the creation of an asset for the purchaser (the right to receive the goods) and a liability (the amount due for the goods). This is because there is evidence (the contract) that a future inflow and outflow of benefit will occur.

This would be a significant change in accounting practice and it is doubtful whether the ASB actually intends this approach to be applied to the majority of transactions.

The Statement of Principles gives some guidance. What constitutes sufficient evidence is a matter of judgement in the particular circumstances of each case. The main source of evidence is experience, including:

- evidence provided by the event that has given rise to the item

- past experience with similar items

- current information directly relating to the item

- evidence provided by transactions of other entities in similar items.

4.2   Recognition – measurement of items

An item should be recognised if it can be measured at a monetary amount with sufficient reliability. FRS 5 states that the effect of prudence is that less reliability of measurement is acceptable when recognising items that involve increases in liabilities than when recognising increases in assets. Where a reasonable estimate of the amount of an item is available, the item should be recognised.

4.3   Derecognition of assets

FRS 5 only addresses derecognition of assets. Derecognition of liabilities is not discussed.

- **Continued recognition of assets** – Where a transaction results in no significant changes to either the benefits or the risks relating to the asset in question the asset should continue to be recognised. For example, if risk is eliminated by financing the asset on a non-recourse basis the asset remains on the balance sheet because the entity still has the benefits attaching to the asset. Any transaction that is in substance a form of financing (e.g. a sale and leaseback) means that the asset cannot be derecognised.

- **Ceasing to recognise an asset in its entirety** – Where a transaction transfers to others all significant rights to benefits and all significant exposure to risks that relate to a previously recognised asset, the entire asset should cease to be recognised.

The difficulty here is interpreting 'significant'. FRS 5 states that it should be judged in relation to those benefits and risks that are likely to occur in practice. The importance of the risk retained must be assessed in the context of the total risk relating to the asset.

4.4   Partial derecognition of assets: special cases

In some cases there may be a significant change in the entity's rights to benefits and exposure to risks, but not a complete transfer.

- **Transfer of only part of an asset** – An identifiable part of an asset can be transferred. For example, an entity might sell a proportionate part of a loan, so that future receipts are shared proportionately between the buyer and the seller. Another example is the sale of part of a freehold property.

  Alternatively, an asset could comprise rights to two or more separate benefit streams, each with its own risks. An entity could dispose of one of these streams. An example would be the 'strip' of an interest bearing loan into rights to cash flow from interest and rights to cash flow from repayment of the principal. The entity disposes of the right to receive interest but retains the right to receive the principal.

  In both these cases, the entity ceases to recognise the part of the original asset that has been transferred, but continues to recognise the remainder.

- **Transfer of an asset for only part of its life** – An example of this is where an entity sells a property and agrees to repurchase it from the buyer in several years' time. The entity's original asset changes from being the original property to a residual interest in the property. In addition, the entity has a liability for the obligation to pay the repurchase price.

  It is not clear how much of the life of the asset must be disposed of in order to justify derecognition of the asset and the recording of a sale. FRS 5 states that both the benefits and the risks retained must be significantly different from those which were held before the transaction took place. For example, selling an asset and buying it back after only a very short time would not allow any part of the asset to be removed from the balance sheet.

KEY POINT

In order to justify derecognition of an asset and the recording of a sale, FRS 5 states that both the benefits and the risks retained must be significantly different from those which were held before the transaction took place.

- **Transfer of an asset for all or part of its life with some benefit or risk retained** – FRS 5 gives examples as follows.

  (a) An entity may sell an investment in a subsidiary with the consideration including an element of deferred performance-related consideration. The asset is no longer an investment in a subsidiary, but a debtor for the performance-related consideration (although under FRS 12 the debtor may be a contingent asset that is not recognised). The effect is that a sale is recognised.

  (b) An entity may sell equipment subject to a warranty in respect of the condition of the equipment at the time of sale. This transfers all significant rights to benefits and some significant exposure to risks to the buyer (i.e. those arising from the equipment's future use) but leaves the seller with some significant risk. The seller ceases to recognise the equipment as an asset (and recognises a sale), but recognises a liability for its warranty obligation or guarantee (subject to the requirements of FRS 12).

- **Measurement and profit recognition** – Where there is partial derecognition, it is necessary to measure the change in the entity's assets and liabilities and any resulting profit or loss. The previous carrying value of the asset is apportioned into an amount relating to those benefits and risks disposed of and an amount relating to those retained.

  This is reasonably straightforward in some cases, particularly in cases where a proportionate share in an asset has been retained. In other cases, there are practical problems. FRS 5 states that a prudent approach should be adopted, with full provision being made for any probable loss, but recognition of any gain being deferred to the extent that it is in doubt. This area of the standard has been criticised as being vague and unsatisfactory.

Example

On 1 January 20X1 the Amber Bank plc made a loan of £5 million to Carnelian Ltd for 4 years. The loan carries a fixed interest rate of 10%. On 31 December 20X1 Amber Bank sold the right to receive interest payments for the remaining three years to the National Bank plc for £1.5 million. The Amber Bank retains the right to repayment of the principal.

How should the partial derecognition be accounted for in the financial statements of the Amber Bank?

Solution

The £5 million debtor in Amber Bank's balance sheet is apportioned between the amount sold and the amount retained. The amount retained is the present value of £5 million receivable in three years' time, discounted at 10% – the interest rate implicit in the arrangement.

Net present value: £5 million × 0.826 = £4,130,000. This amount remains in the balance sheet as a debtor.

Net present value of three annual payments of £500,000: £500,000 × 2.487 = £1,243,500.

The profit on sale is £256,500 (1,500,000 – 1,243,500).

5   International standards

There is no equivalent IAS or IFRS to FRS 5. However, the principle that an enterprise should report the substance of its transactions, rather than their legal form, is included in IAS 1. What are missing though are the detailed provisions and examples of FRS 5.

The IASB has issued an entire IAS on the topic of revenue (IAS 18) which gives more comprehensive guidance on this area than the Application Note in FRS 5.

The IASB has devised some de-recognition criteria that will probably have the same effect as those in FRS 5. The IASB proposes that a disposal that will probably be reversed should not be recognised as a sale. Instead, it would probably be treated as a secured loan. How these criteria will work in practice has yet to be seen.

SELF-TEST
QUESTIONS

The 'off balance sheet' problem

1   What might be said to be the perceived benefits of 'off balance sheet' finance? (1.1)

FRS 5 *Reporting the substance of transactions*

2   What are the general principles of FRS 5? (2.2)

3   When should assets and liabilities be recognised in the balance sheet? (2.5)

Applying FRS 5

4   What is the key factor set down by FRS 5 regarding the inclusion or exclusion of consignment stock in the holder's balance sheet? (3.2)

5   How does FRS 5 treat sale and re-purchase arrangements? (3.3)

6   What is the key factor set down by FRS 5 regarding the inclusion or exclusion of factored debts in the seller's balance sheet? (3.4)

7   How should a PFI contract be analysed? (3.9)

Problem areas

8   What problem areas remain regarding the recognition of transactions? (4.1)

9   How does FRS 5 handle the derecognition of liabilities? (4.3)

EXAM-TYPE
QUESTION

S Ltd

FRS 5 *Reporting the substance of transactions* requires that a reporting entity's financial statements should report the substance of the transactions into which it has entered.

During the most recent financial year (ended 31 August 20X8), S Ltd has entered into a debt factoring arrangement with F plc. The main terms of the agreement are as follows:

1   On the first day of every month S Ltd transfers (by assignment) all its trade debts to F plc, subject to credit approval by F plc for each debt transferred by S Ltd.

2   At the time of transfer of the debtors to F plc, S Ltd receives a payment from F plc of 70% of the gross amount of the transferred debts. The payment is debited by F plc to a factoring account which is maintained in the books of F plc.

3   Following transfer of the debts, F plc collects payments from debtors and performs any necessary follow-up work.

4   After collection by F plc, the cash received from the debtor is credited to the factoring account in the books of F plc.

5   F plc handles all aspects of the collection of the debts of S Ltd in return for a monthly charge of 1% of the total value of the debts transferred at the

beginning of that month. The amount is debited to the factoring account in the books of F plc.

6   Any debts not collected by F plc within 90 days of transfer are regarded as bad debts by F plc and re-assigned to S Ltd. The cash previously advanced by F plc in respect of bad debts is recovered from S Ltd. The recovery is only possible out of the proceeds of other debtors which have been assigned by S Ltd. For example if, in a particular month, S Ltd assigned trade debts having a value of £10,000 and a debt of £500 was identified as bad, then the amounts advanced by F plc to S Ltd would be £6,650 [(70% × £10,000) – (70% × £500)].

7   On a monthly basis, F plc debits the factoring account with an interest charge which is calculated on a daily basis on the balance on the factoring account.

8   At the end of every quarter, F plc pays over to S Ltd a sum representing any credit balance on its factoring account with S Ltd at that time.

Required:

Write a memorandum to the Board of Directors of S Ltd which outlines:

(a)   how, under the principles set out in FRS 5, the substance of a transaction should be determined   **(10 marks)**

(b)   how the debt factoring arrangement will be reported in the financial statements of S Ltd.   **(10 marks)**

(Total: 20 marks)

For the answer to this question see the 'Answers' section at the end of the book.

<table>
<tr><td>FEEDBACK TO
ACTIVITY 1</td><td>The key issue is whether Canterbury plc has purchased the machines from Gillingham plc or whether they are merely on loan. It is necessary to determine whether Canterbury plc has the benefits of holding the machines and is exposed to the risks inherent in those benefits.</td></tr>
</table>

Gillingham plc can demand the return of the machines and Canterbury plc is able to return them without paying a penalty. This suggests that Canterbury plc does not have the automatic right to retain or to use them.

Canterbury plc pays a rental charge for the machines, despite the fact that it may eventually purchase them outright. This suggests a financing arrangement as the rental could be seen as loan interest on the purchase price. Canterbury plc also incurs the costs normally associated with holding stocks.

The purchase price is the price at the date the machines were first delivered. This suggests that the sale actually takes place at the delivery date. Canterbury plc has to purchase any stocks still held six months after delivery. Therefore the company is exposed to slow payment and obsolescence risks. Because Canterbury plc can return the stocks before that time, this exposure is limited.

It appears that both parties experience the risks and benefits. However, although the agreement provides for the return of the machines, in practice this has never happened.

Conclusion: the machines are assets of Canterbury plc and should be included in its balance sheet.

As Lewis plc retains the risk of slow payment and bad debts the substance of the transaction is that of a financing arrangement and the company has not disposed of the debtors.

Under the terms of the factoring agreement, finance will be repaid only from the proceeds generated by the debtors. There appears to be no possibility of any claim against Lewis plc being made other than against proceeds generated from the debtors. The finance appears to be non-returnable. There is only recourse for losses up to a fixed amount. These are indications that linked presentation is appropriate.

Balance sheet (extract)

	£m	£m
Current assets		
Gross debts (after providing for bad debts)	9.7	
Less: non returnable proceeds ((90% × 9.7) – 0.1)	(8.63)	
		1.07
Cash		8.73
Creditors: amounts falling due within one year		
Recourse under factored debts		0.1

Sarton plc manages the factory, which means that it controls its policies. Sarton plc also very clearly stands to suffer or gain from the financial performance of Bypass plc. The bank's return is limited to that of a secured lender. The commercial effect of the arrangement is exactly the same as if Bypass plc were a subsidiary of Sarton plc.

Bypass plc should be consolidated by Sarton plc. All transactions between the two companies should be eliminated from the accounts. The factory should be included in the consolidated balance sheet at its cost to the group (£12 million) and the loan should also be included in the consolidated balance sheet. The loan interest should be included in the consolidated profit and loss account.

Chapter 14

LEASES

This chapter begins by revising the accounting treatment and disclosure of operating and finance leases in the accounts of the lessee, with which you should already be familiar. We then move on to consider accounting for leases in the books of the lessor and the treatment of sale and leaseback agreements.

Lastly, we consider the proposals of a recent Discussion Paper on lease accounting. This has been developed by the 'G4+1' group of standard setters, rather than by the ASB, but the ASB supports its general approach. Exam questions could focus on the proposals in the Discussion Paper and the weaknesses of SSAP 21 *Accounting for leases and hire purchase contracts*.

Objectives

When you have studied this chapter you should be able to:

- discuss the problem areas in lease accounting

- account for sale and leaseback transactions and recognition of income by lessors

- discuss and account for proposed changes in lease accounting.

1 Background and definitions

1.1 Types of lease

SSAP 21 distinguishes between two types of lease:

- finance leases, which in substance are considered similar to hire purchase contracts; and

- operating leases, which are essentially leases of a short-term nature.

1.2 Legal requirements

Although there is no explicit requirement to disclose leasing commitments, Sch 4 CA85 requires particulars to be given of financial commitments which:

- have not been provided for; and

- are relevant to assessing the company's state of affairs.

If such commitments are material then this requirement, together with the overriding true and fair view requirement, will mean disclosure of significant non-cancellable leasing commitments.

DEFINITION

A **lease** is a contract between a lessor and a lessee for the hire of a specific asset. The lessor retains ownership of the asset but conveys the right to the use of the asset to the lessee for an agreed period of time, in return for the payment of specific rentals.

1.3 Definitions in SSAP 21

- A **finance lease** is a lease that transfers substantially all the risks and rewards of ownership of an asset to the lessee. It should be presumed that such a transfer of risks and rewards occurs if, at the inception of a lease, the present value of the minimum lease payments, including any initial payment, amounts to substantially all (normally 90% or more) of the fair value of the leased asset. The present value should be calculated by using the interest rate implicit in the lease (as defined below). If the fair value of the asset is not determinable, an estimate thereof should be used.

Notwithstanding the fact that a lease meets these conditions, the presumption that it should be classified as a finance lease may, in exceptional circumstances, be rebutted if it can be clearly demonstrated that the lease in question does not transfer substantially all the risks and rewards of ownership (other than legal title) to the lessee. Correspondingly, the presumption that a lease which fails to meet these conditions is not a finance lease may in exceptional circumstances be rebutted.

- An **operating lease** is a lease other than a finance lease.

- A **hire purchase contract** is a contract for hire of an asset which contains a provision giving the hirer an option to acquire legal title to the asset upon the fulfilment of certain conditions stated in the contract.

- The **lease term** is the period for which the lessee has contracted to lease the asset and any further terms for which the lessee has the option to continue to lease the asset, with or without further payment, which option it is reasonably certain at the inception of the lease that the lessee will exercise.

- The **minimum lease payments** are the minimum payments over the remaining part of the lease term (excluding charges for services and taxes to be paid by the lessor) and:

    (a) in the case of the lessee, any residual amounts guaranteed by him or by a party related to him; or

    (b) in the case of the lessor, any residual amounts guaranteed by the lessee or by an independent third party.

- The **interest rate implicit in a lease** is the discount rate that, at the inception of a lease, when applied to the amounts which the lessor expects to receive and retain, produces an amount (the present value) equal to the fair value of the leased asset.

2 The requirements of SSAP 21 in the lessee's accounts

2.1 The effect on the financial statements of treating a lease as a finance or operating lease

KEY POINT

SSAP 21 requires capitalisation of finance leases by lessees.

SSAP 21 requires capitalisation of finance leases by lessees. No major change in accounting treatment is required for operating leases. The effect on the lessee's financial statements may be summarised as follows:

	Hire purchase contracts	*Finance leases*	*Operating leases*
P/L account	(a) Depreciation (b) Finance charge	(a) Depreciation (b) Finance charge	Rental payments
Balance sheet - asset	Fixed asset less depreciation	Fixed asset less depreciation	-
- liability	Obligations under hire purchase contracts	Obligations under finance leases	-

2.2 Applying the requirements to given situations to classify leases as finance or operating

A finance lease is defined as a lease that transfers substantially all the risks and rewards of ownership of an asset to the lessee. To decide whether there is a presumption of transfer of risks and rewards of ownership it is necessary to complete the following steps.

Step	*Comment*
(1) Calculate minimum lease payments (MLPs) inclusive of initial payment.	MLPs = minimum payments plus any residual amounts guaranteed by lessee.
(2) Discount (1) to determine present value of MLPs.	Discount factor is either: (i) rate of interest implicit in lease (if known); or (ii) a commercial rate of interest (for a similar lease).
(3) Calculate fair value of asset at beginning of lease.	Fair value = arm's length price less any government grants receivable by lessor.
(4) Presumption is satisfied if (2) amounts to 90% or more of (3).	

However, the '90% test' is not always conclusive. SSAP 21 states that even if a lease fails the '90% test' it should be classified as a finance lease if it can be demonstrated that the lease in fact does transfer the risks and rewards of ownership to the lessee.

A lease is probably a finance lease if:

* the lessee is able to use the asset for all or most of its useful economic life

* the lessee is responsible for repairing and insuring the asset (the lessee has the risk of breakdown or theft)

* the nature of the asset is specialised so that only the lessee can use it, or

* there is an option for a secondary lease term at a nominal rent (if so, the lessee is reasonably certain to exercise it, with the effect that the lessee has the asset for its useful economic life).

2.3 Finance leases – initial entries

At the start of the lease:

* the present value of the MLPs should be included as a fixed asset, subject to depreciation

* the obligation to pay rentals should be included as a liability.

In practice the fair value of the asset or its cash price will often be a sufficiently close approximation to the present value of the MLPs and therefore can be used instead.

2.4 Finance leases – depreciation

The related fixed asset should be depreciated over the shorter of:

- the economic useful life of the asset (as in FRS 15); and

- the lease term, which is essentially the period over which the lessee has the use of the asset. It includes:

  (a) the primary (non-cancellable) period; plus

  (b) any secondary periods during which the lessee has the contractual right to continue to use the asset, provided that it is reasonably certain at the outset that this right will be exercised.

2.5 Finance leases – allocation of finance charges

- Over the period of the lease, the total finance charge is the amount by which the rentals paid to the lessor exceed the present value of the MLPs.

- Each individual rental payment should be split between:

  (a) finance charge (P/L account item); and

  (b) repayment of obligation to pay rentals (thus reducing the balance sheet liability).

- How should finance charges be allocated over the term of the lease? The basic aim is to allocate the charge in such a way as to produce a reasonably constant periodic rate of return on the remaining balance of liability. There are three main methods:

  (a) actuarial method (the most accurate method)

  (b) sum of the digits method (a reasonable approximation to the actuarial method)

  (c) straight-line method (a poor approximation to the actuarial method).

ACTIVITY 1

A company has two options. It can buy an asset for cash at a cost of £5,710 or it can lease it by way of a finance lease. The terms of the lease are as follows:

(1) primary period is for four years from 1 January 20X2 with a rental of £2,000 pa payable on the 31 December each year

(2) the lessee has the right to continue to lease the asset after the end of the primary period for an indefinite period, subject only to a nominal rent

(3) the lessee is required to pay all repair, maintenance and insurance costs as they arise

(4) the interest rate implicit in the lease is 15%.

The lessee estimates the useful economic life of the asset to be eight years. Depreciation is provided on a straight-line basis.

Is the lease a finance lease? How should it be accounted for in the books of the lessee?

Feedback to this activity is at the end of the chapter.

2.6 Hire purchase contracts

The depreciation and the finance charges should be allocated in the same way as for finance leases.

2.7 Operating leases

Rentals under operating leases should be charged to the profit and loss account on a straight-line basis over the term of the lease, unless another systematic and rational basis is more appropriate. Any difference between amounts charged and amounts paid should be adjusted to debtors or creditors.

3 Disclosure requirements for the lessee

3.1 Disclosure – finance leases and hire purchase contracts

For disclosure purposes finance leases and hire purchase agreements are treated as one group.

- **Balance sheet: assets**

  There is a choice of disclosure for assets. Either:

  (a) show by each major class of asset the gross amounts of assets held under a finance lease and related accumulated depreciation; or

  (b) integrate the finance lease assets with owned fixed assets and disclose the net amount of assets held under finance leases.

- **Balance sheet: obligations under finance leases**

  The amounts of obligations related to finance leases (net of finance charges allocated to future periods) should be disclosed separately from other obligations and liabilities, either on the face of the balance sheet or in the notes to the accounts.

  These net obligations under finance leases should then be analysed between amounts payable in the next year, amounts payable in the second to fifth years inclusive from the balance sheet date, and the aggregate amounts payable thereafter.

- **Profit and loss account**

  The total depreciation charge and the aggregate finance charges for the period in respect of finance leases should be disclosed.

3.2 Disclosure – operating leases

- **Balance sheet: obligations under operating leases** – In respect of operating leases, the lessee should disclose the payments which he is committed to make during the next year, analysed between those in which the commitment expires within that year, in the second to fifth years inclusive and over five years from the balance sheet date, showing separately the commitments in respect of leases of land and buildings and other operating leases.

- **Profit and loss account** – Total operating lease rentals are charged as an expense in the profit and loss account, split between hire of plant and machinery rentals and other operating leases.

3.3 Disclosure – accounting policies

Disclosure should be made of the policies adopted for accounting for operating and finance leases.

Gills Ltd has entered into three agreements to acquire machines, X, Y and Z.

The agreement details were as follows:

Agreement date	Subject of agreement	Length of lease	Lease terms	Payable
1 March 20X8	Machine X	18 months	£15,000 pa	Six months in advance
1 January 20X7	Machine Y	6 years	£12,025 pa	Annually in advance
1 January 20X8	Machine Z	5 years	£3,700 pa	Annually in arrears

The accountant of Gills Ltd made further enquiries and discovered that at the time of entering into the agreements the following information was correct

	Age when leased	Useful remaining life at date of agreement	Cost to purchase at date of agreement
Machine X	3 years	6 years	£92,500
Machine Y	New	6 years	£46,250
Machine Z	New	5 years	Cost not available

Assume:

(a) that Gills Ltd could borrow funds throughout 20X7 and 20X8 at 12% per annum

(b) that interest is allocated using the sum of the digits method.

You are required:

(a) to prepare calculations to show the effect on the profit and loss account of Gills Ltd for the year ended 31 December 20X8 and the balance sheet as at 31 December 20X8 of treating the three leases in accordance with the provisions of SSAP 21 *Accounting for leases and hire purchase contracts.*

(b) to prepare calculations to show the effect on the profit and loss account of Gills Ltd for the year ended 31 December 20X8 and the balance sheet as at 31 December 20X8 if the leases were not being treated in accordance with SSAP 21 but were all being treated as operating leases.

12% discount factors are shown below.

Years (t)	Present value of £1 to be received after t years	Present value of £1 per year for each of t years
1	0.893	0.893
2	0.797	1.690
3	0.712	2.402
4	0.636	3.038
5	0.567	3.605
6	0.507	4.112

Feedback to this activity is at the end of the chapter.

4   Accounting for lessors and finance companies

4.1   Introduction

From the viewpoint of the lessor, the substance over form argument regards a finance lease as being equivalent to the provision of finance, rather than the hiring out of a fixed asset. Conversely an operating lease should be accounted for by the lessor capitalising and depreciating the leased asset.

The two types of lease may be compared for the lessor as follows:

	Finance leases	*Operating leases*
Balance sheet	Net investment in finance lease	Property held for operating leases (cost - depreciation)
Profit and loss account	Finance charge (allocated on basis which gives constant periodic return on net cash investment)	Rental income (straight-line basis) Depreciation

4.2 Accounting for finance leases

SSAP 21 deals with calculation of the carrying value of the finance lease receivables and with lessors' profit recognition. It requires the receivables to be carried on a balance sheet at an amount based on the net investment in the lease. Additionally, it requires that profit recognition should normally be based on the lessor's net cash investment.

The **net investment** in a lease is initially the cost of the asset to the lessor, less any government or other grants receivable (i.e. the fair value).

The rentals paid by the lessee should be apportioned by the lessor between (a) gross earnings (i.e. the lessor's interest earned) and (b) a repayment of capital.

Over the period of the lease the net investment in the lease (i.e. the carrying value of the receivables) will therefore be the fair value of the asset less those portions of the rentals which are apportioned as a repayment of capital.

For the purposes of profit recognition, however, the total gross earnings should normally be allocated to accounting periods to give a constant periodic rate of return on the lessor's **net cash investment** (NCI) in the lease in each period. The NCI is based on the funds which the lessor has invested in the lease. The amount of funds invested in a lease by a lessor is different from the net investment in the lease because there are a number of other cash flows which affect the lessor in addition to those which affect net investment. In particular, tax cash flows are an important component of the NCI.

SSAP 21 permits a reasonable approximation to be made in arriving at the constant period rate of return. Hence there are a number of different methods of profit recognition which may comply with the standard. Traditionally, the two main methods used have been the actuarial method after tax and the investment period method, but following changes to UK tax law these are rarely used in practice and are unlikely to be examined. Instead, the 'pre-tax' methods used in lessee accounting (i.e. the straight line method, the sum of the digits method and the actuarial method) will usually give an acceptable answer.

The lessor's profit and loss account

A simple outline of the lessor's profit and loss account might appear as follows:

	£	£	*Note*
Rentals received		X	1
Capital repayments		(X)	
		—	
Finance income		X	2
Interest payable	X		3
Overheads	X		3
Bad debts	X		4
	—		
		(X)	

Profit before tax	X	
Tax	(X)	3
Profit after tax	X	
Dividends	(X)	3
Retained profit	X	

Notes

(1) Rentals received are the aggregation of rental income for all leases.

(2) To compute this figure it is necessary to calculate, for each major type of leasing arrangement that the lessor enters into, the finance income within the total rental receipts using one of the methods which will approximate to the constant period rate of return.

Item 2 is the total of the finance income calculated for all leases for an accounting period.

(3) All these items are the normal expenses incurred by the lessor in the accounting period.

(4) This is assessed in the usual way.

4.3 Illustration of lessor accounting for a finance lease

The lessor in Activity 1 will account for the leased asset as follows:

(a) Confirm that the terms of the lease satisfy the conditions to be a finance lease. This is the same as in Activity 1.

(b) Recognise the £5,710 value of the asset as a receivable (debtor), 'investment in finance lease'.

(c) Recognise the finance income receivable each year on the same basis that the lessee recognised the finance charge payable:

Year	Finance income receivable £
20X2	856
20X3	685
20X4	488
20X5	261
	2,290

(d) At the end of the primary period of the lease, the total lease payments received (4 × £2,000) will exactly equal the original receivable (£5,710) plus the total finance income recognised (£2,290).

4.4 Accounting for hire purchase contracts

In the case of hire purchase, profit recognition should also, in principle, be based on net cash investment. However, since the capital allowances under a hire purchase contract accrue to the hirer, the finance company's net cash investment is often not significantly different from its net investment; hence allocation of gross earnings (i.e. finance charges) based on net investment will again in most cases be a suitable approximation to allocation based on net cash investment.

This will again have the result that the entries in the finance company's accounts will be a mirror image of the entries in the hirer's accounts if the hirer is using the actuarial method before tax.

4.5   Presentation in accounts

SSAP 21 requires disclosure of the net investment in (a) finance leases and (b) hire purchase contracts at each balance sheet date. The amounts should be described as receivables. Whereas in lessee accounting the figures in respect of leases and hire purchase contracts may be aggregated, in the case of lessors and finance companies the amounts in respect of each should be shown separately.

For companies subject to Sch 4 CA85 the net investment in finance leases and hire purchase contracts should be included in current assets under the heading 'debtors' and described as 'finance lease receivables' and/or 'hire purchase receivables' as appropriate. It should be analysed in the notes to the accounts between those amounts receivable within one year and those amounts receivable thereafter.

A suitable form of disclosure would be as follows:

Balance sheet as at 31 December

	20X7	20X6
	£	£
Current assets:		
Finance lease and hire purchase receivables	1,200	1,100

Notes to the accounts: The amounts receivable under finance leases and hire purchase contracts comprise:

	£	£
Finance leases	900	820
Hire purchase contracts	300	280
	1,200	1,100

Included in the totals receivable is £900 (20X6 £850) which falls due after more than one year.

SSAP 21 requires that the gross amounts (i.e. original cost or revaluation) and accumulated depreciation of assets held for use in operating leases should be disclosed. This information could be incorporated into tables showing the amounts for other fixed assets or could be shown as a separate table. It is recognised that, for banks, assets held for use in operating leases are different in nature from a bank's infrastructure (e.g. its own premises). Hence it may not be appropriate to combine assets held for use in operating leases with a bank's infrastructure for capital adequacy purposes.

4.6   Manufacturer/dealer lessor

A manufacturer or dealer may offer customers the option of either outright purchase or rental of an asset. The rental option is thus a means of encouraging sales and may be packaged to appear attractive, e.g. cars sold with 0% finance option.

The question then arises as to whether the total profit on a transaction is split into a trading profit (and thus recognised at the date the agreement is signed) and finance income (spread over the lifetime of the agreement).

SSAP 21 states: 'A manufacturer or dealer/lessor should not recognise a selling profit under an operating lease. The selling profit under a finance lease should be restricted to the excess of the fair value of the asset over the manufacturer's or dealer's cost less any grants receivable by the manufacturer or dealer towards the purchase, construction or use of the asset.'

The fair value of the asset can be taken to be the cash selling price as long as the credit terms reflect a reasonable level of interest. However where, for example, a car dealer is offering 0% finance deals it is not reasonable to record all the profit as trading profit and no finance income. Clearly the trader in this situation is reducing the fair value of the car. An approach that could be taken in this situation is to discount the lease payments using a reasonable estimate of the implicit rate of interest. The PV of the MLPs thus becomes the fair value for determining trading profit.

4.7   Tax-free grants to lessors

Lessors may be able to obtain tax-free grants against the purchase price of assets acquired for leasing.

One possible method of accounting for tax-free grants is 'grossing up'. The pre-tax profit and the tax charge are changed by the same amount so that a standard tax charge is reported. 'Grossing up' fails to reflect the true nature of the transactions that have occurred in the period.

SSAP 21 prohibits the grossing up of tax-free grants to lessors. It requires that the grants should be spread over the period of the lease. The grant is treated as non-taxable income.

5   Sale and leaseback transactions

5.1   Introduction

A common example of a sale and leaseback is a company selling the freehold interest in its office/factory to a financial institution.

Before dealing with how to account for the sale and leaseback transaction itself, the carrying value of the asset in question should be reviewed. If the asset has suffered an impairment in value below its carrying amount it should be written down immediately to its fair value. This is nothing to do with sale and leaseback specifically, but is a step which should be taken so that the sale and leaseback accounting is not distorted.

The subsequent steps will depend on whether the leaseback is an operating lease or a finance lease.

If the asset is land and buildings then it is likely to be an operating lease.

5.2   Operating lease

If the leaseback is an operating lease, the seller-lessee has disposed of substantially all the risks and rewards of ownership of the asset and so has realised a profit or loss on a genuine disposal. Provided that the transaction is established at fair value, the profit or loss should be recognised. However, it is possible that a sale and leaseback transaction can be arranged at other than fair value. If the sale price is above fair value, the excess will not be genuine profit, but will arise solely because the operating lease rentals payable in the ensuing years will also be at above fair value. SSAP 21 therefore provides that the excess of sale price over fair value should not be recognised as profit in the year but should be credited to income, over the shorter of the remainder of the lease term and the period to the next rent review (if any) so as to reduce the rentals payable to a level consistent with the fair value of the asset.

Example

The NBV of an asset is £70,000, the fair value is £100,000. Alternative sale prices and annual rentals (for five years) are:

	(a) £	(b) £
Sale price	120,000	100,000
Rental per annum	28,000	23,000

The recognition of the profit will be as follows:

	(a) £	(b) £
Recognise profit on sale (100,000 – 70,000)	30,000	30,000
Excess proceeds	20,000	
Credit excess proceeds to P & L account over five years	(4,000)	
Rentals	28,000	23,000
Net rental	24,000	23,000

The net rentals charged to P & L account in (a) are higher than (b), reflecting the interest cost of the 'loan' of £20,000 (i.e. the artificially higher selling price).

If the sale price is below fair value then, if it is a bad bargain (e.g. because seller/lessee had to raise cash quickly), the profit/loss should be recognised immediately. If the price is artificially low to compensate for lower than market value rentals, any book profit should be recognised immediately and any book loss should be deferred and amortised over the lease term.

Continuing the previous example, alternative figures for the sale/leaseback deal are as follows:

	(c) £		(d) £
Sale price	80,000		60,000
Rental pa	19,000		15,000

Solution

Profit (80,000 – 70,000)	10,000	Loss (60,000 – 70,000)	(10,000)
No recognition of difference between sale price and fair value		Debit P & L account over five years with	2,000

5.3   Finance lease

If the leaseback is a finance lease, the seller-lessee is in effect re-acquiring substantially all the risks and rewards of ownership of the asset. In other words, he never disposes of his ownership interest in the asset, and so it would not be correct to recognise a profit or loss in relation to an asset which (in substance) never was disposed of.

However, it is possible that a sale and leaseback resulting in a finance lease may be arranged on terms reflecting a higher or lower capital value than the book value of the asset (i.e. so as to reflect an apparent profit or loss).

For example, an asset which has a carrying value of £70 may be sold at £120 and leased back on a finance lease. In such a case, the lease payments would (other things being equal) be higher than if the sale and leaseback had been arranged at carrying value. SSAP 21 therefore provides that the £50 apparent profit should be deferred and amortised (i.e. credited to income) over the lease term. This will have the effect of reducing the rentals, which are shown as interest and depreciation of the leased-back asset, to a level consistent with the previous carrying value of the asset.

Where the asset is carried at below fair value, it may be appropriate to revalue it. If, in the same example, the fair value of the asset were £100, the asset could be revalued to that amount, and there would remain only £20 of apparent profit to be deferred and amortised over the lease term. The effect would then be to reduce the rentals to a level consistent with the fair value of the asset.

As an alternative to calculating the apparent profit and deferring and amortising that amount, the same result can be achieved by leaving the previous carrying value unchanged, setting up the amount received on sale as a creditor, and treating the lease payments partly as principal and partly as a finance charge. This treatment will reflect the substance of the transaction, namely that it represents the raising of finance secured on an asset which is held and not disposed of. Following the issue of FRS 5 this second method should arguably now always be used.

6 Termination of leases

6.1 Termination payments

Most lease contracts provide for a payment to the lessor in the event of early termination. This payment is normally equivalent to most or all of the rentals that the lessor would have received if the agreement had proceeded as planned.

6.2 Operating leases

Accounting for the termination of an operating lease is straightforward. The termination payment is treated as income in the accounts of the lessor and as an expense in the accounts of the lessee.

6.3 Termination of a finance lease in the books of the lessee

- **Early termination**

  This gives rise to the following:

  (a) disposal of the capitalised asset by the lessee

  (b) a termination payment made to the lessor by the lessee.

  The termination payment reduces the lease creditor. The difference between the termination payment and the lease creditor is treated as a gain or loss on disposal of the leased asset.

- **Residual value**

  Some leases provide for the lessee to guarantee the residual value of an asset on termination. This will apply if the lease terminates at the expected date.

  The accounting treatment is very similar to the treatment on early termination.

Example

A Ltd leases a motor vehicle under a finance lease. The vehicle is capitalised at its fair value of £16,000. Under the terms of the lease agreement, A Ltd must guarantee the vehicle's residual value of £4,000. This guarantee will be called upon if the vehicle's actual residual value is less than £4,000.

The lease term is four years and A Ltd depreciates the vehicle using the straight line method.

At the end of the lease period, A Ltd is required to make a payment of £2,000 to the lessor.

Show the journal entry to record the disposal of the vehicle.

Solution

		£	£
Dr	Motor vehicles: Accumulated depreciation	12,000	
	Cr Motor vehicles: Cost		16,000
Dr	Lease obligation: Guarantee	2,000	
Dr	Loss on disposal	2,000	

The motor vehicle is depreciated down to its estimated residual value.

6.4   Termination of a finance lease in the books of the lessor

The lessor will receive a termination payment which will reduce the net investment in the lease. The difference between the net investment in the lease and the termination receipt is treated as a gain or a loss in the profit and loss account.

The treatment of the leased asset depends on the course of action to be taken by the lessor.

- If the lessor expects to sell the asset or to re-lease it under a finance lease it is treated as a current asset.

- If the lessor expects to lease the asset under an operating lease, it is treated as a fixed asset.

7   Tax variation clauses

7.1   Introduction

Tax variation clauses are designed to protect the lessor from any adverse changes in the capital allowance or corporation tax rates. The lessor determines the level of lease rentals on the basis of the tax rates existing at the inception of the lease. When there is a tax variation, the lease rentals are adjusted for the remaining period of the lease. This means that the lessee pays higher or lower rentals than previously.

7.2   Accounting for tax variation clauses in the accounts of the lessee

Any change in total rentals represents a change in the finance charges payable under the lease. This should be dealt with by allocating the revised finance charges over the remaining lease term. The allocation is done in the usual way (e.g. by using the actuarial method).

If there is a reduction in rentals and this exceeds the finance charges that were expected previously, the excess should be deducted from the capitalised cost of the leased asset. This will reduce depreciation charges in future periods. SSAP 21 does not permit negative finance charges.

8   The usefulness of SSAP 21

8.1   Introduction

SSAP 21 has been useful in cutting down the use of off balance sheet financing through the use of lease finance. It should be appreciated that by the time of the issue of SSAP 21, leasing was a very important method of obtaining the use of fixed assets in a business. Leasing remains an important method, but generally is now fairly shown in the financial statements. Its main usefulness has been to disclose the true liabilities of a business.

8.2   The definition of finance leases

There has been some manipulation of the 90% test so that leases have been classified as operating rather than finance leases. The main ploy has been to write the lease agreement leaving a significant residual payment at the end of the lease but the residual payment is not a guaranteed sum. As a consequence, the present value of the expected residual payment does not fall within the definition of the lessee's minimum lease payments.

A further consequence of this can be that the lease is still defined as a finance lease in the books of the lessor (which is probably what the lessor company would prefer). Some examples will illustrate this point.

Examples

Peanuts Ltd has entered into a lease with Almond Ltd for plant with a fair value of £70,000. The lease term is 5 years, and the agreement specifies 5 annual payments of £10,000 each. Peanuts Ltd has not contracted to pay any other amounts to Almond Ltd under the lease.

This lease is an operating lease for Peanuts Ltd as the minimum lease payments are £50,000 and the fair value of the plant is £70,000, i.e. the minimum lease payments are less than 90% of the value of the asset even before discounting. (The present value of the minimum lease payments is not known here as we cannot calculate the interest rate implicit in the lease, but it is clearly less than £50,000.)

Using the facts above, suppose also that Almond Ltd has a guarantee for the residual value of £30,000 from the manufacturer of the plant. There is no unguaranteed residual value.

Amounts receivable

Under the lease	£50,000
Guaranteed residual value	£30,000

There is no unguaranteed residual value, so if these amounts were discounted at the interest rate implicit in the lease, the result would be the fair value of the asset i.e. the lease is a finance lease for the lessor.

Using the original facts above, suppose that the manufacturer of the plant has made a guarantee of £25,000 against the residual value of £30,000.

In this case the minimum lease payments include

Under the lease	£50,000
Guaranteed residual value	£25,000

These amounts should be discounted to present value and compared with the fair value of £70,000 to assess whether or not the lease is a finance lease.

An alternative method is to consider the unguaranteed residual value. If this is less than 10% of the fair value of the asset (even before discounting) then the lease will be a finance lease because so little of the value of the asset is unguaranteed.

In this example the present value of the unguaranteed residual value, which must be less than £5,000, is also less than 10% of the fair value. Hence the lease is a finance lease.

The examples above illustrated that the 90% test can result in different answers for the lessee and the lessor. This occurs because the lessor receives a significant guarantee against the residual value of the asset by a party other than the lessee.

8.3 Further problems of classification

In practice a further problem arises because the lessee may not have adequate information to classify the lease. The difficulties relate to the following areas.

(a) Fair value   –   lessee may be unaware of the cost of the leased asset, and will have to use an estimate

(b) Implicit interest rate   –   lessee may have no estimate of residual value or simply uses a known interest rate for a similar lease.

8.4 Property transactions

SSAP 21 applies to property transactions in the same way as for other leases. Many property leases are classified as operating leases due to the long expected life of the building compared to the length of the lease. The FRRP subsequently noted in reviewing a case that the existing standard did not provide unequivocal guidance for reverse premiums and the UITF developed an Abstract on this topic. This is covered below.

Property transactions are also the major type of asset subject to sale and leaseback arrangements. Some commentators feel that these transactions are too open to manipulation by the lessee company.

8.5 UITF Abstract 28 *Operating lease incentives*

The issue

An operating lease agreement may include incentives for the lessee to sign the lease. Such incentives may take various forms, such as an up-front cash payment to the lessee (a reverse premium), a rent-free period or a contribution to certain lessee costs (such as relocation).

The issue is how an incentive for an operating lease should be recognised in the financial statements of the lessee and of the lessor.

UITF Consensus

All incentives for the agreement of a new or renewed operating lease should be recognised as an integral part of the net payment agreed for the use of the leased asset.

Lessees should recognise the aggregate benefit of incentives as a reduction of rental expense. The benefit should be allocated on a straight line basis over the shorter of the lease term and the period to the date from which the prevailing market rental will be payable.

Lessors should recognise the aggregate cost of incentives as a reduction of rental income. The cost should be allocated on a straight line basis over the shorter of the lease term and the period to the date from which the prevailing market rental will be payable.

9 Current proposals

9.1 Introduction

The ASB has published a Discussion Paper *Leases: Implementation of a new approach*, which reproduces the text of a Position Paper that was developed by the 'G4 + 1' group of accounting standard setters. The proposals in the Discussion Paper will eventually form the basis of a new standard to replace SSAP 21.

9.2 The problem

As we have seen, SSAP 21 states that a lease should be presumed to be a finance lease if, at the inception of the lease, the present value of the minimum lease payments amounts to 90% or more of the fair value of the leased asset. The remainder of the definition implies that even if the lease fails to meet the '90% test' it should be treated as a finance lease if it clearly transfers the risks and rewards of ownership of the asset to the lessee.

Despite this, agreements that are in substance finance leases are often deliberately structured so that they narrowly fail the '90% test'. The leased asset and the obligation to make future payments can therefore be kept off the balance sheet.

One possible solution to this problem would be to redraft the definitions so that the threshold for treating a lease as a finance lease was lower. Another would be to bring leases within the scope of FRS 5, so that leases would have to be treated according to the substance of the agreement.

The ASB and other standard setters believe that any attempt to redefine the difference between operating and finance leases would still be arbitrary. It is unsatisfactory because it is an 'all or nothing' approach. In theory, a lessee recognises all of an asset if the minimum lease payments amount to 91% of its value, but nothing at all if the minimum lease payments are 89% of its value.

Instead, the ASB proposes to abolish the distinction between operating leases and finance leases.

9.3 The main proposal

The main proposal is that all material leases should give rise to assets and liabilities for lessees, and these must be recognised on the balance sheet.

- Assets and liabilities should be recognised by a lessee when the lessor has substantially performed its obligation to provide the lessee with access to the leased property for the lease term. This is normally when the leased property is delivered or made available to the lessee.

- Until the lease is recognised, a lessee should account for a lease contract in a similar way to any contract to purchase property that has not yet been delivered.

- At the beginning of the lease term, lessees should record the fair value of the rights and obligations that are conveyed by the lease. Fair value is measured by the fair value of the consideration given, except where the fair value of the asset received is more clearly evident.

- The fair value of the rights obtained by a lessee would normally be the present value of the minimum payments required by the lease. It cannot be less than this amount.

What is recognised in the balance sheet would not be the leased asset itself, but the right to use the leased asset for the term of the lease. According to the Statement of Principles and other conceptual frameworks used by 'G4+1' group members, these rights in themselves are an asset.

The amount recognised would not necessarily be the full value of the asset. Under many leases that are at present classified as operating leases, an asset is leased for only a small part of its useful economic life. Only the value of that part would be recognised in the lessee's balance sheet. The obligation to make the future payments required by the lease would be recognised as a liability.

After the lease was recognised in the lessee's balance sheet, it would be treated in a similar way to a finance lease under SSAP 21.

9.4   Renewal and purchase options

A lease may include options to extend the minimum term of the lease or to purchase the asset at the end of the lease term. The Discussion Paper proposes that the exercise of these should not be anticipated when the assets and liabilities are recognised by the lessee at the inception of the lease. Options should only give rise to additional assets and liabilities when they are exercised. This is because the fair value of the options will be reflected in the minimum payments required by the lease.

In circumstances where the fixed non-cancellable term of the lease is clearly unrepresentative of the time period that the lessee is compelled to occupy or possess the property, the asset and liability recognised at the beginning of the lease term should reflect the rights and obligations that exist on the assumption that the lease is renewed (or not cancelled).

9.5   Sale and leaseback transactions

Under SSAP 21, the accounting treatment of sale and leaseback transactions depends on whether the leaseback is a finance or an operating lease. Where the leaseback is a finance lease, the lessee continues to recognise the asset in the balance sheet and also recognises a liability for lease payments. Where the leaseback is an operating lease the transaction is treated as the sale of an asset.

The Paper considers two possible approaches to accounting for sale and leaseback transactions.

- The 'one transaction' approach views a sale and leaseback as one transaction with a double purpose: the raising of finance and the partial disposal of an interest in property.

- The 'two transactions' approach views a sale and leaseback as two separate transactions: a sale of property followed by a lease of different property rights. The two transactions are accounted for separately.

The main difference between the two approaches is the carrying amount of the leased asset. Under the 'one transaction' approach it is based on the previous carrying amount (either historic cost or revalued amount). Under the 'two transactions' approach it is based on the fair value of the rights acquired under the lease.

Example

An entity sells a property with a carrying value of £100,000 and a fair value of £120,000. It receives cash of £120,000 and leases back the asset.

Under the 'one transaction' approach the accounting entries are:

Dr Cash	£120,000	
Cr Lease creditor		£120,000

The asset remains in the balance sheet at its carrying value of £100,000. This is very similar to the current treatment for a sale and finance leaseback, following the principles in FRS 5.

Under the 'two transactions' approach the accounting entries are:

Sale:

Dr	Cash	£120,000	
	Cr Asset		£100,000
	Cr Profit on disposal		£20,000

Leaseback:

Dr	Asset	£120,000	
	Cr Lease liability		£120,000

The asset is effectively revalued to its fair value of £120,000.

The Paper proposes that the 'one transaction' approach be used. Because the asset in the balance sheet represents the right to use the leased asset (not the leased asset itself) a sale and leaseback will normally result in the partial disposal of the asset. There are two possible extremes:

(a) a financing arrangement, with an immaterial part of the asset sold (i.e. almost no material residual interest for the lessor); or

(b) a sale, with an immaterial amount of finance raised.

Most sale and leaseback transactions will fall somewhere between these two extremes.

The accounting treatment should therefore be as follows.

(a) A liability is recognised in respect of the payments required by the lease. This is measured using the same methods as for any other lease.

(b) The amount by which the cash received exceeds the liability in respect of the payments required by the lease would be deemed to be consideration for the part of the asset that is sold.

(c) The carrying amount of the asset immediately before the transaction is apportioned between the amount sold and the amount retained.

(d) A gain (or loss) would be recognised for the difference between the amounts calculated in (b) and deemed to be sold in (c) above.

(e) As a result, the part of the asset that is retained (i.e. the right to use the property for the term of the lease) would be carried at a proportion of the previous carrying amount, based on the calculation in (c).

The main reason for adopting the 'one transaction' approach is that a sale and leaseback may consist of two transactions, but these are negotiated as a package.

Example

An entity sells a property with a carrying value of £100,000 and a fair value of £120,000. It receives cash of £120,000 and leases back the asset. The liability for lease payments is £70,000.

This transaction results in a partial disposal of the asset. It is necessary to calculate the carrying amount of the asset as a proportion of the part sold and the part retained. The lease liability is £70,000, so £50,000 of the proceeds of £120,000 has been received for selling part of the asset.

The accounting entries are as follows:

Dr	Cash	£120,000	
	Cr Lease liability		£70,000
	Cr Asset (100 × 50/120)		£41,667
	Cr Profit on disposal		£8,333

The carrying value of the asset is £58,333 (100,000 – 41,667). The profit recognised is 50/120 of the profit of £20,000 that would arise if the whole asset had been sold.

9.6   Accounting by the lessor

The main proposals are as follows:

- Two separate assets should be reported on the balance sheet:

    - amounts receivable from the lessee (under debtors); and

    - an interest in the residual value of the asset (under fixed assets).

    This presentation reflects the fact that these amounts are subject to quite different risks.

- Amounts receivable from the lessee would be recorded initially at fair value and would normally be the converse of the amounts reported as liabilities by lessees.

The Discussion Paper does not address the method by which lessors should recognise income from leases. The ASB proposes that the net cash investment method should continue to be used.

9.7   Leases of land and buildings

Under SSAP 21, leases of land and buildings are almost always treated as operating leases, because the lessor retains a significant interest in the residual value of the property.

Abolishing the distinction between finance leases and operating leases would be particularly contentious for leases of land and buildings. Land and buildings are normally held on long leases and therefore lessees would have to recognise significant additional assets and liabilities in their balance sheets.

The Discussion Paper recommends that leases of land and buildings should not be exempt from the proposed new approach and the ASB supports this recommendation. The Paper points out that a lessee's interest in a leased property could be revalued and would also come within the scope of accounting standards on impairment. This would be a considerable improvement on current financial reporting practice.

The proposals would mean that the financial statements of lessors would be more understandable. In particular, there would be two assets in the lessor's financial statements: a financial asset representing the payments required by the lease and an interest in the residual value of the property. This would enable users of the financial statements to appreciate the extent to which the lessor is primarily at risk from default by the lessee and the extent to which the lessor is at risk from (and may benefit from) future changes in the value of the property.

SSAP 19 *Accounting for investment properties* would continue to apply to residual interests in investment properties held by lessors. These would be reported as the difference between the amount of the lease receivable and the fair value of the property.

9.8   Implications of the proposals

The ASB believes that abolishing the distinction between finance leases and operating leases would improve the consistency and comparability of financial statements.

Further arguments for abolishing the distinction between operating and finance leases include the following.

- Analysts now commonly adjust financial statements to show the effect of recognising the fair values of rights and obligations under operating leases.

- Many leases are now extremely complex and difficult to classify because they have characteristics of both types of lease.

- It avoids the use of an arbitrary threshold that can be manipulated by preparers of accounts.

However, the proposals have some disadvantages.

- Many lessees' gearing will increase significantly if these proposals are adopted. Some commentators believe that leasing may become less attractive as a result.

- Recognising rights to assets, rather than actual assets, may make financial statements less understandable to users.

- Some commentators claim that the proposals can be exploited to leave most leased assets off the balance sheet. For example, suppose that a lessee leases an asset for one year, a very small proportion of its useful economic life. The lessee has an option to renew the lease each year, which it exercises, so that in practice it uses the asset for the whole of its useful economic life. The lessee clearly has the risks and benefits relating to the asset, but because the renewals are not anticipated, the assets and liabilities are deemed immaterial and are kept off the balance sheet. Applying FRS 5 to leases would avoid the possibility of abuses such as this.

SELF-TEST QUESTIONS

Background and definitions

1   How does SSAP 21 define leases, finance leases and hire purchase contracts? (1.3)

2   What are the minimum lease payments? (1.3)

3   What is the interest rate implicit in the lease? (1.3)

The requirements of SSAP 21 in the lessee's accounts

4   How do operating leases differ from finance leases in the way they are accounted for in the books of the lessee? (2.1)

5   How should the finance charges under a finance lease be allocated in the accounts of the lessee? (2.5)

6   How do operating leases differ from finance leases in the way they are accounted for in the books of the lessee? (2.7)

Accounting for lessors and finance companies

7   'For the purposes of profit recognition, the total gross earnings should normally be allocated to accounting periods to give a constant periodic rate of return on the lessor's net .... investment in the lease in each period.' Fill in the blank. (4.2)

8   How should a manufacturer or dealer lessor quantify and recognise a selling profit under (a) an operating lease and (b) a finance lease? (4.6)

9   How should tax-free grants to lessors be accounted for? (4.7)

Sale and leaseback transactions

10   What is a sale and leaseback transaction? (5.1)

Termination of leases

11 How are termination payments accounted for in (a) the books of a lessor with an operating lease and (b) the books of a lessee with a finance lease? (6.2, 6.3)

The usefulness of SSAP 21

12 What are the main weaknesses of SSAP 21? (8)

Current proposals

13 What are the main proposals of the ASB's Discussion Paper on leases? (9)

EXAM-TYPE
QUESTION

Trendy Clothes

Trendy Clothes plc manufactures a machine at a cost of £126,000 that prints on sports shirts. It either sells the machine for £160,748 cash or leases the machine on a three-year lease.

Lease with Sporty Shirts plc

On 1 January 20X8 Trendy Clothes plc entered into a three year non-cancellable lease with Sporty Shirts plc on the following terms:

(i)   lease rentals were £56,000 payable annually in advance

(ii) initial direct costs of £8,400 incurred in commission and legal fees were borne by Trendy Clothes plc and charged to the profit and loss account on a systematic basis

(iii) there was a guaranteed residual value of £28,000

(iv) the interest rate implicit in the lease with Sporty Shirts plc was 18%.

Transaction with Optimistic Sales Ltd

On 1 January 20X8 Trendy Clothes plc entered into an arrangement with Optimistic Sales Ltd. Optimistic Sales Ltd had purchased a machine from Trendy Clothes plc but, having run into cash flow problems, the company arranged a sale and leaseback of the machine to Trendy Clothes plc.

The arrangement was that Optimistic Sales Ltd sold the machine to Trendy Clothes plc for £124,575 and immediately leased it back for four years at a rental of £37,500 payable yearly in advance. At the time of the sale the book value of the machine was £75,000 which was arrived at after the provision of depreciation on the company's normal straight-line basis. It was agreed that the machine should revert to Trendy Clothes plc at the end of the four year period when its scrap value was estimated to be nil. The lease is non-cancellable and Trendy Clothes plc is reasonably confident that the lease payments will be met. The interest rate implicit in the lease with Optimistic Sales was 14%. For the purpose of this question, taxation is ignored and therefore the net cash investment in the lease is equivalent to the net investment.

Required:

(a) In respect of the lease with Sporty Shirts plc:

    (i)   draft the entries that would appear in the profit and loss account of Trendy Clothes plc for the year ended 31 December 20X8   **(8 marks)**

    (ii) draft the entries that would appear in the balance sheets of Trendy Clothes plc as at 31 December 20X8 and 20X9.   **(4 marks)**

(b) In respect of the transaction with Optimistic Sales Ltd draft the journal entries to record the transaction in the books of Optimistic Sales Ltd for the year ended 31 December 20X8.   **(8 marks)**

(Total: 20 marks)

Present value factors to discount from end of the year

End of year	14%	16%	18%
1	0.877	0.862	0.848
2	0.769	0.743	0.718
3	0.675	0.641	0.609
4	0.592	0.552	0.516
5	0.519	0.476	0.437

For the answer to this question see the 'Answers' section at the end of the book.

FEEDBACK TO ACTIVITY 1

Is the lease a finance lease?

Referring to the steps in the earlier paragraph:

Step 1

(1)   MLPs = 4 × £2,000 = £8,000

(2)   Present value of MLPs:

From discount tables – present value of four annual sums – first receivable at the end of the first year:

£2,000 × 2.855 = £5,710

(3)   Fair value of asset is £5,710.

(4)   Present value of MLPs is more than 90% of fair value of asset.

The lease is thus a finance lease.

Step 2

The asset is shown in the balance sheet at £5,710 (subject to depreciation). Depreciation is over eight years (presumably there is no residual value to the asset at the end of eight years).

Annual depreciation charge = 1/8 × £5,710 = £714

Step 3

The liability is shown in the balance sheet at £5,710 but is subsequently reduced by the capital portion of the leasing payments.

The total finance charge is £(8,000 – 5,710) = £2,290. The allocation of this to each rental payment and the consequent capital sum outstanding is calculated as follows:

Period (year ended 31 December)	Capital sum at start of period	Finance charge at 15% pa	Sub-total	Rental paid	Capital sum at end of period
	£	£	£	£	£
20X2	5,710	856	6,566	(2,000)	4,566
20X3	4,566	685	5,251	(2,000)	3,251
20X4	3,251	488	3,739	(2,000)	1,739
20X5	1,739	261	2,000	(2,000)	-
		2,290		8,000	

Step 4

The effect on the financial statements of the lessee may be summarised as follows:

Profit and loss account Year ended 31 December	Finance charge	Depn.	Fixed asset (NBV)	Total	Obligation Non-current	Current
	£	£	£	£	£	£
20X2	856	714	4,996	4,566	3,251	1,315
20X3	685	714	4,282	3,251	1,739	1,512
20X4	488	714	3,568	1,739	-	1,739
20X5	261	714	2,854	-	-	-
20X6	-	714	2,140	-	-	-
20X7	-	714	1,426	-	-	-
20X8	-	714	712	-	-	-
20X9	-	712	-	-	-	-
		2,290	5,710			

The finance charge each year is a constant periodic rate of return (15%) on the remaining balance of liability, e.g. £856 is 15% of £5,710, etc.

FEEDBACK TO ACTIVITY **2**

(a) **Machine X**

Treat as an operating lease.

Profit and loss account   10 months' rental charge   = £12,500
Balance sheet   Prepayment, 2 months' rental charge = £2,500

Disclosure in notes to the accounts, operating lease commitment of £7,500 for next year under heading of lease with a commitment finishing next year.

Machine Y

Treat as a finance lease.

Workings re interest allocation   £

Total purchase price, 6 years × £12,025   72,150
'Cash' purchase price   46,250

Interest   25,900

Sum of digits = 5 + 4 + 3 + 2 + 1 + 0 = 15

For year 20X8 interest allocated to profit and loss account would be:

$$\frac{4}{15} \times £25,900 = £6,907$$

Depreciation charged (straight line) to profit and loss account would be:

$$\frac{£46,250}{6 \text{ years}} = £7,708$$

This would give a fixed asset value of £46,250 less accumulated depreciation of £15,416 in the balance sheet.

Other balance sheet figures would be as follows:

Obligations under finance lease

Less than one year $£12,025 - \left(\dfrac{3}{15} \times £25,900\right)$ = £6,845

More than one year $(£12,025 \times 3) - \left(\dfrac{2+1+0}{15} \times £25,900\right)$ = £30,895

Machine Z

Treat as a finance lease.

Workings using discounted rentals to calculate fair value at time of purchase

$£3,700 \times 3.605 = £13,338.50$

Interest allocation

	£
Total purchase price, 5 years × £3,700	18,500.00
Fair value	13,338.50
Interest	£5,161.50

Sum of digits = 5 + 4 + 3 + 2 + 1 = 15

For year 20X8 interest allocated to profit and loss account would be:

$$\dfrac{5}{15} \times £5,161.50 = £1,720.50$$

Depreciation charged (straight line) to profit and loss account would be:

$$\dfrac{£13,338.50}{5 \text{ years}} = £2,667.70$$

This would give a fixed asset value of £13,338.50 less accumulated depreciation of £2,667.70 in the balance sheet.

Other balance sheet figures would be as follows:

Less than one year $£3,700 - \left(\dfrac{4}{15} \times £5,161.50\right)$ = £2,323.60

More than one year $(£3,700 \times 3) - \left(\dfrac{3+2+1}{15} \times 5,161.50\right)$ = £9,035.40

(b) **Machine X**

No change, as per answer to part (a) above.

Machine Y

Profit and loss account charge of £12,025 annual rental.

Disclose in the notes to the accounts operating lease commitment of £12,025 for next year under heading of lease with a commitment expiring after five years.

Machine Z

Profit and loss account charge of £3,700 annual rental.

Disclose in notes to the accounts operating lease commitment of £3,700 for next year under heading of lease with a commitment finishing in the second to fifth years.

Chapter 15

SEGMENTAL REPORTING

This chapter begins by revising the requirements of SSAP 25 *Segmental reporting*. It then moves on to look at the problem areas in segmental reporting and to examine possible alternative approaches to disclosing segmental information.

Objectives

When you have studied this chapter you should be able to:

- discuss the problem areas in segmental reporting
- understand the different approaches used to disclose segmental information
- discuss the importance of segmental information to users of financial statements.

1   SSAP 25 *Segmental reporting*

1.1   Requirements of SSAP 25 in relation to segmental reporting

If an entity has two or more classes of business or operates in two or more geographical segments it should:

(a) define its classes of business and geographical segments in its financial statements; and

(b) for each class of business and geographical segment, disclose:

   (i)   turnover, distinguishing:

   - turnover derived from external customers; and

   - turnover derived from other segments

   (ii) result before tax, minority interests and extraordinary items

   (iii) net assets.

The standard distinguishes:

(a) **origin** of turnover – the geographical segment **from which** products or services are supplied; and

(b) **destination** of turnover – the geographical segment **to which** products or services are supplied.

The geographical segmentation of turnover should be done by origin and also by destination where the latter is different.

Results should normally be given before interest unless the interest income or expense is central to the business, in which case the result should be given after interest.

The net assets should normally be non-interest bearing unless the results are after interest in which case the interest bearing assets and liabilities should be included.

Segmental information should be presented on the basis of the consolidated financial statements.

> **DEFINITION**
>
> A **class of business** is defined as a distinguishable component of an entity that provides a separate product or service or a separate group of related products or services.

> **DEFINITION**
>
> A **geographical segment** is a geographical area comprising an individual country or group of countries in which an entity operates or to which it supplies products or services.

1.2 Requirements of the Companies Act in relation to segmental reporting

Notes to the profit and loss account must show turnover broken down by classes of business and by geographical markets, having regard to the manner in which the company's activities are organised, in so far as these classes and markets differ substantially.

Classes or markets which do not differ substantially must be treated as one class or market. Immaterial amounts may be combined with those of another class or market.

This additional information on turnover may be omitted if disclosure would be seriously prejudicial to the company's interests. The fact that such information has not been disclosed must be stated in the notes.

1.3 Determining reportable segments under SSAP 25

The directors identify the **reportable segments** having regard to differences in:

- return on capital employed
- risk
- rate of growth
- potential for future development for both classes of business and geographical areas.

All significant segments should be identified as reportable segments.

1.4 Preparing segmental reports in accordance with current requirements

The illustrative example in SSAP 25 is a useful format to follow when preparing a statement.

DEFINITION

A **significant segment** is a segment where:

- third party turnover is 10% or more of the total third party turnover; or
- the segment result is 10% or more of the combined result of all segments in profit, or in loss (whichever is greater)
- net assets are 10% or more of the total net assets.

Class of business	Industry A 20X1 £'000	Industry A 20X0 £'000	Industry B 20X1 £'000	Industry B 20X0 £'000	Other 20X1 £'000	Other 20X0 £'000	Group 20X1 £'000	Group 20X0 £'000
Turnover								
Total sales	33,000	30,000	42,000	38,000	26,000	23,000	101,000	91,000
Inter-segment sales	(4,000)	-	-	-	(12,000)	(14,000)	(16,000)	(14,000)
Sales to third parties	29,000	30,000	42,000	38,000	14,000	9,000	85,000	77,000
Profit before taxation								
Segment profit	3,000	2,500	4,500	4,000	1,800	1,500	9,300	8,000
Common costs							300	300
Operating profit							9,000	7,700
Net interest							(400)	(500)
							8,600	7,200
Group share of the profits before taxation of associated undertakings	1,000	1,000	1,400	1,200	-	-	2,400	2,200
Group profit before taxation							11,000	9,400
Net assets								
Segment net assets	17,600	15,000	24,000	25,000	19,400	19,000	61,000	59,000

Unallocated assets						3,000	3,000
						64,000	62,000
Group share of net assets of associated undertakings	10,200	8,000	8,800	9,000	–	–	19,000	17,000
Total net assets						83,000	79,000

A similar analysis must also be shown by geographical segments, again showing the breakdown of:

- turnover

- profit before tax

- net assets.

Common costs refer to costs where allocation between segments could mislead. Likewise, the segmental disclosure of net assets might include unallocated assets.

The following detailed points from the standard should also assist.

- **Associates** – The share of the results and net assets of associates should be shown separately by segment if the associate accounts for at least 20% of the total result or total net assets of the reporting entity.

  This need not be shown where the information is unobtainable or where publication would be prejudicial to the business.

- **Reconciliation** – The total of the amounts disclosed by segment should agree with the total in the financial statements. If it does not, the reporting entity should provide reconciliation between the two figures. Reconciling items should be properly identified and explained.

- **Comparatives** – Comparatives should be provided. If a change is made to the definitions of the segments or to the accounting policies that are adopted for reporting segmental information, the nature of the change should be disclosed.

- If the directors consider that disclosure of any information required by the standard would be seriously prejudicial to the interests of the reporting entity, the information need not be disclosed.

ACTIVITY 1

Industry and geographical segmental reports

Industry segment	Fruit growing		Canning		Bureau		Group	
	20X2 £'000	20X1 £'000	20X2 £'000	20X1 £'000	20X2 £'000	20X1 £'000	20X2 £'000	20X1 £'000
Total sales	13,635	15,188	20,520	16,200	5,400	4,050	39,555	35,438
Less inter-seg. sales	1,485	1,688	2,970	3,105			4,455	4,793
Third party sales	12,150	13,500	17,550	13,905	5,400	4,050	35,100	30,645
Segment operating profit	3,565	3,375	4,725	3,600	412	540	8,702	7,515
Segment assets	33,750	32,400	40,500	33,750	18,765	17,563	93,015	83,713
Unallocated (common) assets							13,500	11,003
TOTAL ASSETS							106,515	94,716

Geographical segment	UK 20X2 £'000	UK 20X1 £'000	USA 20X2 £'000	USA 20X1 £'000	Other 20X2 £'000	Other 20X1 £'000	Group 20X2 £'000	Group 20X1 £'000
Total sales	29,700	26,190	8,910	6,345	1,350	1,215	39,960	33,750
Inter-seg. sales	2,700	1,890	2,160	1,215			4,860	3,105
Third party sales	27,000	24,300	6,750	5,130	1,350	1,215	35,100	30,645
Segment operating profit	5,130	4,590	2,430	1,890	1,142	1,035	8,702	7,515
Segment assets	43,200	40,500	32,400	24,300	18,360	19,683	93,960	84,483
Unallocated (common) assets							12,555	10,233
TOTAL ASSETS							106,515	95,716

Using the segmental report provided above for illustration if you wish, identify areas in which the requirements of SSAP 25 do not necessarily result in the disclosure of useful information.

Feedback to this activity is at the end of the chapter.

1.5 Problem areas in segmental reporting

- **Defining segments** – Segments are defined by the directors. SSAP 25 gives some guidance on how to define segments, but this is very general. The standard also states that the directors should review the definitions annually and redefine segments when appropriate.

  In practice there are two main approaches to defining segments: the risks and returns approach and the managerial approach. These are discussed in more detail later in the chapter.

  There can be particular practical problems in defining geographical segments where a company operates globally. Operations may be so integrated that it is difficult to determine the destination and the origin of turnover.

- **Common costs** – Common costs normally consist of central administration overheads. Common costs may be allocated to different segments on whatever basis the directors believe is reasonable. Where the apportionment of common costs would be misleading, SSAP 25 requires that they should not be apportioned, but the total should be deducted from the total of the segment results. Despite this, some entities do carry out arbitrary allocation of common costs.

- **Inter-segment sales** – The basis of transfer pricing between group companies need not be disclosed. This limits the usefulness of the segmental information provided.

- **Allocation of interest income and interest expense** – In most companies, the interest earned or incurred by the individual segments reflects the way in which the holding company raises finance rather than the results of individual segments. SSAP 25 requires that in these circumstances the results should exclude interest.

  However, SSAP 25 suggests that interest should be included in arriving at the segment result where interest is fundamental to the nature of the business. This is likely to apply to companies involved in the financial sector. It may also apply where some segments or divisions in a group are cash generative and finance the others.

- **Exceptional items** – There is no guidance on how to treat exceptional items. As these are part of results before tax, they should in theory be allocated between segments. However, some entities analyse their results before exceptional items.

- **Changes within a group** – SSAP 25 does not address the effect of changes within a group on the segmental results. However, FRS 3 requires that 'where an acquisition, sale or termination has a material impact on a major business segment this should be disclosed and explained'.

  In practice, some companies show discontinued operations separately in their segmental analyses while others show discontinued operations as a residual category.

- **Net assets** – SSAP 25 does not define net assets. It does state that in most cases these are non-interest bearing operating assets less non-interest bearing operating liabilities. If interest is included in the segment results, interest bearing assets and liabilities should be included in the calculation of net assets.

  Operating assets of a segment should not normally include loans or advances to or investments in another segment unless interest from these has been included in arriving at the segment result.

  Operating liabilities should exclude liabilities in respect of proposed dividends and corporation tax and interest bearing liabilities (e.g. loans, overdrafts and debentures).

  Non-operating assets and liabilities should be shown as reconciling items between the total of the individual segment net assets and the figure for net assets appearing in the balance sheet.

ACTIVITY 2

An airline operates services both within the United Kingdom and throughout the world. Its flights are sold to customers resident in the United Kingdom and throughout the world.

Its main asset is its aircraft fleet, the large part of which is registered in the United Kingdom.

How might it analyse turnover and net assets by geographical segment for the purpose of segmental reporting?

Feedback to this activity is at the end of the chapter.

2   The different approaches used to disclose segmental information

KEY POINT

The 'risks and returns' approach identifies segments on the basis of different risks and returns arising from different lines of business and geographical areas.

2.1   Approaches to segmental reporting

There are two main approaches to segmental reporting:

- the 'risks and returns' approach
- the 'managerial' approach.

The 'risks and returns' approach identifies segments on the basis of different risks and returns arising from different lines of business and geographical areas. This is broadly similar to the SSAP 25 approach and has also been adopted by the IASC in IAS 14 *Segment reporting*.

KEY POINT

The 'managerial' approach identifies segments corresponding to the internal organisation structure of the entity.

The 'managerial' approach identifies segments corresponding to the internal organisation structure of the entity.

2.2 The 'risks and returns' approach

The 'risks and returns' approach is believed to have the following advantages:

- it produces information which is more comparable between companies and consistent over time than the 'managerial' approach

- it assists in the assessment of profitability and the risks and returns of the component parts of the enterprise

- it reflects the approach taken in the financial statements for external reporting.

The main disadvantage of the approach is that defining segments can be difficult in practice and also subjective. This affects comparability. Some commentators believe that it would be possible to amend SSAP 25 so that it was less flexible. Although IAS 14 adopts the same approach to defining segments, it provides more detailed definitions.

2.3 The 'managerial' approach

The 'managerial' approach bases both the segments reported and the information reported about them on the information used internally for decision-making. This means that management define the reportable segments.

An identifiable segment can be defined as a component of an entity:

- that engages in business activities from which it earns revenues and incurs expenses

- whose operating results are regularly reviewed by senior management to assess the performance of the individual segment and make decisions about resources to be allocated to the segment

- for which discrete financial information is available.

Arguments for the 'managerial approach' include the following.

- Segments based on an entity's internal structure are less subjective than those identified by the 'risks and returns' approach.

- It highlights the risks and opportunities that management believes are important.

- It provides information with predictive value because it enables users of the financial statements to see the entity through the eyes of management.

- The cost of providing the information is low (because it should already have been provided for management's use).

- It will produce segment information that is consistent with the way in which management discuss their business in other parts of the annual report (e.g. in the Chairman's Statement and the OFR).

- Interim reporting of segmental information would be feasible.

Arguments against the 'managerial approach' include the following:

- Segments based on internal reporting structures are unlikely to be comparable between enterprises and may not be comparable from year to year for an individual entity. (For example, organisation structures, or the way in which they are perceived, may change as a result of new managers being appointed.)

- The information is likely to be commercially sensitive (because entities are organised strategically).

- Segmental information given other than by products or services or geographically may be more difficult to analyse using macroeconomic models.

- Using the managerial approach could lead to segments with different risks and returns being combined.

- Analysts define their area of expertise by industry segment, usually based on product or service. The SSAP 25 version of segmental reporting is more likely to reflect these.

2.4 Evaluating the two approaches

It has been suggested that the choice between the risks and returns approach and the managerial approach cannot be made on the basis of principle alone. This is because the results of applying the approaches in practice may differ from that expected.

The risks and returns approach provides information about the major sources of the different risks and opportunities that face an entity. The managerial approach provides information on the way an entity manages its business. The preferences of users depend on which they believe is the most important.

The choice between the two approaches may be influenced by the degree to which the amounts reported to management for the running of the business are consistent and comparable between segments and businesses.

3   The importance of segmental information

3.1 Purpose of segmental information

Many companies and groups carry on several classes of business or operate in several geographical areas. These different parts of the business are likely to have different rates of profitability, different opportunities for growth and different degrees of risk.

For example, a segment trading abroad may be subject to particular problems such as a falling exchange rate or hyper-inflation. Awareness of the environment in which a business is trading is becoming increasingly important as business itself becomes more global.

SSAP 25 states that the purpose of segmental information is to provide information to assist the readers of financial statements:

- to appreciate more thoroughly the results and financial position of the enterprise by permitting a better understanding of the enterprise's past performance and thus a better assessment of its future prospects

- to be aware of the impact that changes in significant components of a business may have on the business as a whole.

3.2 The usefulness of segmental information in practice

Most commentators agree that segmental information is useful to users of the financial statements. However, as we have seen, there are several areas in which SSAP 25 is arguably too flexible.

One of the main problems is that management define the segments. This means that segmental information is only useful for comparing the performance of the same entity over time, not for comparing the performance of different entities.

Another weakness of SSAP 25 is that directors are able to circumvent it. They need not disclose any information if they believe that it would be prejudicial to the entity's interests. For example, directors may resist disclosing segmental information on the grounds that it will provide information to competitors.

3.3　Interpreting segmental information

It is possible to compute return on capital employed (ROCE), profit margin and asset turnover for each segment based on the segmental information disclosed. This provides information on the profitability, efficiency and overall performance of each segment.

However, it may not be possible to compute ratios validly for each segment under SSAP 25 as:

- common costs may or may not be included in the segment result (this is a decision of the directors)

- net assets may have an element of commonality across segments

- segment results may be distorted by transfer pricing policies.

SELF-TEST
QUESTIONS

SSAP 25 *Segmental reporting*

1　What is a significant segment? (1.3)

2　When should a share of the results and net assets of associates be shown separately by segment? (1.4)

3　What are the main problem areas in segmental reporting? (1.5)

The different approaches used to disclose segmental information

4　Distinguish between the 'risks and returns approach' and the 'managerial approach' to segmental reporting. (2.1)

EXAM-TYPE
QUESTION

TAB plc

TAB plc has recently acquired four large overseas subsidiaries. These subsidiaries manufacture products which are totally different from those of the holding company. The holding company manufactures paper and related products whereas the subsidiaries manufacture the following:

	Product	Location
Subsidiary 1	Car products	Spain
Subsidiary 2	Textiles	Korea
Subsidiary 3	Kitchen utensils	France
Subsidiary 4	Fashion garments	Thailand

The directors have purchased these subsidiaries in order to diversify their product base but do not have any knowledge on the information which is required in the financial statements, regarding these subsidiaries, other than the statutory requirements. The directors of the company realise that there is a need to disclose segmental information but do not understand what the term means or what the implications are for the published accounts.

Required:

(a)　Explain to the directors the purpose of segmental reporting of financial information.　　　　　　　　　　　　　　　　　　　　　**(4 marks)**

(b) Explain to the directors the criteria which should be used to identify the separate reportable segments (you should illustrate your answer by reference to the above information).   **(6 marks)**

(c) Advise the directors on the information which should be disclosed in financial statements for each segment..   **(7 marks)**

(d) Critically evaluate SSAP 25 *Segmental reporting*, setting out the major problems with the standard.   **(8 marks)**
                                                                        (Total: 25 marks)

For the answer to this question see the 'Answers' section at the end of the book.

**FEEDBACK TO
ACTIVITY 1**

Your answer may have included some of the following:

(i) Definition of segments

It would be particularly helpful to know whether there are any other classes of business included within the three classifications supplied by the company which are material and subject to different trends or different risks. This is particularly important when one looks at the Canning segment and notices that it comprises 50% of the total sales to customers outside the group.

(ii) Inter-segment sales

The inter-segment sales in the US are relatively high at 24% (£2,160/8,910). In assessing the risk and economic trends it might well be that those of the receiving segment are more useful in predicting future prospects than those of the segment from which the sale originated.

(iii) Analysis of assets

One of the objectives of the reader is often to calculate a return on capital employed for each segment. It is important therefore to ensure that the segmental operating profit and assets are appropriately defined so that segmental operating profit can be usefully related to the assets' figure to produce a meaningful ratio. This means that both the operating profit and assets' figure need to be precisely defined. If, for example, the assets are the gross assets, then the operating profits should be before deduction of interest. This means that the preparer of the segmental report needs to be aware of the reader's information needs.

(iv) Unallocated items

The information provided includes unallocated assets which represent around 12% of the total assets. It is not clear what these assets represent.

(v) Treatment of interest

It would be useful to know if there has been any interest charge incurred and to ascertain whether it is material and whether it can be reasonably identified as relating to any particular segment. As mentioned in (iii) above, the profit is given as operating profit and it is not clear how this is defined or how it has been derived.

A possible approach is illustrated by this extract from an accounting policy note.

Turnover by destination

Turnover from domestic services within the United Kingdom is attributed to the United Kingdom. Turnover from inbound and outbound services between the United Kingdom and overseas points is attributed to the geographical area in which the relevant overseas point lies.

Turnover by origin

Revenue is allocated to the area in which the sale is made.

Geographical analysis of net assets

The major revenue-earning asset of the company is its aircraft fleet, the large part of which is registered in the United Kingdom. Since the group's aircraft fleet is employed flexibly across its worldwide route network, there is no suitable basis of allocating such assets and related liabilities to geographical segments.

Chapter 16

ACCOUNTING FOR RETIREMENT BENEFITS

Many employers provide pension schemes for their employees. A pension scheme is normally a separate entity from the employer itself and therefore it prepares its own accounts. Pension scheme accounts are not included in your syllabus. However, the employer still has to account for the cost of providing pensions in its own financial statements and this can give rise to particular accounting problems.

The chapter begins by explaining the different types of pension scheme and some of the terminology involved. You are unlikely to be examined on the detail of this, but you need a general awareness of the way in which pension schemes operate in order to understand the problems of accounting for pension costs.

The most important part of the chapter concerns the requirements of FRS 17 *Retirement benefits*. FRS 17 contains some complicated definitions of which you should be aware, but exam questions will test your understanding of the main principles involved and ability to apply them in a practical situation using simple numbers.

Objectives

When you have studied this chapter you should be able to:

- understand the nature of defined contribution, multi-employers and defined benefits schemes

- explain the recognition of defined benefit schemes under current requirements

- understand the measurement of defined benefit schemes under current requirements

- account for defined benefit schemes

- discuss perceived problems with current requirements on accounting for retirement benefits.

1 The conceptual nature of pension rights and pension costs

1.1 Pension rights

DEFINITION

Defined benefit schemes – Under these schemes employees' pension benefits are specified, typically as a percentage of final salary.

Under a defined benefit scheme an actuary calculates the size of the fund required to provide the employees with the specified pensions on retirement. The calculation is based on a set of carefully chosen assumptions. The employer then makes the contributions required to ensure that, on the retirement of each employee, the required fund exists. Traditionally, defined benefit schemes comprise a large proportion of the larger UK employee pension schemes.

Under a defined contribution scheme the contributions are simply invested, and the size of the fund accumulated by the retirement date, including investment income, determines the size of the pension payable. The great advantage of such schemes is that it is possible to identify a pool of funds attributable to each individual member, therefore greatly enhancing the portability of the pension. The portability advantage is one reason why an increasing number of employee schemes, particularly in smaller firms, are defined contribution schemes.

1.2 The main problems

The provision of pensions creates two separate decisions for a company.

- **Funding** – This is the level and pattern of cash contributions to provide for the eventual payment of pensions. Funding is normally based on advice given to the employer by a professional actuary.

- **Accounting** – This is the way in which the expense of pensions is charged to the company's profit and loss account.

Because funding and accounting are separate issues, the actual cost of providing a pension is not necessarily the same as the cash contributions made by the employer.

2 Funding

2.1 Funded and unfunded schemes

There are two approaches to funding the provision of pensions.

- **Unfunded pensions** – In some cases the employer appropriates a certain level of funds each year to a separate pool of assets earmarked for the payment of pensions, whereas in other cases he simply pays pensions due out of current revenues. This means that pension payments may be affected if the company experiences problems.

- **Funded pensions** – These pension funds are either administered by trustees or, as in the case of many smaller funds, administered by an insurance company. Funded schemes have the advantage that contributions are accumulated externally to the employing company and thus will not be lost if the company gets into difficulties.

2.2 Calculation of contributions: defined contribution schemes

In defined contribution schemes the liability of the employer is for a set level of contributions. There is no further liability.

The precise amount of the contributions is therefore a matter for negotiation between employer and employee.

2.3 Calculation of contributions: defined benefit schemes

- **Actuarial involvement** – In these schemes the liability of the employer is to provide a set level of pension benefits, typically a percentage of final pre-retirement salary, and is therefore a very long-term commitment. An actuary calculates the contributions which will be required to ensure that sufficient funds will have been accumulated to meet pension liabilities as and when they fall due.

- **Actuarial assumptions** – The calculation of contributions entails taking into account a number of uncertain future factors. Therefore the actuary has to make assumptions to cover factors including the following:

  (a)   future rates of inflation and pay increases

  (b)   increases to pensions already being paid

  (c)   earnings on investments

  (d)   the number of employees joining the scheme

  (e)   the age profile of the employees

  (f)   the probability that employees will die or leave the company's employment before reaching retirement age.

- **Actuarial objectives** – In choosing the level and pattern of contributions the actuary has two major objectives:

  (a)   to build up assets in the scheme in a prudent and controlled manner in advance of the retirement of the members of the scheme

  (b)   to avoid undue distortion of the employer's cash flows.

2.4   Surpluses and deficiencies in defined benefit schemes

The funding plan is based on assumptions about the future which may not be borne out in practice. Therefore most pension schemes are formally valued by an actuary every three years. The valuation may reveal a surplus (the fund assets exceed the liability to pay future pensions) or a deficit (the liability to pay future pensions exceeds the fund assets).

(a)   **Reasons for surpluses and deficits**

The main causes of surpluses and deficits are as follows.

- Variations between reality and the assumptions made at the last valuation. Surpluses and deficits on this basis are referred to as experience surpluses or deficits.

- The effect of changes in actuarial assumptions on the actuarial valuation of accrued benefits.

- Retroactive changes in benefits or in conditions for membership.

- Increases to pensions in payment or to deferred pensions for which provision has not previously been made.

(b)   **Elimination of surpluses and deficits**

Surpluses and deficits need to be eliminated. Surpluses represent needlessly idle funds and deficits mean that the employer may not be able to meet its obligations to pay pensions in future. The actuary recommends an appropriate course of action.

   (i)   **Correction of surpluses**
   - improvement of benefits
   - refunds to the employer
   - contribution holidays (periods of reduced or nil contribution).

(ii) **Correction of deficits**

- an increase in the normal contribution rate

- additional special payments over a limited period

- lump sum contributions.

The decision as to which method to use is made on the advice of the actuary, taking into account the cash flow position of the employer company. For instance a refund would be very suitable for a company in a situation of financial stringency but less so for one which already has cash surpluses.

3 Accounting

3.1 The accounting problem

Defined contribution schemes present few accounting problems. The charge to the profit and loss account is the same as the amount of contributions payable in the period because this is the cost to the employer of providing pensions.

As we have seen, the cost to the employer of providing pensions under a **defined benefit scheme** for an accounting period is not necessarily the same as the contributions payable. There are two main issues in accounting for a defined benefit scheme:

- **measurement**: the method used to value the assets and liabilities of the scheme

- **recognition**: the way in which the amounts relating to the scheme are included in the financial statements.

3.2 Measurement

In order to arrive at the cost of providing pensions under a defined benefit scheme, the scheme assets and liabilities must be valued. There are a number of different methods but these fall into two main groups as follows:

- **actuarial methods:** assets and liabilities are valued by an actuary at the present value of their future cash flows, on the basis of estimates of future interest rates, salary increases and service lives of employees

- **the market value method:** assets and liabilities are stated at their market values or fair values.

Until a few years ago, there was little support in the UK for the use of market values and most actuaries and accountants favoured actuarial methods. However, during the last few years substantial changes have taken place in the actuarial profession and most actuaries now favour market values.

3.3 Recognition

It would be possible to account for pension costs on a cash basis. This would have the advantages of being simple and objective. Supporters of this method argue that, because of various tax and other regulations that now apply to employee pension schemes, it is no longer possible for a scheme to be substantially overfunded or underfunded, and in practice the contributions paid each year are equivalent to the pension cost.

However, most accountants recognise that there is still substantial scope for employers to adopt different and varying contribution schedules and that a cash-based method would not result in the recognition of the cost of a pension as it arises over the service lives of the employees.

Therefore it is necessary to use an accruals-based system of accounting for pension costs. There are two main ways in which this can be done: the spreading approach and the balance sheet approach.

The spreading approach

This treats the pension cost as being made up of two elements: regular cost and variations from regular cost.

- Regular cost is the consistent ongoing cost as calculated under the chosen measurement method.

- Variations from regular cost arise when an entity has to change the pattern of its contributions to the scheme in order to eliminate a surplus or a deficit.

Variations from the regular cost are allocated over the expected remaining service lives of current employees in the scheme (in practice a period representing the average remaining service lives is often used). The reasoning for this treatment is that surpluses and deficits are (in most situations) part of the ongoing process of revising the estimate of the ultimate liability which will fall on the employer on the retirement of employees. They therefore cannot be treated as prior period adjustments (in accordance with FRS 3) as they relate to the employees currently in the scheme, nor is it appropriate to recognise them immediately in the profit and loss account.

This approach emphasises the profit and loss account. The balance sheet amounts produced are residual items and represent the difference between the cumulative cost charged to the profit and loss account and the cumulative payments made by the company in respect of pensions.

Example

The actuarial valuation as at 31 December 20X1 of the defined benefit pension scheme of a company showed a deficit of £30 million. The actuary recommended that the deficit be eliminated by lump sum payments of £15 million per annum for two years, in addition to the regular cost of £5 million per annum. The average remaining service life of employees in the scheme was estimated as eight years.

Using the spreading approach, what will be the entries in the accounts for the year ended 31 December 20X2?

Solution

The pension cost charge for the next eight years should be as follows:

$$£5 \text{ million} + \frac{£30 \text{ million}}{8} = £8.75 \text{ million}$$

The funding and accounting policies will therefore be as follows:

	Funding (cash)	Accounting (P&L)	Prepayment (B/S)
	£m	£m	£m
20X2	20	8.75	11.25
20X3	20	8.75	22.50
20X4	5	8.75	18.75
20X5	5	8.75	15.00
20X6	5	8.75	11.25
20X7	5	8.75	7.50
20X8	5	8.75	3.75
20X9	5	8.75	–
	70	70.00	

Therefore the profit and loss account for the year ended 31 December 20X2 will include a charge of £8.75 million for pension costs and the balance sheet will include a prepayment of £11.25 million.

The balance sheet approach

This treats the surplus or deficit as an asset or a liability of the employer and includes it in the balance sheet. The change in the surplus or deficit in the period is adjusted for the contribution paid in the period to arrive at the pension cost.

The reasoning behind this approach is that a surplus is an asset of the employer because the employer has the ability to receive economic benefits from that surplus (e.g. to reduce contributions). A deficit is a liability because the employer has an obligation to transfer economic benefits (increase contributions) to the scheme.

In this case the balance sheet is emphasised and the profit and loss account contains residual items.

Example

The actuarial valuation as at 31 December 20X1 of the defined benefit pension scheme of a company showed a deficit of £30 million. The actuary recommended that the deficit be eliminated by lump sum payments of £15 million per annum for two years, in addition to the regular cost of £5 million per annum. The average remaining service life of employees in the scheme was estimated as eight years.

Using the balance sheet method, what will be the entries in the accounts for the year ended 31 December 20X2?

Solution

	Liability b/d (B/S) £m	Funding (cash) £m	Accounting (P&L) £m	Liability c/d (B/S) £m
20X2	30	20	5	15
20X3	15	20	5	–
		40	10	

Therefore the profit and loss account for the year ended 31 December 20X2 will include a charge of £5 million for pension costs and the balance sheet will include a liability of £15 million.

4   FRS 17 *Retirement benefits*

4.1   Objectives

The objective of FRS 17 is to ensure that:

- financial statements reflect at fair value the assets and liabilities arising from an employer's retirement benefit obligations and any related funding

- the operating costs of providing retirement benefits to employees are recognised in the accounting period(s) in which the benefits are earned by the employees, and the related finance costs and any other changes in the value of the assets and liabilities are recognised in the accounting periods in which they arise

- the financial statements contain adequate disclosure of the cost of providing retirement benefits and the related gains, losses, assets and liabilities.

4.2   Background to the development of the FRS

FRS 17 was issued in 2000 and replaced SSAP 24 *Accounting for pension costs.* SSAP 24 required scheme assets and liabilities to be valued using actuarial methods. It also adopted the 'spreading' approach described above, with variations in regular pension costs being allocated over the average remaining service lives of the employees in the scheme.

Several factors led to the replacement of SSAP 24, as follows.

- **Weaknesses in SSAP 24**

   The ASB carried out a review of SSAP 24 which highlighted the following problems.

   (a)   Too many options were permitted, leading to inconsistency between companies. For example, SSAP 24 allowed a choice of actuarial valuation method. This provided companies with flexibility to adjust results on a short-term basis.

   (b)   Its disclosure requirements were insufficient to explain the pension cost and related amounts in the balance sheet.

- **The need for international harmonisation**

   One possible solution to the problem would have been to revise SSAP 24, retaining its general approach but eliminating many of the options and improving the disclosure requirements. Instead, the ASB developed a radically different standard.

   When the ASB began its review of accounting for pension costs, the method used to value scheme assets and liabilities was not a major issue. Most respondents to the ASB's earlier Discussion Papers were in favour of retaining the actuarial method. However, the IASC then issued IAS 19 *Employee benefits* which requires the use of market values on the grounds that these give the most objective and comparable information. Most other major standard setters also require the use of market values.

   The ASB came to the conclusion that there were insufficient reasons to go against the global trend towards a market value approach, particularly given the increasing use of market values by the actuarial profession.

4.3   Scope of FRS 17

FRS 17 covers all retirement benefits that an employer is committed to providing, whether the commitment is statutory, contractual or implicit in the employer's actions.

For example, retirement benefits include pensions and medical care during retirement.

4.4 Defined contribution schemes

The cost of a defined contribution scheme is equal to the contributions payable to the scheme for the accounting period. The cost should be recognised within operating profit in the profit and loss account.

4.5 Multi-employer schemes

Multi-employer schemes expose participating employers to the actuarial risks associated with the current and former employees of other entities. Defined contribution multi-employer schemes do not pose a problem because the employer's cost is limited to the contributions payable.

However, if the scheme is a defined benefit scheme an employer may be unable to identify its share of the underlying assets and liabilities on a consistent and reasonable basis. If this is the case, it is difficult to account for the scheme.

FRS 17 states that a multi-employer scheme should be accounted for as a defined benefit scheme unless:

- the employer's contributions are set in relation to the current service period only (i.e. are not affected by any surplus or deficit in the scheme relating to past service of its own employees or any other members of the scheme); or

- the employer's contributions are affected by a surplus or deficit in the scheme but the employer is unable to identify its share of the underlying assets and liabilities in the scheme on a consistent and reasonable basis.

Many group defined benefit schemes are run on a basis that does not enable individual group companies to identify their share of the underlying assets and liabilities.

- Individual group companies should account for the scheme as a defined contribution scheme in their own accounts.

- In the group accounts, the scheme should be treated as a defined benefit scheme as usual.

4.6 Defined benefit schemes

Defined benefit scheme assets

FRS 17 requires that scheme assets should be measured at their fair value at the balance sheet date. The Standard stipulates how fair value should be arrived at for each type of asset

- quoted securities: mid-market value

- unquoted securities: an estimate of fair value should be used

- property: open market value or another appropriate basis of valuation determined in accordance with professional practice.

Scheme assets include current assets as well as investments. Any liabilities such as accrued expenses should be deducted.

Scheme liabilities

Scheme liabilities should be measured on an actuarial basis using the projected unit method. Scheme liabilities comprise:

- any benefits promised under the formal terms of the scheme

- any constructive obligations for further benefits where a public statement or past practice by the employer has created a valid expectation in employees that such benefits will be granted.

In theory, scheme liabilities should also be valued at fair value, but this is not possible as there is no active market for most defined benefit scheme liabilities. Fair value must therefore be estimated using actuarial techniques. Unlike SSAP 24, FRS 17 stipulates the method to be used. It also sets out the following requirements for the valuation.

- The benefits should be attributed to periods of service according to the scheme's benefit formula, unless this attributes a disproportionate share of the total benefits to later years of service (in which case the benefit should be attributed on a straight line basis over the period during which it is earned).

- The assumptions underlying the valuation should be mutually compatible and lead to the best estimate of the future cash flows that will arise under the scheme liabilities. Any assumptions that are affected by economic conditions (financial assumptions) should reflect market expectations at the balance sheet date.

- The actuarial assumptions should reflect expected future events that will affect the cost of the benefits to which the employer is committed (either legally or through a constructive obligation) at the balance sheet date.

Discounting

FRS 17 requires that defined benefit scheme liabilities should be discounted at a rate that reflects the time value of money and the characteristics of the liability. Such a rate should be assumed to be the current rate of return on a high quality corporate bond of equivalent currency and term to the scheme liability.

Scheme liabilities are normally long-term. The requirement to discount them is consistent with other recent FRSs and FREDs and with the Statement of Principles, and means that they will be stated at the best estimate of the present value that will actually be paid out.

Full actuarial valuations by a professionally qualified actuary should be obtained for a defined benefit scheme at intervals not exceeding three years. At each balance sheet date the actuary should review the most recent actuarial valuation and update it to reflect current conditions.

In practice this means that the fair values of assets and the discount rate will be updated annually. Other assumptions, such as the expected leaving rate and the mortality rate, may not need to be updated annually.

4.7   Recognition of defined benefit schemes in the balance sheet

The general rule

- A surplus should be recognised as an asset to the extent that the employer is able to recover the surplus either through reduced contributions in the future or through refunds from the scheme.

- A deficit should be recognised as a liability to the extent of the employer's legal or constructive obligation to fund it.

Although the actual assets and liabilities of a pension scheme do not belong to the employing company, pension scheme surpluses and deficits meet the ASB's definitions of assets and liabilities in the Statement of Principles.

Assets

FRS 17 explains that a surplus gives rise to an asset if the employer has the ability to use the surplus to generate future economic benefits for itself (by reducing future contributions or obtaining a refund from the scheme), and this ability arises as a result of past events (contributions paid by the employer and investment growth in excess of rights earned by the employees).

In determining the asset to be recognised:

- the amount that can be recovered from reduced contributions in the future is the present value of the liability expected to arise from future service by current and future scheme members less the present value of future employee contributions

- the amount to be recovered from refunds from the scheme should reflect only refunds that have been agreed by the pension scheme trustees at the balance sheet date.

Liabilities

The employer has a liability if it has a legal or constructive obligation to make good a deficit in a defined benefit scheme. The employer normally has a legal obligation under the terms of the scheme's trust deed or will have created a constructive obligation by its past actions and statements.

Where employees as well as the employer make contributions, any deficit should be assumed to be borne by the employer unless the scheme rules require members' contributions to be increased to help fund a deficit. In this case, the deficit recognised by the employer should be reduced by the present value of the members' required additional contributions.

Presentation

- Unpaid contributions to the scheme should be presented as a creditor due within one year.

- The defined benefit asset or liability should be presented separately on the face of the balance sheet after other net assets (after accruals and deferred income but before capital and reserves).

- The deferred tax relating to the defined benefit asset or liability should be offset against the defined benefit asset or liability. It should not be included with other deferred tax assets or liabilities.

An Appendix to FRS 17 gives an example of the presentation, as follows:

	20X1 £m	20X0 £m
Net assets excluding pension asset	700	650
Net pension asset	335	143
Net assets including pension asset	1,035	793

The effect of SSAP 24 was potentially confusing. A surplus often gave rise to a creditor in the balance sheet (particularly where a contribution holiday was taken) while a deficit often resulted in a prepayment (because contributions were increased to meet it before they were recognised in the profit and loss account). The ASB believes that the new approach, whereby surpluses are treated as assets and deficits are treated as liabilities, will be more understandable.

4.8   Recognition of defined benefit schemes in the performance statements

Periodic costs

The pension 'cost' is the change in the defined benefit asset or liability in the period (other than that arising from contributions paid). It should be analysed into the following elements:

- current service cost

- interest cost

- expected return on net assets

- actuarial gains and losses.

In the exam, you will probably be given most of these figures. It is unlikely that you will be expected to calculate expected return on assets or interest cost.

Each component of the periodic cost is presented in a way that reflects its characteristics.

- Current service cost is included within operating profit in the profit and loss account, net of any contributions from employees.

- The interest cost and the expected return on assets are included as other finance costs (or income) adjacent to interest.

- Actuarial gains and losses arising from any new valuation, and from updating the latest actuarial valuation to reflect conditions at the balance sheet date, are recognised in the statement of total recognised gains and losses (STRGL) for the period. Once they have been recognised in the STRGL, they are not subsequently recognised in the profit and loss account.

This approach reflects the ASB's current thinking on reporting financial performance, which is that items with similar characteristics should be grouped together in the statements of financial performance. The ASB's Discussion Paper on this subject is discussed in a later chapter.

The ASB accepts that a major disadvantage of the market value approach is that it leads to volatile results. This problem should be avoided because actuarial gains and losses will be treated in a similar way to revaluation gains and losses. The profit and loss account will not be distorted by short-term movements in the value of scheme assets.

Past service costs

Past service costs result in an increase in scheme liabilities in the current period that relates to employee services in prior periods. They arise when scheme benefits are improved – for example, an employer might decide to extend the scheme to provide pension benefits for employees' spouses. They do not include increases in the expected cost of benefits that the employer is already statutorily, contractually, or implicitly committed to, for example cost of living increases to pensions in payment and deferred benefits

FRS 17 states that past service costs should be recognised in the profit and loss account on a straight line basis over the period in which the increases in benefit vest. If the benefits vest immediately, the past service cost should be recognised immediately.

Settlements and curtailments

Settlements include:

- a lump sum cash payment to scheme members in exchange for their rights to receive specified pension benefits

- the purchase of an irrevocable annuity contract sufficient to cover vested benefits

- the transfer of scheme assets and liabilities relating to a group of employees leaving the scheme.

Curtailments include:

- termination of employees' services earlier than expected, for example as a result of closing a factory or discontinuing a segment of a business

- termination of, or amendment to the terms of, a defined benefit scheme so that some or all future service by current employees will no longer qualify for benefits or will qualify only for reduced benefits.

Settlements and curtailments often arise when individual employees retire or transfer out of the scheme and these are normally allowed for in actuarial assumptions. Where they arise from major changes in the circumstances of the scheme they will not have been allowed for in the actuarial assumptions. In this case they are treated in the same way.

- Losses arising on a settlement or curtailment which have not been allowed for in the actuarial assumptions should be measured at the date on which the employer becomes demonstrably committed to the transaction, and be recognised in the profit and loss account covering that date.

- Gains arising on a settlement or curtailment which have not been allowed for in the actuarial assumptions should be measured at the date on which all parties whose consent is required are irrevocably committed to the transaction, and be recognised in the profit and loss account covering that date.

Example

Admiral Ltd operates a defined benefit pension scheme for its employees. At 1 January 20X1 the scheme had a deficit of £20 million. The following information relates to the year ended 31 December 20X1.

	£m
Current service cost	8
Contributions paid	10
Expected return on assets	7
Interest on pension scheme liabilities	5

An actuarial valuation of the scheme assets and liabilities was carried out on 31 December 20X1. This revealed a deficit of £25 million.

Explain how the pension scheme will be treated in the financial statements of Admiral Ltd for the year ended 31 December 20X1.

Solution

Admiral Ltd almost certainly has a legal or constructive obligation to make good the deficit of £25 million and so this will be recognised as a liability in the balance sheet at 31 December 20X1.

The movement between the deficit at the beginning of the year and the deficit at the end of the year is analysed into its component parts.

	£m
Deficit at 1 January	20
Current service cost	8
Contributions paid	(10)
Expected return on assets	(7)
Interest on pension scheme liabilities	5
Actuarial loss (balancing figure)	9
Deficit at 31 December	25

The current service cost of £8 million is included in operating profit. The net figure of the expected return on assets and the interest cost are disclosed as 'other finance income' of £2 million. The actuarial loss of £9 million is reported in the statement of total recognised gains and losses.

ACTIVITY 1

Fox plc operates a defined benefit pension scheme. The following information is relevant:

- At 1 January 20X8 there was a deficit on the scheme of £15 million.

- Contributions paid for the year ended 31 December 20X8 were £2 million.

- At 31 December 20X8 there was a deficit of £20 million. This has largely arisen due to an actuarial loss of £3 million.

How will this information be reported in the financial statements for the year ended 31 December 20X8?

Feedback to this activity is at the end of the chapter.

4.9   Disclosure: defined contribution schemes

The following disclosures are required:

- the nature of the scheme (i.e. defined contribution scheme)

- the cost for the period

- any outstanding or prepaid contributions at the balance sheet date.

4.10 Disclosure: defined benefit schemes

FRS 17 requires extensive disclosures of which the main ones are as follows:

- the nature of the scheme (i.e. defined benefit scheme)

- the date of the most recent full actuarial valuation on which the amounts in the financial statements are based

- the contribution made in respect of the accounting period and any agreed contribution rates for future years

- the main financial assumptions used at the beginning of the period and at the balance sheet date:

    (a)   the inflation assumption

    (b)   the rate of increase in salaries

    (c)   the rate of increase for pensions in payment and deferred pensions

    (d)   the rate used to discount scheme liabilities

- an analysis of the fair value of scheme assets at the beginning and end of the period between equities, bonds and other assets, together with the expected rate of return on each class

- an analysis of the amounts included:

  (a) within operating profit

  (b) as other finance costs

  (c) within the statement of total recognised gains and losses

- a five-year history of:

  (a) the difference between expected and actual return on assets

  (b) experience gains and losses on scheme liabilities

  (c) the total actuarial gain or loss

- the fair value of the scheme assets, the present value of the scheme liabilities and the resulting surplus or deficit. Where the asset or liability in the balance sheet differs from the surplus or deficit in the scheme, an explanation of the difference should be given

- an analysis of the movement in the surplus/deficit in the scheme over the period

- the analysis of reserves in the notes to the financial statements should distinguish the amount relating to the defined benefit asset or liability net of the related deferred tax.

4.11 Illustrations of disclosure

An Appendix to FRS 17 includes disclosure examples. Some of these are reproduced below. You will probably find it helpful to study the way in which the notes interrelate.

Reserves note	*20X2* £m	*20X1* £m
Profit and loss reserve excluding pension asset	400	350
Pension reserve	335	143
Profit and loss reserve	735	493

Pension cost note

The group operates a defined benefit pension scheme in the UK. A full actuarial valuation was carried out at 31 December 20X1 and updated to 31 December 20X2 by a qualified independent actuary. The major assumptions used by the actuary were:

	At *31/12/X2*	*At* *31/12/X1*	*At* *31/12/X0*
Rate of increase in salaries	4.0%	5.5%	6.5%
Rate of increase in pensions in payment	2.0%	3.0%	3.5%
Discount rate	4.5%	7.0%	8.5%
Inflation assumption	2.5%	4.0%	5.0%

Analysis of the amount charged to operating profit

	20X2 £m	*20X1* £m
Current service cost	34	25
Past service cost	12	–
Total operating charge	46	25

Analysis of the amount credited to other finance income

	20X2 £m	20X1 £m
Expected return on pension scheme assets	73	68
Interest on pension scheme liabilities	(53)	(57)
Net return	20	11

Analysis of amount recognised in statement of total recognised gains and losses (STRGL)

	20X2 £m	20X1 £m
Actual return less expected return on pension scheme assets	480	138
Experience gains and losses arising on the scheme liabilities	(58)	(6)
Changes in assumptions underlying the present value of the scheme liabilities	(146)	(41)
Actuarial gain recognised in STRGL	276	91

Movement in surplus during the year

	20X2 £m	20X1 £m
Surplus in scheme at beginning of the year	204	92
Movement in year:		
Current service cost	(34)	(25)
Contributions	25	35
Past service costs	(12)	–
Other finance income	20	11
Actuarial gain	276	91
Surplus in scheme at end of the year	479	204

The full actuarial valuation at 31 December 20X1 showed an increase in the surplus from £92 million to £204 million. Improvements in benefits costing £12 million were made in 20X2 and contributions reduced to £25 million (8 per cent of pensionable pay). It has been agreed with the trustees that contributions for the next three years will remain at that level.

4.12 Perceived problems with the FRS 17 approach

The following criticisms of FRS 17 have been made.

- Market values may be volatile. Even though actuarial gains and losses bypass the profit and loss account there may be significant fluctuations in the balance sheet.

- Market values are not relevant to the economic reality of most pension schemes. FRS 17 requires that assets and liabilities are valued as if they will be realised in the short term, but most pension scheme assets and liabilities are held for the long term. Actuarial valuation would better reflect the long-term costs of funding a pension scheme.

- The treatment of pension costs in the profit and loss account and STRGL is complex and may not be easily understood by users of the financial statements. It has been argued that all the components of the pension cost are so interrelated that it does not make sense to present them separately. One commentator has said that the ASB's approach will report 'budgeted figures in the profit and loss account and variances in the STRGL and pretend that they have nothing to do with each other'.

If actuarial gains and losses are taken to the STRGL it is possible that the profit and loss account will not reflect the true cost of providing pensions.

- Actuarial gains and losses are treated in a similar way to revaluation gains and losses on fixed assets. It has been argued that they are more similar to long-term provisions, such as those for environmental rectification costs. FRS 12 requires that all adjustments to provisions are taken to the profit and loss account.

- A pension scheme surplus meets the ASB's definition of an asset and so FRS 17 treats it as if it 'belongs' to the employer. However, in practice the situation is that the surplus 'belongs' to the members of the scheme and must be applied for their benefit. FRS 17 does not reflect the legal and economic reality of the situation.

ACTIVITY 2

One of the consequences of valuing pension scheme assets at market values is that the amounts in the financial statements may be volatile. What practical consequences might follow from this?

Feedback to this activity is at the end of the chapter.

4.13 Transitional arrangements

The ASB has recognised that most entities will find it difficult to implement FRS 17 and therefore it will become effective in stages. Only some of the **disclosures** are required for financial statements relating to accounting periods ending on or after 22 June 2001, others for statements ending on or after 22 June 2002, and others still for statements ending on or after 22 June 2003. Entities will not have to adopt the **accounting** requirements of the FRS until accounting periods beginning on or after 1 January 2005 (although earlier adoption is encouraged). Gains and losses arising on the initial recognition of items in the primary statements should be treated as prior period adjustments.

5 UITF Abstract 4 *Presentation of long-term debtors in current assets*

The issue – Both for liabilities and for debtors the Companies Act requires a distinction to be drawn between the amounts payable or receivable within one year and those due to be settled or received after more than one year. Although the distinction is disclosed in the notes for each of the items forming part of debtors, unlike in the case of liabilities it is not required to be carried through to the total of current assets nor to the significant Format 1 sub-total of net current assets (liabilities).

In consequence, there is a certain imbalance between the items that the formats require to be classified under current assets or current liabilities. Examples of long-term debtor items include much of the trade debtors of lessors and pension fund surpluses. Under FRS 17 *Retirement benefits* the pension asset or liability will be shown separately rather than under these format headings.

UITF Consensus – There will be some instances where the amount is so material in the context of the total net current assets that, in the absence of disclosure of debtors due after more than one year on the face of the balance sheet, readers may misinterpret the accounts. In such circumstances the amount should be disclosed on the face of the balance sheet.

6   UITF Abstract 35 *Death in service and incapacity benefits*

Abstract 35 relates to death in service and incapacity benefits that are provided through a defined benefit pension scheme. These costs may or may not be insured against. If they have not been insured, then the uninsured scheme liability, and the cost for the current accounting period, should be measured using the projected unit method. This is in line with other retirement benefits.

SELF-TEST
QUESTIONS

The conceptual nature of pension rights and pension costs

1   What is the difference between defined benefit and defined contribution schemes? (1.1)

Funding

2   What is the difference between a funded scheme and an unfunded scheme? (2.1)

3   How are contributions calculated under a defined benefit scheme? (2.3)

4   How can surpluses and deficits in a defined benefit scheme be eliminated? (2.4)

Accounting

5   Distinguish between the actuarial and the market value methods of valuing defined benefit scheme assets and liabilities. (3.2)

6   What is the difference between the spreading and the balance sheet approaches to accounting for pension costs? (3.3)

FRS 17 *Retirement benefits*

7   What are the objectives of FRS 17? (4.1)

8   State the accounting difficulty presented by multi-employer schemes. (4.5)

9   How should defined benefit scheme assets be measured? (4.6)

10   How should defined benefit scheme assets and liabilities be recognised in the balance sheet? (4.7)

11   How should defined benefit scheme periodic costs be recognised in the performance statements (profit and loss and STRGL)? (4.8)

12   What are settlements and curtailments? (4.8)

13   What are the main criticisms that have been made of FRS 17? (4.12)

EXAM-TYPE
QUESTION

Provident plc

FRS 17 *Retirement benefits* was issued by the Accounting Standards Board in November 2000. It is the result of many years' deliberation by the ASB in which a number of factors were influential, in particular: concerns about the previous Standard, SSAP 24 *Accounting for pension costs*; the trend internationally towards the use of fair values for pension cost accounting; and the move within the UK actuarial profession away from traditional actuarial methodologies to a greater use of market values.

Required:

(a)   Explain the problems of accounting for a defined benefit scheme.   **(6 marks)**

(b)   Explain how FRS 17 requires defined benefit scheme assets and liabilities to be valued.   **(6 marks)**

(c) Provident plc operates a defined benefit pension scheme for its employees. An actuarial valuation of the scheme at 31 March 20X4 showed a surplus of £48 million. The actuary confirmed that the surplus could be recovered by taking a contribution holiday for three years. The actuary also explained that £5 million of the surplus had arisen as the result of a reduction in employees because of the closure of one of the company's factories during the year. As the closure did not have a material effect on the nature and focus of the company's operations the costs of closure were charged against operating profit for the year.

The annual current service cost for the scheme has been calculated as £12 million. The actuary has also determined that the expected return on scheme assets for the year is £20 million and the interest cost is £10 million.

At 1 April 20X3 the scheme had a surplus of £23 million.

Required:

Describe the way in which the defined benefit scheme will be treated in the financial statements of Provident plc for the year ended 31 March 20X4. (Note: you are not required to discuss the disclosures in the notes to the financial statements.)   **(8 marks)**

       (Total: 20 marks)

For the answer to this question see the 'Answers' section at the end of the book.

FEEDBACK TO ACTIVITY 1

FRS 17 requires the following treatment:

The deficit of £20 million is recognised as a liability in the balance sheet at 31 December 20X8.

The actuarial loss of £3 million is reported in the statement of total recognised gains and losses for the year.

The charge to the profit and loss account is £4 million (W). This amount should be analysed between the current service cost (which is charged against operating profit) and the interest cost and the expected return on assets (the net amount is reported in the profit and loss account as a financing item).

Working

	£m
Deficit at start of year	15
Contributions paid	(2)
Actuarial loss	3
Profit and loss account (balancing figure)	4
Deficit at end of year	20

FEEDBACK TO ACTIVITY 2

The introduction of FRS 17 is expected to affect the reported performance of most companies that operate defined benefit schemes. There will be greater volatility in the statement of recognised gains and losses. Partially as a result of this, many companies have announced that they will close their defined benefit schemes and operate defined contribution schemes instead.

Chapter 17

TAXATION

This chapter focuses on deferred tax. You will have covered the basic principles of accounting for deferred tax in your earlier studies but at this level it is necessary to study the topic in more detail.

We begin by looking at the principles of accounting for deferred tax, including the alternative methods of calculation. We then move on to cover the ASB's recent accounting standard FRS 19 *Deferred tax*. You will need to understand the reasons why FRS 19 was issued and the principles underpinning it.

Objectives

When you have studied this chapter you should be able to:

- understand the different approaches to accounting for deferred taxation

- understand current regulations for the recognition of deferred taxation in the balance sheet and performance statements

- explain the nature of the measurement of deferred taxation under current regulations

- understand the differences between the recognition requirements of the International Accounting Standard and current UK regulation.

- calculate deferred tax amounts in financial statements under current regulations.

1   Accounting for deferred taxation

1.1   Why taxable and accounting profits are different

There are two types of difference:

- **Permanent differences** – An example of a permanent difference is disallowable entertaining expenditure. This is charged against accounting profits in the period in which it is incurred, but is never allowed against taxable profit.

- **Timing differences** – Timing differences arise from four main sources:

  (a) short-term timing differences (These arise because accounts are prepared using the accruals basis while some items are allowed for tax purposes only when cash is received or paid)

  (b) accelerated (or decelerated) capital allowances

  (c) revaluation surpluses on fixed assets (the gain only becomes taxable when the asset is sold)

  (d) losses (these can be used to reduce taxable profits in subsequent periods).

1.2   Deferred tax

Deferred tax represents tax which will become payable when a present deferral of tax is reversed and the potential liability crystallises.

Example

A company purchases a single item of plant for £240,000. It is entitled to writing down allowances of 25% per annum. It is estimated that the plant will have a useful life of four years after which it will be sold for £76,000. Depreciation will be on a straight-line basis.

Pre-tax profits for the next four years are as follows:

Year	Profit £'000
1	100
2	120
3	140
4	150

Show pre-tax profit, tax charge and post-tax profit on the alternative bases of:

(a) providing only for the tax payable in each period

(b) allocating the total tax charge equitably over the four accounting periods.

Assume corporation tax at 35%.

(a)   Tax payable basis

Year	1 £'000	2 £'000	3 £'000	4 £'000	Total £'000
Pre-tax profit	100	120	140	150	510
Tax payable	(28)	(41)	(51)	(58)	(178)
Post-tax profit	72	79	89	92	332
Effective tax %	28	34	36	39	35

Workings

Year	1 £'000	2 £'000	3 £'000	4 £'000
Profit after depreciation	100	120	140	150
Add: Depreciation	41	41	41	41
	141	161	181	191
Less: Capital allowances (W)	(60)	(45)	(34)	(25)
	81	116	147	166
Tax at 35%	28	41	51	58

Capital allowances

	1	2	3	4
Cost/written down value	240	180	135	101
WDA (25%) (Balancing allowance in year 4)	(60)	(45)	(34)	(25)
	180	135	101	76

Note: the balancing allowance in year 4 is the difference between the tax WDV and the sale proceeds on disposal.

(b) **Tax allocation basis**

Year	1	2	3	4	Total
	£'000	£'000	£'000	£'000	£'000
Pre-tax profit	100	120	140	150	510
Tax charge					
Current tax payable	(28)	(41)	(51)	(58)	(178)
Deferred tax	(7)	(1)	2	6	–
Post-tax profit	65	78	91	98	332
Effective tax %	35	35	35	35	35
Workings					
Depreciation	41	41	41	41	
Capital allowances	(60)	(45)	(34)	(25)	
Timing difference	(19)	(4)	7	16	
Tax at 35%	(7)	(1)	2	6	

2   Bases for accounting for deferred tax

2.1   Introduction

There are three possible approaches to providing for deferred tax. These are:

- nil provision (also known as flow-through or cash basis) method
- full provision (or comprehensive allocation) method
- partial provision (or true rate) method.

You should already be familiar with these methods from your earlier studies.

2.2   Nil provision

This approach is based on the argument that tax is more of an appropriation of profit than a cost. Accordingly, whatever tax happens to be payable in a period should be debited against those profits. Therefore, no attempt is made to 'smooth' tax liabilities over various periods and no liability is set up in the balance sheet for deferred taxation.

Nil provision is straightforward and objective. However, it has many disadvantages.

- It can result in large fluctuations in the tax charge.
- It may understate tax liabilities.

- It does not allow tax relief relating to long-term liabilities such as pension costs to be recognised in the same period as the costs themselves.
- It is inconsistent with international practice.

The earnings per share statistic is calculated using after-tax profits. It is argued that investors and other users of accounts look to the after-tax profit figure as a measure of performance and it is therefore very important to ensure that the tax charge is realistic in relation to profits for a period. For all these reasons nil provision has been consistently rejected by standard setters.

2.3   Full provision

This is based on making provision for all timing differences whether or not they are ever likely to crystallise. It is based on a rigid application of the accruals concept. It is an attractive approach because the amount of the provision can be ascertained with complete certainty and requires no subjective assessment of the likely future crystallisation of the liability.

In computing the full potential liability for deferred tax, it is necessary to consider the historical position. This involves identifying all items in the accounts to date which give rise to a timing difference.

ACTIVITY 1

Patler plc prepares accounts to 31 December annually. At 31 December 20X8 a full provision for deferred tax had been made and the account comprised the following balances

	Timing differences £'000	Tax £'000
Excess of capital allowances claimed over depreciation (for periods up to 31 December 20X8)	150 (30%)	45
Chargeable gain, on sale of freehold, rolled over	100 (30%)	30
	250	75

(Note that the accumulated timing difference on fixed assets is the difference between accounting NBV and tax WDV.)

For the year ended 31 December 20X9 the timing differences comprise:

	£'000
Excess capital allowances for the year	20

The company's budgets, etc. show that it is probable that a liability will arise on reversal of the timing differences.

Required:

Produce the deferred taxation account for 20X9.

Feedback to this activity is at the end of the chapter.

2.4   Partial provision

It is possible for an entity to build up a 'hard core' of timing differences which are unlikely to reverse in practice. This may be the case if there are generous capital allowances or high inflation. Both these conditions applied in the early 1980s, when SSAP 15 *Accounting for deferred tax* was issued. In this situation full provision for deferred tax results in a significant provision for tax which is unlikely ever to be paid. It was argued that these balances were meaningless and also that they distorted the view given by the financial statements.

Under partial provision, an entity only provides for deferred tax which can reasonably be expected to be paid in the foreseeable future. The computation of the partial deferred tax provision can be problematic because preparers of accounts must assess the effect of expected future transactions. Most entities base their assessment on information provided by budgets and forecast capital expenditure.

3   Computing deferred taxation

There are two possible methods of dealing with deferred taxation:

DEFINITION

The **deferral method** shows deferred tax at the amount of the benefit to the company, in historic cost terms, of being able to defer taxation.

DEFINITION

The **liability method** is a method of computing deferred tax whereby it is calculated at the rate of tax that it is estimated will be applicable when the timing differences reverse.

KEY POINT

Most major standard setters (including the ASB) require the use of the liability method.

- **Deferral method for deferred tax** – Under this method the deferred taxation account records the originating timing differences at the rates of taxation in operation when those originating timing differences occurred. No adjustment is made to the existing deferred taxation account when changes in taxation rates occur.

- **Liability method for deferred tax** – Usually the current tax rate is used as the best estimate, unless changes in tax rates are known in advance. As a result, deferred tax provisions are revised to reflect changes in tax rates. Thus, the tax charge or credit for the period may include adjustments of accounting estimates relating to prior periods.

Most major standard setters (including the ASB) require the use of the liability method.

4   Problems in accounting for deferred tax

4.1   Why partial provision is unsatisfactory

Until recently, UK companies used the partial provision method to account for deferred tax (as required by SSAP 15 *Accounting for deferred tax*). Partial provision was a pragmatic response to conditions in the 1980s, but since then inflation has fallen and 100% capital allowances are no longer widely available. There is now a far greater likelihood that timing differences will reverse.

Partial provision is subjective and potentially complicated to apply because it involves predicting future events, such as changes in the taxation system, capital expenditure and the useful economic lives of assets.

There were other problems with partial provision and SSAP 15.

- There were inconsistencies within the SSAP. Full provision was required for timing differences in respect of post-retirement benefits, but partial provision was required for all other timing differences.

- There were inconsistencies in the application of partial provision (e.g. some entities provided deferred tax on fair value adjustments on acquisition while others did not). There was evidence that some entities made full provision on grounds of simplicity. This reduced the comparability of financial statements.

KEY POINT

The most important disadvantage of partial provision is that it is inconsistent with international practice. Almost all other major standard setters require full provision.

However, arguably the most important disadvantage of partial provision is that it is inconsistent with international practice. Almost all other major standard setters (including the FASB and the IASB) require full provision.

4.2   Full provision

As we have seen, the 'full provision' basis is based on the principle that financial statements for a period should recognise the tax effects, whether current or deferred, of all transactions occurring in that period.

Advantages of the full provision basis are as follows:

- It is straightforward to apply and objective.

- It has the effect of smoothing out distortions in the tax charge caused by timing differences. This means that it may provide more useful information for users of the financial statements because it is easier to make inter-temporal comparisons.

- It can be argued that the full provision basis matches the tax liability against the revenue to which it relates.

- It is consistent with international practice.

There are also important conceptual arguments for full provision.

- Every tax difference represents a real liability since every one reverses. Whatever else happens, an entity will pay more tax in future as a result of the reversal than it would have done in the absence of the timing difference.

- Only the impact of new timing differences arising in future prevents the total liability from reducing. Partial provision takes account of these future differences, but this is inconsistent with the principle that only past transactions and events can be taken into account when measuring a liability. (The Statement of Principles defines a liability as an obligation arising from **past** transactions and events and FRSs 5 and 12 are based on this definition.)

- Partial provision relies on management intentions regarding future events. This is inconsistent with the principle that a liability can only arise from an obligation, rather than management decisions or intentions.

4.3   Possible approaches to full provision

Full provision could, in theory, be implemented in different ways.

Timing differences and temporary differences

Earlier in this chapter we saw that there are two types of difference between profit before tax in the financial statements and the profit chargeable for tax: permanent differences and timing differences. In the UK, deferred tax has not been provided on permanent differences, but only on timing differences.

In contrast, IAS 12 *Income taxes* and the US accounting standard require deferred tax to be provided on 'temporary differences'. Temporary differences are the differences between the carrying values of the assets and liabilities in the balance sheet at the end of the period and the amounts that will actually be taxable or recoverable in respect of these assets and liabilities in future.

Most temporary differences are timing differences, but they can include permanent differences, for example:

- non-taxable grants received for the purchase of fixed assets that are deferred and recognised as income over the lives of the fixed assets

- foreign exchange differences on consolidation under the temporal method (non-monetary assets of foreign subsidiaries are translated at historic rates).

One obvious advantage of adopting this approach would be international harmonisation. However, there are several disadvantages. The main one is that identifying and measuring temporary differences is difficult in practice. For example, temporary differences can arise where the financial statements of an overseas subsidiary are consolidated. These can be difficult to quantify because some assets are eliminated on consolidation and others may or may not be taxable.

Other disadvantages of the 'temporary differences' approach include the following.

(a) It is believed to be conceptually wrong. In theory, deferred tax would have to be provided as soon as assets or liabilities were recognised.

For example, say an entity acquires an asset for £100. This asset is subject to tax at 30% and therefore a deferred tax provision of £30 is recognised. The net value of the asset is understated, and this is misleading, because the entity would not have acquired the asset if its value had been less than its cost. The asset should still be recognised at its cost of £100.

(b) Because of the problems described in point (a), in practice there would have to be exceptions for at least some permanent differences. It is more logical to require deferred tax to be provided on timing differences only.

(c) It would lead to the build-up of liabilities that would only crystallise in the distant future, if ever.

Therefore the ASB does not favour the temporary differences approach.

Liabilities and valuation adjustments

There are two very distinct views as to how full provision based on timing differences should be provided in practice.

- Timing differences should be recognised only if they represent rights or obligations at the balance sheet date, that is, only if the critical events that will cause their future reversal have occurred by the balance sheet date.

- Timing differences should be recognised even if the critical events causing their reversal have not occurred by the balance sheet date. This view holds that timing differences are similar to valuation adjustments, even though they may not be liabilities in their own right. A deferred tax liability is recognised in respect of accelerated capital allowances on a fixed asset because that fixed asset is worth less than an otherwise equivalent fixed asset that is still fully tax-deductible.

The choice of approach is important, because it determines which timing differences are recognised.

4.4   Should deferred tax be provided on revalued assets?

There are two points of view, which reflect the two views held as to the nature of deferred tax.

- If deferred tax is regarded as an increase or decrease in a future tax liability it is argued that deferred tax should not be provided on a revaluation gain unless there is a commitment to dispose of the asset. If there is no commitment to dispose of the asset the revaluation gain is a permanent difference, rather than a timing difference, and will never affect taxable profit.

- If deferred tax is regarded as a valuation adjustment it is argued that deferred tax should be provided on all revaluations. This reflects the difference in value between an asset which carries a potential tax liability and one which does not.

For example, if a company revalues land costing £1 million to £1.5 million, that land cannot be worth as much to the company as land acquired separately for £1.5 million (which would be fully tax-deductible). Because the historic cost of the land is only £1 million, the tax cost must only be £1 million.

4.5 Should deferred tax be provided on fair value adjustments?

FRS 7 *Fair values in acquisition accounting* requires the assets and liabilities of an acquired entity to be stated at fair values. Again, there are two points of view.

- If deferred tax is viewed as an increase or decrease in a future tax liability it is believed that deferred tax should not be provided for on fair value adjustments. This is because the new reporting entity's actual tax liability is not altered as a result of the acquisition. For example, if a company attributes a fair value of £600,000 to the stock of an acquired company whose cost to the acquired company was £500,000, the cost of the stock for tax purposes will always be £500,000 and the actual amount of tax that will be payable by the acquired entity on the sale of the stock is not altered as a result of the acquisition.

- If deferred tax is viewed as a valuation adjustment it is believed that deferred tax should generally be provided for on fair value adjustments, where these relate to assets or liabilities that are expected to be realised or settled. Taking the same example as above, the stock which has a fair value of £600,000 and a tax cost of £500,000 cannot be worth as much to the company as stock acquired separately for £600,000 (which would be fully tax-deductible).

5 FRS 19 *Deferred tax*

5.1 Full provision

FRS 19 was issued in December 2000 and replaced SSAP 15 *Accounting for deferred tax*. SSAP 15 was coming under increasing criticism, mainly because of problems arising from the fact that it required deferred tax to be accounted for using the partial provision method.

FRS 19 states that deferred tax:

- should be recognised in respect of all timing differences that have originated but not reversed by the balance sheet date

- should not be recognised on permanent differences.

In other words, **full provision** should be made for all deferred tax assets and liabilities arising from timing differences.

5.2 The incremental liability approach

However, there are some exceptions to the general rule above. Deferred tax assets or liabilities only arise if the transactions or events that increase or decrease future tax charges have occurred by the balance sheet date.

- This means that deferred tax is recognised on timing differences arising from:

    (a) accelerated capital allowances

    (b) accruals for pension costs and other post retirement benefits that will be deductible for tax purposes only when paid

    (c) elimination of unrealised intra-group profits on consolidation

    (d) unrelieved tax losses

    (e) other sources of short-term timing differences.

KEY POINT

Full provision should be made for all deferred tax assets and liabilities arising from timing differences.

- Deferred tax should not be recognised on timing differences arising when fixed assets are revalued, unless, by the balance sheet date, the reporting entity has:

  (a) entered into a binding agreement to sell the revalued assets; and

  (b) recognised any gains and losses expected to arise on sale.

- Deferred tax should not be recognised on timing differences arising when fixed assets are revalued or sold, if, on the basis of all available evidence, it is more likely than not that the taxable gain will be rolled over, being charged to tax only when the assets into which the gain has been rolled are sold.

- Tax that could be payable on any future remittance of the past earnings of a subsidiary, associate or joint venture should be provided for only to the extent that, at the balance sheet date:

  (a) dividends have been accrued as receivable; or

  (b) a binding agreement to distribute the past earnings in future has been entered into by the subsidiary, associate or joint venture.

The principle behind these rules is that deferred tax is only provided where it represents an asset or a liability in its own right. This is the incremental liability approach. The Statement of Principles defines a liability as an obligation to transfer economic benefits as the result of a past transaction or event.

For example, if an entity has capital allowances in excess of depreciation it has an obligation to pay more tax in future. It cannot avoid this obligation. Therefore it has a liability. In contrast, if an entity revalues a fixed asset, it will not have an obligation to pay more tax unless it enters into a binding agreement to sell the asset. Therefore it does not have a liability.

5.3   Fixed assets and deferred tax

FRS 19 includes some detailed points:

- If an asset is not being depreciated (and has not been written down to a carrying value less than cost) the timing difference is the amount of capital allowances received.

- Deferred tax recognised on accelerated capital allowances should be reversed if and when all conditions for retaining the allowances have been met.

  Most capital allowances are repayable via a balancing charge if the related asset is sold for more than its tax written down value. However, some allowances (e.g. industrial buildings allowances) are repayable only if the asset is sold within a specified period. When this period has elapsed, the conditions have been met and any deferred tax that has been recognised should be reversed.

- Deferred tax should be recognised on timing differences arising when an asset is continuously revalued to fair value with changes in fair value recognised in the profit and loss account.

For example, some investments and current assets are 'marked to market' with fluctuations in their market value being recognised in the profit and loss account. FRS 19 anticipates a future standard on the measurement of financial instruments. This will almost certainly require that financial instruments are continuously revalued to fair value.

5.4 Fair value adjustments

As we have seen, timing differences arise when an acquired entity's assets and liabilities are adjusted to their fair values as required by FRS 7 *Fair values in acquisition accounting*. FRS 7 is amended to state that fair value adjustments are treated in the same way as they would be if they were timing differences arising in the entity's own accounts. In other words, fair value adjustments are treated as if they were revaluation adjustments. Deferred tax is not recognised on fair value adjustments unless before the acquisition the acquired entity has entered into a binding agreement to sell the asset and rollover relief is not available.

5.5 Deferred tax assets

Deferred tax assets can arise on most types of timing differences.

For example, a company incurs an accounting loss of £400,000 for the year ended 31 December 20X4. Due to various items of expenditure not being allowed (permanent differences), the taxable loss is £360,000. The relevant tax rate is 30%.

The timing difference here is the amount of loss that can be carried forward to reduce future taxable profits, i.e. £360,000.

The deferred tax asset is £360,000 × 30% = £108,000.

FRS 19 states that deferred tax assets should be recognised to the extent that they are regarded as recoverable. They should be regarded as recoverable to the extent that, on the basis of all available evidence, it can be regarded as more likely than not that there will be suitable profits from which the future reversal of the underlying timing differences can be deducted.

5.6 Recognition and measurement

*   Deferred tax should be recognised in the profit and loss account for the period, unless it is attributable to a gain or loss that is or has been recognised in the statement of total recognised gains and losses (STRGL), in which case the deferred tax should also be recognised in the STRGL.

*   Deferred tax should be measured at the average tax rates that are expected to apply in the periods in which the timing differences are expected to reverse, based on tax rates and laws that have been enacted or substantively enacted by the balance sheet date.

In practice this means that the **liability method** is used.

5.7 Discounting

The main disadvantage of the full provision method is that it is likely to give rise to large liabilities that are never significantly reduced. It gives no indication of when (or whether) the liability will be paid. Discounting deferred tax balances would be a possible method of reducing the effect of full provision.

FRS 19 allows entities to discount deferred tax assets and liabilities to reflect the time value of money.

There are theoretical arguments for discounting deferred tax, as the effect of the time value of money will normally be material. In addition, the Statement of Principles states that discounting should be used where carrying amounts are based on future cash flows.

The ASB has recognised that some entities might wish to discount deferred tax provisions. However:

- for many entities the practical problems of discounting outweigh the benefits

- discounting is not consistent with international practice

and therefore the ASB has made discounting optional.

The ASB has concluded that there will not be a serious lack of comparability if not all entities discounted deferred tax provided that:

- discounting is applied consistently from one period to the next (as implicitly required by FRS 18 *Accounting policies*)

- the impact is clearly highlighted in the financial statements (see the disclosure requirements discussed below).

If a reporting entity adopts a policy of discounting:

- all deferred tax balances for which the impact of discounting is material must be discounted

- the discount period should be the number of years between the balance sheet date and the date on which it is estimated that the underlying timing differences will reverse

- the discount rates used should be the post-tax yields to maturity that could be obtained at the balance sheet date on government bonds with maturity dates similar to those of the deferred tax assets or liabilities.

FRS 19 has adopted the 'full reversal' approach to discounting. Future cash flows are treated as occurring when the timing differences constituting the deferred tax balance at the year end are expected to reverse. This means that in order to calculate a discounted deferred tax provision it is necessary to:

- schedule all timing differences at the balance sheet date by their year of reversal

- apply the discount rate to these individual timing differences.

Example based on a single fixed asset

A company purchases a fixed asset for £500,000 on 1 January 20X0. The asset has a useful economic life of five years and no residual value. Capital allowances of 50% of cost can be claimed for each of the first two years of the asset's life. The rate of corporation tax is 30% and the post-tax discount rate is expected to be 5% throughout the life of the asset.

Calculate the required deferred tax liability at 31 December 20X0 assuming:

(a)   no discounting

(b)   the liability is discounted.

Solution

(a)   At 31 December 20X0:

tax written down value	$= 50\% \times £500,000$	$= £250,000$
carrying value	$= 80\% \times £500,000$	$= £400,000$
Therefore taxable timing difference	$= £150,000$	
Required deferred tax liability	$= 30\% \times £150,000$	$= £45,000$

(b)　We need to stand at 31 December 20X0 and forecast when the timing difference of £150,000 will reverse. The relevant forecast of the future is:

Year	Difference in year £'000	Undiscounted liability at 30% £'000	Discount factor at 5%	Discounted liability £'000
20X1	(150)	(45)	0.952	(43)
20X2	100	30	0.907	27
20X3	100	30	0.864	26
20X4	100	30	0.823	25
		45		35

The discounted deferred tax liability at 31 December 20X0 would be £35,000.

5.8　Presentation

- Deferred tax liabilities should be classified as provisions for liabilities and charges.

- Deferred tax assets should be classified as debtors, as a separate subheading of debtors where material.

- Deferred tax assets and liabilities should be separately disclosed on the face of the balance sheet if the amounts are so material in the context of the total net current assets or net assets that readers might misinterpret the accounts otherwise.

- All deferred tax recognised in the profit and loss account should be included within the heading 'tax on profit or loss on ordinary activities'.

5.9　Disclosure

Profit and loss account and STRGL

The notes to the financial statements should disclose the amount of deferred tax charged or credited within:

(a) tax on ordinary activities in the profit and loss account, separately disclosing changes in deferred tax balances arising from:

- the origination and reversal of timing differences

- changes in tax rates and laws

- adjustments to the estimated recoverable amount of deferred tax assets arising in previous periods

- changes in the amounts of discount deducted in arriving at the deferred tax balance (if applicable).

Note that the effect of discounting is treated as part of the tax charge rather than being disclosed separately as a financing item.

(b) tax charged or credited in the STRGL, separately disclosing the same items as in (a) above.

KEY POINT

The effect of discounting is treated as part of the tax charge rather than being disclosed separately as a financing item.

Balance sheet

Disclose:

- the total deferred tax balance (before discounting, where applicable) showing the amount recognised for each significant type of timing difference separately

- the impact of discounting on, and the discounted amount of, the deferred tax balance

- the movement between the opening and closing net deferred tax balance.

Other disclosures

These include:

- circumstances that affect, or may affect, the current and future tax charges or credits

- a reconciliation of the current tax charge or credit on ordinary activities for the period to the current tax charge that would result from applying a relevant standard rate of tax to the profit on ordinary activities before tax

- where fixed assets have been revalued and deferred tax has not been recognised on the gain, an indication of the amount that may become payable in the foreseeable future and the circumstances in which the tax would be payable.

5.10　Illustrations of disclosures

An Appendix to FRS 19 includes the following illustrations:

Tax on profit on ordinary activities

(a) **Analysis of charge in period**

	200Y		*200X*	
	£m	£m	£m	£m
Current tax:				
UK corporation tax on profits of the period	40		26	
Adjustments in respect of previous periods	4		(6)	
		44		20
Foreign tax		12		16
Total current tax (see (b))		56		36
Deferred tax:				
Origination and reversal of timing differences	67		60	
Effect of increased tax rate on opening liability	12		–	
Increase in discount	(14)		(33)	
Total deferred tax		65		27
Tax on profit on ordinary activities		121		63

(b) Factors affecting tax charge for period

The tax assessed for the period is lower than the standard rate of corporation tax in the UK (31 per cent). The differences are explained below:

	200Y £m	200X £m
Profit on ordinary activities before tax	361	327
Profit on ordinary activities multiplied by standard rate of corporation tax in the UK of 31% (200X: 30%)	112	98
Effects of:		
Expenses not deductible for tax purposes (primarily goodwill amortisation)	22	10
Capital allowances for period in excess of depreciation	(58)	(54)
Utilisation of tax losses	(17)	(18)
Rollover relief on profit on disposal of property	(10)	–
Higher tax rates on overseas earnings	3	6
Adjustments to tax charge in respect of previous periods	4	(6)
Current tax charge for period (see (a))	56	36

(c) Provision for deferred tax

	31.12.200Y £m	31.12.200X £m
Accelerated capital allowances	426	356
Tax losses carried forward	–	(9)
Undiscounted provision for deferred tax	426	347
Discount	(80)	(66)
Discounted provision for deferred tax	346	281
Provision at start of period	281	
Deferred tax charge in profit and loss account for period	65	
Provision at end of period	346	

6   Evaluating FRS 19

6.1   International harmonisation

The most important perceived advantage of full provision is that it is consistent with international practice. This issue is important enough to outweigh the ASB's admission that it is not wholly convinced by the arguments for the full provision method. Despite this, the ASB does not believe that this is one of the areas where a good case can be made for going against international opinion. It believes that continuing with the partial provision method would damage the credibility of UK financial reporting.

One possible view of FRS 19 is that it achieves broad consistency with international practice while mitigating some of the disadvantages of full provision by adopting the incremental liability approach and allowing the use of discounting. FRS 19 is also consistent with the Statement of Principles and other recent FRSs such as FRS 12.

A more critical view of the FRS is that it is necessarily a compromise. It introduces a version of full provision, ostensibly for the sake of international harmonisation. Yet there are significant differences between FRS 19 and IAS 12. Under FRS 19, accounting for deferred tax will still be different from that in the rest of the world.

Because of this most commentators believe that FRS 19 will only be a 'holding standard'. Within a few years it will have to be superseded by a new standard that takes the same approach as IAS 12.

6.2   The practical effects of full provision

Full provision is unpopular because it gives rise to larger tax charges and deferred tax provisions than the partial provision method. For most companies profits will be reduced and gearing will be increased.

This has further implications. The Companies Act states that distributable profits include all realised losses. A provision for deferred tax is a realised loss. This means that the change to full provision may dramatically reduce profits available for dividends. Because the change from partial provision to full provision has to be applied retrospectively (by means of a prior year adjustment) some companies' distributable profits may be virtually eliminated in the period in which they implement the standard.

Preparers of accounts will have to decide whether or not to discount deferred tax assets and liabilities. FRS 19 suggests that they should take the following into account:

- how material the impact of discounting would tend to be to the entity's overall results and financial position

- whether the benefits to users would outweigh the costs of collating the necessary information and performing discounting calculations

- whether there is an established industry practice, adherence to which would enhance comparability.

As we have seen, the discounting calculations are complicated. Discounting involves scheduling individual reversals of timing differences. This may be a very difficult and time consuming exercise, particularly for large multinationals which operate under several different tax regimes. To a certain extent, preparers of accounts will have to base their calculations on estimates and assumptions.

Preparers of accounts will also need to select and apply a suitable discount rate. The yields to maturity on government bonds can be obtained from published sources (e.g. the *Financial Times*). The post-tax yield is estimated by deducting tax at the rate at which it would be paid by the entity if it held the bond.

In practice the post-tax rates for government bonds are likely to be low single figure rates. This means that the effect of discounting may not be sufficiently material to justify the time and cost of performing the calculations.

Critics of the ASB have suggested that the decision to allow (but not require) discounting will lead to a much greater lack of comparability between entities than existed under SSAP 15.

6.3   A further problem

FRS 19 states that deferred tax should not be recognised on timing differences resulting from revaluation of fixed assets unless the entity has entered into a binding sale agreement before the balance sheet date.

In theory it is possible for an entity to choose whether or not to provide for deferred tax on a revaluation gain and therefore to manipulate its reported results and financial position.

Example

A company with a year end of 31 December decides to sell a building that originally cost £1 million. On 30 December 20X1 it receives and accepts an offer for £2 million. The building is revalued to £2 million at 31 December 20X1. Tax of £300,000 is payable on the gain on disposal.

If the company signs a binding sale agreement on or before 31 December 20X1, it recognises deferred tax of £300,000 in that year. If it signs the agreement on or after 1 January 20X2 it recognises current tax of £300,000 in the accounts for the year ended 31 December 20X2.

Accounting for deferred taxation

1 Distinguish between permanent differences and timing differences. (1.1)

2 Why does deferred taxation arise? (1.2)

Bases for deferred tax

3 What are the three possible approaches to providing for deferred tax? (2)

Problems in accounting for deferred tax

4 What basis of providing for deferred tax was required by SSAP 15? (4.1)

5 Why is partial provision unsatisfactory? (4.1)

6 What are the arguments in favour of full provision? (4.2)

7 Should deferred tax be provided on revalued assets? (4.4)

FRS 19 *Deferred tax*

8 Under FRS 19, how far should deferred tax assets be recognised? (5.5)

EXAM-TYPE QUESTION

CS plc

Until now CS plc has provided for deferred tax using the partial provision basis. The directors of CS plc have decided to determine the impact that the introduction of FRS 19 *Deferred tax* will have on the company's financial statements for the year ending 31 December 20X1. The amounts of deferred taxation provided and unprovided in the group financial statements for the year ending 31 December 20X0 were as follows:

	Provided £m	*Unprovided* £m
Capital allowances in excess of depreciation	57	18
Other timing differences	17	21
Pensions and other post retirement benefits	93	–
Losses available for offset against future taxable profits	(51)	(63)

Corporation tax on capital gains arising on the disposal of property which has been deferred under the roll-over provisions	–	240
Tax that would arise if properties were disposed of at their revalued amounts	–	210
	116	426

The following notes are relevant to the calculation of the deferred tax provision under FRS 19 as at 31 December 20X1:

(i)   The excess of capital allowances over depreciation is £270 million as at 31 December 20X1. It is anticipated that the timing differences will reverse according to the following schedule:

	31 Dec 20X2	31 Dec 20X3	31 Dec 20X4
	£m	£m	£m
Depreciation	1,650	1,650	1,650
Capital allowances	1,575	1,560	1,545
	75	90	105

Other timing differences amount to £135 million as at 31 December 20X1. It is anticipated that they will all reverse in the year to 31 December 20X2.

(ii)   The amount of the deferred tax provision required for pensions and other post retirement benefits has risen to £135 million as at 31 December 20X1.

(iii) It is envisaged that any unrelieved tax losses will be offset in equal proportion against taxable profits for the years ending 31 December 20X2 and 20X3. The auditors have concurred with the directors of the company as regards the future recovery of the unrelieved tax losses. No further losses arose in the year to 31 December 20X1. The tax losses provided for at 31 December 20X0 were offset against profits for the year ended 31 December 20X1.

(iv) Corporation tax on the property disposed of becomes payable on 31 December 20X4 under the roll-over relief provisions. There had been no sales or revaluations of property during the year to 31 December 20X1.

(v)   CS plc acquired a 100% holding in an overseas company several years ago. The subsidiary has declared a dividend for the financial year to 31 December 20X1 of £12 million. The dividend has been accrued but no account has been taken of the tax liability on this dividend of £3 million payable on 31 December 20X2. During the year CS plc had supplied the subsidiary with stock amounting to £45 million at a profit of 20% on selling price. This stock had not been sold by the year end and the tax rate applied to the subsidiary's profit was 25%. No other adjustments to deferred taxation are required for the subsidiary other than those required by this note.

(vi) Corporation tax is assumed to be 30% for the foreseeable future and the company wishes to discount any deferred tax liabilities at a rate of 5%.

Required:

(a) Explain why the Accounting Standards Board has produced a Financial Reporting Standard which requires the use of the full provision basis.

(7 marks)

(b) Calculate the provision for deferred tax required in the Group Balance Sheet of CS plc at 30 December 20X1 using FRS 19, commenting on the effect that the application of FRS 19 will have on the financial statements of CS plc.

(13 marks)

(Total: 20 marks)

For the answer to this question see the 'Answers' section at the end of the book.

FEEDBACK TO
ACTIVITY 1

Deferred taxation account

	Memo timing differences £'000	Tax £'000		Memo timing differences £'000	Tax £'000
Balance c/d			Balance b/d (accelerated		
(ACAs (150 + 20))	170	51	capital allowances		
(gain rolled over)	100	30	(ACAs))	150	45
			(gain rolled over)	100	30
				250	75
			P&L a/c 20X9 - (charge		
			for deferred tax excess		
			capital allowances)	20	6
	270	81		270	81

The calculation is relatively straightforward because it involves analysing actual transactions to identify the liability. The total timing difference in respect of accelerated capital allowances is simply the difference between the tax written down value and the net book value of the relevant assets.

Chapter 18

REPORTING FINANCIAL PERFORMANCE AND EARNINGS PER SHARE

FRS 3 *Reporting financial performance* should be familiar to you from your earlier studies. Exam questions in this paper will either focus on the more detailed aspects of the standard, such as accounting for reorganisations and the definition of discontinued operations, or on the current proposals for a revised standard. If these are adopted, there will be major changes to the format of the profit and loss account and the statement of total recognised gains and losses.

Earnings per share is a widely used measure of a company's performance, particularly over a number of years, and it is a component of the very important Stock Exchange yardstick – the price/earnings (P/E) ratio. Exam questions will almost certainly require calculations; they will probably also require you to explain the reasoning behind your calculations and to discuss the usefulness (or otherwise) of earnings per share as a performance measure. The emphasis is on diluted earnings per share.

Objectives

When you have studied this chapter you should be able to:

- understand the proposed changes to reporting financial performance
- explain the rationale behind the proposed changes in reporting financial performance
- calculate basic and diluted earnings per share.

1   Requirements of FRS 3

1.1   Objective of FRS 3

The objective of the FRS is to require companies to highlight a range of important components of financial performance to aid users in understanding the performance achieved by a reporting entity in a period and to assist them in forming a basis for their assessment of future results and cash flows.

It attempts to achieve the objective by requiring all gains and losses recognised in the financial statements for the period to be included in the profit and loss account or the statement of total recognised gains and losses.

Gains and losses may be excluded from the profit and loss account only if they are specifically permitted or required to be taken directly to reserves by an accounting standard or by law.

1.2   Format of the profit and loss account

A layered format must be used for the profit and loss account to highlight the following important components of financial performance:

(a) results of continuing operations (including the results of acquisitions)

(b) results of discontinued operations

(c) profits or losses on the sale or termination of an operation, costs of a fundamental reorganisation or restructuring and profits or losses on the disposal of fixed assets

(d) extraordinary items.

The thrust of this approach can be illustrated diagrammatically as follows:

CONTINUING	**DISCONTINUED**
Normal operations	Normal operations
The items listed in (c) above	The items listed in (c) above

Extraordinary items – being unusual items outside ordinary activities

Note that exceptional items will comprise the items listed in (c) above, which are disclosed separately on the face of the profit and loss account, and other items which are disclosed separately by way of note only (and are thus within the normal operations boxes).

A sample format is shown below.

Profit and loss account for the year ended 30 June 20X3

	Continuing operations 20X3	Acquisitions 20X3	Discontinued operations 20X3	Total 20X3	Total 20X2 as restated
	£m	£m	£m	£m	£m
Turnover	550	50	175	775	690
Cost of sales	(415)	(40)	(165)	(620)	(555)
Gross profit	135	10	10	155	135
Net operating expenses	(85)	(4)	(25)	(114)	(83)
Less: 20X2 provision			10	10	
Operating profit	50	6	(5)	51	52
Profit on sale of properties	9			9	6
Provision for loss on operations to be discontinued					(30)
Loss on disposal of discontinued operations			(17)	(17)	
Less: 20X2 provision			20	20	
Profit on ordinary activities before interest	59	6	(2)	63	28
Interest payable				(18)	(15)
Profit on ordinary activities before taxation				45	13
Tax on profit on ordinary activities				(14)	(4)

Profit on ordinary activities after taxation	31	9
Minority interests	(2)	(2)
Extraordinary items (included only to show positioning)	-	-
Profit for the financial year	29	7
Dividends	(8)	(1)
Retained profit for the financial year	21	6
Earnings per share	39p	10p

1.3 Continuing and discontinued operations

The analysis between continuing operations, acquisitions (as a component of continuing operations) and discontinued operations should be disclosed to the level of operating profit. The analysis of turnover and operating profit is the minimum disclosure required in this respect on the face of the profit and loss account.

The example above thus provides more than the minimum disclosure. The minimum disclosures for the top section of the profit and loss account could be shown as follows:

	20X3	20X3	20X2 as restated
	£m	£m	£m
Turnover			
Continuing operations	550		500
Acquisitions	50		
	600		
Discontinued operations	175		190
		775	690
Cost of sales		(620)	(555)
Gross profit		155	135
Net operating expenses		(104)	(83)
Operating profit			
Continuing operations	50		40
Acquisitions	6		
	56		
Discontinued operations	(15)		12
Less: 20X2 provision	10		
		51	52

(a) In either example, as the full statutory headings have not been shown, a note to the accounts needs to show an analysis of the statutory cost headings between continuing operations, acquisitions (as a component of continuing operations) and discontinued operations.

(b) The analysis in respect of continuing operations, acquisitions and discontinued operations is required only to the profit before interest level because interest payable is usually a reflection of a company's overall financing policy, involving both equity and debt funding considerations on a group-wide basis, rather than an aggregation of the particular types of finance allocated to individual segments of the reporting entity's operations. Any allocation of interest would involve a considerable degree of subjectivity that could leave the user uncertain as to the relevance and reliability of the information.

(c) The comparative figures should be based on the status of an operation in the financial statements of the period under review and should, therefore, include in the continuing category only the results of those operations included in the current period's continuing operations. The comparative figures appearing under the heading 'continuing operations' may include figures which were shown under the heading of acquisitions in that previous period. No reference needs to be made to the results of those acquisitions, since they are not required to be presented separately in the current year.

The comparative figures for discontinued operations will include both amounts relating to operations discontinued in the previous period and amounts relating to operations discontinued in the period under review, which in the previous period would have been included as part of continuing operations.

The analysis of comparative figures between continuing and discontinued operations is not required on the face of the profit and loss account.

1.4 Discontinued operations

Discontinued operations are those operations of the reporting entity that are sold or terminated and that satisfy all of the following conditions.

(a) The sale or termination is completed either in the period or before the earlier of three months after the commencement of the subsequent period and the date on which the financial statements are approved.

(b) If a termination, the former activities have ceased permanently.

(c) The sale or termination has a material effect on the nature and focus of the reporting entity's operations and represents a material reduction in its operating facilities resulting either from its withdrawal from a particular market (whether class of business or geographical) or from a material reduction in turnover in the reporting entity's continuing markets.

(d) The assets, liabilities, results of operations and activities are clearly distinguishable, physically, operationally and for financial reporting purposes.

Operations not satisfying all these conditions are classified as continuing.

Note the timing restriction. If the termination is not completed within the time stated, the turnover and costs of the operations remain in continuing operations.

This does not mean, however, that an exceptional item should not be shown in respect of the actual profit/loss or anticipated loss on disposal. This point is discussed below after the definition of exceptional items has been considered.

Note also part (c) of the definition. The nature and focus of a reporting entity's operations refers to the positioning of its products or services in their markets including the aspects of both quality and location. For example, if a hotel company which had traditionally served the lower end of the hotel market sold its existing chain and bought luxury hotels then, while remaining in the business of managing hotels, the group would be changing the nature and focus of its operations. A similar situation would arise if the same company were to sell its hotels in (say) the USA and buy hotels in Europe.

The regular sales and replacements of material assets which are undertaken by a company as part of the routine maintenance of its portfolio of assets should not be classified as discontinuances and acquisitions. In the example, the sale of hotels and the purchase of others within the same market sector and similar locations would be treated as wholly within continuing operations.

2   Classification of items

2.1   Exceptional items

All exceptional items, other than those stated below, should be included under the statutory format headings to which they relate. They should be separately disclosed by way of note or, where it is necessary in order that the financial statements give a true and fair view, on the face of the profit and loss account.

There are in effect two types of exceptional items: those that are exceptional but are still included in the statutory format headings, and those which are separately identified.

The view of the ASB is that exceptional items should not be transferred to a single heading of 'exceptional', because profit before exceptional items could then become the focus of financial statement presentations, with the implication that no exceptional items are expected in the future.

2.2   Items to be shown separately

The following items, including provisions in respect of such items, should be shown separately on the face of the profit and loss account after operating profit and before interest:

- profits or losses on the sale or termination of an operation
- costs of a fundamental reorganisation or restructuring
- profits or losses on the disposal of fixed assets.

Note that these items may or may not be exceptional. Thus a disposal of a fixed asset may be a normal trading transaction but it may also, due to its size, be an exceptional item. The practical effect of the distinction is that details of each exceptional item need to be disclosed in the notes to the profit and loss account.

Each of the three specific items will be examined in turn.

2.3   Profits or losses on the sale or termination of an operation

The 'sale or termination of an operation' is not defined in FRS 3. It encompasses but is not restricted to the term 'discontinued operation'. Thus the item may be part of continuing operations or discontinued operations and therefore needs to be disclosed under its correct heading. It is likely to be an exceptional item as well.

Often the sale or termination straddles two accounting periods. In the first period a provision may have been established for losses expected to arise in the following period (under the prudence concept). However, there has been much criticism in recent years on the 'excessive' use of provisions by companies and thus FRS 3 imposes the following restrictions.

- A provision should not be made unless the company is demonstrably committed to the sale or termination, e.g. public announcement of specific plans or a binding contract for sale has been entered into after the balance sheet date.

DEFINITION

Exceptional items are material items which derive from events or transactions that fall within the ordinary activities of the reporting entity and which individually or, if of a similar type, in aggregate, need to be disclosed by virtue of their size or incidence if the financial statements are to give a true and fair view.

- The provision should cover only:
    - (a) the direct costs of the sale or termination; plus
    - (b) operating losses up to the sale date; less
    - (c) anticipated trading profits (if any).

Example

X plc has a calendar year end. On 30 October 20X7 the board of directors decide to withdraw from a market which is a significant part of the company's existing business. Plans are disclosed to the workforce on 30 November with a termination set at 31 March 20X8.

Actual and projected results of the operation are as follows:

	Actual to 31 December 20X7 £'000	Projected to 31 March 20X8 £'000
Sales	45,000	8,000
Operating costs	44,000	12,000
Redundancy and other costs		3,000

The accounts for the year ended 31 December 20X7 are expected to be approved by 18 March 20X8.

Therefore in the accounts for the year ended 31 December 20X7 the operation is not classified as a discontinued operation (due to the timing of the date on which the accounts are approved). FRS 3 suggests that a provision should be set up at 31 December 20X7 totalling:

	£'000
Projected loss	4,000
Redundancy	3,000
	7,000

If, in the 20X8 accounting period, actual results of the operation are:

	£'000
Sales	9,400
Operating costs	11,600
Redundancy	3,000

the profit and loss account for the year ended 31 December 20X8 would show:

	Continuing operations 20X8 £'000	Discontinued operations 20X8 £'000	Continuing operations 20X7 £'000	Discontinued operations 20X7 £'000
Turnover	X	9,400	X	45,000
Operating costs	X	(11,600)		(44,000)
Less: 20X7 provision		4,000		
Operating profit	X	1,800		1,000
Provision for loss on operations to be discontinued				(7,000)
Loss on termination of discontinued operation		(3,000)		
Less: 20X7 provision		3,000		
Profit (loss) on ordinary activities before taxation	X	1,800		(6,000)

2.4   Costs of a fundamental reorganisation

Only a reorganisation or restructuring which has a material effect on the nature and focus of the company's operations qualifies for separate disclosure as a fundamental reorganisation. This item will therefore be classified as exceptional as well.

2.5   Disposals of fixed assets

This heading is not intended to include profits and losses that are no more than marginal adjustments to depreciation previously charged.

If an asset has previously been revalued, FRS 3 has now ruled on the method of computation of the profit or loss on disposal. Examples of the computation were shown in an earlier chapter.

ACTIVITY 1

Do the following situations meet the definition of discontinued operations as defined by FRS 3?

(a) X plc, an office furniture and equipment manufacturer, runs separate divisions of approximately equal size for the two activities. It has now decided to sell the less profitable equipment division and use the funds received to expand the furniture division by growth and acquisition. The decision to sell was made in October 20X5 and the sale was completed on 21 March 20X6. The accounts for the year 20X5 were approved on 15 March 20X6.

(b) Y plc, as a result of a recession, has suffered a downturn in demand and now has productive over-capacity. In order to reduce costs Y plc has decided to transfer production into one of its two factories and to 'moth-ball' the other factory. This decision was made in April 20X3 and the transfer was completed in August 20X3. The company has a September year end.

(c) Z plc, a printing company, also carries out specialised book binding. This part of the business is carried out in a separate workshop and comprises approximately 0.5% of the total assets of the company and contributes approximately the same proportion of profits. During 20X4 Z plc sold the bookbinding business to a consortium of the workforce and sold the workshop to the local council. The profit arising from this transaction amounted to £100,000 on profits of £2,400,000 for 20X4.

Feedback to this activity is at the end of the chapter.

2.6   Extraordinary items

DEFINITION

Extraordinary items are material items possessing a high degree of abnormality which arise from events or transactions that fall outside the ordinary activities of the reporting entity and which are not expected to recur.

As discontinued activities are shown as ordinary activities and exceptional items include profit/loss on disposals of operations, extraordinary items are now extremely rare. In reality there are expected to be no extraordinary items ever appearing in a set of UK accounts.

2.7 Prior period adjustments

Prior period adjustments are rare. An entity may change its accounting policy only if the new policy will give a fairer presentation of its results and of its financial position. To be fundamental, an error must be so significant that it destroys the true and fair view and hence the validity of the financial statements.

The following are not prior period adjustments and should be dealt with in the profit and loss account of the period in which they are identified:

- corrections and adjustments to estimates made in prior periods (e.g. provisions for doubtful debts)

- modifications of an existing accounting treatment which are necessary because the entity is undertaking different transactions.

FRS 3 requires the following accounting treatment for prior period adjustments.

- Restate the comparative figures for the preceding period in the primary statements and the notes.

- Adjust the opening balance of reserves for the cumulative effect of the adjustments. This adjustment should be clearly disclosed in the reserves note and should also be disclosed in the reconciliation of movements in shareholders' funds (see below).

- Disclose the effect of prior period adjustments on the results for the preceding period where practicable.

- Disclose the cumulative effect of the adjustments at the foot of the statement of total recognised gains and losses for the current period (see below).

3 Other statements required

3.1 The statement of total recognised gains and losses

The statement of total recognised gains and losses (STRGL) is a primary statement, i.e. it is required for a true and fair view.

As the name suggests, this statement brings together all the gains and losses for the period, including items which do not pass through the profit and loss account.

The STRGL reflects the ASB's concept of financial performance, as discussed in the Statement of Principles. The financial performance of an entity comprises the return it obtains on the resources it controls, the components of that return and the characteristics of those components. In other words, performance is wider than simply profit, it also includes items such as changes in the value of assets and gains and losses on currency translation.

An illustrative statement is shown below.

Statement of total recognised gains and losses for the year ended 30 June 20X3

	20X3	20X2 as restated
	£m	£m
Profit for the financial year	29	7
Unrealised surplus on revaluation of properties	4	6
Unrealised (loss)/gain on trade investment	(3)	7
	—	—
	30	20

Currency translation differences on foreign currency net investments	(2)	5
Total recognised gains and losses relating to the year	28	25
Prior year adjustment (as explained in note X)	(10)	
Total gains and losses recognised since last annual report	18	

3.2 Other statements

FRS 3 requires two other statements to be shown as notes to the accounts.

(a) **Reconciliation of movements in shareholders' funds** – The reconciliation of movements in shareholders' funds brings together the performance of the period, as shown in the STRGL, with all the other changes in shareholders' funds in the period, including capital contributed by or repaid to shareholders.

Example

Reconciliation of movements in shareholders' funds for the year ended 30 June 20X3

	20X3	20X2 as restated
	£m	£m
Profit for the financial year	29	7
Dividends	(8)	(1)
	21	6
Other recognised gains and losses relating to the year (net)	(1)	18
New share capital subscribed	20	1
Net addition to shareholders' funds	40	25
Opening shareholders' funds (originally £375m before deducting prior year adjustment of £10m)	365	340
Closing shareholders' funds	405	365

(b) **Note of historical cost profits and losses** – The note of historical cost profits and losses is a memorandum item, the primary purpose of which is to present the profits or losses of companies that have revalued assets on a more comparable basis with those of entities that have not. It is an abbreviated restatement of the profit and loss account which adjusts the reported profit or loss, if necessary, so as to show it as if no asset revaluation had been made.

Note of historical cost profits and losses for the year ended 30 June 20X3

	20X3	20X2 as restated
	£m	£m
Reported profit on ordinary activities before taxation	45	13
Realisation of property revaluation gains of previous years	9	10
Difference between a historical cost depreciation charge and the actual depreciation charge of the year calculated on the revalued amount	5	4
Historical cost profit on ordinary activities before taxation	59	27

Historical cost profit for the year retained after taxation, minority interests, extraordinary items and dividends	35	20

3.3 Critical evaluation of FRS 3

FRS 3 adopts an 'information set' approach. Users of the financial statements are encouraged to analyse and interpret the profit and loss account as a whole, rather than concentrating on one particular profit figure.

FRS 3 is generally believed to have improved financial reporting in the following ways.

- Reporting entities are required to highlight a range of important components of financial performance. Operating profit is placed in the context of the profit and loss account (and financial performance) as a whole.

- Analysing the profit and loss account between continuing operations, acquisitions and discontinued operations enables users to assess the future performance of an entity. For example, turnover and costs arising from a discontinued operation will not occur in the future.

- Disclosure of exceptional items also provides useful information. Profits or losses from non-trading activities (such as the sale of fixed assets or restructuring costs) can have a dramatic impact on the overall performance of a company. The disclosure draws attention to the fact that they will not recur.

- The STRGL combines information about operating and related performance with other aspects of financial performance and provides information that is useful for assessing the return on investment.

- Standardisation of treatment and disclosure of items (including the note of historical cost profits and losses) has made it easier to compare the performance of different companies.

- The extensive disclosure requirements and the virtual elimination of extraordinary items mean that the profit on ordinary activities is far less likely to be manipulated by preparers of accounts.

However, FRS 3 has been criticised for the following reasons.

- Elimination of extraordinary items means that profit on ordinary activities may fluctuate from year to year and it may be difficult to interpret trends.

- Some commentators believe that the definition of discontinued items is too restrictive and therefore unhelpful. Others believe that preparers of financial statements may still try to manipulate the profit and loss account by arranging sales and terminations so that they fit (or do not fit) the definition.

- It has been argued that the profit and loss account does not highlight operating exceptional items such as stock write-downs or bad debt provisions. In addition, there is no analysis of the components of the tax charge or the minority interest.

- The extensive disclosures required may actually obscure the view given by the profit and loss account and make it more difficult to understand, particularly for less sophisticated users. There is evidence that users may want to concentrate on a single performance figure and may be unwilling or unable to analyse financial information in detail.

4 Reporting financial performance: current developments

4.1 Background

FRED 22 *Revision of FRS 3 Reporting financial performance* was issued in December 2000. FRED 22 has been developed from proposals in the 'G4+1' group Position Paper *Reporting financial performance: proposals for change.*

The reasons for reviewing FRS 3 centre on the operation of the statement of total recognised gains and losses (STRGL):

- Since FRS 3 was first issued, financial reporting practice has developed. The ASB's recent and current projects on derivatives, impairment and pensions have highlighted the need to reconsider the purpose of the statement of total recognised gains and losses (STRGL). When fixed assets, financial instruments or pension scheme assets and liabilities change in value some gains and losses arise that could in theory be reported in either the profit and loss account or in the STRGL. There is a need for firm principles on which to base the distinction.

- There is also some evidence that users and preparers of accounts are confused by the existence of two performance statements. Therefore they concentrate on the profit and loss account and largely ignore the STRGL.

4.2 New statement of performance

FRED 22 proposes that the profit and loss account and STRGL should be replaced by a single performance statement. This would be divided into three sections:

- operating
- financing and treasury
- other gains and losses.

The main principle behind the new statement of financial performance is that items with similar characteristics are grouped together.

The 'operating' section of the statement would be the 'default' section and most gains and losses would be reported here. Only items specified by accounting standards or UITF Abstracts would be reported in the other sections. FRED 22 lists the items that would be reported in the other sections under the requirements of current accounting standards.

- **Financing and treasury:**

    (a) interest payable and receivable

    (b) the unwinding of the discount on long-term items, e.g. pensions

    (c) income from investments held as part of treasury activities

    (d) gains and losses arising on the repurchase or early settlement of debt

    (e) any other recognised gain or loss identified for inclusion by another accounting standard or by a UITF Abstract.

- **Other gains and losses:**

    (a) revaluation gains and losses on fixed assets (including investment properties)

    (b) gains and losses on disposal of properties in continuing operations

    (c) actuarial gains and losses arising on defined benefit schemes

(d)   profits and losses on disposal of discontinuing operations

(e)   exchange translation differences on foreign currency net investments

(f)   any other recognised gain or loss as determined in accordance with or identified by another accounting standard or UITF Abstract.

Some of these items are currently reported in the STRGL while others are currently reported as exceptional items on the face of the profit and loss account.

An Appendix to FRED 22 contains an illustration of the new statement:

Statement of financial performance

	2001		2000 Restated
	£m	£m	£m
Operating			
Turnover			
Continuing operations	600		525
Acquisitions	50		
	650		
Discontinued operations	175		190
		825	715
Cost of sales		(650)	(570)
Gross profit		175	145
Net operating expenses		(124)	(93)
Operating profit			
Continuing operations	60		40
Acquisitions	6		
	66		
Discontinued operations	(15)		12
Operating income/profit		51	52
Financing and treasury			
Interest on debt		(26)	(15)
Financing relating to pension provisions		20	11
Financing and treasury income/profit		**(6)**	**(4)**
Operating and financing income before taxation		**45**	**48**
Taxation on operating and financing income		(5)	(10)
Operating and financing income after taxation		40	38
Minority interests		(5)	(4)
Income from operating and financing activities for the period		**35**	**34**

Other gains and losses

Revaluation gain on disposal of properties in continuing operations	6	4
Revaluation of fixed assets	4	3
Actuarial gain on defined benefit pension scheme	276	91
Profit on disposal of discontinued operations	3	-
Exchange translation differences on foreign currency net investments	(2)	5
Other gains and losses before taxation	**287**	**103**
Taxation on other gains and losses	(87)	(33)
Other gains and losses after taxation	200	70
Minority interests	(30)	(10)
Other gains and losses of the period	**170**	**60**
Total gains and losses of the period	**205**	**94**

4.3 Discontinuing operations

As at present, entities would be required to analyse their operating results between continuing operations, acquisitions and discontinued activities. Entities may also disclose information on continuing and discontinued operations in the financing and treasury section and the other gains and losses section. If they choose to make these extra disclosures they should also disclose the underlying assumptions used in making any allocations (for example, of interest payable).

Under FRS 3, an operation can only be classified as discontinued if the sale or termination is completed within three months after the year end. An operation that is purposely discontinued gradually over a long period must be reported under continuing operations. This means that users of the financial statements may not be aware that an operation is being discontinued until it is actually terminated. This is potentially misleading.

FRED 22 proposes that the definition of discontinued operations is changed, so that they become discontinu*ing* operations.

A **discontinuing operation** is a component of a reporting entity that:

- represents a separate major line of business or geographical area of operations

- can be distinguished operationally and for financial reporting purposes

- pursuant to a single plan, is:

   (a) being disposed of substantially in its entirety, such as by selling the component in a single transaction or by demerger or spin-off of ownership of the component to the entity's shareholders; or

   (b) being disposed of piecemeal, such as by selling off the component's assets and settling its liabilities individually; or

   (c) being terminated through abandonment.

FRED 22 proposes that information about discontinuing operations should be disclosed from the period in which the initial disclosure event occurs.

An **initial disclosure event** is the occurrence of one of the following, whichever occurs earlier:

- the entity has entered into a binding sale agreement for substantially all the assets attributable to the discontinuing operation; or

- the entity's board of directors or similar governing body has both:

    (a) approved a detailed, formal plan for the discontinuance; and

    (b) made an announcement of the plan

    and the actions of the entity are such that they have raised a valid expectation in those affected that it will carry out the planned termination.

4.4 Exceptional items

FRED 22 makes the following proposals.

- Exceptional items should be included in the appropriate section of the performance statement under the format headings to which they relate and analysed under continuing or discontinuing operations as appropriate. As at present, the amount of each exceptional item should be disclosed separately in the notes to the financial statements or on the face of the performance statement if this is necessary in order to give a true and fair view. An adequate description of each exceptional item should be given to enable its nature to be understood.

- A history of exceptional items should be shown in the notes to the performance statement. This should give a breakdown of the exceptional items reported during each of the last five years with a description of each item.

This new disclosure is intended to enable users to see the nature and pattern of exceptional items reported and to assist them in forecasting future results and cash flows.

4.5 Other proposed changes to FRS 3

- The reconciliation of movements in shareholders' funds (reconciliation of ownership interests) would become a primary statement. (FRS 3 allows it to be presented as either a primary statement or a note.)

- The note of historical cost profits and losses would become optional. This is because the ASB has reservations about its usefulness. The note is supposed to enable users to compare the results of different reporting entities where some revalue fixed assets and others do not. Historical cost gains and losses are only truly comparable when the same sorts of assets were bought and sold at the same points in time. This is unlikely to be the case in practice. In addition, full historical cost information may not be available without unreasonable expense or delay.

- Entities would be required to disclose total dividends and dividends per share as memorandum items at the foot of the performance statement.

Most of the other requirements of FRS 3 would remain unchanged. In particular, recycling of gains and losses would continue to be prohibited.

For example, a gain could be recognised in the STRGL or 'other gains and losses' section when a fixed asset is revalued and the same gain could be reported in the profit and loss account or operating section when the asset is sold. FRS 3 and FRS 15 prohibit recycling by requiring that a gain on disposal of a revalued asset is calculated as the sales proceeds less the net carrying amount.

DEFINITION

Recycling is the reporting of an item of financial performance in more than one accounting period because the nature of the item is deemed to have changed in some way over time.

4.6 Dividends

Dividends would no longer be shown in the performance statement but instead would be reported as a movement in ownership interest for the period. The ASB believes that dividends are not part of financial performance but appropriations of profit. It has requested an amendment to the Companies Act 1985 so that dividends paid and proposed no longer have to be disclosed on the face of the profit and loss account.

5   Implications of the proposals

5.1   Providing better information for users

The ASB believes that the new performance statement will be clearer than the existing profit and loss account and STRGL and will enable users to appreciate the performance of the entity as a whole. Items will be classified according to their nature rather than according to whether they are realised or unrealised (as is largely the case at present). Users will be able to focus on the particular aspects of an entity's performance that they judge to be the most important.

5.2   What is performance?

The main criticism of FRED 22 has been its view of performance.

The definition of financial performance is based on the 'balance sheet approach' taken in the Statement of Principles. Critics of the ASB argue that this definition is flawed, because unrealised items such as revaluation gains and exchange differences arising from the retranslation of foreign subsidiaries under the closing rate method are not performance at all. Instead they should be viewed as capital maintenance adjustments.

In fact the ASB's view of performance has not changed significantly since it issued FRS 3. By introducing the STRGL it showed that it believes that items such as revaluation gains are components of performance. However, it will be more difficult for users of the financial statements to disregard unrealised items if they are brought into the main performance statement rather than being included separately in the STRGL.

5.3   What are earnings?

The ASB wishes to discourage users and preparers of financial statements from focusing on one number (e.g. profit on ordinary activities after taxation) as a measure of performance.

Despite this, there is some evidence that users and preparers want a single measure of performance, at least as a starting point for further analysis. (Earnings per share is discussed later in this chapter.) FRED 22 proposes that the earnings figure used to calculate basic earnings per share should be the combined total of the operating section and the financing and treasury section after related taxation and minority interests, less preference dividends. As at present, entities would be able to calculate and disclose an additional earnings per share figure if they chose.

'Other gains and losses' would not be included in earnings. This is a change from current practice, as 'other gains and losses' include some exceptional items, as well as unrealised gains and losses. This means that earnings per share would be less volatile and that it would be easier for users to compare the results of different entities.

5.4   Exceptional items

There are several implications of the proposals.

- Costs of a fundamental reorganisation or restructuring would be included in the operating section.

- Profits and losses on sale or termination of an operation and profits and losses on disposal of fixed assets would be included in 'other gains and losses'. This means that these items would not be treated as part of the company's 'normal' operations and would not be included in earnings per share. Some commentators believe that this is wrong; companies make strategic decisions in buying and selling assets and therefore gains and losses are part of operating activities.

- It will be more difficult for entities to emphasise 'profit before exceptional items'. (This has been common practice but can be misleading because it implies that no exceptional items are expected in the future.) The additional disclosure of the history of exceptional items should enable users to judge the extent to which different types of exceptional items are reported year on year and thus be better able to predict future results and cash flows.

5.5   Investment properties

Some entities (for example, property investment companies) generate profit by trading in assets. SSAP 19 requires that gains and losses on revaluation of investment properties are treated in a similar way to revaluation gains and losses arising on other assets. This means that according to the strict letter of the FRED (and SSAP 19) they should be reported under 'other gains and losses'.

However, the ASB accepts that gains and losses on revaluation of investment properties are operating items and that therefore in theory they should be reported in the operating section. The ASB is considering whether to amend SSAP 19 so that revaluation gains and losses on investment properties are included in the profit and loss account/operating section of the performance statement.

5.6   Groups

Some companies and groups may have practical problems in implementing FRED 22. For example, a retail group may run a property management division or company that manages the properties from which the retail operations trade. The property management company would report gains and losses on revaluation and disposal of properties in the operating section of the performance statement.

However, FRED 22 states that group financial statements should reflect the operations of the group as a whole, not its constituent parts. At the group level, the property management division is subordinate to the retail operation. Therefore in the group financial statements holding gains on properties should be shown in 'other gains and losses', although depreciation and impairment losses will be included in the operating section.

Groups with diverse operating activities may have particular problems. If the financial statements are simply consolidated by adding items together line by line as usual the resulting performance statement may be unhelpful. Segmental information is likely to be very important in these cases.

FRED 22 gives the example of a manufacturing group that owns an insurance company. Neither the three section format proposed by FRED 22 nor the insurance company format required by the Companies Act will enable the performance of the group to be reported fairly on the face of the performance statement. It may be necessary to adapt the structure of the performance statement. In the absence of further guidance (for example, in a

Statement of Recommended Practice (SORP)) management should resolve the issue by considering statutory obligations and the need to show a true and fair view.

5.7   Taxation

FRED 22 proposes that the tax arising from items in the operating section and the financing and treasury section should be shown after the total combined result of the operating and the financing and treasury section. The tax charge or credit arising on items in other gains and losses should be shown as a single item within that section.

This means that entities would have to allocate the total tax charge between 'profit on ordinary activities' and 'other gains and losses'. FRED 22 states that this should be done by calculating the tax charge as if other gains and losses did not exist. The difference between this notional tax charge and the total tax charge is the tax charge relating to other gains and losses.

In most cases it should be possible to identify the tax effects of 'other gains and losses' such as profits or losses on disposal. These are often unusual or material and separate analysis helps users to understand post-tax results and cash flows.

However, it is possible that some entities may need to allocate items between the two parts of the overall result.

5.8   Discontinuing activities

FRED 22 proposes that discontinu*ing* operations should be disclosed, rather than discontinued operations. Disclosure of discontinuing activities reflects the economic decision-making process of management and gives timely information to users of the financial statements.

The change has the further advantage that the new UK standard would be more consistent with the requirements of IAS 35 *Discontinuing operations*. The two definitions of discontinuing operations are almost identical. However, FRED 22 differs from IAS 35 in one important respect: FRED 22 states that if there is a formal plan for discontinuance the actions of the entity must be such that they have raised a valid expectation in those affected that it will carry out the planned termination. This narrower definition means that the circumstances under which a discontinuance can be reversed are extremely rare.

This narrower definition should prevent management from manipulating the reporting of results by identifying activities as 'discontinuing' in a loss making period and then retaining the activities and including them again in 'continuing activities' when the loss making period is over.

5.9   Further proposed changes to FRS 3

In July 2003 the ASB issued FRED 32 *Disposal of non-current assets and presentation of discontinued operations* proposing further changes to FRS 3. The FRED was triggered by the IASB's development of IFRS 5 that covers the same topics.

UK accounting standards currently include no specific requirements for fixed assets held for disposal, other than FRS 11's general requirement to carry out an impairment review if there is any indication of impairment. The effect of FRED 32 would be to introduce a new class of fixed asset:

- FRS 15 continues to apply to assets held for consumption
- SSAP 19 continues to apply to assets held for investment
- FRED 32 would apply to assets held for disposal.

FRED 32 proposes the following practices.

(a)   Fixed assets held for sale should be presented separately on the face of the balance sheet. An asset should be classified as 'held for sale' if it is highly probable that the asset will be sold within one year.

(b)   Fixed assets held for sale should be measured at the lower of existing carrying value and fair value less costs to sell. In practice, 'fair value less costs to sell' is the same as net realisable value.

(c)   Fixed assets held for sale should not be depreciated, regardless of whether they are still in use. This is a controversial proposal that the ASB is not entirely happy with.

(d)   A component part of the reporting entity that is held for sale would qualify as a discontinued operation, requiring separate disclosure under the usual rules for such operations. Again this is controversial, since the FRED's definition of discontinued operations contains no requirement for them to have a material effect. There would be many more discontinued activities under FRED 32 than under FRS 3, since even minor parts of the entity that were terminated would qualify as discontinued activities.

5.10 Conclusion

FRS 3 currently requires financial performance to be reported in a profit and loss account and a STRGL. FRED 22 proposes the radical idea that the current two statements should be combined into a single statement of financial performance. FRED 32 proposes limited revisions to current practice, following IFRS 5 that requires fixed assets held for sale to be presented separately on the face of the balance sheet, and components held for sale to qualify as discontinued activities.

An FRS based on FRED 32 is likely to be produced in due course. The ideas of FRED 22 are so wide-reaching that no FRS based on its ideas is likely in the near future.

6   Earnings per share

6.1   FRS 14 *Earnings per share*

Earnings per share (EPS) is a widely used measure of a company's performance, particularly over a number of years, and is a component of a very important Stock Exchange yardstick – the price/earnings (P/E) ratio.

The objective of FRS 14 *Earnings per share* is to improve the comparison of the performance of different entities in the same period and of the same entity in different accounting periods, by prescribing methods for determining the number of shares to be included in the calculation of earnings per share and other amounts per share, and by specifying their presentation.

FRS 14 applies to public companies. Private companies that voluntarily disclose earnings per share must also comply with FRS 14.

6.2   The calculation of basic EPS

$$\text{Earnings per share (in pence)} = \frac{\text{net profit or loss for the period attributable to ordinary shareholders}}{\text{weighted average number of ordinary shares outstanding in the period}}$$

The net profit or loss attributable to ordinary shareholders is the net profit or loss after deducting non-equity dividends and other appropriations in respect of non-equity shares (normally preference shares).

6.3   Shares in issue

Where several classes of shares are in issue, then earnings should be apportioned according to dividend rights.

6.4   When to include shares in the calculation

Where there has been an issue of ordinary shares during the period, shares are normally included in the weighted average number of shares from the date consideration is receivable, which is generally the date of their issue. For example:

- ordinary shares issued in exchange for cash are issued when cash is receivable

- ordinary shares issued as a result of the conversion of a debt instrument are included as of the date that interest ceases to accrue

- ordinary shares issued as part of the purchase consideration for an acquisition are included as of the date of the acquisition

- ordinary shares issued as part of the purchase consideration for a business combination accounted for as a merger are included for all periods presented.

Ordinary shares that are issuable upon the satisfaction of certain conditions (contingently issuable shares) are not included in the computation until all the necessary conditions have been satisfied.

Partly paid shares are treated as a fraction of an ordinary share to the extent that they were entitled to participate in dividends relative to a fully paid up ordinary share during the period.

For example, a company issues 100,000 ordinary shares of £1 each. Throughout the year to 31 December 20X1 the shares were 50% paid and dividend participation is to be 50% until the shares are fully paid. 50,000 ordinary shares are included in the earnings per share calculation for the year.

6.5   Issue at full market price

Earnings should be apportioned over the weighted average equity share capital (i.e. taking account of when shares are issued during the year).

Example

A company issued 200,000 shares at full market price (£3.00) on 1 July 20X8.

	20X8	20X7
Ordinary profit attributable to the ordinary shareholders for the year ending 31 Dec.	£550,000	£460,000
Number of ordinary shares in issue at 31 Dec.	1,000,000	800,000

Solution

$$20X7 = \frac{£460,000}{800,000} = 57.5p$$

$$20X8 = \frac{£550,000}{800,000 + (\frac{1}{2} \times 200,000)} = 61.11p$$

Since the 200,000 shares have only contributed finance for half a year, the number of shares is adjusted accordingly. Note that the solution is to use the earnings figure for the period without adjustment, but divided by the average number of shares weighted on a time basis.

6.6   Bonus issues

When there has been an event that has changed the number of ordinary shares outstanding without a corresponding change in resources (inflow or outflow of cash), the comparative earnings per share figure should also be adjusted.

Example

A company makes a scrip issue of one new share for every five existing shares held on 1 July 20X8.

	20X8	*20X7*
Ordinary profit attributable to the ordinary shareholders for the year ending 31 Dec.	£550,000	£460,000
Number of ordinary shares in issue at 31 Dec.	1,200,000	1,000,000

Solution

$$20X7 \quad = \quad \frac{£460,000}{1,200,000} = 38.33p$$

$$20X8 \quad = \quad \frac{£550,000}{1,200,000} = 45.83p$$

In the 20X7 accounts, the EPS for the year would have appeared as 46p (£460,000 ÷ 1,000,000). In the example above, the computation has been reworked from scratch. However, to make the changes required it would be simpler to adjust directly the EPS figures themselves.

Since the old calculation was based on dividing by 1,000,000 while the new is determined by using 1,200,000, it would be necessary to multiply the EPS by the first and divide by the second. The fraction to apply is, therefore,

$$\frac{1,000,000}{1,200,000} \quad \text{or} \quad \frac{5}{6}$$

Consequently $46p \times \frac{5}{6} = 38.33p$

Given that the scrip issue has not increased the assets in the company, similarly the market value of each share would be expected to be only 5/6 of the former price, since for every five shares previously held, the shareholder now has six.

Assuming a pre-issue market price of £3.00, five shares would have a market value of £15.00.

After the issue six shares would, other things being equal, have the same value. Therefore, one share would have a theoretical post-issue price of £15.00 ÷ 6 = £2.50. The new EPS could in consequence equally well have been calculated by multiplying the old EPS by the theoretical new share price divided by the actual old price:

$$\frac{£2.50}{£3.00} = \frac{5}{6}$$

Since there are now six shares in issue for every five previously held, the number of shares after the issue is:

$$1,000,000 \times \frac{6}{5} \quad = 1,200,000$$

or alternatively:

$$1,000,000 \times \frac{3.00}{2.50} = 1,200,000$$

These interrelationships are important when considering a rights issue.

6.7   Rights issues

Rights issues present special problems, because they are normally below full market price and therefore combine the characteristics of issues at full market price and bonus issues above. Determining the weighted average capital, therefore, involves two steps as follows:

Step 1

Adjust for bonus element in rights issue, by multiplying capital in issue before the rights issue by:

$$\frac{\text{Actual cum rights price}}{\text{Theoretical ex rights price}}$$

Step 2

Calculate the weighted average capital in issue as above.

Example

A company issued one new share for every two existing shares held by way of rights at £1.50 per share on 1 July 20X8. Pre-issue market price was £3.00 per share.

	20X8	20X7
Ordinary profit attributable to the ordinary shareholders for the year ending 31 Dec	£550,000	£460,000
Number of ordinary shares in issue at 31 Dec	1,200,000	800,000

Solution

20X7   Original per 20X7 accounts:

$$\frac{£460,000}{800,000} = 57.5\text{p}$$

Adjusted for rights issue:

$$57.5\text{p} \times \frac{2.50}{3.00} = 47.92\text{p}$$

20X8   Based on weighted average number of shares:

1st half-year   –   actual in issue 800,000

–   adjusted for bonus element $800,000 \times \frac{3.00}{2.50}$

=   960,000

2nd half-year   –   actual in issue, including bonus element, 1,200,000

Therefore, EPS $= \dfrac{£550,000}{(960,000 + 1,200,000) \div 2}$

=   50.92p

Notes on solution

(1) 20X7

Pre-rights, two shares would be worth £6.00. Ex-rights, three shares would theoretically be worth £6.00 + £1.50 = £7.50, or £2.50 each. The appropriate fraction for the adjustment of comparatives is, therefore, £2.50 divided by £3.00.

The revised EPS figure could have been obtained by dividing the earnings figure of £460,000 by a share number adjusted for the bonus element, i.e:

$$800,000 \times \frac{3.00}{2.50} = 960,000$$

$$\frac{£460,000}{960,000} = 47.92p$$

(2) 20X8

The calculation must take account of the quasi-capitalisation. The share number used must, therefore, reflect the bonus element for the whole year and the increase in the fund of capital for the half year.

(3) Relationship of rights issue to issue at full market price and capitalisation.

Each of the examples used a pre-issue share price of £3.00. Both the rights issue and the issue at full market price raised £600,000 from shareholders. However, after the rights issue there were 1,200,000 shares in issue, whereas following the issue at full market value there were only 1,000,000.

If the latter had been followed immediately by a capitalisation to bring the number of shares issued up to 1,200,000, the EPS figures would have become:

20X7 $57.5p \times \dfrac{2.50}{3.00}$ = 47.92p

20X8 $61.11p \times \dfrac{2.50}{3.00}$ = 50.92p

These are, as would be expected, the same as those calculated for the rights issue.

7 Diluted earnings per share

7.1 The existing circumstances that will cause a company's future EPS to be diluted

As well as basic earnings per share, FRS 14 requires entities to disclose diluted earnings per share. To calculate diluted earnings per share, the net profit attributable to ordinary shareholders and the weighted average number of shares outstanding are adjusted for the effect of all dilutive potential ordinary shares.

Examples of potential ordinary shares:

- convertible loan stock

- convertible preference shares

- share warrants and options

- partly paid shares

- rights granted under employee share schemes

- rights to ordinary shares that are conditional upon the satisfaction of conditions.

Diluted earnings per share shows to what extent the amount available for ordinary dividends per share would have been affected if all the potential ordinary shares had been issued under the greatest possible dilution.

To calculate diluted earnings per share:

- the net profit or loss for the period attributable to ordinary shareholders is adjusted for:

    - dividends on potential shares (e.g. on convertible preference shares)

    - interest (e.g. on convertible loan stock)

    - any other changes in income and expense that would result from the conversion

- the weighted average number of ordinary shares that would be issued if all the potential ordinary shares were converted is added to the weighted number of ordinary shares. (Potential ordinary shares should be assumed to have been converted at the beginning of the period or, if they were not in existence at the beginning of the period, the date of issue.)

7.2 Convertibles

The principles of convertible loan stock and convertible preference shares are similar and will be dealt with together.

Example

On 1 April 20X1, the company issued £1,250,000 8% convertible unsecured loan stock for cash at par. Each £100 nominal of the stock will be convertible in 20X6/20X9 into the number of ordinary shares set out below:

On 31 December 20X6	124 shares
On 31 December 20X7	120 shares
On 31 December 20X8	115 shares
On 31 December 20X9	110 shares

Issued share capital:

£500,000 in 10% cumulative preference shares of £1

£1,000,000 in ordinary shares of 25p = 4,000,000 shares

Corporation tax is 30%.

Trading results for the year ended 31 December

	20X2 £	20X1 £
Profit before interest and tax	1,100,000	991,818
Interest on 8% convertible unsecured loan stock	100,000	75,000
Profit before tax	1,000,000	916,818
Corporation tax	300,000	275,045
Profit after tax	700,000	641,773

Solution

		20X2	20X1
(1)	**Basic earnings per share**	£	£
	Profit after tax	700,000	641,773
	Less: Preference dividend	50,000	50,000
	Earnings	650,000	591,773
	Earnings per share based on 4,000,000 shares	16.2p	14.8p

			20X2	20X1
(2)	**Diluted earnings per share**			
	Earnings as above		650,000	591,773
	Add: Interest on the convertible unsecured loan stock	100,000		75,000
	Less: Corporation tax	30,000		22,500
			70,000	52,500
	Adjusted earnings		720,000	644,273
	Earnings per share based on 5,550,000 shares (20X1 – 5,162,500)		13.0p	12.5p

Notes:

(A) Up to 20X5 the maximum number of shares issuable after the end of the financial year will be at the rate of 124 shares per £100 of loan stock, viz: $((1,250,000/100) \times 124) = 1,550,000$ shares, making a total of 5,550,000.

(B) The weighted average number of shares issued and issuable for 20X1 would have been one-quarter of 4,000,000 plus three-quarters of 5,550,000, i.e. 5,162,500.

7.3   Options and warrants

The total number of shares issued on the exercise of the option or warrant is split into two:

- the number of shares that would have been issued if the cash received had been used to buy shares at fair value (using the average price of the shares during the period)

- the remainder, which are treated like a bonus issue (i.e. as having been issued for no consideration).

The number of shares issued for no consideration is added to the number of shares when calculating the diluted earnings per share.

Example

On 1 January 20X7 a company issues 1,000,000 shares under option. The net profit for the year is £500,000 and the company already has 4,000,000 ordinary shares in issue at that date.

During the year to 31 December 20X7 the average fair value of one ordinary share was £3 and the exercise price for the shares under option was £2.

Solution

Basic earnings per share: $\dfrac{£500,000}{4,000,000} = 12.5\text{p}$

Diluted earnings per share:

Number of ordinary shares in issue	4,000,000
Number of shares under option	1,000,000
Number of shares that would have been issued at fair value:	
(1,000,000 × 2/3)	(666,667)
	4,333,333

Diluted earnings per share: $\dfrac{£500,000}{4,333,333} = 11.5\text{p}$

7.4   Partly paid shares

When computing basic earnings per share, partly paid shares are treated as a fraction of an ordinary share.

When computing diluted earnings per share, partly paid shares are treated in the same way as options and warrants, to the extent that they are not entitled to participate in dividends. The unpaid consideration is treated as the exercise price for the proportion of the partly paid shares not included in the basic EPS.

Example

On 1 January 20X7 a company issues 1,000,000 £1 ordinary shares. The net profit for the year is £500,000 and the company already has 4,000,000 £1 ordinary shares in issue at that date.

The full price of the shares is £1.50 and they are 50% paid up on issue. Dividend participation is to be 50% until the shares are fully paid. The shares remained 50% paid at 31 December 20X7. During the year to 31 December 20X7 the average fair value of one ordinary share was £2.

Solution

Basic earnings per share: $\dfrac{£500,000}{4,500,000} = 11.11\text{p}$

Diluted earnings per share:

Number of fully paid ordinary shares in issue	4,000,000
Proportion of partly paid ordinary shares in basic EPS (50%)	500,000
Proportion of partly paid ordinary shares not in basic EPS (50%)	500,000
Number of shares that would have been issued at fair value:	
(1,000,000 × 75p/£2.00)	(375,000)
	4,625,000

Diluted earnings per share: $\dfrac{£500,000}{4,625,000} = 10.8\text{p}$

The exercise price is treated as being 75p (50% × £1.50). Notice that the dilutive effect depends on the fair value of the shares. If this were the same as the actual issue price (i.e. £1.50 per share) there would be no dilutive effect.

7.5　Employee share schemes

Share option and similar schemes are becoming increasingly common. The accounting treatment of these is covered by FRS 20 (see Chapter 20).

For the purpose of calculating diluted EPS, there are two types of scheme:

- where the award is based on performance

- other schemes.

Performance-based awards are treated as contingently issuable shares (see below). All other awards are treated as options. The assumed proceeds of the potential ordinary shares may need to be adjusted to reflect the fact that they have been earned by past services. The assumed proceeds consist of the consideration (if any) that the employee must pay upon exercise of the award and the cost of the shares not yet recognised.

Example

A company operates an employee share option scheme that awards share options to employees and their dependants on the basis of period of service with the company. The shares were granted on 1 January 20X7 and are due to vest in the employees at 31 December 20X9. The company has 5 million ordinary shares in issue at 1 January 20X7. The following details are also relevant.

- The market price of the shares at 1 January 20X7 was £2.00.

- The exercise price of the option is £1.25.

- There are 1 million shares under option.

- The net profit for the year ended 31 December 20X7 is £600,000.

- The average fair value of an ordinary share during 20X7 is £2.50.

Calculate basic and diluted EPS for the year ended 31 December 20X7.

Solution

Step 1

Calculate the assumed proceeds per option.

FRS 20 requires that the cost of the shares to the company is recognised over the period of the scheme. This is calculated as follows:

	£
Market price at 1 January 20X7	2.00
Less: Exercise price	(1.25)
	0.75

This is allocated over the life of the scheme so that 25p per option per year is charged to the profit and loss account. Therefore the assumed proceeds per option are:

	£
Exercise price	1.25
Compensation cost attributable to future service, not yet recognised (2 × 25p)	0.50
	1.75

Step 2

Calculate earnings per share.

$$\text{Basic earnings per share:} \quad \frac{£600,000}{5,000,000} = 12\text{p}$$

Diluted earnings per share:

Number of ordinary shares in issue	5,000,000
Number of shares under option	1,000,000
Number of shares that would have been issued at fair value:	
$(1,000,000 \times 1.75/2.50)$	(700,000)
	5,300,000

$$\text{Earnings per share:} \quad \frac{£600,000}{5,300,000} = 11.3\text{p}$$

7.6   Contingently issuable shares

Contingently issuable shares are included in the calculation of diluted earnings per share from the beginning of the period or, if they were not in existence at the beginning of the period, from the date of the relevant financial instrument or the granting of the rights.

The number of shares to include in the calculation is based on the number of shares that would be issuable if the end of the accounting period was the end of the contingency period.

- Where a condition is expressed as an average over a period the performance achieved to date is deemed to be that achieved over the whole of the contingency period. For example, if the number of shares to be issued depends on whether profits average £100,000 over a three year period, the condition is expressed as a cumulative target of £300,000 over the three year period. If, at the end of the first year, profits are £150,000, no additional shares are brought into the calculation.

- Where the number of shares to be issued depends on the market price of the shares of the issuing company, the number of shares to be included in the calculation is based on the number that would be issued based on the market price at the end of the current accounting period or the average over a specified period, depending on the terms of the underlying contract.

- If the contingency is based on a condition other than earnings or market price, it should be assumed that the status of the condition at the end of the reporting period will remain unchanged until the end of the contingency period. For example, if a further issue of shares is generated on the opening of the tenth new retail outlet and at the year end only five have been opened, no additional shares are included in the calculation.

Example

A company has 500,000 ordinary shares outstanding at 1 January 20X7. It has agreed to issue additional shares as follows:

(a) 10,000 additional ordinary shares for every new retail outlet opened in each of the three years 20X7 to 20X9

(b) 1,000 additional ordinary shares for each £1,000 of total net profit in excess of £350,000 over the three years ending 20X9.

The company opened one new retail outlet on 1 July 20X7 and another on 1 January 20X9. Net profit for the three years was £150,000, £240,000 and £175,000 respectively.

Calculate basic and diluted earnings per share for each of the three years ended 31 December 20X9.

Solution

Basic earnings per share

One retail outlet is opened during 20X7 and another during 20X9. Therefore 10,000 additional shares are issued in each of those two years. Because the earnings condition is not actually met until the last day of 20X9, no further additional shares are issued.

20X7 $\dfrac{£150,000}{505,000} = 29.7p$

(Number of shares: $(500,000 \times 6/12) + (510,000 \times 6/12)$)

20X8 $\dfrac{£240,000}{510,000} = 47.1p$

20X9 $\dfrac{£175,000}{520,000} = 33.7p$

Diluted earnings per share

Contingently issuable shares are included in the diluted earnings per share calculation from the beginning of the period in which the condition is met. Therefore a further 5,000 potential shares are included in 20X7 as a result of the opening of the retail outlet on 1 July.

Additional shares are included in respect of the earnings contingency as follows:

20X7   Earnings for the period were less than £350,000, therefore no additional shares.

20X8   Cumulative earnings for the two years are £390,000, therefore 40,000 additional shares are included.

20X9   Cumulative earnings for the three years are £565,000, therefore a further 175,000 additional shares are included (565,000 – 390,000).

Number of shares:

	20X7	*20X8*	*20X9*
Basic	505,000	510,000	520,000
Retail outlet contingency	5,000	–	–
Earnings contingency	–	40,000	215,000
	510,000	550,000	735,000

Earnings per share:

20X7 $\dfrac{£150,000}{510,000} = 29.4p$

20X8 $\dfrac{£240,000}{550,000} = 43.6p$

20X9 $\dfrac{£175,000}{735,000} = 23.8p$

7.7 The order in which to include dilutive securities in the calculation

Only potential ordinary shares that would dilute basic earnings per share should be taken into account when computing the diluted figure.

Where there is more than one issue of dilutive share the calculation is in two stages as follows.

1   For each issue, calculate earnings per incremental share.

2   Adjust basic earnings per share for each issue from the most dilutive to the least dilutive.

The diluted earnings per share is the worst possible diluted figure.

Example

The net profit attributable to ordinary shareholders is £500,000. There are 100,000 ordinary shares in issue. The average fair value of one ordinary share during the year was £50.

The following potential ordinary shares must be taken into consideration.

(i)	Options	5,000 share options with an exercise price of £40 per share.
(ii)	Convertible preference shares	40,000 shares entitled to a cumulative dividend of £8 per share. Each preference share is convertible to two ordinary shares.
(iii)	5% convertible bonds	Nominal amount £5,000,000. Each £1,000 bond is convertible to 20 ordinary shares.

The tax rate is 40%.

Solution

Step 1

Calculate the increase in earnings attributable to ordinary shareholders on conversion of potential ordinary shares.

	Increase in earnings £	Increase in number of ordinary shares	Earnings per incremental share £
Options			
Increase in earnings	NIL		
Shares issued for no consideration:			
$(5,000 \times (50 - 40)/50)$		1,000	NIL
Convertible preference shares			
Increase in earnings $(40,000 \times 8)$	320,000		
Increase in shares $(2 \times 40,000)$		80,000	4.00
5% convertible bonds			
Increase in earnings $(5,000,000 \times 5\% \times 60\%)$	150,000		
Incremental shares $(5,000 \times 20)$		100,000	1.50

The lower the incremental earnings per share, the higher the dilutive effect. This calculation shows that the most dilutive potential ordinary shares are the options, followed by the 5% convertible bonds and then the convertible preference shares. This is the order in which they should be considered in the diluted earnings per share calculation.

Step 2

Calculate diluted earnings per share.

	Net profit attributable £	Ordinary shares	Earnings per share £
Basic earnings per share	500,000	100,000	5.00
Options	–	1,000	
	500,000	101,000	4.95
5% convertible bonds	150,000	100,000	
	650,000	201,000	3.23
Convertible preference shares	320,000	80,000	
	970,000	281,000	3.45

Because diluted earnings per share is increased when taking the convertible preference shares into account, the convertible preference shares are antidilutive and are therefore ignored.

The diluted earnings per share is £3.23.

ACTIVITY 2

On 1 January 20X3 Tentsmuir plc granted options to its key employees to subscribe for 500,000 ordinary shares in the company at a price of £2 per share, and on 30 September they issued £1,000,000 of 12% convertible debentures. These debentures could be converted into ordinary shares on 31 December 20X8 at a rate of 60 per £100 of debentures, or on 31 December 20X9 at a rate of 55 per £100 of debentures. The average fair value of one ordinary share during the year was £2.50. The profit (after interest, tax, preference dividends and extraordinary items) for the year ended 31 December 20X3 was £50,000. There were 1,000,000 ordinary shares in issue throughout 20X3. None of the options had been exercised by 31 December 20X3. Assume that the rate of corporation tax is 40%. Calculate the basic EPS and DEPS figures for the year ending 31 December 20X3.

Feedback to this activity is at the end of the chapter.

7.8 Losses per share

In most cases, if basic earnings per share is a loss, diluted earnings per share will be the same as basic earnings per share.

KEY POINT

Potential ordinary shares are only included in the calculation of diluted earnings per share if they decrease a net profit or increase a net loss per share.

This is because potential ordinary shares are only included in the calculation of diluted earnings per share if they decrease a net profit or increase a net loss per share. Potential ordinary shares increase the denominator of the earnings per share calculation and therefore would decrease a loss per share. In these circumstances, potential ordinary shares are antidilutive and therefore excluded from the calculation.

There is one situation where a diluted loss per share could be different from the basic loss per share. FRS 14 requires that shares should be treated as dilutive when their conversion to ordinary shares would decrease net profit or increase net loss per share *from continuing operations*. A company might have an overall net loss that consisted of a profit on continuing operations and a significant loss on discontinued operations. In this case, potential ordinary shares could be brought into the calculation, because they would decrease the net profit per share from continuing operations.

7.9   Presentation

- Basic and diluted earnings per share should be presented on the face of the profit and loss account for each class of ordinary share.

- Basic and diluted earnings per share must be presented with equal prominence.

- Basic and diluted earnings per share should be presented even if the amounts are negative (i.e. a loss per share).

The following information should be disclosed for both basic and diluted earnings per share:

- the amounts used as numerators and a reconciliation of those amounts to the net profit or loss for the period

- the weighted average number of ordinary shares used as the denominator and a reconciliation of the denominators to each other.

If an alternative measure of earnings per share is disclosed this should be:

- calculated using the weighted average number of ordinary shares determined in accordance with FRS 14

- presented consistently over time

- reconciled to the amount required by FRS 14; the reconciliation must list the items for which an adjustment is being made and disclose their individual effect on the calculation

- not presented more prominently than the version required by FRS 14.

The reason for calculating the additional version should be explained.

The reconciliation and explanation should appear adjacent to the earnings per share disclosure, or a reference should be given to where they can be found.

Where ordinary share transactions or potential ordinary share transactions occur after the balance sheet date, a description of these should be disclosed where they are of such importance that non-disclosure would affect the ability of the users of the financial statements to make proper evaluations and decisions.

7.10 The usefulness of FRS 14

DEFINITION

PE ratio =

$$\frac{\text{Market value of share}}{\text{EPS}}$$

The 'earnings per share' (EPS) figure is used to compute the major stock market indicator of performance, the Price Earnings ratio (PE ratio).

Rightly or wrongly, the stock market places great emphasis on the earnings per share figure and the PE ratio. FRS 14 sets out a standard method of calculating EPS, which enhances the comparability of the figure.

However, EPS has limited usefulness as a performance measure. Many of these limitations are inherent in the calculation itself.

- An entity's earnings are affected by its choice of accounting policies. Therefore, it may not always be appropriate to compare the EPS of different companies.

- Where new shares are issued for cash or as consideration for an acquisition, FRS 14 requires the additional shares to be taken into account from the date of issue. In practice, it may be years before the additional capital begins to generate earnings. A new share issue is often accompanied by a decrease in EPS.

- EPS is not an appropriate measure of performance for a small owner-managed company. This is because earnings may be materially affected by policy decisions, for example as to the level of directors' remuneration.

- EPS does not take account of inflation. Apparent growth in earnings may not be true growth.

- EPS does not provide predictive value. High earnings and growth in earnings may be achieved at the expense of investment which would have generated increased earnings in the future.

- EPS cannot be used as a basis of comparison between companies as the number of shares in issue in any particular company is not related to the amount of capital employed. For example, two companies may have the same amount of capital employed, but one company has 100,000 £1 shares in issue and reserves of £4,900,000. Another company may have 5 million 50p shares in issue and reserves of £2,500,000. The same level of earnings will produce different EPS.

- EPS is based on historic information, yet it is used to calculate the PE ratio, which is a forward-looking figure.

- The diluted EPS (DEPS) is a theoretical measure of the effect of dilution on the basic EPS. There is no evidence to suggest that even the most sophisticated analysts use DEPS. This is because of its hypothetical nature.

  In theory, diluted EPS serves as a warning to equity shareholders that the return on their investment may fall in future periods. However, diluted EPS as currently required by FRS 14 is not intended to be forward-looking but is an additional past performance measure. For example, when calculating diluted EPS where there are warrants or options, fair value is based on the average price of an ordinary share for the period, rather than the market price at the period end. Therefore diluted EPS is only of limited use as a prediction of future EPS.

- EPS is a measure of profitability. Profitability is only one aspect of performance. Concentration on earnings per share and 'the bottom line' arguably detracts from other important aspects of an entity's affairs, for example, cash flow and stewardship of assets.

7.11 Earnings per share and FRS 3

The issue of FRS 3 had a significant impact on the usefulness of EPS.

Ever since FRS 3, EPS is computed on earnings after extraordinary items. This means that EPS is now much more volatile than previously and may fluctuate significantly from year to year, for example, following reorganisations or sales of property.

FRS 3 and FRS 14 permit companies to publish more than one EPS figure. This means that EPS can be calculated at different levels of profit.

The ASB believes that it is not possible to distil the performance of a complex organisation into a single measure. It wishes to shift the emphasis away from profit after tax and EPS and to encourage more analysis of the profit and loss account as a whole. The standard EPS figure is the starting point for this analysis.

In practice, many companies do publish an additional version of EPS.

The Institute of Investment Management and Research (IIMR) reacted to the issue of FRS 3 by developing their own alternative to the standard EPS. This is set out in SOIP 1 *The definition of IIMR headline earnings*. It suggested that the figure should be calculated as follows.

(a) Include:

- trading profits and losses (including exceptional items)
- interest
- trading results of acquired or discontinued operations as reported
- tax and minority interest adjustments.

(b) Exclude:

- profits and losses on sales and terminations
- provisions for exceptional items required to be disclosed on the face of the profit and loss account
- profits and losses on the sale of fixed assets
- exceptional profits and losses on the reorganisation or redemption of long-term debt
- any impact of goodwill
- pension cost impact of discontinuations
- extraordinary items (if any) net of tax.

The IIMR figure has now been widely adopted by financial institutions, including the *Financial Times* and Extel. It appears that, despite the efforts of the ASB, users of accounts still want to concentrate on a single measure of performance.

7.12 FRED 26 and IAS 33

FRS 14 was based on IAS 33, and so there are few changes to be made as part of the convergence project. The main change proposed in FRED 26 is the requirement to disclose basic and diluted EPS for both net profit (or loss) for the period **and** for profit (or loss) from continuing operations. This revision brings with it a complication. In the UK, continuing operations exclude discontinued activities (i.e. activities that stopped during the year, or within three months of the year-end). Under IAS 35, continuing operations exclude discontinuing operations (i.e. those that the management plan to dispose of in the foreseeable future). Therefore, the continuing EPS under IAS 33 will be more subjective than the UK version.

SELF-TEST QUESTIONS

Requirements of FRS 3

1 What is the objective of FRS 3? (1.1)

2 Define discontinued operations. (1.4)

Classification of items

3 When can a provision be made in respect of a sale or termination of a business? (2.3)

4 Why are extraordinary items now so rare? (2.6)

Other statements required

5 What is the purpose of the statement of total recognised gains and losses? (3.1)

Reporting financial performance: current developments

6   How is it proposed that FRS 3 will be amended? (4.2)

7   What three sections will be included in the proposed new statement of financial performance? (4.2)

8   Describe the proposed changes to the reporting of exceptional items. (4.4)

Earnings per share

9   What is the objective of FRS 14? (6.1)

10   What is the basic EPS calculation? (6.2)

Diluted earnings per share

11   How are diluted EPS calculated? (7.1)

12   What are contingently issuable shares? (7.6)

13   In what order should dilutive securities be included in the DEPS calculation? (7.7)

EXAM-TYPE
QUESTION **1**

NBS plc

NBS plc is the parent company of a manufacturing group with a wide range of products in its portfolio. You are the chief accountant of the parent company and your assistant has prepared the following draft consolidated profit and loss account for the year ended 31 October 20X7:

	£m
Turnover	2,678
Cost of sales	(1,673)
Gross profit	1,005
Other operating expenses	(361)
Operating profit	644
Abnormal profit on sale of property	100
Interest payable	(264)
Profit before taxation	480
Taxation	(140)
Profit after taxation	340
Minority interests	(61)
Profit for the year attributable to the group	279
Proposed dividends	(99)
Retained profit	180
Retained profit b/fwd	460
Retained profit c/fwd	640

The financial statements are due to be formally approved by the directors on 31 January 20X8.

Your assistant is unsure about the treatment of three transactions which have taken place during the year.

Required:

Write a memorandum to your assistant which explains how EACH of Transactions One to Three below should be treated in the consolidated accounts of NBS plc for the year to 31 October 20X7. Your memorandum should refer to the provision(s) of the relevant accounting standard(s) which support your explanations.

You do NOT need to produce the consolidated profit and loss account.

Transaction One

On 15 September 20X7, the directors of NBS plc decided to dispose of its shareholding in a subsidiary whose draft accounts for the year to 31 October 20X7 showed:

- Turnover   £380 million
- Cost of sales   £340 million
- Other operating expenses   £31 million

You further ascertain that the business of the subsidiary which is being disposed of is not carried on by the rest of the group. The disposal is expected to take place on 31 December 20X7 at a loss of £50 million. No provision has been made for this loss in the draft accounts.   **(10 marks)**

Transaction Two

During the year the group undertook a fundamental restructuring of part of its operations. The cash costs incurred by the group were £28 million. The costs were debited to a suspense account as the assistant was not sure how to treat them.

Upon investigating the situation further, you ascertain that the restructuring operation revealed a number of old sales ledger balances totalling £8 million which must now be regarded as bad debts, and obsolete stock which had cost £5 million to manufacture but should now be scrapped. The bad debts and obsolete stock have not yet been adjusted in the accounts.

Transaction Three

During the year the group disposed of a large number of properties which it had been using for warehouse premises. The disposals were made following a decision to reduce stockholding periods, and therefore storage requirements. The profit on sale of these properties, which is included in the draft accounts, is made up as follows:

	£m
Difference between sales proceeds and written-down value	40
Revaluation surpluses now treated as realised	60
	100

(5 marks)

(Total: 20 marks)

Pilum

Draft profit and loss account for the year ended 31 December 20X4

	£	£
Profit before tax		2,438,000
Less: Taxation		
Corporation tax	1,035,000	
Under-provision for 20X3	23,000	
		1,058,000
		1,380,000
Less: Transfer to reserves	115,000	
Dividends		
Paid – Preference interim dividend	138,000	
Paid – Ordinary interim dividend	184,000	
Proposed – Preference final dividend	138,000	
Proposed – Ordinary final dividend	230,000	
		805,000
Retained		575,000

On 1 January 20X4 the issued share capital of Pilum plc was 4,600,000 6% preference shares of £1 each and 4,140,000 ordinary shares of £1 each.

You are required to calculate the earnings per share (on basic and diluted bases) in respect of the year ended 31 December 20X4 for each of the following circumstances. (Each of the five circumstances (a) to (e) is to be dealt with separately.)

(a) On the basis that there was no change in the issued share capital of the company during the year ended 31 December 20X4. **(5 marks)**

(b) On the basis that the company made a bonus issue on 1 October 20X4 of one ordinary share for every four shares in issue at 30 September 20X4. **(5 marks)**

(c) On the basis that the company made a rights issue of £1 ordinary shares on 1 October 20X4 in the proportion of 1 for every 5 shares held, at a price of £1.20. The middle market price for the shares on the last day of quotation cum rights was £1.80 per share. **(5 marks)**

On the basis that the company made no new issue of shares during the year ended 31 December 20X4, but on that date it had in issue £1,150,000 10% convertible loan stock 20X6 to 20X9. This loan stock will be convertible into ordinary £1 shares as follows:

20X6	90	£1	shares for £100 nominal value loan stock
20X7	85	£1	shares for £100 nominal value loan stock
20X8	80	£1	shares for £100 nominal value loan stock
20X9	75	£1	shares for £100 nominal value loan stock

(5 marks)

(d) On the basis that the company made no issue of shares during the year ended 31 December 20X4, but on that date there were outstanding options to purchase 460,000 ordinary £1 shares at £1.70 per share. The fair value of ordinary £1 shares was £2.00 per share throughout the year.

Assume where appropriate that the corporation tax rate is 50%. **(5 marks)**

(Total: 25 marks)

For the answers to these questions see the 'Answers' section at the end of the book.

(a) This situation meets three of the four criteria laid down by FRS 3 but fails to meet the timing restriction. FRS 3 states that the sale should be completed before the earlier of three months after commencement of the subsequent period and the date on which the financial statements are approved.

(b) This would not be treated as a discontinued operation as the activities have not ceased permanently. The purpose of this decision is to reduce productive capacity temporarily until there is an upturn in the market.

(c) This situation appears to meet the FRS 3 criteria for discontinued operations except that the loss of this part of the business will have no material effect on the operations of Z plc. Therefore it will not be treated as a discontinued operation.

(The size of the profit arising on the sale is not taken into account in the FRS 3 criteria.)

Basic EPS = (50,000 × 100)/1,000,000 = 5p

Diluted EPS:

	Net profit attributable £	Ordinary shares	Earnings per share
Basic earnings per share	50,000	1,000,000	5p
Options (500,000 x 0.5/2.50)	–	100,000	
	50,000	1,100,000	4.5p
12% convertible debentures			
(120,000 x 3/12 x 60%)	18,000		
(600,000 x 3/12)		150,000	
	68,000	1,250,000	5.4p

The convertible debentures are antidilutive and are therefore ignored. The diluted EPS is 4.5p.

(Note that options or warrants must be considered first, because they have no effect on earnings and are therefore always the most dilutive share issue.)

Chapter 19

POST BALANCE SHEET EVENTS, PROVISIONS AND CONTINGENCIES

This chapter looks at two accounting standards: SSAP 17 *Accounting for post balance sheet events* and FRS 12 *Provisions, contingent liabilities and contingent assets.*

You should already be able to apply the requirements of both these standards to practical situations. As well as revising the basic rules, we look at some of the problem areas. FRS 12 is a particularly important standard. It has been heavily based on the ideas in the Statement of Principles and it has also been very controversial.

Objectives

When you have studied this chapter you should be able to:

- understand the problems of accounting for post balance sheet events
- understand the issues relating to recognition and measurement of provisions
- explain the use of restructuring provisions and other provisions
- understand the problems with current standards on provisions and contingencies.

1 The requirements of SSAP 17

1.1 SSAP 17 *Accounting for post balance sheet events*

There are two types of post balance sheet event: adjusting and non-adjusting events.

1.2 Adjusting events

These events provide additional evidence on conditions existing at the balance sheet date. For example, bad debts arising one or two months after the balance sheet date may help to quantify the bad debt provision as at the balance sheet date. Adjusting events may, therefore, affect the amount at which items are stated in the balance sheet.

Examples include the following:

- provisions for stock and bad debts
- amounts received or receivable in respect of insurance claims which were being negotiated at the balance sheet date
- certain special items occurring after the balance sheet date which, for various reasons, are reflected in the current year's financial statements

  (a) proposed dividends

  (b) appropriations to reserves

  (c) dividends receivable from subsidiary companies.

DEFINITION

Post balance sheet events are those events, both favourable and unfavourable, which occur between the balance sheet date and the date on which the financial statements are approved by the board of directors.

DEFINITION

Adjusting events are post balance sheet events which provide additional evidence of conditions existing at the balance sheet date.

1.3 Non-adjusting events

These are events arising after the balance sheet date but which, unlike those events above, do **not** concern conditions existing at the balance sheet date. Such events will not, therefore, have any effect on items in the balance sheet or profit and loss account. However, in order to prevent the financial statements from presenting a misleading position, some form of additional disclosure is required if the events are material, say by way of memorandum note or pro forma consolidated balance sheet indicating what effect the events would have had on the year end balance sheet.

Examples of non-adjusting events include the following:

- the issue of new share or loan capital

- major changes in the composition of the business (for example, acquisitions of new businesses)

- financial consequences of losses of fixed assets or stock as a result of fires or floods.

1.4 Standard accounting practice – SSAP 17

SSAP 17 *Accounting for post balance sheet events* requires that:

'Financial statements should be prepared on the basis of conditions existing at the balance sheet date.

A material post balance sheet event requires changes in the amounts to be included in financial statements where:

- it is an adjusting event; or

- it indicates that application of the going concern concept to the whole or a material part of the company is not appropriate.

A material post balance sheet event should be disclosed where:

- it is a non-adjusting event of such materiality that its non-disclosure would affect the ability of the users of financial statements to reach a proper understanding of the financial position; or

- it is the reversal or maturity after the year end of a transaction entered into before the year end, the substance of which was primarily to alter the appearance of the company's balance sheet.

In respect of each post balance sheet event which is required to be disclosed the following information should be stated by way of notes in financial statements:

- the nature of the event; and

- an estimate of the financial effect, or a statement that it is not practicable to make such an estimate.

The estimate of the financial effect should be disclosed before taking account of taxation, and the taxation implications should be explained where necessary for a proper understanding of the financial position.

The date on which the financial statements are approved by the board of directors should be disclosed in the financial statements.'   *Paras 21 – 26 SSAP 17*

1.5   Companies Act 1985

Para 6 Sch 7 CA85 requires the directors' report to contain:

- particulars of any important events affecting the company or any of its subsidiaries which have occurred since the end of the year

- an indication of likely future developments in the business of the company and of its subsidiaries.

1.6   Reclassification

The Appendix to SSAP 17 states that, in exceptional circumstances, to accord with the prudence concept, an adverse event which would normally be classified as non-adjusting may need to be reclassified as adjusting. Full disclosure of the adjustment is required in these circumstances.

The Appendix does not provide any guidance as to the circumstances under which an event should be reclassified. As this provision is in the Appendix, rather than the standard itself, it has limited force.

One commentator has suggested that events should only be reclassified when the loss due to the post balance sheet event is of such magnitude that the financial statements would be misleading if they were not adjusted.

Otherwise, full disclosure of the event should be adequate to enable users of the financial statements to evaluate its effect. If a non-adjusting event is particularly significant, the disclosures could include pro-forma financial data showing the effect on the financial statements as if the event had occurred on the balance sheet date.

1.7   Window dressing

DEFINITION

Window dressing is the practice of entering into certain transactions before the year end and reversing those transactions after the year end.

If a company has engaged in window dressing, then no real transaction has occurred (i.e. no substance, only legal form) but the balance sheet reflects the transaction (as it primarily records the legal form of assets and liabilities). The hoped-for effect is to improve the appearance of the balance sheet.

SSAP 17 requires a disclosure of such transactions if they are material. They are not, however, adjusting events.

Example

UK plc is concerned that it has over-lent to customers in the year to 31 December 20X8 and that its liquid assets to total assets ratio is too low. It thus arranges a loan of £40 million from another company in December. The loan is repaid in January.

	(a) £m	(b) £m
Liquid assets	10	50
Investments:		
Advances to customers	200	200
Fixed assets	20	20
Less: Creditors – amounts falling due within one year	(10)	(50)
Total assets less current liabilities	220	220

$$\frac{\text{Liquid assets}}{\text{Total assets less current liabilities}} \qquad \frac{10}{220} \times 100 \qquad \frac{50}{220} \times 100$$

$$= 5\% \qquad = 23\%$$

(a) refers to the balance sheet if the transaction had not been entered into

(b) shows the actual balance sheet at the year end.

Clearly (b) looks better if an accepted measure of security/solvency is a 'liquidity' ratio such as calculated above.

One problem is that 'window dressing' can include both:

(a) the fraudulent falsification of the accounts to make things look better than they are

(b) the lawful arrangement of affairs over the year end to make things look different from the way they usually are.

At the time that SSAP 17 was originally issued, the ASC stated that deliberate falsification of the accounts was clearly unacceptable and not a subject for an accounting standard. This suggests that 'window dressing' has the meaning in (b) above.

It has been suggested that this definition of 'window dressing' is flawed. Many companies deliberately (and legitimately) choose a year end when stock levels are at their lowest, often for practical reasons. SSAP 17 could be interpreted as suggesting that the balance sheet should reflect the typical position throughout the year, rather than at the year-end.

It could also be argued that artificial transactions should be adjusted, rather than merely disclosed, following the logic of FRS 5.

1.8   Other problem areas with SSAP 17

These mainly arise from the need to determine whether an event is adjusting or non-adjusting, in other words, whether or not it took place before the balance sheet date or whether or not it provides evidence of conditions existing at the balance sheet date.

Suppose that a fixed asset is valued shortly after the year end. This reveals a significant fall in value. Although the valuation took place after the balance sheet date, it is probably reasonable to assume that the fall in value occurred over a period of several months beforehand. However, there may be sufficient evidence to show the fall occurred after the year end, in which case it is a non-adjusting event.

The following points are relevant.

- **Disposals of fixed assets after the balance sheet date**

  These are generally treated as non-adjusting events if they were not contemplated at the balance sheet date. However, a large loss on disposal indicates that the asset might have become impaired before the balance sheet date. An impairment review should be carried out and the financial statements adjusted if necessary.

- **Sale or termination of an operation after the balance sheet date**

  FRS 3 states that provisions for losses on disposal of operations cannot be set up until the entity is demonstrably committed to the sale. This suggests that no provisions can be made unless a binding sale agreement has been entered into before the balance sheet date. However, FRS 3 also suggests that a contract entered into after the balance sheet date may provide evidence of commitments at the balance sheet date. This can be interpreted as meaning that if there is a demonstrable commitment to sell and a binding sale agreement is entered into before the accounts are signed, a provision can be set up (i.e. the loss may be treated as an adjusting event).

FRS 12 (discussed next) only allows provisions to be made where there is an obligation at the balance sheet date as a result of a past event. No obligation can exist unless there is a binding sale contract at the balance sheet date. However, FRS 3 has not been amended as a result of the issue of FRS 12 and so the situation is unclear.

1.9　FRED 27

FRED 27 proposes that SSAP 17 should be replaced by the revised IAS 10 "Events after the Balance Sheet Date". The main change will be a stricter definition of the term "adjusting event". A liability will only be recognised if an obligation exists at the balance sheet date. Therefore dividends on equity shares proposed after the year-end will no longer be recognised in the balance sheet. (Currently, the Companies Act requires proposed dividends to be treated as liabilities. The Act will have to be amended to allow this, and some other IAS requirements, to be adopted.)

2　FRS 12 *Provisions, contingent liabilities and contingent assets*

2.1　The problem

DEFINITION

A **provision** is a liability of uncertain timing or amount. This definition means that provisions are a sub-class of liabilities.

A **liability** is an obligation to transfer economic benefits as a result of past transactions or events. Uncertainty is what distinguishes a provision from another type of liability (such as a trade creditor or an accrued expense).

Provisions may be made for items such as environmental liabilities, reorganisation costs, litigation and future losses. Although FRS 3 (discontinued operations), FRS 7 (reorganisation costs and future losses) and SSAP 18 (contingencies) partly addressed the problem, there was no accounting standard covering the general topic of provisions.

This led to various problems as follows:

- Provisions were often recognised as a result of an intention to make expenditure, rather than as an obligation to do so.

- Several items were aggregated into one large provision that was reported as an exceptional item (the 'big bath').

- Inadequate disclosure meant that in some cases it was difficult to ascertain the significance of the provisions and any movements in the year.

FRS 12 has been issued to prevent abuses and to ensure that users of the financial statements are provided with sufficient information to understand the nature, timing and amount of provisions.

Note that the FRS 12 definition is narrower than the Companies Act definition. The Companies Act defines provisions as 'amounts retained as reasonably necessary to cover any liability or loss which is either likely or certain to be incurred'. For a provision to be recognised under FRS 12 there must be an obligation to incur expenditure.

Although 'provisions' are often made for items such as depreciation and doubtful debts, these are not provisions within the meaning in FRS 12, but normal accounting estimates.

DEFINITIONS

A **contingent liability** is:

* a possible obligation that arises from past events and whose existence will be confirmed only by the occurrence of one or more uncertain future events not wholly within the entity's control; or

* a present obligation that arises from past events but is not recognised because:
  (i) it is not probable that a transfer of economic benefits will be required to settle the obligation; or
  (ii) the amount of the obligation cannot be measured with sufficient reliability.

A **contingent asset** is a possible asset that arises from past events and whose existence will be confirmed only by the occurrence of one or more uncertain future events not wholly within the entity's control.

DEFINITIONS

A **legal obligation** is an obligation that derives from:
* a contract
* legislation
* other operation of law.

A **constructive obligation** is an obligation that derives from an entity's actions where:

* by an established pattern of past practice, published policies or a sufficiently specific current statement, the entity has indicated to other parties that it will accept certain responsibilities; and

* as a result, the entity has created a valid expectation on the part of those other parties that it will discharge those responsibilities.

2.2 Contingent liabilities and contingent assets

A **contingent liability** is a possible or actual obligation that does not meet the recognition criteria in the Statement of Principles to be recognised in the balance sheet as an actual liability.

A **contingent asset** is a possible asset that arises from past events and whose existence will be confirmed only by the occurrence of one or more uncertain future events not wholly within the entity's control.

2.3 Recognition of provisions

A provision should only be recognised when:

* an entity has a present obligation (legal or constructive) as a result of a past event

* it is probable that a transfer of economic benefits will be required to settle the obligation

* a reliable estimate can be made of the amount of the obligation.

FRS 12 explains the following points.

* A past event gives rise to a present obligation if, taking account of all available evidence, it is more likely than not that a present obligation exists at the balance sheet date.

* A transfer of economic benefits is regarded as probable if it is more likely than not to occur.

* Where there are a number of similar obligations (e.g. product warranties) the probability that a transfer will be required in settlement is determined by considering the class of obligations as a whole. For example, if an entity guarantees to refund the cost of faulty goods, the chance of having to make a refund in respect of one specific item is extremely small, but the entity will almost certainly need to make some refunds in respect of its goods as a whole.

* Only in extremely rare cases will it not be possible to make a reliable estimate of the obligation. If it is not possible to make a reliable estimate, the item is disclosed as a contingent liability.

2.4 Recognition of contingent liabilities

Contingent liabilities should not be recognised. They should be disclosed unless the possibility of a transfer of economic benefits is remote.

2.5 Recognition of contingent assets

Contingent assets should not be recognised. (Recognition of contingent assets could result in the recognition of profit that may never be realised.) If the possibility of an inflow of economic benefits is probable they should be disclosed.

How should the following items be treated in the financial statements?

(a) A manufacturer gives warranties at the time of sale to purchasers of its product. Under the terms of the contract for sale the manufacturer undertakes to make good manufacturing defects that become apparent within three years from the date of sale. On past experience it is probable that there will be some claims under the warranties.

(b) A retail store has a policy of refunding purchases by dissatisfied customers, even though there is no legal obligation to do so. Its policy of making refunds is generally known.

(c) During 20X5 A gives a guarantee of certain borrowings of B, whose financial condition at that time is sound.

(d) A furnace has a lining that needs to be replaced every five years for technical reasons. At the balance sheet date, the lining has been in use for three years.

(e) New laws have been passed that require an entity to fit smoke filters to its factories by 30 June 20X6. At 31 December 20X5 (the balance sheet date) the entity has not yet fitted the smoke filters.

Feedback to this activity is at the end of the chapter.

2.6   Measurement

General rules on measurement are as follows:

KEY POINT

The amount recognised as a provision should be the best estimate of the expenditure required to settle the present obligation at the balance sheet date.

- The amount recognised as a provision should be the best estimate of the expenditure required to settle the present obligation at the balance sheet date. (This is the amount that an entity would pay to settle the obligation at the balance sheet date or to persuade a third party to assume it.)

- In measuring a provision, an entity should take into account:

  (a)   the risks and uncertainties surrounding the event (but uncertainty does not justify the creation of excessive provisions or overstatement of liabilities)

  (b)   future events (e.g. technological developments) where there is sufficient objective evidence that they will occur.

KEY POINT

Where the effect of the time value of money is material, the amount of a provision should be discounted.

- Where the effect of the time value of money is material (for example, where a liability will be settled in several years' time), the amount of a provision should be discounted. The rate used should be a pre-tax rate that reflects current market assessments of the time value of money and the risk specific to the liability. The discount rate should not reflect risks for which future cash flow estimates have been adjusted.

- Gains from the expected disposal of assets should not be taken into account in measuring a provision, even if the disposal is linked to the event giving rise to the provision (for example, where assets are sold when a division is closed down).

- Provisions should be reviewed at each balance sheet date and adjusted to reflect the current best estimate. They should be reversed if the transfer of economic benefits is no longer probable.

- A provision should only be used for expenditures for which it was originally recognised. (This requirement effectively prevents entities from using 'big bath accounting'.)

Reimbursements

- A reimbursement should be recognised only when it is virtually certain to be received.

- The reimbursement should be treated as a separate asset (i.e. it should not be netted off against the provision to which it relates).

- In the profit and loss account, the expense relating to a provision may be presented net of the income recognised for a reimbursement.

Methods of dealing with uncertainties

These include:

- weighting the cost of all probable outcomes according to their probabilities ('expected value')

- considering a range of possible outcomes.

Example – expected value

An entity sells goods with a warranty covering customers for the cost of repairs of any defects that are discovered within the first two months after purchase. Past experience suggests that 90% of the goods sold will have no defects, 5% will have minor defects and 5% will have major defects. If minor defects were detected in all products sold, the cost of repairs would be £10,000; if major defects were detected in all products sold, the cost would be £100,000.

The expected value of the cost of repairs is £5,500 ((5% × 10,000) + (5% × 100,000)).

Example – possible outcomes

An entity has to rectify a serious fault in an item of plant that it has constructed for a customer.

In this case, the most likely outcome is that the repair will succeed at the first attempt at a cost of £400,000, but a provision for £500,000 is recognised because there is a significant chance that a further attempt will be necessary.

The most likely outcome may be the best estimate of the liability, but other possible outcomes must be considered. Where other possible outcomes are either mostly higher or mostly lower than the most likely outcome, the best estimate will be a higher or lower amount.

2.7 Disclosure of provisions

For each class of provision, disclose:

- carrying amount at the beginning and end of the period
- additional provisions made in the period
- amounts used during the period
- unused amounts reversed during the period
- effect of discounting during the period
- a brief description of the nature of the obligation and expected timing of any resulting transfers of economic benefit
- an indication of the uncertainties about the amount or timing of those transfers of economic benefit
- the amount of any expected reimbursement.

2.8 Disclosure of contingent liabilities

For each class of contingent liability (unless remote) disclose:

- an estimate of its financial effect
- an indication of the uncertainties relating to the amount or timing of any outflow
- the possibility of any reimbursement.

2.9 Disclosure of contingent assets

For contingent assets (only where probable) disclose:

- a brief description of their nature
- where practicable, an estimate of their financial effect.

2.10 Prejudicial information

In extremely rare cases, some of the above disclosures may prejudice an entity in a dispute with other parties about the subject of the provision or contingency. If this is the case, the entity need not disclose the information, unless it is required by law, but should disclose the general nature of the dispute, together with the fact that, and reason why, the information has not been disclosed.

2.11 Unwinding of discounts

KEY POINT

Unwinding of the discount is similar to interest because it relates to the time value of money.

Where a provision is discounted, its present value increases as time passes. This means that the provision has to be increased accordingly and the profit and loss account charged with the expense. This expense is called 'unwinding of the discount' and should be included in the profit and loss account as a financial item adjacent to interest (i.e. below operating profit). It should be shown separately from other interest either on the face of the profit and loss account or in a note. The reasoning behind this is that unwinding of the discount is similar to interest because it relates to the time value of money, but it is not 'true' interest.

3 Applying FRS 12 to practical situations

3.1 Future operating losses

KEY POINT

Provisions should not be recognised for future operating losses.

Provisions should not be recognised for future operating losses.

However, note that FRS 12 only covers provisions which are not covered by another accounting standard. This means that there are still situations in which entities are required to make provisions for future losses (e.g. discontinued operations (FRS 3), foreseeable losses on long-term contracts (SSAP 9)).

3.2 Onerous contracts

DEFINITION

An **onerous contract** is a contract in which the unavoidable costs of meeting the obligation exceed the economic benefits expected to be received under it.

An example: a lease contract for a property that is no longer required and where the lease cannot be cancelled.

If an entity has an onerous contract, a provision should be recognised for the present obligation under the contract (for example, for the best estimate of unavoidable lease payments).

3.3   Restructuring

Examples of restructuring are as follows:

- sale or termination of a line of business

- the closure of business locations in a country or region or the relocation of business activities from one country or region to another

- changes in management structure, for example, eliminating a layer of management

- fundamental reorganisations that have a material effect on the nature and focus of the entity's operations.

When does an entity have an obligation to restructure?

Provisions for restructuring costs can only be recognised where an entity has a constructive obligation to carry out the restructuring. A Board decision on its own is not sufficient to create an obligation.

This requirement is designed to prevent entities from recognising provisions where there is only an intention to restructure and also from making unnecessary provisions which can then be used to enhance profits artificially in subsequent periods. However, critics of the ASB have argued that in practice most Boards of Directors do not take decisions to restructure lightly.

A constructive obligation to restructure arises only when the entity:

(a) has a detailed formal plan for the restructuring, identifying at least:

- the business or part of the business concerned

- the principal locations affected

- the location, function, and approximate number of employees who will be compensated for terminating their services

- the expenditures that will be undertaken

- when the plan will be implemented; and

(b) has raised a valid expectation in those affected that it will carry out the restructuring by starting to implement the plan or announcing its main features to those affected by it.

For an entity to have an obligation to sell an operation there must be a binding sale agreement.

Expenses of restructuring

A restructuring provision should include only the direct expenditures arising from the restructuring, which are those that are both:

- necessarily entailed by the restructuring

- not associated with the ongoing activities of the entity.

The provision should not include costs that relate to the future conduct of the business such as the cost of:

- retraining or relocating staff who will continue with the business

- marketing

- investment in new systems and distribution networks.

On 1 December 20X8 the board of an entity decided to close down a division on 31 March 20X9. On 31 January 20X9 a detailed plan for closing down the division was agreed, letters were sent to customers informing them of the decision and redundancy notices were sent to the staff of the division.

Should a provision be recognised in the accounts for the year ended 31 December 20X8?

Feedback to this activity is at the end of the chapter.

3.4 Future environmental costs

Future environmental costs are treated according to the normal rules. FRS 12 states that the fact that the entity's activities have caused environmental contamination does not in itself give rise to an obligation to rectify the damage.

The obligation must arise from a past event. This means that a provision can only be set up to rectify environmental damage that has already happened. If an entity needs to incur expenditure to reduce pollution in the future it does not set up a provision. This is because in theory it can avoid the expenditure by its future actions, for example, it could discontinue the particular activity that causes the pollution.

(a) An entity causes contamination but cleans up only when required to do so under the laws of the particular country in which it operates. One country in which it operates has had no legislation requiring cleaning up, and the entity has been contaminating land in that country for several years. At the balance sheet date it is virtually certain that a draft law requiring a clean-up of land already contaminated will be enacted shortly after the year end.

(b) An entity has constructed an oil rig. Under the terms of its licensing agreement it must remove the oil rig at the end of production and restore the seabed. Ninety per cent of the eventual costs of undertaking this work relate to the removal of the oil rig and restoration of the damage caused by building it, and ten per cent will arise through the extraction of oil. At the balance sheet date, no oil has yet been extracted.

State whether a provision should be recognised in each case.

Feedback to this activity is at the end of the chapter.

KEY POINT

When a provision is recognised, an asset should only be recognised when the expenditure provides access to future economic benefits.

3.5 Recognising an asset when recognising a provision

When a provision or change in a provision is recognised, an asset should only be recognised when the expenditure provides access to future economic benefits, otherwise the setting up of the provision should be charged immediately to the profit and loss account.

FRS 12 gives the following example:

'When an oil rig is commissioned, an obligation for decommissioning costs is incurred. The commissioning also gives access to oil reserves over the years of the oil rig's operation. Therefore an asset representing future access to oil reserves is recognised at the same time as the provision for decommissioning costs (i.e. the double entry is Debit Assets, Credit Provisions rather than Debit Profit and loss account, Credit Provisions).'

Sphere plc has built a nuclear power station which is due to become operational on 1 January 20X1. It is estimated that the cost of decommissioning the power station will be £10 million and that decommissioning will take place in fifteen years' time. The risk free cost of capital for the company is 10%. The nuclear power station is depreciated on a straight line basis over its useful economic life of 15 years, starting from 1 January 20X1. Depreciation is based on the cost of the asset at 31 December each year. Sphere plc has recently won an award for the best environmental report published during the year.

State how the cost of decommissioning the power station should be treated in the financial statements for the years ended 31 December 20X0 and 31 December 20X1.

Feedback to this activity is at the end of the chapter.

4   Problem areas with FRS 12

4.1   Definition of contingent liability

The definition of a contingent liability gives particular problems.

'Possible' is not defined. However, FRS 12 says that 'probable' means more likely than not. Because probable means 'more than 50% probable' it is reasonable to assume that 'possible' means 'less than 50% probable'.

A contingent liability is therefore a liability whose existence is less than 50% probable or where the probability of a transfer of economic benefits is less than 50%.

It has been suggested that this definition is flawed because it ignores the meaning of the word contingent. A contingent liability is a liability that is contingent on a future event. This meaning extends beyond the FRS 12 definition as the existence of a contingent liability could be more than 50% probable. In practice probable contingent liabilities are treated as provisions.

4.2   'Virtually certain' and 'remote'

Contingent assets should be recognised if they are virtually certain and contingent liabilities should not be disclosed if they are remote. There is no definition of 'virtually certain' or 'remote'. It is reasonable to assume that 'virtually certain' means more than 95% probable and 'remote' means less than 5% probable.

4.3   Identifying the obligating event

Where an entity has an obligation, particularly if this is a constructive obligation, it is sometimes difficult to identify an obligating event.

The practical examples in FRS 12 illustrate the requirement that obligations from past events must exist independently of an entity's future actions. For example, in Activity 1(d), no provision could be recognised because the entity had an alternative to incurring the expenditure – it could stop operating the furnace.

The entity does not need to know to whom an obligation is owed as it might be owed to the general public (as in the case of a constructive obligation to rectify environmental damage). However, there must be another party for an obligation to exist. For example, a Board decision does not give rise to a constructive obligation unless it is communicated in sufficient detail to those affected by it (for example, in a restructuring or re-organisation).

4.4   Discounting

Where the effect of the time value of money is material, the provision should be discounted to its present value. In practice, discounting is only likely to be required where cash flows will occur in several years time (for example, in the case of a decommissioning provision).

FRS 12 states that a pre-tax rate that reflects current market assessments of the time value of money and the risk specific to the liability should be used.

There are a number of problems connected with discounting.

- There is a choice of discount rates.

  (a) Where future cash flows are expressed in current prices, a real discount rate (which excludes the effect of general inflation) should be used.

  (b) Where future cash flows are expressed in expected future prices, a nominal discount rate (which includes a return to cover expected inflation) should be used.

- FRS 12 suggests that using a discount rate that reflects the risk associated with the liability (a risk adjusted rate) may be the easiest way of reflecting risk. It gives no guidance on how to calculate a risk adjusted rate. However, it does say that cash flows themselves can be adjusted for risk and then discounted using a risk free rate, such as a government bond rate.

- The discount rate should reflect current market assessments of the time value of money. This appears to mean that when interest rates change, the provision should be recalculated and the interest charge adjusted in the period of change. It has been suggested that this may distort the profit and loss account, depending on the materiality of the adjustment and the direction in which interest rates move.

SELF-TEST QUESTIONS

The requirements of SSAP 17

1   Distinguish between adjusting and non-adjusting events. (1.2, 1.3)

2   Are window dressing transactions adjusting events? (1.7)

3   What are the weaknesses of SSAP 17? (1.8)

FRS 12 *Provisions, contingent liabilities and contingent assets*

4   What is the FRS 12 definition of a contingent liability? (2.2)

5   When should (a) a provision, (b) a contingent liability and (c) a contingent asset be recognised in the balance sheet? (2.3, 2.4, 2.5)

6   How can uncertainties in measuring provisions be dealt with? (2.6)

Applying FRS 12 to practical situations

7   What is an 'onerous contract' and how does FRS 12 say it should be accounted for? (3.2)

8   When should a provision for restructuring expenses be recognised? (3.3)

Problem areas with FRS 12

9   What are the problem areas in FRS 12? (4)

Rowsley plc

Rowsley plc is a diverse group with many subsidiaries. The group is proud of its reputation as a 'caring' organisation and has adopted various ethical policies towards its employees and the wider community in which it operates. As part of its Annual Report, the group publishes details of its environmental policies, which include setting performance targets for activities such as recycling, controlling emissions of noxious substances and limiting use of non-renewable resources.

The finance director is reviewing the accounting treatment of various items prior to the signing of the accounts for the year ended 31 March 20X5. All four items are material in the context of the accounts as a whole. The accounts are to be approved by the directors on 30 June 20X5.

(1)   On 15 February 20X5 the board of Rowsley plc decided to close down a large factory in Derby. The board is trying to draw up a plan to manage the effects of the reorganisation, and it is envisaged that production will be transferred to other factories, mainly in Wales. The factory will be closed on 31 August 20X5, but at 31 March this decision had not yet been announced to the employees or to any other interested parties. Costs of the reorganisation have been estimated at £45 million.   **(6 marks)**

(2)   During December 20X4 one of the subsidiary companies moved from Buckingham to Sunderland in order to take advantage of regional development grants. It holds its main premises in Buckingham under an operating lease, which runs until 31 March 20X7. Annual rentals under the lease are £10 million. The company is unable to cancel the lease, but it has let some of the premises to a charitable organisation at a nominal rent. The company is attempting to rent the remainder of the premises at a commercial rent, but the directors have been advised that the chances of achieving this are less than 50%.   **(6 marks)**

(3)   During the year to 31 March 20X5, a customer started legal proceedings against the group, claiming that one of the food products that it manufactures had caused several members of his family to become seriously ill. The group's lawyers have advised that this action will probably not succeed.   **(3 marks)**

(4)   The group has an overseas subsidiary that is involved in mining precious metals. These activities cause significant damage to the environment, including deforestation. The company expects to abandon the mine in eight years time. The mine is situated in a country where there is no environmental legislation obliging companies to rectify environmental damage and it is very unlikely that any such legislation will be enacted within the next eight years. It has been estimated that the cost of cleaning the site and re-planting the trees will be £25 million if the re-planting were successful at the first attempt, but it will probably be necessary to make a further attempt, which will increase the cost by a further £5 million.**(5 marks)**

Required:

Explain how each of the items (1) to (4) above should be treated in the consolidated accounts for the year ended 31 March 20X5.   **(Total: 20 marks)**

For the answer to this question see the 'Answers' section at the end of the book.

FEEDBACK TO ACTIVITY 1

These items are taken from the Appendix to FRS 12. For each of the items, ask two questions.

(i)   Is there a present obligation as the result of a past event?

(ii) Is a transfer of economic benefits in settlement probable?

A provision is recognised if the answer to both questions is yes.

(a) Present obligation? Yes. The past (obligating) event is the sale of the product, which gives rise to a legal obligation (under the contract).

Transfer of benefits probable? Yes. There will probably be claims for the warranties as a whole.

Conclusion – Recognise a provision.

(b) Present obligation? Yes. The past event is the sale of the product, which gives rise to a constructive obligation.

Transfer of benefits probable? Yes.

Conclusion – Recognise a provision.

(c) Present obligation? Yes. The giving of the guarantee has given rise to a legal obligation.

Transfer of benefits probable? No.

Conclusion – Do not recognise a provision. Disclose the guarantee as a contingent liability unless the probability of having to honour it is remote.

(d) Present obligation? – No. No obligation exists independently of the entity's future actions. There is a realistic alternative to incurring the expenditure – the entity could decide not to continue operating the furnace.

Conclusion – Do not recognise a provision. Instead, the cost of the furnace lining should be capitalised and depreciated over five years.

(e) Present obligation? – No. The obligating event would be either the fitting of the filters (which has not happened) or the illegal operation of the factory without the filters (which has not happened because the filters are not yet legally required).

Conclusion – Do not recognise a provision.

FEEDBACK TO ACTIVITY 2

No provision should be recognised. There was no present obligation at the balance sheet date. The obligating event is the announcement of the plan, which creates a constructive obligation. This did not take place until after the balance sheet date.

FEEDBACK TO ACTIVITY 3

As usual, for each of the items, ask two questions:

(a) Is there a present obligation as the result of a past event?

(b) Is a transfer of economic benefits probable as a result?

Recognise a provision if the answer to both questions is yes. In the absence of information to the contrary, it is assumed that any future costs can be estimated reliably.

(a) Present obligation? Yes. Because the new legislation is virtually certain to be enacted the contamination of the land is the past event that gives rise to a present obligation.

Transfer of economic benefits probable? Yes.

Conclusion – Recognise a provision.

(b) Present obligation? Yes. There is a legal obligation to remove the rig and restore the seabed. However, there is no obligation to rectify any damage caused by extraction of the oil, because no oil has yet been extracted.

Transfer of economic benefits probable? Yes.

Conclusion – Recognise a provision for the best estimate of the eventual costs of decommissioning the oil rig. Do not recognise a provision for the cost of cleaning up damage caused by extraction of the oil.

FEEDBACK TO ACTIVITY 4

Although there is no mention of laws requiring decommissioning it is clear that Sphere plc has a constructive obligation to do so. The obligating event (construction of the power station) has taken place and the transfer of economic benefits is certain. Commissioning the power station also gives rights to future economic benefits in the form of the ability to make profits from generating electricity. Therefore the decommissioning costs are part of the cost of constructing the power station and can be capitalised.

Year ended 31 December 20X0

Sphere plc should recognise a provision of £2.39 million (10 × 0.239) for the decommissioning costs in its balance sheet at 31 December 20X0. It should also recognise an asset for the same amount. No depreciation is charged as the power station is not yet operating.

Year ended 31 December 20X1

At 31 December 20X1 the provision for decommissioning costs increases to £2.63 million (10 × 0.263) and this results in a charge of £240,000 to the profit and loss account, representing the unwinding of the discount.

Depreciation of £159,000 (2.39 ÷ 15) is charged to the profit and loss account.

Chapter 20
RELATED PARTIES AND SHARE-BASED PAYMENT

This chapter focuses on two areas relating to a company's relationships and transactions with its directors and employees.

You should already be familiar with the requirements of FRS 8 *Related party disclosures*. We also look at the topic of payments to directors and employees in the form of shares or share options. Although this form of remuneration is becoming increasingly common, until very recently it was not dealt with by any accounting standard. The 'G4+1' group of standard setters issued a Position Paper *Share-based payment* which the ASB has now developed into FRS 20.

Objectives

When you have studied this chapter you should be able to:

- understand the related party issue

- identify related parties and disclose related party transactions

- discuss the effectiveness of current regulations on disclosure of related party transactions

- describe the current requirements for the recognition and measurement of share-based payment

- show the impact of FRS 20 on the performance statements of an entity.

1   Related party transactions

1.1   The distortion that related party transactions can cause to financial statements

When transactions take place between related parties they may not be on arm's length terms. Disclosure of the existence of such transactions, and of the relationships underlying them, gives important information to users of financial statements.

One striking example of the need for disclosure is that related party transactions have been a feature of a number of financial scandals in recent years, many of which have had in common the dominance of the company by a powerful chief executive who was also involved with the related party.

More generally, transactions between related parties, e.g. companies in the same group are now a common feature of business operations. Disclosure of these transactions, some of which may not have been at arm's length, together with information about the underlying relationship, gives the user of accounts an important indication of their significance to the operating results and financial position of the reporting company. For the same reasons disclosure is called for where transactions take place with a wide range of other related parties, e.g. directors, associates, pension funds and key management.

A related party relationship can affect the financial position and operating results of an enterprise in a number of ways as follows:

- Transactions may be entered into with a related party which may not have occurred if the relationship did not exist, e.g. a company may sell a large proportion of its production to its parent company, where it might not have found an alternative customer if the parent company had not purchased the goods.

- Transactions may be entered into with a related party on terms different from those with an unrelated party, e.g. the terms under which a subsidiary leases equipment to another subsidiary of a common parent may be imposed by the common parent and might vary significantly from one lease to another because of circumstances entirely unrelated to market prices for similar leases; indeed, the terms may be such that no financial consideration passes between the parties.

- Transactions with third parties may be affected by the existence of the relationship, e.g. two enterprises in the same line of business may be controlled by a common party that has the ability to increase the volume of business done by each.

1.2 Companies Act and Stock Exchange requirements concerning related party transactions

The Companies Act provisions dealing with related parties are mainly concerned with directors and persons connected to directors (which can include companies).

If a company has a 'significant contract' with one of its directors, there is a need for disclosure if the director has a 'material interest'. 'Material' is decided by the other directors (or the auditor if they cannot decide).

Loans to a director from a company are illegal except for sums up to £5,000 or if they are funds for business expenditure (there needs to be prior approval by members).

The Stock Exchange has numerous provisions relating to transactions between a company and its directors or substantial shareholders. They are referred to as Class 4 parties. Basically a circular to shareholders is required if, for example, there is an acquisition or disposal of assets between the company and a Class 4 party.

The requirements of the Stock Exchange are extensive and can be argued to be effective in reducing the amount of related party transactions that occur. However they only apply to listed companies and the ASB (as did the ASC) consider that an accounting standard is necessary.

1.3 Requirements of FRS 8

FRS 8 *Related party disclosures* was issued in October 1995. It requires that financial statements disclose:

- information on related party transactions

- the name of the party controlling the reporting entity and, if different, that of the ultimate controlling party, whether or not any transactions between the reporting entity and those parties have taken place.

1.4 Related parties

FRS 8 contains a very detailed definition of related parties, as below.

(a) Two or more parties are related parties when, at any time during the financial period:

   (i)   one party has direct or indirect control of the other party; or

   (ii) the parties are subject to common control from the same source; or

   (iii) one party has influence over the financial and operating policies of the other party to an extent that that other party might be inhibited from pursuing at all times its own separate interests; or

   (iv) the parties, in entering a transaction, are subject to influence from the same source to such an extent that one of the parties to the transaction has subordinated its own separate interests.

(b) For the avoidance of doubt, the following are related parties of the reporting entity:

   (i)   its ultimate and intermediate parent undertakings, subsidiary undertakings, and fellow subsidiary undertakings

   (ii) its associates and joint ventures

   (iii) the investor or venturer in respect of which the reporting entity is an associate or a joint venture

   (iv) directors of the reporting entity and the directors of its ultimate and intermediate parent undertakings

   (v)   pension funds for the benefit of employees of the reporting entity or of any entity that is a related party of the reporting entity.

(c) The following are presumed to be related parties of the reporting entity unless it can be demonstrated that neither party has influenced the financial and operating policies of the other in such a way as to inhibit the pursuit of separate interests:

   (i)   the key management of the reporting entity and the key management of its parent undertaking or undertakings

   (ii) a person owning or able to exercise control over 20 per cent or more of the voting rights of the reporting entity, whether directly or through nominees

   (iii) each person acting in concert in such a way as to be able to exercise control or influence over the reporting entity

   (iv) an entity managing or managed by the reporting entity under a management contract.

(d) Additionally, because of their relationship with certain parties that are, or are presumed to be, related parties of the reporting entity, the following are also presumed to be related parties of the reporting entity:

   (i)   members of the close family of any individual falling under parties mentioned in (a) to (c) above

   (ii) partnerships, companies, trusts or other entities in which any individual or member of the close family in (a) to (c) above has a controlling interest.

The definition concludes by stating that this list is not intended to be exhaustive.

1.5 Control and influence

The terms **control** and **influence** are central to the definition of related parties (just as in group accounts). In establishing whether or not a related party relationship exists, it is often necessary to consider **common control** and **common influence**.

Two subsidiaries of the same parent company would obviously be under common control and would therefore be related parties. Common control would also exist where both parties are subject to control from boards having a controlling nucleus of directors in common.

Example

The directors of A Ltd are X, Y and Z. The directors of B Ltd are W, X and Y. A Ltd and B Ltd are related parties.

Influence is not defined. The explanation to the FRS states that, while control brings with it the ability to cause the controlled party to subordinate its separate interests, the exercise of influence has a less certain outcome.

The FRS gives some examples of situations where there may be common influence but where a related party relationship does not necessarily exist:

- two entities are both associated companies of the same investor

- one party is subject to control and another party is subject to influence from the same source (for example, if A has a subsidiary B and an associate C, that situation in itself would not make B and C related parties)

- two entities have a director in common.

In order for there to be a related party relationship in these and similar situations, one or both parties must have subordinated their own separate interests in entering into a transaction.

1.6 Types of transaction

Transactions between related parties are a normal feature of business. FRS 8 gives some examples:

- purchases or sales of goods (finished or unfinished)

- purchases or sales of property and other assets

- rendering or receiving of services, e.g. accounting, management, engineering or legal services

- agency arrangements

- leasing arrangements, e.g. allowing the use of an asset, whether for a rental or not

- transfer of research and development

- licence agreements

- finance (including loans and equity contributions in cash or in kind)

- guarantees or collaterals

- management contracts.

Note that disclosure is required of all material related party transactions.

1.7   Disclosures

- **Disclosure of control** – Where the reporting entity is controlled by another party, there should be disclosure of the related party relationship and, if different, that of the ultimate controlling party. If either of these is not known, that fact should be disclosed.

   These disclosures must be made whether or not any transactions have taken place between the controlling parties and the reporting entity.

- **Disclosure of transactions and balances** – Financial statements should disclose material transactions undertaken with a related party by the reporting entity. Disclosure should be made irrespective of whether a price is charged. The disclosure should include:

   (a)   the names of the transacting related parties

   (b)   a description of the relationship between the parties

   (c)   a description of the transactions

   (d)   the amounts involved

   (e)   any other elements of the transactions necessary for an understanding of the financial statements

   (f)   the amounts due to or from related parties at the balance sheet date and provisions for doubtful debts due from such parties at that date

   (g)   amounts written off in the period in respect of debts due to or from related parties.

Transactions with related parties may be disclosed on an aggregated basis (aggregation of similar transactions by type of related party) unless disclosure of an individual transaction, or connected transactions, is necessary for an understanding of the impact of the transactions on the financial statements of the reporting entity, or is required by law.

1.8   Exemptions

The following transactions do not have to be disclosed.

- Any transactions:

   - in the consolidated financial statements of intra-group items that have been eliminated on consolidation

   - in the parent's own financial statements, where these are presented with the consolidated financial statements

   - in the financial statements of subsidiaries of intra-group items, provided that at least 90% of their voting rights are controlled within the group and provided that the consolidated financial statements have been published.

- Pension contributions paid to a pension fund.

- Emoluments in respect of services as an employee of the reporting entity.

Relationships and transactions with the following do not have to be disclosed:

- providers of finance

- utility companies

- government departments and their sponsored bodies

- customers, suppliers, franchisers, distributors and general agents with whom the entity transacts a significant volume of business.

ACTIVITY 1

Montgomery Ltd has entered into the following transactions during the financial year.

(a) It made sales totalling £500,000 to Cavendish Ltd, a 90% subsidiary.

(b) It sold a property which was included in the accounts at a valuation of £1,000,000 to Mr Carlisle, the brother-in-law of one of the directors, for £750,000.

(c) It paid a salary totalling £55,000 to Mrs Shirley, the personnel manager. Mrs Shirley is married to the managing director of Cavendish Ltd.

(d) It purchased design services worth £500 from Blythe and Co. Blythe and Co is a partnership set up by three design students. One of the partners is the niece of the chairman of Montgomery Ltd.

The directors intend to take advantage of the exemption from preparing consolidated accounts on the grounds that Montgomery Ltd is a small company as defined by the Companies Act 1985.

Which of these transactions would be required to be disclosed in the financial statements of Montgomery Ltd under FRS 8?

Feedback to this activity is at the end of the chapter.

1.9 Identifying related parties

In order to identify related parties it is necessary to apply the definition in FRS 8. There are many situations in which it is obvious that a related party relationship exists. For example, a subsidiary is clearly a related party of a parent.

In more complicated situations it may be necessary to consider whether the parties are included in the list in parts (b) to (d) of the definition and to consider the basic principle of control and influence. What actually happens within a relationship in practice is often important.

ACTIVITY 2

X plc is an 80% owned subsidiary of T plc. The directors of X plc are A, B, C and D. Which of the following are related parties of X plc?

(a) V Ltd, which is not part of the T plc group, but of which A is a director

(b) Y, who owns 20% of the shares in X plc

(c) K, the financial controller of X plc (who is not a director)

(d) M, the live-in partner of the chairman of B plc, a company in the T plc group.

Feedback to this activity is at the end of the chapter.

1.10 How effective is FRS 8?

There are two main ways in which it is possible to deal with transactions between related parties.

- **Adjust the financial statements** to reflect the transaction as if it had occurred with an independent third party and record the transaction at the corresponding arm's length price. However, as a study by the Accountants International Study Group states, 'it often is impossible to establish what would have been the terms of any non-arm's length transaction had it been bargained on an arm's length basis, because no comparable transactions may have taken place and, in any event, the transaction might never have taken place at all if it had been bargained using different values'.

- As a result of the above difficulty, accounting standards internationally have concentrated on the **disclosure** of related party transactions and relationships.

During the development of the standard it was proposed that only abnormal transactions be disclosed. FRS 8 does not make this distinction since, in its view, when transactions with related parties are material in aggregate, they are of interest whether or not they are made at arm's length. There would also have been practical difficulties in applying definitions of 'normal' and 'abnormal' transactions. This view coincides with current international treatment.

Most commentators accepted the need for a standard on disclosure of related party relationships and transactions and have also accepted the approach taken by FRS 8 as pragmatic.

Some commentators have pointed out problems in applying the requirements of the standard. There are particular problems in applying the definition of 'material' because materiality has to be considered in relation to both parties to the transaction. A transaction that is immaterial to a company might be material to one of its directors. The intention is to ensure that transactions that are beneficial to directors and other individuals are disclosed.

In practice the effect is that some companies disclose all transactions relating to directors, whether they are material or not, or beneficial or not. This can be a particular problem where a company trades directly with the general public (e.g. as a bank or a retailer) and directors enter into normal transactions with it in their capacity as private persons. It has been argued that disclosures such as these distract users from genuine related party transactions.

FRS 8 undoubtedly provides useful information to users of the financial statements and makes it more difficult for directors to benefit from related party transactions without users becoming aware of this. However, some commentators argue that FRS 8 would not provide more than 'a mild deterrent' to any powerful individual determined to commit corporate fraud on a large scale.

1.11 FRED 25 *Related party disclosures*

The IASB has recently revised IAS 24 on related parties. FRED 25 proposes to adopt most of this revised standard. However, the revisions to IAS 24 have brought the international standard closer to the UK's FRS 8, and so FRED 25 does not bring great change to UK practice. One change relates to the disclosures that a subsidiary has to make. FRS 8 exempts 90%+ subsidiaries from making detailed disclosures, whereas FRED 25 only exempts 100% subsidiaries from making disclosures.

2   UITF Abstract 25 *National Insurance contributions on share option gains*

2.1   The issue

Following the Social Security Act 1998, UK employers are charged National Insurance on the gains made by employees upon the exercise of options issued under unapproved scheme option schemes (i.e. those not approved by the Inland Revenue). National Insurance contributions are payable on the difference between the share price at the date the options are exercised and the exercise price payable by the employee. This applies to schemes where the shares can be sold on a stock exchange or there are arrangements in place that allow the employees to obtain cash for the shares.

The issue is whether the employer should accrue for the estimated liability between the grant date and the exercise date, which is when it becomes payable, and, if so, how the liability should be calculated.

2.2 UITF Consensus

- Provision should be made for National Insurance contributions on outstanding share options that are expected to be exercised.

- The provision should be allocated over the period from the date of grant to the end of the performance period; from that date to the date of actual exercise the provision should be adjusted by using the current market value of the shares. Where there is no performance period, full provision should be made immediately.

3 FRS 20 *Share-based payment*

3.1 The problem

The use of share-based payment has increased in recent years. For example, part of the remuneration of directors is often in the form of shares or options. An entity's employees may become entitled to shares or share options, provided they remain in the entity's employment for a specific period of time.

Until recently there was no accounting standard that gave comprehensive guidance on accounting for share-based payment. Share options are often granted to employees at an exercise price that is equal to or higher than the market price of the shares at the date the options are granted. This means that the options have no intrinsic value and traditionally the transaction was not recognised in the financial statements. If companies pay their employees in cash, an expense is recognised in the profit and loss account. However, if companies pay their employees in share options, no expense is recognised. This is an accounting anomaly.

In 2000 the 'G4+1' group issued a Position Paper on share-based payments. This work was then developed further by both the IASB and the ASB. The IASB issued IFRS 2 *Share-based payment* in February 2004, along the lines of its earlier exposure draft ED 2. The ASB agreed strongly with the ideas of ED 2 and IFRS 2, not surprisingly since they had provided much of the input into the original Position Paper on which they were based. The ASB therefore issued FRED 31 proposing the same ideas as ED 2, and in April 2004 issued FRS 20 *Share-based payment* requiring that IFRS 2 is adopted in the UK.

3.2 Should share-based payment be recognised in the financial statements?

There are a number of arguments for not recognising share-based payment. However, the IASB rejects them all, arguing in favour of recognising share-based payment.

- **No cost therefore no charge**

  A charge for shares or options should not be recognised because the entity does not have to sacrifice cash or other assets. There is no cost to the entity. (However, the shareholders do suffer a dilution in their wealth.)

  This argument ignores the fact that a transaction has occurred. The employees have provided valuable services to the entity in return for valuable shares or options. If this argument were applied, the financial statements would fail to reflect the economic transactions that had occurred.

- **Earnings per share would be hit twice**

The charge to the profit and loss account for the employee services consumed reduces the entity's earnings. At the same time there is an increase in the number of shares issued (or to be issued).

However, the double impact on earnings per share simply reflects the two economic events that have occurred: the entity has issued shares, thus increasing the denominator of the EPS calculation, and it has also consumed the resources it received for those shares, thus reducing the numerator. Issuing shares to employees, instead of paying them in cash, requires a greater increase in the entity's earnings in order to maintain its earnings per share. Recognising the transaction ensures that its economic consequences are reported.

- **Adverse economic consequences**

Recognition of employee share-based payment might discourage entities from introducing or continuing employee share plans.

If this were the case, this might be because the requirement for entities to account properly for employee share plans had revealed the economic consequences of such plans. This would correct the present economic distortion, whereby entities are able to obtain and consume resources by issuing valuable shares or options without having to account for such transactions.

3.3 FRS 20 *Share-based payment*

FRS 20 requires that the IASB's IFRS 2 is adopted into UK accounting.

- UK listed companies will already have to comply with IFRS 2 *after* 1 January 2005, following the EU decision to adopt IFRSs for all EU listed companies

- Small companies that follow the FRSSE are exempt from having to comply with FRS 20.

- The scope of FRS 20 therefore focuses on those mid-range companies that prepare their accounts in accordance with UK standards (and do not follow the FRSSE).

IFRS 2 recognises two types of share-based payment transactions:

(a) **equity-settled** share-based payment transactions, in which the entity receives goods or services as consideration for equity instruments of the entity (including shares or share options)

(b) **cash-settled** share-based payment transactions, in which the entity pays cash as consideration for goods or services, but the amount paid is based on the entity's share price.

The IFRS requires an entity to recognise all share-based payment transactions in its accounts, including transactions with employees.

Equity-settled transactions

The goods or services received, and the corresponding increase in shareholders' funds, must be measured *directly*, at the fair value of the goods or services received, unless that fair value cannot be estimated reliably.

If the fair value of the goods or services received cannot be estimated reliably, the value of the transaction must be measured *indirectly* by reference to the fair value of the equity instruments granted.

Examples

(i)   **Direct method**. A company purchases a building with a market value of
        £250,000 by issuing 100,000 £1 shares in consideration. The building will be
        capitalised in fixed assets at its cost of £250,000, the nominal value of the
        shares issued will be £100,000 and there will be a credit to the share premium
        account of £150,000.

(ii)   **Indirect method**. A computer consultant performs some work in exchange for
        10,000 £1 shares with a market value of £3.25 each. The cost of the work done
        is £32,500 (charged as an expense in the profit and loss account), the nominal
        value of the shares issued is £10,000 and the share premium is credited with
        £22,500.

Cash-settled transactions

The fair value of the goods or services acquired must be measured, and a liability
established at this value. Until the liability is settled, the fair value of the liability must
be re-measured at each balance sheet date, with any changes in value recognised in the
profit and loss account.

Example

A computer consultant performs some work in exchange for being paid in six months
an amount of cash equivalent in value to the market value of 10,000 shares then.
Today's share price is £2. An expense of £20,000 is recorded once the work is
complete, together with a corresponding liability of £20,000. This liability will be re-
measured according to changes in the share price at each balance sheet date before it is
settled.

3.4   Determining the fair value of the equity instruments granted

The fair value of shares that are publicly quoted can be determined immediately as the
current market value. For shares in unquoted companies, the usual share valuation
techniques should be used to estimate the fair value (see later in this text).

The fair value of share options is harder to determine. In rare cases there may be
publicly quoted traded options with similar terms, whose market value can be used as
the fair value of the options we are considering. Otherwise the fair value of options
must be estimated using a recognised option pricing model. FRS 20 does not require
any specific model to be used. The most commonly used model to value share options
is the Black-Scholes model, which may produce a reliable option valuation, especially
if the life of the option is relatively short. You do not need any specific knowledge of
option valuation techniques for the purposes of this exam.

3.5   Allocation of the expense

Note the difference in meaning between the *grant date* of options and the *vesting date*.

The *grant date* is the date at which the entity and another party agree to the
arrangement.

The *vesting date* is the date on which the counterparty becomes entitled to receive the
cash or equity instruments under the arrangement.

For example, on 1 January 20X1 A plc might award 1,000 share options to an
employee, on condition that he is still working for the company in two years' time. The
grant date is 1 January 20X1. The vesting period is from 1 January 20X1 to
31 December 20X2. The vesting date is 31 December 20X2.

Once it is agreed that all share-based payments must result in an expense being charged in the profit and loss account, and that the expense should be measured by reference to fair values, the accruals basis can be invoked to decide that the expense must be recognised over the period in which the services are rendered or as the goods are received.

3.6   Impact on the performance statements

The following example illustrates the impact of share-based payment transactions on the performance statements.

Example

CD plc grants 100 share options to each of its 500 employees, each option only maturing if the employee is still working for CD plc in three years' time. Using the Black-Scholes model, at the grant date each option is estimated to have a fair value of £15, assuming that the necessary three year-period is worked.

It is estimated that 20% of employees will leave over the next three years and so will forfeit their option rights.

Assuming that everything turns out as expected, show the accounting entries to be made each year.

Solution

The fair value of options granted and expected to vest = $100 \times 500 \times £15 \times 80\%$

$$= £600,000$$

This expense must be spread over the three-year vesting period, i.e. charged to the profit and loss account at £200,000 p.a.

The impact on each year's financial statements would be:

	Year 1 £	*Year 2* £	*Year 3* £
Profit and loss account			
Staff costs (expense)	200,000	200,000	200,000
Balance sheet			
Included in equity	200,000	400,000	600,000

3.7   Commentary on the FRS 20 requirements

Some commentators argue that implementing FRS 20 will have serious adverse economic consequences (as explained earlier), since many companies (including struggling e-businesses and young companies which cannot afford to remunerate key employees wholly in cash and therefore instead offer large amounts of share options) will see an additional charge in the profit and loss account.

However, the principle of recognising the cost of share-based payment is sound. There may be practical difficulties, for example in determining the fair value of share options at the grant date, but a reasonable estimate is better than omitting the expense entirely.

Related party transactions

1 How do related party transactions distort financial statements? (1.1)

2 Define 'related party transaction' and 'control'. (1.4, 1.5)

3 What does FRS 8 require to be disclosed about related party transactions? (1.7)

4 What items are exempted from the disclosure requirements of FRS 8? (1.8)

UITF Abstract 25 *NI contributions on share option gains*

5 Should NI contributions be provided on outstanding share options? (2.2)

FRS 20 *Share-based payment*

6 State the problem posed by share-based payment to employees. Does FRS 20 require that these payments be charged to the profit and loss account, or merely disclosed in the notes? (3.1, 3.2)

Ace plc

FRS 8 *Related party disclosures* was issued in October 1995. Prior to its existence, there were specific requirements for related party disclosures contained in the 1985 Companies Act and the Listing Rules of the London Stock Exchange.

On 1 April 20X7, Ace plc owned 75% of the equity share capital of Deuce Ltd and 80% of the equity share capital of Trey Ltd. On 1 April 20X8, Ace plc purchased the remaining 25% of the equity shares of Deuce Ltd. In the two years ended 31 March 20X9, the following transactions occurred between the three companies:

(i) On 30 June 20X7 Ace plc manufactured a machine for use by Deuce Ltd. The cost of manufacture was £20,000. The machine was delivered to Deuce Ltd for an invoiced price of £25,000. Deuce Ltd paid the invoice on 31 August 20X7. Deuce Ltd depreciated the machine over its anticipated useful economic life of five years, charging a full year's depreciation in the year of purchase.

(ii) On 30 September 20X8, Deuce Ltd sold some goods to Trey Ltd at an invoiced price of £15,000. Trey Ltd paid the invoice on 30 November 20X8. The goods had cost Deuce Ltd £12,000 to manufacture. By 31 March 20X9, Trey Ltd had sold all the goods outside the group.

(iii) For each of the two years ended 31 March 20X9, Ace plc provided management services to Deuce Ltd and Trey Ltd. Ace plc did not charge for these services in the year ended 31 March 20X8 but in the year ended 31 March 20X9 decided to impose a charge of £10,000 per annum to each company. The amounts of £10,000 are due to be paid by each company on 31 May 20X9.

Required:

(a) Explain why related party disclosures are needed and why FRS 8 was considered necessary given the existing requirements of the 1985 Companies Act and the Listing Rules of the London Stock Exchange. **(6 marks)**

(b) Summarise the related-party disclosures which will be required in respect of transactions (i) to (iii) above for BOTH of the years ended 31 March 20X8 and 31 March 20X9 in the financial statements of Ace plc, Deuce Ltd and Trey Ltd.

(14 marks)

You may assume that Ace plc presents consolidated financial statements for BOTH of the years dealt with in the question.

(Total: 20 marks)

For the answer to this question see the 'Answers' section at the end of the book.

FEEDBACK TO ACTIVITY 1

(a) Sales to the subsidiary must be disclosed. Although this is an intra-group transaction and would normally be exempt from disclosure, Montgomery Ltd does not prepare consolidated accounts and therefore cannot take advantage of the exemption.

(b) The sale of the property is clearly a related party transaction and must be disclosed. Mr Carlisle falls within the definition of 'close family' of a director.

(c) Mrs Shirley's salary need not be disclosed. Although Mrs Shirley may be a related party, the payment of emoluments is specifically exempt from disclosure.

(d) Blythe and Co probably falls within the definition of a related party as this includes partnerships and other entities in which any member of the 'close family' of a related party has a controlling interest. It could be argued that the purchase need not be disclosed on the grounds that the sum of £500 is unlikely to be material in the context of the financial statements of Montgomery Ltd. However, FRS 8 states that in some situations the materiality of a transaction should be considered, not only in relation to the reporting entity, but of the other party to the transaction. As £500 is almost certainly material to Blythe and Co, the spirit of FRS 8 suggests that this transaction should be disclosed.

FEEDBACK TO ACTIVITY 2

(a) V Ltd and X plc are subject to common influence from A, but V Ltd is not a related party unless one or both companies have subordinated their own separate interests in entering into a transaction. (This assumes that A is the only director to serve on both boards; if there were a common nucleus of directors, a related party relationship would almost certainly exist.)

(b) Y is almost certainly not a related party. According to the definition Y is presumed to be a related party, but the existence of a parent company means that Y is unlikely to be able to exert influence over X plc in practice.

(c) K may be a related party, despite the fact that he or she is not a director. A financial controller would probably come within the definition of **key management** (i.e. 'those persons in senior positions having authority or responsibility for directing or controlling the major activities and resources of the reporting entity'). The issue would be decided by the extent to which K is able to control or influence the policies of the company in practice.

(d) M may be a related party. B plc and X plc are under common control and M falls within the definition of close family of a related party of B plc. (**Close family** means 'those family members, or members of the same household, who may be expected to influence, or be influenced by, that person in their dealings with the reporting entity.') M is not a related party if it can be demonstrated that she has not influenced the policies of X plc in such a way as to inhibit the pursuit of separate interests.

Chapter 21
SHARE VALUATION

There are a number of different methods that can be used to value shares in an unquoted company and the suitability of each method depends on the situation. You will need to be able to apply the various methods and to discuss the results. You will also need to be able to give advice to potential purchasers of shares or business entities based on the results of your calculations.

Objectives

When you have studied this chapter you should be able to:

- calculate and appraise a range of acceptable values for shares in an unquoted company

- advise a client on the purchase of a business entity

- analyse the impact of accounting policy changes on the value and performance of an entity.

1 Assessing the valuation of shares in unquoted companies

1.1 Introduction

Unquoted companies may be required to be valued for various reasons. The two main reasons in the context of this syllabus are:

- for a balance sheet valuation for a company which has a minority shareholding in an unquoted company (i.e. a trade investment)

- for determining a value of a company being acquired by another company.

In the second situation, the final value is negotiated between the acquirer and the acquiree. The share valuation is an opening reference point in the negotiations.

1.2 Calculating a range of acceptable values for shares in an unquoted company

Shareholdings may be valued in two different ways – either asset based value or income based value. Each of these may be further subdivided as follows:

Asset based	– book value
	– replacement cost/deprival value
	– break up value.
Income based	– dividend yield
	– PE ratio
	– NPV of future earnings.

Additionally methods based on a mixture of 'assets' and 'income' may be used.

Although from a theoretical point of view, the only sustainable valuation model is that based on the Net Present Value of future earnings, this model is generally impossible to apply because of the practical difficulties associated with estimating future earning streams, choosing an appropriate discount rate, etc. Accordingly in practice the other methods are more widely used, and may in any event be considered as surrogates for the one theoretically sound method.

Each method is generally considered appropriate to certain sets of circumstances. However, it is common that several valuations of the shares are computed using different bases, and an 'average' of these will form the basis of the figure for final negotiation between the interested parties.

1.3   Dividend yield

The gross dividend yield is defined as:

$$\frac{\text{Total annual dividend (gross)}}{\text{Share price}} \times 100\%$$

Note that it is the gross dividend, inclusive of tax credit (where this applies), that is taken into account in computing the gross dividend yield. This is done in order to ease comparison by investors with yields on other securities which are subject to income tax on the whole amount of the income (e.g. quoted loan stock).

Thus, for unquoted companies the formula is turned around to give:

$$\text{Share value} \quad = \quad \frac{\text{Total annual dividend}}{\text{Suitable dividend yield}}$$

There are then two elements to determine: the total annual dividend to be paid by the private company and what is a 'suitable dividend yield'.

It is essential to compare like with like and consequently it is the current annual dividend which is taken into account irrespective of any growth prospects, etc.

The dividend yield to be applied is chosen by looking at the dividend yield which may be obtained in 'similar' quoted companies.

Any value so found is then normally adjusted downwards, by between 20% and 40% to take into account the non-marketability of the shares in the private company being valued. Alternatively the suitable dividend yield is uplifted with the same end result.

ACTIVITY 1

You are required to place a value on a 2% holding of shares in Claygro Ltd, a privately owned company manufacturing flowerpots.

You establish the following additional information.

   Issued share capital: 100,000 £1.00 shares

   Current dividend (gross): 4p per share

Quoted companies involved in the manufacture of flowerpots generally have a gross dividend yield of 4%.

Feedback to this activity is at the end of the chapter.

1.4   Level of future dividends

The simple formula above considers only the current year's dividend. For a fair comparison the expected rate of growth of dividends of the private and public companies should be similar. Whilst these figures themselves are rarely available a comparison of 'dividend cover' (earnings after tax available to pay dividends ÷ net dividend paid) between the companies may be readily computed, and this may indicate whether a similar level of funds is being retained within the business to finance future growth.

KEY POINT

An additional problem with
private companies is that
typically the shareholders are
the same as management and
therefore profits may be paid out
as salaries, or high pension
contributions rather than
dividends.

KEY POINT

Dividend yields to be applied
are those prevailing for quoted
companies in the same sector.
These may need to be adjusted
before being used to value
shares in private companies.

KEY POINT

Value per share =
EPS x a suitable PE ratio.

An additional problem with private companies is that typically the shareholders are the same as management and therefore profits may be paid out as salaries, or high pension contributions rather than dividends. This can mean that dividends are often held at an artificially low level in shareholder managed companies compared with what might reasonably be expected by a provider of risk capital.

1.5   Dividend yield to apply

Dividend yields to be applied are those prevailing for quoted companies in the same industrial sector. However, there are a number of reasons why these may need to be adjusted before being used to value the shares.

- Quoted companies are often more diversified in their activities than private companies, consequently it may be difficult to find a quoted company with a similar range of activities.

- Quoted companies are often bigger than private companies. Because of the generally accepted benefits which size brings, a higher dividend yield should be sought from a smaller, but otherwise comparable company.

- Levels of gearing may differ between companies and hence affect the dividend yield.

- Other specific factors may need to be taken into account. Although a small shareholding is being valued it may hold particular importance to either or both parties (e.g. a 2% shareholding being acquired by a 49% shareholder). In such cases the purchaser may be prepared to pay far more than would be indicated by a valuation based on dividend yield.

1.6   Earnings yield or PE ratio

As with dividend yield the PE ratio is turned around to value shares in unquoted companies:

Value per share = EPS × a suitable PE ratio

Again, any value thence computed is then normally reduced to take into account the non marketability of the shares.

The earnings yield is the reciprocal of the PE ratio. Thus if given a suitable earnings yield, the formula becomes:

$$\text{Value per share} = \frac{\text{EPS}}{\text{Yield}\%}$$

The basic choice for a suitable PE ratio will be that of a quoted company of comparable size in the same industry, and the same difficulties apply as when a suitable dividend yield is sought.

In addition there is a tendency for dividends to be more stable than earnings, consequently since share prices are broadly based on expected future earnings a PE ratio, based on a single year's reported earnings, may be very different for companies in the same sector.

For example, a high PE ratio may indicate the following.

- **Growth stock** – The share price is high because continuous high rates of growth of earnings are expected from the stock.

- **No growth stock** – The PE ratio is based on the last reported earnings, which perhaps were exceptionally low yet the share price is based on future earnings which are expected to revert to a 'normal' relatively stable level.

- **Takeover bid** – The share price has risen pending a takeover bid.

- **High security share** – Shares in property companies typically have low income yields but the shares are still worth buying because of the prospects of capital growth and the high level of security.

Similarly a low PE ratio may indicate the following.

- **Losses expected** – Future profits are expected to fall from their most recent levels e.g. in cyclical industries.

- **Share price low** – As noted previously, share prices may be extremely volatile - special factors, such as a strike at a manufacturing plant of a particular company may depress the share price and hence the PE ratio.

Consequently the main difficulty in trying to apply the model is finding a similar company, with similar growth prospects – which again may perhaps be estimated by considering dividend cover, and hence the level of retained profits.

A further difficulty is that the reported earnings are based on historical cost accounts which in general makes a nonsense of trying to compare two companies.

In spite of these serious shortcomings the PE ratio is regarded as an important measure by investment analysts, etc. and cannot therefore be disregarded. As a broad brush measure, and as long as exceptional items are identified and treated as such, it may be used to value shares.

It is generally considered to be appropriate where the size of the shareholding is sufficient to influence dividend policy – and therefore the shareholder is more concerned with the underlying level of earnings, rather than just dividends.

ACTIVITY 2

You are given the following information regarding Accrington Ltd, an unquoted company

(a) Issued ordinary share capital is 400,000 25p shares.

(b) Extract from profit and loss account for the year ended 31 July 20X4

	£	£
Profit before taxation		220,000
Less: Corporation tax		80,000
Profit after taxation		140,000
Less: Preference dividend	20,000	
Ordinary dividend	36,000	
		56,000
Retained profit for the year		84,000

(c) The PE ratio applicable to a similar type of business (suitable for an unquoted company) is 12.5.

Value 200,000 shares in Accrington Ltd on an earnings yield basis.

Feedback to this activity is at the end of the chapter.

1.7 Asset based measures

Asset based measures are generally considered appropriate as a 'check' on the PE basis when shareholdings greater than 50% are being valued. Such shareholdings give the holder the right to control the acquisition and disposal of the underlying assets, therefore, if there are assets not needed for generation of income the controlling shareholder may cause these to be realised to generate cash.

As described above there are several possible asset based measures which could be used.

- **Book value** – this will normally be an irrelevant figure as it will be based on historical costs.

- **Replacement cost/deprival value** – this should provide a measure of the maximum amount that any purchaser should pay for the whole business, since it represents the total cost of forming the business from scratch. However, a major element of any business as a going concern is likely to be the 'goodwill'. Since this can only be defined as 'income based value of business, less value of tangible assets' it may be seen that there is no real way of applying a pure 'asset based value' to a business – it is always necessary to consider an 'income based value' as well.

- **Break up value** – the break up value of the assets in the business will often be considerably lower than any other computed value. It normally represents the minimum price which should be accepted for the sale of a business as a going concern, since if the income based valuations give figures lower than the break up value it is apparent that the owner would be better off by ceasing to trade and selling off all the assets piecemeal.

However, when a break up is considered in this way it must be remembered to include such items as redundancy costs, liquidator's expenses, etc. which may have a significant effect on the final position.

In spite of these difficulties an asset value per share, based on deprival value, perhaps excluding goodwill, often provides a useful comparison with valuations based on capitalisation of income streams.

ACTIVITY 3

The following is an abridged version of the balance sheet of Grasmere Contractors Ltd, as at 30 April year 4

	£
Fixed assets (net book value)	450,000
Net current assets	100,000
	550,000

Represented by	
£1 ordinary shares	200,000
Reserves	250,000
6% Debentures year 19 (Repayable at 102)	100,000
	550,000

You ascertain that:

(a) market value of goodwill (not recorded in the books) is £50,000

(b) current market value of freehold property exceeds book value by £30,000

(c) all assets, other than property, are estimated to be realisable at their book value.

Value an 80% holding of ordinary shares on an assets basis.

Feedback to this activity is at the end of the chapter.

1.8   Other methods of valuation

- **Berliner method** – This attempts to take into account both the asset value of a company and its earnings potential. Two values of the company are obtained:

    (a) based on capitalising expected future profits at an acceptable rate of return

    (b) based on the going concern value of the company's net tangible assets.

    The value placed is then calculated as $\dfrac{(a)+(b)}{2}$ i.e. the mean of the two values.

    This is a compromise which has no particular theoretical support but it may produce an acceptable purchase figure.

- **Dual capitalisation method** – This is similar to the Berliner method, but it recognises the two different types of asset - tangible and intangible; the latter, such as goodwill, are often risky investments.

    The method used is to determine acceptable yields for both types of asset. Tangible assets are then valued and application of the yield determined for such assets gives a figure representing return on tangible assets. This is deducted from the profits figure to arrive at profit attributable to intangible assets, which is capitalised at the appropriate rate and added to the tangible assets value previously calculated to produce an overall company value.

Example

Flynch Ltd has estimated maintainable profits of £1,400 pa. Its net tangible assets are valued at £10,000 and the required rate of return on such assets is 10%. On intangible assets the required rate of return is 16%.

What is the value of Flynch Ltd under the dual capitalisation method?

	£
Estimated maintainable profits	1,400
Estimated return from tangible assets at 10% = £10,000 × 10%	1,000
Return attributable to intangible assets	£400
Capitalised value of intangible assets @ 16% = £400 ÷ 16%	£2,500
Total value of Flynch Ltd = Value of tangible assets + Value of intangible assets = £(10,000 + 2,500)	£12,500

1.9   Summary of valuation methods

Method	Dividend yield	Earnings yield	Assets basis
Share value	$\dfrac{\text{Dividend (gross)} \times 100}{\text{Dividend yield \% (gross)}}$	Earnings × PE ratio	Net asset value
Required information	(1) Annual dividend (2) Dividend yield expected	(1) Future earnings (2) PE ratio expected	Asset & liability valuations
Advantages	(1) Cash paid out is the key figure (2) Objective	Independent of management's dividend policy	Useful check on other methods
Problems	(1) Forecasting dividends (2) Deciding on dividend yield (3) Management's dividend policy	(1) Forecasting earnings (2) Deciding on PE ratio (3) Subjectivity of earnings (4) Effect of inflation on earnings	(1) Assigning values to individual assets (2) Limited applicability
Suitable for	(1) Quoted companies (2) Small shareholdings (up to approx 20%) in companies with stable dividend policies	(1) Quoted companies (2) Shareholdings in private companies of a size which enables the holder to influence dividend policy (e.g. 20% → 100% holding)	(1) Going concern basis – as a check on earnings yield method. (2) Asset-stripping – useful information if assets are valued at disposal value

2   Advising a client on the valuation of shares in a business entity

2.1   Introduction

This topic is illustrated by working through an example.

Example

You are asked to value a 60% holding in Shade Ltd for the purposes of share transfer. The company manufactures high quality children's toys, and is well known in this field.

The management of the company is regarded as satisfactory, having passed from the hands of the original founding family (a senior member of which is selling his shares) into the hands of professional management. The continuity of management is, at present, well organised.

Net asset position, per balance sheet at 31 January 20X6

	£'000	£'000	£'000
Fixed assets			
Freehold land and buildings, at cost			430
Plant and machinery, at cost less depreciation			60
			490
Current assets			
Stock		200	
Debtors		350	
		550	
Current liabilities			
Creditors	165		
Taxation	50		
Dividends	18		
Overdraft	50		
	283		
		283	267
Total assets less current liabilities			757
8% debenture 20X9			50
			707

Profit and dividend record (approximate figures)

Year to 31 Jan	Turnover £'000	Pre-tax profit £'000	Dividend %	£
20X4	900	150	5	7,500
20X5	1,000	165	10	15,000
20X6	1,200	210	12	18,000

(1) A note to the accounts indicates that the freeholds have this year been revalued, on an existing use basis, at £600,000.

(2) Share capital at 31 January 20X6 consists of 150,000 £1 ordinary shares.

(3) Assume corporation tax at 30%.

You ascertain the following data from the *Financial Times*.

	(Net) dividend yield %	PE ratio
500 share index	6.2	9.7
Consumer goods (non-durable)	6.7	10.0
Toys and games	8.1	6.6

Indicate how you would value:

(a) the 60% holding;

(b) a 5% holding.

Note: Since there can never be a perfect solution, what follows are the suggested steps that would be worked through.

2.2   60% holding

- The normal bases of valuing a holding of this size are by reference to assets and to earnings. Assuming the purchaser wished to continue the business of the company, the earnings basis is more relevant.

- The assets basis should include the revaluations of the property, less, arguably, taxation. Being prudent, the full liability of 30% on a chargeable gain should be allowed for.

	£'000	£'000
Net assets, per balance sheet		707
Revaluation of freeholds (600 – 430)	170	
Less: 30% thereof	51	
	——	119
		——
		826

Value per share £826,000 ÷ 150,000 =   £5.51 per share

- The earnings basis requires the PE, which would have applied to the shares had they been quoted, to be determined and applied to the likely future earnings per share. The PE for a similar quoted company is 6.6; a similar unquoted company would operate on a lower PE of, say, 4.5. (Remember, however, that PE ratios of companies quoted on the Stock Exchange relate to dealings in relatively small parcels of shares, so a higher PE than 4.5 may be more appropriate.)

Earnings per share must be calculated from past figures. There seems little point in averaging past years, since they reveal an increasing trend. The figure of EPS required is that for future years - the past is merely a guide to the future. In the circumstances, the results of the most recent year (to 31 January 20X6) appear to be the best to use as a guide to the future.

	£
Pre-tax profit	210,000
Less: Corporation tax at 30%	63,000
	———
Earnings	£147,000
	———

Earnings per share $= \dfrac{£147,000}{150,000} =$ 98 pence

Value per share 4.5×98 pence =   £4.41 per share

- Other factors which can be extracted from the information given are as follows:

Current ratio	$\dfrac{550}{283} = 1.94$	Satisfactory
Liquid ratio	$\dfrac{350}{28.} = 1.24$	Satisfactory, if debtors are all recoverable and overdraft limit not yet reached

- The range of prices indicated for this majority holding is approximately £4 to £6 per share. The higher end of the range reflects the high asset backing, and perhaps a continuation of the profit trend upwards. The assets, however, are unlikely to be realised, so that a more prudent valuation would be towards the lower end of the scale.

2.3   5% holding

- The normal basis of valuing a holding of this size is by reference to dividends.

- High asset backing, favourable ratios and trend of profits, all discussed above, are factors which would again influence the valuation.

- Dividend cover is important when valuing shares on a dividend basis. An impressive level of distributions may be marred, and be unlikely to continue, if there is low cover. Earnings were taken as £147,000, and the most recent dividend is £18,000, indicating what would be regarded as very good cover of 8.2.

- The yield obtainable on similar quoted securities is 8.1%. It is normal to uplift this by 25% to 40% to compensate for the unmarketability of unquoted securities. One must also allow, at this stage, for the impressive factors referred to above - dividend cover, profits trend and asset backing. Accordingly, the lower uplift (25% × 8.1%) may be appropriate, producing a yield of 10%.

- The dividend yield valuation would thus be:

$$\frac{100}{10} \times 12 \text{ pence} = \underline{120 \text{ pence per share}}$$

This is considerably lower than the value per share of the majority holding - and this is always so when valuing unquoted shares.

3   Related matters

3.1   The impact on profit reporting and balance sheet of share valuations

As we have seen, the available methods of valuation are based on dividends, earnings and assets. If a company has purchased an investment in another company and negotiated the price paid in line with one of these methods, the profits reported subsequent to the acquisition should reflect the method of valuation.

Thus the purchase of a small minority holding will have been negotiated on a dividend yield basis. In the profit and loss account of the investing company, it will be appropriate to record the dividends received and if the investing company prepares group accounts there will be no change to the balance sheet statement of the investment or the amount of income recorded in the profit and loss account.

If a larger percentage of the share capital has been acquired, the investing company will have negotiated a price based on the earnings potential of the investee company. In the individual accounts of the investing company, the different method of arriving at a value will not affect reported profits however. Only dividends will be accounted for rather than a share of profits as only dividends will be realised profits in the context of the individual company. In the group accounts however the share of profits accounted for either under the equity method or the consolidation method will reflect the earnings basis of valuation.

3.2   The impact of legislation allowing companies to purchase their own shares

Company law allows any type of share to be redeemed or purchased by the company which issued the shares. For private companies, the redemption or purchase can exceed the amount of distributable profits in the company, i.e. a repayment out of capital can be made. You will have come across the provisions earlier in your studies.

Situations where the provisions are of a particular advantage include the following.

- In a family business, a shareholder who has worked for the company and wishes to retire can effectively sell his shares to other members of the family. As the company buys back his shares the interest of the remaining shareholders is automatically increased without them having to find funds themselves to buy out the 'retiring' shareholder.

- Venture capitalists are more ready to accept an equity stake in the company rather than have debt. In the venture capital agreement, provisions can be included requiring repayment to the venturer in X years time. The advantage to the company is that it is not burdened with interest payments in the financing period.

- Employee share schemes are attractive to employees as the provisions provide an exit route for the sale of shares without the need for the company to go public.

4 Analysing the impact of accounting policy changes on the value and performance of an entity

4.1 Disclosure of changes in accounting policy

KEY POINT

Changes in accounting policy result in prior period adjustments.

FRS 3 states that a change in accounting policy can only be made if it will give a fairer presentation of the reporting entity's results and financial position. Changes in accounting policy result in prior period adjustments.

FRS 18 requires entities to disclose an indication of the effect of the change on the current year's results. Where it is not practicable to give the effect on the current year, that fact, together with the reasons, should be stated.

Because these disclosures are required, it should be possible to assess the impact of a change in accounting policy on the balance sheet and performance statement of an entity.

4.2 Accounting policies and share valuation

The accounting policies adopted by an entity may affect the value placed on its shares. To arrive at a realistic valuation it may be necessary to adjust earnings or asset values to reflect different accounting policies.

This is particularly likely to be the case where an entity's accounting policies will change following an acquisition. Past earnings figures and asset values should be revised to bring them into line with those that would have been reported under the new policies.

SELF-TEST QUESTIONS

Assessing the valuation of shares in unquoted companies

1   Define gross dividend yield. (1.3)

2   How is the PE ratio used to value unquoted companies? (1.6)

3   Describe three asset based measures that could be used to value a shareholding. (1.7)

4   What are (a) the Berliner and (b) the dual capitalisation methods of valuation? (1.8)

Related matters

5   Are companies permitted to purchase their own shares? (3.2)

R Johnson

R Johnson inherited 810,000 £1 ordinary shares in Johnson Products Ltd on the death of his uncle in 20X5. His uncle had been the founder of the company and managing director until his death. The remainder of the issued shares were held in small lots by employees and friends with no one holding more than 4%.

R Johnson is planning to emigrate and is considering disposing of his shareholding. He has had approaches from three parties as follows:

(i) **A competitor – Sonar Products Ltd**

Sonar Products Ltd considers that Johnson Products Ltd would complement its own business and it is interested in acquiring all of the 810,000 shares. Sonar Products Ltd currently achieves a post-tax return of 12.5% on capital employed.

(ii) **Senior employees**

Twenty employees are interested in making a management buy-out with each acquiring 40,500 shares from R Johnson. They have obtained financial backing, in principle, from the company's bankers.

(iii) **A financial conglomerate – Divest plc**

Divest plc is a company that has extensive experience of acquiring control of a company and breaking it up to show a profit on the transaction. Its policy is to seek a return of 20% from such an exercise.

The company has prepared draft accounts for the year ended 30 April 20X9.

The following information is available:

(1) **Past earnings and distributions**

Year ended 30 April	Profit/(loss) after tax £	Gross dividends declared %
20X5	79,400	6
20X6	(27,600)	-
20X7	56,500	4
20X8	88,300	5
20X9	97,200	6

(2) **Balance sheet of Johnson Products Ltd as at 30 April 20X9**

	£	£
Fixed assets		
Land at cost		376,000
Premises at cost	724,000	
Aggregate depreciation	216,000	
		508,000
Equipment at cost	649,000	
Aggregate depreciation	353,000	
		296,000
Current assets		
Stock	141,000	
Debtors	278,000	
Cash at bank	70,000	
	489,000	
Current liabilities		
Creditors	(335,000)	

Net current assets	154,000
Non current liabilities	(158,000)
	1,176,000

Represented by	
Share capital and reserves	
Ordinary shares of £1 each	1,080,000
Profit and loss account balance	96,000
	1,176,000

(3) **Information on the nearest comparable listed companies in the same industry**

Company	Profit after tax for 20X9 £	Retention %	Gross dividend yield %
Eastron plc	280,000	25	15.0
Westron plc	168,000	16	10.5
Northron plc	243,000	20	13.4

Profit after tax in each of the companies has been growing by approximately 8% per annum for the past five years.

(4) **Net realisable values**

The following is an estimate of the net realisable values of Johnson Products Ltd's assets as at 30 April 20X9

	£
Land	480,000
Premises	630,000
Equipment	150,000
Debtors	168,000
Stock	98,000

Required:

(a) As accountant for R Johnson, advise him of the amount that could be offered for his shareholding with a reasonable chance of being acceptable to the seller, based on the information given in the question, by each of the following:

(i)   Sonar Products Ltd   **(6 marks)**

(ii) the 20 employees   **(6 marks)**

(iii) Divest plc.   **(6 marks)**

(b) As accountant for Sonar Products Ltd, estimate the maximum amount that could be offered by Sonar Products Ltd for the shares held by R Johnson.

(4 marks)

(c) As accountant for Sonar Products Ltd, state the principal matters you would consider in determining the future maintainable earnings of Johnson Products Ltd and explain their relevance.   **(8 marks)**

(Total: 30 marks)

For the answer to this question see the 'Answers' section at the end of the book.

FEEDBACK TO ACTIVITY **1**	

Basic value $= \dfrac{\text{Dividend}}{\text{Dividend yield}}$

$$= \dfrac{4p}{4\%} = \qquad\qquad\qquad £1.00$$

Less: Discount for non-marketability – say 25%   (0.25)

Value per share   £0.75

∴ value of 2,000 shares is estimated to be £1,500.

This figure might well form a reasonable basis for valuing a small holding of shares, where the owner has little or no influence over the affairs of the company, and is or will be simply the passive recipient of dividends.

FEEDBACK TO ACTIVITY **2**	

Valuation of 200,000 shares

$= \quad 200,000 \times \text{PE ratio} \times \text{EPS}$

$= \quad 200,000 \times 12.5 \times £\, \dfrac{(140,000 - 20,000)}{400,000}$

$= \quad £750,000$

FEEDBACK TO ACTIVITY **3**	

Calculation of value of 200,000 shares on an assets basis, as at 30 April year 4

	£	£
Fixed assets per balance sheet		450,000
Add: Unrecorded goodwill	50,000	
Undervalued freehold property	30,000	
		80,000
Adjusted value of fixed assets		530,000
Net current assets		100,000
Net assets		630,000
Less: Payable to debenture holders on redemption		102,000
		£528,000
Valuation of 80% holding $= \dfrac{80}{100} \times £528,000$		£422,400

Note: The debentures have been taken at redemption cost in Year 19. Since this is some years distant, a fairer valuation might be produced by calculating the net present value, based on market rates of interest, of the future interest payments and redemption cost.

Chapter 22
PERFORMANCE MEASUREMENT

This chapter focuses on performance measurement. It begins by covering ratio analysis and most of this should be revision from your earlier studies. We then look at non-financial performance measures and at the problems of assessing performance based on accounting information. Again, much of this should be familiar from your earlier studies for the management accounting and organisational control papers. However, the emphasis for this paper is slightly different because we are assessing performance from the financial statements rather than from management accounting information.

Lastly, we look at some other financial measures which entities are using as alternatives to the more traditional ratios.

Objectives

When you have studied this chapter you should be able to:

- discuss the financial and non-financial measures of performance

- describe the procedures in designing an accounting based performance measurement system

- appraise the different performance measures

- compare target levels of performance with actual performance

- discuss the usefulness of failure prediction models.

1   Financial measures of performance

1.1   Introduction

You should already be familiar with the traditional financial measures of performance. In the examination you may be asked to use these to interpret financial information by calculating and commenting on ratios.

1.2   The aspects of financial performance that each ratio is intended to assess

The variety of ratios that could be calculated is vast, so it is important to restrict the calculations by being selective. The ratios chosen should be the key ones relevant to the requirements of the question. These may be further limited by the available information (i.e. there may be some you are simply unable to calculate). This point is considered further below.

Ratios can be classified into three main groups. These are summarised in the table below.

Type	Reflects	Examples
Profitability	Performance of company and its managers including the efficiency of asset usage	ROCE, Gross profit %, Stock turnover Debtors and creditors days
Financial	Financial structure and stability of the company	Gearing, Current and liquidity ratios

| Investment | Relationship of the number of ordinary shares and their price to the profits, dividends and assets of the company | EPS, P/E ratio, Dividend yield Dividend cover, Net assets per share |

The managers of the company are likely to be concerned about all aspects of the company and therefore may want to know about all of the key ratios in each category.

Shareholders or potential investors are concerned primarily with the investment ratios though certain financial stability and profitability measures are also likely to be of interest (for example gearing and ROCE).

Creditors are most likely to be concerned about financial stability, though a bank, acting as a major source of finance, will usually also look at profitability.

1.3   Commenting on the ratio

Ratios are of limited use on their own, thus most of the marks in an exam question will be available for sensible, well explained and accurate comments on key ratios.

If you doubt that you have anything to say, the following points should serve as a useful checklist:

- What does the ratio literally mean?

- What does a change in the ratio mean?

- What is the norm?

- What are the limitations of the ratio?

1.4   The acceptable range of values that a healthy company should achieve for those ratios

There is little that can be stated in general terms about the acceptable range of values. Profitability rates will vary between industry sectors and within industries for many reasons. The financial structure of a business can also vary considerably and yet the business operates 'healthily'. An oft quoted norm for the current ratio is 2 and the quick ratio is 1 but a supermarket for example with no credit customers and strong influence on its suppliers will have ratios far lower than this. In general the most meaningful analysis of ratios in terms of their acceptability is how well a business does in relation to its competitors.

1.5   Further information required

Any analyst in practice will be limited in the analysis he can perform by the amount of information available. He is unlikely to have access to all the facts which are available to a company's management.

In the examination the information which can be provided about a company in any one question will be limited. Part (a) of such a question could well ask you to interpret the available information. Part (b) could then ask you to state what further information you require.

2   Profitability ratios

2.1   Return on capital employed (ROCE)

The absolute figure of profit earned is not, in itself, significant since the size of the business earning that profit may vary enormously. It is significant to consider the size of the profit figure relative to the size of the business, size being expressed in terms of the quantity of capital employed by that business.

The return on capital employed is the ratio which measures this relationship. It is a key business objective, and is thus the key ratio in assessing financial achievement. It reflects the earning power of the business operations.

The ratio in simple form is:

$$\frac{\text{Profit}}{\text{Capital employed}} \times 100\%$$

ROCE is also known as the primary ratio because it is often the most important measure of profitability.

The ratio shows how efficiently a business is using its resources. If the return is very low, the business may be better off realising its assets and investing the proceeds in a high interest account! (This may sound extreme, but should be considered particularly for a small, unprofitable business with valuable assets such as freehold property.) Furthermore a low return can easily become a loss if the business suffers a downturn.

Once calculated, ROCE should be compared with:

- **previous years' figures** – provided there have been no changes in accounting policies unless suitable adjustments have been made to facilitate comparison (note, however that the effect of not replacing fixed assets is that their book value will decrease and ROCE will increase)

- **company's target ROCE** – where the company's management has determined a target return as part of its budget procedure, consistent failure by a part of the business to meet the target may make it a target for disposal

- **the cost of borrowings** – if the cost of borrowing is say 10% and ROCE 7%, then further borrowings will reduce EPS unless the extra money can be used in areas where the ROCE is higher than the cost of borrowings

- **other companies in same industry** – care is required in interpretation, since there may be:

  (a) different accounting policies, e.g. research and development expenditure, stock valuation and depreciation

  (b) different ages of plant - where assets are written down to low book values the ROCE will appear high

  (c) leased assets which may not appear in the balance sheet at all. (SSAP 21 requires assets held under finance leases to be on the balance sheet but not those held under operating leases.)

2.2 The problem of defining profit and net assets

Return on capital employed can be calculated in a number of different ways.

One version is the return on shareholders' equity which is more relevant for existing or prospective shareholders than management.

$$\text{Return on equity} = \frac{\text{Profit after interest after preference dividends}}{\text{Ordinary share capital} + \text{reserves}} \times 100\%$$

Profit may be before or after tax. After tax is a more accurate reflection of profits (management should seek to minimise tax) however as you will know deferred tax provisions can be subjective so profit before tax may be more objective.

The other commonly used ROCE is:

$$\text{Overall return} = \frac{\text{Operating profit}}{\text{Share capital} + \text{reserves} + \text{all borrowings}} \times 100\%$$

This is used by managers assessing performance.

Further problems with defining profits and net assets are as follows:

- **Treatment of associates and investments** – Where the profit excludes investment income, the balance sheet carrying amounts for associates and investments should be deducted from the capital employed.

  This gives an accurate measure of trading performance. If associates and investments are not deducted, the overall profit figure should include income from investments and associates.

- Large cash balances are not contributing to profits and some analysts therefore deduct them from capital employed (to compare operating profits with operating assets). However it is usually acceptable not to make this adjustment as ROCE is a performance measure and management have decided to operate with that large balance.

Note that any upwards revaluation of fixed assets causes a reduction in ROCE by:

- increasing the capital employed; and

- decreasing profits, by a higher depreciation charge.

2.3   Gross profit percentage

$$\text{Gross profit percentage} = \frac{\text{Gross profit}}{\text{Turnover}} \times 100\%$$

This is the margin that the company makes on its sales.

It is expected to remain reasonably constant. Since the ratio consists of a small number of components, a change may be traced to a change in:

- selling prices – normally deliberate though sometimes unavoidable for example, because of increased competition

- sales mix – often deliberate

- purchase cost – including carriage or discounts

- production cost – materials, labour or production overheads

- stock – errors in counting, valuing or cut-off, stock shortages.

Inter-company comparison of margins can be very useful but it is especially important to look at businesses within the same sector. For example food retailing is able to support low margins because of the high volume of sales. A manufacturing industry would usually have higher margins.

Low margins usually suggest poor performance but may be due to expansion costs (launching a new product) or trying to increase market share. Lower margins than usual suggest scope for improvement.

Above average margins are usually a sign of good management although unusually high margins may make the competition keen to join in and enjoy the 'rich pickings'.

A trading profit margin is:

$$\frac{\text{Operating profit}}{\text{Turnover}} \times 100\%$$

KEY POINT

Low margins usually suggest poor performance but may be due to expansion costs or trying to increase market share.

This is affected by more factors than the gross profit margin but it is equally useful and if the company does not disclose a cost of sales (perhaps using format 2) it may be used on its own in lieu of the gross profit percentage.

One of the many factors affecting the trading profit margin is depreciation, which is open to considerable subjective judgement. Inter-company comparisons should be made after suitable adjustments to align accounting policies.

ACTIVITY 1

X plc and Y plc are both involved in retailing.

Relevant information for the year ended 30 September 20X5 was as follows:

	X plc £'000	Y plc £'000
Sales	50,000	200,000
Profit before tax	10,000	10,000
Capital employed	50,000	50,000

Prepare the following ratios for both companies and comment on the results:

(i) ROCE

(ii) Profit margin

(iii) Asset turnover.

Feedback to this activity is at the end of the chapter.

2.4 Stock turnover

$$\text{Stock turnover ratio} = \frac{\text{Cost of sales}}{\text{Stocks}}$$

This yields a multiple expressed as, say, 10 times per annum.

An alternative is to express this as so many days stock:

$$\frac{\text{Stocks}}{\text{Cost of sales}} \times 365 \text{ days}$$

Sometimes an average (based on the average stock) is calculated which has a smoothing effect but may dampen the effect of a major change in the period.

An increasing number of days (or a diminishing multiple) implies that stock is turning over less quickly. This is usually regarded as a bad sign:

- it may reflect lack of demand for the goods

- it may reflect poor stock control, with its associated costs such as storage and insurance

- it may ultimately lead to stock obsolescence and related write-offs.

However, it may not necessarily be bad where:

- management are buying stock in larger quantities to take advantage of trade discounts

- management have increased stock levels to avoid stockouts

- the increase is slight and due to distortion of the ratio caused by comparing a year end stock figure with cost of sales for the year and that year has been one of increasing growth.

Stock turnover ratios vary enormously with the nature of the business. For example, a fishmonger would have a stock turnover period of 1-2 days, whereas a building contractor may have a stock turnover period of 200 days. Manufacturing companies may have a stock turnover ratio of 60-100 days. This period is likely to increase as the goods made become larger and more complex.

For large and complex items (for example rolling stock or aircraft) there may be sharp fluctuations in stock turnover according to whether delivery took place just before or just after the year end.

A manufacturer should take into consideration:

- reliability of suppliers: if the supplier is unreliable it is prudent to hold more raw materials

- demand: if demand is erratic it is prudent to hold more finished goods.

2.5 Debtors turnover

$$\text{Debtors turnover ratio} = \frac{\text{Trade debtors}}{\text{Turnover}} \times 100\%$$

This can be expressed as a percentage as above or as a number of days:

$$\frac{\text{Trade debtors}}{\text{Turnover}} \times 365 \text{ days}$$

The trade debtors used may be a year-end figure or the average for the year. Where an average is used to calculate a number of days the ratio is the average number of days' credit taken by customers.

For cash-based businesses like supermarkets, debtors days is unlikely to exceed one as there are no true credit sales.

For other businesses the result should be compared with the stated credit policy. A period of 30 days or 'at the end of the month following delivery' are common credit terms.

Increasing debtors days is usually a bad sign as it suggests lack of proper credit control. However, it may be due to:

- a deliberate policy to extend the stated credit period to attract more trade

- one major new customer being allowed different terms.

Falling debtors days is usually a good sign, though it could indicate that the company is suffering a cash shortage.

The debtors days ratio can be distorted by:

- using year end figures which do not represent average debtors

- debt factoring which results in very low debtors

- other credit finance agreements such as hire purchase, where there is insufficient analysis of turnover (HP debtors should be shown separately) to calculate proper ratios.

2.6   Creditors days

The creditors days ratio is usually expressed as:

$$\frac{\text{Trade creditors}}{\text{Purchases}} \times 365 \text{ days}$$

and represents the credit period taken by the company from its suppliers. An average of trade creditors may also be used.

Where purchases are not known, cost of sales is used, or failing that, sales.

The ratio is always compared to previous years. Once again there are two main contrasting points:

- a long credit period may be good as it represents a source of free finance; or

- a long credit period may indicate that the company is unable to pay more quickly because of liquidity problems.

Note that if the credit period is long:

- the company may develop a poor reputation as a slow payer and may not be able to find new suppliers

- existing suppliers may decide to discontinue supplies

- the company may be losing out on worthwhile cash discounts.

3   The liquidity position of companies

3.1   Ratios

Two ratios are used to measure a business's ability to meet its own short-term liabilities.

- Current or (working capital) ratio

$$\frac{\text{Current assets}}{\text{Current liabilities}}$$

- Liquidity, acid test or quick assets ratio

$$\frac{\text{Current assets - stock}}{\text{Current liabilities}}$$

3.2   Current ratio

The current ratio measures the adequacy of current assets to meet its short-term liabilities. It reflects whether the company is in a position to meet its liabilities as they fall due.

Traditionally a current ratio of 2 or higher was regarded as appropriate for most businesses to maintain creditworthiness, however more recently a figure of 1.5 is regarded as the norm.

A higher figure should be regarded with suspicion as it may be due to:

- high levels of stocks and debtors (check working capital management ratios); or

- high cash levels which could be put to better use (for example by investing in fixed assets).

The current ratio should be looked at in the light of what is normal for the business. For example, supermarkets tend to have low current ratios because:

- there are no trade debtors; and

- there is usually very tight cash control as there will be considerable investment in developing new sites and improving existing sites.

It is also worth considering:

- availability of further finance, for example is the overdraft at the limit? – very often this information is highly relevant but not disclosed in the accounts

- seasonal nature of the business – one way of doing this is to compare the interest charges in the profit and loss account with the overdraft and other loans in the balance sheet. If the interest rate appears abnormally high this is probably because the company has had higher levels of borrowings during the year

- long-term liabilities and when they fall due and how will they be financed

- nature of the stocks – as stated above where stocks are slow moving, the quick ratio probably provides a better indicator of short-term liquidity.

3.3   Quick ratio

This is also known as the acid test ratio because by eliminating stocks from current assets it provides the acid test of whether the company has sufficient resources (debtors and cash) to settle its liabilities. Norms for the quick ratio range from 1 to 0.7.

Like the current ratio it is relevant to consider the nature of the business (again supermarkets have very low quick ratios).

Sometimes the quick ratio is calculated on the basis of a six week time frame (i.e. the quick assets are those which will turn into cash in six weeks; quick liabilities are those which fall due for payment within six weeks). This basis would usually include the following in quick assets:

- bank, cash and short-term investments

- trade debtors

thus excluding prepayments and stocks.

Quick liabilities would usually include:

- bank overdraft which is repayable on demand

- trade creditors, tax and social security

- proposed dividends.

Corporation tax may be excluded.

When interpreting the quick ratio, care should be taken over the status of the bank overdraft. A company with a low quick ratio may actually have no problem in paying its creditors if sufficient overall overdraft facilities are available.

Both the current and quick ratio may be distorted by window dressing. For example, if the current ratio is 1.4 and trade creditors are paid just before the year end out of positive cash balances, the ratios improve as shown below:

	Before	*Payment of £400 trade creditors*	*After*
Current assets	£1,400	-£400	£1,000
Current liabilities	£1,000	-£400	£600
Current ratio	1.4		1.7

3.4   The component cause of changes in liquidity

'Financial balance' is the balance between the various forms of available finance relative to the requirements of the business.

A business must have a sufficient level of long-term capital to finance its long-term investment in fixed assets. Part of the investment in current assets would also be financed by relatively permanent capital with the balance being provided by trade credit and other short-term borrowings. Any expansion in activity will normally require a broadening of the long-term capital base, without which 'overtrading' may develop.

Suitability of finance is also a key factor. A permanent expansion of a company's activities should not be financed by temporary, short-term borrowings. A short-term increase in activity such as the 'January sales' in a retail trading company could ideally be financed by overdraft.

A major addition to fixed assets such as the construction of a new factory would not normally be financed on a long-term basis by overdraft. It might be found, however, that the expenditure was temporarily financed by short-term loans until construction was completed, when the overdraft would be 'funded' by a long-term borrowing secured on the completed building.

3.5   The importance of maintaining a healthy liquid position: overtrading

Overtrading arises where a company expands its turnover fairly rapidly without securing additional long-term capital adequate for its needs. The symptoms of overtrading are:

- stocks increasing, possibly more than proportionately to sales

- debtors increasing, possibly more than proportionately to sales

- cash and liquid assets declining at a fairly alarming rate

- creditors increasing rapidly.

The above symptoms simply imply that the company has expanded without giving proper thought to the necessity to expand its capital base. It has consequently continued to rely on its creditors and probably its bank overdraft to provide the additional finance required. It will reach a stage where creditors will withhold further supplies and bankers will refuse to honour further cheques until borrowings are reduced. The problem is that borrowings cannot be reduced until sales revenue is earned, which in turn cannot be achieved until production is completed, which in turn is dependent upon materials being available and wages paid. Overall result – deadlock and rapid financial collapse!

ACTIVITY 2

Calculate the liquidity and working capital ratios for P plc for the year ended 31 December 20X7.

	£m
Turnover	1,867.5
Gross profit	489.3
Stock	147.9
Trade debtors	393.4
Trade creditors	275.1
Cash	53.8
Short-term investments	6.2
Other creditors	284.3

Feedback to this activity is at the end of the chapter.

4 Long-term financial stability

4.1 Gearing

DEFINITION

'**Gearing**' is the relationship between a company's equity capital and reserves and its fixed return capital.

A company is highly geared if it has a substantial proportion of its total capital in the form of preference shares or debentures or loan stock.

A company is said to have low gearing if only a small proportion of its total capital is in the form of preference shares, debentures or loan stock.

A company financed entirely by equity shares has no gearing.

KEY POINT

A company financed entirely by equity shares has no gearing.

4.2 The implications of high or low gearing

The importance of gearing can be illustrated by an example as follows:

Example

Two companies, A plc and B plc, both have capital of £10,000. A plc has it all in the form of equity shares of £1 each, B plc has 5,000 £1 equity shares and £5,000 of 10% debentures.

Both companies earn profits of £5,000 in year 1 and £2,000 in year 2. Tax is assumed at 35% and the dividend paid is 10p per share.

The position will be as follows:

	A plc £	B plc £
Shares	10,000	5,000
Debentures	-	5,000
	£10,000	£10,000

	A plc		B plc	
	Year 1	Year 2	Year 1	Year 2
	£	£	£	£
Profit before tax and debenture interest	5,000	2,000	5,000	2,000
Debenture interest	-	-	500	500
			4,500	1,500
Taxation (35%)	1,750	700	1,575	525
Earnings	3,250	1,300	2,925	975
Dividend (10%)	1,000	1,000	500	500
Retained profits	£2,250	300	£2,425	475
Earnings per share	32.5p	13p	58.5p	19.5p

The effects of gearing can be seen to be as follows:

(a) debenture interest is an allowable deduction before taxation, whereas dividends are paid out of profits after taxation. Company B has consistently higher retained profits than Company A

(b) earnings of a highly geared company are more sensitive to profit changes. This is shown by the following table:

Company	A plc	B plc
Change in profit before interest and taxation	–60%	–60%
Change in earnings	–60%	$-66\frac{2}{3}\%$

The reason for the fluctuation is obviously the element of debenture interest which must be paid regardless of profit level.

This more than proportionate change in earnings is important in relation to the share price of the companies. Many investors value their shares by applying a multiple (known as the P/E ratio) to the earnings per share. Applying a multiple of say 10 to the EPS disclosed above would indicate share valuations as follows:

Company	A plc		B plc	
Year	1	2	1	2
Share price	£3.25	£1.30	£5.85	£1.95

Thus the price of a highly geared company will often be more volatile than a company with only a small amount of gearing.

Not all companies are suitable for a highly geared structure. A company must have two fundamental characteristics if it is to use gearing successfully. These are as follows:

• **Relatively stable profits** – Debenture interest must be paid whether or not profits are earned. A company with erratic profits may have insufficient funds in a bad year with which to pay debenture interest. This would result in the appointment of a receiver and possibly the liquidation of the company.

• **Suitable assets for security** – Most issues of loan capital are secured on some or all of the company's assets which must be suitable for the purpose. A company with most of its capital invested in fast depreciating assets or stocks subject to rapid changes in demand and price would not be suitable for high gearing.

The classic examples of companies which are suited to high gearing are those in property investment and the hotel/leisure services industry. These companies generally enjoy relatively stable profits and have assets which are highly suitable for charging. Note that nonetheless these are industries that could be described as cyclical.

Companies not suited to high gearing would include those in the extractive industries and high-tech industries where constant changes occur. These companies could experience erratic profits and would generally have inadequate assets to pledge as security.

4.3 Methods of computation

There are two methods commonly used for expressing gearing.

(a) The debt/equity ratio, calculated by taking:

$$\frac{\text{Loans} + \text{preference share capital}}{\text{Ordinary share capital} + \text{reserves} + \text{minority interest}} \times 100\%$$

This is more sensitive than (b).

(b) The percentage of capital employed represented by borrowings:

$$\frac{\text{Loans} + \text{preference share capital}}{\text{Total capital}} \times 100\%$$

where total capital is loans, preference share capital, ordinary share capital, reserves and minority interests.

Advanced aspects of computing the gearing ratio are dealt with below.

4.4 Ways in which the application of GAAP affects the gearing of an individual company

GAAP affects the gearing of an individual company because the variation in accounting policies affects the amount at which debt and equity are stated. An accounting standard of particular relevance here is FRS 4 which attempts to restrict the past ability of companies to classify debt as equity and to state debt at lower than its repayable amount. Other GAAP which affect gearing include the following.

- Treatment of development expenditure under SSAP 13 may result in the creation of an intangible asset. Alternatively, development expenditure may be written off as it is incurred.
- Revaluation of assets changes the value of equity but revaluation may not be undertaken by all companies.
- Non-recording of assets as they fall within the definition of operating leases. A company may have engineered a lease to ensure that it does fall within the operating lease definition rather than the finance lease definition.

5 Ratios relevant to potential investors

5.1 Earnings per share (EPS)

The calculation of EPS was covered earlier.

The EPS is used primarily as a measure of profitability, thus an increasing EPS is seen as a good sign. The EPS is also used to calculate the price earnings ratio which is dealt with below.

5.2   The relationship between the market price of a share and its EPS

$$\text{P/E ratio} = \frac{\text{Share price}}{\text{EPS}}$$

The price earnings ratio is the most widely referred to stock market ratio, also commonly described as an earnings multiple. It is calculated as the 'purchase of a number of years' earnings' but it represents the market's consensus of the future prospects of that share. The higher the P/E ratio, the faster the growth the market is expecting in the company's future EPS. Correspondingly, the lower the P/E ratio the lower the expected future growth.

Another aspect of interpreting it, is that a published EPS exists for a year and therefore the P/E ratio given in a newspaper is generally based on an increasingly out of date EPS.

Example

For the year ended 31 December 20X6:

- EPS for X plc = 10p

- Overall market P/E ratio = 10

- P/E ratio for X plc = 20 (because market expects above average growth)

- Market price at 30 April 20X7 (date of publication of previous year's accounts) = £2

- During the year X plc does even better than expected and by 29 April 20X8 the share price is up to £3, therefore giving a P/E ratio of 30 (based on EPS for year ended 31 December 20X6)

- Year ended 31 December 20X7 EPS = 15p, announced on 30 April 20X8. This is in line with expectations so share price is unchanged and P/E ratio drops again to 20 (£3/15p).

5.3   Dividend yield

This is the percentage of the dividend to the market price. In calculating the gross dividend yield, the dividends are grossed up to show the amount including tax credit (at the rate of $^{10}/_{90}$ of the net amount).

Z plc declared an interim dividend of 3.5 pence a share on 15 July 20X4. The final dividend for the year ended 30 September 20X4 was 5.5 pence. The ex-dividend share price was 265p.

What was the net dividend yield?

Feedback to this activity is at the end of the chapter.

5.4   Dividend cover

This is the relationship between available profits and the ordinary dividends payable out of those profits, reflecting how sustainable the dividend level is likely to be in the future. The *Financial Times* adjusts profits to exclude exceptional profits and losses.

6   Non-financial measures of performance

6.1   Introduction

Not all an entity's activities can be expressed in monetary terms. Although the overriding objective of most entities is to maximise profit, there may be other objectives, such as the efficient provision of a service to the public. Ratio analysis and other interpretation techniques based on the financial statements cannot necessarily measure all aspects of performance.

For example, the effect of a business on the environment cannot easily be measured using financial criteria, but is increasingly regarded as an aspect of performance.

6.2   Examples of non-financial performance measures

(a) **Marketing effectiveness**

- trend in market share
- customer visits per salesperson
- client contact hours per salesperson
- number of customers.

(b) **Production performance**

- number of suppliers
- manufacturing lead times
- output per employee
- material yield percentage
- proportion of output requiring correction
- adherence to schedules (e.g. delivery dates met).

(c) **Personnel**

- staff turnover
- training time per employee
- days lost through absenteeism (e.g. accidents or sickness)
- number of complaints received.

(d) **Service quality**

- proportion of repeat business
- customer waiting time
- proportion of deliveries on time
- client turnover.

As with financial ratio analysis, acceptable values may depend on the type of organisation.

Non-financial performance measures are likely to be particularly relevant to 'not for profit' organisations as these organisations need to measure the effectiveness with which services have been provided.

Examples of non-financial performance indicators for public sector bodies could include:

- pupil:teacher ratios

- population per police officer

- serious offences per 1,000 of the population

- proportion of trains arriving on time

- number of patients who wait more than six months for treatment.

6.3   Advantages of non-financial indicators

The advantages of non-financial measures over accounting measures include the following:

- they are easy to calculate

- they are more directly comparable with results of previous periods (e.g. they do not suffer from inflation)

- they are more easily understood by non-financial managers

- they are less likely to be manipulated.

The disadvantage to the external analyst of a business is the lack of non-financial information available in the annual report. They are often therefore of more use to a person within the business.

7   Designing an accounting based performance measurement system

7.1   Introduction

Management use both financial and non-financial indicators to measure the performance of the business as a whole and the performance of individual managers. You will have already studied the detailed principles of performance measurement for the management accounting papers. The general principles are considered below.

7.2   Objectives

The first stage in designing a system is to determine the objectives of the entity. If the entity is a profit-making organisation, maximising profit is normally the most important objective as this maximises the return to investors. Capital growth is also important to investors.

However, many businesses are increasingly recognising that they have wider responsibilities and that companies should be run for the benefit of all their 'stakeholders'.

An entity might set itself objectives of satisfying the needs of some or all of the following stakeholders:

- Customers: Service, value for money, product quality

- Suppliers: Regular and prompt payment, continuity of business

- Management: Remuneration, prestige

- Employees   Job security, job satisfaction, adequate wages and salaries

- The community: Preservation of the natural environment, providing employment.

KEY POINT

Management use both financial and non-financial indicators to measure the performance of the business as a whole and the performance of individual managers.

It is now recognised that, although satisfying the needs of other stakeholders may reduce profit in the short term, it may contribute to a successful business in the longer term.

DEFINITIONS

Quantitative measures are those which may be expressed in numerical terms; examples include profit and market share.

Qualitative measures are those which cannot be expressed in numerical terms, but which may be supported by numerical data. For example quality may be evidenced by the number of complaints.

7.3 Measures

The next step is to decide what is to be measured. It has been said that 'what gets measured gets done'. If something cannot be measured it cannot be improved.

The measures adopted are affected by:

- the competitive environment

- the business's chosen strategy, e.g. cost leadership or product differentiation

- the type of business.

Performance measures may be classified into various groups: financial and non-financial measures, and quantitative and qualitative measures.

7.4 Potential problems

KEY POINT

If something cannot be measured it cannot be improved.

Accounting measurements may be used in a simplistic way when setting targets and measuring the organisation's performance. This may have adverse consequences. Directors and managers may pursue short-term profit at the expense of longer-term growth and this may destroy the longer-term value of the business. Management may meet targets by manipulating performance measures, either by 'creative accounting' or other means.

These problems may be avoided by:

- adopting measures of short-term performance that are consistent with longer-term objectives; and

- not attaching undue significance to any one performance measure, but using a variety of financial and non-financial measures that are consistent with the organisation's objectives.

8   Other measures of performance

8.1 Limitations of traditional measures

KEY POINT

Ratio analysis has many limitations, particularly where it is based on traditional accounting measures such as operating profit margin and earnings per share.

Ratio analysis has many limitations, particularly where it is based on traditional accounting measures such as operating profit margin and earnings per share. These limitations include the following:

- Profit and capital employed are arbitrary figures. They depend on the accounting policies adopted by an entity.

- The accounting periods covered by the financial statements may not reflect representative financial positions. Many businesses produce accounts to a date on which there is relatively low amounts of trading activity. As a result the items on a balance sheet are not representative of the items throughout the accounting period.

- Ratios based on historic cost accounts do not give a true picture of trends from year to year. An apparent increase in profit may not be a 'true' increase, because of the effects of inflation.

- Ratios based on the financial statements only reflect those activities which can be expressed in money terms. They do not give a complete picture of the activities of a business.

- Ratios based on the financial statements reflect historical information. Investors and other users of financial statements are likely to be more interested in an entity's future prospects.

8.2   Other performance measures

Return on investment (ROI)

$$\text{Basic ROI} = \frac{\text{Profit before interest and tax}}{\text{Capital employed}} \times 100\%$$

This is similar to ROCE. It can also be calculated as:

$$\frac{\text{Average annual profit}}{\text{Average book value of capital invested}} \times 100\%$$

and be used to forecast the return on an investment or a project.

ROI measures the efficiency of an entity, a division or a project in generating profits. It is widely used by external analysts and has the advantage of being simple to understand and to calculate from a company's financial statements.

It also has similar drawbacks to ROCE, as both the numerator and the denominator can be affected by the entity's choice of accounting policies.

Residual income (RI)

RI is sometimes known as economic profit.

$$\text{RI} = \text{Profit} - (\text{notional interest charge} \times \text{capital employed})$$

The interest charge deducted represents the opportunity cost of using the capital. The deduction is made because to be 'truly' profitable, a company must generate a return in excess of that required by all its providers of capital, both shareholders and lenders. Although the profit and loss account includes a deduction for debt interest, it does not include a similar deduction for the cost of shareholders' capital. (Equity dividends are determined by the directors and the amount paid does not necessarily reflect the cost of shareholders' capital.)

RI is widely used, particularly to assess the performance of individual units or managers within an entity. Many academics believe that RI is superior to ROCE and ROI, because it takes into account the level of an entity's or a manager's capital expenditure and other investment as well as the profit generated from that investment. RI may be used to assess the performance of individual managers, but this is not appropriate unless the manager is able to influence significantly the level of capital investment.

However, there are some significant problems associated with RI.

- It can be difficult to calculate. For example, what rate should be used? The entity's weighted average cost of capital is often used, but there are also arguments for using current long-term money rates, and/or rates that take risk into account.

- Because RI is based on profits, it has the same limitations as more traditional profit based measures, for example, it is affected by the choice of accounting policies and does not take account of inflation.

- Like EPS, ROCE and ROI, it can be manipulated so that short-term targets are met at the expense of the company's long-term prospects. For example, it can be increased by reducing long-term investment.

- Because rapidly growing companies use large amounts of capital employed, they may have low RI.

ACTIVITY 4

ACTIVITY 4

A company has operating profit of £500,000 and capital employed of £2,500,000. Its weighted average cost of capital (WACC) is 12%.

Calculate ROI and RI using this information.

Feedback to this activity is at the end of the chapter.

8.3 The idea of shareholder value

Shareholder value is created by generating future returns for equity investors which exceed the returns that those investors could expect to earn elsewhere. It is believed that the creation of shareholder value will be reflected in the share price of the company. Many companies are adopting the enhancement of shareholder value, rather than the generation of profit, as their primary objective.

A number of ways of measuring shareholder value have been developed as follows:

- **Shareholder Value Analysis (SVA)**

  SVA calculates a value for the company that is based on projected future cash flows, discounted to their present value at the company's cost of capital. The market value of debt is deducted from this figure to give shareholder value.

- **Economic value added (EVA)**

  This is a variation on RI.

- **Market value added (MVA)**

  MVA is the additional value that is added to a company by its management in excess of the actual value of the funds invested by the shareholders.

The market value of the company is the market share price multiplied by the number of shares in issue. Performance can be measured by calculating the yearly change in MVA.

Measures of shareholder value have a number of common features.

- They focus on cash flow rather than on profit.

- They emphasise the 'whole' business. The idea behind the concept of shareholder value is that there are several 'drivers' within a business that can be managed to create value, e.g. growth in sales; increase in the operating profit margin; reduction in the effective tax rate. These are summarised into a single performance measure.

- They are forward-looking. In particular, calculating SVA involves estimating future performance.

For the purpose of your examination, the most important of these measures is EVA, as this can be calculated from accounting information by external users.

8.4 Economic value added (EVA)

EVA was developed by an American consultant, Stern Stewart, and is a sophisticated version of RI. It is calculated as follows:

EVA = adjusted net operating profit after tax – (WACC × adjusted invested capital)

Stern Stewart argued that the basic RI calculation was distorted by the following factors:

- the effect of accruals based bookkeeping, which tends to hide the true 'cash' profitability of a business

- the effect of prudence, which often leads to conservative bias and affects the relevance of reported figures

- the effect of 'successful efforts accounting' whereby companies write off costs associated with unsuccessful investments. This tends to understate the 'true' capital of a business and subject the profit and loss account to 'one off' gains and losses.

Therefore adjustments are made to operating profit and asset values. Stern Stewart identified over 100 potential adjustments but in practice only adjustments that have a material effect are made (normally 5 to 10). They include the following:

- removing non-recurring gains and losses such as restructuring costs
- capitalising intangible assets such as research and development expenditure
- adding back 'unnecessary' provisions
- capitalising the net present value of future operating lease payments.

Notice that adjustments for provisions should be less frequent following the issue of FRS 12 and that the ASB is currently proposing to bring operating leases onto the balance sheet. However, further adjustments will need to be made now that FRS 19 requires full provision for deferred tax. Full provision is believed to distort profits and capital employed for the purpose of calculating EVA.

Example

	£m
Profits available to ordinary shareholders (from the accounts)	865
Add: interest expense	249
Net operating profit after tax before EVA adjustments	1,114
Less: non-recurring income	(120)
Add: net R&D expense	10
Add: net movement in provisions	101
Net operating profit after tax	1,105
Shareholders' funds (from the accounts)	5,998
Add: cumulative goodwill written off	1,093
Add: capitalised R&D	258
Add: provisions	439
Less: cumulative non-recurring items	(47)
Adjusted shareholders' funds	7,741
Total debt (from the accounts)	1,775
Present value of operating lease commitments	4,528
Total capital	14,044

WACC is 10%.

EVA: $1,105 - (14,044 \times 10\%) = (299)$.

EVA has all the advantages of the RI calculation and addresses some of the problems associated with using profit-based measures. It is becoming increasingly popular as a performance measure.

However, it has several drawbacks:

- it can be difficult and time-consuming to calculate
- it does not address the effect of inflation
- it does not adjust for the effect of depreciation, which is an arbitrary figure
- managers may be encouraged to take decisions which boost EVA in the short term at the expense of long-term value creation.

A positive EVA for a single year does not necessarily mean that value has been created and a negative EVA for a single year does not necessarily mean that value has been destroyed. EVA is probably most helpful when it is used to interpret an entity's performance over a period of several years.

9 Failure prediction

9.1 The importance of corporate failure prediction

A number of user groups would like advance warning of corporate failure. For example, banks and suppliers need to assess the creditworthiness of their customers, and auditors must assess the going concern of their clients. Managers should also be alerted to problems before they become terminal.

Insolvency arises from the inability to pay debts when they fall due. This can be caused by overtrading, borrowing too much, losing customers, bad debts and failing to adapt to market changes.

9.2 Going concern models

A number of models have been developed that use key ratios to determine whether an enterprise may go out of business. Most models calculate a 'score' for the enterprise, which is then compared to a 'pass mark'.

The original model was developed by the American Professor Altman in 1968 and is known as the Z score. The Z score equation consists of five ratios and each ratio is given a weighting. The ratios and weightings were derived from an empirical study of American enterprises and were the ratios and weightings that best discriminated between failed and successful enterprises.

9.3 Altman's Z score

$$Z = 1.2X_1 + 1.4X_2 + 3.3X_3 + 0.6X_4 + 1.0X_5$$

$$\text{where} \quad X_1 = \frac{\text{Working capital}}{\text{Total assets}}$$

$$X_2 = \frac{\text{Retained earnings}}{\text{Total assets}}$$

$$X_3 = \frac{\text{Profit before interest and tax}}{\text{Total assets}}$$

$$X_4 = \frac{\text{Market capitalisation}}{\text{Book value of debts}}$$

$$X_5 = \frac{\text{Sales}}{\text{Total assets}}$$

The pass mark for the Z score is 3.0. Above that level enterprises should be safe (for two or three years anyway!). A score below 1.8 indicates potential problems.

Altman's work in the US was followed by Professor Taffler in the UK, who produced his own version of a 'Z' score equation in 1977.

9.4 Criticisms of Z scores

Criticisms have included:

(a) As with all financial analysis, comparisons are hindered by different companies using **different accounting policies**.

(b) Z scores are based upon **historical information**. By the time that financial statements are published it may be too late for user groups to take corrective action.

(c) There is **no underlying theory** to these Z scores. They merely codify symptoms of past failures. These symptoms may not be useful in predicting failures in the future.

(d) They do not indicate any **time scale** for failure.

(e) They tend to give a large number of **false readings**. Companies identified as potential failures by a Z score often survive. This reduces confidence in any predictions based on Z scores.

Provided that the models are used as an additional analytical resource by a skilled financial analyst, they serve a useful purpose.

9.5   Argenti's failure model

Argenti developed a failure model only partly based on financial information. It was developed from a wide review of actual cases and discussions with bankers, business executives and receivers. It lacks the robustness of Z scores as it has no precise definitions.

The model is summarised below. Points are either given in full or a nil is scored.

The scores are interpreted as follows:

Below 25 in total	The enterprise is not in danger of failing.
Over 25 in total	The enterprise may fail within five years. The higher the mark, the sooner it will fail.
Over 10 for defects	The management may make a fatal mistake.
Over 15 for mistakes but below 10 for defects.	A competent management is running a risky business.

Argenti's model	Score	Danger mark
Defects		
Management		
Autocratic chief executive	8	
Chief executive is also the chairman	4	
Unbalanced skill and knowledge on the board	2	
Passive board	2	
Weak finance director	2	
Lack of professional managers below the board	1	
Poor accounting systems	9	
Slow response to change	15	
Sub-total	43	*10*
Mistakes		
Over-trading	15	
Over-geared	15	
Over reliant on a single project	15	
Sub-total	45	**15**

Symptoms

Worsening ratios etc	4
Creative accounting	4
Non-financial signs: declining quality, morale, market share	3
Terminal signs: writs, rumours, resignation	1
Sub-total	12

Total	**100**	**25**

The management defects identified by Argenti cover some of the weaknesses that have been identified by the recent reports into corporate governance.

<table>
<tr><td>

SELF-TEST
QUESTIONS

</td><td>

Financial measures of performance

1   State four ratios that measure (a) profitability and (b) investment value. (1.2)

Profitability ratios

2   What should ROCE typically be compared with? (2.1)

3   Changes in which factors will affect the gross profit percentage? (2.3)

4   In which circumstances might a decrease in stock turnover be a healthy sign? (2.4)

The liquidity position of companies

5   What should be included in quick liabilities for the purpose of calculating the quick ratio? (3.3)

6   What are the symptoms of overtrading? (3.5)

Long-term financial stability

7   What two fundamental characteristics must a company have if it is to use gearing successfully? (4.2)

Non-financial measures of performance

8   Give seven examples of non-financial performance measures. (6.2)

Other measures of performance

9   What is the advantage of ROI as a performance measure? (8.2)

10   What are shareholder value analysis and economic value added (8.3, 8.4) ?

Failure prediction

11   What are the weaknesses of Z score failure prediction models? (9.4)

</td></tr>
</table>

<table>
<tr><td>

EXAM-TYPE
QUESTION

</td><td>

Provincial Motor Spares Ltd

The trial balance of Provincial Motor Spares Ltd as at 31 December 20X3 was:

	Dr £'000	Cr £'000
Ordinary shares of £1 each		3,600
10% cumulative preference shares of £1 each		1,000
General reserve		1,820
Profit and loss account at 1 January 20X3		2,250
8% Debentures		500
Profit for 20X3		3,780
Debenture redemption reserve		290
Creditors		4,130
Tax payable on 1 January 20X4		700
Deferred taxation on 1 January 20X3		1,655
Investment income		14

</td></tr>
</table>

Premises	7,200	
Equipment	3,800	
Investments	251	
Stock	6,580	
Debtors	1,480	
Bank	428	
	19,739	19,739

(a) Profits accrue evenly throughout the year.

(b) Provision is to be made for

(i)   tax of £1,900,000 on the profits of the current year, payable in 20X5

(ii) the preference dividend

(iii) the proposed ordinary dividend of 10%.

(c) A transfer of £170,000 is to be made to the general reserve.

(d) Sales for the year totalled £21,000,000 of which £1,000,000 was value added tax.

One of the directors had recently read an article on methods of predicting company failure. One of the methods combined five variables and calculated a Z score by multiplying each variable by a discriminant coefficient.

The five variables (labelled X1, X2, X3, X4, X5) were as follows

X1 =   net working capital/total assets (%)

X2 =   retained earnings/total assets (%)

X3 =   earnings before interest and taxes/total assets (%)

X4 =   market value of equity/book value of total debt securities (%)

X5 =   sales/total assets (times)

The Z score was calculated using the following formula

Z score = 0.012 X1 + 0.014 X2 + 0.033 X3 + 0.006 X4 + 0.999 X5

The score was interpreted on the basis that all companies with a score less than 1.81 were likely to become bankrupt; all companies with a score greater than 2.99 were unlikely to become bankrupt; companies with scores between 1.81 and 2.99 were likely to consist of companies that may become bankrupt.

The market value of equity is calculated using a PE ratio of 5:1 applied to earnings before tax and investment income, but after debenture interest.

Required:

(a) Briefly explain the possible reasons for selecting each of the five variables that have been included in the formula given above.   **(5 marks)**

(b) Calculate the Z score for Provincial Motor Spares Ltd using the formula provided.   **(9 marks)**

(c) Briefly give your own views, with supporting calculation, of the company's liquidity and suggest what further reports you would advise the company to prepare.   **(11 marks)**

(Total: 25 marks)

For the answer to this question see the 'Answers' section at the end of the book

	X plc	*Y plc*
ROCE	$\dfrac{10,000}{50,000} \times 100\%$	$\dfrac{10,000}{50,000} \times 100\%$
	$= 20\%$	$= 20\%$
Profit margin	$\dfrac{10,000}{50,000} \times 100\%$	$\dfrac{10,000}{200,000} \times 100\%$
	$= 20\%$	$= 5\%$
Asset turnover	$\dfrac{50,000}{50,000}$	$\dfrac{200,000}{50,000}$
	$= 1$	$= 4$

The ROCE for both companies is the same. X plc has a higher profit margin, whilst Y plc shows a more efficient use of assets. This indicates that there may be a trade-off between profit margin and asset turnover.

Current ratio $\dfrac{147.9 + 393.4 + 53.8 + 6.2}{275.1 + 284.3}$ $= \dfrac{601.3}{559.4}$

$$= 1.07$$

Quick ratio $\dfrac{601.3 - 147.9}{559.4}$ $= 0.81$

Debtors' collection period $\dfrac{393.4}{1,867.5} \times 365 = 77$ days

Stock turnover period $\dfrac{147.9}{1,867.5 - 489.3} \times 365 = 39$ days

Creditors' payment period $\dfrac{275.1}{1,867.5 - 489.3} \times 365 = 73$ days.

Dividend yield $= \dfrac{3.5 + 5.5}{265} \times 100 = 3.4\%$

ROI: $\dfrac{500,000}{2,500,000} \times 100 = 20\%$

RI: $500,000 - (2,500,000 \times 12\%) = £200,000$

Chapter 23

VALUATION AND CHANGING PRICES

This chapter looks at alternatives to historic cost accounting. You will already have studied the alternative systems of accounting for changing prices: current cost accounting (CCA); and current purchasing power accounting (CPP) and the text revises the main principles, advantages and disadvantages of each.

It is now very unlikely that a full system of inflation accounting will be introduced in the foreseeable future. However, the ASB favours greater use of current values in financial statements and several of its recent standards reflect this. We look at the ASB's approach to measurement in financial statements.

Objectives

When you have studied this chapter you should be able to:

- understand the alternative definitions of capital employed and measurement bases for assets

- discuss the impact of price level changes on business performance

- appraise the alternative methods of accounting for price level changes.

1 Alternative views of capital employed

1.1 The deficiencies of a historic cost balance sheet

The pure HC balance sheet ignores the current value of assets and thus the amounts reported are unlikely to be realistic up-to-date measures of the resources employed by the business. The main problems will be unrecorded assets such as goodwill and undervalued assets such as land and buildings.

There is a general consensus that users of financial statements would like details of the current worth of assets which is why many balance sheets do include revaluations.

As no account is taken of the changing value of money over time, it is also difficult to interpret trends. Revaluing assets will not remedy this defect as the valuations reflect prices ruling at a balance sheet date, whereas previous years' accounts will reflect valuations at previous years' prices.

1.2 The ways in which historic cost accounts can be misleading for decision-making purposes

HC accounts can be misleading in a period of changing prices in a number of ways.

(a) **Matching current revenues with out of date costs**

If a business buys an item of stock for £10 and sells it for £20, historic cost accounting would allow distribution of the profit of £10. However if the replacement cost of that item has now risen to £13 that would leave insufficient funds to remain in business.

The concept of operating capital maintenance would only distribute a maximum of £7, arrived at by comparing the current cost of sales of £13 with the current revenue of £20. This would leave £13, sufficient to continue in business.

(b) **Distorted ratios**

With profits overstated in (a) and the balance sheet understated (see above) key ratios such as ROCE can be misleading.

(c) **Fixed monetary items**

No attempt is made to recognise the loss that arises through holding assets of fixed monetary value and the gain that arises through holding liabilities of fixed monetary value during a period of rising prices.

(d) **Time series information**

If no account is taken of changes in the real value of money a misleading impression may be given by trend information. A company may appear to be increasing turnover and profits but this may only be in monetary, not in real terms.

1.3 General and specific price changes

The argument for an alternative to HC accounting has revolved around the question of whether accounting for the effects of inflation should be directed towards:

(a) presenting accounts in the same real terms from one year to another; or

(b) protecting the operating capabilities of companies; or

(c) some combination of the two.

Option (a) involves accounting for general price changes. The owners of the business are shareholders who may suffer from general inflation as the purchasing power of their investment in the business declines. Changes in general prices are thus used to record the effect. This system is known as current purchasing power accounting (CPP).

Option (b) involves the consideration of specific price changes. Here the perspective of the business as a separate entity is paramount. The effects of price changes on the specific assets owned by the business are therefore used. This system is known as current value accounting or current cost accounting (CCA).

1.4 Current purchasing power – the mechanics

CPP accounts are prepared by adjusting all monetary amounts in the accounts to reflect the value of money at one point in time. Thus, the unit of measurement is the 'CPP unit' rather than the monetary unit. In principle the CPP unit can be based on the value of money at any point in time.

CPP accounts are prepared by updating all items in the profit and loss account, and all non-monetary items in the balance sheet, by the CPP factor:

$$\frac{\text{Index at the balance sheet date}}{\text{Index at date of entry in accounts}}$$

Depreciation is adjusted by reference to the date of acquisition of the related fixed asset item.

Monetary items in the balance sheet are not adjusted, because their value in CPP units is their monetary amount.

In the CPP accounts it is necessary to compute a gain or loss from holding monetary items in times of inflation. In principle this can be found by adjusting all entries in the accounts for each monetary item by the CPP factor, so that the difference between the 'CPP balance' and the actual monetary balance represents the gain or loss on holding that item.

KEY POINT

CPP accounts are prepared by adjusting all monetary amounts in the accounts to reflect the value of money at one point in time (normally the balance sheet date).

A C T I V I T Y **1**

C plc owns plant and machinery with an expected useful life of eight years. The plant was purchased in January 20X1 and cost £80,000. You are provided with the following index numbers.

	Plant cost index	Retail price index
1 January 20X1	120	100
1 January 20X5	280	180
Average 20X5	365	202
31 December 20X5	440	220

You are required to show the fixed asset note for the year ended 31 December 20X5 using current purchasing power accounting.

Feedback to this activity is at the end of the chapter.

1.5   Appraising CPP

Advantages

- CPP accounting is both simple and objective, because it relies on a standard index.

- Because it adjusts for changes in the unit of measurement, it is a true system of inflation accounting.

- It measures the impact on the company in terms of shareholders' purchasing power.

Disadvantages

The ASB has rejected CPP on three grounds:

- its complexity

- its failure to capture economic substance when specific and general price movements diverge

- the unfamiliarity of information stated in terms of current purchasing power units.

There are other disadvantages. CPP does not show the current values (value to the business) of assets and liabilities. RPI is not necessarily appropriate for all assets in all businesses. In addition, the physical capital of the business is not maintained.

K E Y   P O I N T

The current cost profit and loss account is charged with the value to the business of assets consumed during the period. The current cost balance sheet reflects the current value of stock and fixed assets.

1.6   Current cost accounting – the mechanics

Current cost (or replacement cost) accounting is not a single system of accounting – there are several variants. These are the general principles.

- The current cost profit and loss account is charged with the value to the business of assets consumed during the period. In particular, the charges for consuming stocks (cost of sales) and fixed assets (depreciation) are based on current rather than historical values.

- The current cost balance sheet reflects the current value of stock and fixed assets. These are included in the balance sheet at their value to the business, i.e. their deprival value.

U plc buys and sells sprocket-flanges. During the three months ended 31 March 20X6 the company enters into the following transactions:

1 Jan 20X6   Buy 500 units costing a total of £750.
31 Jan 20X6   Sell 400 units for £2,000. Replace them with units costing £1,400.
28 Feb 20X6   Sell 200 units for £1,000. Buy 50 units costing £200.
31 Mar 20X6   Sell 200 units for £1,100. Buy 100 units costing £500.

The retail price index during the period was as follows:

1 Jan 20X6   200
31 Jan 20X6   220
28 Feb 20X6   230
31 Mar 20X6   240

You are required to prepare a trading account at 31 March 20X6 using current cost accounting.

Feedback to this activity is at the end of the chapter.

1.7   Appraising current cost and current value accounting

Advantages

The ASB has stated that the most important advantage of current value is its relevance to users who wish to assess the current state or recent performance of the business.

Under CCA, physical capital is maintained, assets are stated at their value to the business and holding gains are eliminated from profit.

Disadvantages

The main disadvantages of current value are its possible greater subjectivity and lower reliability than historic cost. A further disadvantage is its lack of familiarity.

There may also be practical problems in operating current cost accounting, such as the following.

- It is not always easy to obtain an index which is perfectly suitable for measuring the movement in the current cost of a particular type of asset.

- It is often difficult to obtain a suitable market value for specialist items, but indices may be constructed as an alternative.

- There may be no intention to replace an asset, possibly due to a change in the nature of the business.

- There may be no modern equivalent asset due to the advance of technology.

It has also been argued that CCA is not a system of inflation accounting as such, because it only adjusts for changes in the value of assets. It does not take account of general inflation.

1.8   Capital maintenance concepts

Total gains and losses accruing to the owners in a period must equal the difference between capital employed (net assets) at the beginning and end of the accounting period. The valuation method for recording the net assets therefore determines total gains and losses. However it is important to distinguish 'profit' from other gains and losses as users need information about the quality of particular gains and losses, e.g. whether they are realised or relate to assets essential to the entity's operations which are likely to be sold.

The determination of profit is determined by the concept of capital employed (capital maintenance concept) which is adopted.

Capital maintenance concepts can be classified as follows:

- **Money financial capital maintenance**

  If closing shareholders' funds equal opening shareholders' funds in pounds, then capital has been maintained. This concept is associated with historic cost accounting.

- **Real financial capital maintenance** (sometimes called current purchasing power capital maintenance).

  This measures capital employed as a fund of general purchasing power. Closing shareholders' funds are compared with opening shareholders' funds uplifted by the general inflation rate. This concept is associated with current purchasing power accounting.

- **Physical capital maintenance**, alternatively known as operating capital maintenance.

  Physical capital maintenance measures capital as the productive capacity of a company's assets in terms of the volume of goods and services capable of being produced. Profit is only measured after providing for any increases needed to maintain the company's physical capital. Physical capital maintenance is associated with current cost accounting.

Example

A company begins with share capital of £100 and cash of £100. At the beginning of the year one item of stock is bought for £100. The item of stock is sold at the end of the year for £150. Its replacement cost at that time is £120 and general inflation throughout the year is 10%. Any 'profit' is distributed to shareholders at the end of the year.

	Financial capital maintenance		Physical capital maintenance
	'Money'	CPP	
	£	£	£
Sales	150	150	150
Less: Cost of sales	100	100	120
Operating profit	50	50	30
Less: Inflation adjustment (alternatively shown by increasing cost of sales to £110)	-	10	-
Profit for year	50	40	30
Dividend	50	40	30
	-	-	-
Capital and non-distributable reserves at year end	100	110	120

The increase in capital and reserves of £10 for CPP is the credit entry for the £10 inflation adjustment. The £20 for physical capital maintenance is the credit entry for the increased cost of sales. The £20 is known as a 'realised holding gain'. It is a gain (the stock was worth more in money terms when it was used in the business compared to when it was purchased), it arose purely from holding onto the stock in a period of rising prices and it is realised as the product has been sold by the firm.

Under 'money' financial capital maintenance there is no attempt to adjust for inflation, i.e. the accounts are historic cost accounts.

Under real (CPP) financial capital maintenance the emphasis is on maintaining the purchasing power of the opening capital. The shareholders require funds of £110 in order to maintain their purchasing power. (£110 buys the same quantity of goods at the year end as £100 at the beginning of the year.)

Notes

(a) The physical capital maintenance adjustment is based on the specific price changes affecting stocks. This can be calculated by reference to an index for the industry but strictly the company should calculate its own index based on stock purchases during the year. Thus the calculations can be very complex and time-consuming (and hence expensive) to perform.

(b) The physical capital maintenance balance sheet total figure is sufficient to replace the stock which is the whole objective.

1.9 Providing equivalent information in a supplementary form

Where the profit and loss account is not inflation adjusted, supplementary information can be provided in the notes by way of 'adjusted earnings statements'.

Using the numbers in the example above:

Adjusted earnings statement under

	CPP financial capital maintenance £	Physical capital maintenance £
Historical cost operating profit (i.e. before dividend)	50	50
Less: Current cost operating adjustments	-	(20)
Less: Inflation adjustment to opening shareholders' funds	(10)	-
Profit/current cost profit	£40	£30

1.10 Real terms accounting

Real terms accounting is a further capital maintenance concept based on combining real financial capital maintenance and physical capital maintenance.

There are in fact several variations of real terms accounting but the basic idea is to show in the operating profit statement the figures as in the physical capital maintenance statement and to show the inflation adjustment to shareholders' funds in the statement of total recognised gains and losses.

Thus the figures would be as follows:

Profit and loss account

	£
Sales	150
Less: Cost of sales	120
Current cost operating profit	30
Dividend	30

Statement of total recognised gains and losses

	£
Current cost operating profit	30
Gain from holding stock (i.e. credit entry for the increased cost of sales)	20
Nominal money profit	50
Less: Amount to maintain purchasing power of shareholders' investment	10
Real terms profit	40

As with the real financial capital maintenance concept above, it does not follow that the real terms gain (£40) could be fully distributed if the company wishes to continue in business at the same level of activity. This is because the maintenance of a company's real financial capital does not guarantee the maintenance of its operating capital.

2   Asset valuation

2.1   The case for current value accounting

The objective of financial statements is to provide information about the reporting entity's financial performance and position that is useful to a wide range of users for assessing the stewardship of management and for making economic decisions.

If we consider the traditional historical cost basis of measurement used by accountants, we can see that it fails to relate directly to any of the three decisions that might reasonably be made about an asset.

- Another, similar asset might be purchased. In this case management will need to know the current replacement cost, which might have changed substantially since the present asset was purchased.

- The asset might be sold. In this case management will need to know the amount which would be realised from sale, less any costs involved in disposal, i.e. the net realisable value. Again this bears no relationship to historical cost.

- The asset might be used in the business. In this case management will need to estimate the future cash flows arising from the asset and discount these to their present value i.e. their 'economic value'. Clearly, there is no relationship with historical cost in this case.

Historical cost does have the merit of being easily ascertained and objective, but as we have seen it does not relate directly to any decision that might be taken in relation to an asset. There are alternative ways of valuing assets.

- **Entry values**

  Current entry value, often referred to as replacement cost, has been widely considered as a possible basis of measurement to value assets and to determine the cost of items consumed.

- **Current exit value accounting**

    Another value-based approach has been current exit value accounting, based on the use of net realisable values.

- **Deprival value**

    Deprival value can be defined as being the loss a business would suffer if deprived of an asset.

Of these three alternatives, deprival value, also known as 'value to the business', has been accepted as being the most relevant for accounting purposes. The ASB has made use of the 'value to the business' model in its Statement of Principles and in FRSs 11 and 15.

2.2 Deprival value

To identify deprival value we need to identify all three of the measures of value discussed above. Then we can identify two important relationships between values:

Recoverable amount = The higher of net realisable value and economic value

This is because if management own an asset, they have control over the choice between use and disposal, and if it is economically rational they will choose the option having the highest value.

Deprival value   = The lower of replacement cost and recoverable amount

This is because if deprived of an asset, management have a choice as to whether or not to replace it. If they are economically rational they will replace the asset only if they can generate a surplus either by resale or by use.

(a) **Normal business**

A company owns a machine with a five year useful life and no residual value. At 31 December 20X2 the machine is two years old. The replacement cost at that date of a brand new machine of the same type is £100,000.

If the machine were sold it would fetch about £30,000 but there would be dismantling costs of about £5,000.

It is estimated that the machine could generate cash flows of £40,000 per annum if it were used in the business for the next three years. The net present value of these cash flows is £99,000.

Calculate the deprival value of the asset.

(b) **Company anticipating closure**

Assume that the facts are as in (a) above but that the business is in such a poor state that there are no positive cash flows to be obtained from continuing to use the asset.

Calculate the deprival value of the asset.

(c) **Company with low NPV**

Assume that the facts are as in (a) above but that the net present value of the cash flows associated with the continued use of the asset is £55,000.

Calculate the deprival value of the asset.

Feedback to this activity is at the end of the chapter.

3   The usefulness of the alternative capital maintenance concepts

Financial information based on alternatives to money financial capital maintenance may provide useful information.

Real financial capital maintenance (FCM)

All holding gains, whether realised or unrealised, are included in profit for the year. This provides users with information about changes in the value of assets. It also shows whether there has been a gain on borrowing or a loss on holding money in real terms. However, it does not show whether physical capital has been maintained and does not reflect specific price changes.

Physical capital maintenance

This provides information about the ability of the entity to generate profits from its current operations. It also identifies holding gains and treats them as being undistributable. It enables users to make meaningful comparisons between businesses operating in the same business sector. However, it is associated with current cost accounting and shares the disadvantages of this system, particularly its subjectivity. It also ignores the fact that the mix of an entity's assets may change as a result of changes in prices and technology. This means that trend information may be distorted.

The usefulness of the information provided is affected by the needs of users and the nature of the entity's business.

- **The needs of users**

    Shareholders will generally be interested in maximising the purchasing power of their investment. Thus a financial capital maintenance view may seem the most appropriate choice. (This could be CPP capital maintenance or a real terms approach.)

    Managers and employees may consider that the company's major objective is perpetuating its existence by maintaining its ability to produce similar quantities of goods and services as those produced at the present time. This viewpoint is compatible with PCM. If the company does not maintain its operating capacity, there will be a reduction in the scale of its activities which may mean that employees are made redundant.

- **Nature of business**

    Real terms accounting is more suitable for companies in which asset value increases are viewed as an alternative to trading as a means of generating profits. The true measure of the performance of such companies is their ability to produce 'real' profits above the profits which arise from general inflation. The best measure of the success of such companies is based on real terms i.e. opening capital is adjusted by a general index and the change in specific values of assets is assessed.

KEY POINT

Real terms accounting is more suitable for companies in which asset value increases are viewed as an alternative to trading as a means of generating profits.

4　The ASB's contribution to the debate

4.1　Measurement systems

Chapter 6 of the ASB's Statement of Principles considers measurement in financial statements. The first draft of this chapter considered historic cost and the alternatives: a system of measurement based on current values (CCA); and adjustments for the effects of general inflation (CPP).

Although the ASB conceded that the historic cost basis has several important advantages (objectivity, reliability, familiarity and understandability) its main disadvantage is its lack of relevance to the current state of the business, because:

- the balance sheet does not provide an accurate representation of the current financial position; and

- the profit and loss account reports gains on holding assets when they are realised rather than when they occur: one effect is that no distinction is drawn between gains that have been made in past periods but are realised in the current period and those that are both made and realised in the current period.

The ASB drew the following conclusions.

- The use of current values for both assets and liabilities provides the information that is most relevant to the decisions of users.

- In the case of assets, the appropriate current value is stated according to the value to the business rule. In the case of liabilities, market values may be used.

- A real terms capital maintenance system improves the relevance of information because it shows current operating margins as well as the extent to which holding gains and losses reflect the effect of general inflation, so that users of real terms financial statements are able to select the particular information they require.

- Practice should develop by evolving in the direction of greater use of current values to the extent that this is consistent with the constraints of reliability and cost.

4.2　The ASB's current position on measurement

The chapter on measurement in financial statements was arguably the most controversial part of the initial draft of the Statement of Principles. Many commentators interpreted the conclusions, particularly the final one, to mean that the ASB intended to reintroduce a form of current cost accounting.

The ASB subsequently denied this and stated that it accepts that the existing modified historical cost system will be used for the foreseeable future. Significant changes were made to this part of the Statement before the second draft was issued in 1998. The final version of the Statement emphasises the need to choose the most appropriate basis of measurement in specific circumstances. It no longer suggests that current values should be used in preference to historic cost.

4.3　Asset valuation – the basic principles

The final version of Chapter 6 of the Statement of Principles contains the following points.

- A measurement basis (historic cost or current value) must be selected for each category of assets or liabilities. The basis selected should be the one that best meets the objective of financial statements and the demands of the qualitative characteristics of financial information, bearing in mind the nature of the assets or liabilities concerned and the circumstances involved.

- An asset or liability being measured using the historical cost basis is recognised initially at transaction cost. An asset or liability being measured using the current value basis is recognised initially at its current value at the time it was acquired or assumed.

- Subsequent remeasurement will occur if it is necessary to ensure that:

  (a) assets measured at historic cost are carried at the lower of cost and recoverable amount

  (b) monetary items denominated in foreign currency are carried at amounts based on up-to-date exchange rates

  (c) assets and liabilities measured on the current value basis are carried at up to date current values.

- Such remeasurements are only recognised if:

  (a) there is sufficient evidence that the monetary amount of the asset or liability has changed

  (b) the new amount of the asset or liability can be measured with sufficient reliability.

4.4   Choosing a measurement basis

- The carrying amounts of assets and liabilities need to be sufficiently reliable. If only one of the measures available is reliable, it should be the one used if it is also relevant. If both historic cost and current value are reliable, the better measure to use is the one that is most relevant.

- Current value is not necessarily less reliable than historic cost. For example, debtors stated at historical cost may need to be adjusted to allow for bad or doubtful debts and this involves a degree of estimation similar to that involved in estimating current values not derived from an active market. The hurdle that a measure must clear to be deemed reliable is set at the same height for current value measures as for historical cost measures.

4.5   Measurement issues

- The value to the business rule should be used to select from alternative measures of current value. This is the same as deprival value (discussed earlier in this chapter).

- When basing carrying amounts on future cash flows, those cash flows should be discounted.

- The only way to determine an appropriate monetary amount for an asset or liability may be through estimates. This is acceptable provided that a generally accepted estimation method is used and the measure is supported by a reasonable amount of confirmatory evidence.

4.6   The influence of the Statement of Principles on recent standards

Many recent financial reporting standards and exposure drafts reflect the ASB's wish to encourage greater use of current values and its thinking on measurement issues, particularly subsequent remeasurement (revaluation and impairment).

- FRS 10 *Goodwill and intangible assets* and FRS 11 *Impairment of fixed assets and goodwill* require that assets are not stated at more than their recoverable amount.

- FRS 15 *Tangible fixed assets* was introduced to overcome many of the problems associated with the modified historical cost basis. It requires that once an asset has been revalued, it must continue to be stated at current value.

- The definition of recoverable amount in FRS 11 and the definition of current value in FRS 15 are based on the value to the business model.

- FRS 7 *Fair values in acquisition accounting* and FRS 12 *Provisions, contingent liabilities and contingent assets* require the use of discounted cash flows in some circumstances. FRS 19 *Deferred tax* permits deferred tax liabilities to be discounted if the effect is material.

- The ASB is expected to decide that derivatives and most other financial instruments should be stated at current value.

SELF-TEST QUESTIONS

Alternative views of capital employed

1   In what ways could it be said that historic cost accounts are misleading in a period of changing prices? (1.2)

2   What is the basis of CPP accounting? (1.3)

3   What are the advantages and disadvantages of CPP accounting? (1.5)

4   What is 'real terms accounting'? (1.10)

Asset valuation

5   What is deprival value and what is its significance? (2.2)

The usefulness of the alternative capital maintenance concepts

6   What is the difference between money financial capital maintenance and real financial capital maintenance? (3)

The ASB's contribution to the debate

7   What has been the influence of the Statement of Principles on recent UK accounting standards? (4.6)

FEEDBACK TO ACTIVITY 1

Step 1

Calculate the cost of assets at 31 December 20X5 in CPP units

$$£80,000 \times \frac{220}{100} = 176,000$$

Step 2

Calculate accumulated depreciation at 31 December 20X5 in CPP units

$$£80,000 \times \frac{5}{8} \times \frac{220}{100} = 110,000$$

Step 3

Calculate annual charge for depreciation for 20X5 in CPP units

$$£80,000 \times \frac{1}{8} \times \frac{220}{100} = 22,000$$

Step 4

Prepare fixed asset note

	CPP units
Valuation	
At 1 January and 31 December 20X5	176,000
Depreciation	
At 1 January 20X5	88,000
Charge for year	22,000
At 31 December 20X5	110,000
Net book value	
At 31 December 20X5	66,000
At 31 December 20X4	88,000

FEEDBACK TO
ACTIVITY 2

	£	£
Sales 31 Jan		2,000
28 Feb		1,000
31 Mar		1,100
		4,100
Current cost of sales		
31 Jan	1,400	
28 Feb ($\frac{200}{50} \times 200$)	800	
31 Mar ($\frac{500}{100} \times 200$)	1,000	
		3,200
Gross profit		900

FEEDBACK TO
ACTIVITY 3

		£
(a) NRC =	Gross replacement cost	100,000
	Less: Accumulated depreciation $\frac{2}{5}$	40,000
		60,000
NRV =	Sale proceeds	30,000
	Less: Costs to sell	5,000
		25,000
NPV =		99,000

DV =   lower of £60,000 and (higher of £25,000 and £99,000)

Deprival value is the net replacement cost of £60,000

(b) RC as before   60,000

    NRV as before   25,000

    NPV when there are no cash flows =   Nil

    DV = lower of £60,000 and (higher of £25,000 and nil)

    Deprival value is the net realisable value of £25,000

(c) RC as before   60,000

    NRV as before   25,000

    NPV =   55,000

    DV = lower of £60,000 and (higher of £25,000 and £55,000)

    Deprival value is the net present value of £55,000

Chapter 24

THE IMPACT OF ENVIRONMENTAL, SOCIAL AND CULTURAL FACTORS ON CORPORATE REPORTING

Public interest in protecting the natural environment has grown significantly during the last ten years. This has led many large companies to disclose information about the effect of their activities on the environment, even though there is no specific legal requirement to do so. This practice is called environmental reporting and it is increasingly regarded as important both by the general public and by companies themselves.

Social and ethical reporting is the disclosure of information about the ways in which a business attempts to fulfil its responsibilities towards the wider community. It has developed partly as an extension of environmental reporting and partly as a result of factors such as increasing public concern about business ethics and changes in the political climate during the 1990s. Information can be disclosed either within the published annual report (which includes the financial statements) or in separate environmental or social reports.

Objectives

When you have studied this chapter you should be able to:

- appraise the impact of environmental, social and ethical factors on performance measurement

- describe current reporting requirements and guidelines for environmental reporting

- prepare an environmental report in accordance with current practice

- understand the effect of culture on accounting

- understand why entities might include socially oriented disclosures in performance statements

- understand the concept of a social contract and organisational legitimacy

- evaluate ethical conduct in the context of corporate reporting.

1 Environmental, social and ethical reporting

1.1 The wider meaning of performance

Large companies are increasingly accepting the idea that a business is not only responsible to its shareholders, but to several different 'stakeholders', which are usually taken to be:

- customers

- suppliers

- employees

- the government

- the local community

- society as a whole.

Shareholders require dividends and capital growth and so a public company's performance has traditionally been equated with the profits that it generates. If the needs of other stakeholders are taken into account, performance may encompass:

- providing fair remuneration and an acceptable working environment

- paying suppliers promptly

- minimising the damage to the environment caused by the company's activities

- contributing to the community by providing employment or by other means.

1.2   Environmental reporting

During the late 1980s and early 1990s there were several well publicised environmental disasters, including the Exxon Valdez oil spill and the explosion at the Bhopal chemical factory. In addition, the 1992 Rio Earth Summit and the activities of organisations such as Greenpeace and Friends of the Earth drew the general public's attention to issues such as global warming.

There are now considerable incentives for businesses to take action to preserve the environment, such as controlling pollution, using recyclable materials, choosing renewable materials and developing environmentally friendly products. Public interest in safeguarding the environment affects businesses in two main ways.

- They may suffer direct losses as a result of their actions, for example, they may be legally or constructively obliged to incur the expense of rectifying environmental damage, or they may have to pay additional taxes or suffer financial penalties if they cause pollution.

- If a business is believed to cause damage to the environment or to otherwise act in an unethical way it may attract considerable adverse publicity. This leads to loss of customers. There is a positive side: a business can attract customers if it has a 'green' image. One obvious example of this is The Body Shop.

As a result of these factors, the number of companies disclosing information about the effect of their operations on the environment is steadily increasing.

1.3   Environmental reporting in practice

There are two main vehicles that companies use to publish information about the ways in which they interact with the natural environment:

- the published annual report (which includes the financial statements)

- a separate environmental report (either as a separate paper document or simply posted on the company's website).

The published annual report

In 1996 the journal *Corporate Reporting* published a report *Corporate Environmental Reporting in the UK*. This report presented the results of a survey of nearly 700 major UK companies.

The survey discovered that, of the companies in the sample, 71% did not disclose any environmental information at all. Of the remaining 29%, nearly half confined themselves to a general statement about the environment. Only 18% of the sample made any disclosure of policies, achievements or costs. Of these, a significant proportion simply stated their environmental policies, with no attempt to quantify either targets or costs.

Where targets or achievements were quantified, these tended to be in non-monetary terms, for example:

- 'Our factories in the US have reduced corrugated packaging use by 70%.'

- 'We have converted 225 delivery trucks from leaded gasoline to cleaner burning liquid propane and have installed catalytic converters.'

Very few companies in the sample disclosed the amount of environmental costs and provisions made. Disclosure of the amounts of penalties suffered for non-compliance with regulations was very rare.

The study did, however, show that the percentage of companies making some sort of environmental disclosure had almost doubled in the five years between 1991 and 1996.

A survey conducted in 1999 showed that by that date a high proportion of the FTSE 350 and 92 of the FTSE 100 made some kind of environmental disclosure in the annual report. The most common place for disclosure was the directors' report, followed by the operating and financial review.

Separate environmental reports

Many large public companies now publish environmental reports that are completely separate from the annual report and financial statements. The environmental report is often combined with information about other social and ethical issues. Notable examples of companies which produce such reports are The Body Shop, Thorn EMI plc, The Co-operative Bank, British Airways plc and BT plc. There are several awards for good environmental reports, for example, ACCA's 'UK Environmental Reporting Award'.

A company may publish an environmental report for a number of reasons:

- to differentiate it from its competitors

- to acknowledge responsibility for the environment

- to demonstrate compliance with regulations

- to obtain social approval for its activities.

Most environmental reports take the form of a combined statement of policy and review of activity. They cover issues such as waste management, pollution, intrusion into the landscape, the effect of a company's activities upon wildlife, use of energy and the benefits to the environment of the company's products and services. Generally, the reports disclose the company's targets and/or achievements, with direct comparison between the two in some cases. They may also disclose financial information, such as the amount invested in preserving the environment. Many reports are very detailed and may run to over 50 pages.

Because the environmental report is separate from the published annual report, there is no prescribed content and no accepted code of practice. Companies can publish whatever they wish. Environmental reports do not have to be audited. However, many organisations do submit the information in their report to some kind of independent review or audit process.

Public and media interest has tended to focus on the environmental report rather than on the disclosures in the published annual report and financial statements. This separation reflects the fact that the two reports are aimed at different audiences.

Shareholders are the main users of the annual report, while the environmental report is designed to be read by the general public.

1.4   Examples of disclosure in published annual reports

Below are two examples taken from published annual reports. Both are extracts from the Operating and Financial Review. Notice that both draw readers' attention to their forthcoming environmental or social reports.

Example 1: BT 1999 Annual Report

Environment

BT takes its responsibility to the environment very seriously. We were one of the first major British companies to produce an environmental policy and an annual environmental report. We were also among the first to introduce comprehensive environmental management systems and to form a policy on sustainable development. We are confident that we are leading the way in this area and we have committed BT in the UK to achieve ISO14001 registration, the international environmental management system standard, progressively from March 1999. BT has a long and widely recognised record of energy management. We reduced our energy consumption by more than 13% in the five years to April 1997 and are now aiming for a further 11% reduction by March 2002. We have an extensive programme for recycling and recovering materials, including metal from redundant exchange units, cables, toner cartridges, office paper and electronic waste.

BT's first social report, *An issue of responsibility*, which reviews the social impact of BT's activities, will be published shortly.

Example 2: The Boots Company plc Annual Report and Accounts 1999

Environmental performance

Over the past year preparations have continued for the launch of the first Boots annual environmental report. Although the company has prepared internal reports on its environmental performance for some years, this is its first commitment to regular external publication. Preparations have included the development of a set of Key Performance Indicators to provide a consistent basis for tracking performance improvement year on year.

Boots has long recognised that environmental sense and business sense go hand in hand. The company has a long history of environmental management; it built its first combined heat and power plant in Nottingham in 1915, introduced bottle salvage in the 1930s, packaging and office paper recycling in the 1950s and reusable transit boxes also in the 1950s. The company appointed its first senior manager with exclusive responsibility for the environment in 1972.

Today the gap between environmental and business efficiency is closing as governments in the UK and abroad introduce 'polluter pays' measures such as landfill taxes and higher fuel duties.   Boots will continue to enhance its environmental performance accordingly, with each business setting its own targets and reporting annual progress against them.

1.5   The present situation

The first environmental reports were largely a public relations exercise and the aim was to demonstrate a company's commitment to the environment. Some entities continue to view them in this light. However, many others now view the environmental report as a vehicle for communicating an entity's performance in safeguarding the natural environment.

Some commentators believe that 'stand alone' environmental reports are not a substitute for clear disclosure of environmental costs in the financial statements. A business cannot be regarded as successful if it earns its profits by misusing natural resources and does not disclose the cost of these activities. There is an argument that a requirement to disclose environmental costs would encourage responsible behaviour.

There is also an argument that investors need information about environmental costs and potential liabilities, because environmental disasters can harm businesses, as well as society in general. For example, the Exxon Valdez oil spillage reduced the company's profits by almost nine-tenths in one quarter alone.

1.6   Social accounting and reporting

A business may interact with society in several ways:

(a) it employs human resources in the form of management and other employees

(b) its activities affect society as a whole, for example, it may:

- be the reason for a particular community's existence

- produce goods that are helpful or harmful to particular members of society

- damage the environment in ways which harms society as a whole

- undertake charitable works in the community or promote particular values.

In theory, the social accounts of an entity would consist of a social income statement which measured and disclosed the benefits and costs of its activities to various sections of society and a social balance sheet which measured and disclosed the entity's human assets and its use of natural resources and public goods. In practice, any attempt to set a monetary value on these items can only be subjective. There would also be problems in establishing the boundary of the reporting entity: how far do its social responsibilities extend?

Until a few years ago social and ethical reporting was almost non-existent, but several large public companies now publish information about their interaction with society. As with environmental reporting, there are two main vehicles for presenting information: the published annual report; and separate 'social reports'. Most of the attention of preparers and users of information is focused on the latter.

2   Current reporting requirements for environmental reporting

2.1   Environmental disclosures in the financial statements

At present there is very little direct regulation of environmental reporting in the UK. The Companies Acts do not require companies to disclose the effect of their actions on the environment and there is no accounting standard dealing specifically with environmental issues.

KEY POINT

The Securities and Exchange
Commission in the USA
requires listed companies to
disclose estimates of current
and future environmental
expenditure and the effects that
compliance with environmental
regulations may have on profits
and the position of the business.

This contrasts with the position in some other countries. For example, in the Netherlands, Sweden and Denmark large companies are required to present environmental information either in their annual report or in a separate environmental report. The Securities and Exchange Commission in the USA requires listed companies to disclose estimates of current and future environmental expenditure and the effects that compliance with environmental regulations may have on profits and the position of the business. Listed companies in the US are also required to disclose legal proceedings relating to environmental issues.

However, there are several sources of non-mandatory guidance of which the most important is the ASB's Statement on the Operating and Financial Review. This encourages companies to disclose the main factors and influences that may have a major effect on future results, whether or not they were significant in the period under review. This may include information about the way that the company manages risks and uncertainties relating to environmental protection costs and potential environmental liabilities. Companies are also encouraged to explain the nature of the potential impact of these costs and liabilities upon results.

The ASB appears to have no immediate plans to issue a standard or statement of best practice that specifically covers environmental reporting.

This lack of regulation leads to several potential problems.

- Because disclosure is largely voluntary, not all businesses disclose information. Those that do tend to do so either because they are under particular pressure to prove their 'green' credentials (for example, large public utility companies whose operations directly affect the environment) or because they have deliberately built their reputation on environmental friendliness or social responsibility.

- The information disclosed may not be complete or reliable. Many businesses see environmental reporting largely as a public relations exercise and therefore only provide information that shows them in a positive light. Environmental disclosures normally appear in the Chairman's Statement, in the Operating and Financial Review or in a 'stand alone' environmental report. Therefore they do not have to be audited and can be framed in very general terms.

- The information may not be disclosed consistently from year to year.

- Some businesses, particularly small and medium sized entities, may believe that the costs of preparing and circulating additional information outweigh the benefits of doing so.

2.2 Environmental reports

There are a number of non-mandatory codes of practice and guidelines. Some examples of these are as follows:

DEFINITION

Sustainability reporting
comprises the environmental,
social and economic aspects of
performance.

- The Global Reporting Initiative (GRI) has published a document *Sustainability reporting guidelines*. The guidelines are intended to develop sustainability reporting practices worldwide so that they are comparable with financial reporting practices in terms of verification and comparability, and are intended to apply to all entities that prepare sustainability reports, including small and not-for-profit entities. A number of international companies tested the guidelines in draft form.

The guidelines state that the report should include the following sections.

(a) A statement by the Chief Executive Officer (CEO) or equivalent senior management person, describing key elements of the report.

(b) An overview of the reporting organisation and scope of the report to provide a context for understanding and evaluating information in subsequent sections.

(c) An executive summary and details of the key performance indicators used.

(d) A discussion of the vision and strategy of the reporting organisation, including how that vision integrates economic, environmental and social performance.

(e) Policies, organisation and management systems: an overview of the organisation's governance structure and the management systems that are in place to implement its vision, including information on stakeholders and their involvement with the organisation.

(f) The reporting organisation's economic, environmental and social performance, including management explanations and commentary on trends and unusual events. Organisations are asked to report information for the current reporting period, at least two previous periods and a target period. Information should be provided in absolute terms, as well as in ratio form. Organisations should report their performance in a very wide range of areas, including: use of energy, materials and water; emissions, effluents and waste; transport; suppliers; products and services; land use; health and safety; non-discrimination; training; human rights and community development.

The guidelines also set out the content of each section and are extremely detailed.

- The Fédération des Experts Comptables Européens (FEE) has issued an Abstract *Towards a generally accepted framework for environmental reporting*. The object of the paper is to allow environmental reporting to gain the same degree of public acceptance as financial reporting. It discusses users' information needs and the qualitative characteristics of environmental reporting information, based on the IASC *Framework for the preparation and presentation of financial statements* (which was the main source for much of the ASB's Statement of Principles and uses similar terminology). The Paper also includes the United Nations Environmental Program (UNEP)/SustainAbility 50 core reporting elements which entities may wish to consider when developing environmental reports.

- The Confederation of British Industry (CBI) has published a guideline entitled *Introducing Environmental Reporting*.

- The Coalition of Environmentally Responsible Economies (CERES) has published formats for environmental reports and developed a set of principles by which investors and others can assess the environmental performance of organisations.

- ACCA has issued a Guide to environment and energy reporting. It also publishes the criteria by which it judges the environmental reports submitted for its annual Awards scheme.

- The United Nations Conference on Trade and Development (UNCTAD) has published a report *Environmental Financial Accounting and Reporting at the Corporate Level*.

In addition, a large number of academic and governmental bodies have published reports and guidelines that are available on the Internet.

Companies may register under the Eco-Management and Audit Scheme (EMAS). EMAS is an accredited environmental management system which certifies companies that meet its standard. To be certified, a company must develop an environmental policy, environmental programme and environmental management system for each of its sites, carry out an annual audit and publish an independently verified report of its performance.

3 Preparing environmental reports and accounting for environmental issues

3.1 Introduction

In the examination, you may be asked to prepare an environmental report from information provided in the question, or to suggest information that could or should be included in an environmental report. It is important to be aware of:

- information that is normally disclosed either in the Operating and Financial Review or in a separate environmental report
- transactions and events that affect the financial statements themselves.

3.2 What information should be disclosed?

The information below would be included either in the Operating and Financial Review or in a separate report. The list is not exhaustive.

Note that details of environmental provisions and contingencies would also be disclosed in the notes to the financial statements, as required by FRS 12.

(a) Environmental issues pertinent to the company and industry

- The entity's policy towards the environment and any improvements made since first adopting the policy.

- Whether the entity has a formal system for managing environmental risks.

- The identity of the director(s) responsible for environmental issues.

- The entity's perception of the risks to the environment from its operations.

- The extent to which the entity would be capable of responding to a major environmental disaster and an estimate of the full economic consequences of such a future major disaster.

- The effects of, and the entity's response to, any government legislation on environmental matters.

- Details of any significant infringement of environmental legislation or regulations.

- Material environmental legal issues in which the entity is involved.

- Details of any significant initiatives taken, if possible linked to amounts in financial statements.

- Details of key indicators (if any) used by the entity to measure environmental performance. Actual performance should be compared with targets and with performance in prior periods.

(b) Financial information

- The entity's accounting policies relating to environmental costs, provisions and contingencies.

- The amount charged to the profit and loss account during the accounting period in respect of expenditure to prevent or rectify damage to the environment caused by the entity's operations. This could be analysed between expenditure that the entity was legally obliged to incur and other expenditure.

- The amount charged to the profit and loss account during the accounting period in respect of expenditure to protect employees and society in general from the consequences of damage to the environment caused by the entity's operations. Again, this could be analysed between compulsory and voluntary expenditure.

- Details (including amounts) of any provisions or contingent liabilities relating to environmental matters.

- The amount of environmental expenditure capitalised during the year.

- Details of fines, penalties and compensation paid during the accounting period in respect of non-compliance with environmental regulations.

3.3   Environmental costs

The term 'environmental costs' can have a wide range of meanings, depending on the items included.

They can include:

- capital expenditure

- closure or decommissioning costs

- clean-up costs

- development expenditure

- costs of recycling or conserving energy.

This classification is not rigid. For example, closure costs could be classified as either environmental measures or environmental losses, depending on the way in which they arise.

There can be practical problems in deciding whether a particular cost is an environmental cost. For example, a company may replace its motor vehicles with others that use less fuel. These will pollute the environment less and use fewer natural resources, but the company will also make cost savings on fuel as a result. Is the cost of the vehicles an environmental cost or simply normal capital expenditure? Where environmental costs are disclosed in the annual report, there should be a clear explanation of which items are included.

3.4   Accounting for environmental costs

Environmental costs are treated in accordance with the requirements of current accounting standards:

- Most expenditure is charged in the profit and loss account in the period in which it is incurred. Material items may need to be disclosed as exceptional items in the notes to the accounts as required by FRS 3 *Reporting financial performance*.

- Entities may have to undertake fundamental reorganisations or restructuring or to discontinue particular activities in order to protect the environment. If a sale or termination meets the definition of a discontinued operation its results must be separately disclosed in accordance with the requirements of FRS 3. Material restructuring costs may meet the definition of an exceptional item and if so, they must be separately disclosed on the face of the profit and loss account.

- Fines and penalties for non-compliance with regulations are charged to the profit and loss account in the period in which they are incurred. This applies even if the activities that resulted in the penalties took place in an earlier accounting period, as they cannot be treated as prior period adjustments.

- Expenditure on fixed assets is capitalised and depreciated in the usual way (FRS 15 *Tangible fixed assets*). Any government grants received for expenditure that protects the environment are treated in accordance with SSAP 4 *Accounting for government grants*.

- Fixed assets and goodwill may become impaired as a result of environmental legislation or new regulations. FRS 11 *Impairment of fixed assets and goodwill* lists events that could trigger an impairment review; one of these is a significant adverse change in the statutory or regulatory environment in which the business operates.

- Research and development expenditure in respect of environmentally friendly products, processes or services is covered by SSAP 13 *Accounting for research and development*. Note that even where development expenditure is not specifically connected with the environment it must be commercially viable taking into account environmental legislation before it can be deferred.

There are two areas which are potentially more complicated. These are provisions for future environmental costs and the capitalisation of environmental expenditure. These are dealt with below.

3.5   Provisions for future environmental costs

FRS 12 *Provisions, contingent liabilities and contingent assets* states that three conditions must be met before a provision may be recognised:

- the entity has a present **obligation** as a result of a past event; and

- it is **probable** that a transfer of economic benefits will be required to settle the obligation; and

- a **reliable estimate** can be made of the amount of the obligation.

FRS 12 was covered in detail in an earlier chapter, but some points are particularly relevant to provisions for environmental costs:

- The fact that the entity's activities have caused environmental contamination does not in itself give rise to an obligation to rectify the damage. However, even if there is no legal obligation there may be a constructive obligation. An entity almost certainly has a constructive obligation to rectify environmental damage if it has a policy of acting in an environmentally responsible way and this policy is well publicised.

- The obligation must arise from a past event. This means that a provision can only be set up to rectify environmental damage that has already happened. If an entity needs to incur expenditure to reduce pollution in the future it does not set up a provision. This is because in theory it can avoid the expenditure by its future actions, for example, it could discontinue the particular activity that causes the pollution.

- As some environmental liabilities only crystallise several years after the provision is set up, the amount provided may have to be discounted to its present value.

- If the entity cannot recognise a provision it may still need to disclose a contingent liability (apply the normal principles to determine whether this is the case).

- FRS 12 requires disclosure of the nature of the obligation or contingent liability for each separate class. This means that users of the financial statements will be made aware of the existence of any provisions or contingent liabilities relating to environmental matters. Provisions for environmental costs should be analysed separately from other provisions in the note showing movements during the year.

ACTIVITY 1

New legislation has been passed that requires an entity to fit smoke filters in its factories by 30 June 20X0. At 31 December 20X0 (the balance sheet date) the filters have not yet been fitted. According to the company's legal advisers, the new law is not yet being stringently enforced. In practice, provided that the filters are fitted within the next few months, there is a reasonable chance that the company will escape penalties for non-compliance.

State whether a provision should be recognised.

Feedback to this activity is at the end of the chapter.

3.6   Capitalisation of environmental expenditure

The issue here is whether environmental expenditure provides access to future economic benefits. If it does, then it meets the ASB's definition of an asset. For example, the cost of the smoke filters in the Activity above would normally be capitalised and depreciated over the useful economic lives of the filters. The expenditure will enable the factory to generate profits without the risk of penalties in future periods.

An asset may also arise as the result of recognising a provision. FRS 12 states that when a provision or change in a provision is recognised, an asset should also be recognised when, and only when, the incurring of the present obligation gives access to future economic benefits; otherwise the setting up of the provision should be charged immediately to the profit and loss account.

ACTIVITY 2

Carson plc operates a chemical reprocessing plant. The plant is due to close on 31 December 20X4 but will be fully operational up to that date. On 15 December 20X0, the government passed new environmental legislation. This legislation requires that companies operating chemical reprocessing plants leave the site environmentally safe when the plant is closed. Given the expected date of closure, it is estimated that the legislation will require the group to spend £50 million on rendering the plant environmentally safe.

A suitable discount rate for evaluating investments of this nature is 12% per annum.

How should the proposed expenditure be treated in the financial statements for the year ended 31 December 20X0?

Feedback to this activity is at the end of the chapter.

DEFINITION

Culture can be defined as a body of beliefs, traditions and guides for behaviour shared among members of a society, an organisation, or a group.

4   Social and ethical reporting

4.1   Culture and accounting

The culture of a society or a country affects the development of business practices, including financial accounting and reporting.

As we have seen, the business culture in the UK and the USA has tended to emphasise the interests of shareholders over those of other stakeholders in a business, such as employees and the wider community. This has led to an emphasis upon generating profits in the short term.

This contrasts with the traditional business culture in countries such as Japan. One of the main features of Japanese business practice is the idea of *keiretsu*, a web of interdependent relationships between various stakeholders. Until fairly recently, most salaried workers have been guaranteed jobs for life. Companies tend to focus on longer-term goals, such as market share, rather than on profit. In some European countries there is a similar emphasis on the business within society.

Accounting practice develops to meet the information needs of the dominant stakeholders in a particular society. The original reason for producing accounts was so that the management of a company could 'account for' their stewardship of the shareholders' assets. In the UK, financial statements are prepared to enable investors and potential investors to make economic decisions about their investment. In other countries, they may be prepared to meet the needs of different stakeholders.

4.2   Why entities might make socially orientated disclosures

Social and ethical reporting would seem to be at variance with the prevailing business culture in the UK. However, there are a number of reasons why entities publish social reports:

- they may have deliberately built their reputation on social responsibility (e.g. Body Shop, Traidcraft) in order to attract a particular customer base

- they may perceive themselves as being under particular pressure to prove that their activities do not exploit society as a whole or certain sections of it (e.g. Shell International plc and some other utility companies)

- they may be genuinely convinced that it is in their long-term interests to balance the needs of the various stakeholder groups

- they may fear that the government may eventually require them to publish socially oriented information if they do not do so voluntarily.

In other words, entities generally make socially oriented disclosures because it is expedient to do so. Proponents of this view see social reporting and the implied acceptance of very limited social and ethical responsibilities as 'enlightened self interest'.

4.3   The social contract

In contrast, some academics believe that social and environmental accounting should develop in such a way that it reflects the existence of the 'social contract'.

Proponents of the social contract argue that every business is a social institution whose existence can only be justified in so far as it serves society in general and the particular groups from which it derives its power. Businesses are accountable to the communities in which they operate and to grow and survive they must demonstrate:

- that society requires their services

- that the groups benefiting from its rewards (e.g. earnings) have society's approval.

Social reporting is one means by which an entity demonstrates its accountability.

DEFINITIONS

Stakeholder theory views social reporting as a means by which organisations attempt to manage and negotiate their relationships with their stakeholders. The nature of the reporting reflects the importance which an organisation attaches to the various stakeholder groups.

Legitimacy theory views social reporting as a means by which organisations attempt to demonstrate that they reflect the same social value system as the society in which they operate.

4.4   The legitimacy of an organisation

Academics have developed theories to explain corporate social reporting practices.

Legitimacy theory is a development of stakeholder theory. It argues that organisations cannot continue to exist unless the society in which they are based perceives them as operating to the same values as that society. If an organisation feels that it is under threat (for example, because there has been a financial scandal or a serious accident causing major pollution) it may adopt one or more legitimation strategies by attempting to:

- 'educate' stakeholders about its intentions to improve its performance

- change stakeholders' perceptions of the event (without changing its actual performance)

- distract attention away from the issue (by concentrating on positive actions not necessarily related to the event)

- manage expectations about its performance (for example, by explaining that certain events are beyond its control).

Legitimacy theory can explain several aspects of social and environmental reporting as it exists in practice. For example, entities tend to report positive aspects of their behaviour and not to report negative ones.

5   Social reporting in practice

5.1   Social reporting in the financial statements

The Companies Acts require disclosure of the following information about the company and its relationship with the wider community:

- In the notes to the financial statements:

    (a) the average number of employees during the financial year and the average number employed within particular categories to be determined by the directors

    (b) staff costs analysed between wages and salaries; social security costs; and other pension costs

    (c) unquoted companies must disclose detailed information about directors' emoluments, including the amounts payable analysed between fees, salaries and bonuses, gains on share options, pension contributions, long-term incentive schemes and compensation for loss of office and the numbers of directors accruing benefits under pension schemes. Where total directors' emoluments are more than £200,000 information must also be disclosed in respect of the amounts payable to the highest paid director.

- In the directors' report:

    (a) information about directors and their share interests during the period

    (b) total of political and charitable donations (if over £200); details of individual political donations over £200 must also be given

    (c) if the average number of UK employees exceeds 250, a statement of its policy relating to disabled employees

(d) if the average number of UK employees exceeds 250, a statement of its policy relating to employee involvement

(e) a statement of its policy relating to the payment of its suppliers (public companies and some large private companies only).

In addition, listed companies must publish additional information about corporate governance and directors' remuneration.

In practice, most companies make the minimum necessary disclosure, with statements on disabled employees and employee involvement normally being framed in very general terms.

5.2 Other information that might be disclosed in the annual report

The Operating and Financial Review

The ASB's Statement of best practice on the Operating and Financial Review recommends that entities provide information about the main factors and influences that may have a major effect on future results. This may include the existence of major suppliers or customers, health and safety issues, product liability and skill shortages.

Companies that make additional voluntary disclosures in the annual report normally include these in the Operating and Financial Review. These disclosures often include details of charitable initiatives or community involvement, as well as the type of information described above.

5.3 Separate social reports

'Stand alone' social and ethical reports do not have to be audited and there are no regulations prescribing their content. However, there are some sets of non-mandatory guidelines and codes of best practice, for example, the standard AA1000, which has been issued by the Institute of Social and Ethical Accountability (ISEA). Some organisations have the data in their reports independently verified and include the 'auditor's report' in their published document. The social report may or may not be combined with the environmental report.

It has been suggested that there should be three main types of information in the social report:

* Information about relationships with stakeholders, e.g. employee numbers, wages and salaries, provision of facilities for customers and information about involvement with local charities

* Information about the accountability of the entity, e.g. sickness leave, accident rates, noise levels, numbers of disabled employees, compliance with current legal, ethical and industry standards

* Information about dialogue with stakeholders, e.g. the way in which the entity consults with all stakeholders and provides public feedback on the stakeholders' perceptions of the entity's responsibilities to the community and its performance in meeting stakeholder needs.

SELF-TEST
QUESTIONS

Environmental, social and ethical reporting

1   What incentives are there for businesses to take environmental and social reporting seriously? (1.2)

Current reporting requirements for environmental reporting

2   How far does a company have to report on environmental matters in its annual report and accounts? (2.1)

Preparing environmental reports and accounting for environmental issues

3   Define (a) environmental costs and (b) environmental measures. (3.3)

4   On what basis can an entity provide for future environmental costs? (3.5)

5   When can environmental expenditure be capitalised? (3.6)

Social and ethical reporting

6   What is corporate social reporting? (4.2)

7   What is legitimacy theory? (4.4)

EXAM-TYPE
QUESTION

Redstart plc

You are the chief accountant of Redstart plc and you are currently finalising the financial statements for the year ended 31 December 20X1. Your assistant (who has prepared the draft accounts) is unsure about the treatment of two transactions which have taken place during the year. She has written you a memorandum which explains the key principles of each transaction and also the treatment adopted in the draft accounts.

Transaction One

One of the corporate objectives of the company is to ensure that its activities are conducted in such a way as to minimise any damage to the natural environment. It is committed in principle to spending extra money in pursuit of this objective but has not yet made any firm proposals. The directors believe that this objective will prove very popular with customers and are anxious to emphasise their environmentally friendly policies in the annual report.

Your assistant suggests that a sum should be set aside from profits each year to create a provision in the financial statements against the possible future costs of environmental protection. Accordingly, she has charged the profit and loss account for the year ended 31 December 20X1 with a sum of £500,000 and proposes to disclose this fact in a note to the accounts.

Transaction Two

A new law has recently been enacted that will require Redstart plc to change one of its production processes in order to reduce the amount of carbon dioxide that is emitted. This will involve purchasing and installing some new plant that is more efficient than the equipment currently in use. To comply with the law the new plant must be operational by 31 December 20X2. The new plant has not yet been purchased.

In the draft financial statements for the year ended 31 December 20X1 your assistant has recognised a provision for £5 million (the cost of the new plant). This has been disclosed as an exceptional item in the notes to the profit and loss account.

The memorandum from your assistant also expresses concern about the fact that there was no reference to environmental matters anywhere in the published financial statements for the year ended 31 December 20X0. As a result, she believes that the financial statements do not comply with the requirements of the Companies Act and Financial Reporting Standards and therefore must be wrong.

Required:

Draft a reply to your assistant which:

(a) reviews the treatment suggested by your assistant and recommends changes where relevant. In each case your reply should refer to the contents of relevant Accounting Standards   **(12 marks)**

(b) replies to her suggestion that the financial statements for the year ended 31 December 20X0 are wrong because they make no reference to environmental matters.   **(8 marks)**

                                                    (Total: 20 marks)

For the answer to this question see the 'Answers' section at the end of the book.

FEEDBACK TO ACTIVITY 1

There is a present obligation. However, the obligation is not for the costs of fitting the smoke filters, because this has not yet happened. Even though avoiding penalties seems to be linked to the act of fitting the filters in the near future the company can avoid this expenditure (it can cease the activities that generate smoke, or it can continue to operate the factory without the filters at the risk of incurring penalties). The obligating event is the operation of the factory without the filters.

On the basis of the facts above, fines or penalties (transfer of economic benefits) are possible, rather than probable.

Conclusion: Do not recognise a provision, but disclose a contingent liability.

FEEDBACK TO ACTIVITY 2

- The legislation requiring the subsidiary to make the chemical plant environmentally safe was passed before the year end and therefore the company has a legal obligation as the result of a past event. The company will have to incur expenditure to meet this obligation and a reliable estimate of the amount has been made.

- FRS 12 *Provisions, contingent liabilities and contingent assets* requires that full provision is made immediately. The provision should be discounted to its net present value at 12%.

- The amount to be recognised and reported under 'provisions for liabilities and charges' is £31.8 million (50 × 0.636).

- By incurring the expenditure to make the plant safe, the group gains access to future economic benefits (the ability to continue to make profits from operating the plant). Therefore the company should recognise a tangible fixed asset of £31.8 million and this will be depreciated over the next four years in the same way as the plant.

Chapter 25

INTERNATIONAL ISSUES

For much of the 1990s the ASB tried to ensure that its own standards were compatible with international standards. For example, FRS 14 and IAS 33 (on EPS) were developed jointly by the ASB and IASC, as was FRS 12 and IAS 37 (on provisions and contingencies).

From 2005, all quoted companies in the European Union will be required to prepare their consolidated financial statements in accordance with international accounting standards (IASs and IFRSs). In order to maintain consistency between group accounts and company accounts, the ASB in the UK will be amending its own standards to bring them into line with the international standard. At a stroke, the International Accounting Standards Board will become the most important accounting standard setter in Britain, Europe and probably the World. This chapter explains how this has come about.

Objectives

When you have studied this chapter you should be able to:

- evaluate the developments in global harmonisation and standardisation

- assess proposed changes to national and international regulation

- identify the reasons for major differences in accounting practices

- restate overseas financial statements in line with UK accounting policies

- discuss the implications of moving to IFRSs.

1   The need for harmonisation

Increasingly businesses operate on a global scale and investors make investment decisions on a worldwide basis. There is thus a need for financial information to be presented on a consistent basis. In more detail, the advantages of harmonising accounting practices are as follows:

- **Multi-national companies**

  Multi-national companies benefit from closer harmonisation for the following reasons.

  (a) Access to international finance is easier. The international financial markets understand the financial information presented to them more easily if the information is provided on a consistent basis between companies irrespective of their country of origin.

  (b) In a business which is operating in several countries, there tends to be improved management control. Internal financial information is more easily prepared on a consistent basis if externally required financial information is required on a uniform basis.

  (c) There is greater efficiency in accounting departments.

  (d) Consolidation of financial statements is easier.

- **Investors**

  If investors wish to make decisions based on the worldwide availability of investments then better comparisons between companies are required. At present most non-domestic investments are made by public investment companies and unit trusts which employ analysts skilled in the examination of financial statements from different countries.

  An individual investor would have difficulty making an informed investment decision with the present differences in international financial reporting.

- **International economic groupings**

  International economic groupings, e.g. the EU could work more effectively if there were international harmonisation of accounting policies. Part of the function of international economic groupings is to make cross-border trade easier. Similar accounting regulations would help this process.

2   The IASC Foundation and the IASB

2.1   Introduction

The International Accounting Standards Committee (IASC) was set up in 1973. It consists of representatives from accountancy organisations from around the world.

In 2001 a new Constitution and structure came into force. The new constitution sets out the objectives of the IASC as follows:

(a)   to develop, in the public interest, a single set of high quality, understandable and enforceable global accounting standards that require high quality, transparent and comparable information in financial statements and other financial reporting to help participants in the world's capital markets and other users make economic decisions

(b)   to promote the use and rigorous application of those standards

(c)   to bring about convergence of national accounting standards and International Accounting Standards to high quality solutions.

2.2   The structure of the IASC

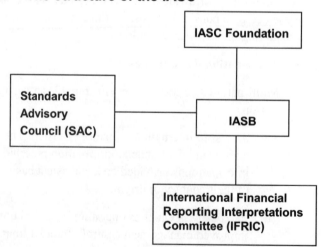

The IASC Foundation is an independent, not-for-profit foundation based in the US. The Trustees of the Foundation appoint the members of the IASB, SAC and IFRIC.

The IASB (International Accounting Standards Board) is responsible for developing and issuing new international standards. These are known as International Financial

Reporting Standards (IFRSs). Its members are meant to be experts, and they do not represent any particular countries or interest groups.

The Standards Advisory Council (SAC) advises the IASB when important decisions have to be taken. Membership of the SAC is drawn from different cultural and industrial backgrounds.

The IFRIC draws up guidance for users in two situations. Firstly if a completely new problem arises, and secondly if existing standards are being interpreted in unsatisfactory or conflicting ways. Its guidelines are called IFRIC Interpretations.

Before 2001, the standards issued by the IASC were called International Accounting Standards (IASs), and the guidelines were called SICs. In future, new standards issued by the IASB will be called International Financial Reporting Standards (IFRSs) and the guidelines issued by the IFRIC will be called IFRIC Interpretations.

However, all the existing IASs and SICs will remain in force until amended or withdrawn in the future. In this book the generic term 'international accounting standards' is used to refer to both IASs and IFRSs.

2.3   The authority attached to IFRSs and IFRIC Interpretations

A set of financial statements can only be described as complying with IFRSs if they comply with all existing IFRSs and IFRIC Interpretations, plus all existing IASs and SICs.

The IASC itself has no power to enforce or police compliance because it is not a government institution. However, some countries have given legal backing to IFRSs, and from January 2005 all listed groups in the European Union will prepare their consolidated financial statements using IFRSs.

2.4   Other international bodies

International Federation of Accountants (IFAC)

The IFAC has the same membership as the IASC and works closely with it. The IFAC does not set accounting standards but it does have committees that play a part in the process of harmonisation.

The main committee of relevance is the International Auditing and Assurance Standards Board (IAASB). Its objective is to produce generally accepted international standards on auditing. The standards effectively perform a similar function to IASs, i.e. they do not override national standards.

Organisation for Economic Co-operation and Development (OECD)

Membership of the OECD consists of most of the 'developed' countries. It has a 'Committee on International Investment and Multi-national enterprises' which has established guidelines regarding the disclosure of information for multi-national companies. It also has a 'Working group on accounting standards' which supports the efforts of the IASC and publishes reports on the harmonisation of accounting standards.

United Nations (UN)

The UN has a 'Commission on Transnational Reporting Corporations' which gathers information concerning the activities and reporting of multi-national companies. It seeks to improve the availability and comparability of information disclosed by multi-national companies and has initiated a number of special projects aimed at improving comparability.

There is some criticism of its work as to its political nature. The conclusions drawn may overly reflect the general suspicions that developing countries have to multi-national companies.

The 'G4 + 1' group

The 'G4 + 1' group consisted of representatives of the ASB, the Financial Accounting Standards Board of the United States (FASB), the standard setting bodies of Canada, Australia and New Zealand and the IASC. The group had the objective of seeking common solutions to financial reporting issues, based on a common conceptual framework. It did not issue accounting standards but, through its Discussion Papers (called Position Papers), it sought to influence the development of accounting standards of the member organisations. The group has discontinued its activities, with the member bodies now acting directly with the IASB.

3   Harmonisation: the current situation

3.1   The acceptance of international standards

Big multinational corporations operate in many different countries. They also need to raise finance globally on different stock exchanges. Until recently this meant that a multinational would have to prepare financial statements complying with the accounting standards of each of the countries that they operated in or raised finance in. This was obviously time consuming and costly, but it also created uncertainty in the investment community. This was illustrated in 1993 when Daimler Benz was first listed on the New York Stock Exchange. It had reported a profit of DM168m using German accounting standards, but this became a loss of DM949m when restated using US accounting standards. The investing community obviously did not know which set of results was 'correct'. This uncertainty increases risk, which in turn increases the cost of capital.

Companies, like Daimler Benz, that are quoted on more than one stock exchange, have traditionally prepared 'reconciliation statements' which explain the differences in the reported profits on the various stock exchanges. This helps a bit, but it does not eliminate the uncertainty, nor the embarrassment for the accounting profession of having two different profit figures. This incident spurred the international accounting community into action.

The investing community was also worried, and so in 1995 the International Organisation of Securities Commissions (IOSCO) and the IASC agreed to develop a set of core accounting standards that could be used by companies that wanted to obtain a share-listing in a foreign country. This process was completed successfully in 2000. See Section 4 below.

Although companies can now use international standards for cross-border listings, they still have to prepare a set of accounts using their own national standards in order to comply with their own national laws. This problem will be solved within the European Union in January 2005, when international standards will be adopted within the EU for the consolidated accounts for all listed groups. Most European nations are taking this opportunity to harmonise their own national standards with international standards at the same time.

3.2   The evolution of international standards

One reason why it has taken so long for international standards to be accepted is that in the early days of the IASC, International Accounting Standards had a poor reputation. This was because the IASC wanted its standards to be as inclusive as possible in order to encourage new countries to subscribe to them. As a result standards often included so many alternative accounting treatments that they were hardly standards at all.

From 1990 the IASC began to reduce the permitted alternatives and to highlight a preferred 'benchmark' treatment, although other methods were still permitted.

The 1990s also saw a new wave of accounting standards that were based on a theoretical 'Framework for the Preparation and Presentation of Financial Statements'.

The IASC's new body of accounting standards have won over IOSCO and the European Union. In addition, many countries in the developing world have already adopted International Standards as their own.

4   The IASC and the International Organisation of Securities Commissions (IOSCO)

IOSCO, the International Organisation of Securities Commissions, is an influential organisation of the world's stock market regulators, in which the US Securities and Exchange Commission (SEC) is a key member.

Although many stock exchanges have accepted IASs for cross border listing purposes, the US did not. This means that overseas companies seeking a listing in the US must prepare accounts in line with US Generally Accepted Accounting Principles (US GAAP), or reconcile their accounts to US GAAP. As US GAAP is both extremely prescriptive and very conservative, this can result in significant additional costs and other problems.

In 1995 IOSCO agreed to consider endorsing IASs for multinational listings in all global markets, including the US, once the IASC had completed a core set of standards. The standards were completed in 1999. In May 2000 IOSCO agreed to endorse the core standards. In theory, this should mean that all stock exchanges will now accept accounts prepared in compliance with IASs from overseas companies seeking a listing.

Unfortunately the endorsement was not unconditional. IOSCO recommended that its members permit incoming multinational issuers to use the core standards to prepare their financial statements for cross-border offerings and listings. However, this should be supplemented where necessary to address outstanding substantive issues at a national or regional level. Supplementation may take any of the following forms:

- reconciliation of certain items to show the effect of applying a different accounting method, in contrast with the method applied under IASC standards

- additional disclosures, whether in the financial statements or in the notes

- specifying use of a particular alternative provided in an IAS, or a particular interpretation in cases where the IAS is unclear or silent.

Individual IASs may also be waived under exceptional circumstances.

KEY POINT

Overseas companies seeking a listing in the US had to prepare accounts in line with US Generally Accepted Accounting Principles (US GAAP), or reconcile their accounts to US GAAP.

KEY POINT

In May 2000, IOSCO agreed to endorse the core IASs for multi-national listings.

5   The impact on the UK

5.1   Background

Until recently, it was relatively easy to ensure that most UK standards complied with the requirements of IASs. This was because IASs were very simple and permitted many alternative treatments. In only a very few cases were there differences between the requirements of a SSAP or FRS and the requirements of an IAS.

However, as IASs become more authoritative, they are also becoming more detailed and prescriptive, with fewer alternatives permitted. This means that there are now significant differences between UK GAAP and IASs in a number of areas, notably in accounting for proposed dividends and pensions.

The ASB will be revising its own standards over the next two years to bring them as closely into line with international standards as possible. To this end FREDs 23 to 30 have been issued, which have all been discussed in the appropriate part of this text.

5.2   The future of the ASB

Until 1 January 2005, all UK companies will continue to prepare their financial statements in accordance with UK law and UK accounting standards. From 1 January 2005, listed companies must use IASs to prepare their consolidated accounts, and the relevant EU Regulation permits governments to allow or require the wider use of IASs. The UK government is consulting on this matter, but its likely policy will be to permit (but not require) any company to elect to adopt IASs.

This leaves the ASB in a difficult position in terms of its future role. Is there any future for UK domestic accounting standards, or should the ASB accept the inevitable, scrap SSAPs and FRSs, adopt IASs wholesale, and simply become a pressure group contributing to the development of future IASs?

There are some arguments for retaining UK standards, not least that they have been developed in response to the UK economic environment and business practices. There is also the problem of small companies. Compliance with international practice mainly influences the financial statements of large and listed companies. In the UK, small private companies are able to take advantage of a growing range of exemptions from Companies Act disclosure requirements. They are also exempt from the requirements of some accounting standards. The ASB has issued a Financial Reporting Standard for Smaller Entities (FRSSE), which effectively introduces a separate reporting regime for small companies. There is no international equivalent of the FRSSE or any similar project, although there are signs that small companies may now be on the IASBs agenda.

In March 2004 the ASB issued a Discussion Paper *UK accounting standards: a strategy for convergence with IFRS* considering these matters. The ASB believes that:

- in the medium term, there is no case for the use in the UK of two sets of different accounting standards

- no new UK standard should be issued that is more restrictive that the equivalent international standard.

The ASB intention therefore is to adopt a phased approach over a number of years, bringing in UK standards based on IASs. This approach has already resulted in FRS 20 implementing IFRS 2 on share-based payment, as covered earlier.

The ASB intends to maintain the UITF to address emerging issues, and to maintain the FRSSE, but otherwise there should be no difference between UK standards and international standards in the medium term.

KEY POINT

There are significant differences between UK GAAP and IASs in a number of areas, notably in accounting for proposed dividends and pensions.

KEY POINT

Until 1 January 2005 all UK companies will continue to prepare their financial statements in accordance with UK law and UK accounting standards.

KEY POINT

There is no international equivalent of the FRSSE.

6   Reasons for differences in accounting practice

6.1   Introduction

Several factors may influence the development of financial reporting practice within a country. The most important of these are the legal system, the main providers of finance and to a lesser extent the prevailing type of business organisation. It is important to remember that a number of influences may work together and some may have greater importance than others in a particular situation.

6.2   Legal systems

There are two basic forms of legal system.

- A common law system: there is relatively little statute law, but this is interpreted by the courts which build up case law to supplement the statutes. Therefore the law evolves over time in response to individual cases.

- A codified system: statute sets out firm rules.

Common law systems are found in the UK, the USA, Canada, Australia and New Zealand. In these countries company law tends not to prescribe financial reporting practice in detail. This is left to the profession, which develops accounting standards to meet the needs of users and preparers of financial statements. Financial reporting practice evolves over time in response to changes in the business environment.

In contrast, most European countries and Japan have codified legal systems. Accounting practices and the content of financial statements are prescribed in detail by company law. In these countries companies often have to prepare their financial statements to comply with a chart of accounts or uniform format. Accounting standards are less important and there is very little scope for flexibility or for individual judgement.

6.3   Finance

The main providers of finance are normally the most important users of financial statements.

In some countries, such as the UK and the USA, many companies are publicly listed and rely on large numbers of equity shareholders who do not take any active part in the management of the company. Although there are also small family owned companies, the regulatory framework is designed to ensure that external investors are provided with the information that they need in order to assess the performance of their investment and the stewardship of management. For example:

- There is an emphasis upon disclosure and upon presenting information fairly. (The requirement to present a true and fair view and the concept of substance over form are important where external investors are the main users of accounts.)

- There is also a need for generally accepted principles such as accruals and consistency, because investors need to be able to compare one year with another and one company with another.

- The format of the performance statement emphasises gross profit, net profit and earnings; the format of the balance sheet emphasises working capital and net assets and groups shareholders' funds together. There is normally a requirement to disclose earnings per share and to prepare a cash flow statement.

In other countries, such as France, Germany and Japan, most finance is provided by banks, rather than by equity investors. There are relatively few large public listed companies and even these tend to be controlled by large institutional investors. This means that there is normally one powerful provider of finance who is likely to have access to internal information. Therefore the main objective of financial reporting is to protect creditors.

It is common for companies in such regimes to be required to transfer a proportion of their profits to a legal reserve. This is non-distributable and ensures that there are extra funds available to repay creditors.

Accounting estimates tend to be conservative, provisions or reserves for general risks may be set up, upward revaluations of fixed assets may be banned, companies may be required to use the depreciation method that produces the highest charge.

It is less important to present information in a way which highlights certain figures. Therefore the performance statement and the balance sheet may be two sided, with the debits and credits grouped together (although this has become less common since the implementation of the EC Fourth and Seventh directives).

6.4   Taxation

In the UK tax regulations have very little impact on financial reporting. Profit before tax in the accounts has to be adjusted for items such as disallowable expenses and capital allowances to arrive at profit chargeable to corporation tax.

In other countries, for example Germany, the financial statements must be drawn up in accordance with tax regulations, so that profit before tax in the accounts is the same as taxable profit. This is often the case where a country has a 'codified' legal system or where the government is one of the main users of the accounts. This has several implications as follows.

- Depreciation rates are standardised and may well be much higher than is normal in the UK as companies will charge the maximum allowed.

- There are prescribed methods for valuing assets such as stocks. Upward revaluation of fixed assets is either prohibited or compulsory.

- Deferred tax is almost non-existent.

- Preparers of accounts have an incentive to make reported profit as low as possible.

6.5   Politics

The political system of a country influences its financial reporting practices. Where there is a strong central government and most or all business is nationalised, the main objective of financial statements is normally to provide the government with the information that it needs in order to control the economy. Accounts are used to assess the size of industries and resources, to measure the performance of various sectors, control prices and allocate funds. Until recently this was the case in much of Eastern Europe and in China and may now apply in some developing countries.

Accounts prepared in a centrally controlled economy are generally standardised, based on strict rules and presented in a uniform format. There is no concept of a 'true and fair view' or 'fair presentation' and in some cases accounting is little more than double entry bookkeeping.

6.6   Inflation

Where there is very high inflation, historical cost accounts are of very limited value and financial statements may be prepared using a form of current purchasing power accounting (CPP). This has been the case in several South American countries. Another possible approach to dealing with inflation is a compulsory 'one off' revaluation of fixed assets using government indices: this was done in France in the late 1970s and still affects financial reporting in that country.

6.7   Historical 'accidents'

Former colonies tend to have accounting systems based on those of their mother countries. For example, Australia, New Zealand, India, Pakistan and Hong Kong all have accounting systems similar to that of the UK.

The accounting system in France has been influenced by the German occupation in the Second World War. In Nazi Germany accounts were used as a tool to control the economy and were highly standardised. After the war the French economy had to be tightly controlled and therefore a version of the German 'accounting plan' was adopted.

Economic and trading links or the desire to form them can also shape accounting practice. Examples include:

- the influence of the US on Canadian financial reporting practice

- the way in which the EU countries have adopted similar accounts formats as a result of the EC Directives

- the adoption of International Accounting Standards (IASs) by some developing countries

- the adoption of UK and US style accounting practices by some Eastern European countries and by China.

6.8   The profession

KEY POINT

Countries which have a system of common law and strong equity markets generally have a strong and highly regarded accounting profession.

Countries which have a system of common law and strong equity markets generally have a strong and highly regarded accounting profession. Countries which have codified legal systems and few public listed companies have less need for highly educated accountants and therefore the profession tends to be weak.

The strength of the accountancy profession in turn influences the development of financial reporting. This influence is both direct (the development of accounting standards) and indirect. For example, it could be argued that the UK is able to have a sophisticated, principles based, system of financial reporting because it has a large number of accountants capable of developing and implementing such a system. In contrast, some countries may keep a prescriptive system of accounting based on rules because there is a relative shortage of accountants capable of developing alternatives or influencing regulatory bodies to adopt them.

Some developing countries have been able to overcome these problems by adopting IASs. Eastern European countries have been assisted by the international accounting firms in developing accounting practices suitable for a market economy.

6.9   Culture and local custom

Financial reporting practice may be influenced by cultural factors in a number of ways.

- Some nationalities are naturally conservative and this may affect their attitude to accounting estimates, particularly providing for liabilities.

- Religion may affect accounting practices, for example Islamic law forbids the charging or accepting of interest.

- Different nationalities have different attitudes to risk. For example in Japan high gearing is usual and is a sign of confidence in a company.

- Attitudes to disclosure also vary. Some cultures value openness while others have a strong tradition of confidentiality.

- In the UK and the USA the main objective of management and shareholders is generally to maximise profit in the short term. However, in some countries investors and management may have different or wider objectives, such as long-term growth, stability, benefiting the community and safeguarding the interests of employees.

6.10 International harmonisation

Lastly, the need for international harmonisation has itself affected financial reporting practice in some countries. In the 1980s and 1990s, UK financial reporting practice was influenced by the implementation of the EC Fourth and Seventh Directives. This meant that UK company accounts must follow prescribed formats similar to those in accounting 'codes' used in other EU countries. The EC Directives also introduced the concept of the 'true and fair view' into company law throughout the EU. Many countries are now adopting IASs in order to secure stock exchange listings abroad.

The current trend is for national standard setters to be under increasing pressure to comply with international practice. The way in which this has affected the work of the ASB in the UK was discussed earlier in this chapter.

7 Restating overseas financial statements in line with UK GAAP

7.1 Summary of differences between UK GAAP, IASs and US GAAP

We have considered in general terms the issues involved and work that has taken place in the international harmonisation of accounting standards. In this section we examine what the major differences are at the present time. You are not required to know what international practices are in detail but, if you have an appreciation of the differences, you will be better able to understand some of the current controversies being tackled by the ASB. You may also be required to restate overseas accounts to UK practice and here familiarity with international practice before the exam will help you in the exam.

	UK GAAP	IAS	US GAAP
True and fair view override	Permitted in exceptional circumstances	Permitted in exceptional circumstances	Not permitted
Extraordinary items	Effectively prohibited	Effectively prohibited	Permitted, but limited to a few events outside the control of the company
Purchased goodwill	Capitalise and amortise over useful economic life; maximum period normally 20 years but can be longer or indefinite if certain criteria met	Capitalise but do not amortise, subject to annual impairment review	Capitalise but do not amortise, subject to annual impairment review
Development costs	Either treat as expense *or* capitalise and amortise if criteria met	Must capitalise and amortise if criteria met	Must be treated as expense

	UK GAAP	IAS	US GAAP
Tangible fixed assets	Carry at historic cost or valuation	Carry at historic cost or valuation	Must carry at historic cost; revaluations not permitted. (N.B. this applies to all assets with the exception of some securities and derivatives)
Investment properties	Carry at open market value; do not depreciate	Carry at fair value or historic cost	Treat as tangible fixed asset (must be at historic cost)
Capitalisation of borrowing costs	Optional (but policy must be applied consistently)	Optional (but policy must be applied consistently)	Compulsory for certain qualifying assets. Prohibited if assets do not qualify.
Stocks	Carry at lower of cost and NRV. FIFO and weighted average method permitted; LIFO not normally permitted	Carry at lower of cost and NRV. FIFO and weighted average methods all permitted. LIFO not permitted	Carry at lower of cost and market (market is the lower of replacement cost and NRV minus normal profit margin)
Deferred tax	Full provision, liability method	Full provision, liability method	Full provision, liability method
Pension costs	Assets valued at market value Recognise surpluses and deficits in balance sheet; recognise actuarial gains and losses immediately in STRGL	Assets valued at fair value Recognise cumulative actuarial gains and losses over average remaining service lives of employees if these fall outside limits based on 10% of present value of defined benefit obligation or 10% of fair value of plan assets, otherwise they can be deferred. Faster amortisation or immediate recognition is permitted, provided policy is applied consistently	Assets valued at fair value or market value. Similar to IAS approach

	UK GAAP	**IAS**	**US GAAP**
Capital instruments	All shares shown within shareholders' funds, analysed between equity and non-equity. All preference shares are non-equity	Capital instruments classified according to substance. Redeemable preference shares normally treated as liabilities	Shareholders' funds analysed between common stock and other categories. Redeemable preference shares normally in separate category between debt and equity
	Convertible debt is treated as a liability	Convertible debt split between debt and equity	Convertible debt is treated as a liability
	No standard on measurement of derivatives	Derivatives measured at fair value; changes in fair value taken to income statement	Derivatives measured at fair value; changes in fair value taken to income statement
Dividends	Must provide for dividends relating to a financial year even though not declared until after the year end	Do not provide for dividends that are not declared at the year end	Do not provide for dividends that are not declared at the year end

ACTIVITY 1

Extracts from the notes to the financial statements of a multinational company are shown below.

The following are the main US accounting principles which differ from those generally accepted in the United Kingdom.

Revaluation of land and buildings

Periodically land and buildings are revalued by professionally qualified external valuers and such assets are written up to the appraised value. Depreciation is, where applicable, calculated on these revalued amounts. When revalued properties are sold, the gain or loss on sale is calculated based on revalued carrying amounts. Under US GAAP such revaluations would not be reflected in financial statements and the gain or loss on sale would be calculated based on original cost.

Foreign currencies

Revenues, expenses, assets and liabilities relating to overseas subsidiaries are translated at the year-end rate. Under US GAAP assets and liabilities are translated as under UK GAAP; however, revenues and expenses are translated at average rates for the year.

Ordinary dividends

Final ordinary dividends are provided in the year in respect of which they are proposed on the basis of the recommendation by the directors which requires subsequent approval by the shareholders. Under US GAAP dividends are not provided for until formally declared.

For each of these three accounting policies, state whether the policy results in:

(a)   an increase in UK profits, or

(b)   a decrease in UK profits, or

(c)   the effect of the policy depends on the circumstances, or

(d)   the policy does not affect UK profits.

Feedback to this activity is at the end of the chapter.

7.2   Reconciliation statements

Due to the differences referred to, a company with a large group of international investors and, as a likely consequence, a listing on more than one stock exchange, may need to produce financial information which is expressed in terms of the domestic accounting policies of the investors.

UK companies with a listing on a US stock exchange may be required to produce figures following US GAAP which consists of a reconciliation statement between UK and US GAAP. In addition a narrative statement summarising the differences in policies is required.

7.3   Restatement of overseas accounts

The Examiner may ask you to prepare a reconciliation statement, or to restate overseas accounts to comply with UK GAAP. You should clearly state any assumptions that you make about accounting policies followed.

The two special problems you may have if the accounts presented in the examination question are non-UK are:

- the description and order of items in the financial statements may be different. Part of the mark allocation may be therefore for the reordering and change in narrative of the items

- if the accounts are stated in a foreign currency (which is, of course, to be expected!), the easiest approach is to perform your workings and reconciliation statement in that currency so that the accounts will balance and then translate all items using a suitable and the same exchange rate. Look at the example above.

ACTIVITY 2

The summarised financial statements of Exodus Inc, a company trading in Erewhon, are shown below.

	20X3 $ million	20X2 $ million
Revenue	4,231.4	2,999.2
Income after tax	268.3	404.6
Assets	$ million	$ million
Cash	435.9	336.4
Marketable securities	-	51.8
Accounts receivable	719.1	427.4
Inventories	522.0	309.4
Prepaid expenses	38.0	16.3
Income taxes	44.7	25.9
Other receivables	77.3	17.4
Total current assets	1,837.0	1,184.6
Property, plant & equipment	1,071.0	291.8

Investment in associated companies	6.1	4.9
Goodwill	116.4	124.4
Total assets	3,030.5	1,605.7
Liabilities		
Bank loans & overdrafts	113.3	89.1
Short-term debt	29.8	12.0
Accounts payable	518.7	236.8
Other accounts payable and accrued expenses	346.1	155.3
Income taxes	186.7	95.9
Dividends	82.2	40.0
Total current liabilities	1,276.8	629.1
Long-term debt	103.6	62.1
Other liabilities	275.4	88.4
Total liabilities	1,655.8	779.6
Equity share capital	87.4	22.1
Retained earnings	1,287.3	804.0
Total equity	1,374.7	826.1
Total liabilities & equity	3,030.5	1,605.7

The major accounting policies adopted and relevant figures are as follows:

(a) The goodwill relates to two acquisitions of subsidiaries. Goodwill is amortised over 20 years. The original amounts are $58 million and $102 million.

(b) Interest has been capitalised on certain properties which the group constructed for its own use. The total capitalised interest is $4.5 million and $3.1 million in 20X3 and 20X2 respectively.

(c) Dividends to shareholders are accounted for in the year the directors propose to pay the dividends. Proposed dividends at 31 December 20X2 and paid in 20X3 were $48 million. Proposed dividends at 31 December 20X3 and paid in 20X4 were $56 million.

(d) The assets of the group are stated under the HC convention as required by local GAAP. Land is estimated to be worth $150 million more than its book value at both balance sheet dates.

Produce a balance sheet as at 31 December 20X3 under UK GAAP. You are required to amortise goodwill over 20 years but to adjust for other items to present the highest amount of shareholders' funds.

Show the results in dollars.

Feedback to this activity is at the end of the chapter.

8   IFRS 1 *First-time Adoption of International Financial Reporting Standards*

8.1   Introduction

From 2005, International Financial Reporting Standards dominate UK financial reporting. EU Regulations require UK quoted companies to apply international standards for periods beginning on or after 1 January 2005. These companies and their subsidiaries will therefore be first-time adopters that year. Non-quoted companies are expected to have the option to adopt IFRSs, but do not have to.

IFRS 1 sets out the procedures for making the transition from national accounting standards to international standards.

You may think it odd that you have to study an IFRS as part of the UK accounting exam, but many UK companies will be choosing to switch to IFRSs soon, and it is IFRS 1 that explains how the switch should be carried out.

8.2   Date of transition: comparative figures

When IFRSs are adopted, they must be applied from the first day of the first accounting period, when there has to be an *opening IFRS balance sheet*. For example, for a UK quoted company with a year ending 31 December 2005, because comparative statements must be published, the opening IFRS balance sheet for an entity adopting IFRSs for the year ending 31 December 2005 will be 1 January 2004, which is the first day of the comparative period. Consequently, for many UK quoted companies and their subsidiaries, international standards will have to be applied from the beginning of 2004, and applied for the whole period from 1 January 2004.

The opening IFRS balance sheet must comply with international standards.

(a)   It must recognise all assets and liabilities required by international standards and must not recognise any assets or liabilities not permitted by the standards.

(b)   All assets, liabilities and components of equity must be re-classified and valued in accordance with international standards.

Any gains or losses arising on the adoption of IFRSs should be recognised directly in retained earnings as at the date of transition.

8.3   Standards to adopt

Accounting policies for first-time adopters must comply with IFRSs in force at the reporting date. This means that for UK quoted companies with a year ending 31 December, international standards in force at 31 December 2005 must be applied to the whole period commencing 1 January 2004.

8.4   Reconciliations in the year of transition

IFRS 1 requires companies to provide a reconciliation between the figures produced for the first time under international standards and the comparable figures produced using the previous national standards ('previous GAAP').

Equity computed under previous GAAP should be reconciled to its IFRS equivalent. The profit reported in the final previous GAAP accounts should also be reconciled to the IFRS profit. This means, for example, that if a company publishes IFRS accounts for the first time on 31 December 2005, it must present a statement reconciling the previous GAAP equity and IFRS equity as at both 31 December 2004 and 1 January 2004. It must also reconcile the previous GAAP profit with the IFRS profit for 2004.

8.5 Exemptions

IFRS 1 grants limited exemptions in situations where the cost of compliance would outweigh the benefits to the user. For example:

- Previous business combinations do not have to be restated in accordance with IFRS. This relates to classifying combinations as mergers or acquisitions, fair valuing assets and liabilities, and the treatment of goodwill.

- If it is not possible to establish the cost of an asset, then fair value at the date of transition can be used as deemed cost. (This exemption is unlikely to be used in a developed country where accurate accounting records have been kept.)

- Some actuarial gains and losses on pension schemes are left unrecognised under the 10% 'corridor' approach required by the relevant IAS. A first-time adopter may find it easier to recognise all gains and losses at the date of transition.

- Past currency translation gains and losses included in revenue reserves need not be separated out into the currency translation reserve.

- Under the relevant IAS, part of the proceeds of convertible debt is classified as equity. If the debt had been repaid at the date of transition no adjustment is needed for the equity component.

- If a subsidiary adopts IFRS later than its parent, then the subsidiary may value its assets and liabilities either at its own transition date or its parent's transition date (which would normally be easier).

There are also three situations where retrospective application of IFRS is prohibited. These relate to derecognition of financial assets and liabilities, hedging and estimates. The IASB thought that it would be impractical to obtain the information necessary to restate past financial statements, and that restating past fair values and estimates was open to manipulation.

Example

Channel plc is adopting IFRSs for the first time in the year ending 31 December 2005. It has previously prepared its financial statements under UK GAAP.

The balance sheets shown below for 31 December 2003 and 2004, together with a profit and loss account for 2004 have been prepared under UK GAAP.

Required:

(a) Restate the balance sheets and profit and loss accounts in accordance with IFRSs.

(b) Prepare the Statement of Changes in Equity for 2004. This will record the adjustments to opening reserves caused by the adoption of IFRSs.

(c) Prepare the reconciliations of equity and profit required by IFRS 1.

Channel plc: UK GAAP balance sheets

		31 Dec 2004		31 Dec 2003	
		£m	£m	£m	£m
Fixed assets			800		700
Current assets					
Investments	Note 1	180		180	
Sundry		198		160	
		378		340	

Creditors due within one year

		£m		£m
Proposed equity dividend	Note 2	150		120
Sundry		73		89
		(223)		(209)
Net current assets		155		131
Capital employed		955		831
Convertible debt	Note 3	(200)		(200)
Provision for deferred tax	Note 4	(95)		(81)
Net assets		660		550

Capital and reserves

Ordinary shares		250	250
Retained profits		290	180
		540	430
Preference shares	Note 5	120	120
		660	550

Channel plc: UK GAAP profit and loss account 2004

		£m	£m
Operating profit			358
Interest paid			(20)
Profit before tax			338
Taxation			
Corporation tax		50	
Deferred tax	Note 4	14	
			(64)
Profit after tax			274
Preference dividend	Note 5		(14)
Ordinary dividend	Note 2		(150)
Retained profit for the year			110
Opening reserves			180
Closing reserves			290

Notes:

(1) **Investments**

These are available-for-sale equity securities. They are held at cost under UK GAAP. IAS 39 requires them to be carried at fair value with any gain or loss during the year reported in the income statement. Their fair values were:

31 December 2003	£150m
31 December 2004	£170m

(2) Proposed equity dividend

The Companies Act requires proposed equity dividends to be provided for as a liability. IAS 10 states that proposed equity dividends are not liabilities. Dividends are recognised in the Statement of Changes in Equity when they are paid.

2003's proposed equity dividend was paid during 2004.

(3) Convertible debt

Under FRS 4 convertible debt is recognised as a liability until it is converted or redeemed. IAS 32 requires these compound instruments to be split between their equity and liability components. This debt would be split as follows:

Equity	£16m
Debt	£184m

(4) Deferred tax

Channel plc has discounted its deferred tax liabilities. This is not allowed under IAS 12. The undiscounted deferred tax provisions will be as follows:

31 December 2003	£90m
31 December 2004	£108m

(5) Preference dividends

The Companies Act requires preference shares to be classified as part of Capital and Reserves and for their dividends to be treated as an appropriation of profit.

FRS 32 classifies these preference shares as liabilities and their dividends as charges against profit.

Solution

Channel plc: IFRS balance sheet

	31 Dec 2004		31 Dec 2003	
Assets	£m	£m	£m	£m
Fixed assets		800		700
Current assets				
Investments	170		150	
Sundry	198		160	
		368		310
Total assets		1,168		1,010
Equity and liabilities				
Capital and reserves				
Ordinary shares		250		250
Other equity components		16		16
Retained profits		417		261
		683		527
Non-current liabilities				
Convertible debt	184		184	
Preference shares	120		120	
Deferred tax	108		90	
		412		394

Current liabilities

Sundry	73	89
Net assets	1,168	1,010

Channel plc: IFRS income statement 2004

	£m	£m
Operating profit		358
Increase in value of investments (170 – 150)		20
Finance costs		
Preference dividend		(14)
Interest paid		(20)
Profit before tax		344
Taxation		
Corporation tax	50	
Deferred tax (108 – 90)	18	
		(68)
Profit for the year		276

Channel plc: IFRS statement of changes in equity 2004

	Ordinary shares £m	*Other equity* £m	*Retained earnings* £m	*Total* £m
1 January 2004 as previously reported	250	–	180	430
Adjustments to apply IFRS				
Reclassification of part of convertible debt	–	16	–	16
Decrease in value of investments	–	–	(30)	(30)
Increase in deferred tax provision	–	–	(9)	(9)
Add back of equity dividend	–	–	120	120
1 January 2004 restated for IFRS	250	16	261	527
Profit for the year	–	–	276	276
Equity dividends paid	–	–	(120)	(120)
31 December 2004	250	16	417	683

Reconciliation of equity under UK GAAP and IFRS

	Date of transition 1 Jan 04 £m	*Final reported balance sheet 31 Dec 04* £m
As previously reported under UK GAAP	430	540
Reclassification of part of convertible debt	16	16
Change in value of investments	(30)	(10)
Increase in deferred tax provision	(9)	(13)
Add back of equity dividend	120	150
As restated for IFRS	527	683

Reconciliation of profit for 2004 under UK GAAP and IFRS

	£m
Profit after tax as previously reported under UK GAAP	274
Increase in value of investments during the year	20
Increase in deferred tax charge (18 – 14)	(4)
Less: Preference dividend charge	(14)
As restated for IFRS	276

The income statement for 2005 and the balance sheet as at 31 December 2005 will be prepared under IFRS only. There is no requirement to reconcile them to what would have been reported under UK GAAP.

SELF-TEST QUESTIONS

The need for harmonisation

1   What are the advantages of closer international harmonisation of accounting practices for (a) multi-national companies and (b) for investors? (1)

Harmonisation: the current situation

2   Will all companies in the European Union be required from 2005 to prepare financial statements under international standards? (3.1)

The impact on the UK

3   What measures are being taken by the UK's ASB to bring UK GAAP into line with international standards? (5.2)

Reasons for differences in accounting practice

4   Why are there differences between accounting practices in different countries? (6)

EXAM-TYPE QUESTION

Dixie Inc

You are the accountant of Widespread plc, a company that is incorporated in the United Kingdom, prepares its accounts using UK accounting standards, and has a number of subsidiaries located in various countries around the world. One of these subsidiaries is Dixie Inc, a company based in the USA. Your managing director, who is not an accountant, has decided to take an interest in the preparation of the consolidated financial statements. Some time later he calls you into the office because he is confused by a number of the documents he has seen. He is particularly confused by the reconciliation statement that the chief accountant of Dixie Inc has prepared. This statement is shown below.

	$'000
Profit before taxation per local accounts	56,000
Capitalisation of development costs net of related amortisation	7,000
Write-off capitalised interest net of related amortisation	(4,000)
Restatement of stock on the FIFO basis from the LIFO basis	7,500
Profit before taxation for consolidation	66,500
Taxation per local accounts	22,400
Write-back of deferred taxation	(4,400)
Taxation for consolidation	18,000

The managing director does not really understand why this reconciliation statement is necessary. He is wondering whether the group should adopt international accounting standards in an effort to avoid having to prepare it.

Required:

Write a report to your managing director that:

(i)   explains in general terms why the reconciliation statement is necessary;

(5 marks)

(ii)   identifies the accounting issue that underpins each of the four items in the statement;   **(10 marks)**

(iii)   evaluates the suggestion of the managing director that the group should adopt international accounting standards.   **(5 marks)**

(Total: 20 marks)

For the answer to this question see the 'Answers' section at the end of the book.

FEEDBACK TO
ACTIVITY 1

Revaluation of land and buildings

This results in a decrease in UK profits due to the higher depreciation charge and lower gains on disposal.

Foreign currencies

The effect on profits depends on the direction in which the exchange rate is moving.

Ordinary dividends

This has no effect on profits; all dividends are eventually charged against profit, whether in the year they are declared or the year in which they are paid.

FEEDBACK TO
ACTIVITY 2

Tutorial note: Interest may be capitalised under UK GAAP. As this increases assets and therefore shareholders' funds, no adjustment has been made.

Dividends require adjustments but the statement provided is at the pre-dividend level.

Balance sheet as at 31 December 20X3 under UK GAAP

	$ million	$ million	$ million
Fixed assets			
Intangible			116.4
Tangible (1,071 + 150)			1,221.0
Investment in associated undertakings			6.1
			1,343.5
Current assets			
Stocks		522.0	
Debtors:			
Trade	719.1		
Prepayments	38.0		
Other (44.7 + 77.3)	122.0		
		879.1	
Cash at bank and in hand		435.9	
		1,837.0	

Creditors: amounts falling due within one year			
Bank loans and overdrafts	113.3		
Other loans	29.8		
Trade creditors	518.7		
Other creditors including taxation	186.7		
Accruals	346.1		
Dividends (82.2 + 56)	138.2		
		1,332.8	
Net current assets			504.2
Total assets less current liabilities			1,847.7
Creditors: amounts falling due after more than one year			
Loans	103.6		
Other	275.4		
			379.0
			1,468.7
Capital and reserves			
Called up share capital			87.4
Revaluation reserve			150.0
Profit and loss account (W1)			1,231.3
			1,468.7

Workings

Effect of adjustments on retained earnings	*$ million*
Per accounts	1,287.3
Dividends proposed not recorded	(56.0)
	1,231.3

Chapter 26

CURRENT ISSUES AND DEVELOPMENTS

The big issue at the moment is, of course, the European adoption of IASs in 2005. This was looked at in the previous chapter. This chapter looks at a number of other recent exposure drafts, statements of best practice and discussion papers covering:

- year-end financial reporting

- proposed changes to company law

- interim reports and preliminary announcements

- disclosure of accounting policies

- discounting.

Objectives

When you have studied this chapter you should be able to:

- identify ways of improving communication of corporate performance

- understand current proposals relating to year-end financial reports and business reporting on the internet

- discuss the problem areas in interim reporting

- discuss current issues in corporate reporting including disclosure of accounting policies and discounting.

1   Year-end financial reports: improving communication

1.1   Reasons for reviewing present practice

The financial statements that listed companies prepare each year for their shareholders have become much longer and more complex in recent years. Recent changes in financial reporting requirements are widely acknowledged to have improved the quality of information provided. However, there is evidence that much of the more detailed information now required to be disclosed is aimed at and understood only by institutional investors and other expert users. There are two potential disadvantages of this:

- the cost of preparing and distributing annual financial statements may exceed the benefit to shareholders

- the majority of shareholders, who have less time and expertise, are worse off than before because the information that is of interest and importance to them is lost in the detail.

Listed companies are permitted to send summary financial statements to shareholders who choose to receive them instead of the full financial statements, but in practice many companies do not do so.

The ASB has responded to these concerns by issuing a Discussion Paper *Year-end financial reports: improving communication*. The Paper reviews the ways in which financial statements of listed companies could be simplified for private shareholders. It also considers the implications of the growing importance of the Internet, although it does not make any firm proposals.

The publication of the Discussion Paper coincides with a review of company law by the Department of Trade and Industry (DTI). One of the issues that this review is considering is possible changes to reporting requirements.

1.2   Is there a need for change?

It has been suggested that the problem of information overload could be addressed without changing the reporting framework.

Good referencing within the financial statements and possibly colour coding different sections might enable private shareholders who have a serious interest in the performance of a company to identify the information of interest to them. However, there is evidence that many shareholders read only a small proportion of the full financial statements and would prefer a shorter document. In addition, it is not necessarily easy to highlight key financial information of general interest within the full financial statements. If key disclosures are placed together they are out of context within the full financial statements and if they are colour coded shareholders still have to read through the full financial statements in order to find them.

Unnecessary disclosures could be eliminated from the full financial statements. This would benefit professional users, as well as private shareholders. Research has been undertaken to identify required disclosures that were not used in the decisions made by financial analysts. As a result of this, the ASB has concluded that there was very limited scope for reducing the content of the full financial statements.

Summary financial statements may already be sent to shareholders who prefer them to the full financial statements. However, many listed companies choose not to prepare them partly because of the additional cost and partly because it was felt that it was unwise to reduce the information provided to shareholders in a post-Cadbury climate where fuller disclosure is being emphasised. There is also evidence that in practice summary financial statements are not as user friendly as legislation intended.

1.3   Possible solutions

As a result of the problems outlined above, the ASB considered ways in which the process of producing summary financial statements might be made attractive to companies.

The law could be reframed so that summary financial statements become the main reports sent to shareholders. This would have the advantage of overcoming concern that shareholders might be deprived of information. Although it would not in itself reduce costs, the role of the full financial statements would probably change, so that they became either 'plain paper' or electronic documents. This would be in tune with current developments, such as the growth of reporting via the internet.

A single two-part document could be prepared, instead of two stand-alone documents. The first part would contain the summary financial statements and would be sent to all shareholders. The second would contain the additional information required to make up the full financial statements and would be available only on request. This alternative would reduce both costs and administrative problems associated with preparing two separate documents, but also has disadvantages.

The notes to the financial statements might not be easy to allocate to either one of the two parts. Some would have to be split between the two, making the financial statements less comprehensible.

It could be especially difficult to divide the operating and financial review between the two parts. Therefore the whole of the operating and financial review would be included in the summary financial statements, obscuring the information of particular interest to private shareholders.

1.4 Main proposals

The ASB proposes the following.

- The law should be reframed so that summary financial statements become the main report for shareholders. All listed companies would prepare them.

- The full audited financial statements should continue to be produced for those who request them and for filing purposes. They could become less important as promotional documents and in time might evolve into 'plain paper' formats.

- Summary financial statements should be required by legislation to contain at least the financial information recommended by the Statement of best practice on preliminary announcements (discussed later) together with details of directors' remuneration.

The advantages of basing the requirements and recommendations for summary financial statements on those for preliminary announcements would be the following.

- The preliminary announcement is carefully designed to provide a focused summary of the key aspects of the company's financial performance for the period. Although it is prepared for institutional investors, its succinct format could be an ideal basis for the summary financial statements.

- Costs and administrative efforts would be minimised if the contents of the two reports were similar.

- Because only a very basic financial content would be prescribed, companies would retain the flexibility to adapt the summary financial statements to best reflect their widely varying circumstances and the needs of their particular shareholders.

The Discussion Paper also proposes that companies legislation should be amended to permit (but not require) companies to offer their shareholders the option of receiving a simplified financial review instead of summary financial statements. This would comprise a few pages of narrative highlighting key financial measures and explaining them in a readily understandable manner.

1.5 The impact of the internet on financial reporting

The internet has several implications for financial reporting:

- on-line trading is relatively cheap and this means that the number of private investors may grow in the future

- information about companies and other organisations is being accessed by an increasing number of people, many of whom are private investors

- the technology itself allows information to be presented in innovative ways.

KEY POINT

Most large companies already place their annual report on their website.

The DTI is at present considering whether to allow companies to communicate with their shareholders via the internet if their shareholders so wish. It is likely that in the near future annual reports, interim reports and preliminary announcements will have to be published on the company's website as well as, or instead of being distributed to shareholders in printed form. Most large companies already place their annual report on their website. The ASB believes that entities should also be encouraged to post on their websites preliminary announcements and other financial information given to analysts and institutional investors. This means that there should be more equality between investors in terms of the information that is available.

At present, most companies simply post the printed annual report and accounts. There are other possibilities however.

- 'Hyperlinks' enable users to jump from one area of the financial statements to other areas where the same topic is discussed. This means that users can easily find the information that they need. Use of hyperlinks could help to overcome 'information overload' without removing detailed disclosures that are useful to analysts.

- Some companies already post financial statements on spreadsheets that can be downloaded and merged with those of other companies. This enables comparisons to be made. In future, companies may be able to place a database of audited financial information on the internet from which users could prepare their own reports, presented in a way that best meets their particular needs.

Another possibility not highlighted by the ASB is that companies may report to shareholders at much more frequent intervals, so that much less emphasis is placed on the traditional annual report. Some commentators (although not all) believe that eventually companies will report in 'real time' so that annual financial statements will become obsolete.

The ASB believes that users will benefit from financial reporting on the internet, but in its Discussion Paper *Year-end financial reports* it also draws attention to the potential risks.

- There is an increased risk that information will be inaccurate. Even if electronic financial statements are checked when they are first published, in the absence of adequate controls they might be selectively updated subsequently.

- It may be unclear which information is regulated (prepared in accordance with statutory or other requirements) and which is unregulated. Because information can be placed on a website very easily it is likely that companies will supplement their standardised reports to shareholders with further information, for example, alternative presentations or additional analyses. Users might be misled into thinking that information is regulated when it is not.

- Information that is inconsistent with the audited financial statements might be given. Users have no guarantee that unregulated information is consistent with standard financial reports sent to shareholders.

1.6   Responses to the proposals

Although the Discussion Paper has been broadly welcomed, it has been criticised for concentrating on conventional reporting channels. Commentators have pointed out that it does not fully address the possibilities of the internet, nor does it consider developments such as environmental and social reporting.

The ASB has now analysed the responses to the Discussion Paper and has communicated these to the DTI. The ASB is monitoring the progress of the Company Law Review and will in due course seek to develop best practice guidance within the new legal framework.

2   Further proposals: review of company law

2.1   Introduction

In March 2000 the Company Law Review Steering Group published a consultation document *Modern Company Law for a Competitive Economy: Developing the Framework*. This was followed by a further paper *Modern Company Law for a Competitive Economy: Completing the Structure*. The final report was issued in July 2001. The consultation document proposes a large number of changes to the current framework for company accounting and reporting. These proposals are intended to lead to a new Companies Act.

Whereas the ASB's proposals concentrate on ways of dealing with 'information overload', the Steering Group's proposals address wider issues. The Steering Committee believes that change is needed for the following reasons.

- Because the annual reports of listed companies have become so long and complex, financial statements only meet the needs of institutional investors and analysts. The resulting 'information overload' obscures the overall view of a company's performance for other users.

- Information is not provided in a sufficiently timely manner for today's economic conditions.

- Company reporting is essentially backward looking and based on financial indicators. There are few statutory requirements to report on the main factors which influence past and future performance (for example, opportunities and risks, key business relationships and intangible assets).

- Despite the exemptions now available to small companies, the assumption underlying much of the current requirements is that 'one size fits all' – regardless of the nature or size of the company.

2.2   The main proposals

Listed companies

- All listed companies should publish their preliminary announcements on the company website as soon as they are released.

- Listed companies should also be required to file a 'full annual report' at Companies House within 6 months of the year-end (the current time limit is 7 months). This report would be published on the company's website within 4 months of the year-end.

- The directors' report would be replaced by an expanded Operating and Financial Review.

    This requirement means that listed companies would be legally required to publish an Operating and Financial Review (at present it is merely best practice). Companies would be required to provide:

    (a)   a fair review of the development of their business over the year and position at the end of it, including material post year-end events, operating performance and material changes

    (b)   the company's purpose, strategy and principal drivers of performance.

They would also be required to provide information on: key relationships (e.g. with employees, customers and suppliers); corporate governance; dynamics of the business (e.g. key risks faced); environmental policies; policies and performance on community, social, ethical and reputational issues; and receipts from and returns to shareholders.

This requirement is intended to address the lack of forward-looking and non-financial information needed by users of financial statements to assess fully a company's performance and prospects.

Other companies above the small company threshold

- All unlisted companies above the small company threshold should continue to file and distribute a full annual report to all shareholders.

- Large private companies would be required to prepare an Operating and Financial Review.

- All companies above the small company threshold should file their annual report within 7 months of the year-end (the current limit for private companies is 10 months).

Small companies

There would be completely separate accounting and reporting rules for small companies. This contrasts with the current situation, where small company accounts are based on the full requirements for large companies, but with extensive exemptions. The approach adopted by the Steering Group is to 'think small first'.

(a) The turnover and assets thresholds to qualify as a small company should be increased to the maximum amounts permitted under European law.

(b) The category of medium-sized company would be effectively abolished.

(c) Small companies would be required to file the same accounts as they prepare for shareholders. The distinction between abbreviated accounts (for filing) and 'simplified' small company accounts (for distribution to shareholders) would be abolished.

(d) The time limit for preparing and filing small company accounts should be reduced from 10 months to 7 months.

3   Interim reports

3.1   Introduction

Interim reports covering the first six months of each financial year are required by the London Stock Exchange as a condition of listing. They play an important role as a progress report in the continuing reporting process of the operating, financing and investing activities of a business.

Apart from the London Stock Exchange requirements, there has been little guidance for preparers of UK interim reports.

In September 1997 the ASB issued a Statement *Interim Reports*. Like the Statement on Operating and Financial Review it is intended to be a statement of best practice and its adoption is voluntary.

One of the recommendations of the Committee on the Financial Aspects of Corporate Governance (the Cadbury Committee) was that the ASB and the London Stock Exchange should clarify the accounting principles to be adopted by companies when preparing their interim reports. It also recommended that balance sheet information should be included with the interim report. The Statement has been developed in response to these recommendations.

3.2   Approaches

There are two possible approaches to the preparation of interim reports:

- the 'discrete' approach, which treats the interim period as a distinct accounting period and therefore applies the same accounting principles as are applied at the year end

- the 'integral' approach, which treats the interim period as part of the larger financial reporting period, meaning that revenues and expenses are recognised as a proportion of estimated annual amounts.

The ASB has adopted the 'discrete' approach. The only exception to this is taxation, which can only be determined at the end of the financial year.

3.3   Main recommendations

(a) Interim reports should be drawn up using the same measurement and recognition bases and accounting policies as are used in the preparation of annual financial statements.

(b) The interim period's tax charge should be based on an estimate of the annual effective tax rate, applied to the interim period's results.

(c) Interim reports should contain the following items:

- management commentary (an explanation of significant events and trends since the previous annual financial statements)

- summarised profit and loss account (including segmental analysis and disclosure of discontinued operations and acquisitions). Basic earnings per share should be derived from the results for the interim period and calculated and disclosed in the same manner as at the year end

- statement of total recognised gains and losses, where relevant

- summarised balance sheet (based on similar classifications to those used in the annual financial statements)

- summarised cash flow statement (including reconciliation of operating profit to net operating cash flow and reconciliation of cash flow to the movement in net debt).

(d) Companies are encouraged to make their interim reports available within 60 days of the period end (the Stock Exchange Listing Rules require publication within four months of the end of the period to which they relate).

3.4   Problem areas in interim reporting

Seasonal businesses

Some companies, for example holiday companies and domestic fuel suppliers, operate in businesses which are heavily seasonal. These companies often choose their financial year to fit their annual operating cycle. This means that their first six months may give very little indication of their likely annual results.

The Statement says that fluctuations of seasonal businesses are generally understood by the marketplace and it is appropriate to report them as they arise. However, this ignores the fact that although direct costs usually arise (or can legitimately be treated) in line with sales, indirect costs must be recognised on a time basis. This means that an interim report for a seasonal business could show a loss for the first six months, while showing a substantial profit for the year.

The management commentary should describe the nature of any seasonal activity and provide enough information for the performance of the business to be understood in the context of the annual cycle. Comparative figures for the half year and the full year also help the user to interpret the information.

Taxation

Taxation is assessed on an annual basis. This makes the discrete approach difficult to apply. Companies generally predict the effective tax rate for the whole year and apply it to the interim result. The Statement endorses this approach.

Other items determined on an annual basis

These include staff bonuses, profit sharing, sales commissions and some discounts. In practice, these are usually calculated by reference to the expected amount for the full year.

The Statement distinguishes between items where there is a recognisable obligation at the period end and those where there is not. The approach is similar to that taken by FRS 12 on provisions. For example, a provision could be made for a profit related bonus where the staff's expectations gave rise to a constructive obligation, but not for a one-off discretionary payment given at the end of the year.

Non-recurring items

Some major items of expenditure arise in the first half of the year and are not repeated in the second, or vice versa. For example, there may be reorganisation costs or cyclical expenses such as major repairs during the annual shutdown of a plant.

The Statement says that exceptional items should be included in the period in which they are incurred. It seems reasonable to extend this approach to all non-recurring items, but to make adequate disclosure in the management commentary.

Valuations

Using the discrete approach, it would be logical to revalue assets and assess them for impairment at the half-year. However, the Statement says that revalued properties may be left at the amounts shown at the previous year end (although this should be disclosed). Quoted investments carried at market value should be updated to values ruling at the end of the interim period.

3.5 Evaluation of the recommendations

Although the recommendations are not mandatory, they are expected to generally improve the standard of interim reporting. In particular, companies are encouraged to present balance sheet and cash flow information and a statement of total recognised gains and losses. (In the past, some companies did not provide this information.)

The recommendations have other advantages:

- Most companies will prepare interim statements using the discrete approach and comparability of information between entities should be improved. Previously, some companies have taken the discrete approach and some have taken the integral approach.

- Use of the discrete approach should mean that companies will be unable to hide the impact of seasonal trends on their results.

However, the recommendations have been criticised on the following grounds:

- Some commentators believe that the recommendations in the Statement should be compulsory, rather than simply a statement of best practice.

- Many preparers of interim reports dislike the discrete approach. They argue that the integral approach provides more useful information because it uses the interim results to predict and explain the full year's results. It enables users to assess trends.

4   Preliminary announcements

4.1   Introduction

The London Stock Exchange requires quoted companies to notify the Exchange of their preliminary statement of annual results immediately after Board approval. The preliminary announcement is the first external communication by companies of their financial performance and position for the year. However, there has been very little guidance on their content.

The ASB has issued a Statement on Preliminary Announcements. Like the Statement on Interim Reports, the Statement on Preliminary Announcements is intended to be a non-mandatory guide to best practice.

4.2   Main recommendations

Content – The content should be similar to that recommended for interim reports, i.e.:

(a)   a narrative commentary

(b)   a summarised profit and loss account

(c)   a statement of total recognised gains and losses

(d)   a summarised balance sheet

(e)   a summarised cash flow statement.

As well as the results for the full year, data for the final interim period (i.e. the second half-year) should be separately presented and commented upon.

Timeliness – Companies are encouraged to issue their preliminary announcement within 60 days of the year end.

Reliability – Information given should be reliable and consistent with the 'yet to be published' audited financial statements. It should therefore be based on material upon which the audit is substantially complete.

The recommendation that the second half-year's results should be presented in addition to results for the full year has been controversial. The reasoning behind this is that the market tends to react more quickly to previously unreported information about the second half-year (the period not covered by the interim report). However, many preparers of accounts may believe that the usefulness of the second half-year's results does not outweigh the additional cost of presenting the extra information unless it is particularly relevant (e.g. where the business is highly seasonal).

5 FRS 18 *Accounting policies*

5.1 Background

FRS 18 sets out the principles to be followed in selecting and disclosing accounting policies. It replaces SSAP 2 *Disclosure of accounting policies*.

FRS 18:

- updates the discussion of the four fundamental accounting concepts of SSAP 2 (going concern, accruals, consistency and prudence) so that they are consistent with the *Statement of Principles for Financial Reporting*

- clarifies the distinction between accounting policies and estimation techniques (which SSAP 2 did not explicitly address)

- makes explicit many of SSAP 2's implicit requirements

- incorporates the disclosures required by UITF Abstract 7 *True and fair view override disclosures* and UITF Abstract 14 *Disclosure of changes in accounting policy* (so that these two Abstracts are withdrawn).

5.2 Accounting policies

The requirements of FRS 18 restate current best practice.

(a) An entity should adopt accounting policies that enable its financial statements to give a true and fair view. Those accounting policies should be consistent with the requirements of accounting standards, Urgent Issues Task Force (UITF) Abstracts and companies legislation.

(b) If in exceptional circumstances compliance with the requirements of an accounting standard or UITF Abstract is inconsistent with the requirement to give a true and fair view, the requirements of the accounting standard or UITF Abstract should be departed from to the extent necessary to give a true and fair view.

(c) Where it is necessary to choose between accounting policies, an entity should select whichever of those accounting policies is judged by the entity to be most appropriate to its particular circumstances for the purpose of giving a true and fair view.

(d) An entity should prepare its financial statements on a going concern basis, unless

- the entity is being liquidated or has ceased trading; or

- the directors have no realistic alternative but to liquidate the entity or to cease trading.

Directors should assess whether there are significant doubts about an entity's ability to continue as a going concern.

(e) An entity should prepare its financial statements, except for cash flow information, on the accrual basis of accounting.

(f) An entity should judge the appropriateness of accounting policies to its particular circumstances against the objectives of:

- relevance

- reliability

- comparability

- understandability.

These objectives are the qualitative characteristics of useful financial information discussed in Chapter 3 of the Statement of Principles.

(g) An entity should take into account the following constraints:

- the need to balance the different objectives above

- the need to balance the cost of providing information with the likely benefit of such information to users of the entity's financial statements.

(h) An entity's accounting policies should be reviewed regularly to ensure that they remain the most appropriate to its particular circumstances. In judging whether a new policy is more appropriate than the existing policy, an entity will give due weight to the impact on comparability.

Frequent changes to accounting policies do not enhance comparability over the longer term, because they make it difficult for users to compare an entity's financial statements with those of earlier periods. Entities must consider the impact of past and expected future changes. Accounting policies should not be changed unless the benefit to users outweighs the corresponding disadvantages. However, consistency is not an end in itself, and should not prevent the introduction of improved accounting practices.

5.3   The role of the fundamental accounting concepts

Unlike SSAP 2, FRS 18 does not emphasise the fundamental concepts of going concern, accruals, consistency and prudence.

Note that the Companies Acts and EC Directives still require companies to observe the four fundamental concepts, unless there are special reasons for departing from them.

Going concern and accruals

FRS 18 requires entities to observe the going concern concept and the accruals concept. It goes further than SSAP 2, which only required disclosure of any departure from them.

The ASB has stated that going concern and accruals are part of the bedrock of accounting and that therefore they are critical to the selection of accounting policies.

Consistency

FRS 18 takes the view that consistency is a desirable quality of financial information, rather than a concept as such. Consistency is an aspect of comparability, which is one of the qualitative characteristics of useful financial information. Consistency is important, but it should not be used to justify retaining an existing accounting policy when a new policy is more appropriate to an entity's circumstances.

Prudence

Like consistency, prudence is viewed as a desirable quality of financial information, rather than as a fundamental concept. Prudence is one aspect of the overall objective of reliability.

SSAP 2 defined prudence partly in terms of realisation. The ASB believes that this is out of date as markets have developed so that it is often possible to be reasonably certain that a gain exists, and to measure it with sufficient reliability, even if no disposal has occurred. Prudence is now much more concerned with uncertainty. The notes to FRS 18 explain that, in conditions of uncertainty, prudence requires:

- more confirmatory evidence about the existence of an asset or gain than about the existence of a liability or loss; and

---

DEFINITION

The **accruals** concept: revenue and costs are accrued (that is, recognised as they are earned or incurred, not as money is received or paid), matched with one another so far as their relationship can be established or justifiably assumed, and dealt with in the profit and loss account of the period to which they relate.

DEFINITION

Prudence is the inclusion of a degree of caution in the exercise of the judgements needed in making the estimates required under conditions of uncertainty, such that gains and losses are not overstated and losses and liabilities are not understated. (Statement of Principles)

- a greater reliability of measurement for assets and gains than for liabilities and losses.

The Companies Act states that only profits realised at the balance sheet date should be included in the profit and loss account and these requirements **continue to apply** to companies unless there are special reasons for departing from them. FRS 18 states that this may be the case if it is possible to be reasonably certain that, although a gain is unrealised, it nevertheless exists, and to measure it with sufficient reliability.

5.4 Estimation techniques

Examples of estimation techniques:

- methods of depreciation (such as straight line and reducing balance)

- different methods used to estimate the proportion of trade debts that will not be recovered, particularly where such methods consider a population as a whole rather than individual balances.

SSAP 2 did not cover the selection of estimation techniques (as opposed to accounting policies). The requirements of FRS 18 are as follows.

- Where estimation techniques are required to enable the accounting policies adopted to be applied, an entity should select estimation techniques that enable its financial statements to give a true and fair view and are consistent with the requirements of accounting standards, UITF Abstracts and companies legislation.

- Where it is necessary to choose between estimation techniques, an entity should select whichever of those estimation techniques is judged by the entity to be most appropriate to its particular circumstances for the purpose of giving a true and fair view.

- A change to an estimation technique should not be accounted for as a prior period adjustment, unless:

    (a) it represents the correction of a fundamental error; or

    (b) another accounting standard, a UITF Abstract or companies legislation requires the change to be accounted for as a prior period adjustment.

In other words, a change in estimation technique is not the same as a change in accounting policy.

5.5 Applying the definitions in practice

A change in accounting policy gives rise to a prior period adjustment (as required by FRS 3), while a change in an estimation technique does not. This means that it is necessary to distinguish between the two in practice. FRS 18 gives the following examples.

- An entity has previously stated assets at historic cost and it now states them at replacement cost. This is a change in a measurement base and is therefore a change in accounting policy.

- An entity has previously measured the current disposal value of an asset by reference to recent disposals of similar assets and it now does this by reference to prices quoted in advertisements. This is a change in the method of estimation, not a change in accounting policy.

Accounting policies are used to determine which facts about a business are to be presented in financial statements and how those facts are to be presented. Estimation techniques are used to establish what those facts are.

FRS 18 makes further points:

- Some accounting standards allow a choice over what is to be recognised For example:

  (a) FRS 15 allows finance costs of constructing an asset to be capitalised or charged as an expense

  (b) SSAP 13 allows development expenditure to be treated as an asset or as an expense.

  Where there is a choice, that choice is a matter of accounting policy.

- A change in the way in which an entity presents particular items is a change in accounting policy. However, if an entity merely presents additional information, this is not a change in accounting policy.

<table>
<tr><td>

ACTIVITY 1

</td><td>

Which of the following is a change in accounting policy as opposed to a change in estimation technique?

(1) An entity has previously charged interest incurred in connection with the construction of tangible fixed assets to the profit and loss account. It now capitalises this interest (as permitted by FRS 15).

(2) An entity has previously depreciated vehicles using the reducing balance method at 40% per year. It now uses the straight line method over a period of five years.

(3) An entity has previously shown certain overheads within cost of sales. It now shows those overheads within administrative expenses.

(4) An entity has previously measured stocks at weighted average cost. It now measures stocks using the FIFO method.

</td></tr>
</table>

Feedback to this activity is at the end of the chapter.

5.6   Disclosures

FRS 18 requires the following disclosures, which are more extensive than those required by SSAP 2.

(a) A description of each of the accounting policies followed for material items.

(b) A description of estimation techniques used that are significant. An estimation technique is significant only if the range of reasonable monetary amounts is so large that the use of a different amount from within that range could materially affect the view shown by the entity's financial statements. To judge whether an estimation technique is significant, an entity should consider the impact of varying the assumptions underlying that technique.

(c) Details of any changes to accounting policies that were followed in preparing financial statements for the preceding period.

(d) Where the effect of a change to an estimation technique is material, the effect and a description of the change.

(e) In relation to the going concern assessment required by the FRS:

  - any material uncertainties that may cast significant doubt upon the entity's ability to continue as a going concern

  - where the foreseeable future considered by the directors has been limited to a period of less than one year from the date of approval of the financial statements, that fact

- when the financial statements are not prepared on a going concern basis, that fact, together with the basis on which the financial statements are prepared and the reason why the entity is not regarded as a going concern.

(f) Where there has been a material departure from the requirements of an accounting standard, a UITF Abstract, or companies legislation, particulars of the departure, the reasons for it and its effect should be disclosed by including the following in the financial statements:

- a clear and unambiguous statement that there has been a departure from the requirements of an accounting standard, UITF Abstract or companies legislation, and that the departure is necessary to give a true and fair view

- a statement of the treatment that the accounting standard, UITF Abstract or companies legislation would normally require and a description of the treatment actually adopted

- a statement of why the treatment prescribed would not give a true and fair view

- a description of how the position shown in the financial statements is different as a result of the departure, normally with quantification, except where quantification is already evident in the financial statements themselves or where the effect cannot reasonably be quantified, in which case the directors should explain the circumstances.

5.7 Effect of the standard

Most commentators appeared to accept the need to replace SSAP 2 once the Statement of Principles had been issued in its final form.

FRS 18 clarifies the distinction between accounting policies and estimation techniques. It abandons the SSAP 2 terminology of accounting bases, which some users and preparers of accounts found confusing in practice.

Most criticisms of the FRS have reflected criticisms of the Statement of Principles itself, particularly the 'downgrading' of the prudence concept. It has been argued that the change to the definition of prudence (discussed above) implies that unrealised profits can be recognised. In reply, the ASB has pointed out that the Companies Act still requires that only realised profits are included in the profit and loss account.

However, FRS 18 acknowledges that in some circumstances it may be possible to include unrealised profits in the profit and loss account. This will happen if a new standard requires financial instruments to be measured at fair value or current value.

6   Discounting in financial reporting

6.1   Introduction

In April 1997 the ASB published a Working Paper *Discounting in financial reporting*. The Working Paper sets out the ASB's approach to discounting.

A number of the ASB's recent projects (e.g. provisions, pension costs and impairment of fixed assets) raise the issue of discounting. Some commentators have expressed concern about the apparently piecemeal introduction of discounting into financial reporting. The Working Paper has been issued in order to respond to this concern.

6.2   Discounting

DEFINITION

Discounting is a method of reflecting the time value of money and risk in the value of an asset or a liability.

The time value of money and the risk inherent in the item can have a significant effect on long-term items in the balance sheet that are measured by future cash flows, for example, long-term provisions and impaired assets. If such items are recorded in the financial statements at an amount based on undiscounted cash flows, unlike items will appear alike. For example, a riskless cash inflow of £1 million due tomorrow, a riskless cash inflow of £1 million due in ten years and a risky cash inflow of £1 million due in ten years would all be recorded at £1 million. However, no company would regard these assets as equal, nor would they cost the same to acquire. If they are recorded at £1 million, relevant information is lost to the user of the financial statements and misleading information is given instead.

6.3   The ASB's approach

The ASB does not intend to make discounting a requirement for every balance sheet item. There is no need to discount the vast majority of current assets and current liabilities.

For this reason, the ASB does not intend to issue a general financial reporting standard on discounting. The decision on whether discounting will be prescribed in any specific circumstance will be considered as and when individual standards are developed.

In order to determine what discount rate should be used in any particular situation, it is necessary to consider:

- the implications of risk

- the accounting objective being sought.

7   Recent UITF Abstracts

7.1   UITF Abstract 24 *Accounting for start-up costs*

- **The issue**

  Start-up costs include costs arising from one-time activities relating to opening a new facility, introducing a new product or service, conducting business in a new territory, conducting business with a new class of customer, initiating a new process in an existing facility, starting some new operation and similar items. They include costs of relocating or reorganising all or part of an entity, costs relating to organising a new entity and expenses and losses incurred both before and after opening.

  The issue is whether start-up costs can be treated differently from similar costs that are incurred as part of an entity's on-going activities. For example, can costs that would normally be recognised as incurred be capitalised or deferred?

  FRS 15 *Tangible fixed assets* states that certain start-up costs cannot be included in the cost of a fixed asset. However, it does not specify how these costs should be accounted for.

- **UITF Consensus**

  (a) Start-up costs should be accounted for on a basis consistent with the accounting treatment of similar costs incurred as part of the entity's on-going activities.

  (b) In cases where there are no such similar costs, start-up costs that do not meet the criteria for recognition as assets under a relevant accounting standard should be recognised as an expense when they are incurred.

If start-up costs meet the definition of exceptional items they should be disclosed in accordance with FRS 3 *Reporting financial performance*. Disclosure regarding start-up costs in the Operating and Financial Review is also encouraged.

7.2   UITF Abstract 26 *Barter transactions for advertising*

- **The issue**

An entity such as a publisher or broadcaster may agree to provide advertising in exchange for advertising services provided by its customer, rather than for cash. For example, companies often display advertising on their websites in exchange for advertising of their own services on another website.

The issue is what amount, if any, should be included in reported turnover and expense. Although the profit or loss of an entity is not affected, turnover is affected. Turnover is often used as a key performance measure for internet companies.

The Abstract is not mandatory for barter transactions for services other than advertising, although its principles may be relevant to such transactions.

- **UITF Consensus**

Turnover and costs in respect of barter transactions for advertising should not be recognised unless there is persuasive evidence of the value at which the advertising would have been sold for cash in a similar transaction. In these circumstances, that value should be included in turnover and costs.

Persuasive evidence of the value of advertising exchanged will exist only where it can be demonstrated that similar advertising has been sold for cash. This will be the case only where the entity has a history of selling similar advertising for cash and where substantially all the turnover from advertising within the accounting period is represented by cash sales.

7.3   UITF Abstract 29 *Website development costs*

- **The issue**

The Abstract addresses the accounting for the development costs of a website for the company's own use.

The cost of developing a website includes planning costs, application and infrastructure development costs, design costs and content costs. Planning costs do not give rise to future economic benefits controlled by the entity, but the remaining costs could give rise to an asset, which should be capitalised if the relationship between the expenditure and the future economic benefit is sufficiently certain.

However, there is often substantial uncertainty regarding the viability, useful economic life and value of a website. There is also uncertainty as to whether capitalised website development costs should be treated as tangible assets or intangible assets.

- **UITF Consensus**

Planning costs should be charged to the profit and loss account as incurred.

Provided that they meet the criteria below, other website development costs should be capitalised as tangible fixed assets and treated in accordance with the requirements of FRS 15.

Expenditure to maintain or operate a website once it has been developed should be charged to the profit and loss account as incurred.

Design and content development costs should be capitalised only to the extent that they lead to the creation of an enduring asset delivering benefits at least as great as the amount capitalised. This will be the case only to the extent that:

(a) the expenditure is separately identifiable

(b) the technical feasibility and commercial viability of the website have been assessed with reasonable certainty

(c) the website will generate sales or other revenue directly and the expenditure makes an enduring contribution to generating revenue

(d) there is a reasonable expectation that the present value of the future cash flows to be generated by the website will be no less than the amounts capitalised

(e) adequate resources exist, or are reasonably expected to be available, to enable the website project to be completed and to meet any consequential need for increased working capital.

7.4   UITF Abstract 34 *Pre-contract costs*

- **The issue**

In some industries, entities incur significant costs in bidding for and securing contracts. Where a bid is successful, the entity will often have incurred significant costs before the contract is signed. The questions to be decided are:

(a) Should such pre-contract costs be recognised as an asset, or written off as incurred?

(b) If recognised as an asset, at what value should they be measured?

- **UITF Consensus**

Pre-contract costs can be differentiated from start-up costs which are dealt with by Abstract 24. Instead, pre-contract costs are part of the ongoing costs of obtaining contracts. The activity of bidding for contracts is unlikely to result in an asset, since an asset requires rights to benefits that are *controlled* by the entity. While there may be an expectation that benefits will accrue, until the contract is signed there is no control. Only when it is virtually certain that a contract will be awarded can an asset be recognised.

All costs incurred before the recognition criteria are satisfied must be written off as incurred, and not subsequently reinstated. Directly attributable costs incurred after the recognition criteria are satisfied should be recognised as an asset if they can be separately identified and measured reliably.

7.5   UITF Abstract 36 *Contracts for sales of capacity*

- **The issue**

In some industries, entities enter into contracts that convey the right to use some or all of the capacity of a physical asset. For example, in the telecommunications industry or electricity distribution industry, entities can buy capacity on another provider's network. The capacity provider retains ownership of the network assets, but rights of use are conveyed to the purchaser for an agreed period of time.

The UITF wished to give guidance on how such purchases and sales of capacity should be accounted for. Are they the sale of an asset or for part of an asset (in which case the seller should derecognise all or part of an asset from its balance sheet), or should the seller continue to recognise its assets in full and recognise income over the life of the contract?

- **UITF Consensus**

A seller of capacity should not report the transaction as the sale of an asset (or the sale of part of an asset) unless:

(a) the asset sold is specific and separable

(b) the purchaser's right of use is exclusive and irrevocable; and

(c) the term of the contract is for a major part of the asset's useful life.

Otherwise no sale of an asset should be recognised. Income from the contract is then recognised over the life of the contract.

If the transaction is reported as the sale of an asset, then the proceeds should only be reported as turnover if the asset was designated as held for resale (and included in stocks). Otherwise such a transaction should be reported as the disposal of a fixed asset.

7.6   UITF Abstract 37 *Purchases and sales of own shares*

- **The issue**

Until recently, companies that purchased their own shares had to cancel them. However changes in UK law (the Companies Acquisition of Own Shares Regulations 2003) now permit companies to purchase their own shares and then hold them (when they are known as treasury shares) before either cancelling or reissuing them in the future.

The issue is how to account for purchases and sales of own shares. The Abstract does not apply to an entity's own shares held by an ESOP trust; that is covered by Abstract 38.

- **UITF Consensus**

An investment in own shares is a deduction in ownership interest, not an asset. An asset requires economic benefits to be received from some third party. An expectation of being paid dividends to yourself is not an asset. The required accounting is therefore:

(a) consideration paid for an entity's own shares should be deducted in arriving at shareholders' funds

(b) no gain or loss should be recognised (in either the profit and loss account or the STRGL) on the purchase, sale or cancellation of an entity's own shares. Such transactions are purely movements in shareholder' funds, so any consideration paid or received in such transactions must be shown separately in the reconciliation of movements in shareholders' funds.

SELF-TEST QUESTIONS

Year-end financial reports: improving communication

1   What are the ASB's current proposals for summary financial statements? (1.4)

2   How has the internet affected financial reporting? (1.5)

Further proposals: review of company law

3   What changes are proposed to company law? (2)

Interim reports

4   What are the differences between the 'discrete' and the 'integral' approach to interim reports? Which does the ASB favour? (3.2)

Preliminary announcements

5 What are the ASB's main recommendations regarding preliminary announcements? (4.2)

FRS 18 *Accounting policies*

6 On what basis should an entity select its accounting policies? (5.2)

7 What are the FRS 18 requirements regarding estimation techniques? (5.4)

Discounting in financial reporting

8 How should the discount rate to be used in particular circumstances be chosen? (6.3)

EXAM-TYPE
QUESTION

Sterndale plc

In December 1999 the ASB issued the final version of its *Statement of Principles for Financial Reporting*. At the same time, it issued FRED 21 which was subsequently developed into FRS 18 *Accounting policies*. FRS 18 addresses the selection, application and disclosure of accounting policies and supersedes SSAP 2 *Disclosure of accounting policies*.

Required:

(a) Explain the reasons why the ASB has withdrawn SSAP 2. **(6 marks)**

(b) Explain the way in which FRS 18 requires that an entity should select accounting policies. **(6 marks)**

(c) Sterndale plc engages in diverse activities. The company has made a number of changes to the way in which it deals with particular items in the financial statements for the year ended 31 December 20X2.

   (i) The company previously wrote off development expenditure to the profit and loss account in the period in which it was incurred. It now proposes to capitalise development expenditure where it meets the criteria for deferral set out in SSAP 13 *Accounting for research and development* and to amortise it on a systematic basis over the life of the products being developed.

   (ii) During the year the company used forward exchange contracts to hedge its exposure to foreign currency exchange risks. It has never before used any kind of derivative financial instrument. As a result it will have to make additional disclosures in the notes to the financial statements, as required by FRS 13 *Derivatives and other financial instruments: disclosures*.

   (iii) On 1 January 20X0, the company recognised a provision for the cost of dismantling an oil rig and cleaning up any contamination resulting from the extraction of oil in accordance with FRS 12 *Provisions, contingent liabilities and contingent assets*. This provision was not discounted because the directors were of the opinion that the effect of discounting was not material. During the year the provision was revised upwards and as a result, the effect of discounting is now material. Therefore Sterndale plc is now required to report the provision at the discounted amount for the first time.

Required:

For each of the three items above:

   (1) explain, with reasons, whether the change is a change in accounting policy, and

   (2) state how the change should be treated in the financial statements for the year ended 31 December 20X2. **(8 marks)**

(Total: 20 marks)

For the answer to this question see the 'Answers' section at the end of the book

---

**FEEDBACK TO
ACTIVITY 1**

These examples are taken from an Appendix to FRS 18. For each of the items, ask whether this involves a change to:

- recognition?
- presentation?
- measurement basis?

If the answer to any of these is yes, the change is a change in accounting policy.

(1) This is a change in recognition and presentation. Therefore this is a change in accounting policy.

(2) The answer to all three questions is no. This is only a change in estimation technique.

(3) This is a change in presentation and therefore a change in accounting policy.

(4) This is a change in measurement basis and therefore a change in accounting policy.

Answers to exam-type questions

Accounting framework for small companies

The main aim of developing an accounting framework for small companies is to provide users with a reporting framework which generates reliable, relevant and useful information. It is important that the accounting standards which are used by small companies are of value to them and therefore it is necessary to determine which companies are to be within the definition of a small company. Very few accounting issues need to be addressed by a small company simply because of its size. The criteria for a small company need not be determined by reference to size but would be more meaningful if the definition were based on the relationship between the shareholders and management. Small companies could be defined by reference to the ownership and management of the company. It is inaccurate to assume that small companies are simply smaller versions of large public companies.

The basis for developing an accounting framework for small companies ought to be based around the issues of recognition, measurement and disclosure. The question to be answered is whether alternative standards should be developed in recognising, measuring and disclosing transactions of small companies.

The objectives of financial reporting differ between large companies and owner managed companies. The nature of accountability is different between large and small companies and thus there is a major distinction between the objectives of financial reporting for the two types of company. The needs of users of financial statements should determine the nature of those statements. It is intellectually and commercially sound to develop an accounting framework on the basis of the objectives of the financial statements.

The ASB has developed an accounting standard 'Financial Reporting Standard for Smaller Entities' (FRSSE) which uses size criteria to determine the nature of a small company.

It is often stated that the purpose of producing an accounting framework for smaller companies is to reduce the administrative burden on those companies. In reality the financial statements are produced by external accountants and thus the production of such a framework on the pretext of reducing the administrative costs is an unrealistic objective. Additionally many of these accounting standards will have a negligible impact on a small company and those standards which are selected for application to small companies may apply to some and not to others. It might appear that an approach which takes existing accounting standards and eliminates those which are thought not to be applicable to small companies is going to result in a framework which is simply a hybrid version of the large company's regulatory system.

The FRSSE in the UK has been received with mixed feelings as it aims to simplify and reduce the financial reporting requirements of small companies. It selects certain elements of certain accounting standards as a basis of reporting for small companies and exempts entities from compliance with the other extant accounting standards and UITF Abstracts. It applies the size criteria set out in the Companies Acts for a small company and utilises the same measurement bases as for large companies. Measurement requirements of a complex nature have been omitted but small companies do undertake complex transactions and in these cases they are referred to the full standard. It is not surprising that this accounting standard will in fact increase the amount of work involved in preparing financial statements in the short term whilst companies change the nature of the information disclosed and become expert in the application of the standard.

| CHAPTER 2 | EXAM-TYPE QUESTION |

Daxon plc

(a) Memo to the Board of Directors

From:　Accountant

Dated:　4 December 20X5

Subject:　Directors' responsibilities

Following an enquiry concerning the directors' responsibilities statement that I included in the draft of the 20X5 annual accounts, I have set out the following information to explain how the need for the statement has arisen in order for the company to be following best practice.

The background to the inclusion in the annual report of a directors' responsibilities statement

Major changes in corporate governance disclosures were recommended in the report of the Committee on the Financial Aspects of Corporate Governance (published by the Cadbury Committee in December 1992). In the report, the committee recommended that listed companies should state in their annual report whether they comply with a Code of Best Practice drafted by the committee, giving reasons for non-compliance.

The recommendations included a statement by the directors of their responsibility for preparing the accounts; a report on the effectiveness of their system of internal control; and a report explicitly on whether the business is a going concern. These have subsequently been incorporated into the *Principles of Good Governance and Code of Best Practice* (The 'Combined Code'). The Stock Exchange Listing Rules require all UK listed companies to include the following in their annual report and accounts:

(a)　a statement explaining how they have applied the principles set out in the Combined Code; and

(b)　a statement as to whether or not they have complied throughout the accounting period with the Code provisions.

The requirement to include a statement of directors' responsibilities is to give emphasis to the fact that the financial statements are the responsibility of the directors and, in this way, to reduce the misunderstandings of some readers.

There is a view that users of the annual report have not distinguished between the directors' responsibilities and the auditors' responsibilities and have assumed that the audit responsibility was far greater than was actually the case. The statement should educate these users so that they appreciate the actual position.

How the board can determine whether the financial statements give a true and fair view

There has always been a duty on the board to ensure that the financial statements are true and fair. However, it has in the past been the practice to regard this as a matter for the auditor. Inclusion in the directors' responsibility is merely recognition of a long standing duty.

Perhaps it would be helpful to first review the criteria for determining whether financial statements provide a true and fair view which is a step that we have not previously taken. The criteria are:

(i) They are prepared in accordance with accepted accounting principles.

(ii) The accounting principles applied are appropriate to the business, i.e. it is not sufficient to be able to demonstrate that such principles have been applied by other companies and other accounting firms – they also need to be appropriate to the particular company.

(iii) They exhibit the qualitative characteristics of financial information set out in Chapter 3 of the Statement of Principles, i.e. relevance, reliability, comparability and understandability.

(iv) They provide sufficient information for the intended users to be able to comprehend and interpret, i.e. there is an implication that the financial statements are a reflection of the economic position, regardless of particular accepted accounting policies and rules, which convey the nature of the business to a prospective or current shareholder with no inside knowledge of the company.

This latter criterion is generally referred to as reflecting the substance of transactions.

It is in order to reflect the substance of transactions that there is a requirement that, where the application of existing standards or statutes is not considered by the directors to result in a true and fair view, they are not to be applied. In such a case, there is a requirement to explain the departure.

The board's responsibility is therefore to ensure that the accountant in preparing the accounts has had regard to statutory, mandatory and voluntary pronouncements. The board's responsibility would be discharged by ensuring that the company employs appropriate professional staff and ensuring that their technical knowledge and competence is kept current.

(b) (i) The principal aim of the financial review section is to explain to the user of the annual report the capital structure of the business, its treasury policy and the dynamics of its financial position – its sources of liquidity and their application, including the implications of the financing arising from its capital expenditure plans.

The discussion should concentrate on matters of significance to the position of the business as a whole. It should be a narrative commentary supported by figures where these assist understanding of the policies and their effect in practice.

(ii) Specific matters that should be addressed when discussing capital structure and treasury policy include the following.

Discuss the capital structure in terms of the maturity profile of debt, type of capital instruments used, currency, and interest rate structure including comments on relevant ratios such as interest cover and debt/equity ratios.

The policies and objectives covering the management of the maturity profile of borrowings, exchange rate and interest rate risk and the implementation of such policies in the period under review in terms of:

- the manner in which the treasury activities are controlled

- the use of financial instruments for hedging purposes

- the extent to which foreign currency net investments are hedged by currency borrowings and other hedging instruments

- the currencies in which borrowings are made and in which cash and cash equivalents are held

- the extent to which borrowings are at fixed interest rates

- the purpose and effect of major financing transactions undertaken up to the date of approval of the financial statements

- the effect of interest costs on profits and the potential impact of interest rate changes.

| CHAPTER 3 | EXAM-TYPE QUESTIONS |

Question 1: P Group

(a) **Consolidation schedules**

   (1)   **Goodwill on acquisition of Q Ltd**

	£	£
Cost of investment		95,000
Less: Net assets acquired		
Share capital	80,000	
Profit and loss account	20,000	
	100,000	
Group share (75%)		75,000
		20,000

   (2)   **Goodwill on acquisition of R Ltd**

	£	£
Cost of investment		79,000
Less: Group share of Q's profit on sale		
(75% × (79,000 – 50,000))		(21,750)
		57,250
Less: net assets acquired		
Share capital (80% × 49,000)	39,200	
Pre acquisition profits:		
(75% × 80% × 12,000)	7,200	
(25% × 80% × 20,000)	4,000	
		(50,400)
		6,850

   (3)   **Unrealised profit on stock**

	£	£
Dr Consolidated profit and loss account		
(20% × 7,000)	1,400	
Cr Stocks		1,400

(4) **Transfer of fixed asset**

	£	£
In the books of Q Ltd:		
Dr Profit and loss account	5,000	
Cr Tangible fixed assets		5,000
In the books of P Ltd:		
Dr Tangible fixed assets $(2 \times \frac{1}{4} \times 5,000)$	2,500	
Cr Profit and loss account		2,500
Net book value of fixed asset in P's books		
$(30,000 \times \frac{1}{4} \times 2)$		15,000
Net book value to the group $(25,000 \times \frac{1}{4} \times 2)$		(12,500)
Adjustment		2,500

(5) **Cancellation of inter-company balances**

	£	£
Dr Cash in transit	7,500	
Dr Creditors	17,500	
Cr Debtors		25,000

(6) **Consolidated profit and loss account**

	£	£
P Ltd		197,450
Provision for unrealised profit		(1,400)
Depreciation		2,500
		198,550
Q Ltd (42,950 – 20,000)	22,950	
Profit on transfer of fixed asset	(5,000)	
	17,950	
Group share (75%)		13,462
Group share of profit on sale of R Ltd		
$(75\% \times 29,000)$		(21,750)
R Ltd $(80\% \times 22,760)$	18,208	
Less: Pre-acquisition profits		
$(7,200 + 4,000)$	(11,200)	
		7,008
Goodwill fully amortised: (20,000 + 6,850)		(26,850)
		170,420

(7) **Minority interest**

	£	£
Q Ltd		
Share capital	80,000	
Profit and loss account		
$(42,950 – 5,000)$	37,950	
	117,950	
MI share (25%)		29,488

R Ltd

Share capital	49,000	
Profit and loss account	22,760	
	71,760	
MI share (20%)		14,352
		43,840

(b) **P Ltd**

Consolidated balance sheet as at 31 December 20X7

	£	£
Fixed assets		
Tangible assets (775,000 + 125,750 + 67,920 − 2,500)		966,170
Current assets		
Stocks (22,950 + 11,890 + 7,440 − 1,400)	40,880	
Debtors (55,960 + 12,530 + 6,510 − 25,000)	50,000	
Cash at bank and in hand (1,250 + 750 + 7,500)	9,500	
	100,380	
Creditors: amounts falling due within one year		
(31,710 + 27,220 + 10,860 − 17,500)	(52,290)	
Net current assets		48,090
		1,014,260
Capital and reserves		
Called up share capital		800,000
Profit and loss account		170,420
		970,420
Minority interests		43,840
		1,014,260

(c) **Control and ownership**

The operations of a group can be viewed in different ways, according to whether control or ownership is considered to be most important. The entity or control concept implies that the group is a single economic unit and that minority interests are an integral part of the group. The financial statements reflect the resources controlled by the group. The proprietary or ownership concept implies that minority interests are completely external to the group. The financial statements reflect the resources owned by the parent company.

In their present form, consolidated financial statements are a hybrid of these two concepts and reflect both control and ownership.

The net assets side of the balance sheet and the first part of the profit and loss account (down to profit after tax) include all the balances and transactions of the subsidiary, whether or not the subsidiary is wholly owned. This reflects the resources controlled by the group.

The share capital and reserves side of the consolidated balance sheet distinguishes between the resources owned by the group and the resources owned by the minority interest. The minority interest's share of the profit for the year is deducted from profit after tax in the consolidated profit and loss account to show retained profits attributable to the group.

This is illustrated by considering intra-group transactions. Q Ltd has sold a fixed asset to P Ltd and has made a profit of £5,000 on the transfer. The adjustment is as follows.

Dr	Consolidated profit and loss account	£3,750	
Dr	Minority interest	£1,250	
	Cr Tangible fixed assets		£5,000

The removal of the whole of the profit on sale from tangible fixed assets, means that the balance sheet reflects the resources controlled by the group at their cost to the group. The profit on sale was made by the subsidiary and so the profit on sale is deducted from the reserves of the group and the minority to reflect their respective ownership shares.

Question 2: A plc

(a) Goodwill in C Ltd

	£'000	£'000
Cost (3,000 × £1.90)		5,700
Less: fair value of net assets acquired:		
Book values	6,200	
Increase in tangible fixed assets		
(8,295 – 7,875)	420	
Increase in stocks (2,100 – 2,000)	100	
	6,720	
Group share (75%)		(5,040)
		660

The treatment of items in Notes 2 to 7

Note 2 FRS 7 states that the cost of acquisition is the cash paid and the fair value of any other purchase consideration given. In the absence of further information, it is assumed that the consideration was paid entirely in cash and that the fair value of the shares in C Ltd is their agreed market value.

Note 3 The goodwill calculation must reflect the fair values of the separable net assets acquired at the date of acquisition. The summary balance sheet shows the book values of C Ltd's net assets and is the starting point for the fair value calculation. The fair value of short term monetary items (e.g., debtors, creditors and cash) is normally their carrying value.

Note 4 FRS 7 states that the fair value of tangible fixed assets should be their market value or their depreciated replacement cost. The fair value should not exceed the recoverable amount of the asset. The fixed assets are valued at their net replacement cost (depreciated replacement cost) of £8,295,000 as this is lower than their recoverable amount of £9,000,000.

Note 5 The fair value of stocks is their replacement cost or net realisable value, whichever is the lower. In this case, stocks are valued at their replacement cost of £2,100,000 as this is lower than their net realisable value of £2,400,000.

Note 6   The fair value of the long-term loan is the present value of the amount expected to be paid. In this case, this is the same as its carrying value as interest of 10% per annum will be paid until the loan matures.

Note 7   FRS 7 states that fair values must reflect conditions at the date of acquisition. Changes arising from the acquirer's intentions (such as rationalisation) cannot affect fair values at the date of acquisition. The provision for rationalisation costs can only be taken to the profit and loss account once the rationalisation has been publicly announced.

(b) Consolidated balance sheet at 30 September 20X6

	£'000	£'000
Fixed assets		
Intangible assets (660 – 165)		495
Tangible assets (9,100 + 9,000 + 8,000 + 360)		
(W4)		26,460
		26,955
Current assets		
Stocks (4,000 + 3,000 + 2,500 + 25) (W5)	9,525	
Debtors (3,000 + 2,500 + 2,000 – 400) (W6)	7,100	
Cash at bank and in hand (800 + 700 + 600)	2,100	
	18,725	
Creditors: amounts falling due within one year		
Bank overdraft (3,200 + 2,800 + 2,450)	8,450	
Trade creditors (2,500 + 2,000 + 1,700)	6,200	
Taxation (600 + 500 + 450)	1,550	
Proposed dividends: parent undertaking	600	
minority interests (W6)	100	
	16,900	
Net current assets		1,825
Total assets less current liabilities		28,780
Creditors: amounts falling due after more than one year		
Long-term loan (8,000 + 2,000 + 2,000)		(12,000)
Provisions for liabilities and charges: rationalisation costs		(1,500)
		15,280
Capital and reserves		
Called up share capital		5,000
Profit and loss account (W2)		7,079
		12,079
Minority interests (W3)		3,201
		15,280

Workings

(W1) **Group structure**

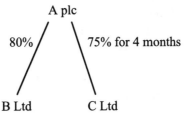

(W2) **Consolidated profit and loss account**

	£'000	£'000
A plc		5,900
B Ltd (80% × 3,400)		2,720
C Ltd:		
At 30 September 20X6	2,500	
At acquisition	(2,200)	
	300	
Depreciation (W4)	(60)	
Stock (W5)	(75)	
Group share (75%)	165	124
Less: provision for rationalisation		(1,500)
Less: goodwill (part (a)) (660 ÷ 4)		(165)
		7,079

(W3) **Minority interests**

	£'000	£'000
B Ltd (20% × 7,400)		1,480
C Ltd: Net assets at balance sheet date	6,500	
Fixed asset adjustment (W4)	360	
Stock adjustment (W5)	25	
	6,885	
MI (25%)		1,721
		3,201

(W4) **Tangible fixed assets**

	£'000	£'000
Net replacement cost		8,295
Net book value		7,875
Fair value adjustment at acquisition		420
Additional depreciation:		
Gross replacement cost	14,220	
Historic cost	13,500	
Adjustment to cost	720	
Depreciation (720 × 25% × 4/12)		(60)
Fair value adjustment at balance sheet date		360

(W5) Stock adjustment

	£'000	£'000
Fair value adjustment at acquisition (2,100 – 2,000)		100
Less: adjustment relating to stock sold (assuming pro-rata basis) fair value of stock sold (2,100 × 1,500 ÷ 2,000)	1,575	
cost of stock sold	(1,500)	
		(75)
Fair value adjustment at balance sheet date		25

Reduction in profit on sale of stock (proof):	
Profit based on cost (1,800 – 1,500)	300
Profit based on fair values (1,800 – 1,575)	(225)
	75

(W6) Proposed dividends

	£'000
Minority interests (20% × 500)	100

Debtors are reduced by £400,000 (80% × 500).

CHAPTER 4   EXAM-TYPE QUESTIONS

Question 1: H Ltd

Group structure

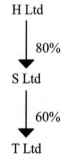

H Ltd

80%

S Ltd

60%

T Ltd

Shareholdings	*S Ltd*		*T Ltd*	
Group – direct	80%	– indirect	80% of 60% =	48%
Minority	20%	– direct		40%
		– indirect	20% of 60% =	12%
				52%

(a) **Goodwill**

	S Ltd £	S Ltd £	T Ltd £	T Ltd £
Cost of investment		95,000		
80% × £48,000				38,400
Less: Share of net assets acquired				
Share capital	75,000		50,000	
Profit and loss account	10,000		8,000	
	85,000		58,000	
	(80%)	(68,000)	(48%)	27,840
Goodwill		27,000		10,560

Consolidated profit and loss account

	£
H Ltd:	120,000
S Ltd: 80% (60,000 − 10,000)	40,000
T Ltd: 48% (40,000 − 8,000)	15,360
	175,360

Minority interest

	£
S Ltd: 20% × (135,000 − 48,000)	17,400
T Ltd: 52% × 90,000	46,800
	64,200

(b) **Goodwill**

	S Ltd £	S Ltd £	T Ltd £	T Ltd £
Cost of investment		95,000		
80% × £48,000				38,400
Less: Share of net assets acquired				
Share capital	75,000		50,000	
Profit and loss account	12,000		18,000	
	87,000		68,000	
	(80%)	(69,600)	(48%)	(32,640)
Goodwill		25,400		5,760

Consolidated profit and loss account

	£
H Ltd:	120,000
S Ltd: 80% (60,000 − 12,000)	38,400
T Ltd: 48% (40,000 − 18,000)	10,560
	168,960

Minority interest

		£
S Ltd:	20% × (135,000 − 48,000)	17,400
T Ltd:	52% × 90,000	46,800
		64,200

(c)

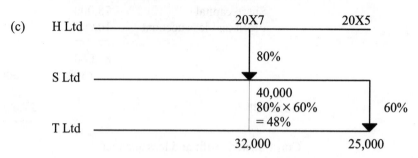

Goodwill

	S Ltd		T Ltd	
	£	£	£	£
Cost of investment		95,000		
80% × £48,000				38,400
Less: Share of net assets acquired				
Share capital	75,000		50,000	
Profit and loss account	40,000		32,000	
	115,000		82,000	
	(80%)	92,000	(48%)	39,360
Goodwill/(negative goodwill)		3,000		(960)

Consolidated profit and loss account

		£
H Ltd:		120,000
S Ltd:	80% (60,000 − 40,000)	16,000
T Ltd:	48% (40,000 − 32,000)	3,840
		139,840

Minority interest

		£
S Ltd:	20% × (135,000 − 48,000)	17,400
T Ltd:	52% × 90,000	46,800
		64,200

Consolidated balance sheets as at 31 December 20X8

	(a) £	(b) £	(c) £
Goodwill on consolidation	37,560	31,160	2,040
Sundry net assets	302,000	302,000	302,000
Minority interests	(64,200)	(64,200)	(64,200)
	275,360	268,960	239,840
Capital and reserves			
Called up share capital	100,000	100,000	100,000
Consolidated revenue reserves	175,360	168,960	139,840
	275,360	268,960	239,840

Question 2: Hale, Rein and Snowe

Tutorial notes: We first determine the percentage holdings in each company:

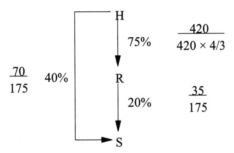

Rein is a subsidiary of Hale.

Snowe is a subsidiary of Hale, by virtue of Hale controlling 20% of Snowe via Rein and 40% directly, i.e. Hale controls a majority of Snowe's ordinary shares.

Group interest in Snowe

Hale (direct)	40%
Via Rein (indirect) 75% × 20%	15%
	55%
Therefore minority interest is	45%

Cost of control/minority interest adjustment regarding indirect holding

MI in Rein × Rein's cost of investment in Snowe

25% × 24,500 = £6,125

Dr   Minority interest   £6,125
    Cr   Cost of control (Snowe)   £6,125

Let us now proceed straight to the answer! Consolidated reserves can be the balancing figure.

This is a good exam technique.

Hale, Rein and Snowe

Consolidated balance sheet as at 30 November 20X7

	£	£
Fixed assets		
Land and buildings		730,450
Plant and machinery		662,250
Fixtures and fittings		104,300
		1,497,000
Current assets		
Stock* +12,500 – (25/125 × (12,500 + 10,400))	783,520	
Debtors* –25,500	375,850	
Bank* +8,000	109,030	
	1,268,400	
Current liabilities		
Creditors* – 5,000	265,730	
Net current assets		1,002,670
Minority interest (W1)		(191,625)
		2,308,045
Share capital		1,750,000
Consolidated reserves (balancing figure)		558,045
		2,308,045

Tutorial note

*Stock	Add stock in transit less provision for unrealised profit (PURP)
Debtors	Less current account
Bank	Add cash in transit
Creditors	Less current account

Workings

(W1)   **Minority interest**

	£
Rein	
Share capital (25% × 420,000)	105,000
Profit and loss account [25% × (70,000 + 17,500)]	21,875
Less: Indirect holding adjustment (25% × 24,500)	(6,125)
Snowe	
Share capital (45% × 175,000)	78,750
Profit and loss account [45% × (17,500) LOSS]	(7,875)
	191,625

Tutorial notes: The PURP is not charged against the minority as Hale reported the profit.

This answer can be produced fairly quickly.

Let us now prove the consolidated reserves figure. First calculate the goodwill arising on both acquisitions.

Let us assume for illustrative purposes that the pre-acquisition dividend received by Hale Ltd has caused a permanent diminution in the value of its investment in Rein so a correction is required:

Dr Hale reserve	£26,250	
Cr Cost of investment		£26,250

(W2) Goodwill – Rein

	£
Cost of investment	367,500
Less pre-acquisition dividend [75% × (70,000 × ½)]	(26,250)
Less group share of net assets at acquisition [75% × (420 + 0)]	(315,000)
	26,250

Tutorial note: Although at acquisition Rein had a P&L reserve of £35,000 this has all been distributed. The investment is recorded net of the pre-acquisition distribution so the net assets acquired must also be stated thus.

(W3) **Goodwill – Snowe**

	£
Cost of investment	
Direct	49,000
Indirect	24,500
Less minority interest/indirect adjustment (25% × 24,500)	(6,125)
Less group share of net assets at acquisition	
55%[175,000+(35,000loss)]	(77,000)
∴ Negative goodwill	(9,625)

(W4) **Consolidated reserves**

	£
Hale (other)	350,000
Hale (P&L)	180,250
Adjustment for pre-acquisition dividend incorrectly credited	(26,250)
Goodwill	
Rein (positive – fully amortised)	(26,250)
Snowe (negative – fully amortised)	9,625
Provision for unrealised profit	
25/125 × (12,500 + 10,400)	(4,580)
Group share of post-acquisition reserves	
Rein – other 75% (70,000 – 0)	52,500
Rein – P&L 75% (17,500 – 0)	13,125
Snowe – 55% [(17,500) – (35,000)]	9,625
	558,045

Tutorial note: The detail of the bottom half of the balance sheet therefore appears as follows.

	£
Share capital	1,750,000
Other reserves (350,000 + 52,500)	402,500
Profit and loss account	155,545
	2,308,045

Question 3: Apricot

(a)

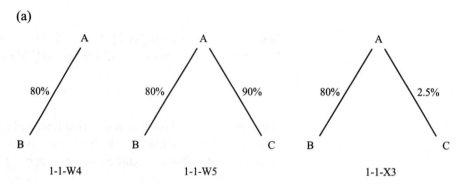

1-1-X3

Sale of 350,000 shares leaves a holding of just 10,000 shares = 2.5%.

From 1-1-X3, C is treated as a trade investment of A. The trade investment is valued at cost in the individual balance sheet of A. However, the group still owns 2.5% of the post-acquisition reserves of C and so the investment is 'frozen' at its carrying amount under the equity method at the date of disposal (i.e. 2.5% of its net assets at 1.1.X3).

A plc
Consolidated profit and loss account for the year ended 31 December 20X3

	£'000
Operating profit (W1)	1,434
Profit on sale of shares in C Ltd (W2)	700
Profit before tax	2,134
Tax (W3)	(629)
Profit after tax	1,505
Less: Minority interests (20% × 190)	(38)
Profit for the financial year	1,467
Less: Dividends	(50)
Retained profit for the financial year	1,417

A plc
Consolidated balance sheet as at 31 December 20X3

	£'000
Trade investment at cost (2.5% × 1,400)	35
Other net assets (W4)	6,452
	6,487
Share capital	1,500
Reserves (W5)	4,701
	6,201
Minority interests (20% × (1,260 + 170))	286
	6,487

(b) **A plc**

Reconciliation of opening and closing consolidated reserves for 20X3

	A plc £'000	B Ltd £'000	C Ltd £'000	Adjustments £'000	Consolidated reserves £'000
Balance b/f	3,300	272 (W6)	612 (W7)	(900) (W8)	3,284
Retained profits for the year	790	136 (W9)	-	-	926
Profit on disposal	627 (W10)	-	-	-	627
Elimination of C's reserves and write-back of goodwill	-	-	(595) (W7)	459 (W8)	(136)
	4,717	408	17	(441)	4,701

Workings

(W1) We are told that A plc accounts for dividends when received. B Ltd has paid a dividend of 20 during the year, so it is assumed that A's 80% share of this has already been included in A's operating profit and must now be eliminated.

Group operating profits are calculated as:

	£'000
A plc (1,200 – 16 dividend elimination)	1,184
B Ltd	250
	1,434

(W2)

	£'000
Proceeds	1,925
Net assets disposed of (87.5% × 1,400)	(1,225)
	700

	£'000	£'000
(W3)		
A's corporation tax		360
B's corporation tax		60
Tax on disposal		
Proceeds	1,925	
Cost in A's books $(\frac{350}{360} \times 1,120)$	(1,089)	
Gain in A's books	836	
Taxed at 25%		209
		629

(W4) Group net assets as at 31 December 20X3

	£'000
A plc as at 31.12.X2	2,516
Add: Retained profits for year per draft P&L a/c	790
B Ltd as at 31.12.X2	1,260
Add: Retained profits for year per draft P&L a/c	170
Proceeds of sale of shares	1,925
Less: Tax payable thereon (W3)	(209)
	6,452

(W5) In an exam it might be best to leave reserves as the balancing figure on the consolidated balance sheet, and prove it in part (b). However the figure of 4,697 can be proved as follows:

A plc	£'000
Reserves at 1 Jan X3	3,300
Retained profits for 20X3	790
Net profit on disposal (see Working 10)	627
B Ltd	
Reserves at 1 Jan X3 (see Working 6)	272
Retained profits for 20X3 (see Working 9)	136
Less: Elimination of goodwill when A bought B (see Working 8)	(428)
	4,697

(W6) A's share of B's post-acquisition profits $= 80\% \times (760 - 420)$

$= £272,000.$

(W7) A's share of C's post-acquisition profits $= 90\% \times (1,000 - 320)$

$= £612,000.$

Elimination of reserves in C $(\frac{350}{360} \times 612) = £595,000$

(W8) Accumulated goodwill write-offs are as follows:

	£'000
Investment in B (1,164 − (80% × (500 + 420)))	428
Investment in C (1,120 − (90% × (400 + 320)))	472
	900
Elimination of goodwill in C ($\frac{350}{360} \times 472$)	459

(W9) 80% × 170 = £136,000.

(W10)

	£'000
Gain in A's books (W3)	836
Less: Tax at 25%	(209)
Net gain	627

CHAPTER **5**   EXAM-TYPE QUESTION

Charlie plc

(a) The proposed combination must be accounted for as a merger if the criteria set out in both the Companies Act 1985 and FRS 6 are met.

The Companies Act conditions are.

(i)   The subsidiary was acquired by an arrangement providing for the issue of equity shares by the parent company.

(ii)   The group has obtained at least 90% of the equity shares in the subsidiary.

(iii)   The fair value of the consideration other than equity shares does not exceed 10% of the nominal value of the equity shares issued.

(iv)   The adoption of merger accounting complies with generally accepted accounting principles or practice.

The first two conditions are clearly met and the last condition helps give weight to the criteria set out in FRS 6.

Let us consider whether condition (iii) is met. The fair value of the non-equity consideration (in this case cash, but it could be preference shares or debentures for example) is £1.25 million, whereas the nominal value of the shares issued is £10 million and so the criteria that the non-equity consideration does not exceed 10% of the nominal value of the equity shares issued is not met.

Cash consideration	5,000,000 × 25p	=	£1,250,000
Nominal value of shares issued	2 × 5,000,000	=	£10,000,000

$$\frac{1,250,000}{10,000,000} = 12.5\%$$

Tutorial note: It would be wrong now not to discuss the FRS 6 criteria and whether they are met just because the CA 1985 criteria are not met.

The FRS 6 criteria are as follows.

(1) No party to the combination is portrayed as either acquirer or acquired, either by its own board or management.

Both management teams appear to regard the combination as a merger, to counter foreign competition. However no indication is given of what the new entity will be called and as the only proposed rationalisations concern Alex Ltd, this criteria appears not to be met.

(2) All parties to the combination participate in establishing the management structure for the combined entity and in selecting the management personnel.

The proposed redundancies affect Alex Ltd only, an indication that this criteria has not been met.

(3) The relative sizes of the combining entities are not so disparate that one party dominates the combined entity by virtue of its relative size.

The shareholders of Alex Ltd will be issued with 10 million shares, and therefore after the share issue will control 45% ($^{10}/_{22} \times 100\%$). It would appear this criteria is met.

(4) The fair value of the consideration received by equity shareholders will only contain an immaterial proportion of non-equity consideration.

$$\frac{\text{Cash}}{\text{Cash + Fair value of shares}} = \frac{1,250,000}{1,250,000 + £3 \times 10,000,000} = 4\%$$

i.e. 96% of the consideration received by equity shareholders in relation to their shareholding comprises equity shares. This criteria appears to be met.

(5) No equity shareholders of any of the combining entities retain a material interest in the future performance of only part of the combined entity.

In the absence of any minority interest and no earn out clauses this criteria is definitely met.

Conclusion

This combination must be accounted for as an acquisition. It neither meets the statutory nor FRS 6 criteria.

(b) **The Charlie plc group balance sheet as at 31 December 20X5**

	£'000	£'000
Fixed assets		
Intangible (W4)		17,708
Tangible (9,715 + 10,000 + 5,000)		24,715
		42,423
Current assets		
Stock (8,000 + 2,500)	10,500	
Long-term debtors (W1)	1,196	
Investments (W2)	980	
Debtors (600 + 875)	1,475	
	14,151	

Creditors: Amounts falling due within one year

(1,100 + 3,200 + 1,250) (W5)   (5,550)

     8,601

Total assets less current liabilities   51,024

Creditors: Amounts falling due after more than one year

(1,000 + 3,809) (W3)   (4,809)

     46,215

Called up share capital (12,000 + 10,000)   22,000

Merger reserve (W5)   20,000

Other reserves   4,215

     46,215

Note: fair value table

Acquisition – Alex Ltd – 31 December 20X5

	Book value £'000	Revaluations £'000	Provisions £'000	Fair value £'000
Fixed assets				
Freehold offices (i)	8,000	2,000		10,000
Plant (ii)	6,250		(1,250)	5,000
Current assets				
Stock (iii)	2,000	500		2,500
Long-term debtors (iv)	1,500		(304)	1,196
Investments (v)	500	480		980
Debtors	875			875
Total assets	19,125	2,980	(1,554)	20,551
Current liabilities	(3,200)			(3,200)
Long-term liabilities (vi)	(4,000)		191	(3,809)
Total liabilities	(7,200)		191	(7,009)
Net assets	11,925	2,980	(1,363)	13,542

Explanation of adjustments

(i)   increases in value of freehold property since last revaluation

(ii)   write down of plant to its net replacement cost

(iii)   adjustment of stock to its net replacement cost

(iv)   write down of long-term debtors to their present value

(v)   revaluation of investments to their market value

(vi)   adjustment of long-term liabilities to their present value.

Workings

(W1)   **Long-term debtors**

The fair value is the present value of the amount expected to be received; two years at a discount rate of 12%. The discount rate of 12% is relevant as it is the current interest rate.

$$1,500 \times 0.797 = 1,196$$

(W2)   **Current asset investments**

	£
Market value	980,000
Cost	500,000
Fair value adjustment	480,000

(W3)   **Long-term liabilities**

The fair value of the long-term liability is the present value of the amount expected to be paid. Where the current rate of interest commanded by the new group (in this question 12%) is materially different to the coupon rate (in this question 10%) a fair value adjustment is required.

			£'000
31.12.X6	Interest	400×0.893	357
31.12.X7	Interest	400×0.797	319
31.12.X8	Interest and capital	$4,400 \times 0.712$	3,133
			3,809

(W4)   **Calculation of goodwill**

	£'000
Cost of investment $(5,000 \times 2 \times £3) + (25p \times 5,000)$	31,250
Less: Group share of the fair value of the net assets at acquisition $(100\% \times 13,542)$ (see fair value table)	(13,542)
Premium arising on consolidation/goodwill	17,708

Note: The combination is treated as taking place on 31 December 20X5, and so no amortisation of goodwill has yet occurred.

(W5)   **Charlie plc will record the cost of the investment in Alex**

	£'000	£'000
Dr Cost of investment	31,250	
Cr Share capital		10,000
Merger reserve (in lieu of share premium)		20,000
Bank $(25p \times 5,000)$		1,250

(c) Prior to the introduction of FRS 7 it was relatively common for acquirers to evaluate the fair value of the net assets acquired from their perspective, i.e. after making provision for post combination reorganisation costs and losses and writing down assets which they considered to be of little value in the light of integration/reorganisation plans.

This had the beneficial effect of reducing the fair value of the net assets acquired thus increasing the goodwill, which was then normally written off immediately against reserves under SSAP 22.

When the post-combination reorganisation costs were incurred, etc. they were charged not against the profit and loss account for the period, but against the provision.

FRS 7 has effectively curtailed this creative accounting practice. Therefore if FRS 7 had not been in force the plant could have been written down by £3,750,000 to £2,500,000 and provision made for the other costs of closing Alex Ltd's regional distribution network.

CHAPTER 6	EXAM-TYPE QUESTION

S plc

(a) Consolidated balance sheet of T Group plc at 31 May 20X7

		£m
Intangible assets: goodwill (W1)		12
Tangible assets		732
Net current assets		564
Creditors due after one year		(48)
Minority interest (W2)		(29)
		1,231
Called up share capital		120
Share premium account		120
Profit and loss account (W3)		991
		1,231

Workings

	£m	£m
(W1) Goodwill		
Cost of investment		108
Less: Share of net assets acquired:		
Share capital	36	
Share premium	12	
Profit and loss account	72	
	120	
Group share (80%)		(96)
		12
(W2) Minority interest		
Share capital	36	
Share premium	12	
Profit and loss account	96	
	144	
MI share (20%)		29

(W3) Group profit and loss account

T plc		972
U Ltd:		
At year-end	96	
At acquisition	(72)	
	24	
Group share (80%)		19
Less: goodwill amortisation to date		(–)
		991

(b)

S Group plc
Consolidated profit and loss account for the year ended 31 May 20X7

	Continuing operations £m	Discontinued operations £m	Total £m
Turnover	10,236	3,990	14,226
Cost of sales	(6,384)	(2,634)	(9,018)
Gross profit	3,852	1,356	5,208
Net operating expenses	(2,550)	(552)	(3,072)
Operating profit	1,302	834	2,136
Goodwill on discontinued operations (W5)		(552)	(552)
Profit on ordinary activities before taxation	1,302	282	1,584
Taxation			(678)
Profit on ordinary activities after taxation			906
Minority interests (W4)			(42)
Profit for financial year			864
Dividends (W6)			(1,255)
Retained loss for financial year			(391)

S Group plc (after demerger)
Consolidated balance sheet at 31 May 20X7

	£m
Intangible assets: negative goodwill (W1)	(34)
Tangible assets	4,308
Net current assets	2,268
Creditors due after one year	(162)
Minority interest (W2)	(70)
	6,310
Called up share capital	1,620
Share premium account	1,860
Profit and loss account (W3)	2,830
	6,310

Workings

	£m	£m
(W1) Goodwill		
Cost of investment		60
Less: Share of net assets acquired:		
Share capital	24	
Share premium	24	
Profit and loss account	108	
	156	
Group share (60%)		(94)
		(34)
(W2) Minority interest		
Share capital	24	
Share premium	24	
Profit and loss account	126	
	174	
MI share (40%)		70
(W3) Group profit and loss account		
S plc		3,900
V Ltd:		
At year-end	126	
At acquisition	(108)	
	18	
Group share (60%)		10
Less: demerger (cost of investment in T plc)		(1,080)
		2,830
(W4) Minority interest – S Group profit/loss account		
Minority interest in V 40% of 72		29
Minority interest in U 20% of 66		13
		42
(W5) Goodwill		
Cost of investment – T plc	1,080	
Net assets acquired – T plc (120 + 120 + 300)	(540)	
		540
Goodwill on acquisition of U		12
Goodwill on discontinued operations		552
(W6) Demerged assets		
DR Profit/loss a/c (dividend in specie)		1,219
CR Separable net assets of T group plc (1,231 − 12)		
BEFORE demerger		1,219

There will be no profit or loss on the demerger of T group plc as the demerger involves simply a distribution of assets effectively to existing shareholders in the form of a dividend in specie.

Dividends	- dividend paid	36
	- dividend in specie	1,219
		1,255

(W7) Consolidated reserves (for information only)

At 1 June 20X6	3,221
Loss for period	(391)
At 31 May 20X7	2,830

(W8) Opening balance on reserves

S	(3,900 − 820)	3,080
T	(972 − 473 − 300)	199
U	80% of (96 − 60 − 72)	(29)
V	60% of (126 − 66 − 108)	(29)
		3,221

(c) W Group plc

Share capital and reserves at 31 May 20X7

	£m
Ordinary shares of £1	360
Profit and loss account (see below)	859
	1,219

Profit and loss account

T Group's Profit and loss account (991 − 12)		979
Less difference on consolidation		
W's share capital	360	
T's share capital	(120)	
T's share premium	(120)	
		120
		859

CHAPTER 7

EXAM-TYPE QUESTION

Bold plc

Tutorial notes: For part (a) (i) eliminate only the group's share (25%) of the unrealised profit. Provide only two or three notes based on your workings for part (a) (i) when answering part (a) (ii).

For part (b) concentrate on the lack of information disclosed when using equity accounting when compared with full consolidation.

For part (c) consider the drop in percentage holding. For part (c) (i) consider this as a post balance sheet event and for part (c) (ii) consider the carrying value of the (now) trade investment.

(a) (i) **Consolidated profit and loss account for year ended 31 August 20X1**

	£	£
Turnover		175,000
Group operating profit	88,000	
Share of operating profit of associate (including amortisation of goodwill £5,800) (£60,000 × 25% − 5,800)	9,200	
Profit on sale of property to associate (£13,000 − 5,000)	8,000	
Profit on ordinary activities before tax		105,200
Tax on profit on ordinary activities: group	22,000	
Share of taxation of associate (£20,000 × 25%)	5,000	
		27,000
Profit on ordinary activities after tax		78,200
Proposed dividends		61,000
Retained profit for the year		17,200

Tutorial note: With only the group's share of net assets of Face plc being incorporated in the consolidated balance sheet it is only necessary to eliminate 25% of the profit made on the sale of the property i.e. 25% × (£60,000 − £40,000) = £5,000.

Consolidated balance sheet as at 31 August 20X1

	£	£	£
Fixed assets			
Tangible			135,000
Investment in associated undertaking (W1)			53,200
			188,200
Current assets	Stock	72,000	
	Debtors	105,000	
		177,000	
Current liabilities	Creditors	95,000	
	Bank	14,000	109,000
Net current assets			68,000
			256,200
Ordinary shares			135,000
Reserves (W3)			121,200
			256,200

Workings

(W1) Goodwill on acquisition

	£	£
Cost of investment		54,000
Share of ordinary shares (25% × £50,000)	12,500	
Share of pre acq reserves (25% × £50,000)	12,500	
		25,000
		29,000
Amortisation (29,000 ÷ 5)		(5,800)
		23,200

(W2) Investment in associate

	£
Share of net assets (25% × £140,000)	35,000
Elimination of share of unrealised profit	(5,000)
	30,000
Goodwill not yet amortised	23,200
	53,200

(W3) Reserves

	£
Bold	122,000
Face (25% × £40,000)	10,000
Unrealised profit	(5,000)
Goodwill	(5,800)
	121,200

(ii) Notes to the accounts

Investment in associated undertaking

The group holds 25% of the ordinary shares of Face plc, a property investment company. The amounts shown in the consolidated profit and loss account and consolidated balance sheet can be expanded as follows.

	£'000
Share of turnover (200 × 25%)	50
Share of profit before tax (60 × 25%)	15
Share of taxation (20 × 25%)	(5)
Share of profit after tax	10
Share of assets	
Share of fixed assets (200 × 25%)	50
Share of current assets (260 × 25%)	65
	115

Share of liabilities

Share of liabilities due within one year (120 × 25%)	30
Share of liabilities due after one year or more (200 × 25%)	50
	(80)

Share of net assets at 31 August 20X1	35
Less: share of unrealised profit on sale of property within the group	(5)
	30
Goodwill	23
	53

Tutorial note: Face plc clearly exceeds the '25% threshold' and therefore FRS 9 requires the additional disclosures shown above.

(b) **Defect relating to equity accounting in the profit and loss account**

The results of the associate are incorporated without giving any indication as to whether or not the income reported will ever be received, by way of dividend, by the investing group. The group while having a degree of influence may not be able to guarantee the receipt of the reported profit, and in any case the associate may be in no position to make such a distribution.

For example, Face plc appears to have a serious liquidity problem with current liabilities in excess of double the company's debtors, and loans which are nearly double the equity investment. This level of gearing could result in serious problems if the associate were to suffer a reduction in the level of pre-interest profits. This problem could only be remedied by an extension of the disclosure requirements to cover details of the associate's liquidity position and gearing ratio.

FRS 9 requires disclosure where there are significant restrictions on the ability of an associate to distribute its reserves.

Defect relating to equity accounting in the balance sheet

The inclusion of only a single figure covering the group's share of net assets makes it very difficult to analyse the financial position of the associate. A considerable amount of the net assets may be represented by intangible fixed assets carried at a subjective valuation. In addition it is not possible to ascertain the make up of the tangible fixed assets, which in the case of Face plc total £200,000. Finally any liquidity or gearing problems are not apparent.

FRS 9 now requires additional disclosures where associates are material in the context of the group, but even these may not go far enough to provide a full picture of the financial position of the associate.

(c) (i) It may be necessary to include a note in the 20X1 accounts informing readers that the interest of the group in the associate has fallen from 25% to 15.625% $\left(\dfrac{£12,500}{£80,000} \right)$, and is therefore not automatically an associate. In fact with a single third party holding a 37.5% interest, it is unlikely that the group would have the level of significant influence for its investment in Face plc to be accounted for under the equity method as an associate. This event should probably be disclosed as a non-adjusting post balance sheet event in line with the requirements of SSAP 17. This should avoid misleading the users of the financial statements as to the investments held by the group.

(ii) The investment should be carried at the value attributed to the investment at the date it ceased to be considered an associate company. The investment in Face plc should be recorded at a valuation, i.e. $25\% \times £140,000 + 23,200 = £58,200$. This valuation may be updated to $15.625\% \times (£140,000 + \text{Cash from issue } £120,000) + \text{goodwill } 23,200$, £63,825 with the increase in valuation of £5,625 probably treated as an unrealised revaluation gain. This amount should be reviewed for impairment and written down to its recoverable amount if necessary.

CHAPTER **8**	EXAM-TYPE QUESTION

UK plc

(a) SSAP 20 *Foreign currency translation* describes two methods of translating the financial statements of a subsidiary: the closing rate (net investment) method and the temporal method. The nature of the relationship between the parent and the subsidiary determines the method of translation.

France SA

France SA has been wholly owned since its incorporation and it acts as a selling agent for UK plc. In addition, UK plc is actively involved in the management of France SA as it provides or arranges all its funding and has guaranteed its overdraft. France SA appears to operate as an extension of UK plc's trading activities and is more dependent on the economic environment of sterling than on its own reporting currency, the Euro. Therefore the temporal method of translation should be used.

Under the temporal method, the subsidiary's financial statements are translated as if the parent had entered into all its transactions in its own currency. Assets, liabilities, income and expenditure are translated at the exchange rate ruling on the date when the transaction occurred. Monetary items in the balance sheet are re-translated at the closing rate at the year end and the exchange difference is taken to the profit and loss account. Non-monetary items in the balance sheet are not re-translated at the year end.

US Inc

US Inc operates in such a way that it is independent of its parent company. It arranges its own finance and sells its own products. It appears that US Inc is held for its investment potential, rather than as an extension of the parent's operations. Therefore the closing rate method of translation should be used.

Under the closing rate method, it is the net investment in the company which is translated into sterling, rather than the individual assets and liabilities. This is achieved by translating all balance sheet items at the exchange rate ruling at the year end (the closing rate). Profit and loss account items may be translated at either the closing rate or the average rate during the year and the alternative selected must be applied consistently from year to year. The opening net investment in the subsidiary is retranslated at the closing rate and the resulting exchange difference is taken to reserves. Therefore the exchange difference does not affect the group's profit for the year.

(b) Consolidated balance sheet at 30 September 20X8: Working schedule

	UK plc	France SA	US Inc	Adjustments	Total
	£'000	£'000	£'000	£'000	£'000
		(W2)	(W3)		
Goodwill	–	–	–	1,750 (W4)	1,750
Tangible assets	26,000	10,000	31,111		67,111
Investments	25,500	–	–	(25,500)	–
Stock	15,000	4,000	13,889	(400) (W5)	32,489
Debtors	10,000	2,500	8,889	(1,000) (W6)	
				(1,917) (W7)	18,472
Cash in hand	2,000	500	1,667		4,167
Bank overdraft	(8,000)	(833)	(5,000)		(13,833)
Trade creditors	(6,000)	(1,000)	(4,444)	1,000 (W6)	(10,444)
Tax	(3,000)	(500)	(2,222)		(5,722)
Proposed dividend	(2,000)	(667)	(1,667)	1,917 (W7)	(2,417)
Long term loans	(20,000)	–	(13,889)		(33,889)
	39,500	14,000	28,334	(24,150)	57,684
Share capital	20,000	8,000	16,000	(24,000)	20,000
Reserves:					
Pre-acquisition	–	–	4,000	(4,000) (W4)	–
Post-acquisition	19,500	6,000	8,334	(3,234) (W8)	30,600
Minority interest	–	–	–	7,084 (W9)	7,084
	39,500	14,000	28,334	(24,150)	57,684

Workings

(W1) **Group structure**

UK plc

100% $\frac{24,000}{32,000} = 75\%$

France SA   US Inc

(W2) **Translation of France SA**

	€'000	Rate	£'000
Tangible assets	95,000	(W10)	10,000
Stocks	44,000	11	4,000
Debtors	30,000	12	2,500
Cash in hand	6,000	12	500
Bank overdraft	(10,000)	12	(833)
Trade creditors	(12,000)	12	(1,000)
Tax	(6,000)	12	(500)
Proposed dividend	(8,000)	12	(667)
	139,000		14,000

Share capital	80,000	10	8,000
Post-acquisition reserves	59,000	(bal. fig.)	6,000
	139,000		14,000

(W3) **Translation of US Inc**

	$'000	*Rate*	£'000
Tangible assets	56,000	1.8	31,111
Stocks	25,000	1.8	13,889
Debtors	16,000	1.8	8,889
Cash in hand	3,000	1.8	1,667
Bank overdraft	(9,000)	1.8	(5,000)
Trade creditors	(8,000)	1.8	(4,444)
Tax	(4,000)	1.8	(2,222)
Proposed dividend	(3,000)	1.8	(1,667)
Long term loans	(25,000)	1.8	(13,889)
	51,000		28,334
Share capital	32,000	2	16,000
Pre-acquisition reserves	8,000	2	4,000
Post-acquisition reserves	11,000	(bal. fig.)	8,334
	51,000		28,334

(W4) **Goodwill**

	£'000	£'000
US Inc		
Cost of investment (35,000 @ 2)		17,500
Net assets acquired:		
Share capital (32,000 @ 2)	16,000	
Reserves (8,000 @ 2)	4,000	
	20,000	
Group share (75%)		(15,000)
		2,500
Less: amounts amortised $(2,500 \div 20 \times 6)$		(750)
		1,750

	£'000
France SA	
Cost of investment (25,500 – 17,500)	8,000
Net assets acquired: (Group share 100%)	
Share capital (80,000 @ 10)	(8,000)
	–

(W5) Intra-group stock

	£'000
Sales (44,000 @ 11)	4,000
Cost of sales	3,600
Unrealised profit	400

	£'000	£'000
Dr Post acquisition reserves	400	
Cr Stocks		400

(W6) Inter-company balances

	£'000	£'000
France SA		
Dr Trade creditors (12,000 @ 12)	1,000	
Cr Debtors		1,000

(W7) Proposed dividends

	£'000
France SA (8,000 @ 12)	667
US Inc (3,000 × 75% @ 1.8)	1,250
	1,917

	£'000	£'000
Dr Proposed dividends	1,917	
Cr Debtors		1,917

(W8) Post acquisition reserves (proof)

	£'000
UK plc	19,500
France SA (W2)	6,000
US Inc (75% × 8,334 (W3))	6,250
Amortisation of goodwill (W4)	(750)
Provision for unrealised profit (W5)	(400)
	30,600

(W9) Minority interest

	£'000
US Inc:	
Share of net assets at balance sheet date (25% × 28,334)	7,084

(W10) Tangible fixed assets: France SA

	€'000	*Rate*	£'000
20X0	10,000	10	1,000
20X3	45,000	9	5,000
20X7	40,000	10	4,000
	95,000		10,000

Orchard group

Tutorial note: A fairly straightforward question based on the presentation of the cash flow data in line with FRS 1. The only major problem is in dealing with the £100,000 and £30,000 exchange differences. Assume the amounts charged to the consolidated profit and loss account for labour and expenses are equal to the cash payments made during the period for such items.

(a) **Cash flow statement for the year ended 31 December 20X1**

	£'000	£'000
Operating activities		
Cash received from customers (W4)	4,416	
Cash paid to suppliers (W5)	(2,369)	
Expenses paid	(863)	
Cash paid to employees	(805)	
Net cash inflow from operating activities (Note 1)		379
Returns on investments and servicing of finance		
Other income (assumed to be interest)	55	
Dividends paid to minority interests (W3)	(18)	
		37
Taxation		
Corporation tax paid (W6)		(120)
Capital expenditure		
Plant purchases (W1)	(1,090)	
Plant disposals (W2)	173	
		(917)
Equity dividends paid		(200)
Net cash outflow before use of liquid resources and financing		(821)
Management of liquid resources		
Purchase of current asset investments (804 – 737)		(67)
Financing		-
Decrease in cash in the period		(888)

Reconciliation of net cash flow to movement in net funds (Note 2)

	£'000
Decrease in cash in the period	(888)
Cash outflow from purchase of current asset investments	67
Change in net funds resulting from cash flows	(821)
Exchange differences	(5)
Net funds at 1 January 20X1	645
Net debt at 31 December 20X1	(181)

Notes to the cash flow statement

(1) **Reconciliation of operating profit to net cash inflow from operating activities**

	£'000
Operating profit (354 – 55 + 172)	471
Depreciation charges	161
Increase in stocks (576 – 403 – 20)	(153)
Increase in debtors (1,145 – 919 – 42)	(184)
Increase in creditors (681 – 550 – 47)	84
Net cash inflow from operating activities	379

(2) **Analysis of changes in net funds**

	At 1 January 20X1 £'000	Cash flows £'000	Exchange differences £'000	At 31 December 20X1 £'000
Cash at bank/bank overdraft	58	(888)	25	(805)
Long-term loan	(150)		(30)	(180)
Current asset investments	737	67		804
Total	645	(821)	(5)	(181)

Tutorial note: An alternative is to show all £100,000 exchange differences in the movement in cash with the following balances operating in the statement.

	£'000
Cash received from customers	4,374
Cash paid to suppliers	(2,342)
Purchases of plant	(1,150)

(b) The exchange gain has no effect on the actual cash flows for the period but it would be necessary to take account of the differences that arise from using an average rate in the profit and loss account and the closing rate in the balance sheet. The calculations based on the movements in certain accounts, e.g. debtors would have to be adjusted to reflect the exchange differences. It is possible to make a single adjustment of £10,000 as described in the tutorial note above instead of making adjustments to all calculations for the individual figures in the cash flow statement.

Workings

(W1) **Plant purchases**

	£'000	£'000
Opening balance	1,150	
Exchange gain	60	
Cost of disposals	(690)	
		520
Closing balance		(1,610)
Purchases (assume on cash basis)		1,090

(W2) Plant sale proceeds

Book value of disposal (after dep'n)	345
Loss on sale	(172)
Proceeds	173

(W3) Dividend to MI

Opening balance	300	
Share of profits	42	
Share of exchange gain	20	
		362
Closing balance		(344)
Dividends paid		18

(W4) Cash received from customers

Debtors opening balance	919	
Adjustment for exchange gain	42	
Plus sales	4,600	
		5,561
Debtors closing balance		(1,145)
Cash received		4,416

(W5) Cash paid to suppliers

Cost of sales	2,300	
Opening stock balance	(403)	
Adjustment for exchange gain	(20)	
Closing stock	576	
Purchases		2,453
Creditors opening balance		550
Adjustment for exchange loss		47
Creditors closing balance		(681)
Cash paid		2,369

(W6) Taxation paid

Opening balance	140	
Tax incurred	105	
		245
Closing balance		(125)
Tax paid		120

CHAPTER **10**   EXAM-TYPE QUESTION

Invest plc

(a) Key factors which lay behind the decision to prohibit the write off of purchased goodwill to reserves

Immediate elimination against reserves was the preferred treatment under SSAP 22, which preceded FRS 10. There are many disadvantages of using this method:

- Immediate elimination of goodwill gives the impression that the acquirer's net worth has been depleted or even eliminated. This is misleading, because an acquisition normally increases the net worth of the group.

- Goodwill is not taken into account when measuring the assets on which a return must be earned and therefore management is not held accountable for the amount that it has invested in goodwill. If there is a loss in the value of goodwill, this does not have to be disclosed. Return on capital employed and similar measures are overstated.

- There are inconsistencies in the treatment of goodwill in the profit and loss account. Costs attributed to building up internally generated goodwill are offset against profits in the profit and loss account, but the costs of purchased goodwill are not charged in the profit and loss account. This means that companies that grow by acquisition may appear to be more profitable than those that grow organically.

- Immediate elimination of goodwill is inconsistent with the Accounting Standards Board's (ASB's) Statement of Principles. It defines assets as 'rights or other access to future economic benefits controlled by an entity as a result of past transactions or events'. It can be argued that, although goodwill is not an identifiable asset, it is part of a larger asset, the investment, and therefore it should be included in the balance sheet.

- Immediate elimination is also prohibited by International Accounting Standards.

Because the balance sheet was weakened by elimination of goodwill against reserves, some entities valued brand names and similar intangible assets separately from goodwill. In this way they reduced the amount of purchased goodwill. This was possible because before the issue of FRS 10 there was no accounting standard covering the treatment of intangibles other than goodwill and development costs. The ASB believes that intangible assets such as brands have similar characteristics to goodwill and should therefore be accounted for in the same way, particularly as the allocation of value between the two is rather subjective.

(b) **Charge to the consolidated profit and loss account for the year ended 30 April 20X9**

	£'000	£'000
Cost of investment		31,000
Less: net assets acquired:		
Included in the balance sheet	30,000	
Brand name (note)	3,000	
	33,000	
Group share (80%)		(26,400)
Goodwill		4,600
Amortisation charge (4,600÷40)		115

Note

FRS 10 states that intangible assets acquired with a business can be capitalised separately from goodwill if their value can be measured reliably on initial recognition. The question refers to 'a reliable estimate' of its value to the group and therefore it has been included in the net assets acquired at its fair value of £3 million.

(c) **Action to be taken in 20X8/9 and in future years**

FRS 10 states that goodwill should normally be amortised over a period of 20 years or less. The goodwill arising on the acquisition of Target Ltd is to be amortised over 40 years.

Under FRS 10, this treatment is allowed, provided that the durability of Target Ltd can be demonstrated and justifies this estimate of the goodwill's useful economic life. The goodwill must also be capable of continued measurement, as the directors of Invest plc are required to review the goodwill for impairment at the end of each reporting period. The impairment reviews must be carried out in accordance with the requirements of FRS 11 *Impairment of fixed assets and goodwill*.

The carrying value of the goodwill must be compared with its recoverable amount. FRS 11 defines recoverable amount as the higher of net realisable value and value in use. If carrying value is greater than the recoverable amount, the goodwill must be written down accordingly and an impairment loss recognised in the profit and loss account. The revised carrying value of the goodwill should be amortised over its remaining useful economic life and the investment held in the accounts of the parent undertaking should also be reviewed for impairment.

CHAPTER 11	EXAM-TYPE QUESTION

Properties (London) Ltd

(a) If depreciation is charged in 20X6, then the balance sheet entries should be as follows.

Either	£
Additions	160,000
Cost c/d	160,000
Depreciation charge	2,500
Depreciation c/d	£2,500

or	£
Additions	160,000
Revaluation	40,000
Valuation c/d	200,000
Depreciation charge	2,500
Revaluation	(2,500)
Depreciation c/d	-

Since the property is an asset in the course of construction, depreciation need not be charged at all in 20X6.

Appropriate entries for 20X7 would be as follows.

Either	£
Cost b/d	160,000
Additions	40,000
Cost c/d	200,000
Depreciation b/d	2,500
Depreciation charge	3,300
Depreciation c/d	5,800
or	
Valuation b/d	200,000
Additions	40,000
Revaluation	35,000
Valuation c/d	275,000
Depreciation b/d	-
Depreciation charge	3,800 being 2% × (150,000 + 40,000)
Revaluation	(3,800)
	-

(b) (i)   If the units are not used as a head office for Properties (Brighton) Ltd then, once completed, they will be investment properties and will not be subject to depreciation. Any revaluation surpluses will be included in the investment property revaluation reserve.

	20X7	20X6
Profit and loss account	£	£
Rental income	2,500	-
Interest payable	(24,000)	(17,500)
Depreciation	-	-
Balance sheet		
Fixed assets in the course of construction	-	160,000
Fixed assets – investment properties	275,000	-
Investment property revaluation reserve	75,000	-

(ii)   **Accounting policies for the year ended 31 December 20X6**

Income available for distribution

The balance on the profit and loss account is available for distribution. The investment property revaluation reserve is not available for distribution.

Properties and depreciation

Properties are included at cost. No depreciation has been charged as the properties are in the course of construction and are to be used as investment properties on completion.

Tutorial note: If an accounting policy note for 20X7 for properties and depreciation had been a requirement of this question, then it would state that no depreciation was charged on investment properties in accordance with SSAP 19 and that this was a departure from the requirements of the Companies Act 1985 so as to give a true and fair view.

Hartington plc

(a) Why a financial reporting standard was needed

In recent years, large companies have made increasing use of a wide range of complex financial instruments. These have included traditional primary financial instruments (for example, shares and debentures), and derivative financial instruments. A derivative financial instrument is a financial instrument that derives its value from the price or rate of some underlying item, such as interest rates, exchange rates and stock market and other indices. Derivatives include futures, options, forward contracts, interest rate swaps and currency swaps.

- The Companies Act and FRS 4 *Capital Instruments* already require entities to provide some information about their use of financial instruments, in particular, about the maturity of debt and the interest rate terms of indebtedness. However, the ASB believed that these disclosures were inadequate where derivatives were used. This is because the use of derivatives poses particular problems.

  (a) Many derivatives have no cost. This means that they may represent substantial assets and liabilities of the company and yet they might not appear in the balance sheet.

  (b) Gains and losses are normally not recorded until cash is exchanged. Because gains and losses can be easily realised, management may be able to choose when to report gains and losses on realisation.

  (c) Because the value of a derivative depends on the value of underlying items it can change very rapidly, thus exposing an entity to the risk of large profits or losses. Derivatives can rapidly transform the position, performance and risk profile of an entity, yet the financial statements often contained little or no information about the impact of derivatives on the risks faced by an entity.

- There have been a number of well publicised financial disasters involving derivatives and these have highlighted the inadequacies of traditional accounting practices, including disclosure, in this area.

- A further reason why the ASB wished to undertake work on derivatives is that the increasing globalisation of financial markets has meant that derivatives and other financial instruments have become a topic of international concern. The ASB wishes to be able to make an effective contribution to the international debate.

- The ASB decided to address the disclosure issues as a priority, so that users of the financial statements would have information about the main aspects of the entity's risk profile and an understanding of how this risk profile is being managed.

(b) Index linked loan

The loan will be included in the balance sheet at a value of £2,095,238 (2,000,000 × 110/105) and the change in value is treated as an additional finance cost in accordance with the requirements of FRS 4 which states that finance costs contingent on uncertain events should be recognised only once the events have occurred. Total finance costs are £195,238 and consist of interest paid of £100,000 (2,000,000 × 5%) plus the change in value of the principal amount.

Zero coupon bonds

Although no interest is paid during the term of the bonds, there is a finance charge which represents the difference between the issue proceeds and the amount to be paid on redemption. FRS 4 requires that this is allocated to periods over the term of the debt at a constant rate on the carrying amount. The effective rate of interest on the bonds is 10% (see working) and therefore they will be included in the balance sheet at £5,500,000. The finance cost of £500,000 is charged to the profit and loss account.

(c) **Notes to the financial statements: extracts**

	£'000
Creditors: Amounts falling due after more than one year:	
Debenture loans	5,500
Bank loans and overdrafts	2,095
	7,595

On 1 July 20X2 the company issued zero coupon bonds of £5,000,000. The total consideration received for this issue amounted to £5,000,000.

	£'000
Interest rate profile:	
Fixed rate financial liabilities	5,500
Floating rate financial liabilities	2,095
	7,595

All liabilities are denominated in sterling. The weighted average interest rate for the fixed rate financial liabilities is 10%. The floating rate financial liabilities comprise a bank loan that bears interest at rates based on an index.

Maturity of financial liabilities

The maturity profile of the group's financial liabilities at 30 June 20X3 was as follows:

	£'000
In more than one year, but not more than two years	2,095
In more than two years, but not more than five years	5,500
	7,595

In addition to the disclosures above, the aggregate fair values of the long term borrowings should also be disclosed.

Working

Interest rate on zero coupon bonds: $\frac{5,000}{8,051} = 0.621$, which is the discount factor for five years at 10%.

CHAPTER **13**	EXAM-TYPE QUESTION

S Ltd

MEMORANDUM

To: The Board of Directors

From: Accountant

Subject: Debt factoring arrangement

Date: 25 November 20X8

(a) **Determining the economic substance of a transaction**

FRS 5 *Reporting the substance of transactions* states that in order to determine the economic substance of a transaction it is necessary to identify its effect on the assets and liabilities of the entity.

FRS 5 defines assets and liabilities very widely. Assets are 'rights or other access to future economic benefits controlled by an entity as a result of past transactions or events'. Control means the ability to obtain the future economic benefits relating to an asset and to restrict the access of others to those benefits. Evidence of whether an entity has benefits (and therefore has an asset) is given by whether it is exposed to the risks inherent in those benefits. A liability is 'an obligation to transfer economic benefits as a result of past transactions or events'. If an entity cannot avoid an outflow of resources, it has a liability.

Therefore to determine the substance of a transaction it is necessary to identify the asset or assets involved and then to identify the risks and benefits associated with them. The details of the transaction or arrangement are then analysed to establish which party is actually exposed to the risks and benefits in practice, regardless of the legal position. Provided that the asset(s) can be measured reliably in monetary terms and that there is sufficient evidence of their existence, the party exposed to the risks and benefits recognises the asset in its financial statements.

(b) **How the debt factoring arrangement will be reported in the financial statements**

The legal form of the transaction is that S Ltd has transferred the title to the debtors to the factor, F plc. However, the key issue is whether S Ltd has actually assigned its debtors to F plc in practice or whether S Ltd has merely raised a secured loan from F plc. In order to determine the substance of the arrangement it is necessary to establish which party bears the risks and enjoys the benefits associated with the debtors.

The main benefit of holding debtors is normally an eventual cash inflow, while the main risks are slow payment and non-recovery (i.e. bad debts).

The terms of the agreement can be analysed as follows.

- F plc only accepts debts subject to credit approval, so that S Ltd bears the risk of slow payment and bad debts.

- S Ltd receives only 70% of the debts at the time of assignment. The remaining sums, less interest charged by F plc, are only paid to S Ltd after the debtors have been collected by F plc. Again, S Ltd bears slow payment risk.

- Although F plc administers the scheme and collects the debts, S Ltd must pay a fee for this service. Additionally, all debts not paid within 90 days are re-assigned to S Ltd and S Ltd must repay any monies advanced in respect of those debts. S Ltd is bearing the risk of bad debts.

- F plc charges further interest based on the balance on the factoring account, the size of which depends on the speed with which debts are collected. S Ltd is bearing slow payment risk.

From this analysis it is clear that S Ltd is bearing all the risks associated with the debtors and that the commercial substance of the relationship is that F plc has provided a loan secured on the debtors. The risks to S Ltd are mitigated to some extent, because F plc can only recover bad debts out of the proceeds of other debtors assigned to it.

S Ltd should recognise the debtors as an asset until they have been collected by F plc. The sum advanced from F plc should be treated as a loan, but a linked presentation is appropriate, so that the loan is deducted from the debtors on the face of the balance sheet. S Ltd should record expenses for interest, administration charges and bad debts in its profit and loss account.

CHAPTER 14	EXAM-TYPE QUESTION

Trendy Clothes

Tutorial notes

(1) Part (a) is a straightforward leasing question once it is recognised that Trendy Clothes is a manufacturer/lessor and is thus entitled to take immediate credit for 'normal' trading profit provided that the lease is a finance lease.

(2) Part (b) is a sale and leaseback transaction. Before the issue of FRS 5, the finance arrangement would have resulted in a profit to the lessee which would have been spread over the life of the lease to reduce the lease rentals to those that would have (roughly) applied had the asset been 'sold' at its current net book value. However, the substance of the agreement is that Optimistic Sales Ltd has taken out a loan to finance its continued use of the asset.

(a) The lease is a finance lease if the present value of the minimum lease payments (MLPs) is more than 90% of the fair value of the asset.

The gross investment in the lease is the MLPs either guaranteed (£28,000) or rentals payable (£56,000 × 3 years = £168,000) plus any unguaranteed residual value (for this lease, nil), i.e. £196,000. These MLPs should be discounted, at the implicit interest rate of 18%, to give the net investment in the lease.

£		Discount factor	Present value £
56,000	×	1.000	56,000
56,000	×	0.848	47,488
56,000	×	0.718	40,208
28,000	×	0.609	17,052
Net investment in finance lease			160,748

PV of MLPs is therefore 100% of fair value.

Trendy Clothes should take immediate credit for the trading element of profit.

	£
PV of MLPs	160,748
Less: Cost	126,000
Trading profit	34,748

Gross earnings allocated over the period of the lease are (£196,000 – £160,748) = £35,252. Allocation based on finance provided is as follows.

Period (year)	Net cash investment at start of period	'Cost'	Rentals	Average cash investment in period	Interest (18%)	Net cash investment at end of period
	£	£	£	£	£	£
20X8	-	(160,748)	56,000	(104,748)	18,855	(123,603)
20X9	(123,603)	-	56,000	(67,603)	12,169	(79,772)
20Y0	(79,772)	-	56,000	(23,772)	4,228 *	(28,000)
					£35,252	

* figure rounded.

(i) **Profit and loss account extracts (year ended 31 December 20X8)**

	£
Turnover	160,748
Cost of sale	(126,000)
Gross profit	34,748
Interest receivable under finance lease	18,855
Direct lease expense (straight line allocation over three year lease period)	(2,800)

(ii) **Balance sheet extracts (as at 31 December)**

	20X8 £	20X9 £
Investment in finance lease		
Current	43,831	51,772
Non-current	79,772	28,000
Prepaid expenses	5,600	2,800

(b) Given the value of the rentals compared to a reasonable estimate of fair value the lease appears to be a finance lease. Although the seller/lessee appears to have made a 'profit' of £49,575 (124,575 – 75,000) the substance of the arrangement is that the seller/lessee has taken out a loan of £124,575 on which it will pay finance charges. The asset remains in the balance sheet at £75,000.

Relevant journal entries in the books of Optimistic Sales Ltd

	£	£
Dr Bank account	124,575	
Cr Obligations under finance lease account		124,575

being sale of asset under leaseback agreement and recognition of liability under such contract.

Dr Obligations under finance lease account	25,309	
Dr Profit and loss account	12,191	
Cr Bank account		37,500

being rental paid, to pay interest and part clear liability
   under lease contract.

Dr Profit and loss account	18,750	
Cr Accumulated depreciation account		18,750

being the depreciation charge for the year
   (75,000 ÷ 4)

Workings

	£
'Sale'	124,575
Net book value	75,000
Profit on 'sale'	£49,575

Total finance charges = (£37,500 × 4) − £124,575	=	£25,425
Average cash invested in lease for 20X8 = £124,575 − £37,500	=	£87,075
Finance charge = 14% × £87,075	=	£12,191

CHAPTER 15   EXAM-TYPE QUESTION

TAB plc

Tutorial note: Parts (a) to (c) can be answered directly from SSAP 25. The emphasis in part (d) should be on the problems of the standard.

(a) Para 1 SSAP 25 details the purpose of segmental information. Overall this is to provide users of financial statements with sufficient details for them to be able to appreciate the different rates of profitability, different opportunities for growth and different degrees of risk that apply to an entity's classes of business and various geographical locations. The segmental information should enable users to:

   (i) appreciate more thoroughly the results and financial position of the entity by permitting a better understanding of the entity's past performance and thus a better assessment of its future prospects

   (ii) be aware of the impact that changes in significant components of a business may have on the business as a whole.

(b) Para 8 SSAP 25 states that 'in identifying separate reportable segments, the directors should have regard to the overall purpose of presenting segmental information and the need of the user of the financial statements to be informed where an entity carries on operations in different classes of business or in different geographical areas that

   • earn a return on investment that is out of line with the remainder of the business, or

   • are subject to different degrees of risk, or

   • have experienced different rates of growth, or

   • have different potentials for future development.'

Each significant segment should be reported.

A segment may be presumed significant where the turnover, profit or net assets exceed 10% of the business as a whole.

TAB plc could classify on a geographical basis under the headings 'Europe' and 'The Far East'.

TAB plc has five types of products and more information is really required on the commonality of any of these five. A product split could thus be for five segments.

Likely candidates for grouping together are textiles and fashion garments, perhaps under the heading 'textiles' or 'textiles and clothing'. In addition it may be reasonable to group car products and kitchen utensils under the heading 'domestic products'.

(c) Disclosures required by SSAP 25 are as follows.

Definition of each reported class of business and geographical segment.

By class of business

For all companies	–	External turnover
For public and large companies only	–	Profit before tax (before or after interest)
	–	Inter-segment turnover
	–	Net assets
	–	Share of associate's profit before tax and net assets

By geographical segment

For all companies	–	External turnover, destination basis
For public and large companies only	–	External turnover, origin basis
	–	Inter–segment turnover
	–	Profit before tax (before or after interest)
	–	Net assets
	–	Share of associate's profit before tax and net assets

(d) SSAP 25 appears to have been adopted by the affected companies quite easily. The case for increased disclosure had been argued for many years by users, particularly investment analysts, who required more information about the trading operations of large groups. The delay in issuing a standard was caused by the perceived problem of companies not wishing to disclose 'sensitive' information about their operations.

Perhaps the reason that companies have accepted the standard is because it is flexible as to the groupings shown and therefore the requirements are not seen as too demanding.

Problems of segmental disclosure under SSAP 25 are as follows:

(i) Defining segments is not always easy. Differences will exist in segment identification making it difficult to make comparisons between organisations.

Directors have the responsibility for defining classes of business and geographical segments. Guidance is given in the standard but the decision of the basis is left with the directors. This could lead to bias in the selection of segments. Decisions may be influenced by a desire not to make any class or segment look unduly secure or at risk.

(ii) There are problems in the measurement of segmental performance if the segments trade with each other. Disclosure of details of inter-segment pricing policy is often considered to be detrimental to the good of a company.

There is little guidance on the policy for transfer pricing.

(iii) Common costs may be so significant that to ignore them would result in an incomplete picture, but to incorporate them would result in misleading data.

Common costs are to be treated in the way in which directors deem most appropriate. The result of this can be a lack of consistency of treatment.

(iv) Deciding on what segmental data is required is subjective. Various users require differing levels of disclosure and deciding on a level may be to the detriment of certain of these users.

CHAPTER 16   **EXAM-TYPE QUESTION**

Provident plc

(a) In a defined benefit scheme, the benefits to be paid depend upon either the average pay of the employee during his or her career or, more typically, the final pay of the employee. It is impossible to be certain in advance that the contributions to the pension scheme, together with the investment return thereon, will equal the benefits to be paid. The employer may have a legal obligation to make good any shortfall; alternatively, if a surplus arises the employer may be entitled to a refund of, or reduction in, contributions paid into the pension scheme.

The amounts involved are frequently material. Typically many years elapse between making contributions and actually meeting the liabilities.

The pension funds of defined benefit schemes must be regularly valued by a qualified actuary. The valuation should reveal any surplus or deficit of assets over liabilities. The level of contributions is adjusted so that the fund will be adequate to meet the estimated eventual liability or, alternatively, to take advantage of a surplus.

Valuing a pension fund is a complicated exercise requiring specialist knowledge. The actuary must make estimates of matters such as the rate of return on new investments, salary increases and the estimated future service lives of employees.

Because the level of contributions is dependent on the results of the valuation the actual amount paid can fluctuate wildly. Therefore the actual contribution paid in a period does not necessarily represent the true cost to the employer of providing pensions in that period.

(b) The assets of a defined benefit scheme normally consist of investments and current assets. FRS 17 requires that scheme assets should be measured at their fair value at the balance sheet date. In practice the fair value of an asset is generally its market value. Estimates of fair value may have to be used for unquoted securities and some insurance policies.

The liabilities of a defined benefit scheme consist of the benefits promised under the formal terms of the scheme and any constructive obligations for further benefits where a public statement or past practice by the employer has created a valid expectation in employees that such benefits will be granted. In theory, these liabilities should also be valued at market value. This is not usually possible because there is no active market for most defined benefit scheme liabilities. Therefore FRS 17 requires that fair value is estimated by means of an actuarial valuation using the projected unit method. The assumptions underlying the valuation should be mutually compatible and lead to the best estimate of the future cash flows that will arise under the scheme liabilities.

Because pension scheme liabilities are normally long-term, FRS 17 requires them to be discounted at a rate that reflects the time value of money and the characteristics of the liability. Such a rate should be assumed to be the current rate of return on a high quality corporate bond of equivalent currency and term to the scheme liability.

Full actuarial valuations by a professionally qualified actuary should be obtained for a defined benefit scheme at intervals not exceeding three years. At each balance sheet date the actuary should review the most recent actuarial valuation and update it to reflect current conditions.

(c) **Balance sheet at 31 March 20X4**

A surplus of assets over liabilities in a defined benefit pension scheme is an asset of the employing entity to the extent that the employer can recover it through reduced contributions in the future.

However, part of the surplus has been caused by a reduction in employees. This is a curtailment and it must be recognised in the profit and loss account for the period.

Therefore Provident plc will recognise an asset of £43 million (48 – 5) and disclose it separately on the balance sheet below other net assets, as required by FRS 17.

Profit and loss account for the year ended 31 March 20X4

The cost of providing pensions in the period is the movement in the liability during the year. This is analysed into its component parts.

The profit and loss account will include the following amounts.

Charged to operating profit:

	£m
Current service cost	12
Curtailment	(5)
Total operating charge	7

Other finance income (adjacent to interest)

	£m
Expected return on pension scheme assets	20
Interest on pension scheme liabilities	(10)
Net return	10

Statement of total recognised gains and losses for the year ended 31 March 20X4

The statement of total recognised gains and losses will include an actuarial gain of £17 million (W).

***Working*: Movement in surplus during the year**

	£m
Surplus in scheme at beginning of the year	23
Movement in year:	
Current service cost	(12)
Contributions	–
Curtailment	5
Other finance income	10
Actuarial gain	17
Surplus in scheme at end of the year	43

CHAPTER **17**	EXAM-TYPE QUESTION

CS plc

(a) Why the full provision method is now required

SSAP 15 required deferred tax to be calculated by the partial provision method. There were several reasons for reviewing the use of the partial provision method:

- The partial provision method is inconsistent with international practice. Most other countries, including the USA, require the full provision method. In addition, the International Accounting Standards Committee (IASC) has issued an accounting standard which requires full provision. The Accounting Standards Board (ASB) recognises that there is an increasing need for international harmonisation of financial reporting practice.

- SSAP 15 was originally issued over 20 years ago, when the tax system and the economic climate were very different. At that time it was possible to claim capital allowances of 100% on many fixed asset additions and there was also high inflation. As many entities had a 'core' of timing differences that would never reverse, partial provision reflected economic reality. Since then, conditions have changed, and there is now a far greater likelihood that timing differences will reverse.

- The partial provision method is subjective to apply. The ASB also believes that partial provision is conceptually unsound, because deferred tax provisions reflect the effects of future transactions, rather than past ones.

- There is evidence that some entities have provided for deferred tax in full on grounds of simplicity. In addition, there are many variations in the application of the partial provision method in practice. Entities within the same industry and facing similar conditions may take quite different views on the level of provision that is necessary. These inconsistencies have reduced the comparability of financial statements.

The ASB has issued FRS 19 *Deferred tax*, which requires that full provision should be made for deferred tax. The full provision method has several advantages:

- Unlike partial provision, it is straightforward to apply and objective. It does not involve predicting future events, such as changes in the taxation system, capital expenditure and the useful economic lives of assets.

- The maximum potential liability is provided. Because profit after tax and liabilities are calculated prudently it can be argued that full provision provides users of the financial statements with more reliable information about both performance and risk.

- It applies the accruals concept to taxation.

- It also reflects the definition of liabilities in the ASB's Statement of Principles, because the taxation charge is based on the effect of past transactions.

Many UK preparers and users of accounts do not support full provision. Despite this the ASB believes that the disadvantages of full provision do not outweigh the advantage of harmonising UK accounting standards with international financial reporting practice.

(b) Calculation of deferred tax liability

Reversal of timing differences:

	20X2 £m	20X3 £m	20X4 £m
Capital allowances in excess of depreciation reversal	75	90	105
Other timing differences	135		
Tax losses (63 ÷ 0.3 = 210)	(105)	(105)	
Corporation tax on capital gain (240 ÷ 0.3)			800
Inter company profit in stock	(9)		
	96	(15)	905
Tax rate	30%	30%	30%
Deferred tax liability (96 × 30% + 3)	31.8	(4.5)	271.5
Discount factor (5%)	0.952	0.907	0.864
Discounted amount	30.3	(4.1)	234.6

	£m
Total discounted liability (30.3 − 4.1 + 234.6)	260.8
Plus pension provision undiscounted	135.0
Total deferred tax provision	395.8

Notes

1   Taxation should not be provided on the unremitted earnings of subsidiaries unless there are dividends accrued as payable or there is a binding agreement to distribute past earnings. Thus a provision of £3m is required in this case. A provision needs to be set up for the inter-company profit in stock at the rate of tax used by the supplying company (CS plc).

2   Deferred tax should not be provided on revaluation gains or losses unless the company has a binding sale agreement and has recognised the expected gain or loss. If rollover relief is likely to be utilised, then tax on the sale of assets should not be provided for. However, if taxation has merely been postponed then tax should be provided.

3   The pension provision will already have been discounted by reason of the actuarial valuation and therefore does not require further discounting.

Comment

The deferred tax provision of CS plc will rise by £280 million, thus reducing net assets, distributable profits, and post tax earnings. The borrowing position of the company may be affected and the directors may decide to cut dividend payments. However, the amount of any unprovided deferred tax, analysed into its major components, was required to be disclosed under SSAP 15. FRS 19 brings the majority of this liability onto the balance sheet but because the liability has already been disclosed the impact on the share price should be minimal.

CHAPTER **18**	EXAM-TYPE QUESTIONS

Question 1: NBS plc

MEMORANDUM

To:	Assistant Accountant
From:	Chief Accountant
Subject:	Accounting treatment of three transactions
Date:	19 November 20X7

Transaction One

This disposal appears to meet the definition of a discontinued operation in FRS 3 *Reporting financial performance,* provided that the activity does cease permanently and the disposal takes place as planned on 31 December 20X7 (or within three months of the balance sheet date). It represents a withdrawal from a particular market and the operation is clearly distinguishable from the rest of the business. The disposal must be treated as a discontinued operation in 20X7 if the company is demonstrably committed to the sale. This means that there must have been an announcement or an offer from a buyer which would make it difficult for the company to withdraw from the sale. A Board resolution alone would not be sufficient.

If these conditions are met, the profit and loss account must be analysed between continuing operations and discontinued operations down to the level of operating profit, with the amounts relating to the disposal being shown as part of discontinued operations.

FRS 3 also requires that an expected loss is recognised at the time of the decision to sell. Provision should be made for the loss of £50m on disposal provided that there is a binding sale agreement (as required by FRS 12 *Provisions, contingent liabilities and contingent assets*). This should be disclosed on the face of the profit and loss account as an exceptional item, and included in the discontinued operations column.

Transaction Two

The fundamental restructuring does not meet the definition of a discontinued operation and therefore it must be reported as part of continuing operations. The restructuring costs should be disclosed as an exceptional item on the face of the profit and loss account.

The obsolete stock and old sales ledger balances are material and as such also represent exceptional items. The cost of sales figure in the continuing operations column should be adjusted for these items. The exceptional items, together with their effects on taxation (if any) should be disclosed in a note to the financial statements.

Transaction Three

The profit on disposal of the properties should be disclosed as an exceptional item on the face of the profit and loss account, in the continuing operations column. The profit on disposal is the difference between the sale proceeds and the carrying amount (net book value based on the revalued amount).

The revaluation surplus is not taken through the profit and loss account, but is transferred from the revaluation reserve to the general profit and loss account reserve. The realisation of the property revaluation gain is also disclosed as a reconciling item in the note of historical cost profits and losses.

Question 2: Pilum

(a) 26.7p   (W1)

(b) 21.4p   (W2)

(c) 24.4p   (W3)

(d) 22.4p   (W4)

(e) 26.2p   (W5)

Workings

(W1)

	£'000
Profit on ordinary activities after tax	1,380
Preference dividends 138×2	276
Earnings	1,104

$$\text{EPS} \quad \frac{1,104}{4,140} \times 100 = 26.7\text{p}$$

(W2)   Five shares in issue for every four before, multiply answer to (a) by 0.8: 26.7p $\times 0.8 = 21.4$p

(W3)   Value

				£
Before	5	shares at	£1.80 =	9
Rights	1	share at	£1.20 =	1.20
After	6			10.20

$$\text{Theoretical ex rights price} = \frac{£10.20}{6} = £1.70$$

$$\text{Weighted average number of shares} = \left(\frac{9}{12} \times 4,140 \times \frac{1.8}{1.7}\right) + \left(\frac{3}{12} \times 4,140 \times \frac{6}{5}\right)$$

(in 000s)

$$= 3,288 + 1,242$$

$$= 4,530$$

Multiply answer to (a) by $\dfrac{4,140}{4,530}$: $\dfrac{4,140}{4,530} \times 26.7p = 24.4p$

Tutorial note: the last part of the calculation is substituting the new denominator for the old denominator which is a quicker way of producing the figures.

(W4)   £'000

Earnings in working 1	1,104.0
Add: After tax interest saved if converted	
$1,150 \times 10\% \times 50\%$	57.5
	1,161.5

Calculate dilution as if conversion took place issuing the highest number of shares possible i.e. 90 per £100.

No of shares $= 4,140 + \left(\dfrac{90}{100} \times 1,150 \right) = 5,175$

(in 000s)

Diluted EPS $= \dfrac{1,161.5}{5,175} \times 100 = 22.4p$

(W5)

Number of ordinary shares in issue	4,140,000
Number of shares under option	460,000
Number of shares that would have been issued at fair value:	
$(460,000 \times 1.70/2.00)$	(391,000)
	4,209,000

Earnings per share (earnings as in (a)): $\dfrac{1,104}{4,209} \times 100 = 26.2p$

CHAPTER **19**   EXAM-TYPE QUESTION

Rowsley plc

In all four cases, the key issue is whether or not a provision should be recognised. Under FRS 12 *Provisions, contingent liabilities and contingent assets*, a provision should only be recognised when:

(a) there is a present obligation as a result of a past event; and

(b) it is probable that a transfer of economic benefits will be required to settle the obligation; and

(c) a reliable estimate can be made of the amount of the obligation.

Factory closure

As the factory closure changes the way in which the business is conducted (it involves the relocation of business activities from one part of the country to another) it appears to fall within the FRS 12 definition of a restructuring.

The key issue here is whether the group has an obligation to incur expenditure in connection with the restructuring. There is clearly no legal obligation, but there may be a constructive obligation. FRS 12 states that a constructive obligation only exists if the group has created valid expectations in other parties, such as employees, customers and suppliers, that the restructuring will actually be carried out. As the group is still drawing up a formal plan for the restructuring and no announcements have been made to any of the parties affected, there cannot be an obligation to restructure. A board decision alone is not sufficient. Therefore no provision should be made.

If the group starts to implement the restructuring or makes announcements to those affected before the accounts are approved by the directors it may be necessary to disclose the details in the financial statements as required by SSAP 17 *Accounting for post balance sheet events*. This will be the case if the restructuring is of such importance that non-disclosure would affect the ability of the users of the financial statements to reach a proper understanding of the group's financial position.

Operating lease

The lease contract appears to be an onerous contract as defined by FRS 12 (i.e. the unavoidable costs of meeting the obligations under it exceed the economic benefits expected to be received under it).

Because the company has signed the lease contract there is a clear legal obligation and the company will have to transfer economic benefits (pay the lease rentals) in settlement. Therefore the group should recognise a provision for the remaining lease payments. The group may recognise a corresponding asset in relation to the nominal rentals currently being received, if these are virtually certain to continue. (In practice, it is unlikely that this amount is material.) As the chances of renting the premises at a commercial rent are less than 50%, no further potential rent receivable may be taken into account.

The financial statements should disclose the carrying amount at the balance sheet date, a description of the nature of the obligation and the expected timing of the lease payments and the amount of any expected rentals receivable from sub-letting. If an asset is recognised in respect of any rentals receivable, this should also be disclosed.

Legal proceedings

It is unlikely that the group has a present obligation to compensate the customer and therefore no provision should be recognised. However, there is a contingent liability. Unless the possibility of a transfer of economic benefits is remote, the financial statements should disclose a brief description of the nature of the contingent liability, an estimate of its financial effect and an indication of the uncertainties relating to the amount or timing of any outflow.

Environmental damage

It is clear that there is no legal obligation to rectify the damage. However, through its published policies, the group has created expectations on the part of those affected that it will take action to do so. There is therefore a constructive obligation to rectify the damage and a transfer of economic benefits is probable.

The group must recognise a provision for the best estimate of the cost. As the most likely outcome is that more than one attempt at re-planting will be needed, the full amount of £30 million should be provided. The expenditure will take place some time in the future, and so the provision should be discounted at a pre-tax rate that reflects current market assessments of the time value of money and the risks specific to the liability.

The financial statements should disclose the carrying amount at the balance sheet date, a description of the nature of the obligation and the expected timing of the expenditure. The financial statements should also give an indication of the uncertainties about the amount and timing of the expenditure.

CHAPTER 20	EXAM-TYPE QUESTION

Ace plc

(a) Why FRS 8 was considered necessary

In theory, an entity controls its own resources and acts independently of its individual owners, managers and other people connected with it. Unless they have reason to believe otherwise, users of financial statements assume that the transactions included in the financial statements were undertaken on an arm's length basis. In practice, this is not always the case.

When transactions are arranged between related parties, they may not take place on the same terms that could have been obtained in a transaction with an external party. Transactions between related parties are often arranged to obtain a particular result desired by one or both of the parties. Therefore they can have a material effect on the position and performance of one or both parties. Unless users of the financial statements are made aware of the existence of related party relationships and transactions, the view given by the financial statements may be misleading.

Although the Companies Act 1985 and the Stock Exchange Listing Rules do contain requirements to disclose some related party transactions, these are largely limited to transactions between directors and the company or group. The Accounting Standards Board (ASB) recognised that 'related party' relationships are not limited to those between a company and its directors. FRS 8 contains a much wider definition of 'related parties', which is based upon ideas of 'control', 'common control' and 'influence', rather than upon specific categories of people or organisations.

The main objective of the Companies Act and Stock Exchange disclosures is to ensure that shareholders can assess the stewardship of the directors. FRS 8 has a wider objective, which is to ensure that users of the financial statements are provided with information on which to base economic decisions. It extends the Companies Act requirements as entities must disclose all material related party transactions in the notes to the financial statements. When the reporting entity is controlled by another party, there must be disclosure of the relationship, regardless of whether any transactions have taken place.

Lastly, FRS 8 brings UK practice broadly into line with International Accounting Standards.

(b) Disclosure of related party transactions

The first step is to determine whether related party relationships existed between the three companies during each of the two accounting periods.

Year ended 31 March 20X8

Ace plc owns 75% of the equity share capital of Deuce Ltd and 80% of the equity share capital of Trey Ltd. This means that Ace plc is a related party of both subsidiaries, as it controls both of them. (An entity is presumed to be a related party of another entity if that entity owns more than 20% of its equity share capital.)

Deuce Ltd and Trey Ltd are related parties as they are under common control.

Year ended 31 March 20X9

Ace plc owns 100% of the equity share capital of Deuce Ltd and 80% of the equity share capital of Trey Ltd. Therefore all three companies are still related parties of each other. As Ace plc now owns over 90% of the equity shares in Deuce Ltd, Deuce Ltd need not disclose transactions with Ace plc.

Three sets of financial statements are relevant:

- the consolidated financial statements of Ace plc

- the individual financial statements of Deuce Ltd

- the individual financial statements of Trey Ltd.

Ace plc will not prepare individual company financial statements and so there is no distinction between the transactions of Ace plc and the transactions of the Ace Group.

Related party disclosures

The following details of each related party transaction are required:

- name of related party with which the transaction was made

- description of the relationship between the parties

- description of the transaction and the amounts involved (including the fair value of the transaction if this is different from the actual value)

- any amounts due to or from related parties at the year end (including any doubtful debts)

- any amounts written off related party debtors

- any other information necessary for an understanding of the transaction and its effect on the financial statements.

It is assumed that all the related party transactions are material.

The transactions are summarised in the following table:

Year ended 31 March 20X8

	Ace plc: Consolidated financial statements	Deuce Ltd	Trey Ltd
(i) Sale of machine by Ace plc to Deuce Ltd	Disclose intra-group profit on sale of £5,000 Otherwise sale eliminated on consolidation	Disclose purchase of machine from parent at £25,000 and depreciation charge of £5,000. No amounts outstanding at year end	
(ii) Not applicable			
(iii) Management charges made by Ace plc to both Deuce Ltd and Trey Ltd	No disclosure: eliminated on consolidation	Disclose purchase of management services from parent at no charge	Disclose purchase of management services from parent at no charge

Year ended 31 March 20X9

	Ace plc: Consolidated financial statements	Deuce Ltd	Trey Ltd
(i) Sale of machine by Ace plc to Deuce Ltd	No disclosure as transaction completed	Disclose depreciation charge of £5,000 on machine purchased from parent in previous year	
(ii) Sale of goods by Deuce Ltd to Trey Ltd		Disclose sale of goods to Trey Ltd for £15,000 and profit of £3,000. No debt written off or outstanding at year end	Disclose purchase of goods from Deuce Ltd for £15,000. No amounts outstanding at year end. All stock sold at year end

(iii) Management charges made by Ace plc to both Deuce Ltd and Trey Ltd	No disclosure: eliminated on consolidation	No disclosure because more than 90% of equity share capital owned	Disclose purchase of management services from parent for £10,000. Disclose £10,000 due to parent at year end

CHAPTER 21

EXAM-TYPE QUESTION

R Johnson

Tutorial notes

(1) For part (a) look at the position from the point of view of the respective buyers, even though you are the accountant adviser to the seller.

(2) Base your answer to part (b) on the returns currently achieved by Sonar Products Ltd.

(3) For part (c), while listing the principal matters, do not forget to explain the relevance of each to the circumstances of **this** question.

(a) (i) Sonar Products Ltd would achieve a controlling interest in Johnson Products Ltd by this acquisition. This would enable the company to determine the level of payout based on the earnings achieved. Earnings, and not dividends, would therefore be the relevant income measure on which to base a valuation. In the computations below all of the past five years have been taken as relevant, including the loss-making year 20X6, but the later years have been given more relevance by using a weighting factor. (If the early years are not considered to represent feasible future earnings levels, they should be ignored.)

Year	Earnings £'000	Weighting factor	Weighted earnings £'000
20X5	79.4	1	79.4
20X6	(27.6)	1	(27.6)
20X7	56.5	2	113.0
20X8	88.3	2	176.6
20X9	97.2	3	291.6
		9	633.0

Weighted average earnings = £70,000 (round thousands).

To calculate a value these earnings need to be expressed as a percentage return. Using the details concerning the nearest comparable listed companies in the same industry, the following average return can be computed.

If earnings are not retained, they are assumed to be distributed by way of dividend. Therefore, if for Eastron plc 25% is retained, then 75% must be distributed – the dividend yield of 15% therefore represents 75% of the earnings yield, which must have been 20%.

Applying the same argument to Westron plc and Northron plc:

Westron plc $\quad \dfrac{10.5\%}{100\% - 16\%} = 12.5\%$

Northron plc $\quad \dfrac{13.4\%}{100\% - 20\%} = 16.75\%$

The simple average of these three earnings yields is 16.42%. To allow for a marketability reassessment let the earnings return be (say) 18%. This gives a valuation of:

$$\frac{£70,000}{18\%} = £389,000$$

This is the value of the whole company. R Johnson has a 75% holding which on this basis is valued at £290,000.

(ii) With each manager holding only a minority shareholding and probably looking on dividends as a form of periodic return, it is probably more realistic to consider the valuation from a dividend yield point of view rather than from an earnings yield point of view.

The simple average of the three comparable companies' dividend yield is 13%. Allowing for lack of marketability of Johnson Products Ltd's shares, a rounded figure of 15% could be used. Reviewing the five previous years' gross dividends, a dividend of 5p would not appear to be unrealistic. This gives a valuation of

$$\frac{5p}{15\%} \times 810,000 \text{ shares } = £270,000$$

(iii) With 'asset stripping' appearing to be the objective of Divest plc, neither the earnings nor dividend yield based valuations are applicable. Any valuation should be based on the net realisable values of Johnson Products Ltd. This asset based valuation would be as follows

	£'000
Land	480
Premises	630
Equipment	150
Debtors	168
Stock	98
Cash at bank	70
	1,596
To pay creditors	(493)
	1,103
To minority interest shareholders (25%)	276
Value to Divest plc (75%)	827

The amount that Divest plc would pay would be dependent on the return the company would expect on the acquisition at a piecemeal sale. A return of 25% would set the price at $\dfrac{£827,000}{1.25} = £661,600$.

(b) The current post-tax return of 12.5% would need to be at least maintained. If the company accepts that the 20X9 profit of Johnson Products Ltd can be maintained, then Sonar Products plc may consider a price of $\dfrac{97,200}{12.5\%} = £777,600$ as the absolute maximum value of a 100% shareholding. A 75% interest would therefore be valued at £583,200.

Any valuation based on average earnings or an increased risk adjusted rate of return would obviously reduce this maximum.

(c) The future maintainable earnings of Johnson Products Ltd would be dependent on many variables but the important matters to consider would include the following.

(i) Economic predictions of the industrial sector in which Johnson Products Ltd exists; this could include assessment of the 'size' of the sector and the proportion of that market in that sector that is likely to be held by Johnson Products Ltd.

(ii) The level of profitability that the company can achieve in the market share it can expect to hold; this would include an assessment of past performance and its relevance to future performance, and a comparison of the trend of Johnson Products Ltd's performance over years 20X5 to 20X9 with that of other companies in the industrial sector.

(iii) Any changes in the strategic development of the company – possible changes to product mix, manufacturing method, market distribution and financial arrangements would need to be considered.

(iv) The likelihood or otherwise of Johnson Products Ltd maintaining its past management team and organisational structure – are future changes likely to affect future levels of performance and profitability?

(v) The budgets and forecasts produced by management would also be of interest together with variance reports for past periods, so that an assessment of the accuracy of management's plans could be made.

(vi) Any changes to the financial structure of the company, with particular reference to changes in the level of interest-bearing loans.

Finally, the earnings will be based on the accounting policies adopted by the company. If any of the policies are to change, efforts should be made to revise the past earnings figures to bring them into line with those that would have been produced had the new policies been adopted at that time.

CHAPTER **22**　　EXAM-TYPE QUESTION

Provincial Motor Spares Ltd

(a) $X_1 = \dfrac{\text{Net working capital}}{\text{Total assets}}$

Firms with heavier fixed assets proportions are less liquid and more likely to go into liquidation. Companies with negative working capital will be given lower Z scores and traditional analysis would point to liquidation as such companies have low current ratios also.

$$X_2 = \frac{\text{Retained earnings}}{\text{Total assets}}$$

Total assets are financed by debt or equity. Short or long-term borrowings increase the risk of failure to survive through not being able to service debt. Lower geared companies are a lesser risk and should be given a better chance of survival. Companies that can demonstrate high finance by equity particularly through retention of earnings rather than cash calls are even more likely to survive.

$$X_3 = \frac{\text{Earnings before interest and taxes}}{\text{Total assets}}$$

This measures return on capital employed (ROCE). Firms are unlikely to go into liquidation if they earn a good ROCE, as further finance would be made available if there were liquidity problems. Those with low or negative X_3s, will strain their liquidity and struggle to renew finance sources.

$$X_4 = \frac{\text{Market value of equity}}{\text{Book value of total debt}}$$

This ratio will be lowest for those heavily dependent on debt to finance total assets. Highly geared companies are known to be more prone to forced liquidation.

$$X_5 = \frac{\text{Sales}}{\text{Total assets}}$$

To get a good ROCE (see X_3) companies must get high asset turnovers. Companies that do not work their assets intensively will fail.

(b) Z score

0.012	X_1	=	$\dfrac{3,198}{19,739}$	$\dfrac{(W1)}{(W2)} \times 100\%$	=	0.012×16.2	= 0.19
0.014	X_2	=	$\dfrac{5,504}{19,739}$	$(W3) \times 100\%$	=	0.014×27.88	= 0.39
0.033	X_3	=	$\dfrac{3,820}{19,739}$	$(W4) \times 100\%$	=	0.033×19.35	= 0.64
0.006	X_4	=	$\dfrac{18,900}{1,500}$	$(W5) \times 100\%$	=	$0.006 \times 1,260$	= 7.56
0.999	X_5	=	$\dfrac{20,000}{19,739}$	$(W6) \times 100\%$	=	0.999×1.013	= 1.01

Total Z score   9.79

(c) Current ratio $= \dfrac{\text{Current assets}}{\text{Current liabilities}} = \dfrac{8,488}{5,290} = 1.6$

This is less than the 'ideal' of 2

Quick assets (acid) ratio $= \dfrac{\text{Current assets} - \text{stock}}{\text{Current liabilities}} = \dfrac{8,488 - 6,580}{5,290} = 0.36$ which is very much less than the 'ideal' of 1.

The above suggests the company could be at risk of being forced into liquidation. However, the Z score suggests that the company is safe for the time being.

Such summary statistics give only a general picture and do not take account of variation between industries or the availability of future finance. A cash budget month by month would be the most valuable extra information.

Workings

(W1) Net working capital

	£'000	£'000
Stock		6,580
Debtors		1,480
Bank		428
Current assets		8,488
Current tax	700	
Creditors	4,130	
Dividends – pref	100	
Dividends – ord	360	
Current liabilities		5,290
Working capital		3,198

(W2) Total assets

	£'000
Premises	7,200
Equipment	3,800
Investments	251
Current assets (W1)	8,488
	19,739

(W3) Retained profits

	£'000
Profits for 20X3	3,780
Investment income	14
Profit before tax	3,794
Tax	1,900
Profit after tax	1,894
Dividends	460
	1,434
Retained profit – 1 January	2,250
General reserves b/f	1,820
	5,504

(W4) Earnings before interest and tax

	£'000
Profit for 20X3	3,780
Interest 8% × £500	40
	3,820

(W5) Market value of equity

£3,780,000 × 5 = £18,900,000

(W6) **Turnover**

	£'000
Sales	21,000
VAT	1,000
Turnover	20,000

CHAPTER 24   EXAM-TYPE QUESTION

Redstart plc

MEMORANDUM

To: Assistant Accountant

From: Chief Accountant

Subject: Accounting treatment of two transactions and disclosure of environmental matters in the financial statements

Date: 25 March 20X2

(a) **Accounting treatment of two transactions**

Transaction One

FRS 12 *Provisions, contingent liabilities and contingent assets* states that provisions should only be recognised in the financial statements if:

- there is a present obligation as a result of a past event; and

- it is probable that a transfer of economic benefits will be required to settle the obligation; and

- a reliable estimate can be made of the amount of the obligation.

In this case, there is no obligation to incur expenditure. There may be a constructive obligation to do so in future, if the Board creates a valid expectation that it will protect the environment, but a Board decision alone does not create an obligation. There is also some doubt as to whether the expenditure can be reliably quantified. The sum of £500,000 could be appropriated from profit and transferred to an environmental protection reserve, subject to formal approval by the Board. A note to the financial statements should explain the appropriation.

Transaction Two

Again, FRS 12 states that a provision cannot be recognised if there is no obligation to incur expenditure. At first sight it appears that there is an obligation to purchase the new equipment, because the new law has been enacted. However, the obligation must arise as the result of a past event. At 31 December 20X1, no such event had occurred as the new plant had not yet been purchased and the new law had not yet come into effect. In theory, the company does not have to purchase the new plant. It could completely discontinue the activities that cause pollution or it could continue to operate the old equipment and risk prosecution under the new law. Therefore no provision can be recognised for the cost of new equipment.

It is likely that the company will be disposing of the old plant before it would normally have expected to do so. FRS 11 *Impairment of fixed assets and goodwill* requires that the old plant must be reviewed for impairment. If its carrying value is greater than its recoverable amount it must be written down and an impairment loss must be charged in the profit and loss account. This should be disclosed as an exceptional item in the notes to the profit and loss account if it is material, as required by FRS 3 *Reporting financial performance.*

(b) **Reference to environmental matters in the financial statements**

At present companies are not obliged to make any reference to environmental matters within their financial statements. Current UK financial reporting practice is primarily designed to meet the needs of investors and potential investors, rather than the general public. Some companies choose to disclose information about the ways in which they attempt to safeguard the environment, but this is almost invariably carried out as a public relations exercise. Disclosures are often framed in very general terms and appear outside the financial statements proper. This means that they do not have to be audited.

A few companies do publish fairly detailed 'environmental reports'. It could be argued that as Redstart plc's operations affect the wider community, it has a moral responsibility to disclose details of its activities and its environmental policies. However, at present it is not required to do so.

If a company has, or may have, an obligation to make good environmental damage that it has caused it is obliged to disclose information about this commitment in its financial statements (unless the likelihood of crystallisation of the liability is remote). If it is probable (more likely than not) that the company will have to incur expenditure to meet its obligation, then it is also required to set up a provision in the financial statements. In practice, these requirements are unlikely to apply unless a company is actually obliged by law to rectify environmental damage or unless it has made a firm commitment to the public to do so (for example, by promoting itself as an organisation that cares for the environment, as the directors propose that Redstart plc should do in future).

CHAPTER **25**   EXAM-TYPE QUESTION

Dixie Inc

REPORT

To:	Managing Director
From:	Accountant
Subject:	Reconciliation statement of Dixie Inc **Date:** 25 November 20X1

As requested, I set out below my responses to your queries about the financial statements of Dixie Inc and the reconciliation statement.

(i) **Why the reconciliation statement is necessary**

Because Dixie Inc is based in the USA it is subject to the regulatory framework in that country. Therefore it prepares its financial statements in accordance with generally accepted accounting principles in the USA (US GAAP). The financial statements of Dixie Inc are also incorporated into the consolidated financial statements of Widespread plc, its parent undertaking. Widespread plc is registered in the UK and must therefore prepare its financial statements in accordance with generally accepted accounting principles in the UK (UK GAAP). Although US GAAP and UK GAAP are similar in most respects, there are some important differences. Therefore a statement reconciling profit under US GAAP to profit under UK GAAP is prepared.

(ii) The items in the statement

These concern development expenditure, capitalised interest, stock valuation and deferred taxation.

- **Development expenditure**

  Under US GAAP, development expenditure must be treated as an expense in the profit and loss account in the period in which it is incurred. Under UK GAAP development expenditure may be capitalised as an intangible fixed asset and amortised through the profit and loss account over the periods expected to benefit from the expenditure, provided that certain conditions are met.

- **Capitalised interest**

  Under US GAAP, interest must be capitalised where it relates to the construction of certain assets. In the UK, capitalisation of interest incurred in constructing fixed assets is still optional. Widespread plc has evidently adopted a policy of non-capitalisation.

- **Stock valuation**

  Under US GAAP, stock can be valued using the last in, first out method (LIFO). Under UK GAAP this is not normally acceptable, because LIFO often results in stocks being stated at a value that bears little or no resemblance to actual cost. The first in, first out method (FIFO) is an acceptable method in the UK and is the method adopted by the Widespread group.

- **Deferred taxation**

  Under US GAAP full provision must be made for deferred tax on all timing differences. Although UK GAAP also requires full provision, FRS 19 adopts an incremental liability approach. This means that under UK GAAP, deferred tax is not provided on items such as revaluation gains that are not expected to crystallise in the foreseeable future. Alternatively, the adjustments could represent deferred tax on timing differences that have arisen as a result of the other adjustments in the reconciliation.

(iii) Adoption of International Accounting Standards

Each of our subsidiaries must prepare financial statements and these must normally be prepared using GAAP for the country in which the subsidiary is based. In some countries financial statements may be prepared in accordance with International Accounting Standards (IASs), but for now in the US and the UK they must comply with US GAAP and UK GAAP respectively. Although the three financial reporting regimes are broadly similar, there are significant differences and it should be noted that US Financial Accounting Standards are more prescriptive than IASs. Where there are differences between IASs and local GAAP, local GAAP must prevail. Therefore the adoption of IASs would not necessarily remove the need to prepare reconciliation statements.

CHAPTER 26

EXAM-TYPE QUESTION

Sterndale plc

(a) The reasons why the ASB has withdrawn SSAP 2

SSAP 2 was originally issued more than 30 years ago. At that time there were very few accounting standards and no conceptual framework. SSAP 2 was intended to assist in developing accounting policies and in order to do this it defined four fundamental accounting concepts: going concern, accruals, consistency and prudence. The standard was never intended to represent a conceptual framework and SSAP 2 itself made clear that the four concepts were practical rules rather than theoretical ideals. It was recognised that as accounting thought and practice developed, they would be capable of variation and evolution.

Since SSAP 2 was originally issued the business environment and financial reporting practice have become far more sophisticated, so that the approach taken by the standard is out of date. The emphasis in FRS 18 is on selecting accounting policies from those allowed by legislation and accounting standards, rather than on developing them.

In addition, the ASB has now issued its *Statement of Principles for Financial Reporting*. This discusses the four fundamental concepts, but in a context that is rather different from that of SSAP 2. There is now an explicit requirement to observe the concepts of going concern and accruals, but consistency and prudence are now seen as desirable qualities of financial information, rather than accounting concepts. It was generally recognised that SSAP 2 should be revised so that it was consistent with the Statement of Principles.

Although the ASB regarded SSAP 2 as satisfactory in other respects, it recognised that it is not always easy to distinguish between a change of accounting policy and a change in estimate. SSAP 2 did not address this issue. The distinction is important, because changes in accounting policy require prior period adjustments, while changes in estimate do not. FRS 18 contains guidance on how to distinguish between the two.

(b) Selection of accounting policies

To some extent, FRS 18 restates and clarifies existing practice. An entity should adopt accounting policies that enable its financial statements to comply with applicable accounting standards and companies legislation. Where it is necessary to choose between accounting policies that satisfy these conditions, an entity should select whichever policy is most appropriate to its particular circumstances for the purpose of giving a true and fair view.

An entity should prepare its financial statements (except for cash flow information) on the accrual basis of accounting. The going concern convention must also be observed, unless the entity is being liquidated or has ceased trading or there is no realistic alternative to doing so.

An entity should judge the appropriateness of accounting policies to its particular circumstances against the objectives of:

- relevance

- reliability

- comparability

- understandability.

These are the characteristics that financial information should have if it is to be useful and they are described in the ASB's Statement of Principles.

When judging the appropriateness of accounting policies, an entity should take into account the following constraints:

- the need to balance the different objectives above

- the need to balance the cost of providing information with the likely benefit of such information to users of the entity's financial statements.

An entity should review its accounting policies regularly to ensure that they remain the most appropriate to its particular circumstances. If an accounting policy is no longer judged most appropriate, the entity should implement whichever accounting policy is now judged most appropriate. Frequent changes to accounting policies do not enhance comparability in the long term, but consistency is not an end in itself and should not prevent the introduction of improved accounting practices.

(c) FRS 18 explains that accounting policies can be distinguished from estimation techniques. Accounting policies present the same set of facts in different ways or different aspects of the same set of facts. Estimation techniques are used to arrive at the facts to be presented. A change in accounting policy involves a change to the basis on which an item is recognised, measured, or presented.

(i) **Development expenditure**

This is a change to the basis on which development expenditure is recognised and presented. It is therefore a change in accounting policy.

FRS 3 *Reporting financial performance* requires that a prior period adjustment is made. Comparative figures for the preceding period should be restated and opening reserves adjusted for the cumulative effect of the change. The cumulative effect of the change should also be disclosed in the statement of total recognised gains and losses and the reconciliation of shareholders' funds. The effect of prior period adjustments on the results for the current period and the preceding period should be disclosed where practicable.

(ii) **Forward exchange contracts**

At first sight this would appear to be a change in presentation and therefore a change in accounting policy. However, FRS 18 explains that where information is disclosed for the first time or a more detailed analysis of a particular item is presented that is not of itself a change in accounting policy.

(In addition, FRS 3 states that a change in accounting policy does not arise from the adoption or modification of an accounting method necessitated by transactions or events that are clearly different in substance from those previously occurring.)

The company should simply make the disclosures required by FRS 13 and disclose corresponding amounts in similar detail (in practice these will be nil).

(iii) **Provision for dismantling costs**

The practical effect of the increase in the provision is that it has to be discounted for the first time. This is a change in the way that the amount of the provision is measured but not an actual change in the measurement basis used. Therefore it is a change in estimation technique, not a change in accounting policy.

No prior year adjustment should be made. The change should be taken to the profit and loss account and included in financing items. The effect of the change and a description of it should be disclosed in the notes to the financial statements. (This is required by FRS 3, as well as FRS 18.) The company should also make the required disclosures under FRS 12.

Index

FTC Foulks Lynch
A **Kaplan Professional** Company

STUDY TEXT REVIEW FORM
ACCA Paper 3.6 UK

Thank you for choosing the official text for your ACCA professional qualification. As we are constantly striving to improve our products, we would be grateful if you could provide us with feedback about how useful you found this publication.

Name: ....

Address: ....

....

Email: ....

<table>
<tr><td>

Why did you decide to purchase this Study Text?

Have used them in the past ☐

Recommended by lecturer ☐

Recommended by friend ☐

Saw advertising ☐

Other (please specify)...

</td><td>

How do you study?

At a college ☐

On a distance learning course ☐

Home study ☐

Other (please specify)...

</td></tr>
</table>

Within our ACCA range we also offer Exam Kits and Pocket Notes. Is there any other type of service/publication that you would like to see as part of the range?

CD Rom with additional questions and answers ☐

A booklet that would help you master exam skills and techniques ☐

Space on our website that would answer your technical questions and queries ☐

Other (please specify)...

During the past six month do you recall seeing/receiving any of the following?

Our advertisement in *Student Accountant* magazine? ☐

Our advertisement in any other magazine? (please specify) ☐

....

Our leaflet/brochure or a letter through the post? ☐

Other (please specify)...

Overall opinion of this Study Text

	Excellent	*Adequate*	*Poor*
Introductory pages	☐	☐	☐
Syllabus coverage	☐	☐	☐
Clarity of explanations	☐	☐	☐
Clarity of definitions and key terms	☐	☐	☐
Diagrams	☐	☐	☐
Activities	☐	☐	☐
Self-test questions	☐	☐	☐
Practice questions	☐	☐	☐
Answers to practice questions	☐	☐	☐
Layout	☐	☐	☐
Index	☐	☐	☐

If you have further comments/suggestions or have spotted any errors, please write them on the next page.

Please return this form to: Veronica Wastell, Publisher, FTC Foulks Lynch, FREEPOST NAT 17540, Wokingham RG40 1BR

Other comments/suggestions and errors

....
....
....
....
....
....
....
....
....
....
....
....
....
....
....
....
....
....
....
....
....
....
....
....
....
....
....
....
....
....
....
....

Other comments/suggestions and errors

....
....
....

ftc
FTC Foulks Lynch
A **Kaplan Professional** Company

ACCA Order Form

Swift House, Market Place, Wokingham, Berkshire RG40 1AP, UK
Tel: +44 (0) 118 989 0629   Fax: +44 (0) 118 979 7455
Order online: www.financial-training.com
Email: publishing@financial-training.com

Examination Date: Dec 04 ☐ Jun 05 ☐ (please tick the exam you intend to take)	Study Text £23.00	Exam Kit £13.00	Pocket Notes £7.00
Part 1			
1.1 Preparing Financial Statements (UK)	☐	☐	☐
1.1 Preparing Financial Statements (International)	☐	☐	☐
1.2 Financial Information for Management	☐	☐	☐
1.3 Managing People	☐	☐	☐
Part 2			
2.1 Information Systems	☐	☐	☐
2.2 Corporate & Business Law	☐	☐	☐
2.2 Corporate & Business Law (Global)	☐	☐	☐
2.2 Corporate & Business Law (Scottish)	☐		
2.3 Business Taxation – FA 2004	☐	☐	
2.4 Financial Management & Control	☐	☐	☐
2.5 Financial Reporting (UK)	☐	☐	☐
2.5 Financial Reporting (International)	☐	☐	☐
2.6 Audit & Internal Review (UK)	☐	☐	☐
2.6 Audit & Internal Review (International)	☐	☐	☐
Part 3			
3.1 Audit & Assurance Services (UK)	☐	☐	☐
3.1 Audit & Assurance Services (International)	☐	☐	☐
3.2 Advanced Taxation – FA 2004	☐	☐	☐
3.3 Performance Management	☐	☐	☐
3.4 Business Information Management	☐	☐	☐
3.5 Strategic Business Planning & Development	☐	☐	☐
3.6 Advanced Corporate Reporting (UK)	☐	☐	☐
3.6 Advanced Corporate Reporting (International)	☐	☐	☐
3.7 Strategic Financial Management	☐	☐	☐
Research and Analysis Project Guide (supporting Oxford Brookes University BSc (Hons) in Applied Accounting)	£20 ☐		

| Postage, Packaging and Delivery (per item):   **Note**: Maximum postage charged for UK orders is £15 | | | **TOTAL** | |

Study Texts and Exam Kits	First	Each Extra	**Pocket Notes**	First	Each Extra
UK	£5.00	£2.00	UK	£2.00	£1.00
Europe (incl Republic of Ireland and Channel Isles)	£7.00	£4.00	Europe (incl Republic of Ireland and Channel Isles)	£3.00	£2.00
Rest of World	£22.00	£8.00	Rest of World	£8.00	£5.00

Product Sub Total £....................   **Postage & Packaging £**.................... | Order Total £.................... | **(Payments in UK £ Sterling)**

Customer Details

☐ Mr   ☐ Mrs   ☐ Ms   ☐ Miss   Other ....

Initials:....................... Surname: ....

Address: ....

....

....

Postcode: ....

Delivery Address – if different from above

Address: ....

....

Postcode: ....

Telephone: ....

Email: ....

Fax: ....

Delivery please allow:	United Kingdom	– 5 working days
	Europe	– 8 working days
	Rest of World	– 10 working days

Payment

1   I enclose Cheque/Postal Order/Bankers Draft for £.....................................

Please make cheques payable to **'The Financial Training Company Ltd'**.

2   Charge MasterCard/Visa/Switch/Delta no:

| | | | | | | | | | | | | | | | |

Valid from: | | | | | Expiry date: | | | |

Issue no:

(Switch only) | | |

Signature: .... Date: ....

Declaration

I agree to pay as indicated on this form and understand that The Financial Training Company's Terms and Conditions apply (available on request).

Signature: .... Date: ....

Notes: All orders over 1kg will be fully tracked & insured. Signature required on receipt of order. Delivery times subject to stock availability. A telephone number or email address is required for orders that are to be delivered to a PO Box number.

ACCA
Official Publisher

The Financial Training Company
A **Kaplan Professional** Company

SPECIAL OFFER
Increase your chances of success and upgrade your Official ACCA Study Text to a Distance Learning Course for only £80 per paper and gain:
- Personal Tutor Support
- The whole range of Official ACCA Publications including Exam Kits and Pocket Notes
- Programme of Study
- Unique 5-Star-Guide written by a Specialist Tutor
- Two Progress Tests which you can send to us for marking and feedback
- Hints and Tips Audio Tape
- Student Handbook packed with practical information

Our Distance Learning Students consistently achieve pass rates above the ACCA global average.
This offer is only available if you own the Official FTC Foulks Lynch ACCA Study Text for the December 2004 or June 2005 Examinations.

ACCA Distance Learning Enrolment Form

Surname   First Name   Mr / Miss / Mrs / Ms

Home Address

Post Code   Country

Home Tel   Office Tel

Mobile   E-mail

Date of Birth   ACCA Registration Number

Exam sitting: ☐ December 2004   ☐ June 2005

EMPLOYER DETAILS

Company Name

Manager's Name

Address

                                 Post Code   Country

Telephone   Email

SPONSORED STUDENTS: EMPLOYER'S AUTHORISATION
If the above employer is responsible for the payment of fees, please complete the following:
As employer of the student for whom this form is completed, we are responsible for payment of fees due on receipt of the invoice in respect of the student named above and undertake to inform you in writing of any change to this arrangement. We understand that we are fully responsible for the payment of fees due in all circumstances including termination of employment or cancellation of course.

Purchase Order Number _____   Please send reports to the sponsors ☐

Manager's Name _____

Manager's Signature _____   Date _____

DATA PROTECTION ACT:
Your sponsor can be informed of your test results unless we are otherwise notified.

HOW TO ENROL:
By phone: If you are paying by credit card, please telephone 0113 388 9326
By post: Complete this enrolment form and return to:
               FTC Foulks Lynch Distance Learning, 49 St Paul's Street, LEEDS LS1 2TE
By fax: Fax both sides of your completed enrolment form to 0113 242 8889

Distance Learning Courses include VAT and all materials. Add postage & packing – applicable to both Distance Learning options (for rates see below).	Distance Learning		Distance Learning (excluding Official ACCA Study Text applicable for the December 2004 and June 2005 examinations sittings only)	
	£	✓	£	✓
Part 1				
1.1 Preparing Financial Statements (UK)	104		80	
1.1 Preparing Financial Statements (International)	104		80	
1.2 Financial Information for Management	104		80	
1.3 Managing People	104		80	
Part 2				
2.1 Information Systems	104		80	
2.2 Corporate & Business Law	104		80	
2.3 Business Taxation (FA 2003)	104		80	
2.4 Financial Management and Control	104		80	
2.5 Financial Reporting (UK)	104		80	
2.5 Financial Reporting (International)	104		80	
2.6 Audit & Internal Review (UK)	104		80	
2.6 Audit & Internal Review (International)	104		80	
Part 3 Options				
3.1 Audit & Assurance Services (UK)	104		80	
3.1 Audit & Assurance Services (International)	104		80	
3.2 Advanced Taxation (Finance Act 2003)	104		80	
3.3 Performance Management	104		80	
3.4 Business Information Management	104		80	
Part 3 Core				
3.5 Strategic Business Planning & Development	104		80	
3.6 Advanced Corporate Reporting (UK)	104		80	
3.6 Advanced Corporate Reporting (International)	104		80	
3.7 Strategic Financial Management	104		80	

FEES	£
Postage & Packing	£
Total	£

POSTAGE & PACKING

Distance Learning (per paper):

UK & NI £6, Europe & Channel Islands £15, Rest of World £40

DISTANCE LEARNING TERMS AND CONDITIONS OF ENROLMENT:

1. Full payment of fees or employer's authorisation is required prior to despatch of materials.

2. Where an employer's authorisation is received, the full fees are payable within 30 days of the invoice date. The employer is responsible for the payment of fees due in all circumstances including termination of employment or cancellation of course. FTC Foulks Lynch reserves the right to charge interest on overdue accounts.

3. A deferral to the following exam sitting can be processed subject to a deferral fee of £25 if notified in writing. If new study materials are required due to syllabus changes or changes in Finance Acts, they will have to be paid for in addition to the deferral fee.

4. No cancellation or refund can be made after materials have been despatched.

5. Courses are not transferable between students.

6. Distance Learning fees include VAT and all materials but exclude any taxes or duties imposed by countries outside the UK.

METHODS OF PAYMENT:

☐ Please invoice my employer (details completed overleaf).

☐ I enclose a cheque made payable to The Financial Training Company Ltd for £ _____

Payments will only be accepted in UK Sterling.

☐ Please charge my Credit/Debit Card Number for the fees indicated above.

Expiry [ ][ ][ ]   Solo/Switch Issue No [ ][ ]   Security Code [ ][ ][ ]

I agree to the terms and conditions of enrolment which I have read.

Student Signature _____   Date _____